DICTIONARY OF INDO-EUROPEAN CONCEPTS AND SOCIETY

HAU
BOOKS

www.haubooks.com

DICTIONARY OF INDO-EUROPEAN CONCEPTS AND SOCIETY

Émile Benveniste

Foreword by Giorgio Agamben

Translated by Elizabeth Palmer

HAU Books
Chicago

Cover and layout design: Sheehan Moore

Cover image: "The Tower of Babel," Hendrick van Cleve III (ca. 1525–1589), ca. Sixteenth Century, Oil, Kröller-Müller Museum, Netherlands, KM 100.870

Typesetting: Prepress Plus (www.prepressplus.in)

ISBN: 978-0-9861325-9-9
LCCN: 2016955902

HAU Books
Chicago Distribution Center
11030 S. Langley
Chicago, IL 60628
www.haubooks.com

HAU Books is marketed and distributed by The University of Chicago Press.
www.press.uchicago.edu

Printed in the United States of America on acid-free paper.

Table of Contents

FOREWORD

The Vocabulary and the Voice

GIORGIO AGAMBEN

Translation by Thomas Zummer

Émile Benveniste's *Le vocabulaire des institutions indo-européennes* is certainly the *culmination* of twentieth-century linguistics, in both senses of the term.[1] It is here that the nineteenth-century project of comparative grammar had reached its highest point, and, simultaneously, coincided with its end. While there certainly will be further studies that prolong the scientific orientation embodied in the prestigious genealogy of Bréal, Saussure, Meillet, and Benveniste, it is also the case that, after the death of Benveniste, linguistics as a whole has taken quite different paths, whereof the school of transformational-generative grammar is such an outstanding example. It is all the more pressing, then, to understand what gives Benveniste's conception of language such an unusual

1. Works by Benveniste are cited in this foreword with the following abbreviations: Voc. = *Le vocabulaire des institutions indo-européennes*, Minuit, Paris 1969, Vols. 1 and II; Pr. = *Problèmes de linguistique générale*, Gallimard, vol. I, Paris 1966, vol.II, Paris 1974; L. = *Dernières Leçons*, Gallimard-Seuil, Paris 2012. Full bibliographical citations of these texts are also included in the references list at the end of the foreword. —Eds.

character. It is necessary, in other words, to investigate the background, to show what is really diversified, and in this manner, to try to understand upon what seemingly insurmountable obstacle this project has been shipwrecked.

The conception that it was possible to trace, through purely linguistic analysis, the prehistoric, or at least the most archaic stages of social history, was earlier hinted at by Hermann Usener in his book *Götternamen* ([1896] 2000). Usener, whose research concerned the names of the Gods, noted that for such an investigation we have no other documents than those that come from an analysis of language (ibid.: 5). As early as 1859, the Genevan linguist and patrician Adolphe Pictet, who had a likely influence on the young Saussure, published the two volumes of his masterpiece *Les origines indoeuropéennes.* As his subtitle, *Essai de paléontologie linguistique,* suggests, his purpose was to reconstruct "the whole life of a prehistoric people," the Indo-Europeans (or Aryans as he preferred to call them), entirely through the analysis and comparison of words. Because "words last as long as bones" the linguist, like the paleontologist—whose examination of the fossil record "can not only reconstruct the animal, but also instruct us about habits, ways of moving, feeding, etc."—can replenish, through an examination of common linguistic data, "the state of material, social and moral welfare of the people who have produced this primitive idiom." (Pictet 1877: 6).

Still, Benveniste was determined to put himself at a distance from such a model. While not specifically naming Pictet in the Preface to the *Vocabulaire*—probably one of the last texts he wrote (the *Vocabulaire* was published four months after the hemiplegia which rendered him aphasic until his death)—Benveniste refers to his predecessors in these terms:

> *Il est apparu très tôt aux spécialistes de l'indo-européen que les concordances entre les vocabulaires des langues anciennes illustraient les principaux aspects, surtout matériels, d'une culture commune; on a ainsi les receueilli preuves de l'héritage lexical dans les termes de parenté, les numéraux, les noms d'animaux, des métaux, d'instruments agricoles, etc. Plusieurs auteurs successifs, du XIXe siècle jusqu'à ces dernières années, se sont des employés à dresser des répertoires, au demeurant fort utiles, de ces notions communes.*[2] (*Voc.*, I, pg. 9)

2. "Very early on it occurred to specialists in the Indo-European field that correspondences between the vocabularies of ancient languages illustrate the principal aspects of a common culture, particularly of material culture. Thus

Although he adds immediately: "*Notre entreprise est entièrement différente*"[3] (ibid.), and the antithesis is dramatically enhanced in the following pages: "*Nous ne voyons guère des travaux antérieurs auxquels nous aurions pu confronter nos propres raisonnements*"[4] (ibid., pg. 12).

What does this incomparable novelty consist of? Benveniste soon clarifies his purpose. For him, the task is not to make an inventory of the Indo-European institutional realities as they were defined by lexical correspondences between languages, but to investigate the genesis and development of the vocabulary that refers to those realities.

> *L'aspect historique et sociologique de ces procés est laissé à d'autres. Si nous nous occupons du verbe grec* hēgéomai *et de son dérivé* hēgemṓn*, c'est pour voir comment s'est constituée une notion qui est celle d l' 'Hegemonie,' mais sans égard au fait que gr.* hēgemonía *est tout à tour la suprématie d'un individu, ou d'une nation, ou l'équivalent de l'*imperium *romain, etc., seul nous retient le rapport, difficile à établir, entre un terme d'autorité tel que* hēgemṓn *et le verbe* hegéomai *au sens de 'penser, juger.' Nous par éclairons par là la* signification; *d'autres se chargeront de la* désignation.[5] (ibid., pg. 10)

The opposition is reiterated at the end of the Preface of the *Vocabulaire*: "*Il s'agit, par la comparaison et au moyen d'une analyse diachronique, de faire*

---

instances of the lexical inheritance were collected from expressions for family relationships, numbers, names of animals, metals, agricultural implements, etc. A series of authors, ranging from nineteenth century until recent times, devoted themselves to the compilation of such lists of common expressions, which are of an evident utility" (this volume, pg. xxii).

3. "Our enterprise is of a wholly different nature." (this volume, pg. xxiii)

4. "[W]e are not aware of much previous work with which we could have compared our arguments." (this volume, pg. xxv)

5. "I leave to others the historical and sociological aspects of these processes. If we deal with the Greek verb *hēgéomai* [ἡγέομαι] and its derivative *hēgemṓn* [ἡγεμών], this is in order to see how the notion of "hegemony" was established, but without regard to the fact that Greek *hēgmonia* came to mean successively the supremacy of an individual, or a nation, or the equivalent of a Roman *imperium*, etc. What concerns us is the connection, difficult to account for, between an expression of authority such as *hēgemṓn* and the verb *hēgéomai* which means "to think, to judge." In so doing, we explain the *signification*, leaving to others the problem of *designation*" (this volume, pg. xxiii).

apparaître une signification *là où, au départ, nous n'avons qu'une* désignation."[6] (ibid., pg. 12)

In a 1969 article on "Deux modèles linguistiques de la cité," which incorporates and continues a page of the *Vocabulaire*, the distinction between *signification* and *désignation* is further explained. In the inquiries on the relationship between language and society, Benveniste writes, one is usually constrained to correlate an element of the vocabulary to a certain social fact that it designates, on the completely arbitrary assumption that language is a kind of mirror of the society. The elements thus correlated refer to each other indefinitely, "*le terme* désignant *et le terme* désigné *ne contribuant, dans ce couplage un à un, qu'à une sorte d'inventaire lexicologique de la culture*"[7] (*Pr.* II, pg. 272). In the essay, the concept of "city" is apprehended through the relationship between the Latin *civis* and *civitas* and, in Greek, in the relation between the *polis* [πόλις] and *polites* [πολίτης]. The object of linguistic comparison is not here "*une substance, a donné lexical, sur lequel s'exerce socio-linguistique comparaison*"[8] (ibid.), but a purely linguistic relationship between a basic term and a derivative thereof. While in Latin the derivation moves from *civis* (conceived as "citizen") to *civitas* (the totality constituted by *cives*), in Greek this movement proceeds in exactly the opposite direction, from the *polis* (the city as an abstract entity or State) to *polites* (the one defined by the participation in the city, from which offices and privileges are bestowed). It is only through the manner in which this relationship is configured in language that one can possibly draw out enlightening consequences for the understanding of social reality to which these terms refer. This indicates that in Benveniste's research these terms are simply never scrutinized as elements of a *lexicon*, but as parts of a *speech* (*un discorso*). In the title of this *magnum opus*, the term *Vocabulaire* must be appreciated as entirely different from what is usually the case: not as a lexicon, but, according to its etymology, as something that deals with the living voice, a moving image of an enacted speech. This is why, by setting itself apart from works that are only

6. "The task is, by comparison and diachronic analysis, to elicit a 'signification,' whereas our starting point will merely be a 'designation.'" (this volume, pg. xxv)

7. "the designating term (*désignant*) and the designated or referred term (*désigné*) merely contribute, in this coupling, to a kind of lexical inventory of the culture."

8. "a substance, a lexical given, based on which a socio-linguistic comparison is produced"

similar in appearance, the *Vocabulaire* remains a totally unique work, which no research in the humanities could do without.

The opposition between designation and signification, which is the foundation of the *Vocabulaire,* becomes fully intelligible when correlated with the distinction between "semiotic" and "semantic" which Benveniste stubbornly retains, at least from his 1966 article "La forme et le sens dans le langage," and which perhaps found its most accomplished expression in the 1969 essay on "Sémiologie de la langue." At the origin of these novel developments is the recognition, early on in Benveniste, of the insuffiencies of Saussurean semiotics. If the definition of language as a "system of signs" is both at the origin of structuralism and allowed for the birth of a new science of language, according to Benveniste, "this was blocked by the same tool that created it: the *sign*" (*Pr*. II, pg. 66). Human language is, in fact, characterized by the capacity of combining two distinct modes of signification, which Benveniste calls the *semiotic* and the *semantic.*

> *Le sémiotique désigne le mode de signifiance qui est propre au signe linguistique et qui le constitue comme unité. . . . La seule question qu'un signe suscite pour être reconnu et celle de son existence, et celle-ci se décide par oui ou non: arbre, chanson, laver . . . et non orbre, vanson, laner. . . . Pris en lui-même, le signe est pure identité à soi, pure altérité à tout autre, base significant de la langue, matériau nécessaire de l'énonciation. Il existe quand il est reconnu comme signifiant par l'ensemble des membres de la communauté linguistique . . .* (ibid.: 64)[9]

The mode of signification is completely different from the semantic mode, through which one enters into the order of discourse.

> *Les problèmes qui se posent ici sont fonction de la langue comme productrice de messages. Or le message ne se réduit pas à une succession d'unités à identifier*

9. "The semiotic designates the mode of significance that is proper to the linguistic sign, and which constitutes it as a unit. . . . The only question by which the sign and its existence are recognized, is answered by yes or no: yes to *arbre, chanson, laver* . . . and no to *orbre, vanson, laner*. . . . Taken in itself, the sign is pure identity with itself, pure alterity to any other, the signifying basis of language (*langue*), the necessary stuff of enunciation. It exists when it is recognized as significant by all members of a linguistic community . . ."

> *séparément; ce n'est pas une addition de signes qui produit le sens, c'est au contraire le sens ("l'intenté"), conçu globalement, qui se réalise et se divise en "signes" particuliers, qui sont les* mots. (ibid.)[10]

There is a different criterion of validity which defines each of the two orders, and which refers to two distinct mental faculties: for a sign to achieve its validation, it is sufficient that it is *recognized* and perceived as identical; *speech* on the contrary, which implies a novel enunciation each time, must be *understood* (ibid., pp. 64–65).

Ultimately, the thought of Benveniste is defined by the paradoxical attempt to preserve the unity of these two incommensurable orders while at the same time underlining their radical heterogeneity. In his last lecture at the Collège de France, five days before the cerebral incident that was to forever silence him, Benveniste mentions again the opposition "*entre deux mondes et deux linguistiques*"[11] (*L.*, pg. 144). In a handwritten annotation on a loose piece of paper, the sober scholar feels obliged—in order to contrast these two worlds—to forge two nonexistent adjectives: "*Le langage n'est pas seulement* signalique . . . *il est* nuntial"[12] (ibid., pg. 51), it does not merely list signs in place of things, but proclaims or utters the *real.*

It is not surprising that in another handwritten annotation to the article on "Sémiologie de la langue," Benveniste refers to the study of the semantic mode as a "*phénoménologie de l'avenir*"[13] (*Pr.* II, ivi, pg. 50): taken as speech and not as a system of signs, language has to do each time with the production of a novel reality. In this sense there is an unexpected continuity between the late work of Benveniste and Chomskian linguistics. In fact, in an interview of 1968, it is Benveniste who suggests this: "*Lui (Chomsky) considère la langue comme*

10. "The problems posed here are a function of language as producer of messages. But the message is not reduced to a succession of units to be identified separately; it is not an addition of signs that produces meaning, rather it is the sense (the 'intended') conceived as a whole, which is realized and divided into individual 'signs,' i.e. the words."

11. "between two worlds and two linguistics"

12. "Language is not only *signalic* [informational] . . . it is *nuntial* [enunciatory]."

13. "phenomenology to come; phenomenology of the future"

production . . . il part de la parole comme produite"[14] (*Pr.* II, pg. 18). Focusing his attention on syntax, and on the speaker's ability to produce sentences, Chomsky, while decisively abandoning the ground of historical inquiry that had defined comparative grammar, has somehow taken over, and, in some manner embraced the legacy of its last great representative. Just so—and this is the ultimate enigma of the thought of Benveniste, and perhaps the rock on which it was shipwrecked—the essay "Sémiologie de la langue" concludes with the statement that between the two planes in which language is cleaved, between the "signalic" and the "enunciatory," there is no communication or passage: "*En réalité le monde du signe est clos. Du signe à la phrase il n'y a pas transition, ni par syntagmation ni autrement. Un hiatus les sépare*"[15] (*Pr.* II, pg. 65). If we start from language as a system of signs, one cannot speak.

This is the hiatus that Benveniste's last inquiries have so stubbornly addressed and attempted to overcome, although the project—announced at the very end of the essay (ibid., pg. 66)—of an "intralinguistic analysis" of the semantic and a "metasemantics" built on the semantics of enunciation, could not be brought to completion. From this perspective, the *Vocabulaire* is perhaps one of the few genuine attempts made in this direction. It wouldn't be incorrect to consider this comprehensive repertoire of Western institutions as a paradoxical attempt to transform a lexicon into a discourse. This masterpiece of the human sciences of the twentieth century is crossed by a genuinely poetic impulse. Indo-European institutions do not appear so much as "states" or as "substances" but as living relationships in motion in the minds of men who think and speak.

The remark, at the end of the essay, about a "semantic of enunciation" evokes another Benvenistian attempt to suture the fracture between the semiotic and the semantic. In a 1956 article on the nature of pronouns ("La nature des pronoms"), and, later, in a 1969 essay addressing the the formal apparatus of enunciation ("L'appareil formel de l'énonciation"), Benveniste had isolated in language a number of elements—the pronouns "I" and "you," the adverbs "here,"

14. "He (Chomsky) considers language as a production . . . it starts from the ground of speech as produced."

15. "In reality the world of the sign is closed. From the sign to the sentence there is no transition, neither in the syntagmatic sequence, nor otherwise. A dividing hiatus separates them."

"now," "today," "yesterday," "tomorrow," etc., which have the particular function of allowing the implementation of language by a speaker. Common to all of these items, which Benveniste calls "indicators of enunciation," is that they have not, like other symbols (for example the word "tree"), a lexical meaning and a predetermined real referent: they refer to something exclusively linguistic, that is, the instance of discourse that contains them: "'I' means the person who states the present instance of discourse containing 'I' . . . 'here' and 'now' define the spatial and temporal instance coextensive and contemporary with the instance of speech" (*Pr.*, I, pp. 252–53). Lacking, as they are, a material denotation, these particles are "*signes 'vides' . . . qui deviennent 'pleins' dès qu'un locuteur les assume dans chaque instance de son discours. . . . Leur rôle est de fournir l'instrument d'une conversion, qu'on peut appeler la conversion du langage en discours*"[16] (ibid., ivi, pg. 254).

Already in 1956 the difference between *semiotic* and *semantic*, though not thematically formulated, is clearly present in the necessity of the conversion of language into speech. Consistent with these premises, Benveniste's 1969 essay defines the enunciation as "*mise en fonctionnement de la langue par un acte individuel d'utilisation*"[17] (*Pr.*, II, pg. 80). The *enunciation marks*, which Roman Jakobson called *shifters*, specifying that they must be in an "existential relationship" with their subject, form a bridge that, bypassing the gap that divides them, allows for the passage from one to another level of language (Jakobson 1971: 132).

Consider the apparently perspicuous definition: *I* signifies the person who states the present instance of discourse containing "I." In which sense can we speak of an "existential relationship" and a "simultaneity" between the indicator and the instance of discourse that contains it? To merely think about these questions is to realize that contemporaneous and existential relationships are possible only on the assumption of a voice. The enunciation and the instance of speech—and the speaker in question—can be identified only through the speaking voice. As the poet Paul Valéry understood first, and perhaps more clearly than the linguists, the one who enunciates, the speaker, is first of all a voice, and the

16. "'empty' signs . . . that become 'full' when a speaker assumes them in every instance of his speech. . . . Their role is to provide the instrument of conversion, which we may call the conversion of language into discourse."

17. "an implementation of language through an individual act of use"

problem of the shifter is the problem of the relationship between voice and language. ["The I is the word associated with the voice. It is the meaning of the voice, the voice considered as a sign" (Valéry 1974: 466).]

It is strange that Benveniste, who also, when defining the formal apparatus of enunciation, mentions first the "*réalisation vocale de la langue*"[18] (*Pr.* II, pg. 80), considers subsequently the voice solely from the perspective of the individual peculiarities of the uttered sounds without being aware of the constitutive relationship between voice and enunciation. It is on motives of this abeyance that we should now reflect.

Benveniste's final course at the College is largely devoted to the problem of writing. After examining the transition from pictographic to alphabetic and syllabic writing, Benveniste investigates the effects that the introduction of this form of writing has had on language.

Overturning conventional wisdom, also attested to by Saussure, that language would be independent from writing because it is only a sign of speech (*parole*), he contends, on the contrary, that only writing has allowed language to establish itself as a system of signs: "*Elle (l'écriture) permêt à la langue de se sémiotiser elle-même. . . . Seule cette réalisation d'une forme secondaire du discours à permis de prendre conscience du discours dans ses éléments formels et d'en analyser tous les aspects*"[19] (*L.*, pg. 132). Between writing and language the rapport is not one of significance, but of *relays*: "*Le système primaire voix (la bouche)-oreille est relayé par le système secondaire main (l'inscription)-oeil. La main joue le rôle d'émetteur en traçant les lettres, et l'oeil devient récepteur en collectant les traces écrites. Entre la bouche et l'oreille, le lien est la* phonie *émise-entendue; entre la main (l'inscription) et l'oeil, le lien est la* graphie *tracée-lue*"[20] (ibid.). At this point, with a decisive move, Benveniste

18. "vocal realization of language"

19. "It (writing) allows language to "semioticize" itself . . . It is only by this realization of a secondary form of speech that we can get to know speech in its formal elements and analyze all of its aspects."

20. "The primary system, voice (or mouth)-to-ear is relayed by a secondary system, hand (or inscription)-to-eye. The hand acts as a transmitter by drawing letters, and the eye becomes the receiver, collecting written traces. Between the mouth and the ear, the link is *phonic*: emitted-heard; between the hand's inscription and the eye, the link is *graphic*: traced-read."

identifies *reading* as the true criterion of writing: while picture writing can be understood, but not read, writing is such only if you can read: "*tout est là: lire est le critère de l'écriture*"[21] (ibid., pg. 133). One may want to reflect on the implications of this singular reversal of the common perspective: the operation of writing is not simply to create signs for the voice, but to shift the word (*parole*, speech) from one sensory system to another, so as to allow the eye to read in the voice what the hand has written. Writing therefore moves language from the voice to the eye, from listening to reading, but it can do so only on the basis, tacitly accepted, that it is a sign of something that is already in language. The voice is excluded and removed from language, because writing has captured and included it in letters. The voice relayed through the hand and the eye is, as Hegel had suggested at the beginning of the *Phenomenology of Spirit*, an *Aufhebung*, a removal and a reserve.

In any case, the final lecture of Benveniste ends with the announcement of a new research program, one which implied an expansion of the notion of language: "*Nous sommes au début d'une réinterprétation de nombreux concepts (tous ceux qui touchemt à la langue). La notion même de langue doit être plus large: elle doit comprendre plus de notions qu'om ne lui an a attribuées*"[22] (ibid., pg. 135). Although the issue of voice is only negatively placed in these lectures on writing, it is indeed possible that the expansion of the notion of language may go in this direction.

The aphasia that afflicted Benveniste on December 6, 1969 was an *expressive aphasia*, which consequently affected only the vocal expression of language, and not reading and writing. Georges Redard, the student to whom we are indebted for a brief biography of Benveniste, informs us that his teacher, despite having regained the ability to write after some sessions of rehabilitation, had renounced writing "*et ne prendra plus la plume qu'en de rares occasions*"[23] (*L.*, pg. 154). Colleagues had questioned the reasons for this renunciation, which is not easily understood, since writing would have permitted the resumption and

21. "this is key: reading is the criterion of writing"

22. "We are at the very beginning of the reinterpretation of a number of concepts (all of which touch upon language). The very notion of language must be understood more broadly: it must include more notions than what we have usually associated to it."

23. "and only put pen to paper on rare occasions after that"

continuation of an intellectual activity so rudely interrupted. Father Menasce, an old friend from the Freiburg period, explained this reluctance by citing the difficulties in having to relearn the simplest things, things that had previously been done without effort, especially for a "walled-in and self-enclosed character" as Benveniste was (ibid.).

It is possible however, that, by abandoning the field of psychology (which cannot interest us here), we might not offer explanations, but rather point out certain similarities and coincidences. The last lectures on writing show that the loss of voice coincides with the moment that Benveniste understood that the semiotic dimension of language, from which he sought in every way to break away from, was based ultimately on the power of writing to "*relayer la voix*," to replace the voice. He could not ignore that the very idea that resides at the ground of Western reflection on language, that of articulation (*diarthrosis*), already clearly present in Aristotle, implies an obliteration of the voice in favor of *grammata*, of letters. The articulate voice (*phoné enarthros, vox articulata*) with which the ancient grammarians began their discussion, was, in fact, nothing other than a *phone engrammatos*, a voice into which letters have been inscribed (*vox quae scribi potest, quae litteris comprehendi potest*).

The singular power of *grammata* to replace the voice does not apply solely to the register of grammatical analysis. In the Jewish tradition in which Benveniste had been brought up, and that he stubbornly excluded from the scope of its research, this faculty is posited in a fundamental role. Although in *Deutoronomy* 4:19, it is read that "The Lord spoke to you from the fire: you hear the words, but saw no form, only a voice heard," in Judaism the primacy of the acoustic sphere is transferred to the sphere of writing. This is especially evident with regard to the name of God. The true name of God, the *shem-ha-mephorash*, can be written but cannot be pronounced. As Maimonide [Moses Maimonides] observes: "It is called *shem-ha-mephorash*, and it is only the name *tetragrammaton*, which is written, but that you can not pronounce according to the letters. . . . It merely indicates the essence of God" (Maimonide 1979: 148). And yet, according to the Cabbalists, this name *tetragrammaton* is the foundation of the Hebrew language, which can only be spoken by virtue of the unpronounceable name that is contained within it. The relay of the voice, through writing, pervades the entire tradition of the West, from Athens to Jerusalem.

Another Benveniste's student has reported that in one of her last visits to her teacher, he had inexplicably written on a sheet of paper the word "THEO" (*L.*, pg. 39–40). The spontaneous association the student makes at this point with the Hebrew *tetragrammaton* is not, perhaps, so arbitrary as it may seem at first glance.

REFERENCES

Benveniste, Émile. 1966. *Problèmes de linguistique générale*. Vol. I. Paris: Gallimard.

———. 1969. *Le vocabulaire des institutions indo-européennes*. Paris: Minuit.

———. 1974. *Problèmes de linguistique générale*. Vol. II. Paris: Gallimard.

———. 2012. *Dernières Leçons*. Paris: Gallimard-Seuil.

Hermann Usener, Hermann. (1896) 2000. *Götternamen: Versuch einer Lehre von der religiosen Begriffsbildung.* Frankfurt-am-Main: Klostermann.

Jakobson, Roman. 1971. "Shifters, verbal categories and the Russian Verb." In *Selected Wrtitings*. The Hague:

Maimonide, Moïse. 1979. *Le guide des égarés*. Lagrasse: Verdier.

Pictet, Adolphe. 1877. *Les origines indoeuropéennes: Essai de paléontologie linguistique*. Volume 1, 2nd Edition. Paris: Joël Cherbuliez.

Valéry, Paul. 1974. *Cahiers*. Paris: Gallimard.

Preface

This book, as its title indicates, is the outcome of research which had as its object a considerable portion of the Indo-European vocabulary. But the nature of the expressions studied, the method applied, and the analysis carried out, need elucidation.

Among the languages of the world are those belonging to the Indo-European family best lend themselves to wide-ranging study both in space and time. Such studies can also be pursued in the greatest variety and depth, since these languages extend from Central Asia to the Atlantic and are attested for a period of almost four millennia. Further, they are bound up with very ancient civilizations of varying degrees of development, some of them ranking among the richest which have ever existed. Finally, certain of these languages have produced an abundant literature of a very high order, and for this reason were for a long period the exclusive object of linguistic analysis.

Indo-European is defined as a family of languages, issuing from a common language, which have become differentiated by gradual separation. This constitutes a global event, immense in scope, which we are able to grasp in its entirety because in the course of time it broke up into a series of separate histories, each of them that of a particular language.

It is a very remarkable fact indeed that we are able to single out the peoples which partook in the original community and to designate them with certainty as Indo-Europeans to the exclusion of all others, because the stages of their migrations and their settlements remain unknown. The reason for this is language and language alone. The notion "Indo-European" is primarily a linguistic one, and if we are in a position to extend it so as to include other aspects of their civilization, this again is due solely to language. The concept of genetic relationship has in no other linguistic domain so precise a sense and such clear justification. We find in Indo-European a model of the correspondence relationships which delimit a family of languages and which allow us to reconstruct their earlier stages back to the initial one.

For the last hundred years the comparative study of the Indo-European languages has been pursued in two opposed but complementary directions. On the one hand, reconstructions are made from simple or complex elements, be they phonemes, whole words, or inflections, which are susceptible to comparison in different languages and so can make their contribution to a reconstruction of the common prototype. In this manner models are devised which in their turn form the basis of new reconstructions. On the other hand, we may proceed in the opposite direction: we start with a well-established Indo-European form and trace the forms which are descended from it. This method traces the paths of dialectical differentiation which resulted in new unities. At this stage, the elements inherited from a common language are found incorporated in independent structures which constitute individual languages. As such, they are transformed and assume new values within the oppositions by which they are created and which they determine. Thus we must not merely study the possibilities of reconstruction which summarize vast series of correspondences and reveal the structure of common elements; we must also examine the development of individual languages, because it is here that we have the productive medium, the source of the innovations which transform the ancient system. The comparative linguist thus moves between these two poles and his efforts are precisely directed towards distinguishing between conservation and innovation; he must account both for identities and differences.

To these general considerations, which the principle of linguistic comparison imposes, must be added the specific traits within the lexical domain, which are those concerned in the present study.

Very early on it occurred to specialists in the Indo-European field that correspondences between the vocabularies of ancient languages illustrate the principal aspects of a common culture, particularly of material culture. Thus instances of the lexical inheritance were collected from expressions for family relationships, numbers, names of animals, metals, agricultural implements, etc. A series of authors, ranging from nineteenth century until recent times, devoted themselves to the compilation of such lists of common expressions, which are of an evident utility.

Our enterprise is of a wholly different nature. No attempt has been made to compile yet one more inventory of Indo-European "facts" in so far as they are defined by lexical correspondences. On the contrary, most of the material we are concerned with does not belong to the common vocabulary. The forms involved are specifically expressions relating to institutions, but in particular languages; and what we propose to analyze is their genesis and their Indo-European connections. In other words, we propose to study the formation and organization of the vocabulary of institutions.

The expression "institution" is here understood in a wider sense: it includes not only the institutions proper, such as justice, government, religion, but also less obvious ones which are found in various techniques, ways of life, social relationships and the processes of speech and thought. The subject is truly boundless, the aim of our study being precisely to throw light on the genesis of the vocabulary which relates to it. Our starting point is usually one or the other of the Indo-European languages and the examples chosen come from the terms of pregnant value. Round the chosen datum, by an examination of its peculiarities of form and sense, its connections and oppositions, and following this, by comparison with related forms, we reconstruct the context in which it became specialized, often at the cost of profound transformations. In this way, we endeavor to restore a unity dissolved by processes of evolution, bringing buried structures to light and harmonizing the divergencies of technical usages. In so doing, we shall also demonstrate how languages reorganize their systems of distinctions and renew their semantic apparatus.

I leave to others the historical and sociological aspects of these processes. If we deal with the Greek verb *hēgéomai* and its derivative *hēgemṓn,* this is in order to see how the notion of "hegemony" was established, but without regard to the fact that Greek *hēgmonia* came to mean successively the supremacy of an individual, or a nation, or the equivalent of a Roman *imperium*, etc. What concerns us is the connection, difficult to account for, between an expression of authority such as *hēgemṓn* and the verb *hēgéomai* which means "to think, to judge." In so doing, we explain the *signification*, leaving to others the problem of *designation.* When we discuss the Germanic word *feudum* in connection with the terms of animal husbandry, feudalism itself is mentioned merely by preterition. This approach will make it easier for historians and sociologists to see what use they can make of analyses presented here, precisely because no extra-lingusitic presuppositions have intruded.

The task of the linguist is delimited in the following way. He takes his material from the vast store of established correspondences which are transferred without much change from one etymological dictionary to another. This material is of its very nature far from homogenous. Each separate fact comes from a different language and constitutes part of a distinct system which develops along unpredictable lines. The primary task is to demonstrate that these forms correspond to one another and that they are all direct continuations from some original form. This established, we have next to account for the differences, sometimes considerable, which they may present with regard to their phonetic appearance, their morphology, or their meaning. Thus we may equate the Armenian word *kʿun* "sleep" with Latin *somnus* "sleep," because we know the rules of correspondences which allow us to reconstruct a common form **swopno-*. It is possible to connect the Latin verb *carpo* "to gather" with the German noun *Herbst* "autumn," because *Herbst* in Old High German is *herbist*, and *herbist* may be traced back to a pre-Germanic form **karpisto-* which means "(time) most appropriate for harvesting" (cf. Engl. *harvest*); and this is confirmed by a third datum, the Greek noun *karpós* "fruits of the earth, harvest produce." But a simple comparison which seems acceptable at first sight, like the root *teks-* in Latin (in the verb *texo*) and the root *takṣ-* in Sanskrit, two forms which correspond exactly, runs into grave difficulties: Latin *texo* means "weave," whereas Sanskrit *takṣ* means "cut with an ax"; and one cannot see how one meaning can be derived from the other, nor from which original meaning either could have evolved, since "weaving" and "carpentry" seem irreducible to a common technique.

Even within the corpus of a single language, forms of the same word can be divided into distinct groups which seem hardly reconcilable. Thus from the root **bher-*, represented by *fero* in Latin, three separate groups of derivatives have evolved which form as many lexical families: (1) *fero* "to carry" in the sense of gestation, from which *forda* "pregnant female" is derived, linking up with *gesto*; (2) *fero* "carry" in the sense of "bring about, involve, entail" is used with reference to manifestations of chance, hence *fors*, *fortuna*, and their numerous derivatives, which also include the notion of "fortune, riches"; (3) *fero* "carry" in the sense of "carry off" forms a group with *ago* and can be defined as referring to seizure and booty. If we compare with this the forms derived from *bhar-* in Sanskrit, the picture becomes still more varied. To the senses just listed we must add those of "to carry" in the sense of "support, take care of," hence the derivative *bharir-* "husband"; from "carry" in connection with horse riding comes "ride," etc. Thus one only has to study in detail one of these groups to see that in every case they constitute a coherent lexical unit hinging on a central notion, readily supplying institutional expressions.

An attempt has been made to show how words which at first exhibited little differentiation progressively acquired specialized applications and evolved semantic subfamilies what reflect a profound evolution of institutions, as well as the emergence of new activities or ideas. Such developments within a particular language may also come to influence other languages through cultural contact. For instance, lexical relationships established by processes peculiar to Greek served as models through translation or simple borrowing from similar relationships in Latin.

We have tried to bring out the dual character peculiar to the phenomena here described. On the one hand, we are faced with the tangled web of developments which may take centuries ore even millennia and which the linguist must trace back to their primary causation; and on the other hand the investigator must try to bring out certain universal tendencies which govern these individual developments. We can understand them, apprehend their structure, and arrange them in a rational schema (1) if we are able to study them directly and avoid the pitfalls of simplified translations; (2) if we are able to establish certain essential distinctions, notably one on which we have repeatedly insisted, namely that between designation and signification. For without this distinction so many discussions of "meaning" end in confusion. The task is, by comparison and diachronic analysis, to elicit a "signification," whereas our starting point will merely be a "designation." By such a method the chronological approach is tantamount to an explanatory one.

The nature of this research determines the manner of exposition. No discussions of detail or bibliographical references will be found. The material used in the analyses is to be found in all the etymological dictionaries, but we are not aware of much previous work with which we could have compared our arguments. Everything here said stems from first-hand study of the facts used. We have made every effort to be intelligible to the non-specialist reader with strict regard for the exigencies of demonstration. But it must be conceded that the ramifications and complex connections which came to light in the course of this exploration make coherent exposition difficult. It is not easy to make neat distinctions between the various subjects under discussion. Inevitably there will be some overlapping between the various parts of this work because this is inherent in the facts of the vocabulary. All the same, we hope that those who are willing to follow this exposition for our researches to the end will find in it matter for more general considerations, especially on the possibility of applying certain of the proposed models to the study of languages or civilization in which, because of the lack of written documentation there is also a lack of historical perspective.

The present work is based on several series of lectures given at the Collége de France which M. Lucien Gerschel had been kind enough to collect. They have been thoroughly revised and recast, and the first draft has often been entirely rewritten and recent results have been added. Some parts had previously been the subject of detailed treatment in published articles and references to these are given. In order to clarify the exposition, we have followed the suggestion by M. Pierre Bourdieu, who read the whole manuscript and made some useful comments: each chapter is preceded by a brief abstract, which is the work of M. Jean Lallot. This scholar kindly prepared the manuscript for the press and also drew up the tables of languages and made the index.[1] I should like to thank him here for his help and the meticulous execution of his task.

Émile Benveniste

1. This volume contains a new index prepared by Katherine Herman. For M. Lallot's index, please consult previous versions of the English translation published by Faber & Faber, Ltd. (1973) and University of Miami Press (1973). —Eds.

List of Abbreviations

<	comes
>	becomes
Ags.	Anglo-Saxon
Arm.	Armenian
Av.	Avestan
Engl.	English
Fr.	French
Germ.	German
Got.	Gothic
Gr.	Greek
Hitt.	Hittite
Hom.	Homeric Greek
Icel.	Icelandic
I.E.	Indo-European
Il.	Iliad
I.Ir.	Indo-Iranian
Ir.	Iranian
Irl.	Irish
Ital.	Italian
Khot.	Khotanese
Lat.	Latin
Lett.	Lettish

Lith.	Lithuanian
MHG	Middle High German
Myc.	Mycenaean Greek
Od.	Odyssey
OE	Old English
OHG	Old High German
ON	Old Norse
OPruss.	Old Prussian
Osc.	Oscan
OSl.	Old Slavic
Pehl.	Pehlevi
R.V.	Rig-Veda
Skt.	Sanskrit
Sl.	Slavic
Sogd.	Sogdian
Tokh.	Tokharian
Umbr.	Umbrian
Ved.	Vedic Sanskrit

BOOK I

Economy

SECTION I

Livestock and Wealth

BOOK I, CHAPTER ONE

Male and Sire

Abstract. Contrary to traditional etymologies we have to distinguish between two ideas on the Indo-European level: (1) on the physical side that of the "male," i.e. **ers-*, and (2) on the functional side that of the "sire," i.e. **wers-*. A semantic rapprochement between these two roots is found only in Sanskrit and may be regarded as secondary.

We shall first consider some typical expressions relating to stock breeding. The object of study will be the differentiations characteristic of special techniques: on the lexical level, as elsewhere in linguistics, the differences are instructive, whether they are immediately apparent or come to light only after the analysis of a unitary group. An obvious and necessary distinction in a society of stock breeders is that between males and females. This is expressed in the vocabulary by words which can be regarded as common, since they appear in several languages, though not always with the same applications.

For the first word which we are going to study we have a series of correspondences which are relatively stable, although they admit of variations. They concern the word for "male":

Skt.	*r̥ṣabha*	Av.	*arəšan*	Gr.	ársēn, árrēn
	vr̥ṣabha		**varəšan*		

We postulate for Avestan a word which happens not to be attested but which is implied by its derivatives, i.e. Av. *varəšna–* 'masculine', *varəšni-* 'male', 'ram'.

In Greek, again, we find slightly deviant forms in the group *e(w)érsē (ἐ(w) ἑρση), hérsai (ἕρσαι)* (cf. the form with v in Indo-Iranian); the meaning is (1) "rain, dew" (in the singular), whereas (2) the plural is applied to animals. To this family belongs Lat. *verrēs*, the male of a particular species, with its corresponding forms in Baltic, Lit. *veȓšis*, Lett. *versis*. All these derive from the verbal root **wers-* exemplified in the Skt. *varṣati*, which means in the impersonal "it rains" (cf. *eérsē*); we may also adduce Irl. *frass* 'rain' < **wr̥stā.*

There is a morphological difference between the last forms and the preceding nominal forms, but this has not prevented etymologists from grouping them together. But this should give us pause: we have on the one hand forms with and without an initial *w* in Indo-Iranian. Similarly in Greek, whereas árrēn (ἄρρην) never has a *w*, Homeric metre implies that *eérsē* = *ewérsē*, which develops to *hérsai*.

Comparatists have interpreted this disagreement as an alternation. But since there are no compelling reasons to follow them, we should practice the utmost economy in the use of hypothetical "alternations."

In Indo-European morphology there is no principle which would permit us to associate forms without *w-* with those containing a *w-*. To postulate a unified group here is gratuitous; there is no other example of this alternation *w-*/zero. As for the meaning of the words thus associated, where an analysis is possible, it will be seen that there are difficulties in bringing the words together.

In Sanskrit, *vr̥ṣabha-* and *r̥ṣabha-* attest the same manner of formation and the same notion. This is that of the "mythological bull" and "the male in general," the epithet of gods and heroes alike. In Avestan, on the other hand, the two words (with or without *w*) have divergent meanings, and this disaccord is instructive outside Indo-Iranian: in Iranian *arəšan* and **varəšan* are absolutely separate words. *Arəšan* in the Avestan texts is always opposed to a word which designates the female, this being sometimes *xšaθrī* (a purely Iranian term), but usually *daēnu*. This latter expression, which is Indo-Iranian (cf. Skt. *dhenu*), belongs to the group of Greek *thẽlus* (cf. the Sanskrit root *dhay-* 'suckle, nourish'). Thus we have here a specific designation, a functional one, for the female animal.

The opposition of *arəšan-* : *daēnu-* is constant. In the lists of animals we find the two series of terms enumerated in the same order:

"horse"	*aspa-arəšan-*	*aspa-daēnu-*
"camel"	*uštra-arəšan-*	*uštra-daēnu-*
"bovine"	*gau-arəšan-*	*gau-daēnu-*

The Avestan *arəšan* never designates any particular species, as does the Sanskrit *ṛṣabha* which, without being the exclusive word for bull, frequently has this meaning. This is quite different from *arəšan*; it simply denotes the male as opposed to the female.

This opposition male/female may appear in a slightly different lexical guise in Avestan. For human beings, *nar/xšaθrī* are used, where the latter term looks like the feminine form of the adjective meaning 'royal', that is, 'queen'. This may appear somewhat strange, but it is not inconceivable if we think of the correspondence between Greek *gunḗ* 'woman' and English queen. There are some slight variants such as *nar/strī*, where the second term is the Indo-Iranian name for "woman," cf. in the compounds *strīnāman* (cf. Lat. *nōmen*) 'of female sex', while *xšaθrī* is sometimes transferred to the animal world. All this is quite clear; the opposition is unambiguous. Outside Iranian, *arəšan* has an exact equivalent in the Greek ársēn, árrēn with precisely the same sense as in Avestan: it denotes the male as opposed to the female, árrēn contrasts with *thễlus*. The etymological identity of the two terms argues an Indo-European origin.

Let us now consider the Avestan word **varəšan*. It expresses a different notion, that of the sire. It is not the characteristic of a special class of beings, but an epithet of functional value. **Varəšan* (the actual form is *varəšni-*) is used with the name for sheep to designate the "ram": *maēša-varəšni-*. This combination leaves no doubt as to its meaning. Apart from this, there is also historical testimony: **varəšan*, by regular sound development, yielded Persian *gušan*, and this signifies not the "male" (represented in Persian by a form derived from *nar*) but the "sire."

Outside Iranian, Latin *verrēs* is the exact counterpart in form and meaning. It does not denote the "male," the male pig being called *sūs* (a word to which we shall return later) but the "sire." *Verrēs*, 'boar', is used in exactly the same way as the corresponding Avestan form **varəšan*.

What conclusion can we draw from these observations? **Ers-* and **wers-*, which were regarded as identical, are two different forms, absolutely distinct both in meaning and morphology. Here we have two words which rhyme, which may be superimposed, but which in reality belong to two independent families. One designates the "male" as opposed to the "female"; the other denotes a function, that of the "sire" of a flock or herd and not a species, like the first. It is only in Sanskrit that there was a close rapprochement between *ṛṣabha-* and *vṛṣabha-*. Because of a mythology in which the bull has a prominent place and in virtue of a style in which high-flown epithets abound, the two terms became so far assimilated that the first assumed a suffix which belongs properly only to the second.

Such is our first conclusion. It can be given further precision by recourse to a distinct lexical development. There is probably some connection between Greek *eérsē* and *hérsai*. How can this be defined? The singular *eérsē* denotes the light rain of the morning, dew. Apart from this we have the Homeric plural form *hérsai*, which is only attested once (Od. 9,222): in the cave of Polyphemus there is a sheep-fold in which the animals are arranged in age groups, from the adults to the very youngest—the *hérsai*. Now, *hérsai* is the plural of *eérsē*. To understand this peculiar association, we can adduce some parallels in Greek: *drósos* means "dew drop," but in Aeschylus *drósos* in the plural denotes young animals. There is a third example of the same kind: *psakás*, which means "fine rain," has a derivative *psákalon*, 'the newly-born of an animal'. This lexical relationship may be explained as follows. The tiny newly-born animals are like dew, the fresh little drops which have just fallen. Such a development of meaning, peculiar to Greek, would probably not have taken place if **wers-* had first been the name of an animal, considered as the "male." It seems therefore now to be established that we must posit for Indo-European a distinction between the two different notions and two series of terms. It was only in Indic that a rapprochement was effected with the result that they became similar in form. Everywhere else we find two distinct lexical items: one, **ers-*, designating the male, (e.g. Greek *árrēn*), and the other **wers-* in which the original notion of rain as a fertilizing liquid was transformed into that of "sire."

BOOK I, CHAPTER TWO

A Lexical Opposition in Need of Revision
sūs and *porcus*

Abstract. It is usually held that: 1) IE **porko-* (Latin *porcus*) denotes the domestic pig as opposed to the wild animal, **sū-* (Lat. *sūs*); 2) The dialect distribution of **porko-* leads to the conclusion that only the European tribes practiced pig-breeding.

However, a careful examination shows 1) that in all languages, and particularly in Latin, where the opposition **sū-* : **porko-* was maintained, both these terms applied to the domesticated species, **porko-* designating the piglet as opposed to the adult **sū-*; 2) that **porko-* is in fact also attested in the oriental part of the Indo-European world. Consequently pig-breeding must be attributed to the Indo-Europeans, but it was eliminated at an early date in India and Iran.

The Latin term *verrēs* forms part of a group of words which refer to a particular species of animals, the pig. An attempt will be made to define the relations between the terms in this series of animal words in Latin, i.e. *verrēs*, *sūs*, and *porcus*.

Sūs and *porcus* have equal claim to Indo-European status, since both have correspondents in the majority of Indo-European languages. What is the relation between their senses? The distinction is generally held to be between the wild and the domesticated animal: *sūs* meaning the pig-species in general in its wild form, the wild boar, while *porcus* denoted exclusively the domesticated animal.

This is supposed to be a very important distinction from the point of view of the material culture of the Indo-Europeans, because whereas *sūs* is common to all dialects from Indo-Iranian to Irish, *porcus* is restricted to the European area of Indo-European and does not occur in Indo-Iranian. This difference suggests that Indo-Europeans were not acquainted with the domestic pig and that domestication did not take place until after the unity of the Indo-European people had been disrupted and some tribes had established themselves in Europe.

Today we might wonder how it came about that this interpretation was regarded as self-evident so that scholars came to believe that the difference between *sūs* and *porcus* reflected a distinction between the wild and the domesticated pig. Let us scrutinize those Latin authors who wrote on agricultural themes—Cato, Varro, Columella—and who used the language of the countryside. For them, *sūs* denoted both the domestic and the wild animal. *Sūs* is certainly used with reference to the wild pig, but the same word in Varro is always applied to the domestic species: the *minores pecudes*, the small animals, comprise *ovis* 'sheep', *capra* 'goat', *sūs* 'pig', and they are all domestic animals.

A further proof is found in the term *suovetaurilia*, which designated the great sacrifice of the triple lustration, in which three symbolic animals figure. This technical term combines two species (*ovis*, *taurus*), which were certainly domesticated, with *sūs*, and this presumably indicates that this was likewise a domesticated animal. This conclusion is confirmed by the fact that in Rome no wild animals were ever sacrificed.

Similarly in Greek, there is an abundance of examples in which *hûs* (ὗς = Lat. *sūs*) applies to the domestic animal. Certainly a distinction was made between the wild and domestic species, but only by means of an added epithet. The wild pig is called *hûs ágrios* as contrasted with the domesticated animal. We must conclude that it was in prehistoric times before the emergence of Latin that Indo-European **sū-* = Greek *hûs* became applied to the useful species, i.e. the domesticated one.

In the other Indo-European dialects, the word is used in a different way. In Indo-Iranian *sū-* denoted the wild pig. The historic forms Sanskrit *sūkara*, Avestan *hū-* are formed from an identical stem. According to Bloomfield, one must begin with *sūka-*, this being an ancient stem which received a suffix *-ra*, attached on the model of other animal names, such as *vyaghra* 'tiger'. *Sūka-ra* was analyzed as *sū+kara* 'the animal which makes *sū*' by a kind of popular etymology. Besides Av. *hū*, a form *xūk* is met in Iranian, and this presupposes **hūkka*. Thus Indo-Iranian had a form with a suffix *-k* which, over the domain of Indic and Avestan, referred only to the wild species. The reason is that neither in India nor in Persia were pigs bred in ancient times. There is no mention of pig breeding in our texts. Yet against this, from the evidence of Latin, we have seen that in the European sector the domestication of the pig took place well before Latin was constituted, the generic name being already employed for the domesticated animal. It is this sense of "domesticated pig" which is almost exclusively used in Latin. *Sūs* refers to the wild boar only in those contexts where the generic term suffices.

In studying the meaning of words which are peculiar to Latin with reference to the pig, a problem emerges: a minor one at first sight, but with consequences which turn out to be of considerable importance. Since *sūs* designates the species in general and more especially the domestic species, the distinction usually drawn disappears. Since both words refer to the domestic pig, *sūs* and *porcus* become synonymous. This pleonasm is surprising and provokes closer examination of the testimony by which the meaning of *porcus* is established (and not the translations, which are unanimous on this point).

We may begin with one of the terms in which the name of the animal appears in a stock expression, *suovetaurilia*, an expression already quoted, which implies the sacral combination of three animals sacrificed on the occasion of a lustration ceremony. The expression *suovetaurilia* is said to be irregular in a number of ways. We have 1) a compound containing a group of three terms; but similar compounds are attested in the Indo-European languages, cf. Gr. *nukhthḗmeron*, 'a night and a day'. Thus the objection is invalid; 2) a phonetic difficulty, because the form is *ove* instead of *ovi*.

This can be resolved if we give an exact determination of its signification and site it in the conditions in which it was constituted. It is no ordinary compound word, but a juxtaposition comprising not nominal stems, but case forms. It is a series of three ablatives: **sū*, the ancient ablative of *sūs* (cf. *sūbus*, the ancient plural form); *ove*, a regular ablative, and finally *taurō*. There are thus three ablatives in juxtaposition and the whole being treated as a single word with attachment of the adjectival suffix *-ilis*, *-ilia* added to the last word with elision of the case ending. Why this juxtaposition? Because it is taken from the ritual expression in which the name of the sacrificial animal is in the ablative: *sū facere* 'to sacrifice *by means* of an animal' and not the animal itself. *Facere* + the ablative is certainly the ancient construction. Therefore it meant to perform the cult act *by means* of these three animals, an ancient sacrificial grouping of these three species, where *sūs* is the name for the porcine species. We must reread a chapter of the *De Agricultura* by Cato (141), the famous text which describes the way in which the lustration of the fields, a ceremony of a private nature, was carried out. In this text, which has often been read, quoted and used, we are expressly concerned with the *suovetaurilia*. In proceeding to the sacrifice, the owner of the field must pronounce these words: *macte suovetaurilibus lactentibus esto*. This is a prayer of Mars that he should accept these *suovetaurilia lactentia*, three "suckling" animals, that is, young ones. This prayer is repeated a second time in these terms: *Mars pater, eiusdem rei ergo, macte hisce suovetaurilibus lactentibus esto*. Cato continues: "when you sacrifice the *porcus*, the *agnus*, the *vitulus*, you must..." (*ubi porcum immolabis, agnum vitulumque, oportet...*) The sacrifices in fact comprise three animals which this time are called *porcus*, *agnus*, *vitulus*. Let us compare the terms of the nominal sacrifice *sūs*, *ovis*, *taurus* with that of the actual offering, *porcus*, *agnus*, *vitulus*. These expressions follow each other in exactly the same order and they indicate the sacrificial animals. It follows that *vitulus* is the young of the *taurus*, *agnus* the young of the *ovis*, and *porcus* the young of the *sūs*. This is deduced in quasi-mathematical manner by superimposing the ritual expressions on the actual species of the sacrifice. The conclusion is inescapable that *porcus* can only mean piglet. The difference between *sūs* and *porcus* is not between the wild animal and the domesticated one: it is a difference in age, *sūs* being the adult and *porcus* the young animal.

We have another text which makes this point. In the *De re rustica* of Varro (Book II, ch. 1) the author gives advice to breeders on the raising of animals. Some months must elapse before the young animals are weaned: the *agni* at four months, the *haedi* at three months, and the *porci* at two months. Thus *porcus* is paralleled with *agnus* and *haedus*. There are so many examples of this kind that the greater part of the chapter could be quoted. Varro makes the point that one can tell *sues* of good stock *a progenie*: *si multos* ***porcos*** *pariunt*, 'if they produce plenty of *porci*'. As to feeding, it is the custom to leave the *porci* two months *cum matribus*. A little further on we read: ***porci*** *qui nati hieme fiunt exiles propter frigora*, 'the *porci* born in the winter...' Here the association of *porcus* and *mater* speaks for itself.

In an archaic expression of the religious vocabulary, the *porci* which are ten days old *habentur puri* 'are considered pure', and for this reason they are called "*sacres*" (the ancient form, instead of *sacri*, from the adjective **sacris*); *sacres porci*, a very old expression, "the pigs which are ten days old." Similarly, *lactens porcus* appears frequently, but we never encounter **lactens sūs*. A diminutive *porculus* or *porcellus* exists, just as one finds *agnus*/*agnellus*, *vitus*/*vitellus*; but there is no word **sūculus*, since the name for the adult animal does not admit a diminutive. Thus the meaning of *porcus*, which is found perhaps forty times in this text, is constant. The meaning does not vary in later usage. Cicero uses it in the same sense: with reference to a *villa* ('estate') he writes: "*abundat porco, haedo, agno,*" an expression where *porci* figure along with the other young animals, *haedi* and *agni*, kids and lambs. We know two words for swine-herd: *sūbulcus* 'he who occupies himself with *sues*' (parallel with *būbulcus*) and *porculator*. What reason was there to coin two separate expressions if the two words *sūs* and *porcus* had the same meaning? In fact the *porculator* looks after the young pigs (piglets), which need special treatment, while the *sūbulcus* looks after the adult pigs. We have thus established that throughout ancient Latin down to the classical period *porcus* designated only the piglet. The difference is now clear. What is astonishing is that this fact was not seen earlier and that an erroneous translation of such a common term as *porcus* has endured for so long. The relation of *sūs* to *porcus* is exactly the same as that of Greek *hū̂s*, *sūs* (ὗς, σῦς) to *khoîros* (χοῖρος). This difference is of great importance. In public and private cult there were no animals more commonly offered than the *porcus*, the young pig.

The Romans already knew what we have just discovered. Varro gives us, with a fanciful etymology, precisely the equivalents in the two languages: *R.R.* II, 1: "***porcus*** *graecum est nomen…quod nunc eum vocant* ***khoîron***." He thus knew that *porcus* meant the same as *khoîros*. But *porcus* exists not only in Latin; it is also found in Italic. The contrast between *si* and *purka* is the same in Umbrian in a ritual text where both figure. We must see what this opposition signifies in Umbrian.

The translation of the Iguvine Tables is usually expressed in Latin so that it is not particularly lucid. But we must consider the adjectives which accompany *si* and *porko*. *Si* is found with *kumia*, translated as '*gravida*', and also with *filiu*, translated as '*lactens*'; and on the other hand there is *purka*. Now the combination of *lactens* with *sūs* is impossible in Latin and the difference in Umbrian becomes incomprehensible. If the Umbrian word *si* can signify an animal which may be *gravida* 'pregnant' as well as *lactens* 'suckling', what can *porko* mean? If the same word applies both to the adult and to the newly born animal, the difference of designation is no longer justifiable, and the other word *purka* becomes redundant.

In a ritual text of such precision, why is there this difference, in one place *si* and in another *purka*? The crux of the problem lies in the meaning of *filiu*. There is another possibility than that of the traditional translation. Two interpretations of *filiu* are possible: one as *lactens* 'suckling', but it is also possible to think of *lactans* 'in milk' ("she who suckles"). In fact the Umbrian *filiu* is related to Greek *thēlus* and to *fēmina*, which in Latin means "she who suckles," also the meaning of Greek *thēlus*. In Irish and Lithuanian a form with the suffix *l* made from the same root **dhē-* is used with reference to the mother: Lith. *pirm-delú* 'animal which suckles for the first time'. Thus we may take the Umbrian *filiu* not as '*lactens*' but as '*lactans*'. The sow is sometimes spoken of as "*gravida*" and sometimes as "*lactans*," according to whether the animal is still pregnant or has already farrowed. It follows that *purka* is the term for the young pig; it is the piglet, just like the Latin *porcus*, and the situation which at first was quite incomprehensible becomes intelligible. We may thus be assured that the difference illustrated by both Latin and Umbrian is an inherited lexical difference. It is in fact prior to Italic.

In Celtic, the corresponding word for *porcus*, phonetically Irl. *orc*, is always cited with the group of *porcus* and given the translation "pig." But the precision which we expect is given by the detailed dictionary of the Irish Academy, which translates *orc* as "young pig." Thus we see that both Italic and Celtic show solidarity in offering one and the same meaning.

In Germanic, the two corresponding words are represented by derivatives, on the one hand by *swein* (German *Schwein*) and on the other by *farh*, *farhili* (German *Ferkel*). Here the modern forms already indicate the distinction: *Ferkel* is the piglet, specifically a diminutive form, whereas *swein* 'pig', derived from *sū-*, does not show a diminutive formation. The Germanic word corresponding to *porcus* immediately attests the sense of "young pig" which it has preserved. Finally, in Slavic and Baltic, the Lithuanian *paršas*, Sl. *pracęs* (from which comes the Russian *porosënok*, which is a diminutive) is opposed to *svin*. Now the Slavic and Baltic **parša-* corresponding to *porcus* has the sense of "piglet." We thus have the same contrast in Slavic as in Germanic. This demonstration could have been pursued from two different angles, but whether we start from Germanic or Slavic, the same conclusion is reached as emerged from an unprejudiced study of the Latin evidence. At all events the testimony is consistent and the lexical situation seems identical in all western dialects of Indo-European.

It is, however, on the Indo-European level that the contrast between the two terms poses a new problem. The distribution of the two forms is unequal. The form **sū-* is common Indo-European. It is attested in Indo-Iranian as well as all the strictly "European" dialects, whereas **porko-* does not appear in Indo-Iranian but only in the European languages.

From this dialect distribution and from the meaning attributed to **sū-* and **porko-* the conclusion has been drawn that the Indo-European community was not acquainted with the pig except as a wild species. The very meaning of *porcus*, so it was believed, implied that the domestication had only begun in Europe after the settlement of certain ethnic groups.

But the restored signification of these terms transforms the problem. It assumes a new aspect, since the opposition is adult/newly-born and not wild/domesticated. Why then is the name for the newly-born animal (**porko-*) not co-extensive with that of the adult (**sū-*)? But is there in fact this unequal distribution of *sūs* and *porcus*? The whole chain of reasoning rests on the allegation that no trace of *porcus* has been found in Indo-Iranian territory. In fact, the problem has been much advanced and today the traditional affirmation must be challenged.

The same word **porkos* is attested in an area that is geographically adjoining but linguistically quite different, in Finno-Ugrian, by the Finnish word *porsas*, Mordvinian *purts* and Zyrenian *porś*. Scholars are agreed in regarding this as a common borrowing by the Finno-Ugrian languages from a form in *-s* at some stage of Indo-European, but at what date did this word penetrate into Finno-Ugrian?

We may begin by noting that the meaning is certain: "piglet, small pig" in Finnish; in the other languages, the lexica are less precise, but this meaning is probable. The connection with Indo-European forms has been noted and the possible chronology of the borrowing has been discussed. What seems certain is that *porsas* in Finnish presupposes a stem in *-o*; the final *-as* is a Finnish adaptation of a stem in *-o*, replaced by *a*, because, from ancestral Finno-Ugrian times, *o* was not permitted in the second syllable: **porso* becomes *porsa*. The root **porso* exhibits a characteristic palatalization of the *k* into *s*. The original form borrowed into Finno-Ugrian was marked by this palatalization before the change of the root *o* into *a*, which is characteristic of Indo-Iranian. The theoretical Indo-Iranian form is **parśa*, and this would appear in Indic as **parśa* and in Iranian as **parsa*. The phonetic shape of the Finno-Ugrian borrowing takes us back to the stage prior to Indo-Iranian, but posterior to the common Indo-European, where the word possessed *a-k-*. It was therefore an ancient dialect form which would precede the separation of Indo-Iranian. This is the conclusion reached by Finno-Ugrian specialists. But one difficulty has given them pause: the pre-Indo-Iranian form implied by the borrowing is not attested in Indo-Iranian. They have therefore hesitated to draw any firm conclusion.

But now we have the form in the oriental region. A Middle Iranian dialect of Eastern Iranian, called Khotanese, the knowledge of which goes back only a few years, has yielded evidence for the existence and the meaning of a word *pasa*, gen. *pasä*, which designates the pig. The meaning is certain because the texts are translated from Sanskrit or Tibetan, in which there occur expressions for dates borrowed from the animal cycle: there is a year or month of "the pig." Thus Khotanese has restored to us the expected Indo-Iranian form: *parśa*, and it furnishes the proof that **porko-* was also known in Indo-Iranian territory.

The negative argument can thus no longer be sustained. True, there is no trace of **porko-* in Indic, but a word of this kind is exposed to accidents. There are peoples who, for religious reasons, exclude this animal from sacrifice and consumption, whereas it was esteemed by the peoples of Europe. We now know that the word did exist in Iranian. There is now no difficulty in admitting in principle that the Indo-European stem **porko-* was common to all dialects. We have established its presence in Eastern Iranian and confirmation has been given by the Finno-Ugrian borrowings.

True, we are not yet able to define the exact meaning of the term in Khotanese, a language not attested until the seventh or eighth century of our era. But since **sū-* is common to Indo-Iranian and the European languages, if **porko-* was also used in Iranian, it must have been distinct from the word **sū-*. The features which are presumed or are established indirectly accord with those taken from textual usage.

All this, namely the existence of two words employed since the European period, and the difference of sense which we have underlined, allows us to state that the common Indo-European word **porko-* meant "the young pig." The negative conclusion of traditional doctrine can no longer be upheld: there was after all Indo-European domestication of the pig. This is what the vocabulary reveals by the distinction made between *sūs* and *porcus*, which runs parallel with that encountered in the names for the other domestic animals.

Another point may be made, namely that the lexical distinction made between *sūs* and *porcus* may later be expressed by different terms. The opposition *sūs* : *porcus* persists throughout the whole of Latinity until after the classical period; but later the proper sense of *sūs* was transferred to *porcus*, which took over the function of *sūs*. At that moment *sūs* disappeared.

In the Glosses of Reichenau, which give such precious testimony for the transition of Latin to French, the term *sūs* is glossed as '*porcus salvaticus*' (= wild pig). Thus *sūs* had been limited to the meaning of "wild pig" and *porcus* had taken its place as the name for "pig." But it was necessary to coin a term to replace *porcus* in its original sense: hence *porcellus*, French *pourceau*.

Later, under the influence of the language of the Gospels, where *porcellus* means "pig," recourse was had to a technical term for the young animal, French *goret*. There is an innovation in the expression for the distinction, but the distinction is preserved, for it is important to maintain a distinction which is anchored in an extra-linguistic reality—animal husbandry.

BOOK I, CHAPTER THREE

Próbaton and the Homeric Economy

Abstract. It has been maintained that the term *próbaton*, created by the Greeks, meant small animals, especially the "sheep," since in a mixed flock the sheep tend to walk in front (*pro-baínein*).

It will be shown that this thesis is untenable; 1) *próbaton*, to begin with, designated the large as well as the small animals. 2) the Greeks had no mixed flocks. 3) *probaínein* does not mean "walk in front."

In fact, *próbaton*, a singular of *próbata*, is to be connected with *próbasis* '(movable) wealth'. It was because the sheep constituted "movable wealth" par excellence as opposed to possession which were stored in chests (*keimḗlia*), that it was called "*próbaton*."

We have just considered a problem which is raised by the coexistence of several terms which appear to have the same meaning within one and the same language or in a number of Indo-European languages.

An analogous situation is present in Greek, where we also find two terms for the name of another species, the sheep: *ówis* (ὄϝις) and *próbaton* (πρόβατον). The two terms both designate the sheep from the time of the earliest texts.

The first is an ancient word of the common vocabulary, exactly preserved in Greek, Latin and Sanskrit, which is now attested in Luvian in the form of *hawi-*.

The second is confined to Greek and the form itself gives grounds for believing that it is a relatively late creation.

In Homer, *ówis* and *próbaton* coexist, but subsequently *ówis* disappeared in favor of *próbaton*, which was the only one to survive until modern times. The problem which poses itself is why there should be two distinct terms. What was the meaning of the new term? As for the first, we can do no more than note that it was a common Indo-European word of the ancestral Indo-European vocabulary, and is not susceptible to further analysis.

As for the second word, *próbaton*, considered on its own without regard to its meaning, there is an evident connection with *probaínō* (προβαίνω) 'to walk in advance'. But what exactly is this connection between "sheep" and "walking" and how can we interpret it? The explanation given by the comparative linguist Lommel[1] has won general acceptance: *probaínō* means "walk in front"; *próbaton* designates the small animals because they "walk in front"; but in front of what? In certain African countries, we are told, herds and flocks are formed by assembling animals of various species and it is the sheep which walk at the head. As a consequence of this *próbaton* would have designated the animals which walk at the head of a mixed herd of animals. This explanation, approved by Wackernagel, has achieved orthodoxy; for instance, it figures in Liddell and Scott's lexicon.

It is the history of this term which we will now take up again to see whether, from a study of its usage, the development of its meaning in the course of an evolution which we can follow step by step confirms the proposed explanation.

It must be noted at the outset that the form *próbaton* is not the most common one. The first examples are in the plural, *tà próbata*, and the singular is unknown at an early date. Only the plural is used in Homer and Herodotus. Especially in Herodotus, thirty-one examples of the plural are found but not a single one of the singular. In the Homeric poems, if one animal is referred to, it is *óïs* which is used and never *próbaton*; in fact, the only Homeric form is *próbata*—and this is not merely a morphological detail. We should not speak of a plural but rather of a collective: *tà próbata*. It follows that the form *próbaton* is what is called a singulative; we may compare the relationship *tálanta* to *tálanton* and *dákrua* to *dákruon*. The generic names for animals are more frequently collectives, e.g. *tà zōa*, which occurs earlier than *tò zôon*.

1. *Zeitschrift für Vergleichende Sprachforschung*, 1914, 46–54.

A new term of Greek coinage which has persisted down to modern times is *tò álogon* which, early in our era, occurs with the specialized meaning of "horse" in the papyri. We must regard *tò álogon* as the singulative of *tà áloga* 'the beasts', those "deprived of reason," the term given to the most common or most useful of animals, that is, the horse. Similarly, in Latin, *animalia* is older than *animal*. This is a very common type of designation: a large proportion of animal names are collectives.

It remains to give precision to the morphological relationships between *tà próbata* and *probaínō*. At first sight *próbaton* or *próbata* seems to be a compound form in *-batos*, this being a verbal adjective derived from *baínō*. But if this were so, it would not have its normal meaning: for instance, *ábatos*, *dúsbatos*, *diábatos* all have a passive sense, that is to say, "that which is crossed," with a restriction of sense indicated by the first member of the composite word, or rather "that which can be crossed." The passive voice is also apparent in the simple adjective *batós* (βατός) 'accessible'. A different meaning appears in the composites like *hupsíbatos*, where *-batos* has an active meaning ("one who has climbed high, has gone on high").

But neither the active nor the passive sense fits the suggested interpretation of *próbaton*, in which the second element functions as a present participle "which walks." The fact is that the ancient grammarians make a distinction between *próbaton* and the adjectives in *-batos*: according to them, the plural dative of *próbaton* is *próbasi* (πρόβασι). Here we have a consonantal stem: *pro-bat-* (προ-βατ). This is the only form which explains the dative and it is this which must be postulated. Such a form can be justified from a morphological point of view because there are root forms suffixed by *-t-* (cf. Skr. *-jit-*,*kṣit-*) which Greek adapted to a suffixal type and to an inflectional category which was more familiar. Compared with the Sanskrit *pari-kṣit-*, we have Greek *periktit-ai* (*Od.* 11, 288); cf. Lat. *sacer-dōt-*. Where the Greek had *-thet-* this became normalized as *-thét-ēs*, this being one of the processes for converting archaic and aberrant forms to a more normal type. An analogous phenomenon, though by a different process, is seen in the case of *próbaton*: here recourse was had to thematization (facilitated by *probatá*) to normalize the original form in *-bat-* which is implicit in the dative plural *próbasi* and also in the present participial function of the word.

Now that we have considered the morphology with greater precision, we may turn to the problem of meaning. As we have seen, according to Lommel, *próbata* designated small animals, the sheep, so named because "they walk at the head" of the herd. What is thus essential to Lommel's thesis is that *próbata* designated the "small animals." But is this really the use of the word? Far from it! We have at our disposal many examples in the literary texts and in ancient dialect epigraphy.

First in Homer, *Il.* 23, 550: "you have in your house much gold, bronze, *próbata* and servants." What does *próbata* mean here? Evidently "animals" in general, since no species is mentioned. Herodotus writes τὰ λεπτὰ τῶν προβάτων to specify "the small animals," which would be absurd if *próbata* already meant "small animals." Consequently what is meant are animals as such without any specification as to kind of size. After scrutiny of all the examples in Herodotus we can affirm that it is applied to live-stock, large or small. In Hippocrates, who wrote in the ancient Ionian dialect and whose vocabulary is of great interest, we find a clear opposition between *próbata* and *ánthrōpoi*, live-stock and men.

Next comes a decisive fact from an Arcadian inscription relating to Athene Alea at Tegea, τὸ μὲν μέζον πρόβατον…τὸ δὲ μεῖον 'the large and small *próbaton*', and there is another similar example with μεῖος and μεῖζων. All this is a clear indication that the word designates live-stock in general without further specification. It is possible to fix the moment when the sense became restricted to mean "small animals," and it was in Attic that this semantic restriction took place.

There is no need to labor this point further: if *próbata* originally and everywhere designated "live-stock" in general, it becomes impossible to base the prehistory of the term on the sense "small live-stock," this being a comparatively late development. A second point may be made: what warrant have we that in ancient Greece large mixed herds existed, at the head of which the sheep walked? This custom can be observed, we are told, in Africa. But was it pastoral custom precisely in Greece to assemble large herds of different animals?

We have no testimony about the composition of flocks, and all we have to do is to recall some familiar facts of Greek vocabulary. There is no single noun or a single compound for an assembly of animals. Greek uses different specific terms according to the kind of animals, with specific words for the respective herdsmen:

pō̃ü is exclusively a flock of *sheep* (shepherd = *oiopólos*)
agélē ... a herd of *cattle* (cowherd = *boukólos*)
subósion ... a herd of *pigs* (swineherd = *subṓtēs*)
aipólion ... a herd of *goats* (goatherd = *aipólos*)

It should be noted that the name of the shepherd is based on *ówis*, not *próbaton*.

This distinction exists in other languages: in Latin, *pecudes* refers to the sheep (cf. *pō̆ü*), whereas *amenta* are "the large animals." The English *flock* and *herd* may also be compared; indeed, English has a whole series of words for assemblages varying according to the species of animal.

If we only encounter special names for particular assemblages this must mean that mixed herds did not exist. Each species had its own special herdsman and was pastured separately.

This is therefore a decisive objection to Lommel's explanation. The practice of stock breeding was so old in Greece that long before the time of Homer there was a division of labor among the various specialized herdsmen. We find even in Mycenaean Greek a *suqota*, corresponding to Homeric *subṓtēs* and a *qoukoro*, who corresponds to *boukólos*. The name of the goatherd is also known in Mycenaean: *aikipata*. Thus there is nothing either in the traditional practice or in the vocabulary which would allow us to posit the existence of mixed herds: the second argument of Lommel falls to the ground.

However, there is still the etymological relationship between *próbata* and *probaínō*, which would seem to impose on *próbata* the meaning "those who walk at the head of." But even for a verb of so transparent a form as *probaínō* we must not neglect verification. Now if one re-reads the examples, it emerges that *probaínō* never means "walk at the head of" even though all the dictionaries affirm it. We must scrutinize the sort of example from which this sense is deduced. The most frequent sense is in fact "to advance, progress, move forwards." This sense is beyond all argument, for the examples are immediately apparent. In Homer (*Il.* 13, 18) κραιπνὰ ποσὶ προβιβάς 'advancing with rapid steps'; Lysias (169, 38) προβεβηκῶς τῇ ἡλικίᾳ 'of advanced age'. The meaning is thus invariably "to advance."

But a second sense is posited: "to walk in front of somebody"—which is quite a different thing. This meaning is based on three examples from Homer, all of the same type: ὅ τε κράτεϊ προβεβήκῃ (*Il.* 16, 54) 'who surpasses in might the others, who surpasses the others in power', which has to be understood as "superior in might"; cf. *Il.* 6, 125; 23, 890. But it is the perfect tense which occurs in all these passages, and much confusion has arisen between the sense of the perfect and the sense of the verb: *probaínō* 'I advance, I proceed forward'; thus the perfect *probébēka* means "I find myself in an advanced position," e.g. *Il.* 10, 252 ἄστρα δὲ δὴ προβέβηκε, meaning "the night is advanced." So an expression like προβέβηκε ἁπάντων or κράτεϊ means "someone is in an advanced position with respect to all" or "in respect to might." In fact in Homer we find (*Il.* 6, 125) πολὺ προβέβηκας ἁπάντων, which means literally "you are far in advance of all." It is because *probaínō* does not mean "to walk at the head of" but "to advance" that lexicographers have had to rely on these examples in the perfect in order to extract the sense of "to be in front of." That sense does no more than illustrate the normal value of the perfect; as for the notion of superiority this simply results from the genitive-ablative, which indicates the point of departure from which an advanced position has been reached. Thus there is no difference in the meaning of the verb in the phrase ἄστρα προβέβηκε and in the three examples cited. The sense is one and the same, so that there is no need to subdivide into categories to distinguish between univocal examples. There is, however, a difference in Latin between *progredior*, which is the exact equivalent of *probaínō*, and *praegredior* 'I walk ahead of the others'. But *probaínō* corresponds only to *progredior*.

Accordingly *próbata* does not mean "those who walk at the head of the herd." One by one all the reasons which have been advanced in support of this explanation have crumbled: (1) *próbata* does not designate the small animals; (2) the Greeks did not keep mixed herds; (3) the meaning of *probaínō* is not "walk at the head of" but "proceed."

What remains? Simply, a relationship between *próbata* and *probaínō*. To understand this relationship our starting point must be the meaning "advance, proceed": *próbata* are those which advance, or proceed. But what then? The designation appears most peculiar and not a little puzzling. Is this a special attribute of live-stock or do not all animals "proceed" normally?

The solution is given in an expression morphologically related to *próbata* which we have not yet considered. It is the Homeric word *próbasis* (πρόβασις), an abstract word derived by the suffix *-ti-* from the same verb *probaínō*, which occurs only once in Homer, but in conditions which are ideal for our purpose. *Od.* 2, 75: *keimēliá te próbasín te*. The Homeric expression denotes wealth: *próbasis* is a word in *-sis* of the class of abstract nouns capable of expressing collective meaning. This tendency is illustrated by such words as *árosis* which means "plowing" but also "arable land," "corn-land" (cf. the French expression *labour* in "*marcher dans les labours*"); *ktēsis* 'possession' and also 'the totality of *ktḗmata*', just as *árosis* is the totality of ploughed land.

Thus *próbasis* indicates the totality of *próbata*, and the opposition *keimēlia*/*próbasis* refers to possessions of two different categories, a distinction which seems to be essential in the economy of the Homeric world: Immovable or "lying" (*keimēlia* from κεῖμαι 'lie'), i.e. immovable property, and movable property (*hósa probaínei*).

This way of regarding property in its two categories has a rough resemblance to the French distinction between *meubles* (*mobilia*) and *immeubles* (*immobilia*). But *immeubles* are buildings, whereas *meubles* are chattels. In Homeric Greece the division was different: all that "lies" (*keîtai*), *keimēlia*, precious metals in ingots, gold, copper and iron, is opposed to *tà próbata*, property on the hoof, consisting of the herds and live-stock in general. Such is the sense of *próbata* as we have established from the textual evidence.

This explanation puts the economy of the Homeric world in a new perspective. Lommel conjured up an extraordinarily primitive type of herd composed of large numbers of animals. In fact *próbata*, connected as it is with *próbasis*, implies a much more developed social organization. In Homeric society wealth was a composite thing with a broad distinction on two different levels, between *keimēlia* and *próbata*.

The same distinction was preserved until a much later age in Germanic. In the Scandinavian world we find a term which reminds us of *próbata*. This is the Icelandic *gangandi fé*, German *gehendes Vieh* ('walking animals'); but here *fé* represents *pecus* in the Germanic sense, that is to say "wealth." Got. *faihu* translates *argúrion* 'money'. The literal meaning of the expression is "wealth which moves" and this refers to live-stock (see below, Book One, Chapter Four). A further possible parallel, which we do not press, is offered by the Hittite *iyant-* 'sheep', for the word can be analyzed as the participle of the verb *ai-* (cf. Gr. *eîmi*) 'go, walk'. It is however not yet certain that this is the word for sheep in general and not that of a particular variety. If the sense were confirmed, the parallel would be striking.

These are the essential facts. As for the rest of the semantic development, there is little point in illustrating ramifications of meaning represented by many examples in all languages at all periods.

The meaning to which the generic terms becomes restricted is determined by the most important species. This fact is universal and well attested, thus:

Lat. *bestia*	>	Fr. *biche* 'hind, doe'
"	>	Engandine *becha* 'sheep'
Lat. *animal*	>	North Ital. dialects: *nimal* 'pig'
"	>	other regions: *nemal* 'ox'

It is always the animal *par excellence*, the best represented species, the most useful locally which takes the generic name: Ital. *pecora*, 'sheep'.

We may thus cite *próbata* among the groups of words subject to constant innovation. The special sense of *próbaton* derives from the local conditions of animal husbandry. The primary meaning, connected as it is with *probaínō*, cannot be interpreted except within the framework of a definite economic structure.[2]

2. For the whole of chapters 1, 2, 3 reference may be made to our article "Noms d'animaux en indo-européen" in *Bulletin de la Société de Linguistique de Paris*, 1949, pp. 74–103.

BOOK I, CHAPTER FOUR

Livestock and Money
pecu and pecunia

Abstract. For all comparative philologists, Indo-European **peku* means "live-stock" or, in a narrow sense, "sheep." The meaning of "wealth" (e.g. Lat. *pecūnia*) is consequently regarded as secondary and this is explained as the result of a semantic extension of the term which originally referred to the main type of wealth, i.e. live-stock.

A study of **peku* and its derivatives in the three great dialects where it is represented—Indo-Iranian, Italic and Germanic—leads to a reversal of the traditional interpretation: **peku* originally meant "personal chattels, movables" and it was only as a result of successive specifications that it came to mean in certain languages "live-stock," "smaller live-stock" and "sheep." The evolution runs parallel with that of *próbata* (Book One, Chapter Three).

In the vocabulary of the Indo-European economy, which was of a pastoral character, there is one term of central importance, **peku*, attested in three great dialect regions: Indo-Iranian, Italic, and Germanic (Lithuanian *pekus* is most probably a loanword from Germanic or some other occidental language).

All comparative linguists are agreed in regarding **peku* as the Indo-European name for "live-stock" and in deriving it from a root **pek-* 'to shear'. Thus, on this view, the term was applied to the sheep as the bearer of the fleece, and it was only as the result of a secondary development that the term came to be used for "live-stock" in general. Such is the explanation put forward in the early stages of comparative grammar.

An attempt will now be made to show that this conception of **peku* is untenable and that a renewed examination of the evidence is necessary. The investigation will be concerned successively with Indo-Iranian, Latin and Germanic and will lead to conclusions which go beyond the problem under consideration.

I. INDO-IRANIAN

The forms to be studied are Vedic *paśu* and Avestan *pasu*. In Vedic, the meaning is by and large "live-stock," and this is confirmed by the various circumstances of its employment, its connection with *vraja* 'cow-pen, fold, stall', with *gopā* 'shepherd', with *yūtha* 'flock', etc. It must, however, be observed that:

1) *paśu* is a collective term which covers the types of domestic animal (horses, cattle) and only those: *aśvavantam gomantam paśum* (*Rig Veda* I, 83, 4), *paśum aśvyam gavyam* (V, 61, 5), etc.;
2) *paśu* even includes man, who is regarded as a biped *paśu*, on a par with the quadruped *paśu*: *dvipáde cátus padeca paśáve* (III, 62, 14). It is not only from this passage that this can be inferred, it is the explicit teaching of the Satapatha-Brahmana (VI, 2, 1, 2) on the five *paśu*: *puruṣam aśvam gām avim ajam* 'man, horse, ox, sheep, goat'. Other texts transpose this definition into a theory of sacrifice.

The inclusion of man among the *paśu* is indicative of a pastoral society in which movable wealth was composed of both men and animals, and in which the term *paśu*, which at first denoted movables, could stand both for bipeds and quadrupeds.

Iranian confirms this view. The association of men and animals, implicit in the Vedic definition, is expressed by the Avestic formula *pasu vīra* "livestock-men," the antiquity of which has long been recognized.

What is the real meaning of *vīra* 'man' in the Avestic formula *pasu vīra*, which is echoed at the other end of Indo-European by the *uiro pequo* of the Iguvine tables? For Sanskrit, Lüders has shown that *vīra*, in a context where it is connected with livestock, means "slave." This meaning, whether taken in a strict sense or merely as "house personnel, domestics," is also valid for the Avestic *vīra* in *pasu vīra*.

We may adduce further confirmation taken from a *gāthā* of Zarathustra. In a strophe of a pathetic tone (*Y.* 46.2) Zarathustra complains of his impotence in overcoming the hostility which surrounds him on all sides: "I know why I am without power, O Mazda; it is because I am *kamna-fšu* (=I have few *pasu*) and because I am *kamna-nar-* (=I have few men)." The two qualifications *kamna-fšu* 'who has few *pasu*' and *kamna-nar-* 'who has few men' evidently come from the formula *pasu vīra*, with a replacement of *vīra* by *nar-*, which is also known in the Avesta. It is the fact that he has few *pasu* and few *nar-* that makes Zarathustra "powerless." These possessions, which constitute the two species of movable wealth, together confer power. We may now add the Gathic expression *kamna-fšu*, *kamna-nar-* to the Avestan repertory of compounds based on the expression *pasu vīra* with their characteristic pairing.

The diversity of the linguistic evidence reflects the importance of *pasu* for the pastoral society of the northeast of Iran, the ideology of which has inspired the most ancient parts of the Avesta.

We shall restrict ourselves to the most ancient phase without following the later development of *pasu*, which is in any case well known. The ancient term has become today the name for "sheep" in one part of the Iranian world. A further specialization has thus followed on a much earlier one which conferred on *pasu* the meaning "livestock."

All the same, it is in the sense of movable wealth that the Avestan *vīra* in *pasu vīra* has to be understood. This turn of phrase designates the totality of private movable possessions, whether human or animal, the men being sometimes included in *paśu* (*pasu*) but sometimes mentioned separately.

The same interpretation might be extended to *uiro* in Umbrian, not only because the formula *uiro pequo* comes from a common Indo-European heritage, but because of a specific indication peculiar to the two Italic peoples, the Umbrians and the Latins. Not enough attention has been paid to the striking similarity between the Umbrian formula and a passage in an ancient prayer by Cato. In Umbrian a certain ritual expression appears eleven times: *uiro pequo… salua seritu* 'salva servato'. Compare this with Cato: *pastores pecuaque salva servassis*. It suffices to superimpose the two texts:

Umbrian *uiro pequo . . . salua seritu*

Latin *pastores pecuaque salva servassis*

to bring out the close correspondence of the two formulae. All the successive terms are etymologically related, except the first, where the same meaning is expressed by separate terms: it is precisely the Umbrian term *uiro* for which the Latin equivalent is not *viros* but *pastores*. From this we may conclude that Umbrian *uiro*, linked with *pequo*, designated the men whose task it was to look after the livestock. Thus we have in Umbrian an exact parallel to the notion of *vīra* associated with *pasu* in Indo-Iranian.

That *pasu* in the first instance had an economic sense can be confirmed from the term *kṣu*, which, although related to *paśu-* as Av. *fšu-* is to *pasu-*, became detached early on and kept the original sense better. The adjective *purukṣu* means "abounding in riches," "in possessions," but not specifically in livestock. This is an epithet of the gods Agni, Indra, Soma, and is often found associated with words meaning "wealth."

All the indications point to the fact that the sense of "livestock" is a restriction of the more ancient comprehensive term "movable wealth," applied as it was to the principal form of property in a pastoral society.

II. LATIN

The formation of *pecūnia* is unique in Latin. This gives it its value, but also its difficulty. It must be stressed that up to now the problem of its morphology has not been considered. The formal relation of *pecūnia* to *pecū* is that of a secondary derivative, which resulted in a lengthening of the final vowel of the stem. The essential question is that of the suffix. A parallel to the formation of Lat. *pecūnia* has been pointed out by Meillet among others: it is the O.Sl. *-ynji* (< **-unia*). The suffix *-ynji* in Old Slavic makes abstract nouns from adjectives, e.g. *dobrynji* 'goodness': *dobrŭ* 'good'; or female names derived from corresponding male ones: *bogynji* 'goddess': *bogŭ* 'god'. We may even adduce a Slavic derivative in *–ynji* from a stem in **-u-*: this is *lĭgynji* 'lightening' : *lĭgŭkŭ* 'light' (cf. Skr. *laghú-*, *raghú-* 'light').

This connection may be accepted, but we must draw certain conclusions. Since Latin *pecūnia* is an abstract noun, we have to posit an *adjective* as its basic form, just as with the Slavic abstract nouns in *-ynji*. We should then have to regard **peku* as the neuter of a very archaic adjective which has not been preserved in any language. If this conclusion, inescapable as it is, seems too bold and if we think that it postulates a form the existence of which cannot otherwise be demonstrated, there still remains the alternative of explaining *pecūnia* from the resources of Latin.

We can link *pecūnia* with feminine derivatives in *-nus*, *-nā-* which are formed from nouns in *-u-*: thus *fortūna*, which is derived from **fortu-* (cf. *fortuitus*), or *Portūnus*, *opportūnus* from *portu-*. We should then have to admit (1) that the correspondence between Latin *pecūnia* and the Slavic form in *-ynji* is only apparent and is due to a secondary process, and (2) that *pecūnia* is an abstract in *-ia* formed in Latin itself from a derivative *-nus*/*-nā* analogous to *portūnus*, *fortūna* (cf.*portus* and *fortu-itus*), or possibly from a feminine form in *-*nī*-.

This is the dilemma which confronts us in the analysis of this abstract noun for which there exists no parallel in Latin. Either *pecūnia* is an example of the same type of formation as the Slavic words in *-*ūnyā* and it must be linked up with an ancient *adjective* and not with the historical neuter *pecū*; or *pecūnia* is derived directly from the neuter form *pecū*, but by a process of suffixation which is not immediately comparable to the Slavic abstract noun in *-ynji*.

The other substantive which is derived from *pecū* is *pecūlium*. Here again we have an isolated form without analogous formations among the neuter words in *-ium*. Nevertheless it is possible to unravel its formation. Between *pecū* and *peculium* we have to posit an intermediary **pecūlis*, which stands to *pecū* as *īdūlis* stands to *īdūs* and *tribūlis* to *tribus*. For the relationship between **pecūlis* and *pecūlium* we might compare *edūlis* and *edūlia* (whence *edūlium*). From *pecūlium* is formed the denominative verb *peculo*(*r*), from which comes the noun *peculātus*, -*ūs*. Thus the series *pecūlium* : *peculo*(*r*) : *peculātus* becomes parallel with *dominium* : *dominor* : *dominātus*. The whole string of derivatives which are grouped around *pecūlium* are now rationally organized.

Now the essence of the problem is, however, the meaning of *pecūnia*, that of *pecūlium*, and their relation to *pecū*. In the eyes of comparatists, *pecū* means livestock, *pecūnia* 'wealth in the form of livestock' and *pecūlium* 'the animals given to a slave'. This is the information found in all etymological dictionaries and in works on Latin morphology, all of which repeat the interpretation of the three terms *pecū*, *pecūnia*, *pecūlium*, an interpretation which goes back for centuries and even millennia because it comes to us from the Roman etymologists.

The formal relationship between the three words is assured. The problem is how to interpret it. To this end we have to begin by establishing the sense of *pecūnia* and *pecūlium*.

I. Pecūnia

It is not enough to have explained the formal link which exists between *pecūnia* and *pecū*. We must also elucidate the sense relationship which follows from the derivation. Yet we shall peruse in vain the works of early and classical Latinity; equally fruitless will it be to scrutinize the examples quoted in Latin dictionaries; nowhere shall we discover a link between the meaning of *pecūnia* and that of *pecū* 'flock, live-stock'. In all the examples quoted *pecūnia* means exclusively "fortune, money" and it is defined as "copia nummorum." We thus have no option but to proceed by methodical inference without regard for traditional views.

If from the outset *pecūnia* had the exclusive meaning of "money, fortune, χρήματα," this is because *pecū* has exclusively an economic sense and means "movable possessions." Only in this way can we account for the constant meaning of *pecūnia* which as a collective abstract noun generalizes the specific sense of *pecū*.

It was only by a special development of a pragmatic and secondary kind that **peku*, which meant "movable wealth," became applied in particular to an item of the real world, "live-stock." In this analysis we must distinguish two different theoretical planes: (a) that of "signification" and (b) that of "designation." Consequently we must distinguish (a) the proper sense of **peku* as revealed by its ancient derivations and (b) the historical use of the word to designate "live-stock." Once the semantic link between the particular term **peku* and the particular reality "live-stock" was effected, the designation became fixed for a time. But history does not stand still and new specifications can always come about. This is what happened with the differentiations which were effected in Latin between *pecū*; *pecus*, *-oris*; *pecus*, *-udis*. They form part of Latin lexical history and do not affect the fundamental relationships which it is our task to bring to light.

It is precisely these relations which have been misunderstood. The result is that both *pecū* and *pecūnia* have been wrongly interpreted. And these inexact ideas inspired first Romans and then modern scholars to offer the naïve translation of *pecūnia* as "wealth of live-stock," which goes against all the evidence.

On the contrary, we may posit that the real nature of the prehistoric *pecū* is elucidated by the real meaning of the historic *pecūnia*.

The notion "movable possessions," expressed by *pecūnia*, may embrace other types of property than live-stock. Some idea of its original extent can be gained from a notice of Festus which may refer to an archaic expression: *pecunia sacrificium fieri dicebatur cum fruges fructusque offerebantur, quia ex his rebus constant quam nunc pecuniam dicimus* ('a sacrifice was said to be made with *pecūnia*, when fruits and produce were offered, because what we now call *pecūnia* consists of such things').

For this glossator, *fruges fructusque* constituted the *pecūnia*. We record this extended meaning of *pecūnia* without rejecting, but rather by reinterpreting, the definitions of Varro: *pecuniosus a pecunia magna, pecuniam a pecu : a pastoribus enim horum vocabulorum origo* ('"*pecuniosus*" from "great *pecunia*"; "*pecunia*" from "*pecu*": for these words originally belonged to the vocabulary of herdsmen').

We only need to read Varro (*L.L.*) to realize what was understood in his time by *pecūnia* : under *pecūnia* he includes words like *dos* 'dowry', *arrabo* 'deposit', *merces* 'salary', *corollarium* 'tip' (V, 175); then *multa* 'fine' (177); *sacramentum* 'sacred deposit' (180); *tributum* 'tribute' (181); *sors* 'pecūnia in faenore' ('capital bearing interest') (VI, 65); *sponsio* 'a deposit guaranteeing a promise of marriage' (VI, 70). In addition there existed *pecūnia signata* 'minted money' (V, 169), the *nuncupatae pecuniae* of legal texts (VI, 60). In short, *pecūnia* covers all possible uses of money as an economic value or as a monetary symbol; but, we again repeat, it never refers to possession of "live-stock." This means that in Latin usage, *pecū* and *pecūnia* had become separate terms owing to the fact that when *pecū* became specialized as the designation for live-stock this did not affect *pecūnia*, which preserved its original sense of "movable possessions."

II. Pecūlium

What has been said of *pecūnia* is to a large extent also true of *pecūlium*. We have here a term which, we may say straight away, is still further removed from *pecū* than *pecūnia* was. It is known that *pecūlium* denotes possessions granted to those who had no legal right to possessions as such: personal savings granted by the master to his slave and by the father to his son. The notion of "personal possessions" is the key notion, and they always consisted of movable goods:

money or sheep. It is no task of ours to enquire why *pecūlium* refers to the savings of the slave and *pecūnia* to the fortune of the master; this is a problem which concerns the history of institutions and not the linguistic form. The distribution stated, we shall recognize the meaning of *pecūlium* in the derivative *pecūliāris* 'pertaining to *pecūlium*' or 'given as *pecūlium*'. In fact, *pecūliāris* is only an adjective of *pecūlium*, and any movable possession can become *pecūlium*. This is seen as early as Plautus: a young boy can be given as *pecūlium* to the son of the master and will be called his *pecūliāris puer*. This is one of the elements in the comedy of the *Captivi* (v. 20, 982, 988, 1013). In ordinary conditions of life the slave could hardly amass a *peculium* except with what was within his reach: a little money and a few sheep. But this limitation did not imply that *peculium* designated an item of live-stock or a coin.

We thus find in *pecūlium* a second proof that the basic notion, that of *pecū*, did not refer specifically to live-stock. In *pecūlium*, even more than in *pecūnia*, the connection with personal property is underlined, even if it was restricted to a certain social class. But the possessions concerned are invariably movable ones, whether *pecūlium* is taken in the strict sense or in the figurative sense. These two notions, personal possession and movable possessions, also apply to the derived verb *peculo(r)*, which yielded *pecūlātus* '(fraudulent) appropriation of public money'. Between this legal term and the basic term *pecū* a functional continuity can be re-established, *pari passu* with the link of morphological derivation. We may here argue from analogy. In the same way as we work back from *edūlium* 'a tasty dish' to *edūlis* 'edible' and thence to **edu*, roughly "edibles," so from *pecūlium* 'personal movable possessions' we work back to **pecūlis* *'what may be possessed' and from **pecūlis* to *pecū*, which we must now define as "(movable) property." Whatever route we choose, we always arrive at the same conclusion: *pecū* signifies "movable property" (personal chattels).

III. GERMANIC

The word **peku* is attested in all the ancient Germanic languages, but the sense varies according to the dialect and it is precisely these variations which are illuminating for the real sense of the term. We must scrutinize it in the proper context of each of the ancient dialects. It so happens that within the Germanic group the Old High German form *fihu* (variants *feho*, *fehu*) is the only one which denotes "live-stock." In texts translated from Latin this word renders *pecus*, *pecudes*, and more generally *iumenta*. We may deduce further *fëhelîh* 'tierisch' (animal-like), *fihu-stërbo* 'animal-plague', *fîhu-wart* 'Viehhirt' (herdsman), *fihu-wiari* 'Viehweiher' (animal pond). But these are Latinisms and here, as in many other instances, the Latin models were the determining factor. In fact we shall see that Old High German *fihu* was very far separated from the meaning which the word had preserved in the rest of the Germanic group, and the innovation or specialization must be laid at the door of Old High German, contrary to what is generally believed. Otherwise it would be impossible to understand the situation of **peku* in all the other dialects, still to be described. Nor could we understand the role which this Old High German term played in the genesis of mediaeval Latin *feudum* 'fief'.

We must first examine the Gothic evidence. The Gothic neuter *faihu* means only "money," "fortune" and never refers to the animal world. An example follows. *Gahaihaitun imam faihu giban* 'they promised to give him money, *epēggeílanto autôi argúrion doûnai,* promiserunt ei pecuniam se daturos' (Mark 14, 11).

This example should suffice to demonstrate that *faihu*, the term chosen to translate Gr. *khrēmata, argúrion*, Lat. *pecūnia, possessiones* refers exclusively to money, to wealth. This is also shown by the Gothic compounds of *faihu*, such as *faihufriks* 'avaricious, *pleonéktēs, philárguros*', *faihufrikei* 'cupidity, *pleonexía*', *faihugairns* 'desirous of money, *philárguros*', etc.

It is clear that *faihu* was completely foreign to the pastoral vocabulary which includes quite different expressions, such as *hairdo* 'herd, *poímnē, agélē*'; *hairdeis* 'shepherd, *poimēn*'; *aþwei* "flock, *poímnē*'; *wripus* 'flock, *agélē*', *lamb* 'sheep, ewe, *próbaton*'. The semantic associates of *faihu* are the terms which designate money and wealth: *gabei* 'wealth, *ploûtos*', *gabeigs* (*gabigs*) 'rich, *ploúsios*', and the denominative verbs *gabigjan* 'to enrich, *ploutízein*' and *gabignan* 'to enrich oneself, *plouteîn*'; further, *silubr* 'money, *argúrion*' (metal and money), *skatts* 'the coins, *dēnárion, mnâ*', in the plural 'pieces of silver, *argúria*'.

A further proof that Got. *faihu* had no connection with the sphere of animal husbandry is furnished by a lexical relationship which has escaped notice and which must be established.

There exists in Gothic a verb *gafaihon, bifaihon*, which translates the Greek *pleonekteîn*; from this verb is derived the noun *bifaih* '*pleonexía*'. In the Second Epistle to the Corinthians, which contains all the examples, St. Paul uses "*pleonekteîn*" for "getting the better of somebody, to enrich oneself at his expense, to exploit him." This is what the Gothic *bifaihon, gafaihon* renders.

The explanation of *faihon* is to be found within Gothic itself; *faihon* is the denominative of *faihu*. Its morphology is that of verbs made from nouns in *-u-*, e.g. *sidon* : *sidus*, or *luston* : *lustus*. The semantic connection between *faihon* and *faihu* is seen from the use of compounds of *faihu*. Since *faihu* denotes "money, wealth" and since *faihu-friks* translates *pleonektēs*, just as *faihu-frikei* and *faihu-geiro* translate *pleonexía*, a verb *faihon* (*bi-*, *ga-*) was created as the equivalent of *pleonekteîn* in the particular sense of "to enrich oneself (at someone else's expense)."

We now examine the Nordic evidence. The usual translation for Old Norse *fé* 'Vieh, Besitz, Geld' (in German—live-stock, possession, money) must be rectified: basic and primary is the notion of "wealth, movables." This emerges from three circumstances:

1) the expression *gangandi fé* for "live-stock" evidently implies that *fé* alone did not signify "live-stock," but "wealth, possessions"; *gangandi fé* was used with reference to "wealth on the hoof," the "live-stock"; cf. Gr. *próbasis*, *próbaton*.
2) The compound *félag* 'common possession', from which comes *félagi* 'comrade, companion' (this passed into Old English as *feolaga* 'fellow') also required the sense of "fortune, goods," for *fé* and not that of "herd."
3) The denominative verb *féna* means "to enrich oneself," hence "acquire a fortune (*fé*)." From this is derived *fénadr* 'riches', which eventually came to mean "live-stock" as the result of a new specialization.

For Old English, it is sufficient to consult the *Concise Anglo-Saxon Dictionary* by J. R. Clark Hall and Meritt to see that *féoh* in the sense of "cattle, herd," traditionally put at the head of the article, is attested only in a few examples, which incidentally would now require careful reconsideration, while the great majority of the examples are found among the headings "movable goods, property" and especially "money, riches, treasure." We may say, then, that in Old English *féoh* was applied first and foremost to riches in general or to movable goods and only in the second instance, and then very rarely, to that form of movable property which consists of live-stock. In Beowulf it means solely "riches" or "treasure" and in Aelfric the expression *wi liegendum fēo* 'for ready money' confirms the antiquity of the sense. Finally, there are only three compounds where *féoh* means "animals" as against about thirty where it means "money, riches."

The same observation can be made for Middle English by studying the articles on *fę* in the *Middle English Dictionary* of Kurath-Kuhn (III, 430). There are very few examples meaning "live-stock" but many more of *fe* in the sense of "movable property; possessions in live-stock, goods or money, riches, treasure, wealth," and of "money as a medium of exchange or used for taxes, tributes, ransom, bribes etc."

It was necessary to examine afresh the examples and to classify the usages according to their exact contextual value, liberating ourselves from the traditional schema which imposed "live-stock" as the primary meaning at all costs. This revision would probably be of some consequence for the history of English *fee* and that of French *fief*, Old French *feu*. According to the traditional explanation the Frankish *fehu* 'live-stock' is derived from Latin *feus*, 'movable wealth'. It would rather seem that *fihu*, like Gothic *faihu*, designated all forms of movable property and that it kept that sense when it passed into Latin. Here, too, a new examination would appear to be called for.

IV. CONCLUSIONS

What has been outlined above shows that the traditional conceptions of **peku* in Indo-European must be entirely rethought. Our first conclusion is that **peku* signifies "movable personal possession." That this possession may in fact take the form of live-stock is a separate datum which concerns social structure and the forms of production. It is only in virtue of this frequent association between the term **peku* and the material reality of animal husbandry that, by a generalization which took place outside the class of producers, **peku* came to mean "live-stock" (the first specialization), then specifically "small live-stock" (the second specialization), and finally "sheep" (the third and last specialization). But intrinsically **peku* does not designate either the flock or any animal species.

We are now able to establish a correlation between the proper sense of **peku*, thus restored, and its dialect distribution. It is interesting to note the fact that **peku* is lacking in Greek. This is no accident. Such an important notion could not simply disappear. The Indo-European term was in fact replaced in Greek by a new designation, which had the same sense. This is the Homeric *próbasis* with its far more common equivalent, *próbata*. Our study of this term (see above, Book One, Chapter Three) has revealed the evolutionary model which we have posited for **peku*: it was, to begin with, an expression which designated "movable possessions." For extra-linguistic reasons this term was frequently applied to the possession of "live-stock." It thus became the word for live-stock and subsequently for the predominant species, "the sheep."

But as was shown above, this specialization, which took place at an early date in Indo-Iranian, did not take place everywhere. We have in Latin and in a large part of Germanic testimony of great antiquity which shows that the initial meaning was "movable possession" and this explains the derivatives. This evolution is not reversible. It is in the highest degree improbable that **peku*, if it had really signified "live-stock," could have come to designate "money" and "fortune" in general, which is the exclusive meaning of *próbata*. Similarly the specific English term *cattle*, Fr. *cheptel*, goes back to Latin *capitale* 'principal property'; already in a text of 1114, *captale* means "chattel, cattle, movable goods."[1] But in the Middle Ages it still has the meaning "fortune, goods, income," and the Spanish *caudal* signifies "goods, riches." The progress from "movable possession" > "live-stock" is characteristic. But once accomplished, it is irreversible. Thus "livestock" is very often designated by expressions which refer to possessions in general, that is, it is simply called "property"; but the reverse never happens.

Our interpretation of **peku* and its evolution thus conforms to what might be called the norm with regard to the terms of possession: a general or generic term is used by a certain class of producers as the designation for the typical object or element. In this sense it spreads outside its original milieu and becomes the usual designation of the object or element in question. Such is the case here. We have been able by comparative study of the evidence presented in three dialect groups to follow the stages of the process in the case of **peku*, and to verify to a certain extent this internal reconstruction.

A last conclusion concerns the etymology of **peku*. If the present demonstration is considered acceptable, it destroys the traditional rapprochement with **pek(t)-* 'to shear'. It is evident that **peku*, a term with an economic sense which does not denote any animal, can have nothing in common with terms derived from **pek(t)-*, which are concerned with the technique of shearing and combing wool: Gr. *pékō* 'comb, card', *pókos* 'fleece', *pektéō* 'shear', *pékos* n. 'fleece', *pokízō* 'shear the wool', *kteís* 'comb'; Lat. *pecto* 'comb, card', *pectin*

1. Baxter-Johnson: *Mediaeval Latin Word-List*, 1934, p. 64.

'comb', *pexus* 'hairy, downy', Arm. *asr* 'wool'. Between these forms and **peku* the resemblance amounts to no more than simply homophony. The connection must be abandoned, and **peku*-, a vestige of the most ancient Indo-European vocabulary, seems irreducible to any known root.[2]

2. A much more detailed version of the present study has been published in the USA in the conference proceedings entitled *Indo-European and Indo-Europeans*, 1970, University of Pennsylvania Press, 307–20.

SECTION II

Giving and Taking

BOOK I, CHAPTER FIVE

Gift and Exchange

Abstract. Greek has five words that are commonly translated uniformly by "gift." A careful examination of their use shows that they do in fact correspond to as many different ways of envisaging a gift—from the purely verbal notion of "giving" to "a contractual prestation imposed by the terms of a pact, an alliance, a friendship, or a 'guest-host' relationship."

The Gothic term *gild* and its derivatives take us back to a very ancient Germanic tradition in which the religious aspect ("the sacrifice"), the economic aspect (a mercantile association), and the juridical aspect (the atonement for a crime) are closely interwoven.

The varied history of the words related to Gr. *dáptō*, Lat. *daps*, on the one hand discloses the practice of "potlatch" in the Indo-European past, and on the other hand shows how the ancient notion of "prestigious expenditure" became attenuated to mean "expense, damages."

The Hansa, which had become in the form of the guild an economic association, continues the tradition of the *comitatus* of young warriors attached to a chieftain, such as Tacitus described in his *Germania*.

We now approach the study of a complex of economic notions that is difficult to define otherwise than by the sum of their peculiarities: "gift," "exchange," "trade." The terminology relating to *exchange* and *gift* constitutes a very rich chapter of the Indo-European vocabulary.

We begin with the notion of "giving." One might think that this is a simple idea. In fact it comprises some strange variations in the Indo-European languages, and the contrasts found between one language and another merit examination. Furthermore, it is extended to notions which one might not think of associating with it. The activity of *exchange*, of *trade*, is characterized in a specific way in relation to an idea which appears to us different, that of the disinterested *gift*. In this light exchange appears as a round of gifts rather than a genuine commercial operation. The relationship of exchange to purchase and sale emerges from a study of the terms employed for these different processes.

In this field there is great lexical stability. The same terms remain in use for very long periods, and, in contrast to what happens with those for more complex notions, they are often not replaced.

THE VOCABULARY OF "GIVING" IN GREEK

We start from the root **dō-*, for which the consensus of languages guaranteed a constant form and meaning. The nominal forms show an ancient structure, that of derivatives in *-no-* and *-ro-*: Skr. *dānam*, Lat. *dōnum*, Gr. *dō̂ron* (δῶρον), Arm. *tur*, Slavic *darŭ*. These forms clearly attest, in the very constancy of this resemblance or of this difference, an ancient alternation *r*/*n*, this being the mark of an archaic declension, called heteroclitic, which is often revealed by the coexistence of derivatives in *-r-* and *-n-*. We have further a series of nominal forms in Greek, distinguished only by the class of derivation, all of which relate to "the gift." They are: Gr. *dṓs* (δώς), *dō̂ron* (δῶρον), *dōreá* (δωρεά), *dósis* (δόσις), *dōtínē* (δωτίνη), five distinct terms which are uniformly translated as "gift."

The first is very rare: we have only one example. The other four are much more common and may coexist in the same author. Is this a fortuitous lexical redundancy or are there reasons for this multiplicity? Such is the problem which we must investigate.

The first form, *dṓs*, is a stem in *-t-*. It corresponds to Latin *dōs* (stem *dōt-*). In Latin the word is specialized; it is the "dowry," the gift which the woman brings into marriage, sometimes also the gift by the husband in purchase of his bride.

To establish the sense of Greek *dṓs*, which is not yet specialized, we have a verse by Hesiod: δὼς ἀγαθή, ἅρπαξ δὲ κακή, θανάτοιο δότειρα '*dōs* is good, but robbery (*hárpaks*) is bad, because it brings death' (*Works*, 356). This verse is found precisely in a passage where the "gift" is highly praised as a means of establishing advantageous relations. *Dṓs* and *hárpaks* are root nouns, and it is no accident that no other example is found: they represent the idea in its most abstract form: "giving" is good, "robbing" is bad.

Dȏron and *dōreá* seem to have the same sense. But when Herodotus uses them concurrently we can see that he distinguishes them according to a principle which it is not difficult to discern. Thus III, 97: Κόλχοι…ταξάμενοι ἐς τὴν δωρεήν…δῶρα…ἀγίνεον 'the Colchidians having assessed [having imposed payment on] themselves, brought gifts (*dȏra*) for the *dōreá*'. *Dōreá* is strictly the act of offering a *dȏron*. It is an abstract noun derived from *dōréō* (δωρέω), which is itself a denominative of *dȏron*. The verbal force is clearly seen in *dōreá*, and this explains the adverb *dōreán* (δωρεάν) (Attic) 'by a gift, for a gift, gratuitously, for nothing'. Thus *dȏron* is the actual gift and *dōreá* is the act of bringing, of presenting a gift. From *dȏron* are derived *dōreîsthai* (δωρεῖσθαι) 'to make a gift' which governs the name of the thing or the person to whom it is given, and *dṓrēma* (δώρημα) 'the thing which is presented, the present which serves as a recompense'.

Dósis is very different. Our translations do not distinguish it from *dȏron*; but its use in Homer *Il.* 10, 213 makes it clear: καί οἱ δόσις ἔσσεται ἐσθλή. A volunteer is needed for a dangerous mission; he is promised a good *dósis*, not a *dȏron*, because the object itself of the gift does not exist. *Dósis* is a nominal transposition of a verbal form in the present tense or, as here, in the future: "we shall give him, we shall make him a gift." A formula where the verbal force of this abstract is still apparent is found in Homer, *Od.* 6, 208, δόσις δ'ὀλίγη τε φίλη τε—words used by people who give but who excuse themselves for not giving much. "This gift is a small one, but given gladly." Thus *dósis* is "the act of giving." The formation in *-ti* indicates an effective accomplishment of the idea, which may also, but not necessarily, be materialized in an object. *Dósis* may also designate a legal act. In Attic law it is the bestowal of a bequest, by express will, outside the rules of normal inheritance.

There is a further medical usage in which *dósis* denotes the act of giving, whence develops the sense of the amount of medicine given, a "dose." Here the notion of gift or offering is absent. This sense passed by loan translation into German, where *Gift*, like Gr.-Lat. *dosis*, was used as a substitute for *venēnum* 'poison', whereas (*Mit*) *gift* 'dowry' still preserves the original connection with "giving." In the early texts there is no interference of *dósis* either with *dôron* or with *dōreá*.

Finally it remains to define the essential use of *dōtínē*. This is the most specialized term of the whole group. The examples are few but they are well characterized. It is a word of Ionic poetry which appears in Homer and also in Herodotus but soon passed out of use. *Dōtínē* certainly denoted some species of "gift," but precisely what?

To persuade Achilles to return to battle, he is promised, among other things, a grant of land together with its rich inhabitants, who will become his subjects "...who will honor him (*timḗsousi*) like a god with *dōtínai* and who under his scepter will pay the *liparàs thémistas*" (*Il.* 9, 155–156).

The two words *timḗsousi* and *thémistas* are essential for defining *dōtínēsi*. By *thémistas*, an extremely complex notion, is understood the prerogatives of a chieftain; in particular, it is the respect shown, and the tribute brought, to a personage such as a king in accordance with the requirements of divine law. Still more important is the *timḗ*. This expression is derived from *tíō* and belongs to the group of Skt. *cayati* 'to have regard, respect for', from a root which must be strictly distinguished from that which signifies "to avenge, to punish," Gr. *poinḗ*, which is often associated with it. *Poinḗ*, which corresponds exactly to Av. *kaēnā* 'vengeance, hate' is the retribution that compensates for a murder. This also developed the emotional sense of "hate," of vengeance considered as a retribution (cf. the sense in Iranian). The other group, the one which concerns us here, *timḗ*, denotes the honor due to a god, to a king, and the tribute due to them from a community. It is at the same time a mark of esteem and estimation in a social and sentimental, as well as an economic, sense.[1] The value attributed to somebody is measured by the offerings of which he is judged worthy, and these are the terms which elucidate *dōtínē*.

In Homer, *Od.* 9, 266–286, we find: "We are come to your knees to see whether you will offer us a *xeinḗïon* (a gift of hospitality) or whether you will give us a *dōtínē*, as is the law of hospitality (*thémis xeínōn*)." This time, in a text which seems made for our enlightenment, a relationship is established between *dōtínē* and the presents which are exchanged between host and guest according to the traditions of hospitality. Similarly, in *Od.* 11, 350 ff. "let our guest wait

1. On *timḗ* and its group cf. Book 4, Chapter 5.

until tomorrow before leaving us so that I may be able to assemble the whole of his *dōtínē.*"

Fleeing from Athens, the followers of Pisistratus wanted to repossess themselves of the tyranny from which they had been ejected. To this end they travelled through all the towns which might have obligations towards them to assemble the *dōtínai*: ἤγειρον δωτίνας (Herodotus I, 61).

There exists also a verb *dōtinázō*, which is found once in Herodotus (II, 180): on the occasion of the reconstruction of a temple which was incumbent on a group of federated cities, the priests went from town to town collecting gifts: περὶ τὰς πόλις ἐδωτίναζον.

These quotations throw light on a very different notion from the others. It is not merely a present, a disinterested gift: it is a gift *qua* contractual prestation, imposed by the obligations of a pact, an alliance, a friendship, or a bond of hospitality; the obligation of the *xeînos* (of the guest), of the subjects towards their king or god and also the prestation implied by an alliance. Once this meaning has been established it helps us to solve the philological problems posed by the variants in the textual tradition of these words. Thus the manuscript tradition of Herodotus VI, 89 is divided between the reading *dōtínēn* and the reading *dōreḗn*. The Corinthians wanted to aid the Athenians and sold them twenty vessels, but at a very low price, at five drachmas per boat, because the law forbade a gratuitous *gift*. Thus it was a symbolic payment imposed on the Athenians because, according to the law, it was impossible for one city to *give* the vessels to another. Is this *dōtínē* or *dōreḗ*? In fact what was involved was a gratuitous present. The valid reading is therefore *dōreḗn* and not *dōtínēn*, which is excluded because it is a gratuitous gift which the law forbade, not that which is inherent in an alliance.

Such is the way in which the Greek distinguishes for the same notion "gift" between three nouns which, for all that they are derived from the same root, are never for one moment confused. This notion is diversified in accordance with social institutions and what I may call the context of intention: *dōsis*, *dō̂ron*, *dōtínē*, three words for expressing a gift, because there are three ways of conceiving it.[2]

2. For a detailed analysis of the "gift" vocabulary see our article "Don et échange dans le vocabulaire indo-européen," *L'Année Sociologique*, 3rd Series, vol. II, 1951, pp. 7–20.

A GERMANIC INSTITUTION: THE GUILD

To the Greek terms we have reviewed we may now add the Germanic word which has become the name for "money," in German, *Geld*. In Gothic, *gild* translates the Greek *phōros* 'tax', while the compound noun *kaisara-gild* translates the Gr. *kȇnsos* 'tax'. We also have a verb: *fra-gildan*, *us-gildan* 'to render, repay, *apodidónai*, *antapodidónai* ' and a derived noun *gilstr*, which likewise translates *phóros* 'tax'.

In the other Germanic languages the sense is quite different: Old Icel. *gjald* 'recompense, punishment, payment'; OE *gield* 'substitute, indemnity, sacrifice'; Old High German *gelt* 'payment, sacrifice'; in composition *gotekelt* '*Gottesdienst*, divine service, worship'. In Frisian *jelde*, *jold* appears the special sense which was to become generalized in Germanic: "a guild of merchants," implying also "a corporation banquet." The whole notion seems extremely complex within Germanic society; it is simultaneously of a religious, economic and legal character. We are here confronted with a very important question which dominates the whole of the economic history of the Middle Ages: the formation of the guilds, a problem so vast that it cannot be treated here and which in any case is more the concern of the historian than the linguist.

It is not the conception itself which we shall consider but rather the starting point of the great medieval economic associations which developed between the sixth to seventh century and the fourteenth century, especially in the coastal regions of the North Sea, in Frisia, in the south of England and in the Scandinavian countries.

The institutions have both an economic and a religious character. These fraternities were united by economic interests but apparently also by a common cult. They were studied in the work (1921) by Maurice Cahen, *La libation en vieux scandinave*. According to this scholar, toasts, banquets, compotations, were like rites which were celebrated by the members of a fraternity. This finally took on a specific form and became in Germanic countries an economic association.

The author, however, ran into a serious difficulty. According to modern historians of the Middle Ages, the guilds constituted an exclusively economic phenomenon of fairly recent date and did not reach back into the beginnings of the Germanic world. In these economic groupings, in which people were brought together by common interests, one should not look for a survival of older religious associations.

But more recent researches into medieval history have justified these conclusions. M. Coornaert has sketched the history of this institution in broad outline in two articles in the *Revue Historique*, 1948. Not content with confirming the ancient and religious character of the guild, he reproaches Maurice Cahen for deferring to the judgment of earlier historians who rejected any intrusion of comparative studies into this field.

At present the facts can be seen to form part of a continuous history which goes far back in time. It has been claimed that *ghilda*, a Latinized form of a Germanic word, does not go back further than the eighth century. But it is now known from the Gallo-Roman period in a text which is dated to 450 AD.

What is a guild? It is first and foremost a festive occasion, a sacrificial meal within a "fraternity" which has assembled for a voluntary communion, and those who are thus assembled bear the same name. The notion of a sacred banquet is at the very center of this expression. Now, we encounter it in 450, that is to say, shortly after the period when the Gothic text has become fixed in writing (towards 350).

It will thus be relevant to give close scrutiny to the Gothic data. The essential words *gild* and *fra-gildan* have no correspondents except in Germanic. It is a new term which offers no possibility of comparative study.

The Gothic word *gild* is found in the well-known question in Luke XX, 22: "Are we permitted to pay tribute to Caesar or not?" *skuldu ist unsis kaisara* ***gild*** *giban*...? In the same question Mark XII, 14 replaces *gild* with *kaisara-gild*. A neuter *gilstr*, that is to say, **geld-strum* or **geld-trum*, is given with the same sense: Epistle to the Romans, XIII, 6: "That is also why you pay taxes, φόρους τελεῖτε."

The verb *fra-gildan* means "to give back, to restore," Luke XIX, 8: "I give, *gadailja* (*dídōmi*) to the poor (literally: I share my possessions with the poor); if anybody is cheated by me, I repay him *fragilda* (*apodídōmi* 'to make a return payment' in the text) fourfold." Cf. also Luke XIV, 12 and 14: "if you prepare a meal, do not invite your friends or your brothers or other relations, or rich neighbors, lest they invite you in their turn and this will result in an *antapodóma*, an obligation to further requital" (Gothic *usguldan*). The sense is "to render in exchange for what has been received," not to give back the object itself but "to spend as much as is equivalent to the amount by which one has benefited."

In order to understand the value of the terms in Gothic it is necessary to envisage the problem, which must have vexed the translator, of transposing into Gothic Greco-Roman ideas like those of Gr. *phóros*, Lat. *census* 'tax, assessment, the obligation to obey a higher authority', since the Germanic tradition knew only small independent groups, each obeying a particular chieftain, without any idea of a general organization.

Gild may be defined as a "reciprocal tribute"; it is a fee which is paid personally in order to benefit from a collective service within a fraternal grouping: an entrance fee (which is paid for in one way or another) into a fraternity bound by a common cult.

Wulfila thus gave a very special sense to a very different expression of traditional Gothic vocabulary, the word *gild* 'obligatory contribution (paid to a group of which one is a member and a beneficiary)', when he used it as an equivalent of *phóros*. This word evokes "a cult association," a true fraternity which is fulfilled, expressed and reinforced in banquets and common celebrations at which affairs of high importance are decided.

In fact Tacitus (*Germania*, 22) speaks of the *convivial* of the Germans, the banquets which were an essential part of their social and private life. They attended under arms, a fact which simultaneously showed the military and civil character of the matters to be debated: it was there they discussed "the reconciliation of private enemies, the conclusion of family alliances, the choice of chieftains, peace and war, because they believed that there was no more favorable moment for man's spirit to be open to frankness and to be fired to greatness."

We have here the very important idea of the *convivial communion*, which is as it were the symbol and the intensification of the fraternity. The point of departure of the economic groups called *ghildes* lies in such fraternities which were bound together by a common interest, by one and the same activity. And within such a group the banquets, *convivia*, *ghilda* are among the most characteristic institutions of the Germanic world. In thus "paying" (*gildan*) a fee to a fraternity, one pays a "due," a sum which one must pay, and the payment itself is money, the *geld*.

We have here given a resumé of a long and complex history which has led up to institutions and to collective values. But to begin with the word was attached to an idea of a personal kind: the proof of this is the *wergeld* 'the price of a man' (with *wer* 'man'), the price which was paid for the expiation of a crime, the ransom. Let us take up once again the *Germania* of Tacitus, chapter 21: "they are obliged to share the hostilities of the father or their kinsmen as well as their friendships, but they are not prolonged indefinitely. Even homicide can be redeemed with heads of cattle which are a benefit to the household." This *wergeld*, compensation for murder by a certain payment, is equivalent to Gr. *tísis*; it is one of the ancient aspects of the *geld.*

We are thus on three lines of development: first *religious*, the sacrifice, a payment made to the divinity, secondly *economic*, the fraternity of merchants, and thirdly *legal*, a compensation, a payment imposed in consequence of a crime, in order to redeem oneself. At the same time it is a means of reconciliation. Once the crime is over and paid for, an alliance becomes established and we return to the notion of the guild.

It was first necessary to define these ideas in their mutual relations and their peculiar senses in Germanic in order to assess how far apart these terms were in their original meaning from the Greek terms which they were used to translate. This is a fact to which insufficient attention has been paid. Scholars have always tended to proceed by straight interpretation of the Gothic without noting the effort of transposition which must have been involved and the difficulties which resulted from it. These Gothic expressions, when compared with those in Greek, are quite differently structured.

Another difference lies in the manner in which economic ideas became established in the Germanic and classical languages respectively. They are often bound up with facts of religion which make still wider the gulf which separated them from each other in the past, and they took shape in wholly dissimilar institutions.

PRESTIGIOUS EXPENDITURE

We must remember that the fraternities constituted a group of close solidarity and a kind of dining club. The two aspects of this institution could be maintained also in other ways. What was in origin a convivial group might become with the evolution of society an association of an economic, utilitarian, and commercial character.

One of the two aspects, the dining club, recalls a parallel institution in another society. It may be defined with the help of the Lat. *daps* 'banquet'. This word forms part of an etymological group which is well characterized in form, but has divergent meanings. Outside Latin, the root recurs in Greek *dáptō* (δάπτω) with the more general meaning "to devour," but also in a nominal form which is closely connected with *daps* in spite of the apparent difference: *dapánē* (δαπάνη) 'expenditure'. There are corresponding words in other languages: Old Icel. *tafn* 'sacrificial animal, sacrificial meal', Arm. *tawn* 'festival'.

It will be noticed that all the forms have the same suffix *-n*. This formal feature brings in the Lat. *damnum* < **dap-nom*, which is mentioned separately because at first sight it does not seem to be associated with the previous group.

Daps is a term of the religious vocabulary; the Scandinavian and Armenian expressions also belong to the same sphere. At an early date, within the historic period, *daps* had the sense of "banquet offered to the gods, festive meal." The *daps* is described by Cato in *De Agricultura* with a characteristic expression of the old Latin religious vocabulary, *dapem pollucere* 'to offer a sacred banquet'. This archaic expression *pollucere* is applied to the lavish feasts offered to the gods: *polluctum*.

Apart from this, there is evidence that *daps* is associated with the notions of abundance, lavish expenditure, generous offerings. Noteworthy are the adjective *dapaticus* and the adverb *dapatice*, obsolete forms collected and cited by Festus, who translates *dapatice* by *magnifice* 'in a magnificent manner'. A verb *dapino* from *daps* or perhaps from the Greek *dapanân*, which had a closely related meaning, also existed. We have only a single example of *dapino* in Plautus (*Capt.*, 897), but it is characteristic: *aeternum tibi dapinabo victum* '(if you tell the truth) I will offer you in perpetuity a sumptuous feast, I will entertain you royally for ever'.

A direct testimony defines the sense of *daps*, and *dapatice* as well as *dapaticus* confirm it: it is a "magnificent feast." Ovid in the fifth book of the *Fasti* shows us a poor peasant to whom Jupiter appears in disguise. Suddenly, he reveals who he is: the peasant offers him as a *daps* his only possession, an ox, which he roasts whole. This is his most precious possession.

In Greek, *dapanân* means "to spend," *dapánē* is "ostentatious expenditure." In Herodotus the expression is applied to lavish expenditure. The adjectives Gr. *dapsilḗs*, Lat. *dapsilis* (coined on the Greek model) apply to what is abundant, ostentatious. Icel. *tafn* denotes the consumption of food; Arm. *tawn*, a solemn feast. From all this we may abstract a general notion, that of "expenditure on the occasion of a sacrifice which involves the consumption of large amounts of food," expenditure required for a feast, for prestige, to display wealth.

We thus find in Indo-European a social phenomenon which in the language of the ethnologist is called *potlatch*; the display and consumption of wealth on the occasion of a feast. It is necessary to make a show of prodigality in order to demonstrate that one sets no store by it, to humiliate one's rivals by the instantaneous squandering of accumulated wealth. A man conquers and maintains his position if he outdoes his rivals in this reckless expenditure. The *potlatch* is a challenge to others to do likewise in their turn. The competitors make a still more lavish outlay, and this results in circulation of wealth, which is accumulated and expended for the prestige of some and the enjoyment of others, as Mauss has shown so well.

In Indo-European there is no clear notion of rivalry; the agonistic character so prominent in archaic society has here a subordinate role. Nevertheless, emulation is not absent from this expenditure. In fact it is closely connected with hospitality (cf. *daps* and *dapatice*). We see the social roots of an institution which is a necessity in certain communities; its essence is the obligation to make a gift of food, which is understood to impose reciprocity. But these are ideas and terms of great antiquity, which are in the process of fading. In historic times there remains only *damnum* with the derived sense of "injury sustained, what is taken away by forcible seizure." It is the expense to which one is condemned by circumstances or by certain legal stipulations. The peasant spirit and the legal exactitude of the Romans transformed the ancient conception: ostentatious expenditure became no more than an outright expenditure, what constitutes a loss. *Damnare* means to afflict a *damnum* on somebody, a curtailment of his resources; from this stems the legal notion of *damnare* 'to condemn'.

Side by side with the words in which the ancient notion has survived, there are innovations which create a new concept, and this means that we have simultaneously two strongly contrasted aspects of an ancient idea.

THE HANSA AND ITS MILITARY ORIGINS

Among the confraternities, where the participants in the communal banquet enjoy special privileges—those which characterize the guild in its medieval development—we encounter in the same economic and religious vocabulary of the Germanic world a close neighbor of *ghilda*, the *hansa*. This ancient term, which has survived down to modern times, designated in the countries around the North Sea an institution of great historic and economic importance. The Hansas are economic associations of groups of merchants; they constitute a society to which one belongs in virtue of a right which can be purchased, inherited or sold, and which forms part of commercial assets. The workings of this institution have been the object of numerous studies. The results of those who studied the origin of the word are negative: *hansa* has no certain etymology. Since no correspondence is found outside Germanic, it is the history in Germanic of the word which we must try to trace.

The story begins with the Gothic *hansa*, which gives a precise starting point to the analysis, although we have but few examples. In one passage, *hansa* translates, in apparently a vague way, the Greek *plêthos* 'crowd'. But in three other examples, *hansa* corresponds to *speîra* (σπεῖρα) 'cohort'. In Mark XV, 16: "the soldiers took Jesus inside the courtyard, that is to say into the pretorium, and they called together the whole cohort," Got. *alia hansa* 'totam cohortem'. It functions similarly in John XVIII, 3, 12. In the passage where *plêthos* is rendered by *hansa* (Luke VI, 17), if we read it in its entirety, we see that the translator had to translate successively *ókhlos* and *plêthos*. He chose *hiuma* 'turba' for *ókhlos*, and for *plêthos* 'multitudo' he used *hansa* 'cohort'. This unit in fact comprised several hundred men, as many as a thousand, and could represent a "crowd" which in some way had been mobilized to welcome Jesus.

It is not by accident that *hansa* is found in Old High German in Tatian to translate *cohors*. In OE *hōs* is "the follower of a lord." It is not until Middle High German that *hans(e)* assumes the sense of "commercial association" with the sense that it henceforward keeps. In Late Latin or in Latinized German *hansa* means a tax for a trade license as well as a commercial association.

The sense of "(military) cohort" indicates that one has to envisage the *hansa* as a company of warriors. *Hansa* would not have been employed in Gothic to translate *speîra* if it had, for instance, meant a religious group or a group with a common interest. In fact when Tacitus (*Germania* 13–14) describes the societies of young men (*comitatus*) which are attached to the chieftains, he gives us a picture of what the *hansa* must have been. These young men who attach themselves to a chieftain live from his bounty and receive abundant food which serves instead of pay (14, 4). They are always ready to follow him and defend him and to win renown under his orders.

It is probable that these companies of young warriors who vied with each other under their chieftain, while the chieftains competed among themselves to see who would attach to himself the keenest followers, formed the first model of the *hansa*. With the evolution of society, this company of warriors in which privileges and rites were shared was transformed into a society of companions of a different type, devoted to economic activities. The word remained but it was attached to a new reality.

BOOK I, CHAPTER SIX

Giving, Taking, and Receiving

Abstract. 1) Hittite, which attaches to the root *$d\bar{o}$*- the sense of "to take," suggests that in Indo-European the notions "to give" and "to take" converged, as it were, in gesture (cf. English *to take to*).

2) Contrary to the traditional etymologies which find no difficulty in bringing together Lat. *emo* and Got. *niman* (Germ. *nehmen*), but firmly separate *niman* from Gr. *némō*, justifying both decisions by appeal to the sense, it can be shown that:

a) Got. *niman* and Gr. *némō* can be superimposed without difficulty on the basis of their original (technical) sense, which is preserved exactly in the Got. *arbi-numja* and the Gr. *klēro-nómos* "heir."

b) Lat. *emo* "take," in its primitive gestural sense, has no etymological connection with Got. *niman*, which had originally a legal significance.

The expressions for "purchase" and "sale" are not separable from those for "give" and "take." The root **dō*- means "give" in all Indo-European languages. However, there is one language which fails to conform to this definition: in Hittite, *dā*- means "take" and *pai*- "give." We cannot categorically affirm, given the inconsistent notation of Hittite consonants, that *dā*- really corresponds to the Indo-European **dō*-; theoretically it could correspond to **dhē*- 'to place, put,' but this is not very likely. In general there is agreement in recognizing here—whatever the semantic evolution—the root **dō*. The fact is that if we started from **dhē-* to arrive at the sense "take" the semantic evolution would be even more obscure.

We simply have to take it as a fact that in Hittite *dā-* 'take' we have the contrary of the sense "give." To explain this scholars have adduced as a parallel the form *ā-dā* 'take' in Sanskrit. But here the preverb *ā-* is essential; it indicates movement towards the subject. With this preverb and the middle endings, the change to the sense "receive, take" is explicable within Sanskrit itself. Thus Sanskrit is of no direct help in explaining the sense of *dā-* in Hittite.

To explain it we may suppose that semantic shifts comparable to that undergone by the English word *take* in the expression *to take to* occurred within the ancient languages, but in different directions. This comparison may help us to discover the link between the two opposite meanings. Hittite and the other Indo-European languages have specialized in different ways the verb **dō-*, which lent itself, according to the syntactical construction, to either sense. While Hittite *dā-* restricted the sense to "take," the other languages constructed *dō* with the idea of a destination, which results in the sense "to give."[1]

This is not an artificial construction. Indo-European has several expressions for "take," each of which specifies the notion in a different way. If one accepts that the original sense is that preserved in Hittite, the evolution leading to the meaning "give," attested in the rest of the Indo-European domain, becomes intelligible.

Equally archaic is Hittite *pai-* "give." It is explicable as a compound of the preverb *pe-* with **ai-* 'attribute, allocate', a root attested in the Tokharian *ai-* 'give' and by several derived nouns, such as Av. *aēta-* 'part' and Osc. *aeteis* (gen. sing.), which translates Lat. *partis*.

The notion of "give" and "take" are thus linked in prehistoric Indo-European. It may be useful to consider in this connection an etymological problem relating to an already specialized word, Lat. *emo*, which, as will be shown below, once meant "take." In another language a root is encountered with the same sense, which differs from the Latin form by the initial *n-*: this is Germanic **nem-*, Got. *niman*, German *nehmen* 'take'. Here we have two verbs of the same sense, Lat. *em-*, Germanic *nem-*; is there an etymological connection between them? This has often been accepted; but how can it be morphologically justified? Recourse is had to two devices: *nem-* may be composed of **(e)n* + *em* or derived from a reduced form of *ni* + *em*. But in order to practice economy

1. Cf. our article "Don et échange dans le vocabulaire indo-européen," already cited.

in reconstructions, we must first consider what matters most, although the least attention has been paid to it so far, i.e. the meaning.

The most ancient Germanic forms appear in Gothic. They are very frequent and instructive. The form *niman* presupposes **nem-*, and we are acquainted with such a root. It appears in Gr. *némō* (νέμω), but the connection is ruled out because of the meaning of *némō*, which is not "take." For the time being we do no more than point this out and turn our attention to *niman*. We have the simple verb as well as several compounds with numerous preverbs in various applications. The Greek verbs to which it corresponds are *lambánein, aírein* 'take', *déksasthai* 'to receive' (very frequent, especially in the expression "to receive grace"); the compounds with *and-* translate *dékhesthai* (*apo-*, *para-*); those with *ga-* (cf. German *an-ge-nehm* 'pleasant') "to receive, conceive, welcome" and also *mente accipere, matheîn* 'receive with the mind, learn'. There is a considerable preponderance of instances in which *niman* signifies not "take" but "receive." In particular, a compound noun deserves attention because of its special technical meaning: *arbi-numja* 'heir'. The first part, *arbi*, is an independent term which means "heritage," Germ. *Erbe*, and which has considerable importance in the vocabulary of institutions. The form is clear: it is a neuter **orb-hyom*, which links up on the one hand with the Celtic terms of the same sense, e.g. Irl. *Orbe* 'heritage', *com-arbe* 'he who inherits' (the connection is so close that here, as in many other cases, it is possible that this may be a borrowing by Germanic from Celtic). Another connection is with adjectival forms which may serve to throw light on the concept: Lat. *orbus* 'bereft', Arm. *orb* 'orphan', Gr. *orpho-*, *orphanós*. Outside Celtic the terms corresponding to *arbi* designate a person deprived of a parent, and also an orphan. The relationship between "heritage" and "orphan" may seem somewhat strange; but there is an exact parallel of meaning in another family of words. The Latin adjective *hērēd-* 'heir' has a certain correspondent in Greek in the agent noun *khērōstḗs* 'collateral heir' and also in the adjective *khē̂ros* 'deprived of a parent', fem. *khḗra* 'widow'.

How can this etymological relationship be explained? In Homeric Greek, *khērōstḗs* is the member of the family who inherits in the absence of children, the relative who receives a property which has become "abandoned" (*khē̂ros*). Now in Gothic, *arbi* 'heritage', derived from the neuter form **orbhyom*, means literally 'what devolves on the *orbus*', that is to say, the property which is legally bestowed on a person who has suffered the loss of an immediate relative. It is the same idea as in *hērēs*, *khērōstḗs*. According to Indo-European usage property is directly transmitted to the descendant, but he is not for this reason alone qualified as an "heir." At that time, no need was felt for the legal precision which makes us qualify as "heir" the person who enters into possession of material wealth, whatever his degree of relationship with the deceased. In Indo-European, the son was not designated the "heir." Heirs were only those who inherited *in the absence* of a son. This is the case with *khērōstai*, the collaterals who divided an inheritance where there was no direct heir.

Such is the relationship between the notion of "orphan, deprived of a relative" (son or father) and that of "inheritance." It is illustrated by the definition given in a sentence from the *Germania* of Tacitus, Chapter 20: *Herede…successoresque sui cuique liberi, et nullum testamentum*, 'everybody has as heirs and successors his own children, and there is no will and testament'; *si liberi non sunt, proximus gradus in possessions fratres, patrui, avunculi*, 'if there are no children it is the next of kin who enter into possession, the degrees of succession being brothers, paternal uncles and maternal uncles'.

Such are the *arbi-numja*. The literal sense of *arbi-numja* is "he who receives (*numja*) the heritage (*arbi*). We may now ask which Greek term *arbi-numja* translates? It is *klēronómos* (κληρονόμος). There is also an analytical expression *arbi niman* 'to inherit' which translates the Gr. *klēronomeîn* (κληρονομεῖν).

The formation of the Greek compound is instructive. The second term links up with *némō*, *nómos*, *nomós*, a very rich family of words which has been the subject of a study by E. Laroche (*Histoire de la racine nem- en grec ancien*, 1949), in which its uses are examined in detail. This extremely important root has a rich variety of derivatives. The notion which is elicited is that of a legal division or sharing out, exclusively enjoined by law, custom, or by agreement, but not by arbitrary decision. Other verbs in Greek mean "divide"; an example is *datéomai*, but here the difference is this: *némō* is "to divide according to agreement or the law." It is for this reason that pastureland which has been shared out according to customary law is called *nomós*. The meaning of *nómos* 'the law' goes back to "legal apportionment." Thus *némō* is defined in Greek as "to divide legally" and also "to acquire legally by way of apportionment" (this being the sense of the active).

Is it an accident that the Gothic (*arbi-*)*numja* has the same formation as (*klēro-*)*nómos*, seeing that there would be no occasion to use the verb *niman* to translate *kléronomeîn* if it meant "to take"?

We can now see how the correspondence in a technical sense is arrived at between *némō* and *niman*: it is because Gothic *niman* means "take" in the sense of "receive legally" (cf. the use in which it corresponds to the Greek *dékhesthai*); hence comes the sense "receive, receive one's share, take." We may consider this expression *arbi niman* and the compound *arbi-numja* 'heir' as one of those where the ancient meaning of *niman* survives, the same meaning which *némō* had in Greek and which led to the formation of the term *klēronómos* 'heir'. The other usages are easily explicable.[2]

Thus the Germanic *niman* has nothing to do with *emo*. We must postulate a Germanic root *nem-* which, in the light of this interpretation of its sense, links up with the group of Indo-European forms from the root **nem-*, which are also abundantly represented in Greek.

To what result do we come if we subject *emo* to like scrutiny? Correspondences with initial *e-* are found in Old Slavonic *imǫ*, and in Baltic in the Lith. *imù, im̃ti* "take." Latin helps to delimit the meaning of *emo*, which is "to draw back, to take away."*Eximo* is to "take out of," while the meaning of *eximius* corresponds in sense to Gr. *éxokhos* 'outstanding, preeminent'. Further, we have *exemplum* which, by a curious development, means "an object set apart, separated by its very marked characteristics," hence "model, example"; *prōmo* means "draw from (a store)" and its verbal adjective *promptus* 'taken out, drawn, ready to hand'. *Per-imo* (with the meaning of the preverb which we find in *per-do*) means "make disappear, annihilate"; *sūmo* (from **subs-emo*) 'take by lifting'.

All this shows that the Latin sense "take < draw, remove, seize" has no connection with "take < receive, welcome" of Germanic. These are quite different notions in origin, and they reveal their peculiarity if we succeed in grasping their first sense. Each of them has its own domain and history. It is only at the end point of their evolution and in the most watered-down sense that Germanic *niman* and Latin *emo* resemble each other.

We return to *emo* 'buy'. The manner in which *emo* develops a restricted sense in Latin suggests that the meaning "buy" implies a quite different conception from that inherent in the terms belonging to the Greek family of *pérnēmi*, etc. It is clear that *emo* at first meant "take to oneself, draw to oneself." The possession which it affirms is expressed by the gesture of the man who takes the object and draws it to himself. The sense of "buy" must first have evolved with reference to human beings whom one "takes" after having fixed a price. The notion of "purchase" had its origin in the gesture which concluded the purchase (*emo*) and not in the fact of paying a price, handing over the value of the object.[3]

2. For the meaning of *némō* we may refer to our analysis of *némesis* in *Noms d'agent et noms d'action en indo-européen*, Paris, 1948, p. 79.

3. On Gr. *pérnēmi* and Lat. *emo*, see Book One, Chapter Ten.

BOOK I, CHAPTER SEVEN

Hospitality

Abstract. In Latin "guest" is called *hostis* and *hospes* < **hosti-pet-*. What is the meaning of these elements? What is the meaning of the compound?

1) *-pet-*, which also appears in the forms *pot-*, Lat. *potis* (Gr. *pótis*, *despótēs*, Skr. *patiḥ*), and *-pt-* (Lat. *-pte*, *i-pse*?) originally meant personal identity. In the family group (*dem-*) it is the master who is eminently "himself" (*ipsissimus*, in Plautus, means the master); likewise, despite the morphological difference, Gr. *despótēs*, like *dominus*, designated the person who personified the family group *par excellence*.

2) The primitive notion conveyed by *hostis* is that of equality by compensation: a *hostis* is one who repays my gift with a counter-gift. Thus, like its Gothic counterpart, *gasts*, Latin *hostis* at one period denoted the guest. The classical meaning "enemy" must have developed when reciprocal relations between clans were succeeded by the exclusive relations of *civitas* to *civitas* (cf. Gr. *xénos* 'guest' > 'stranger').

3) Because of this Latin coined a new name for "guest": **hosti-pet-*, which may perhaps be interpreted as arising from an abstract noun *hosti* "hospitality" and consequently meaning "he who predominantly personifies hospitality, the one who is hospitality itself."

The study of a certain number of expressions relating to exchange, especially those based on the root **mei-*, like the Latin *mūnus* 'an honorific post implying an obligation to reciprocate', I.-Ir. *Mitra*, the personification of a reciprocal contract (as illustrated in

Iliad VI, 120–246), **mei-t-* in the Latin *mūtuus*, Skt. *mithu-* 'changed (falsely)' > 'lie', Av. *miθwara* 'pair', also leads us to a word for "guest": *mēhmān* in middle and modern Iranian. Another word for "guest" in modern Iranian, *ērmān* < *aryaman*, links up with a very special kind of "hospitality" within a group of the Arya, one of the forms of which is reception by marriage.

The vocabulary of Indo-European institutions throws up some important problems, the terms of which have, in some cases, not yet been posed. We become aware of their existence and even partly create the object of our study by examining words which reveal the existence of an institution, the traces of which we can barely glimpse in the vocabulary of this or that language.

One group of words refers to a well-established social phenomenon, *hospitality*, the concept of the "guest." The basic term, the Latin *hospes*, is an ancient compound. An analysis of its component elements illuminates two distinct notions which finally link up: *hospes* goes back to **hosti-pet-s*. The second component alternates with *pot-*, which signifies "master," so that the literal sense of *hospes* is "the guest-master." This is a rather peculiar designation. In order to understand it better we must analyze the two elements **potis* and *hostis* separately and study their etymological connections.

The term **potis* first merits a brief explanation in its own right. It presents itself in its simple aspect in Sanskrit *pátiḥ* 'master' and 'husband' and in Greek *posís* 'husband', or in composition as in *despótēs*.

In Sanskrit the distinct senses "master" and "husband" correspond to different declensions of one and the same stem; but this is a development peculiar to Sanskrit. As for Gr. *posís*, a poetical word for "husband," it is distinct from *despótēs*, where the sense "master of the house" is no longer felt; *despótēs* is solely an expression of power, whereas the feminine *déspoina* conveys the idea of "mistress," a title of majesty.

The Greek term *despótēs*, like the Sanskrit correspondent *dám pátiḥ*, belongs with a group of ancient compound words, each of which had as its first element the name of a social unit of variable extension:

dám pátiḥ (master of the house)
viś „ (master of the clan)
jās „ (master of the "lineage")

Apart from *despótēs* and *dám pátiḥ*, the only one attested in a number of languages is the compound which is in Sanskrit *viś-pátiḥ* and in Lithuanian *vẽš-pats* 'clan chief'.

In Latin an extensive word family is organized around the word **potis* either as a free form or in composition. Apart from *hospes* it forms the adjectives *impos*, *compos* 'who is not…' or 'who is master of himself, of his senses' and the verb **potire*, the perfect of which, *potui*, survives incorporated into the conjugation of the verb meaning "be able," *possum*, which itself is formed from the adjective *potis* in a predicative use: *potis sum*, *pote est*, an expression which is simplified to *possum*, *potest*.

All this is clear and there would be no problem, the sense being constant and the forms superimposable, had not **potis* at two points of the Indo-European world developed a very different sense. In Lithuanian it provides the adjective *pats* 'himself' and also the substantive *pats* 'master' (in composition *vẽš-pats*). Parallel to this, we find in Iranian the compound adjective x^{u} *aē-paiθya* 'one's own', 'of oneself', which is used without distinction of person: "mine, yours, his"; "one's own." x^{u}*aē* is an Iranian form of the ancient reflexive pronoun **swe*, **se*, literally "of oneself," and *-paiθya* derived from the ancient **poti-*. These facts are well known, but they deserve careful scrutiny because of the singularity of the problem which they pose. Under what conditions can a word denoting "master" end up signifying identity? The primary sense of **potis* is well defined, and it had a strong force: "master," whence in marriage "husband," or in social terminology the "chief of some unit, whether house, clan, or tribe." But the sense "oneself" is also well attested. Here Hittite makes an important new contribution. It offers no form corresponding to **potis*, whether as adjective or substantive. Despite the early date at which it appears, Hittite has a vocabulary which has already been transformed to a considerable extent. Many notions now are conveyed by new terms. The interesting point in the present connection is that Hittite presents an enclitic particle, *-pet* (*-pit*), the sense of which is "precisely (him)self," a particle of identity referring to the object under discussion. An example is the following:

'If a slave flees,	takku IR-iš huwāi
and if he goes to an enemy country,	naš kururi KURe paizzi
the one who brings him back,	kuišan EGIR-pa uwatezzi
that very one takes him.'	nanzan **apāšpit** dai.

In this demonstrative *apāš-pit* 'that one precisely, that very one', the particle *-pit* establishes a relation of identity. It has, incidentally, the same function whether attached to a demonstrative, a noun, or even a verb. It is evident that the use of this particle corresponds to the sense of identity of **potis* found in Lithuanian and in Iranian.

Once the sense, the form and the use is established in these languages, we discover elsewhere other forms which can be linked with them in all probability. The Lithuanian particle *pat* signifies "exactly, precisely," like the Hittite *-pet*. With this may be compared Lat. *utpote*, the analysis of which must be rectified. It does not mean etymologically "as is possible" (with the *pote* of *pote est*) but "precisely inasmuch," with *pote* marking the identity. *Utpote* emphatically identifies the action with its agent, the predicate with the person who assumes it. We may also add the Latin postposition *-pte* in *suopte* (Festus: *suopte* ***pro*** *suo ipsius* 'his very own, what belongs to that very person'). A further example, but this is less certain, is the mysterious *-pse* of *ipse*. In any case, if we confine ourselves to the two Latin facts and to the Lithuanian *pat*, we can establish the survival of a use of **pot-* to designate the person himself, and to assign to him the possession of a predicate affirmed in the sentence. Accordingly, what was considered as an isolated use becomes an important indication and reveals to us the proper signification of *potis*. While it is difficult to see how a word meaning "the master" could become so weakened in force as to signify "himself," it is easy to understand how an adjective denoting the identity of a person, signifying "himself," could acquire the sense of master. This process, which illustrates the formation of an institutional concept, can be corroborated elsewhere: several languages have come to designate "the master" by a term meaning "himself." In spoken Latin, in Plautus, *ipsissimus* indicates the "master (mistress), the patron," the (personage) *himself*, the only one who is important. In Russian, in peasant speech, *sam* 'himself' refers to the "lord." Among a restricted but important community, the Pythagoreans, the formula *autòs éphā* (ἀυτὸς ἔφα) 'he himself has said it', with *autós* referred to the "master" *par excellence*, Pythagoras, was used to specify a dictum as authentic. In Danish, *han sjølv 'er selbst'* has the same meaning.

For an adjective meaning "himself" to develop into the meaning "master" there is one necessary condition: there must be a circle of persons subordinated to a central personage who assumes the personality and complete identity of the group to such an extent that he is its summation: in his own person he is its incarnation.

This is exactly the development we find in the compound **dem-pot*(*i*)- 'master of the house'. The role of the person so named is not to give orders but to assume a representation which gives him authority over the family as a whole with which he is identified.

A verb derived from **poti-*, like Skt. *pátyate*, Lat. *potior* 'to have power over something, have something at one's disposal', already marks the appearance of a sense of "to be able to." With this may be compared the Latin verb *possidēre* 'possess', stemming from **pot-sedēre*, which describes the "possessor" as somebody who is established on something. The same figurative expression has passed into the German word *besitzen*. Again, in Latin we have the adjective *compos* 'he who is master, who has command of himself'. The notion of "power" (theoretical) is thus constituted and it receives its verbal form from the predicative expression *pote est*, contracted to *potest*, which gives rise to the conjugation *possum*, *potest* 'I am capable, I can'.[1]

It is worthwhile pausing for a moment to consider a peculiar fact: as against Skt. *dam pati* and Gr. *despótēs*, Latin has formed from the same root an equivalent expression, but by a different procedure: this is *dominus*, a secondary derivative which belongs to a series of expressions for "chief." Thus *tribunus* 'chief of the tribe', in Gothic *kindins* (< **genti-nos*) 'chief of the *gens*'; **druhtins* (OHG *truhtin*) 'chief of the body'; *þiudans* < **teuta-nos* 'king, chief of the people'. This morphological process, whereby **-nos* is suffixed to the name of a social unit, has furnished in Latin and Germanic expressions for chiefs of political and military groups. Thus, by independent paths, the two series link up: on the one hand by means of a suffix, on the other by a compound word, the term for the master has been coined from the social unit which he represents.

We must return now to the compound which provoked this analysis, *hospes*, this time in order to study the initial term, *hostis*. Among the expressions common to the prehistoric vocabulary of the European languages it is of special interest: *hostis* in Latin corresponds to *gasts* of Gothic and to *gostĭ* of Old Slavonic, which also presents *gos-podi* 'master', formed like *hospes*.

But the meaning of Gothic *gasts* and OSl. *gostĭ* is "guest," whereas that of Latin *hostis* is "enemy." To explain the connection between "guest" and "enemy" it is usually supposed that both derived their meaning from "stranger," a

1. For the semantic study of *pot*(*i*)-, reference may be made to our article "Problèmes sémantiques de la reconstruction," *Word* X, Nos. 2–3, 1954, and *Problèmes de linguistique générale*, Gallimard 1966, pp. 301ff.

sense which is still attested in Latin. The notion "favorable stranger" developed to "guest"; that of "hostile stranger" to "enemy."

In fact, "stranger, enemy, guest" are global notions of a somewhat vague character, and they demand precision by interpretation in their historical and social contexts. In the first place, the signification of *hostis* must be narrowed down. Here we are helped by the Latin authors themselves who furnish a series of words of the same family and also some instructive examples of the use of the term *hostis*. It preserved its ancient value of "stranger" in the law of the Twelve Tables, e.g.: *adversus hostem aeterna auctoritas est(o)*, no word of which, with the exception of the verb "to be," is employed in the same sense as in classical Latin. It must be understood as "vis-à-vis a stranger, a claim for property persists forever," that is, it never lapses when it is against a foreigner that the claim is introduced. Of the word *hostis* itself, Festus says: *eius enim generis ab antiquis* ***hostes*** *appellabantur quod erant* ***pari iure*** *cum populo Romano, atque* ***hostire*** *ponebatur pro* ***aequare*** 'in ancient times they were called *hostes* because they had *the same rights* as the Roman people, and one said *hostire* for *aequare*'. It follows from this note that *hostis* is neither the stranger nor the enemy. We have to proceed from the equivalence of *hostire* = *aequare*, while the derivative *redhostire* is glossed as *referre gratiam* 'repay a kindness' in Festus. This sense of*hostire* is still attested in Plautus: *Promitto hostire contra ut merueris* 'I promise you a reciprocal service, as you deserve' (*Asin.* 377). It recurs in the noun *hostimentum*, explained as *beneficii pensatio* 'compensation of a benefit', and also *aequamentum* 'equalization'. To a more specialized technique belongs *hostus*, an archaic term of the language of agriculture, cited and explained by Varro, *R.R.* 1, 24, 3: ***hostum*** *vocant quod ex uno facto olei reficitur* 'one calls *hostus* the amount of oil obtained in a single operation of the press'. In some way the product is considered as a counterpart. Another technical term is *hostorium*, a stick for use with a bushel measure so as to keep a constant level. The old Roman pantheon, according to S. Augustine, knew a *Dea Hostilina*, who had as her task to equalize the ears of corn or to ensure that the work accomplished was exactly compensated by the harvest. Finally, a very well-known word, *hostia*, is connected with the same family: its real sense is "the victim which serves to appease the anger of the gods," hence it denotes a compensatory offering, and herein lies the distinction which distinguishes *hostia* from *victima* in Roman ritual.

It is a striking fact that in none of these words, apart from *hostis*, does the notion of hostility appear. Primary or derived nouns, verbs or adjectives, ancient expressions of the religious language or of rural vocabulary, all attest or confirm that the first sense is *aequare* 'compensate, equalize'.

How does *hostis* itself fit in with this? This emerges from the definition of Festus already cited: *"quod erant pari iure cum populo Romano."* This defines the relation of *hostis* and *hostire*: "the *hostes* had the same rights as the Romans." A *hostis* is not a stranger in general. In contrast to the *peregrinus*, who lived outside the boundaries of the territory, *hostis* is "the stranger insofar as he is recognized as enjoying equal rights to those of the Roman citizens." This recognition of rights implies a certain relation of reciprocity and supposes an agreement or compact. Not all non-Romans are called *hostis*. A bond of equality and reciprocity is established between this particular stranger and the citizens of Rome, a fact which may lead to a precise notion of hospitality. From this point of view *hostis* will signify "he who stands in a compensatory relationship" and this is precisely the foundation of the institution of hospitality. This type of relationship between individuals or groups cannot fail to invoke the notion of *potlach*, so well described and interpreted by Marcel Mauss in his monograph on "le Don, forme primitive de l'échange," *Année sociologique*, 1924. This system which is known from the Indians of Northwest America consists of a series of gifts and counter-gifts, each gift always creating an obligation of a superior gift from the partner, in virtue of a sort of compelling force. It is at the same time a feast connected with certain dates and cults. It is also an economic phenomenon, insofar as it secures circulation of wealth; and it is also a bond between families, tribes and even their descendants.

The notion of "hospitality" is illuminated by reference to *potlach*, of which it is a weakened form. It is founded on the idea that a man is bound to another (*hostis* always involves the notion of reciprocity) by the obligation to compensate a gift or service from which he has benefited.

The same institution exists in the Greek world under a different name: *xénos* (ξένος) indicates relations of the same type between men bound by a pact which implies precise obligations that also devolve on their descendants. The *xenía* (ξενία), placed under the protection of Zeus Xenios, consists of the exchange of gifts between the contracting parties, who declare their intention of binding their descendants by this pact. Kings as well as private people act in this way: "(Polycrates) had concluded a *xenía* (with Amasis) and they sent each other presents" ξενίην συνεθήκατο (verb of making a compact) πέμπων δῶρα καί δεκόμενος ἄλλα παρ' ἐκείνου (Herodotus III, 39). Mauss (*Revue des Études Grecques*, 1921) finds an example of the same custom among the Thracians.

Xenophon wanted to conclude arrangements for the food supplies of his army. A royal councilor tells him that if he wants to remain in Thrace and enjoy great wealth, he has only to give presents to King Seuthes and he would give him more in return (*Anabasis* VII, 3; X, 10). Thucydides (II, 97) gives much the same testimony apropos of another Thracian king, Sitalkes: for him it is more shameful not to give when one is asked to do so than not to receive when one has asked. In the civilization of Thrace, which seems to have been rather archaic, this system of obligation was still preserved in its full force.

One of the Indo-European expressions of this institution is precisely the Latin term *hostis*, with its Gothic correspondent *gasts* and Slavic *gospodĭ*. In historical times the custom had lost its force in the Roman world: it presupposes a type of relationship which was no longer compatible with the established regime. When an ancient society becomes a nation, the relations between man and man, clan and clan, are abolished. All that persists is the distinction between what is inside and outside the *civitas*. By a development of which we do not know the exact conditions, the word *hostis* assumed a "hostile" flavor and henceforward it is only applied to the "enemy."

As a consequence, the notion of hospitality was expressed by a different term in which the ancient *hostis* nevertheless persists, but in a composition with **pot*(*i*)*s*: this is *hospes* < **hostipe*/*ot-s*. In Greek, the guest (the one received) is the *xénos* and he who receives is the *xenodókhos* (ξενοδόχος). In Sanskrit, *atithi* 'guest' has as its correlate *atithi-pati* 'he who receives'. The formation is parallel to that of Latin *hospes*. The one who receives is not the "master" of his guest. As we have seen, *-pot-* did not have originally the meaning of "master." Another proof of this is the Gothic *brūþ-faþs* 'newly married man, νύμφιος', the German equivalent of which is *Bräutigam* 'bridegroom'. From *bruþ* 'newly married woman' was created the corresponding designation for the "newly married man," either with **potis* as in Gothic *brūþ-faþs*, or with *guma* 'man', like in the German *Bräutigam*.

The formation of **ghosti-* (*hostis*) deserves attention. It looks like an abstract word in *-ti* which has become a personal qualification. All the ancient compounds in *-poti-* have in effect as their first element a general word designating a group: thus **dems-poti*, *jās-pati*. We thus understand better the literal sense of **ghosti-pets*, *hospes* as the incarnation of hospitality. In this way we link up with the above definition of *potis*.

Thus the history of *hostis* recapitulates the change brought about in Roman institutions. In the same way *xénos*, so well characterized as "guest" in Homer, later became simply the "stranger," the non-national. In Attic law there is a *graphḕ xenías*, a lawsuit against a "stranger" who tries to pass for a citizen. But *xénos* did not evolve the sense of "enemy" as did *hostis* in Latin.

The semantic mechanism described for *hostis* has a parallel in another order of ideas and another series of words. It concerns those which come from the root **mei-* 'exchange', Skt. *ni-mayate* 'he exchanges' and especially the Latin term *mūnus* (< **moi-nos*, cf. the archaic form *moenus*). This word is characterized by the suffix *-nes*, the value of which was determined by Meillet (*Mem. Soc. Ling.*, vol. XVII) in *pignus*, *facinus*, *fūnus*, *fēnus*, all words which, like *mūnus*, refer to notions of a social character; cf also Skt. *rek-naḥ* 'heritage', etc. In fact *mūnus* has the sense of "duty, a public office." From it are derived several adjectives: *mūnis*, *immūnis*, *communis*. The last has a parallel in Gothic: *ga-mains*, German *gemein* 'common'.

But how can the notion of "charge, responsibility, public office" expressed by *mūnus* be associated with that of "exchange" indicated by the root? Festus shows us the way by defining *mūnus* as "*donum quod officii causa datur*" (a gift made for the sake of an *officium*). In fact, among the duties of a magistrate *mūnus* denotes spectacles and games. The notion of "exchange" is implied by this. In nominating somebody as a magistrate one confers on him honor and certain advantages. This obliges him to render counter-service in return, in the form of expenditure, especially for games and spectacles. In this way we can better understand the affinity between *gratus* and *mūnis* (Plautus, *Merc.* 105), and the archaic sense of *immūnis* as "*ingratus*" (that is to say, one who fails to make due return for a received benefit). If *mūnus* is a gift carrying the obligation of an exchange, *immūnis* is he who does not fulfill his obligation to make due return. This is confirmed in Celtic by Irl. *moin* (*main*) 'precious objects', *dag-moini* 'presents, benefits'. Consequently *communis* does not mean "he who shares the duties" but really "he who has *munia* in common." Now if the system of compensation is active within one and the same circle, this determines a "community," a group of persons united by this bond of reciprocity.

Thus the complex mechanism of gifts which provoke counter-gifts by a kind of compelling force finds one more expression among the terms derived from the root **mei-*, like *mūnus*. If we did not have the model of this institution, it would be difficult to grasp the meaning of the terms which refer to it, for it is within this precise and technical framework that these terms find their unity and proper relations.

A further question now arises: is there no simple expression for "gift" which does not call for a return? The answer is already given. It emerges from a previous study: there exists an Indo-European root, that of Latin *do*, *dōnum*, Greek *dôron*. It is true, as we have seen above (Book One, Chapter Five), that the etymological prehistory of **dō-* is by no means straightforward but is a criss-cross of apparently contradictory facts.

Nevertheless, in historical times the notion of "give" is everywhere attached precisely to the form of **dō-*, and in each of the languages (except Hittite) it gives rise to parallel formations. If in Greek the term down does not indicate in itself and unequivocally "gift" without reciprocity, the meaning of the adverb *doreán* 'gratuitously, for nothing' is sufficient guarantee that the "gift" is really a disinterested one. We must further mention forms stemming from another root which is little known and represented but which must be re-established in its importance and antiquity: this is the root **ai-*. From it is derived the verb *ai-tsi* 'give' in Tokharian, as well as the Hittite *pai-* (formed by attachment of the preverb *pe-* to *ai-*) 'give'. Greek has preserved a nominal form *aîsa* (αἶσα) 'lot, share'. In Oscan an abstract **ai-ti-* 'part' is attested by the genitive singular *aeteis*, which corresponds in meaning to the Latin genitive *partis*. Finally, Illyrian onomastics presents us with the proper name *Aetor*, which is the agent noun from this same root *ai-*. Here we have evidence for a new expression for "give" conceived as "assigning a portion."

Returning now to the words belonging to the etymological family represented in Latin by *mūnus*, *immūnis*, *communis*, we can pick out in Indo-Iranian a derivative of considerable importance and peculiar formation. This is a divine personification, the Indo-Iranian god *Mitra*, formed from **mei-*, in a reduced form, with the suffix *-tra-*, which generally serves to form the neuter nouns for instruments. In Vedic, *mitra-* has two genders, masculine as the name of the god and neuter in the sense of "friendship, contract." Meillet, in a famous article (*Journal Asiatique*, 1907) defined *Mitra* as a divinized social force, as the personified contract. But both "friendship" and "contract" may be given further precision by siting them in their context: what is concerned is not sentimental friendship but a *contract* in so far as it rests on an *exchange*. To make clear these notions as they were practiced and lived in ancient society, we may recall a Homeric scene which gives what might be called a "sociological" illustration. It is the celebrated episode of the sixth book of the *Iliad*, lines 120–236.

Glaucus and Diomedes, face to face, are trying to identify each other and discover that their fathers are bound by the bonds of hospitality (174). Diomedes defines his own position vis-à-vis Glaucus:

> Yes, you are for me an hereditary guest (*xeînos*) and that for a long time (215)... thus I am your host in the heart of the Argolid and you are mine in Lycia, the day when I shall go to that country. From now on we shall both avoid each other's javelin (224–226)...Let us rather exchange our weapons so that everyone may know here that we declare ourselves to be hereditary guests. (230–231)

This situation gives each of the contracting parties rights of greater force than the common national interest. These rights are in principle hereditary, but should be periodically renewed by means of gifts and exchanges so that they remain personal: it is for this reason that the participants propose to exchange arms. "Having thus spoken, they leap from their chariots, take each other by the hand and pledge their faith. But at that moment Zeus...stole away Glaucos' reason because in exchanging arms with Diomedes...he gives him gold in exchange for bronze, the value of one hundred oxen in exchange for nine" (232–236).

Thus the bard sees here a fool's deal. In reality the inequality of value between the gifts is intentional: one offers bronze arms, the other gives back arms of gold; one offers the value of nine oxen, the other feels himself bound to render the value of one hundred head of cattle.

This episode serves to throw light on the manifestations which in this society accompany the type of engagement which we call a "contract," and to restore its proper value to a term like Skt. *mitra-*. Such is the *mitra-* between Diomedes and Glaucus, an exchange which is binding and contractual. It also makes clear the formal analysis of the term. This suffix *-tra-* may form an *agent* noun as well as an *instrumental* one, the grammatical gender varying according to whether the action is the work of an instrument or a man: hence we have along with the neuter *mitram*, the masculine *mitras*. We might examine mythology and try to discover in the role of Mitra the survivals of its etymological origin. But first we must extend the inventory of notions which were formed from the same root and which are related to those which we have been studying. Closely related to **mei-* is a form **mei-t-* with the suffix *-t-*, which appears in the Latin verb *mūtō* 'change', 'exchange'. The signification may be more precisely delimited if it is compared with the adjective *mūtuus* 'reciprocal, mutual'. We must also consider a particular use of the adjective: *mūtua pecūnia* 'money lent or borrowed', as well as the verb derived from the adjective as thus used, *mūtuāre* 'borrow', i.e. to take money with the obligation to repay it. Thus "loan" and "borrowing" enter in their turn into the cycle of exchange. This is not the end of the matter. "Exchange" here has a close affinity with the "gift." The Gothic correspondent of the Latin from *mūtō*, *mūtuus* is *maidjan* 'exchange'. Now the derived noun *maiþms* (from **mait-mo-*) translates the Greek *dôron* 'gift', but in a passage where it implies "recovery" and to a certain extent "exchange."

The other derivatives are divided into:

1) one group with a specialized sense, e.g. Skt. *mithu-* 'false, lie'; as with Latin *mūtō*, the idea of "changing" leads to that of "altering." When we say of somebody that he has altered, this is rarely to his advantage.
2) A series of other derivatives, however, preserve the proper sense. This is particularly so in Iranian: e.g. Avestan *miθwara-* 'paired'; *maēθman-* < **mei-t-men* 'pairing'. A development of a social character gives to *maēθman* the sense of "mutuality," and this leads to the designation of the "guest" in Middle and Modern Iranian by *mēhmān* < **maēθmānam* (accusative), which by a long detour brings us back to our starting point. Once again we end up by defining the "guest" by the notion of mutuality and the bonds of reciprocity.[2]

There is another term for the "guest" in modern Iranian: *ērmān*, the ancient form of which is attested as *aryaman* 'intimate friend', a term well known in Indo-Iranian. This is also the name of a mythological figure, the name of a god. *Aryaman* is the god of hospitality. In the Rig Veda, as in the Atharva, he is especially associated with marriage.

In whatever way we interpret the formative *-man* (this must be a nominal form), the name of the god *Aryaman* is connected with the term *arya*. We shall see later in this work that *arya* is the common and reciprocal term used by members of a community to designate themselves. It is the name for a man of the same language and the same race. This explains why one of *Aryaman*'s functions was to admit individuals into an exogamic community, called "Aryan," through a marriage ceremony: it is a kind of internal hospitality, a tribal alliance. Aryaman intervenes when a woman taken from outside the clan is introduced for the first time as a wife into her new family.

Aryaman later came to be used in a number of different senses. The Persian *ērmān* 'guest' has been quoted above. In the language of the Ossetes, an Iranian people occupying an enclave in the Caucasus with institutions and vocabulary of great antiquity, the word *limän* means "friend," and this is the regular phonetic development of *aryaman*. The bonds of relationship, of family and tribal

2. On the root *mei-* see our article "Don et échange..." quoted above.

friendship, are redefined in each language accordingly as the terminology remains fixed or evolves. These terms, far removed from one another, came back to the same problem, that of institutions of welcoming and reciprocity, thanks to which the men of a given people find hospitality in another, and whereby societies enter into alliances and exchanges. We have found a profound relationship between these institutional forms as well as a recurrence of the same notions behind a terminology which is sometimes refashioned.

BOOK I, CHAPTER EIGHT

Personal Loyalty

Abstract. For Osthoff, *Eiche und Treue* (1901), the group of Germ. *treu* is related to the Indo-European name for "oak," Gr. *drûs*: to be loyal means to stand as firm as an oak. It will be shown that if the relationship really exists, the affiliation is the reverse: the common root signifies "to be firm" and the adjective designates "tree," literally "what is resistant, the solid one" (the meaning of "oak" is limited to a period of Greek and should not be attributed to the time of Indo-European unity).

Between Germanic **drauhti-* (Got. *ga-drauhts* 'soldier') and **drauhti-no-* (old Icelandic *drottin-* 'chief lord'), the affiliated words in Slavic and Baltic meaning "friend, companion" allow us to establish the link known elsewhere (in *dominus,tribūnus*, etc.) between the nominal expression and its derivative in *-no-*. **drauhti* is a collective designating "company" (in the military sense, as described for us by Tacitus, *Germ.* 13) and *drauhtino-*, the *princeps* who impersonates authority.

In the light thrown both by the Germanic legends concerning Odin *Herjan* and by Tacitus *Germania* 43, Gothic *harjis* (Germ. *Herr*) is revealed as the name of a group of masqueraders who on occasion assembled for plundering expeditions. (Although Gr. *koíranos* may formally correspond to *herjan*, the meaning which emerges from Homeric usage prompts the rejection of this purely formal equation.)

Lat. *fidēs* preserves a very ancient meaning, blurred and simplified in other languages where the root **bheidh* is represented, and altered even in Latin itself after a certain period; its meaning was not "trust" but "the inherent quality of a person which inspired confidence in him and is exercised in the form of a protective authority over those who entrust themselves to him." This notion is very close to that of **kred-* (studied below in Chapter 15). So we can understand why Lat. *fidēs* was at all periods the noun corresponding to *credo*.

The terms which we have studied up to now have all been concerned with the relationships of man to man, in particular the notion of "hospitality." From this point of view, which is both personal and institutional, we shall now consider the notion of *personal loyalty* within a particular group of languages, but with reference to the common Indo-European vocabulary: that is to say, the bond established between a man who possesses authority and the man who is subjected to him by a personal pledge. This "loyalty" gives rise to an institution which is very ancient in the western Indo-European world and which is most clearly apparent in the Germanic world.

I

The designation of this concept appears in an expression represented today by the German *Treue* and which is well attested in all Germanic dialects: in Gothic by the verb *(ga)trauan*, which translates πεποιθέναι 'to have faith', the noun *trauains*, πεποίθησις, 'trust', *trūa* in Icelandic, *truōn* in Old English (German *trauen*), all derived from a nominal stem **truwō*; Icelandic *trū* 'respect, trust bestowed', from which is derived Icelandic *trur* 'loyal, faithful'. The action noun derived from this root has undergone a considerable development and has persisted for a long time in Germanic vocabulary: Gothic *trausti* 'pact, alliance', which translates διαθήκη, Icelandic *traustr* 'reliable, sure, loyal'.

This is the source of the modern derivatives some of which designate a pact of alliance, an agreement, the pledged word, while others, verbs and nouns, have the meaning to "inspire confidence," to "reassure," to "console"; on the one hand we have the group represented by the English "trust" and on the other the group represented by the German *trösten* 'console'. These moral notions are clearly bound up with an institution. In Germanic feudal vocabulary the Latinized form *trustis* designates the bond of fealty and also those who have thus bound themselves and who form the followers of a personage. The Old High German noun *Traue* is the source of the French *trève* 'truce'.

The diversity of the Germanic forms shows the complexity of this idea, which results in terms as different as Germ. *Treue*, *trauen* 'to have trust', *Trost* 'consolation', Engl. *trust*, *true* and *truce*. They all have one and the same origin in a Germanic root **dreu-*, from which stems a Germanic abstract **drou-sto-* (Old Icel. *traust* 'faith, trust', Germ. *Trost* 'consolation'), a derivative **draust-yo-* (Gothic *trausti* 'pact') and an adjective **dreu-wo-* (Gothic *triggws* 'faithful', German *treu*).

This group of words was studied by the etymologist H. Osthoff, in his *Etymologica Parerga* (1901), a collection of different etymological studies, one chapter of which is entitled "Eiche und Treue" ('Oak and Loyalty'). This strange title summarizes the substance of a lengthy study (about a hundred pages) which starts with this word family and connects it up with an Indo-European prototype, which he thought was the name of the "oak." The formal basis of the deduction is a connection of the Indo-European **dreu-wo* with Greek *drûs* (δρῦς) 'oak'. Osthoff considers that the "oak," the hardiest and strongest of the trees, was the symbol of qualities the most abstract expression of which is found in this group of words with reference to the notion of "loyalty." Thus the "oak" on this showing stood as a symbol of institutional "loyalty." This demonstration has found a place in our etymological dictionaries, so it is important to check its foundations. Every etymological reconstruction must give the greatest weight to the dialect distribution of the forms and to the relationships which emerge from them in the classification of the different senses. Now it can be shown that Osthoff's study completely falsifies the whole history of these terms; the true relations of the facts have been reversed.

In effect, if Osthoff is right, the name of the oak should be a common Indo-European one: it must have existed in all languages and in the given sense. We should thus expect to find a primary term in Indo-European, of constant form and sense, designating the "oak." This is far from being the case. This word for "oak" appears only in one language and only at a certain period of that language. Before we begin to discuss it at all, one point of fact must be made. The oak is a tree limited to a specific area. The Indo-Europeans could not have known and designated it with a common name because it does not exist everywhere: there is no word for oak in Indo-Iranian for a very good reason. It is a tree of Central Europe and only the languages of Central and Eastern Europe have a word to denote it.

It would appear that this lexical distribution corresponds to the movement of the Indo-European peoples towards their historical sites. Everything—the historical, linguistic and archaeological facts—indicates that migration took place from east to west and that the Germanic peoples were among the last to be installed in the regions which they now occupy. This migration took place in several stages along a route which we can work out, and it ended in the region where the oak is found. It certainly did not start from that region.

This is confirmed by an examination of the names for the oak. The Indo-European form appears in two guises **de/orw-* and **drew-* with a full and a reduced degree respectively of the root and of the suffixal element, conforming to the well-established pattern of the Indo-European root. From these two forms came respectively the Gr. *dóru* (δόρυ) and *drûs*. In studying the senses, we shall take together the forms which derive from one or the other form of the root. Now it can be seen that the radical **dreu-* with its alternative forms **drū-*, **doru-* exclusively designates "tree." Thus Gothic *triu* translates Gr. *xúlon* 'tree, wood', and this is the sense in most languages. It is easy to establish that the old Slavic *druva* signifies "wood," that the Indo-Iranian forms *drū*, *dāru* denote exclusively "tree," "wood" and "plant." In the Avestan material the adjective *drvaēna*, like the Gothic *triweins* which corresponds to it, is applied to a "wooden" object. In certain languages a secondary differentiation between the derivates took place, such as in Old Slavic between *drevo* 'tree' (from **derwo-*) and *druva* 'wood' (from *druwo*).

The Greek forms are of particular interest in this connection. From the same root Greek has derived two historically distinct, but evidently related, terms: *dóru* '(wood of) the spear' and *drûs* 'oak', which we must consider in greater detail. The first sense of *dóru* is "tree, sapling"; thus in *Od.* 6, 167 Odysseus says to Nausicaa: "I have never seen grow from the earth such a tree (*dóru*)."

It is also the wood used in the construction of ships: δόρυ νήϊον, the keel of a ship; further, it is the "wood" of the spear, the shaft made from ash: δόρυ μείλινον (*Il.* 5, 666); finally, it is the spear itself, inasmuch as it is made of wood. All these are specifications of the sense "wood," just as in French, where *bois* may be applied to a bed, an orchestra or a stag.

On the other hand, *drûs* did not always designate the "oak" in Greek. The ancients tell us so quite explicitly: according to the testimony of a scholiast of the *Iliad* (*ad Il.* 11, 86) δρῦν ἐκάλουν οἱ παλαιοὶ πᾶν δένδρον 'the ancients called any tree *drûs*'. This is confirmed by the usage of writers; thus, Sophocles, *Trach.* 766 δρῦς πίειρα 'the resinous tree, the pine'. The word became specialized at an early date. Already in Homer, *drûs* is the oak, the "tree" *par excellence*, associated with certain cults, like the prophetic oaks of Dodona. But this specialization occurred in the course of the history of Greek and at a recent period, since it did not obliterate the memory of a time when *drûs* designated "tree" in general, in accordance with the testimony of all the other languages, where the corresponding term signifies "wood, tree" and not "oak." Further, we find in Greek itself the original sense of *drûs* in the derivative *drûás*, which designated the mythological beings, the Dryads: these are nymphs which reside in trees, and not in oaks in particular.

There is another Greek form which is connected with *drûs*. This is *déndron* (δένδρον), Homeric *déndreon* (δένδρεον) 'tree', the result of a dissimilation of **der-drewon*, a reduplicated form of the type called broken reduplication (cf. Lat. *carcer* from **karkros*, Gr. *karkínos*).

Here, too, the sense of the root is "wood, tree." Thus we see how all these testimonies converge and locate in a comparatively recent phase of Greek the development of the term *drûs* from the ancient sense "wood, tree," to that of "oak." It follows that Osthoff's account should be exactly the reverse. The sense of "oak" is the latest phase, and one limited to Greek, of an evolution of which the intermediary step is "tree" and which may proceed from an original concept such as "to be firm, solid." We find an exact parallel to this evolution in modern Iranian. The Persian name for "tree" *diraxt*, Middle Iranian *draxt*, is an ancient verbal adjective *draxta-* (the participle of *drang-*), the literal meaning of which is "what is steady, what is firm"; the relationship is the same as that of Greek *drûs* to **dreu-*.

It can be seen that the restriction in sense which leads to "tree" and "oak" depends on local conditions. In fact the development did not take place precisely in Germanic, where **dreu* remains the name for "tree" in general (Got. *triu*, cf. Engl. *tree*), while for "oak" there is a special term **aik-* (German *Eiche*).

We are now able to reconstruct the development of Indo-European forms along different lines. From this root **dreu-* come the adjectives Skt. *dhruva-* (the *dh* is secondary, of analogical origin; it replaces an ancient *d*), Ir. *druva-* 'solid, firm, in good health'; with an initial *su-*, Slavic *sŭdravŭ*, '*salvus*, healthy'; in Baltic, Lith. *drutas* 'strong, solid' (cf. Pruss. *druwis* 'faith, guarantee', *druwit* 'believe', 'to have faith'). In Greek (Argolic dialect) *dro(w)ón* is translated by *iskhurón* 'strong' according to a gloss of Hesychius. This is a development into which the whole family of *Treue* (Gothic *triggws* 'faithful', 'loyalty') naturally fits.

But on the other hand **dreu-* furnishes also an adjective **drū* 'strong, resistant, hard' which has become the word for "tree." It follows from this that the lexical development must be placed at different levels: the sense of "fidelity," peculiar to Germanic, is directly connected with that of the Indo-European root, whereas the sense of "tree" was an early specialization which occasionally, as in Greek, alone survives.

Here we can see in its full force the distinction between *signification* and *designation* and how great the gap between them can be, often so big that the designation gives no clue to the signification, if semantic pointers are not available.[1]

The relationships of "trust" and "fidelity" find other expressions which we shall study particularly in the Germanic languages. One of these words is used as a term of nobility and as a military term. Our study may begin with the Gothic word *ga-drauhts* which in the New Testament translates στρατιώτης 'soldier'. It is composed of a prefix *ga-*, indicating community, and a derivative in *-ti* from the verb *driugan*, which translates στρατεύεσθαι 'to wage war, take the field'. From the same abstract noun *drauhti-* comes the denominative present *drauhtinon* 'στρατεύεσθαι' and the compound *drauhti-witoþ* 'στρατεία, combat', where the second element signifies "rule, law." Outside Gothic, the abstract in Germanic takes on a different sense: Old Icelandic *drōt*, and the corresponding forms in other dialects, designate the "armed retinue," the "troop"; thus Old English *dryht*, Old Saxon *druht*, Old High German *truht*. Especially notable is the nominal derivative of **druhti-*; it furnishes in its turn a form in *-no*-which designates the "chief, "lord": Old Icel. *drottinn*, Old Engl. *dryhten*, Old High Germ. *truhtin*. The Icelandic feminine *drottning* 'queen' is still preserved in the Scandinavian languages.

Such is this Germanic word-family, the morphological relations of which are clearly apparent: an abstract noun, Goth. *drauhti-*, and a derived noun, literally "he who has the same *drauhti-*, to designate the soldier. On the other hand, another derivative in *-no* signifying 'chief' is formed on the basis of the abstract *druhti-*. These are the facts to be sited in the semantic context which will illuminate them.

The proper sense of these terms is recovered by comparison with a neighboring language, Slavic, and to some extent in Baltic. From this it emerges that

1. For **doru-*/**dreu-* see our article "Problèmes sémantiques de la reconstruction" already cited.

"troop" and "chief of the troop" develops from a much more general sense, that of "friend." In Old Slavic and in the modern Slav languages, *drugŭ* 'φίλος', 'ἑταῖρος' signifies "friend, companion." The notion of a bond, of friendship, is so strong that the adjective, when repeated, may render the notion of reciprocity, "the one, the other": Russian *drug, druga.* The same sense is found in Lithuanian, where *draugas*, with a different vocalic grade, signifies "friend, one of a couple, of a pair"; hence the abstract noun *draugẽ* 'friendship, company, group of friends'. Baltic utilizes this nominal stem in a grammatical function, Lithuanian *draugé* 'with'. Thus the Old Prussian compound noun *draugi-waldūnen* signifies 'he who shares the inheritance, the co-heir', German '*Mit-erbe*'.

The interest in this confrontation of German, Slavic, and Baltic is the light it throws on the proper signification of these Germanic words. We have here the notion of "company," specified in the peculiar condition indicated in Germanic: a warrior friendship. Old Slavic preserves a parallel expression, the collective term *družina* 'comrades in arms, συ-στρατιῶται'. The Gothic word for "soldier" *ga-drauhts*, literally "he who is part of a companionship, a friendship," understood as a collective term the group of people who are bound together by common service in war. The abstract word *drauhts* is "warrior companionship"; *drauhti-witoþ* 'στρατεία' is "combat" as the "rule of the **drauhti-*."

Let us now consider Old Icelandic *drottinn* and its group. The Germanic form **druxti-nax*, going back to **drukti-nos*, is an example of a well-defined mode of formation: these are the secondary derivatives formed like Latin *dominus*, which designate the person at the head of a certain social group. In the Germanic languages, this type is represented by several important derivatives: Gothic *þiudans* (from **teuta-nos*) 'king, chief of the community', *kindins* (from **genti-nos*) 'chief of the *gens*', parallel with *tribūnus* from *tribus*. In Old English *dryhten* 'lord' (in the Christian texts 'the Lord') represents **drukti-nos* 'chief of the *drukti*'.

This type of relationship was characteristic of ancient Germanic society. An illustration is found in Tacitus, independent of the terms we are trying to interpret and so all the more precious, in chapters XIII and XIV of the *Germania.* The historian describes the manner in which the Germans fight, how they assemble, how they are organized in companies, and the relations between the companies and their chief:

> Noble birth or the illustrious deeds of their fathers bestow on some the rank of a prince from early childhood; the others attach themselves to chieftains, who are

> in the full vigor of manhood and ripe in experience; and the role of companion is nothing to be ashamed of. It even confers distinction, depending on the esteem of the prince to whose retinue a man belongs. Among these *comites* there exists a singular rivalry to occupy the first place beside their prince; the princes for their part vie with each other as to the most numerous and the most courageous companions.

This reminds us of the relations between the *princeps* and his *comites*: the *princeps* is here called '*drottinn*' and the *comites* '*gadraunts*'. A certain correlation is established between the historian's description and the analysis of the vocabulary.

The formation of *gadrauhts* is repeated in Gothic in the synonym *gahlaiba* 'συ-στρατιώτης', 'companions in arms, comrades', literally 'he who shares the same bread'. It seems evident that there is a close relationship between Gothic *ga-hlaiba* and Latin *companio*: one of the two is a calque of the other. Probably *gahlaiba* is the original and *companio* the imitation.

The name for the "army" is a term common to the Germanic dialects: Gothic *harjis*, Old Icel. *herr*, Old High Germ. *hari*. It appears already in the form *hari-* several times in the Runic inscriptions. It is further also met with as *Hario-*, *Chario-* in the Germanic proper names which have been handed down by classical authors.

This term has a counterpart in Celtic; the form *harja* coincides exactly with Middle Irish *cuire* < **koryo* 'army'. This is confirmed by the names of Gaulish peoples: the *Vo-corii*, *Tri-corii*, *Petru-corii* are so named because they have two, three or four troops; thus they are constituted by a union of groups of variable numbers. Here, too, Baltic, if not Slavic, has a corresponding form: Lithuanian *karias*, Old Prussian *karjis* 'army'.

It is possible that this comparison extends beyond the western world, if we accept the Old Persian *kāra* as related, a word which signifies in certain passages of the Achaemenid inscriptions "the people" and in others "the army" and so denotes "the people in arms." In this case the correspondence is less exact. The vocalic grade is different; it has a long vowel and it is not a form in *-*yo*. Further, *kāra-*, which recurs in the Middle Persian *kārčār*, Persian *kārzār* 'combat' is isolated and peculiar to Persian. There is no comparable Indo-Iranian term.

We may now try to make the meaning of the term in Germanic more precise with the help of an ancient mythological designation: Old Icel. *Herjan*, the name or surname of the great god Odin. This name is remarkable even in its formation; it belongs to the same type of derivatives in *-no-* mentioned above apropos of the words for "chief." *Herjan* rests on **koryo-nos*, 'chief of the army'. The name of Odin himself, i.e. *Wotan*, is also formed in this manner: **Wōda-naz* 'chief of the *Wōda*', 'of the frenzy', or 'the frenzied army'.

Thus in his two names the great god is designated as the chief of a group: as Odin, he is the chief of the frenzied group which perpetrate their misdeeds in his name; as *Herjan*, he is the chief of the troop whose mythological name is also known to us, the *Einherjar*, the dead warriors who inhabit Walhalla and fight under his orders. Odin in this guise is the god of the dead. This is the troop which he commands, which constitute his proper *Heer* 'army'.

How do they fight? There is a correspondence between the practices of the terrestrial *Heer* and those of the same *Heer* of the next world. There is the same grouping, infernal or terrestrial, there are the same relations between the members of that group and its chief.

Here, too, Tacitus throws much light on the sense of the words in question and his text, on the other hand, is illuminated by a study of these words. In chapter XLIII of the *Germania* he describes the appearance which these warrior peoples assume: "Those fierce men improve on their savage nature by enlisting the help of art and time: they blacken their shields, they dye their skin, and they choose the darkest nights for battle. The horror alone and the darkness which envelops that doleful army (*feralis exercitus*) spreads terror: there is no enemy who can withstand that strange and, so to speak, infernal aspect; because in each battle the eyes are the first to be vanquished!" Who are such people? They are the *Harii*. Tacitus here describes what was later called **Wuotanes heri* (German *wütendes Heer*), the "frenzied army" or the "army of Wotan," disguised as the army of the dead: they take on the appearance of infernal beings (it is a *masquerade*) choosing the night for fighting, to strike terror into their enemies; it is an irruption of the dead among the living. Such a masquerade is supposed to represent Odin's army in his character as *Herjan*, imitating on earth the exploits of Odin's band, those which the epic calls *Berserkr*, literally "those who are disguised as bears."

The Germanic name of the "army," Gothic *harjis*, is defined by these conceptions and also in its lexical connections as a devastating troop: the proper activity of the *Heer* is characterized by the derived verb Icel. *herja*, Old High Germ. *herian* 'to make a foray', German *heeren, verheeren* 'to devastate'. In this linguistic, ethnographic, and mythological complex, we discover the structure and function of the *Heer*, which is something quite different from *exercitus* in Latin or *laós* in Greek. It is a grouping of the same kind as that described by Tacitus in chapters XIII and XIV of the *Germania* in the passage cited above to illustrate the notion of *drauhti-*: restricted groups devoted to a common life and a warrior companionship by loyalty to the chief whom they follow, occasionally sallying forth to plunder or to tribal combat. It is quite a different conception from the *philía* of the Hellenic world, which is a normal relationship between the members of large groups, whether family or tribe, sharing the same laws, speaking the same tongue and bound by ties of hospitality. In Germanic we have an exclusive friendship between man and man, in a masculine society, devoted to the practice of arms: *harjis*, *drauhti*, like German *trauen*, all refer to his complex of ideas and institutions.

However, is this term limited to the western European world? The Greek term *koíranos* (κοίρανος) 'chief' has often been connected with *harjis*, etc. It is curious, in fact, that the formation of *koíranos* coincides exactly with Icelandic *herjan* 'chief of the army', and this suggests that we have in Greek the same name for the army, in the form **koryo-*. We must therefore define more closely the sense of *koíranos* which is rather vaguely translated as "chief."

In Homer, the *koíranos* exercises the functions of commander, and the term, taken in this sense, provides a derivative verb *koiranéō* 'to act as *koíranos*'. For instance, *Il.* 2, 207: "Thus *koiranéōn*, he went through the ranks of the army…"; *koiranéōn* (present participle) consists in reprimanding some and encouraging others; in calming down those who are excited and giving confidence to the less courageous. As for those who want to impose their views and to meddle by giving advice to their chief, he reminds them (ibid, v. 204–205): οὐκ ἀγαθόν πολυκοφανίη εἷς κοίρανος ἔστω, είς βασιλεύς…'*polu-koiraníē* is not a good thing: let there be only one single *koíranos*, one *basileús*'. For the poet, different from the *basileús*, the *koíranos*is not a war lord; he never takes part in the battle himself nor is he found at the head of his troops. He goes among the ranks to make his personal authority felt. Nor does he preside over the debates in the assembly. In the *Odyssey* (18, 106) the beggar Iros takes it on himself to chase away those who come to beg in their turn; he provokes from Odysseus the advice not to act as a *koíranos*, that is to say to meddle by giving orders, by administering reprimands. So the *koíranos* is here again different from a fighting chieftain. In Homer, as in non-Homeric texts, *koiraneîn* is the activity of a local potentate exercising his authority over the people of the household rather than over the whole army. If in the *Odyssey* there are several passages in which the suitors *koiranéousi*, this is because they give orders to domestics and behave like masters. But it would seem that we cannot regard the *koíranos* as the military chief at the head of a given unit. The title corresponds to a very different function from that of the Nordic *herjan*.

Another question is the connection which there may be between *koíranos* and the Hittite *kuirwanaš* (variants *kuriwanaš*, *kurewanaš*) 'independent, autonomous, not a vassal'. As far as it can be defined, the Hittite term seems only to have a fortuitous resemblance to *koíranos*. It is even possible, to judge by the variations in form, that it comes from a local language. It is not clear what to make of the fact that the proper name *Koíranos* is borne in Homer by a Lycian and a Cretan. Similarly, it is impossible to interpret in one way or another the absence of the term *koíranos* in Mycenean.

II

The expression *par excellence* for the notion of "loyalty," the one which is the most general and at the same time the best characterized in western Indo-European, is the Latin *fidēs* with its etymological family. It is attested in several spheres of usage, i.e. with religious, moral, philosophical, and even legal senses. We shall now consider this group of words in order to define as far as we may the modalities of the notion by study of the normal relations.

To the family of Latin *fidēs* corresponds in Greek that of *peíthomai* (πείθομαι). The verbal form appears first in the middle, the present active *peíthō* 'persuade' being secondary. It was coined at a fairly late date from *peíthomai* 'obey'. In accordance with an ancient morphological alternation, *peíthomai* has as its perfect the active form *pépoitha*, like *gígnomai*: *gégona*. This root provided an abstract noun *pístis* 'trust, faith', with an adjective *pistós*, 'faithful'. From *pistós* comes a new present tense *pistoûn* 'to make trustworthy, to oblige, to bind by promise' and also *pisteúō* 'to have faith', which has persisted.

Apart from Latin and Greek we can only cite with the same sense a noun form in Albanian *bē* 'oath', from **bhoidā*. There are numerous other phonetically comparable forms, but the sense is so different that we can not justify the relationship which the form suggests: this is where the difficulties of the problem begin. The facts are first those of Germanic: the Gothic form *beidan* goes back to **bheidh-*, that is the same prototype as Latin *fidēs*, *foedus*, but the Gothic verb means 'προσδοκᾶν, to expect, to await, to endure', the same as Old Icel. *biđa*. Further, with another grade of the root, we have Gothic *baidjan*, with a different meaning again, because it translates Greek *anankázein* 'compel', just like Old Saxon *bēdian* 'compel', 'force'. The sense of "constrain" permits however a connection with the Slavic *běditi*, which translates the same verb *anankázein*, and with the noun *běda*, '*anánkē*, necessity, compulsion'.

These connections are registered in all the etymological dictionaries with the uncertainties and doubts imposed by the disparity of the meanings.

We do not venture either a firm rejection or adoption of these correspondences seeing that we have no means of either justifying or refuting them. It is, however, important to know how far we can extend the comparison. Must we limit ourselves to Greek and Latin forms for the reconstruction? But if Germanic and Slavic forms are to be included, this modifies the semantic data. Before coming to a decision it will be necessary to examine the sense of the terms in those languages where it can be rigorously defined.

Let us first consider the Latin words. We must first state that the sense of *fidēs* is defined inaccurately in our dictionaries, so inaccurately as to make it impossible even to understand the construction of its first uses. To study it we must have recourse to the article on *fidēs* in the Latin *Thesaurus*, where the different meanings are correctly classified.

If we continue to translate *fidēs* with "faith," certain essential expressions like *fidem habere*, *fidēs est mihi*, frequently met with in the language of comedy, risk being understood in exactly the opposite sense: thus Plautus, *Pseudolus* 467: *parvam esse apud te mihi fidem ipse intellego*. If we translate *mihi fidēs est* with "I have faith (in you), I give (you) my confidence" we arrive at exactly the opposite of what it actually means, which in fact is "(I have known for a long time that you despise me because) I understand well that you have only very little confidence in me." Another example in Plautus, *Amph.* 555: *facis ut tuis nulla apud te fidēs sit* is to be understood in the same way: "*You have no confidence* in your people."

The context and the authentic syntax of this turn of phrase impose a translation which seems to reverse the expected connections: *fidēs est mihi apud aliquem* signifies "somebody has confidence in me." To translate *fidēs* more literally, let us replace "confidence" with "credit." The literal translation of *fidēs est mihi apud aliquem* becomes "I have credit with somebody"; this is really the equivalent of "I inspire confidence in him" or "he has confidence in me." Thus the Latin notion of *fidēs* establishes between the partners an inverse relationship to that which we generally understand under the notion of "confidence." In the expression "I have confidence in somebody," the confidence is something belonging to me which I can put into his hands and which he disposes of. In the Latin expression *mihi est fidēs apud aliquem* it is the other who puts his trust in me and it is at my disposal.

Thus the term *fidēs* is bound up with the construction *est mihi,* the proper expression of possession; and this "possession" is determined by the preposition *apud* '*chez*', indicating the partner. The "possessor" of the *fidēs* thus holds a security which he deposits "with" (*apud*) somebody: this shows that *fidēs* is really the "credit" which one enjoys with one's partner. All the early examples confirm this.

This term figures in still another well-known turn of phrase where the sense also requires rectification. This is the appeal: *pro divom fidem* made to obtain the help of the gods, or again: *di, obsecro vestram fidem,* 'O gods, I beseech you for your *fidēs*'. Since *fidēs* designates the confidence which the speaker *inspires* in his interlocutor, and which he enjoys with him, it follows that it is for him a "guarantee" to which he can have recourse. The *fidēs* that mortals have with the gods assures them in return of a guarantee: it is this divine guarantee which the speaker invokes in his distress.

Once we have penetrated into these syntactical and semantic relations, it is the French phrase *avoir confiance en quelqu'un* 'to have confidence in someone' which looks peculiar. It is right to say "*je **donne** ma foi, j'accorde ma confiance,*" 'I *give* my trust, I bestow my confidence'. Something of mine is in effect given to somebody who now possesses it ("he *possesses* my confidence"). But how to explain that we also say "to *have* confidence" in somebody? How can one *give* a thing and *have* it at the same time? The answer should not be sought in French or English itself; the expression "*avoir confiance*" 'to have confidence' is incomprehensible except as a translation of the Latin *fidem habere.* We must thus explain *fidēs* in this new construction which is quite different from the other. This time it is the verb which we must consider. In fact, the turn of phrase *fidem habere alicui* is to be understood in the same manner as *honorem habere alicui* 'to bestow honor on somebody', and signifies thus "to bestow on somebody the *fidēs* which belongs to him." Thus Terence, *Eun.* 197: *forsitan hic mihi parvam habeat fidem* 'perhaps this man will have little confidence, will bestow on me slight *fidēs*'.

Here we see the relation between *hic mihi fidem habet* and the ancient *est mihi fidēs apud ilium.* By a natural development we pass in the language of rhetoric to the expression *fidem facere orationi* 'to create *fidēs* in an oration', that is credibility. From now on it is the utterance which possesses a *fidēs* and it is possible to say *est orationi fidēs apud auditorem* 'the speech possesses this *fidēs* vis-à-vis the hearer' and thus becomes capable of persuading him. From this by abbreviation we get *fidem auditori facere*, literally "to make credibility for the hearer."

It is from this that *fidēs* develops into a subjective notion, no longer the confidence which is inspired in somebody, but the trust which is placed in somebody. This conversion was the essential stage in the evolution. It would be possible to follow the development of the notion in familiar phrases: *se in fidem ac dicionem populi Romani tradere* 'to deliver oneself into the *fidēs* and power of the Roman people'; *fidēs* is joined to *dicio*, the power to dispose of somebody; or *se in fidem et potestatem alicuius tradere*, 'to surrender oneself into the *fidēs* and power of someone'. Just like *potestās* and *diciō*, *fidēs* is a quality acknowledged in the victor.

These equivalents bring to light another aspect of *fidēs*. If we review the different words associated with *fidēs* and the circumstances in which they are employed, it will be seen that the partners in "trust" are not in the same situation; the one who holds the *fidēs* placed in him by a man has this man at his mercy. This is why *fidēs* becomes almost synonymous with *diciō* and *potestās*. In their primitive form these relations involved a certain reciprocity: placing one's *fidēs* in somebody secured in return his guarantee and his support. But this very fact underlines the inequality of the conditions. It is authority which is exercised at the same time as protection for somebody who submits to it, an exchange for, and to the extent of, his submission. This relationship implies the power of constraint on one side and obedience on the other. It is seen very clearly in the precise signification of the Latin word *foedus* (from **bhoides-*), a "pact" established originally between two unequal partners. This is shown in certain poetic usages: *omnes foedere naturae certo discrimina servant* 'all, in conformity with the *laws fixed by nature*, preserve the characteristics which differentiate them' (Lucretius V, 923); *has leges alternaque foedera certis imposuit natura locis* 'nature has imposed these laws and eternal pacts on certain localities' (Vergil, *Georgics* I, 60). The constraining power of *foedus* was later extended to both parties.

The Latin forms illuminate the various aspects of the sense thanks to the phraseology of the religious and legal language. Outside Latin, these notions have become laicized and specialized. Nevertheless, the verb *peíthomai* in Greek "I let myself be persuaded, I obey" still enables us to recognize that "persuasion" is equivalent to, or develops to, the sense "obedience" and presupposes a constraint although the institutional form of this submission is no longer apparent.

We may now return to, and make more precise, the etymological relationships with the Germanic and Slavic forms. Up to now etymologists have left open the question whether the sense of Gothic *beidan* 'to wait, bide' should or should not be connected with that of *fidēs*, etc. The same is true of Old Slavic *běda* 'constraint, *anánkē*'. Similar problems often arise if we take too summary a view of the relationships of sense. The first condition is to observe and to define exactly the terms in question in the language itself. If we examine how Gothic employs *beidan* 'to expect, *prosdékhesthai, prosdokân*', it will be noticed, particularly in Luke II, 25 "he was a just and pious man" *beidands laþonais Israelis*, προσδεχόμενος παράκλησιν τοῦ Ἰσραήλ, 'who expected the consolation of Israel'. Here the "expectance" is a "confidence" in the fulfilment of the prophecy of Isaiah (33, 20). Mark XV, 43 *was silba beidands þiudangardjos gudis* (Joseph of Arimathea, a notable member of the Council) 'who also expected the kingdom of God'. Here, also, "expect" is equivalent to "place one's confidence in…" Luke II, 38 *þaim usbeidandam laþon Jairusaulwmos* 'to those who expected the deliverance of Jerusalem'; it is still an event expected with confidence that is given by conviction. This is indirectly confirmed in the context of I Cor. XIII, 7 where *gabeidiþ* 'ὑπομένει, endures' follows *þulaiþ* 'excuses', *galaubeiþ* 'believes', *weneiþ* 'hopes'. There thus is in Gothic no break with the ancient sense of **bheidh-*, but only an evolution from "put one's confidence in somebody or something" to "expect," and even if it is taken in an ordinary sense, this verb always refers to a hopeful expectation.

Nor is there any difficulty in admitting that *beidan* has its causative in *baidjan*. Here, again, scholars have found an insurmountable obstacle in the sense of *baidjan*, which translates Gr. *anankázein* 'constrain'; how could "constrain" be the causation of "expect"? The fact is that the following has not been taken into consideration: Gothic uses two different verbs to render *anankázein*. One is *nauþjan* 'to exercise a physical constraint' and the other *baidjan*, indicating only a moral constraint, which is that of persuasion (cf. II Cor. XII, II; Gal. II, 3, 14). It is thus possible to imagine that the connection between *beidan* and *baidjan* is analogous to that of Gr. *peíthomai* 'to trust somebody' and *peíthō* 'to get somebody to obey'. The same is true of Old Slavic *běda* 'constraint'. In this light the old unity can be restored and we can see that, as between the senses of the Greek and Latin forms and those of Germanic and Slavic, there was a weakening and especially a loss of the institutional sense. This is in the main due presumably to the emergence of another expression for faith and fidelity in Germanic, i.e. *Treue* and the related terms.

The history of *fidēs* goes beyond its etymological relatives. It has long been noticed that *fidēs* in Latin is the abstract noun corresponding to a different verb: *crēdō*. This suppletive relationship has been studied by A. Meillet[2] who has shown that the ancient connection between *credo* and *fidēs* was revived in Christianity: it was then that *fidēs*, a profane expression, evolved towards the sense of "religious faith" and *crēdere* 'believe' towards that of "to confess one's faith."

We must here anticipate the conclusions of an analysis which will be found below (Book One, Chapter 15) in order to demonstrate what predetermined to some extent that *fidēs* and *credo* should function in this suppletive way. *Crēdō*, we shall see, is *literally* "to place one's **kred*," that is "magical powers," in a person from whom one expects protection thanks to "believing" in him. Now it seems to us that *fidēs*, in its original sense of "credit, credibility," implying dependence on the one who *fidem habet alicui*, designates a notion very close to that of **kred*. It is easy to see, once the old root noun **kred* was lost in Latin, how *fidēs* could take its place as a substantive corresponding to *crēdō*. In these two terms we are back once again with notions in which there is no distinction between law and religion: the whole of ancient law is only a special domain regulated by practices and rules which are still pervaded by mysticism.

---

2. *Mémoires de la Société de Linguistique de Paris*, XXII, 1922, 215ff.

SECTION III

Purchase

BOOK I, CHAPTER NINE

Two Ways of Buying

Abstract. Were the roots **wes*- and *kʷrī*-, which have provided the verbs for "to buy," synonymous in Indo-European? Greek, where these two roots coexist and function in suppletion, enables us to determine the first as the designation of *transaction* and the second as that of *payment*.

To designate the "purchase," the agreement of several languages provides us with a well-defined etymological group, that of Skt. *vasna*-, Gr. *ō̃nos* (ὦνος), Latin *vēnum*. The nominal form is everywhere the primary form: Skt. *vasna*- 'purchase price' furnishes a verbal form, which incidentally is rare, the denominative *vasnayati* 'to haggle', 'to bargain'. In Greek, *ō̃nos* furnishes the verb *ōnéomai* (ὠνέομαι), while from Armenian *gin* (< **wesno*-) a verb is derived which is phonetically *gnem* 'I buy'. In Latin the noun *vēnum* is linked with two verbs, *vēnum dare* 'to sell' and *vēnum īre* 'to go for sale, to be sold'. It should be noted that in Latin itself, the phrase *vēnum dare* has produced *vendere* 'sell'. This close connection established between *vēnum* and *dare* is a most remarkable fact: the notion of "selling" in Latin is defined as "giving" in a certain way, the determination being expressed by *vēnum*.

The Indo-European term is **wesno*-, a nominal form: the historical verbal forms are all denominatives either by morphological processes or by syntactic processes (Latin *vēnum dare, ire*); and yet **wesno-* itself cannot be anything other than a derivative. We must therefore posit a prehistoric root **wes-*.

We now have this root **wes-* attested in Hittite; this is a fairly recent confirmation of our reconstructions: the Hittite present*waši* signifies "he buys." From this same root is derived the Hittite verb *usnyazi* 'he sells', which presents the formation in *-n-* of the noun **wesno-*. These Hittite facts are a guarantee that we have in the root **wes* one of the most ancient forms of the Indo-European vocabulary.

There is another confirmation for this, but it is indirect. It is obtained by retracing to its origin the well-known Persian word *bāzār*, which means "market." We have to go very far back to reconstitute the original form: Armenian has preserved the borrowed form *vačaṙ*, with an *ṙ* (trilled *r*) which indicates *r* + consonant. In Middle Iranian we find *wāčarn* 'market street' (Sogdian and Pehlevi), where the group *rn* explains the *ṙ* in Armenian. This permits us finally to reconstruct a compound **wahā-čarana*, the second term denoting the process of walking or circulating, while the first term derived from **wah-* (the root **wes-*). The compound word therefore denotes "the place where one circulates to make purchases," the "bazaar." The constancy of the form is evident.

However, this complicates the Indo-European situation. For it so happens that we have testimonies of equal antiquity for the use of a different root which likewise signifies "buy." This is the root of Skt. *krīṇāmi* (which derives from the root **kʷrt*), of modern Persian *xarīdan*. In lexical usage the forms of *krī-* have even more substance than *vasna-*, which is no more than a Vedic survival.

This root is found again in the language (wrongly) called Tokharian, where "trade" is called *kuryar* or *karyar*, according to the dialect; the connection with the Sanskrit root was immediately recognized. In Greek it is recognizable in the aorist *príasthai*, which functions as a suppletive tense form in the conjugation of *ōnéomai*. In Irish we have *crenim* 'buy', in Slavic, Old Russian *krĭnuti*; the root exists also in Baltic. It is not found in Latin, nor in Germanic, which stands on its own in this sphere of the vocabulary.

The problem thus arises, at least for Indo-Iranian and Greek, how can we explain the coexistence of two distinct etymological families to designate one and the same notion which hardly seems to admit of differentiation? While here the same operation is designated by two different verbs, it so happens that the two notions of "buying" and "selling" may be expressed by the same verb, with a variation which may be the addition of a prefix (German *kaufen* and *verkaufen*) or a tonal variation (Chinese *mǎi-mài* 'buying-selling' with two different tones), the notion itself being somehow differentiated between the two halves of the process.

It may even happen that the determination of the sense can only be made from the context: thus *misthòn pherō*, where *misthón* signifies "wages, pay," may have the two meanings of "to pay a wage, to take a wage to somebody" and "to carry away the wage," when speaking of the one who receives it. Thus in different contexts it may mean "pay" or "receive."

The problem is that here, on the contrary, we have two different verbs for the operation of "buying." The attested sense is the same for **wes-* and for **k^wrī-*, both equally ancient, with a distribution which coincides over part of the territory. **wes-* is Hittite, Indo-Iranian, Greek, Latin, and Armenian; **k^wrt-* is Indo-Iranian, Greek, Celtic, Slavic, and Baltic.

Most of the Indo-European languages have opted for one or the other of the roots. In one language, in Greek, the two function together: *ōnéomai* and *príasthai* are found associated in a single conjugation of complementary forms, the second supplementing the first by providing its aorist. But the two were once used separately and thus each possessed a complete conjugation. In Indo-Iranian *krī-*, *krīṇa-* is in frequent use, practically to the exclusion of the other root, represented only by *vasna-* and some other forms, such as the denominative verb *vasnayati*, which is almost obsolete. The usual verb is *krī-*.

In Greek the facts are more instructive. The examples in Homer and later on those of Ionic prose allow us to determine the proper value of each of these roots. We note that *ōneomai*, that is "buy," after discussion with the vendor, quite often means "to seek to buy"; but *príasthai* has the peculiarity that it appears with an instrumental determination like *kteátessi* 'goods, merchandise, possessions'. Apparently the use of this verb denotes the mode of payment, and on occasion the amount paid. While *ō̃nos*, *ōnḗ*, *ō̃néomai* designate "purchase in general," "the fact of behaving as buyer," *príasthai* is "to actualize the purchase by paying."

This interpretation is confirmed by the derivatives from the two roots which are not constructed in the same way. Thus we have the adjective *ōnētós*, the feminine of which, *ōnētḗ*, is opposed to *gametḗ* in Homer to designate a "bought" wife, as distinguished from one who has been formally married. But **priátē* does not exist: the notion of purchase in this case is specifically expressed by *ōnéomai*. Conversely, we have a negative adjective: *apriátē* 'not bought', which is followed by *anápoinon* in a passage (*Il.* 1, 99) where the father of the young captive whom Agamemnon holds claims his daughter and demands she should be given back to him "without the fact of *príasthai* and without *poinḗ*." He does not want to make a transaction: she is his daughter, she must be given back to him purely and simply, without ransom (*anápoinon*) and also *apriátēn*: she does not provide an occasion for a purchase. A father should not have to pay to obtain his daughter: *apriátē* is on the same level as *anápoinon* 'without *poinḗ*', a material notion, a manner of payment.

It can now be seen how the two verbs are distinguished: *príasthai* is more restricted and more material; *ōnéomai* is the more general expression. This also emerges from the semantic opposition established between the two aspects of the operation: if one wants to say "buy" as contrasted to "sell," it is *ōnéomai* and not *príasthai* which is used.

Purchase and payment are two different operations, or at least two different stages of the same operation in the ancient civilizations and still in some archaic civilizations of our own days: the *payment* follows the conclusions of the *purchase* and agreement on the price.

BOOK I, CHAPTER TEN

Purchase and Redemption

Abstract. Indo-European had words for "to be worth" and "value." But a study of the Homeric usage of *alphánō* 'to bring in, yield, fetch' makes it clear that *alphḗ* designated originally the exchange value of a man put up for sale. Skt. *arhat* 'a man of particular merit' brings confirmation of this ancient sense. With the Germans, the custom of selling a man who had staked and lost his liberty in gambling, enables us to understand how the sense of "sell" of the Gothic verb *saljan* developed from an earlier sense, that of "offering a sacrifice." Numerous concordant linguistic facts indicate that at an early date it was not merchandise but human beings who were bought. Thus buying was originally "redeeming," because by purchase, a man was freed from a precarious situation, for instance being a prisoner of war.

For the notion of "price" and "value" we have in Indo-European a term which is rare in the realm of economy. It is represented by Greek *alphḗ* (ἀλφή) and especially by the denominative verb *alphánō* (ἀλφάνω) 'to get a price, to make a profit', and in Indo-Iranian by Skt. *arh-* 'to be worth', *arghá-* 'value, price'; Av. *arəj-* 'to be worth', *arəǰah-* 'value, price'; Persian *arzīdan* 'to be worth, to have value', *arzān* 'who has worth'.

Elsewhere we have only a correspondence in Baltic: Lith. *algà*, Old Pruss. *algas* 'wage'.

In Greek *alphḗ* is a rare term which has few derivatives; apart from a compound which will be discussed later, in classical Greek the root has produced only the adjective *timalphḗs* which is commonly translated by "precious" but means literally "what is worth its price." It seems that all we have to do is to note the sense, which is assured, moreover, by the correspondents just cited,and to conclude from it that an expression for "value" existed in Indo-European.

But what is interesting is precisely to define "value" and to establish, if it is at all possible, with what kind of conception this notion was associated. What was it the value of? How was it estimated? It will be useful to determine more precisely the sense of *alpháno̅*, of which there are only a few examples in Homer, but all of them significant. In *Il.* 21, 79 the subject is a combat between Lycaon, the son of Priam, and Achilles, who has him at his mercy and is on the point of killing him. The other, who can no longer defend himself, beseeches him to spare his life: "It was in your house that I ate corn, the day that you made me prisoner in my father's house and transported me (*epérassas*, literally "to make me cross over," cf. below) to Lemnos (to sell me)," ἑκατόμβοιον δέ τοι ἦλφον 'I brought you the price of a hundred oxen'.

Thus the sense of *alpháno̅* 'to have a value' will have been more exactly "to fetch a price," "a certain benefit"; it is the price which a man procures by his sale of the one whom he rightly possesses by act of war. *Od.* 15, 453: "This man, I could take him and afterwards bring him to a ship and ὁ δ'ὑμίν μυρίον ὦνον ἄλφοι." It concerns a slave who is taken away to be sold and then would bring in a price (cf. above on *ô̄nos*) 'ten thousand times what he might cost'.

We see here a connection between *alpháno̅* and *ô̄nos*, the price of purchase: in the first example it was linked with *peráo̅* 'sell'. We shall see that *ô̄nos* is also connected with trade in human beings.

Od. 17, 250: a man whom on my ship I shall take far from Ithaca ἵνα μοι βίοτον πολὺν ἄλφοι 'in order that he may bring me an abundant livelihood, one from which I can live well'. *Od.* 20, 383: The suitors, assured of their victory, indulge in insulting remarks about the guests among whom is Ulysses in disguise: "Let us throw the guests out" (360)... "let us take these strangers, throw them on a ship and send them to Sicily..." ὅθεν κέ τοι ἄξιον ἄλφοι... 'where they will fetch a price worthy of them'.

These are all the examples in Homer. There is not the slightest variation in the sense; it is remarkable that this constant application has not been registered: *alpháno̅* signifies "to bring in a benefit" in speaking of a man put up for sale by his owner. This is the proper sense of the verb "to be worth."

We can confirm this by another test. This is the compound *alphesíboios* in the phrase *parthénoi alphesíboiai* (*Il.* 18, 593) 'young girls who bring in oxen' (for their family) because this was the price offered to obtain them in marriage.

The notion of "value" takes its origin from that of a personal worth, the physical value of the man who can be put up for sale: in the Homeric world *alphánō* was still exclusively used for the profit procured by the sale of a prisoner of war.

In Indo-Iranian the corresponding term, Skt. *arh-*, Av. *arəj-*, is much wider. It designates all kinds of value. But in Indian use we have an indication that the signification revealed by the Gr. *alph-* is not a development peculiar to Greek, but an inherited notion. It can be seen in a well-known term of the religious vocabulary of India: this is the participle *arhat* 'a man of peculiar merit, who has acquired merit', especially in Buddhism.

It is worth noting that *arh-* is applied only to a man and never to an object. From Vedic on, this restriction to a human quality, even if it is transposed into the moral sphere, indicates that "merit" is the personal "value" of a human being. Thanks to Greek we may bring the notion of personal "merit" into connection with "value," the latter being associated with verbs signifying "to buy" and "to sell." All this throws light on the same type of society and the same customs.

The right which the captor has over the captive, the transfer of prisoners, the sale of men by auction, such are the conditions in which the notions of "purchase," "sale" and "value" emerged.

In Germanic territory an analogous process can be observed which reveals the correlation between a historical witness and a lexical datum. The testimony is that of Tacitus who, in reporting the taste for certain games among the Germans, shows to what length this passion for games of dice can go:

> Dice are, surprisingly, a serious matter for them to which they apply themselves when sober; they are so carried away by gain or loss that, when they have nothing more, they are capable of staking their liberty and their own person in a last, desperate throw. The loser accepts voluntary servitude: . . . younger or more robust though he be, he allows himself to be bound and sold. Such is the folly of their obsession: they call this keeping their word. They rid themselves of this sort of slaves by trade in order to liberate themselves, too, from the shame of victory. (*Germania*, 24)

We must note the manner in which Tacitus describes the conditions of those who go so far in this game as to stake the liberty of their own person: *servos condicionis huius*. They are not slaves in the Roman sense: there were no slaves in the proper sense in the Germanic world; Tacitus states this clearly elsewhere. They put them up for sale (*per commercia tradunt*) not because they wanted to make a profit thereby but to rid themselves of the shame of thus having reduced a partner to servitude.

This helps us perhaps to a better understanding of the ancient term signifying "to sell" in the Germanic languages of the North and West, which we have not considered so far. As we have seen, it is not uncommon for "sell" to be a variant of "buy": this is the case in modern German *kaufen* and *verkaufen*. It is also the case in other languages where the same term, according to whether it is active or middle, renders the reciprocal notions of "buying" and "selling." But in a large part of the Germanic world we have two different verbs for "to buy": Gothic has *bugjan*, Engl. *buy*, which will be explained a little later. But for "to sell" we find in Old Norse *selja*, Old Engl. *sellan*, Engl. *sell*; the corresponding Got. *saljan* does not signify "sell" but "to offer as sacrifice" (Gr. *thúein*), as in the expression *hunsla saljan* = λατρείαν προσφέρειν τῷ θεῷ 'to accord worship to God', where *hunsl* designates the sacrificial offering.

The Gothic *saljan* 'bring as an offering to a divinity' explains the origin of Old Icelandic *selja* 'to deliver, to sell'; it is properly the "sale" conceived as an offering which is brought. Such is probably the type of sale of which Tacitus speaks, the sale of a man to which one resigns oneself, not in a spirit of gain, but to rid oneself of the shame of having got the better of him; and this is achieved by way of an offering, as a kind of sacrifice of a human being.

The history in Germanic of *saljan* shows that this notion is prior to the vocabulary of commercial relations in the proper sense. At this point we may note that this development is consistent with that of the verb *bugjan* 'to buy', which etymologically means "to liberate, to redeem somebody," to save him from a servile condition. Everything hangs together: these are in fact two notions primarily concerned with persons and still charged with religious values.

If we now pursue our enquiry into the terms for "to sell" in other languages, we find within each one that they are organized as opposites. Thus Greek has *pōleîn* (πωλεῖν) 'sell' and also a verb from the root **per-* represented by the present tenses *pérnēmi* (πέρνημι) and *pipráskō* (πιπράσκω) (aorist *epérasa*, ἐπέρασα). Now it is possible to draw a distinction between the two verbs which, at the same epoch, seemed to have been employed concurrently without any difference as to sense. The meaning of the second group can be accurately deduced thanks to its derivation from the root **per-*; this appears also in the adverb *péran* 'beyond', 'on the other side', so that the verb will have meant "to cause to pass, to transfer." Thus originally the group of *pérnēmi* did not evoke the idea of a commercial transaction, but the act of transferring. It may have been the ancient custom among these people to transfer from one point to another, or in the market-place, what they wanted to sell: thus *epérasa*, with a personal name as object, signifies "transfer" or, as we say, "export" (cf. *Il.* 24, 752, where the connection between *pérnēmi* and *péran* is clear).

The frequent sense "to sell" must be considered as secondary: it is the result of a semantic restriction of the root **per-*. As for the morphological differentiation observable in *pérnēmi*—the present tense in *-nā-* —it is worth noting that it is formally parallel with Skt. *krīṇā-* 'buy', the present in *-nā-* expressing the opposed idea.

The verb *pōleîn* has no etymology as clear as this. At first sight it has a related form in Greek itself; *pōléomai* (πωλέομαι) in Homer seems parallel to *pōleîn*. But the sense of *pōléomai* is entirely different: it is "to go regularly, to frequent, to circulate," with a local determination in the accusative and with prepositions. This form must be linked with *pélomai* (πέλομαι); we must therefore separate it from *pōleîn*, which never had any other sense than "sell." This latter word has been linked with Old High German *fāli* (with an ancient *e*), German *feil* 'venal, what can be bought', Lithuanian *pelnas* 'merit, gain'. The iterative *pōleîn* would then signify "to procure advantages for oneself" and only secondarily "to sell."

If we want to say in Greek "to buy and sell," *pōleîn* is associated with *ōnéomai*. But taken separately each of these notions may be expressed in two ways. For the notion of "buy" we find the two verbs together, *priámenos ōneîsthai* (πριάμενος ὠνεῖσθαι) 'to buy and pay the price'. There are likewise two terms for "sell": *pōleîn* 'put a price on, seek a profit' and *pipráskō* or *pérnēmi* 'to sell by transferring the object (at the market)', generally overseas.

We now turn to the Latin facts. The noun *vēnum* is joined more and more closely to *do* and *eo*: hence *vendo*, *vēneo*. The contraction had already taken place in the classical period, but we still find *vēnum do*. Thus the notion of *vēnum* has served to express the two opposite aspects of "to put up for sale" and "to go to be bought." Since *vēnum* is a supine or more probably a noun, it is from the purchase that the notion of "sell" developed.

We must also note that at an early date the terminology of "purchase" underwent an important innovation through the use of the verb *emo* in the sense "I buy."

It is peculiar on the one hand that it should be precisely the notion of "sell" which received new expression by using the combination of the Latin derivative *vēnum* (from the root for "buy" in Indo-European) with *dare* in the sense "to sell," whereas *emo* was used for "I buy." Here we have a secondary specialization of this verb. The ancients still knew that *emo* signified "take," e.g. Festus: *antiqui* ***emere*** *dicebant pro* ***sumere*** ('the ancients used to say *emere* for *sumere* "to take"'). There are etymological correspondences which confirm this: Lithuanian has *imù* 'take' and in Celtic, Irish has *ar-fo-emat* 'they take', where *ar-* and *-fo-* are preverbs. In Latin itself we have this sense in a series of compounds: *demo* 'take away', *sumo* 'to remove', *promo* 'produce' ('draw wine') etc. We should, therefore, note that *emo* first signified "take" and then "buy."

To interpret this we must call other languages to witness. The facts are very complex in Germanic, where we find new words for "to buy" which have undergone successive transformations. We need not consider the German *kaufen* < Gothic *kaupon* 'to trade', a late borrowing from Lat. *caupo* 'innkeeper', 'trader', the sense of which was "trafficking" in general. From Gothic *kaupon* comes Old Slavic *kupiti*, Russ. *kupit'*, 'buy'. In Germanic this verb has taken the place of a term preserved in Gothic *bugjan* 'buy', first person singular preterite *baúhta*, Engl. *buy*, *bought*. We have here, once again, no convincing etymology of this ancient verb. Feist in his dictionary contents himself with making vague suggestions which do not touch on the true sense of the verb. It is this sense which we must first interpret.

The Gothic verb *bugjan* translates Greek *agorázein* 'to buy at the market', and it also serves for the notion "sell": *fra-bugjan*'*pōleîn, pipráskein*', with the same preverb as the German *ver-kaufen*. Combined with a different preverb, *us-bugjan* renders *exagorázein* 'to repurchase, to redeem'. The root also forms compound noun derivatives: *andabauhts* (abstract in *-ti*), which translates *antílutron* 'purchase price', *faur-bauhts*, which translates *apolútrōsis* 'redemption'. It has long been considered that this root is somehow or other connected with the root **bheug*(*h*) in Indo-European. But the forms listed under this root are so confused and their senses so different that Feist preferred to leave *bugjan* without an etymology. Perhaps it may be possible to constitute a family by bringing together *fungor* 'to discharge a function', *fugiō* 'flee', Gr. *pheúgō* 'flee', *phugḗ* 'flight', Skt. *bhuj-* 'eat' and also 'fold' (cf. Gothic *biugan*, German *beugen* 'bend')?

If all this is to be traced back to a common meaning, it must be one of rare complexity. In reality it is a jumble of irreconcilable forms which are in sore need of discrimination:

1. Lat. *fungor* must be linked with Skt. *bhuṅkte*, present middle, a nasal form (cf. *bhuj-*), the primary sense of which is "enjoy"; but at an early date it became specified in the sense of "enjoying food, consume." This links up with the Armenian *bucanem* 'to nourish, bring up'.
2. Gothic *biugan* 'bend' from **bheugh-* could be compared with Skt. *bhuj-* 'bend', Lat. *fugio*, Gr. *pheúgō*, these last from **bheug-*.
3. Finally, we think that Gothic *bugjan* 'buy' is to be compared with the root attested only, but in a very clear way, by Old Iranian: Av. *baog-*, which has abundant derivatives in Iranian and signifies "undo," "detach" (a girdle or a garment) and later "set free" and finally "save." The Av. verb *baog-* exists with several preverbs; it supplies the agent noun *baoxtar* 'liberator'. It has a material, as well as a religious sense. It was, like other Iranian words, borrowed into Armenian: see the Arm. noun *boyz*, the present tense verb *buzem* 'save' (only from illness), 'cure'.

Very soon the religious sense was emphasized: liberation through the intervention of a god, of a "savior," who must come and deliver captive creation. It was to express the idea of salvation, redemption, liberation, that the word was employed, particularly in the vocabulary of Manichaeism: Parthian *bōžāyar*, Persian *bōzēyar* 'the liberator', and quite naturally it also expressed the notion of "redemption" in Christian texts.

The connection with Got. *bugjan* may be based on the use of the Gothic verb and the Greek equivalents cited above. We have seen that *-bauhts* is equivalent to *-lusis*, *-lutron* 'deliverance, redemption'.

What were the conditions under which this semantic development could take place? It could only be in a situation of buying *persons*, with a view to liberating somebody who is a prisoner and is offered for sale. The only means of liberating him is to buy him. "To buy" is "to liberate." This clearly establishes the relationship with *anda-bauhts* 'repurchase, redemption'.

Let us return to the Latin facts: *vendo*/*emo*. It is of great significance that *vēnum* is supplanted by *emo* in the sense of "buy," for *emo* is "I take" (but in the proper sense "to draw to oneself"). This specialization of sense probably reflects the conditions under which *emo* was employed. It must have been said of a person whom one takes, not of something; to purchase is the act of taking someone put up for sale whom one takes to oneself, once the transaction is concluded.

If we examine the uses of *ōnéomai* (root **wes-*) 'buy' in Homer, it will be seen that all the examples are applied to *persons*: one buys slaves, prisoners who become slaves and who are offered as such. There are scenes in which the prisoner begs to be bought. One must realize that the situation of a slave only becomes to some extent normal when he is bought. In the hands of his captor or the dealer the prisoner is not yet in the position of a servant, a slave, who is after all in possession of certain guarantees: he attains to this position once he is bought.

It is one and the same process which is expressed through different words. Whether it be through the ancient expressions *vēnum*, *ōnéomai*, or more recent ones like *bugjan* for "to buy," there is always some pointer which enlightens us about the nature of the transaction: purchase or sale, not of merchandise or goods, of commodities, but of human beings. The first uses were concerned with the purchase of slaves or those destined to become slaves. Symmetrically *peráō*, *pipráskō*, etc. 'sell', strictly meaning "transfer," is applied to prisoners, to captives. Actual commodities, apart from precious materials, were doubtless not involved in this kind of trafficking and were not subjected to the same procedures of purchase and sale.

Such is the important fact of civilization which seems to emerge from the expressions concerned in one way or another with trade, purchase or sale.

BOOK I, CHAPTER ELEVEN

An Occupation without a Name
Commerce

Abstract. The comparison of Indo-European languages furnishes no common designation for commerce as a specific activity, as distinguished from buying and selling. The particular terms which appeared in different places are usually recognizable as borrowings (Lat. *caupo*, Gr. *kápēlos*), or recent creations (Gr. *émporos*). The Latin *negōtium*, itself a recent word, has a peculiar history:

1) A calque on Gr. *a-skholía, neg-ōtium* conveys the same senses as the Greek model, which are positive despite the negative formation: "occupation, impediment, difficulty."

2) At a later stage *negōtium* is the equivalent of Gr. *prâgma* 'a thing', but also more specifically and especially in derivations "commercial affairs." A calque, semantically this time, on *prâgma, negōtium* becomes the designation for "business."

The specialization in the sense of "commercial affairs" of a term originally meaning "occupation," far from being an isolated phenomenon, recurs in modern languages (Fr. *affaires*, Engl. *business*, etc.); it reveals the difficulty of defining by specific terms an activity without a tradition in the Indo-European world.

One might think that "buy" and "sell" would lead to a study of the terms relating to commercial activities. But here we make a fundamental distinction: buying and selling are one thing, commerce in the proper sense is another.

To begin with we must clarify this point. Commerce is not a concept that is everywhere alike. It allows of some variations according to the type of culture. All those who have studied commercial relations report that in civilizations of a primitive or archaic character, these relations have a very peculiar character: they concern the whole population; they are collectively practiced, there is no individual initiative. They are exchanges which entail entering into a relationship with other populations by a special procedure. Different products are offered in exchange by the partners. If an agreement is reached, religious celebrations and ceremonies may take place.

In Indo-European there is nothing of this character. At the level at which the facts of language allow us to study the social facts, we are very far from the stage of civilization just reported. No term seems to evoke collective exchanges by primitive populations nor the tribal manifestations that take place at such an occasion.

The notion of commerce must be distinguished from that of buying and selling. The man who cultivates the soil thinks only of himself. If he has a surplus, he carries it to the place where other cultivators assemble for the same purpose as well as those who have to buy food for their own sustenance. This is not commerce.

In the Indo-European world commerce is the task of a man, an agent. It constitutes a special calling. To sell one's surplus, to buy for one's own sustenance is one thing: to buy, to sell for others, another. The merchant, the trader is an intermediary in the circulation of produce and of wealth. In fact there are in Indo-European no common words to designate trade and traders; there are only isolated words, peculiar to certain languages, of unclear formation, which have passed from one people to another.

In Latin, for instance, the term *pretium* 'price' is of difficult etymology; its only congener within Latin is *inter-pret-*: the notion may be that of "bargaining, a price fixed by common accord" (cf. *inter-*). For "commerce" Latin, and only Latin, has a fixed expression, constant and distinct from the notions of "buying" and "selling": *commercium*, derived from *merx*, with *mercor*, *mercator*. We have no etymology for *merx*, the sense of which is "merchandise," or more exactly "object of trade." From this comes *mercor* 'to engage in trade, to make an occupation of it', usually in a far-off country, and *mercator* 'trader'.

These terms, as we can see, have no connection with those indicating the process of buying and selling: they are different notions. Besides, such commerce and trade is not practiced by citizens, but generally by persons of inferior status, who often are not natives of the country but foreigners, freedmen, who specialize in this activity. These facts are well known in the Mediterranean, where the Phoenicians practiced trade on a large scale; in fact, several commercial terms, notably *arrha* 'pledge', entered the classical languages via the Phoenicians. Still others came as "wander-words" and by borrowings. Lat. *caupō* perhaps has something to do with Gr. *kápēlos* 'small merchant', 'retailer', although the forms do not exactly coincide. Neither of them can be analyzed, and we might have here a borrowing from some Oriental language. As we have seen, Latin *caupo* has been borrowed into Germanic and given rise to *kaufen* and *verkaufen*, and from Germanic it passed into Slavic.

Large-scale commerce demanded new terms formed within each language. Thus Greek *émporos* designates the large-scale merchant, who carries on his business by sea: *emporeúomai* 'to voyage by sea' is employed for large-scale commerce, which is necessarily of a maritime character: the form *émporos* simply indicates the action of bringing something into port after crossing the sea. It is not a specific term relating to a specific activity. Often we do not even know whether the notion of commerce existed. Thus, while we have for "to buy" and "to sell" ancient terms in Iranian which are partly shared with Indic, in the Avesta there is not a single mention of any term relating to commerce. This is probably not due to chance because, although religious notions predominate in this great work, those of daily life also find a place. We have, therefore, to suppose that commerce had no place in the normal activities of the social classes to which the Mazdian gospel was addressed.

We know that in the Roman world it was otherwise. Besides *commercium*, which has already been cited, Latin has the word *negōtium*, a term which is central to a rich development of economic terms. Here the facts seem so clear that it might seem to be sufficient simply to mention it. In fact, it has a remarkable history, in the first place because it proceeds from a negative expression.

There is no difficulty about the formation itself of the term *negōtium*; it is from *nec-ōtium*, literally "absence of leisure," incidentally a formation which is all the more certain because we have in Plautus an analytical variant of *negōtium*: *fecero quanquam haud otium est* (*Poenulus*, 858) 'I shall do it although I have not the leisure'. The commentators compare it to another passage in Plautus: *dicam si videam tibi esse operam aut otium* (*Mercator*, 286) 'I will tell you if I see that you have the time or that you are prepared to help me' says one character, and the other replies: "I am prepared to, although I have no leisure" *quanquam negōtium est*, that is, "although I have something to do."

In this connection scholars quote *quid negoti est* either as a simple question or with *quin* "what hindrance is there (to doing something)?" Thus it appears that the notion was constituted in historical times in Latin. However, the analysis proposed for *neg-ōtium* leaves out the essential point. How and why did this negative expression become a positive one in meaning? How does the fact of "not having leisure" become the equivalent of "occupation, work, office, obligation"? To begin with, why did Latin have the occasion to coin such a phrase? From the fact that *negōtium* presupposes a verbal phrase, *negōtium est*, which in fact we find, one might conclude that the archaic negative particle *neg-* is exclusively verbal. This would not be altogether true. We have *nec* with a verbal form in ancient texts: thus in the law of the Twelve Tables: *si adgnatus nec escit*, 'if there is no *adgnatus* (to succeed somebody to inherit his possessions)': here *nec* is equivalent to *non*. But *nec* is also used as the negation of a word: thus in Plautus, *nec ullus* = *nullus*, or in the *Ciris*: *nec ullo volnere caedi* 'not to be inflicted with any wound'. Similarly, the term *res* ***nec*** *mancipi* is opposed to *res mancipi*, a familiar legal term which remained in use. *Nec* as a negation of a word survived in the classical language in words like *necopinans*, *neglegens*. There is thus no difficulty in supposing that Latin formed a compound negative, *neg-ōtium*, independent of the sentence *negōtium est*. But the problem remains: why do we have here a negative expression and why did it have such a development?

There is no explanation in Latin itself. The essential fact which we propose to establish is that *negōtium* is no more than a translation of Gr. *askholía* (ἀσχολία). It coincides entirely with *askholía*, which literally means "the fact of not having leisure" and "occupation." The word is ancient. The sense which interests us is attested from the beginning of its use in Greek (the beginning of the fifth century). We find in Pindar a characteristic example: the poet addresses the city of Thebes which he praises:

> ...τό τεόν...
> πράγμα καὶ ἀσχολίας ὑπέρτερον θήσομαι
> – (*Isthm.* I, 2)

"I shall place your interests above all occupation." This is no poetic word: it is employed by Thucydides in the sense of "hindrance, affair." It is also found in colloquial language in Plato. Socrates says when taking leave: ἐμοί τις ἀσχολία ἐστί, of which *mihi negōtium est* could be the Latin translation, with exactly the same sense in which we encounter the expression in Plautus.

Besides, *askholía* 'occupation' signifies also "difficulties, worries" in the expression *askholían parékhein* 'cause worries, difficulties'. Another example from Plato: τὸ σῶμα μυρίας ἡμῖν παρέχει ἀσχολίας 'the body causes innumerable difficulties for us'. This could be translated literally as *negōtium praebere* or *exhibere*, which has the same sense of "creating difficulties for somebody." *Askholía* can also be taken in the sense of "affair" in general: *askholían ágein* 'to pursue an affair', like *negōtium gerere*.

Finally, from *askholía*, we go back to the adjective *áskholos* 'who has no leisure', in fact, "who is occupied with something." In Latin we have, on the contrary, an adjective derived from *negōtium*. On the model of *ōtium*: *ōtiōsus*, *negōtiōsus* was made, which corresponds exactly to all the senses of *áskholos*.

It is therefore Greek which determined the formation and the sense of the Latin word: precisely because of the meaning "leisure" for Greek *skholḗ*, *askholía* was from the outset a positive concept. This is why the analysis of *negōtium* does not necessarily imply a predicative origin *nec-ōtium* (*est*). It is a compound of the type of *nefas* 'not-(divine) law'. Later, fixed in the sense of "commercial affairs, business," *negōtium* gave rise to a series of derivatives, both verbal and substantival: *negōtiārī*, *negōtiātor*, *negōtiāns*.

It is at this point that Greek made its influence felt in another form. The Greek term *askholía* certainly means "private or public business" but without the distinct implication of commercial business which *negōtium* has. The Romans themselves tell us that they coined these terms in imitation of Greek. Aulus Gellius tells us that *negōtiōsitās* was used to render *polupragmosúnē*, while Cicero created *negōtiālis* to render *pragmatikós*. From this time on, in imitation of the Greek *prâgma*, an altogether new system of derivatives from *negōtium* was organized. We can observe a curious semantic process: *negōtium*, from this moment on, takes on all the senses of Greek *prâgma*; it signifies, like *prâgma*, "thing" and even "person."

It has sometimes been suggested that this was a calque on *khrêma*. This is not so. It was *prâgma*, along with its family, which served as a model for *negōtium* and all its family. From this comes the verb *negōtiātor*, imitating *pragmateúesthai* 'to occupy oneself with trade', and the agent noun *negōtiātor*, imitating *pragmateutḗs* 'trader'.

Such were the conditions which, by a complex process, gave rise to a rich lexical development in Latin, producing forms which still live on in many European languages. At two stages there was semantic borrowing from Greek: the first resulted in *negōtium*, a direct and immediate calque on *askholía*; at the second stage certain derivatives were created to apply to commercial transactions on the model of derivatives of *prâgma*. At this first stage the form itself was imitated; at the second there was semantic innovation. Such is the history of this word family, a history which is very much less straightforward than appears in accepted accounts, from which an essential component is missing: the Greek terms which served as inspiration for Latin forms have not been recognized.[1]

It will be useful to glance at the modern equivalents of *negōtium*. The French word *affaires* is no more than a substantivization of the expression *à faire*, *j'ai quelque chose à faire* 'I have something to do', from which comes *j'ai une affaire* 'I have some business'. But the semantic content which *affaire*, *affaire commerciale* has today is foreign to the literal meaning. Already in ancient Greek *prâgma*, the vaguest of words, had taken on this precise sense. In Latin, in the case of *negōtium*, a negative expression was used to express the notion of "commercial affairs": the "absence of leisure" is an "occupation," but the term tells us nothing about the nature of the activity. Modern languages have created the same expressions by independent routes. In English, the adjective *busy* produced an abstract noun *business*. In German the abstract noun *Geschäft* is very vague, too: *schaffen* indicates the action of making, or forming, of creating in general. In Russian *dělo* also signifies "work" and then "affairs" in all the senses of the French word.

We see here a widespread phenomenon common to all these countries and already revealed in the original terms: commercial affairs as such have no special term; they cannot be positively defined. Nowhere do we find a proper expression which denotes them specifically. The reason is that—or at least in the beginning—this was an occupation which did not correspond to any of the hallowed, traditional activities.

Commercial affairs are placed outside all occupations, all practices, all techniques; it is for this reason that they could not be designated in any other way than by the fact of "being occupied," "having something to do."

This highlights the new character of this type of activity, and we are thus in a position to observe this lexical category in all its peculiarity in the process of formation, and to see how it was constituted.

It was in Greece that this terminology was created, but Latin was the intermediary through which it spread, and it remained active in a renewed form in the Indo-European world down to the modern vocabulary of the West.

---

1. On *negōtium* see our article "Sur l'histoire du mot latin *negotium*," *Annali della Scuola Normale Superiore di Pisa*, vol. XX, Fasc. I-II, 1951, pp. 3-7.

Among the concepts in the economic sphere studied here in their most striking or most singular expressions, we note that the clearest terms are often those which have assumed a sense determined by the general evolution of the economy and which denote new activities and techniques.

The difficulties which present themselves in this respect are different from those which we encounter in other spheres of the Indo-European vocabulary. The problem is not so much to identify survival as to interpret innovations. The expressions often belong to a new type of designation which is partly still in current development.

This section took as its point of departure particular terms which had acquired a technical sense or were in the process of doing so. This explains their diversity, their unequal distribution, and the variety of their origins. We are observers of the constitution of a vocabulary which was in some cases already specified in ancient times, but on the whole took shape in the course of the individual history of each language.

The terms for wealth and operations such as exchange, purchase, sale, loan, etc. are found connected with institutions which often developed on parallel lines. Hence the analogies observed between independent processes.

It will also have been noticed that the usages and techniques of the Indo-European peoples were at a different stage of development from those of the people of archaic cultures. In a number of the processes analyzed above the difference of level was considerable.

As the result of the investigation we have been able to discern in the Indo-European world a material civilization of considerable elaboration, existing as early as the period which can be reached by the most ancient word-correspondences. The terms which have been the objects of study are embedded in a highly articulated social structure, which is reflected in features which are often convergent, though at different epochs and at different levels, in Greece and Rome, in the Indo-Iranian world, or in Germanic.

Through some of these terms we can sometimes catch a glimpse of the origins of our modern vocabulary. All this does not merely reconstitute a vanished world of long ago; our study is not limited to relics. By this means we reach back to the origin of notions which still live on in one form or another in the languages of today, whether they persist by direct tradition or whether, by way of loan translations, they have taken on a new semantic life.

SECTION IV

Economic Obligations

BOOK I, CHAPTER TWELVE

Accountancy and Valuation

Abstract. Latin *duco* and Greek *hēgéomai* have the same senses; the literal sense "lead, command" and the figurative sense "believe, judge, estimate." But we must be careful not to deduce from this that there were parallel lines of development in both cases, from the literal to the figurative sense. Whereas with Greek *hēgéomai* 'command' there was a direct passage from "to judge" (with authority), in Latin a concrete intermediary—the practice of addition—intervened between the two senses of *duco*. This intermediary is found again in an almost identical manner between *putare* (*vineam*) 'to prune (the vine)' and *putare* (*deos esse*) 'to think (that the gods exist)'.

From the sense of "lead" the Latin verb *ducere* evolved towards the more abstract and general notion of "judge." The construction may be either predicative or with an infinitive proposition: *aliquem* (with an adjective predicate in the accusative) *ducere* 'to consider somebody as —'; or else *ducere* governing an infinitive proposition in the sense of "believe, judge, estimate."

This specific use has a parallel in the Greek verb *hēgéomai* (ἡγέομαι), which corresponds in its sense to *duco*. It also appears in a transitive construction "lead, conduct," and is also used in the sense of "judge, consider somebody as such." To explain this Greek fact the development of Latin *ducere* is generally invoked as a parallel. But this use of *duco* itself has not been completely clarified. As a general rule, when peculiar senses arise in the course of semantic development, the scholar must look to see whether they may have arisen in particular contexts.

Duco seems hardly cut out to be the designation for a mental operation. Originally it signified exclusively "draw, drag, lead." However, a single example in an archaic poet, Lucilius, *sumptus duc* (imperative) 'make a calculation of expenses, provides us with the explanation we are looking for. The phrase must be interpreted in the proper sense of *duco*, which is here modified by the noun it governs. It indicates an operation of a peculiar type: addition. In the classical civilization this operation was carried out in a different way from ours. Superimposed numbers were counted not downwards, like with us, but upwards, until the operation reached what was called the *summa*, that is to say "the topmost figure." This is why we still talk of the "sum" for the total. *Sumptus ducere* reflects this operation, and *ducere* has the original sense of "draw." The person doing the addition "draws" the series of figures from the bottom to the tops until he arrives at the total.

This is confirmed by an expression of classical Latin: *rationem ducere* 'to draw up an account'. *Ratio* is the technical term for "account, calculation." We have thus the point of departure of the semantic development: this is the operation of counting as it was carried out by practical devices and in writing. No high degree of civilization is required for such terms to become important: even in a rural civilization a proprietor's accounts are an essential element in administration (cf. Cato, Varro).

Through the mediation of an expression where *ducere* signifies "to bring an account to its total" (*rationem ducere*), hence "count," we can understand the phrase *aliquid honori ducere* 'to count something as honorable', or *aliquem honestum ducere* 'to count somebody as honorable'. It is always the idea of "to make a total." The conditions determining the specialization of sense were thus produced by the technique of computing. The computation itself, calculation, is a process which conditions mental operations in general.

But what of the curious parallelism with Greek *hēgéomai*? The line of semantic development looks so similar that one is tempted to assume the same process for Greek. We must, however, make sure that the conditions of usage were the same or that one may in all probability suppose that the initial facts were the same as in Latin.

In fact, not only are the intermediaries missing in Greek, but the initial sense was quite different. It is true that *exercitum ducere* and *stratoû hēgeísthai* are admissible expressions. The sense of *hēgéomai* is certainly also "to lead, to be the chief, to guide, to precede others in some action." From this comes *stratēgós* 'chief of the army', a title of which we probably have a calque in the Germanic compound noun, Old High German *heri-zogo* 'he who leads the army' (a military title which became an aristocratic one, *Herzog*), and this term in its turn has produced in Old Slavic *vojevoda* 'chief of the army', '*voivod*'.

But how can "to be master, to be chief" become "to consider somebody as"? The Latin model provides us with no means of connecting the two senses. *Hēgéomai* conveys no notion of a mathematical operation. In our view, we pass directly from the sense of *hēgéomai* as "to be chief, to lead" to that of the predicative construction. This is to be understood as "to be a guide (in the opinion) that," that is to say, "to think while assuming the responsibility of one's judgment." We have here the notion of an authoritative judgment; in fact *hēgéomai* in the sense of "estimate" is often applied to matters which are the object of faith and decision, for instance the existence of the gods. The authority here is that of individual judgment, not of power. It is interesting to observe that *hēgéomai* in this predicative construction is employed by Herodotus in the perfect "to have authority (in the opinion) that..." What is here expressed is an opinion announced with authority by someone qualified to judge.

We find a true parallel, although under slightly different conditions, in Latin *iudicare*, initially "to judge *qua* sovereign judge," and later simply "to express a judgment (of thought)." Compared to this evolution, which brings *iudicare* into connection with Gr. *hēgéisthai*, we can see how fallacious the apparent parallel between *ducere* and *hēgéisthai* is: the two developments are absolutely independent and do not resemble each other except in their final result.

Latin uses another verb for "judge, consider, estimate," and one of its compounds refers to calculation. This is *puto*. This verb presents a striking peculiarity. We do not yet know whether we must posit one or two verbs *puto*. One has the material sense "to prune." The other is a verb of judgment, of calculation, of belief, which admits several preverbs, particularly *com-*, as in *computo*.

Putare in the sense of "prune" is well attested: it is an agricultural term. The verb is employed by writers on agriculture with "trees," "bushes," "vines"—*vitem, vineam putare* 'to prune the vines' is often encountered in Cato, Varro and Columella. We find not only *puto* but also, with the same objects, *de-puto*, *re-puto* (that is, to repeat the operation), *inter-puto* (this is also used for the olive trees: *oleam interputare*); and better known, because it has survived: *amputare* 'prune all around'. This verb *puto* has a technical sense "to cut by excision," particularly useless branches.

Does this provide an explanation of the other verb? We must start from a metaphorical use, *rationem putare*, and interpret this literally with the technical sense of *puto*: "while following the accounts (from bottom to top) to detach successively all the items which have been verified." Hence the sense "to verify, to audit an account." Once every item has been verified and then cut out, the operation is concluded. From this comes *rationem putare* for "to check an account," where *putare* connects with its material sense: "verify in such a manner that, item by item, the account is considered in order."

In a metaphorical transposition the sense is that which we translated by "judge" or "believe," that is, to come to a conclusion after having verified all the elements of a problem, just as one verifies an account, after successive elimination of all the items. When Cicero says: *deos esse puto*, this is no act of faith. He means: "*all accounts having been made*, I believe that the gods exist." It is thus certainly the same verb but specialized in the operation of accountancy, and so far removed from its agricultural origins that it has become an autonomous verb.

These three verbs resemble each other; they could pass for syntactical synonyms: Lat. *puto*, *duco* and Gr. *hēgéomai* are construed in the same way. But we see how different their origins were and the paths which converged on this common usage.

BOOK I, CHAPTER THIRTEEN

Hiring and Leasing

Abstract. Unlike French, Latin opposes *conducere* 'to hire, take on lease' to *locare* 'let out on hire, to lease'. The specialized sense of *conducere*, which basically signifies "lead," started in the military context of recruiting and becomes specifically "to hire" when a chief (*dux*) engages men for a given sum of money: *conducere mercede*. By a parallel development, *locare* 'to put a thing in the place where it belongs' became specified in the sense of "hire" once it was applied to men or their work, especially when the price of hire was specified, as in Plautus' expression: *locare operam suam tribus nummis*. In the Germanic world the expression for hiring had a quite different origin: the custom, described by Tacitus, which the ancient Germans had of burying in the ground anything they wanted to preserve explains the strange polysemy of Gothic *filhan* 'to bury' and 'to entrust, to let out'.

Our next object of study is a compound of the verb *ducere* 'to lead'. For "hire, take on lease," Latin uses *conducere*; and the complementary expression is *locare* 'to hire out, let', from which French *louer* has developed. Thus Latin has two terms for these different notions, for which French uses only one—*louer*. *Conducere* 'hire, take on lease' can be said of many things: a servant, soldiers, land, houses, furniture, work; even the construction of a building: *conducere templum aedificandum* 'to contract for building a temple'.

This specialized sense of *conducere* is doubtless derived from the general sense "to lead," "conduct": "to lead workers, soldiers," hence "take them for hire." We have here a technical expression in Latin which appears to have been created within the language and taken on its special sense under our eyes. But what eludes us is precisely the transition to the sense "to take for hire." Failing this, "lead" and "hire" remain different notions. It is this transition point which we must elucidate.

We must first consider the simple verb; *duco* signifies "lead," but it corresponds etymologically to Gothic *tiuhan* (German *ziehen*) 'to draw'. The Gothic verb is very common, with numerous preverbs that differentiate the modalities of the action: "draw," "drag," "lead." We can further adduce Gr. δαιδύσσεσθαι· ἕλκεσθαι (*daidússesthai*: *hélkesthai*, 'drag'). This is formed from the root **deuk/duk* with the suffix *-y* and reduplication: *dai-duky-*, meaning "drag vigorously."

The comparison of Gothic and Latin alone enables us to draw the conclusion that the original sense of *duco* was "draw." In fact with *ensem* it signifies "draw the sword." *Duco* is also used with *murum*, *vallum*, 'wall, an entrenchment'. Now there is in Latin another verb meaning "draw": *traho*, which has become *traire* in French. What is the difference between the two verbs?

Whereas *traho* means "to draw towards oneself, to pull something which resists," *duco* is "to lead along an established line"; all uses of *duco* confirm this sense. *Ducere aquam* (cf. *aquae ductus*) 'to draw water', but along a prepared way; *ductus* can be said of *littera* 'a letter' with reference to writing: a letter by its shape conforms to a prescribed model; *dux*, the agent noun, is used of somebody who leads, who "draws on" along a way where others will follow. In the military sense, *duco* is "to draw behind one, towards a definite goal"; the correlative verb is *sequor* 'follow', to comply with a movement or an imparted impulse. There is another familiar phrase *ducere uxorem*, *ducere in matrimonium* 'to lead away a woman in marriage'.

With its preverb, *conducere* is not merely "to lead" but "to lead in such a way as to gather together." From this comes the technical sense of "contract." In medicine, *conducitur aut laxatur* is said of a muscle which contracts or relaxes. To explain *conducere* in the sense of "hire," we must observe how it is used when applied to men. An instructive passage in Caesar (*De Bello Gallico*, I, 4, 2) shows this: a Gaulish chieftain under the impact of a serious accusation seeks to defend himself by all possible means. On the day of the trial *omnem suam familiam coegit…et omnes clientes obaeratosque suos conduxit*: he collected all his connections and those with obligations towards him so that they could lend him their support before the tribunal. For his *suos* 'the members of his household' the verb is *coegit* 'to push before him to assemble them'; but for his clients and his debtors *conduxit* is used. It applies to those over whom one has the rights of a patron *vis-à-vis* a client, or a creditor vis-à-vis a debtor. This is the relationship conveyed by *conducere*: it is not merely "to assemble" but "to assemble in virtue of a certain authority." In fact, in the military language *conducere copias* is "to mobilize one's own troops"; *conducere* always implies the natural authority of the *dux* and, for the men, the duty of gathering together to serve him.

Here we have the conditions of use favoring the semantic transition to the sense "to hire." It must be added that *conducere* when it signifies "hire," "take for hire," is accompanied by *mercede* 'for pay'. This adjunct completes the specialization of the sense. By itself, *conducere* suffices to denote the levying of troops by someone who exercises his right to assemble his own troops. But, apart from this situation, one can recruit men by paying them, *mercede*, and it is the payment that provides the possibility of *conducere*. Hence the expression *mercede milites conducere*—with a number of variants, *auxilia, mercenarios conducere*. To begin with it referred to the action of a chief, the practice of those who disposed of their liege men. It presupposes, as with Greek *laós*, the authority of a chieftain over men pledged to his personal service and always ready to take up arms in his cause.

In this way the sense of "to take for hire" developed originally with reference to the hiring of soldiers. Later it was used of those from whom some difficult or dangerous work was expected; these could be hired assassins, or more often workmen. In popular language, in Plautus, we often find *conducere* for the "hiring" of cooks, musicians, mourners at a funeral, etc. The strictly economic sense thus emerged from the relation of the chief to the men under his authority: but very soon *conducere* was applied to the hiring of labor of any kind. The agent noun shares these various usages. The *conductor* is the man charged with recruiting men for an expedition. He is also a contractor who recruits workers, "hires" them for some work. Once this notion of "hiring" had become established, *conducere* was employed for "leasing" of land, a house (*agrum, fundum*) and not merely for manual work.

We must now turn to the term *locare*. The lexical opposition with *conducere* could not have developed until after *conducere* had assumed the sense of "recruit, take for hire." We must briefly show what prepared *locare* for its function as a correlate of *conducere*. To the expression *ducere in matrimonium* 'to take (a woman) in marriage' there corresponds *locare in matrimonium*, which applies to the father of the girl. The established juridical term in this connection is *dare* 'give'. But *locare* is often found in Plautus, and even as careful a writer as Caesar also used it. We also find *collocare in matrimonium*.

Why is this verb used in this way? Here we have a function of the sense of *locare* which itself depends on the sense of *locus*. In such vague words as those designating "places" we must make an effort to grasp the sense of the word. *Locus* is to be defined as the "natural place of something." This is likewise the sense of the Greek term which *locus* serves to translate: *tópos* (τόπος). It would be easy to establish this, but we content ourselves with the bare assertion.

It follows that *locare* is not simply "to put something somewhere" but "to put something in its proper place, the place to which it naturally belongs." In French one says in the same sense *établir sa file*, i.e. "marry off." Thus *locare* is very different from *ponere* 'to abandon, to leave something just anywhere'.

The transition to the sense of "to put out for hire" came about in the same way as with *conducere*, i.e. when *locare* was applied to men or their work: *locare operam suam tribus nummis* (Plautus, *Trin.* 844), literally "to place his work for three coins," which means "hire out." Similarly, if someone has a *fundus* which he knows he cannot cultivate himself, he "places" it, i.e. "hires it out": *locare fundum*. With the development of cities and public works, the authorities "invited tenders" for municipal works, e.g. *locare viam exstruendam* 'to put out under contract the construction of a road'. In this way, the sense of "let out on hire" became established, complementary to, but not simultaneously with, the technical use of *conducere*.

Both expressions were used together only when it was necessary to specify "taking" and "giving" a lease. If Latin used two different verbs, this was not only because of their solicitude for legal precision, for which the Romans are famed, but because Latin lacked the faculty which Greek had of using the same verb by varying the voice. Greek preserved for a long time the possibility of employing the same verb in the active and middle voice to indicate two correlative notions. Examples are *daneízō* 'lend', *daneízomai* 'borrow'; *misthô̂* 'to put out for hire', *misthoûmai* 'to take for hire'. Latin, once the deponent verbs had gone out of use, lacked this resource. It was made up by lexical means, by specializing *locare* and *conducere*.

This example will serve to illustrate a methodological principle on which we may insist at the risk of repeating ourselves: if the signification of a word is subject to such specialization, we must try to discover the particular usages which determined the new sense.

We may now turn to a quite different term, which connects with the concepts just studied. It is taken from Germanic, in particular from Gothic: this is the verb *filhan* 'to hide' and, with different preverbs *af-*, *ga-*, *us-* *filhan* 'to inter, bury'. But *ana-filhan*, strangely enough, signifies "give," "deliver" and also "hire out." This is why it is of concern to our study. The verb *filhan* translates Greek *krúptō* 'hide' and *tháptō* 'bury': *let filhan, áphes thápsai* 'bury him' (*ga-filhan* is also used). As for *af-filhan*, the sense is "hide, put out of sight": Luke 10, 21 *apékrupsas taûta apò sophō̂n* 'you have hidden (*affalht*) this from the wise'. As for *ga-filhan*, it also translates *tháptō* 'bury': *etáphē* 'he has been buried', *gafulhans war*. This is confirmed by other Germanic evidence: OHG *fel(a)han* 'bury, hide'.

The case of *anafilhan* is quite special. The verb, which is abundantly attested, translates Greek *paradidónai* 'hand over to someone, to entrust to', and *ekdídosthai* 'to hire, lease'. We have a characteristic use in a parable in Luke XX, 9: a man plants a vineyard and leases it out to farmers because he has to go away: *anafalh ina waurstwjam*, ἐξέδοτο γεωργοῖς. The same sense relationship still appears in Middle High German *bevehlen* 'to bury, entrust', cf. German *befehlen, empfehlen*, in which only the notion of "command, recommend" persists.

Nowhere do we find an adequate explanation of this semantic development. Such a change of sense at first seems incomprehensible: how has a verb signifying "hide," when furnished with a preverb denoting movement towards someone, come to mean "transmit, entrust"?

Now the original notion implied by these divergent significations may be found in the description of certain customs of the Germans in Tacitus' *Germania*, 16: "The German peoples do not inhabit towns, and cannot abide contiguous habitations; their villages, different from those of the Romans, are not adjacent and do not adjoin one another; instead, each man surrounds his habitation with a large space." Then, after having stressed that the Germans do not have the same methods of construction as the Romans, Tacitus goes on to say (16, 4):

They have the custom of hollowing out subterranean caverns which they cover from above with large piles of manure, a refuge in the winter and a receptacle for their harvest; in this they mitigate the rigors of their climate, and if ever an enemy happens to approach, he plunders what is to be seen; but what is hidden, or is buried in the ground, either escapes their attention or eludes them precisely because they have to be searched for.

Solent et subterraneos specus aperire eosque multo insuper fimo onerant, suffugium hiemi et receptaculum frugibus, quia rigorem frigorum eius modi molliunt, et si quando hostis advenit, aperta populatur, abdita autem et defossa aut ignorantur aut eo ipso fallunt, quod quaerenda sunt.

Here we have a custom which might explain the use of *filhan*. The original sense of *filhan* is "to hide, to bury"; it would not be surprising if the operation described by Tacitus was precisely the one which the Germans expressed by this verb. The puzzling signification of *anafilhan* (which translates *paradidónai*, *parádosis*) 'to hand out, to deliver somebody or something' will be explained as "to deliver that which has been put into safekeeping and hidden," or "to deliver for putting into safekeeping." What was thus put in a safe place were precious articles and provisions.

In this way the notion "to put into safekeeping" originated in the custom of keeping indispensable resources hidden. Then it evolved towards the sense of "lease," "hire out," which is a specialization of "entrust"; *anafilhan* can then translate *ekdídosthai*, *parádidonai*: 'to deliver to somebody with confidence, to entrust to him, what is kept in reserve'.

Here is a possible explanation of a semantic development peculiar to Germanic, the justification for which cannot be found in etymological considerations. Further on we shall study the connection of *bergen* 'to put under cover' and *borgen* 'lend, borrow' in German.

There are thus no specific expressions for "hire" in Germanic, but only a specialization of the verb "to put into safety, to hand over (a precious possession, one put in reserve)." Financial operations, introduced at a late date, could not have had any particular terminology in Gothic. Once again we grasp the complexity of these usages of economic life which were created at various dates, starting from different notions and which borrowed their vocabulary from previously existing institutions.

BOOK I, CHAPTER FOURTEEN

Price and Wages

Abstract. When studied in their most ancient uses and referred to their Indo-European origin, the words for wages—in particular Gr. *misthós*, Got. *laun* (German *Lohn*)—show that before designating the "price for some piece of work," they signified "reward for a brilliant exploit," "prize in a competition." As for Lat. *merces*, which also does not signify "wage" in the modern sense, its connection with *merx* 'merchandise' reveals the introduction of money into relations between men for the purchase of services just like merchandise.

Among the terms which denote relations of exchange we must include that for "wages," all the more so because, here at least, we have a well-attested Indo-European correspondence and a clear meaning.

It concerns a group of words of which the representatives are Gr. *misthós* (μισθός), Skt. *mīḍha-*, Av. *mižda*, Got. *mizdo*, Old Slavic *mizda*, i.e. a term common to Indo-Iranian, Greek, Germanic and Slavic. The constancy of the forms is remarkable, as is that of the sense. There is merely a slight difference between the words cited and this at first sight throws little light on the genesis of the sense "wage."

All the same it will be useful to study this set of correspondences a little more attentively to try and better define the notion. The form, in itself, does not permit analysis. We have here a derivative, the basis of which is not apparent. If it is a verbal root, we are not in a position to elicit it; we have no means of identifying it. It is, therefore, an isolated noun (the sole connection is that of Ved. *mīḍha-* with *mīḍhvas-* 'generous'), which nevertheless belongs to the most ancient vocabulary.

The Vedic term *mīḍha-* does not properly signify "wage," but "competition." The Avestan facts must be considered here. *Mižda-* is attested several times, notably in the Gāthās, and it is governed by the verb *han-* (this is constant), the Sanskrit correspondent of which is *san-*, the strict sense being "gain." If we study the uses of *han-* with *mižda*, we see that what is concerned is not a wage paid for a piece of work but a recompense—material or otherwise—in exchange for some activity, especially one performed in the service of the faith. It should not cause surprise that the term should have this limitation of sense: the Gāthās of the Avesta are a poetic and theological text, a series of vehement pronouncements in favor of the Zoroastrian faith. All the pregnant terms are charged with a religious value.

It is always by some piece of work or some meritorious action in the service of the faith that one gains the *mižda*. But at least on one occasion this recompense assumes a concrete aspect, *Yasna* 44, 18: "grant us the *mižda* which you have promised us, to wit, ten mares provided with stallions and one camel." This is the only time that a material compensation is mentioned. In all other examples, it is of a spiritual order: felicity, recompense in the future life. It is worth noting that we have a parallel use of Gr. *misthós* in the Gospels. This is due to the identity of the initial conditions: it is the future Kingdom—"the desirable Kingdom," to use the Avestan terminology—which has primacy in the Zoroastrian gospel. The *mižda* is to be found in this kingdom and in the promised felicity.

In comparing Vedic and Avestan terms, we see a more precise signification emerging, with a quite different orientation from what might be expected. This is not concerned with some advantage of an economic character, nor of a regular remuneration, nor again with a wage for an ordinary piece of work, but rather with a recompense—material or otherwise—awarded to the one who emerges victorious from a struggle or a competition. This makes it plausible that, within Vedic, *mīḍha-* is related to *mīḍhvas-* 'generous'.

It is the Greek term which is most abundantly represented. Gr. *misthós* has effectively the signification of "wage," in the sense as we understand it, from the Homeric texts on. The examples are clear: in *Il.* 21, 445, Poseidon reminds Priam that he has worked for him *misthôi epì rētôi*, μισθῷ ἐπί ῥητῷ 'for a stipulated wage'; here we have certainly the meaning "remuneration."

What was this remuneration? In a passage of the *Odyssey* (18, 358ff) a man who works for a *misthós* tells us what he earns: his daily corn, his clothes and shoes; such is the *misthós* of an employee. We learn that there were often protests if the hired man did not receive his wage or if he only received part of it.

However, there are examples in which the sense "wage" does not fit, where the use of *misthós* suggests a probably much older sense: in *Il.* 10, 304, a volunteer is sought in the Trojan camp to carry out a dangerous task of reconnoitering among the Achaeans and he is promised a great recompense: δώρῳ ἐπὶ μεγάλῳ; μισθὸς δέ οἱ ἄρκιος ἔσται 'and he will have an assured *misthós*': a chariot and two beautiful horses.

The position of the man who receives this *misthós* is quite different from one who receives a wage. He will have accomplished some exploit, and the *misthós* is the reward promised for this exploit. Here we come closer to the signification which is suggested by the Indo-Iranian terms; the *misthós* is no regular payment but the prize gained by the victor in a competition, the hero of a hazardous exploit.

We have yet another of these interpretations, one which we must spend some time on, because it has not yet been noticed. A compound verb is made from *misthós* to express the notion "to earn a wage": this is *mistharneîn* (μισθαρνεῖν) 'to work for a wage, to be a wage earner'. The verb *árnumai* (ἄρνυμαι) can be recognized in this compound, and this has clear uses in Homeric Greek, so few that we can scrutinize them all.

First, we have the remarkable fact that the ancient grammarians translated the verb by *antikatallássesthai* 'to obtain as a consequence of a competitive test'; this definition, which modern lexicographers have not noticed, is certainly exact, as is shown by the Homeric examples: right at the beginning of the *Odyssey* (1, 5), where the subject is the tribulations of Odysseus, the hero, of whom the poet asks the muse to sing, ἀρνύμενος ἥν τε ψυχὴν καὶ νόστον ἑταίρων 'he who seeks to gain his own life and the return of his companions'.

By dint of hard struggles, in the course of the many trials over which he triumphs, he wins the*prize*, which is to have saved his life and secured the return of his companions. One sees also, *Il.* 1, 159, *timên árnusthai* 'to win his *timḗ*', i.e. to win that honor due to a chief, to Agamemnon, in war or in a competition (cf. 5, 553); or, again, *árnusthai méga kléos* (6, 446) 'to gain great glory in combat'. Finally, in the pursuit of Hector by Achilles, after their final combat, comes the most significant text (22, 160): οὐχ ἱρήϊον οὐδὲ βοείην ἀρνύσθην ἅ τε ποσσὶν ἀέθλια γίγνεται ἀνδρῶν 'they were not striving to win a prize for which men compete in a race', but the true stake was Hector's life as he was pursued by Achilles.

Thus *árnumai* signifies "to carry off a hard-won prize in a great competition." Is it fortuitous that *mistharneîn* has as a component a verb so specific, which implies precisely the recompense attached to such a test? Incidentally, do not the French say "*gagner*" a wage, just as they "*gagner*" a prize, a victory? Thus, directly or indirectly, *misthós* is certainly the same notion which we have established in Indo-Iranian: a prize, fixed in advance, in a competition. This sense is better preserved in the heroic tradition of the Vedic hymns, but it is still recognizable in Homer. Such is the first use of *misthós*. Even in the sense of "wage" the notion "recompense fixed in advance and paid when the work is finished" survives. The "prize" in a competition becomes the "wage" for a piece of work.

Gothic and Slavic provide little information. Gothic *mizdo* serves to translate Gr. *misthós* and does not present any instructive variation. However, there is in Gothic besides *mizdo* another term which renders Gr. *misthós*: this is *laun* (Old High German *lōn*, German *Lohn*) which goes back to an ancient neuter **launom*. This rival of the ancient Indo-European term deserves our attention in its own right.

The Gothic *laun* is not isolated in the Indo-European vocabulary; however, before studying it together with its correspondences, we shall examine the signification which emerges from its uses. It serves as the equivalent of three Greek words: *misthós*, *opsṓnia*, *kháris*, and probably it does not exactly correspond to any of these three.

One passage in particular shows the semantic relations between *laun* and *mizdo* in Gothic, precisely where the Greek model employs the single term *misthós*. Matthew VI, 1: *laun ni habaiþ fram attin izwaramma* ... 'You have no *laun* (μισθόν οὐκ ἔχετε) from your Father'; then comes "I tell you in truth, the hypocrites receive their wage" (ἀπέχουσι τὸν μισθὸν αὐτῶν) *andnemun mizdon seina*.

To translate the same term Gothic employs two different words within the space of two lines. The second time, *mizdo* is used because it concerns a proper human wage, the wage of those who are called "hypocrites," whose recompense is measured in esteem or other advantages. When the wage is to be received from the Father who is in Heaven, it is *laun*; the word *mizdo* was considered inappropriate.

It is *laun* again which is employed to render a very crude expression, the popular word *opsṓnia*: Romans VI, 23, *Launa frawaurhtais dauþus* (τὰ ὀψώνια τῆς ἁμαρτίας θάνατος) 'the wage of sin is death'. The proper sense of *opsṓnia* is "pay," that is, provisions other than bread: meat and especially fish given to soldiers, hence the pay of a soldier who is paid in kind. In this passage it is used figuratively: it is the wage, the retribution for sin, and *laun* is in the plural because of the Greek plural. Another example: "if you repay what you have been given, if you love those who do good to you, if you etc. . . . where is your *khális*?" (Luke VI, 32–34), where *kháris* 'grace' is translated as *laun*.

We now consider two compounds which will help to narrow down the meaning: *sigis-laun*, German *Siegeslohn*, 'the *laun* of victory', which translates *brabeîon*, the "prize" given by the *brabeús*, the umpire, to the victor in a competition. It is the term employed for the prize gained in a race in the stadium; the text (I Cor. IX, 24) states this expressly: "of all those who run the race, only one wins the *sigislaun*."

The second compound is curious: *launa-wargs* (II Timothy III, 2) translates *akháristos* 'ungrateful, *ingrātus*' (Vulgate). It is *-wargs* which here fulfills the function of a negative preverb, although Gothic had the means of forming a negative adjective with *un-*. The sense of *-wargs* is precise and strong: (*ga-*) *wargjan* signifies "condemn," *wargiþa* 'condemnation', Old High German *warg* 'criminal'. This is a peculiarly Germanic notion: the *warg* is put outside the law and banished from the community. The compound *launa-wargs* thus properly signifies "deprived of *laun*," one to whom *laun* is refused. It is a very forceful expression, much stronger than the term it renders.

Thus we see that *laun* is something quite different from a wage; it is a gift granted as a favor or an advantage gained by an activity which is no ordinary work (for which *mizdo* would have been the right term); it is properly a "grace" obtained or a "prize" gained.

The comparative method provides the means of circumscribing the sense still further: *lau-* is well attested, especially by Lat. *lū-crum* (from **lau-tlom*), *lūcror*.

The sense of *lūcrum* is gain, benefit, with the idea that it represents something unexpected, an unforeseen profit. In other languages, this meaning is more specialized: Skt. *lota, lotra* 'booty' (these are words found in lexicons) and this links up with the Slavic terms: *lovŭ* 'booty', *loviti* 'to catch, to capture in hunting', 'to grasp', Gr. *lēís* (ληΐς) 'booty', *lēízomai* 'to plunder', *lēístōr* 'brigand'.

The spoils of war, a catch in hunting: such are precisely the advantages which cannot be reckoned with in advance, they are "favors" of some kind. This root is found again in Greek in a different semantic family, that of *apolaúō* 'enjoy'. Although "enjoy" is the classical sense of the verb, the ancient sense is still apparent. By connecting it with the idea of "booty," the development is easy to follow: "to secure a booty and to enjoy it," "to draw profit from a prize of war or the chase." The point of departure for Germanic **launom*, Got. *laun* will therefore be "a benefit gained by capture, booty," hence a gain quite different from the wage which is earned by regular work.

We see thus here a convergence and approximation of two radically different notions in Gothic vocabulary with the words *mizdo* and *laun*. The first evokes the idea of competition and the prize attached to it; the second, the spoils of war or the chase, hence favor or recompense in general.

There remains a third term to consider which is limited to Latin: *merces*, genitive *mercedis* 'wage, recompense', from which comes *mercenarius* and all the words attached to it. The peculiarity of *merces* is that it is clearly connected with *merx*, but the senses of the two words have widely diverged. From the morphological point of view, *merces* is a formation in *-ed-*. We have few examples of this formation, and there is no uniformity in these examples; they are generally very unclear terms. We certainly have *hered-*, but this is an adjective, while *merced-* is a noun formed from another noun.

This peculiarity noted, we must try and understand how *merces* is connected with *merx*, and what relation there can be between the notion of "merchandise" (*merx*) and that of "remuneration" (*merces*). It must be stressed that *merces* is something quite different from a "wage." What *merces* remunerates is not the result as such of a working man's labor, but the sweat of his brow, the soldier's service in war, the skill of a lawyer and furthermore, in public life, the intervention of a politician, what one would call a trading in influence.

This particular kind of "remuneration" thus connects up with the terms studied in the commercial vocabulary. But it has nothing to do with "commerce" in the ordinary sense.

The notion which may link *merx* with *merces* is that the remuneration is made in money: *merx*, insofar as it means "merchandise," denotes merchandise obtained *for money*; not barter, the exchange of one thing for another, but a proper commercial purchase, effected by means of money. Such is the foundation of the connection between the two notions of *merx* and *merces*. To understand it better, we may compare the case of French *denrée* 'commodity'. In Old French it was *denerée* 'what one could obtain for one denier', a product which can be paid for, which enters into commerce. This is what constitutes the connection between *merx* and *commercium*.

Merces is therefore a payment which recompenses the temporary services of a man for a particular project. The term denotes quite a new notion, the introduction of money into the relations between men to buy services just as one buys a commodity.

These different terms, considered together here because of their meaning, have connections which must be retraced if we want to understand how it was possible for them to converge from such different origins. They reveal the complexity of the important aspects of civilization which they denote. Here we can see how in the vocabulary and economy of different Indo-European peoples the notion of "wages" was developed from that of "recompense," whether in war or play, in proportion to the gradual establishment of fixed labor relationships, and how the notions of "commerce" and "merchandise" in their turn determined a new type of remuneration.

The same processes are repeated in the terminological innovations in modern languages. For instance, the *solde* (soldier's pay), whence comes *soldat* < Ital. *soldato* 'remunerated by a *solde*', used with reference to men-at-arms. Formerly speakers were conscious of the connection with Lat. *solidum* 'piece of gold' (from which comes Fr. *sol*, *sou*). As with the word *salary*, the words have diverged so far in meaning that present-day speakers have little notion that the "salary" was, in its Latin form, the *salarium* 'the money given to soldiers to buy salt' (Lat. *sal*). Again, *pay* derives from Lat. *pacare* 'to satisfy, to appease (by a distribution of money)'. Further, French *gages* 'wages' is the plural of *gage* 'guarantee, ransom'. The images of war, of mercenary services, preceded and engendered those of work and the legal remuneration attached to it.

BOOK I, CHAPTER FIFTEEN

Credence and Belief

Abstract. The exact formal correspondence between Lat. *crē-dō* and Sanskrit *śrad-dhā-* is a guarantee of ancient heritage. Studies of the uses of *śrad-dhā-* in the Rig Veda show that the meaning of the word is "act of confidence (in a god), implying restitution (in the form of a divine favor accorded to the faithful)." The expression of the same complex notion, the IE **kred-*, recurs in a secular sense in Latin *crēdō* 'to entrust something with the certainty of recovering it'.

Like the designations for "wages," those which relate to the notion of "loan" or "borrowing" did not originally have an economic sense.

A "loan" is money or valuables entrusted to another to be given back subsequently. This definition will be found applicable to certain terms, some of which are common to several Indo-European languages, while others are the result of recent developments.

We shall first consider a Latin term with a wider meaning, which is explained by correspondences of wide extent and antiquity. This is Latin *crēdō* and its derivatives. From the time of the earliest texts the meaning of "credit" is extended to include the notion "belief." The very range of the meaning poses the question of how these notions are connected in Latin, for the corresponding terms in other languages also show the antiquity of the notion and the close association of the two senses.

The dialect distribution of the terms is striking: on the one hand Latin *crēdō* and Irl. *cretim*, and at the far end of the Indo-European territory Skt. *śraddhā*, a verb and a feminine noun, with the parallel Avestan *zrazdā-*, a verbal stem and also a noun. In Indo-Iranian, the sense is likewise "believe" with the same construction as in Latin, i.e. governing the dative. Hans Köhler has studied in detail in his dissertation (Göttingen 1948) the notion of *śraddhā* in Vedic and Buddhistic literature.

We have here one of the most ancient correspondences in the Indo-European vocabulary; it is remarkable because (as has already been noted) it is attested only at the two extremities of the common territory; and, as in the case of a number of important terms relating to beliefs and institutions which have the same distribution, such a survival is indicative of an archaism.

This fact is corroborated by the antiquity of the formation. We are dealing with an ancient verbal compound, formed by means of the verbal root **dhē-*. The prototype is easily restored as **kred-dhē-* 'to put the **kred*'; phonetically *crēdō* comes from **crezdō*, corresponding to Skt. *śraddhā*. In Avestan, where **srazdā* would have been expected, we have *zrazdā* with an initial *z* by assimilation; thus all the forms are in exact agreement. Such an identity of forms under these conditions is a guarantee that we have a lexical heirloom which has been faithfully preserved.

When J. Darmesteter first established this correspondence, he saw in the first element the word for "heart" (Lat. *cor*, *cordis*). This interpretation was quickly abandoned for various reasons which we shall have to reconsider because the etymological problem is again under discussion. In the current view **kred* is regarded as a separate word signifying "magic power"; **kred-dhē-* thus signifies "to put one's **kred* in somebody (which results in trust)." This is not exactly simple but we cannot *a priori* expect such a notion to correspond to modern ideas.

The problem was reconsidered by Köhler, who examined the sense of the verb and the noun in Vedic and has shown what seems to follow therefrom for the Indo-European etymology. According to him, Darmesteter's etymology, positing **kred* as the word for "heart," was wrongly rejected. If we return to the explanation of **kred-dhē-* as "to put one's heart into somebody," we can see without difficulty how the different senses attested could have developed, which remained constant in Indic, both in Vedic and Pāli, including the late sense of "desire." If the Vedic term refers to "belief," this is not a theological *credo*, but the trust which the faithful put in the gods, in their might, particularly in Indra, the god of aid and succor, who is the mightiest of the gods. The central religious conception in a religion of sacrifice, which is what Vedic religion is, is expressed according to Köhler by a succession of three terms: *Treue* (faith), *Hingabe* (devotion), *Spendefreudigkeit* (pleasure in giving, generosity in giving). The evolution from "faith" to "lavish offering (in the sacrifice)" first took place in the noun and then in the verb.

The deified concept is met with in the Vedic texts: *Śraddhā* is the goddess of offering. Subsequently, in an ecclesiastical context, the term came to denote the "trust" of the layman in the brahman and in his power, a trust which correlates with generosity in the offering. In this way we pass from trust in the gods to the power of the offering.

The rest of Kohler's study is concerned with the history of the term in the *Upaniṣad* and the Buddhistic texts, which attest to the survival of the notion of "belief" and the notion of "generosity in offering." The initial sense would therefore have been "to place one's heart," and this is the old etymology which Köhler proposes to revive, and he submits that it is demonstrated by notions culled from Vedic.

How much of this will stand up to examination? Let us leave for the moment the etymology, to which we shall return at the end. If *śraddhā* in Vedic signifies "believe, have trust in," we are not told how "belief" can be defined. It would appear that this notion was similar in Vedic to that of "belief" in Latin or Irish, where it was already established from the beginning. This being so, we have to rely solely on the etymology to reach a conclusion about the original sense.

In fact, with the help of the texts cited exhaustively by Köhler, it is possible to characterize this notion a little more precisely. The term *śrad-* is not combined with verbs other than *-dhā*, except once with *kar-* (*kr̥-* 'make'). But *śrad-kar-* is artificial and unclear: everybody agrees on that. It must also be noted that the verb *śraddhā-* is often treated as a compound with a preverb or one in which the components can be severed, *śrad* and *dhā*. Such belief is never a belief in a thing; it is a personal belief, the attitude of a man vis-à-vis a god; never a relation of man to man, but a relation of man to god; the *śraddhā* is addressed particularly to Indra, the national god, the hero whose exploits fill the Rig Veda. By a well-known transfer, every time a divinity has a function, it is that divinity who is needed by man to accomplish the same function on earth; this is why man has need of Indra in order to be himself victorious in battle.

1. We begin with a text which shows under which conditions this trust is placed in Indra.

> ***śráddhitaṃ*** *te mahatá indriyā́ya*
> *ádhā manye* ***śrát*** *te asmā́* ***adhāyi***
> *vŕ̥ṣā codasva mahaté dhánāya*
> – Rig Veda I, 104, 6

We have trust in your great Indrian might, and it is for this reason that I have thought (*manye*): trust has been put in you, rush forward like a bull to win the great prize of combat.

The subject here is winning the prize in a combat, it is not war, but single combat, a joust. Whether gods or the representatives of the gods are involved, each has his partisans and the cause of the god is that of all those who support him, because they put their faith, their trust in the god.

2. We next have a passage in which, for the first and probably the only time, there appears a question about the origin of the gods and a doubt as to their existence (Rig Veda II, 12, 5): "He of whom they ask 'where is he?' the terrible (god) of whom they also say 'he does not exist,' he diminishes (*mināti*) the possessions of the *ari* (the rival) just like (a player) does the stake; have confidence in him, *só aryáḥ puṣṭī́r víja ivā mināti śrád asmai dhatta.*"

   The subject is a joust, in which the god whose existence some venture to doubt carries all away, reduces the stake of the rival. Therefore, *śrad asmai dhatta* 'believe in him!'

   This god is the champion who carries the hopes of the man whose cause he represents; the man must reinforce his might by making this *śraddhā*; thus he places *śrad* in him so that he may triumph in the combat; the god must justify this trust by his previous exploits.

3. In another text (X, 147, 1) *śrad te dadhāmi* 'I place my trust in you, because you have crushed the dragon and accomplished a manly exploit'. This refers to the combat of Indra with Vr̥tra, a previous exploit which obliges the faithful to give him his trust.

4. Next comes an invocation to the divine twins, the Nāsatyas (the Aśvins, who correspond to the Dioscuri), the twins who are gods of healing and learning (X, 39, 5): "We invoke you to pledge yourselves to renew your favors to us, O Nāsatyas, so that this *ari* (the clan companion) may have *trust* in you."

   They are anxious to obtain proof from these heavenly physicians that they are capable of helping man, so that the "other" (the *ari*) who does not believe in them will henceforward grant them his trust and be their supporter.

5. Why?—a text gives the answer (VII, 32, 14): "Which man, O Indra, would attack him whose treasure you are" (*tvā-vasu* 'who has you as his wealth, his fortune'). "In entrusting himself to you, *śraddhā te*, the hero endeavors to gain the prize (of combat) on the decisive day."
6. "Because I have said: in choosing you, O Indra and Agni, we must take away in combat this *sóma* from the Asuras (who are the enemies of the gods), come to support the *śrad* and drink of the pressed cup of *sóma* (*suta*)." (I, 108, 6).
7. "O Indra, gladdened by the *śraddhā* and by drinking of the *sóma*, you have in favor of Dabhīti (this is the name of a man) put to sleep (the demon) *čumuri*." (VI, 26, 6).

***

The response to our "why?"—cf. (5) above—is therefore: because the god who has received the *śrad* returned it to the faithful in the form of support in victory.

In conformity with the general tendencies of the religious vocabulary, there develops here an equivalence between the abstract action *śrad* and the act of offering: to put one's *śrad* in the god is tantamount to making him an oblation; hence the equivalence between *śrad* on the one hand and *yaj-* and all the other verbs of oblation on the other. We see that there is no need for the "generosity" which Köhler believed was the semantic constituent of the word.

If we ventured to propose a translation for *śrad*, it would be "devotion" in the etymological sense: a devotion of men to a god for a contest, in the course of a combat, or a competition. Such a "devotion" permits the victory of the god who is the champion, and it confers in return essential advantages on the faithful: victory in human contests, healing of sickness, etc. "To have confidence" is to put one's trust (in someone), but with the implied obligation of return service. In Avestan, the notion is defined in the same way: here, too, we find an act of faith manifested towards a god, but specifically in order to obtain his help in combat. The act of faith always implies the certainty of remuneration; it is to secure the benefit of what has been pledged that this devotion is made.

So similar a structure in different religious contexts guarantees the antiquity of the notion. The situation is that of a conflict among the gods, where humans intervene by espousing one or the other of the causes. In this engagement men give a part of themselves to reinforce that god whom they have chosen to support; a return service is always implied, some recompense from the god is expected. Such is apparently the basis of the secularized notion of *credit, trust,* whatever the thing trusted or entrusted.

The same framework appears in all manifestations of trust: to entrust something (which is one of the uses of *crēdo*) is to hand over to another person without considering the risk something that belongs to you, but which for various reasons is not actually given, with the certainty of receiving back what has been entrusted. It is the same process both for a religious faith in the proper sense, and for trust in a man, whether the pledging ("engagement") is performed by words, promises or money.

We thus reach far back into the distant past of prehistory, at least the outlines of which we can discern: trials of strength between clans, between divine and human champions, in which it is necessary to vie in strength or generosity in order to assure victory or to win in gambling (gambling is a truly religious act: the gods gamble). The champion needs people to believe in him, to entrust their **kred* to him, on the condition that he lavishes his benefits on those who have thus supported him: there is some sort of *do ut des* ('I give that you may give') between men and gods.

What is the **kred*? Does the analysis which we have just completed justify the conclusion which Köhler drew that **kred* must come from the word for "heart"? The old objection against this interpretation persists. The form **kred* is not identical with the name for heart in Indo-Iranian: this is a strange, but indisputable fact. Indo-Iranian differs from Latin *cor*(*d*), Gr. *kễr*, *kardía*, Gothic *hairtō*, Sl. *srŭdĭce*, in that the initial consonant reflects a voiced aspirated stop: *hr̥d-*, *hārdi* in Sanskrit, *zəred-* in Avestan.

Whatever the explanation, there is not the least trace in Indo-Iranian of the voiceless dorsal plosive attested everywhere else. Thus the form **kred* cannot be identified with the name for "heart." Even in the western group where the form presents an initial *k-*, we find for "heart" **kerd*, **kord*, **kr̥d* (zero-grade), but never **kred*.

There is a further, and this seems to me a still more serious, difficulty, one of sense: yet this is the aspect of the question to which least attention is paid. What is represented in Indo-European by "heart"? In the first place it is the organ *par excellence*: one throws the heart of a man to the dogs. In the second place, the heart is the seat of a number of emotions. The reader of Homer knows that courage and thought reside in the heart, certain emotions manifest themselves there, especially anger, and this explains the sense of a derivative verb like the Old Slavic *srŭditi*, Russ. *serdit'* 'irritate' (Old Slav. *srŭdĭce*, Russ. *serdce* 'heart').

The derivative nouns are bound up with the same ideas: in Latin *se-cors*, *con-cors*, together with the abstract nouns like *con-cordia*, *ve-cors* 'who is out of his heart, his faculties', as well as the verbal derivative *recordor* 'to remind (oneself)'. The heart is simply an organ, the seat of an affection, a passion, possibly of memory, but no more.

What is *never* attested in any Indo-European language is an analytical phrase like "*to put one's heart into somebody." To anyone who is familiar with the phraseology, the style, the way of thinking of the ancients, this would be just as strange an expression as "to put one's liver." Only an illusion born of modern metaphors could have made anybody imagine such an Indo-European turn of phrase as "to place one's heart into somebody." We would search in vain in ancient texts for the least trace of such a phrase. This interpretation must definitely be discarded. Unfortunately we cannot propose anything definite to put in its place: **kred* remains obscure; it does not appear except in this combination, never as an independent word. From the point of view of etymology, the word is completely isolated.

Thus all we can do is to hazard a conjecture: **kred* may be some kind of "pledge," of "stake," something material but which also involves personal feeling, a notion invested with a magic power which all men possess and which may be placed in a superior being. There is no hope of giving a better definition of this term, but we can at least restore the context which gave rise to this relationship that was first established between men and the gods, and later came to be established between men.

BOOK I, CHAPTER SIXTEEN

Lending, Borrowing, and Debt

Abstract. In contrast to Bartholomae, who distinguishes two roots *par-*, it is shown that the Iranian derivatives (and the Armenian ones) of *par-*, from which comes Iranian **pr̥tu-*, and from it Armenian *partk*^{c} 'debt', can be attached to a single basic meaning "compensate by something levied on oneself, on one's own person or one's own possessions." Lat. *par* 'equal' can be brought together with *par*-in Iranian.

In Latin, *debere* 'to owe' does not imply the receipt of something from someone to which it must be given. The technical expression *pecunia mutua*, on the contrary, designates precisely the twofold movement, i.e. going, coming back of the same sum of money, without any interest.

In Germanic, the specialization of *leihv-* < Indo-European **leik*^{w}- (cf. Gr. *leípō* 'to leave') in the sense of "lend" depends both on the notion of "vacating" attached to this root and on the existence of another verb—*letan*—for "leave." On the other hand, to designate "debt," Gothic, which has a verb for "to be obliged to" (in general), has had to borrow another term from Celtic.

Again in Gothic, the vocabulary of "lending," which apparently was not very precise, in fact comprises two different notions—one is of long standing, that of a loan as a personal transaction, the other is recent, that of a loan on interest as a professional activity. Analogous facts can be observed in Greek.

The purpose of this chapter is to show how, independently in several languages, in Iranian, Latin, Gothic and Greek, the technical terms relating to "debt," "loan" and "borrowing" were constituted by specialization and differentiation of more general terms or those belonging to a different order of ideas. We shall encounter, however, apart from special terms which are the product of an evolution peculiar to each language, on the one hand a term of considerable generality and on the other morphological processes common to the group of words connected with these notions.

DEBT IN IRANIAN

In the eastern Indo-European region, there is a series of Iranian forms without (in the present state of research) sure correspondences elsewhere, which are difficult to differentiate in Iranian itself. These are the derivatives from the Avestan root *par-*.

The distinctions between the words which derive from it are not clearly made in the authoritative dictionary, that of Bartholomae. The first task must, therefore, be to attempt an analysis which will enable us to regroup words dispersed in several articles. Bartholomae in fact distinguishes two roots (1) *par-* 'to pay back equal amounts', (2) *par-* 'to condemn'. In my opinion we must bring together the forms deriving from both roots to make up a single family: these forms are partially congruent in the two articles in Bartholomae's dictionary. They are generally used in the passive: e.g. *pairyete*, the present tense common to both roots *par-*: "to be compensated" or "to be condemned."

An example will show the context in which these forms appear. The derivative *ā-pərəti*, with the preverb *ā* and the suffix *-ti*, occurs in the company of a middle participle *pārəmna-* from the same root in the following passage: "Such is the *čiθā*, such is the *āpərəti* for the faithful who repents (*pārəmnāi*)" (*Vidēvdāt* 8, 107).

The abstract noun *āpərəti* is accompanied by *čiθā* 'expiation, compensation', the two together indicate a reparation made to expiate a sin against religion. *Āpərəti* is also found as equivalent to *yaoždāθra-*, an action to make somebody or something ritually appropriate which is polluted and hence unsuitable for religious use.

Two other derivatives are used especially in the code of purity called *Vidēvdāt*: *pərəθā-* 'corporal punishment', 'fine', something that is given to atone for a sin; and the negative adjective *anāpərəθa-* 'not to be compensated', 'inexpiable' applied to *šyaoθna-* 'action'.

We next have a series of forms which have been linked to another root par-, but which actually ought not to be dissociated from those just discussed. They are legal expressions frequently found in the *Vidēvdāt*: from the neuter *pərəθa* 'expiation, compensation' (which is implied by the adjective *anāpərəθa* which we have just mentioned) certain compounds were made: *tanu-pərəθa*, *pərətō-tanu*, *pəšō-tanu* (the last two forms are merely orthographic variants), the literal meaning of which is "of whom the body (*tanu*) is condemned, serves as a compensation," an adjective qualifying those who have committed certain crimes. Very characteristic, too, is the conjunction in one and the same expression of the compounds *dərəzānō-pərəθa*—'he whose compensation is heavy'—with the noun *pāra-* 'debt'. The Avestan vocabulary enables us to discern a set of ideas which pertain both to religion insofar as they are connected with "expiation" or "compensation," and to economic relations. This is confirmed by the indirect testimony of Armenian, which has borrowed at all periods of its development a considerable number of Iranian words. Given the large gaps in our knowledge of Iranian for certain periods, Armenian helps us to reconstitute lexical families which are defective or insufficiently represented in Iranian.

Such is the case here. We have in Armenian *partk* ᶜ 'debt' (with *k* ᶜ of the plural which is normal in abstract words), genitive *partuc* ᶜ, a stem in *-u*, which is otherwise unknown in Iranian. We have thus an opposition of two abstract formations: *ā-pərəti* and **-pr̥tu*, that is to say the two forms in *-ti* and *-tu* respectively. In Armenian *partk* ᶜ 'debt' designates also "obligation" in general, the fact of "owing," just like German *Schuld.* Hence such expressions as *part ē inj*, literally "there is a debt, a duty for me," i.e. "I owe, I have an obligation to" (negative ᶜ *ē part inj* 'I need not'), whether it concerns a moral obligation or a debt. With the common suffix *-akan,* the adjective *partakan* 'debtor' has been derived from *par-*, which may be construed as a predicate, *partakan ē*. Later the word became specialized also in compounds of which both components are Iranian in formation: *partavor* 'he who bears a debt or an obligation; liable'; and in particular *part-a-pan* 'debtor', literally "he who preserves a debt." From *partapan* was created the opposite term *partatēr* (in which *tēr* is an Armenian word for "master"), literally "master of the debt," that is "creditor." From this comes a number of new derivatives: first the verb *partim* 'I owe, I am obliged to'; then a technical term which may be taken from Iranian, the compound *part-bašxi,* the use of which explains the formation. One says in Armenian "to give one's own fortune as a *partbašxi* for others," which means "to settle the debts of others." This compound **pr̥tu-baxšya-* (this being the original Iranian form of the Armenian loanword) will have meant "the settlement of a debt": this is a technical expression of the legal language.

We thus have at our disposal a fairly considerable collection of forms. We must now pay closer attention to the characteristic suffixes of these terms. The word for "debt," **pr̥tu*, is to be defined literally as "a thing to compensate," hence "obligation" in general. This interpretation is suggested by the suffix *-tu* which implies an aptitude or eventuality. On the contrary, with the suffix *-ti*, the Av. derivative *āpərəti* represents the expected sense of "effective compensation," hence (and this is the attested sense) "debt effectively settled," which is different from **pr̥tu*—"debt" that is still to be settled.

The notion of *par-* in Iranian is much wider than our notion of "debt": it is everything which is owed by way of reparation, by one who is guilty of an offense. Thus there is after all only one root *par-* 'to compensate by something levied upon oneself, one's own person or property'; this meaning accounts for the whole lexical family just reviewed.

We find a correspondence outside Iranian (the root is unknown in Indic as far as I am aware): this is the Latin adjective *par*, *paris*, indicating parity or equality. There is no primary verbal root in Latin: *paro*, *comparo* are derivatives of the adjective *par*. In Umbrian, too, *pars* (Lat. *par*) is only a noun.

The sense permits the equation: it is one of those survivals which connect Latin with the eastern group of the Indo-European languages, and the correspondence is all the more instructive because it supplies the starting point of the technical development which took place only in Iranian and produced the term for "debt." It is largely from religious notions that these legal expressions have been constituted.

We must be careful to distinguish homophonies. The group of Latin and Iranian forms has nothing to do with those which were studied apropos of the notion of "sell," which derive from a root of the same form: *perdō*, *epérasa*, *pipráskō*. As we have seen, the expression for "sell" goes back in Greek itself to the sense "to transfer, to take abroad."

This is far from the sense "to compensate," and the two roots **per-* have nothing in common, either in their sense or their dialect distribution.

"DEBT" AND "LOAN" IN LATIN

The sense of Latin *dēbeō* 'owe' seems to result from the composition of the term *dē* + *habeō*, a compound which is not open to doubt since the Latin archaic perfect is still *dēhibui* (for instance in Plautus). What does *dēbeō* mean? The current interpretation is "to have something (which one keeps) from somebody": this is very simple, perhaps too much so, because a difficulty presents itself immediately: the construction with the dative is inexplicable, *debere aliquid alicui.*

In Latin, contrary to what it might seem, *debere* does not constitute the proper expression for "to owe" in the sense "to have a debt." The technical and legal designation of the "debt" is *aes alienum* in the expressions "to have debts, to settle a debt, in prison for debt." *Debere* in the sense "to have debts" is rare; it is only a derived usage.

The sense of *debere* is different, although it is also translated by "to owe." One can "owe" something without having borrowed it: for instance, one "owes" rent for a house, although this does not involve the return of a sum borrowed. Because of its formation and construction, *debeo* should be interpreted according to the value which pertains to the prefix *de*, to wit: "taken, withdrawn from"; hence "to hold (*habere*) something which has been taken from (*de*) somebody."

This literal interpretation corresponds to an actual use: *debeo* is used in circumstances in which one has to give back something belonging to another and which one keeps without having literally "borrowed" it; *debere* is to detain something taken from the belongings or rights of others. *Debere* is used, for instance, for "to owe the troops their pay" in speaking of a chief, or the provisioning of a town with corn. The obligation to give results from the fact that one holds what belongs to another. That is why *debeo* in the early period is not the proper term for "debt."

On the other hand, there is a close relation between "debt," "loan" and "borrowing," which is called *mutua pecunia*: *mutuam pecuniam solvere* 'pay a debt'. The adjective *mutuus* defines the relation which characterizes the loan. It has a clear formation and etymology. Although the verb *muto* has not taken on this technical sense, the connection with *mutuus* is certain. We may also cite *munus* and so link up with an extensive family of Indo-European words which, with various suffixes, denote the notion of "reciprocity" (see above, Book One, Chapter Seven). The adjective *mutuus* indicates either "loan" or "borrowing," according to the way in which the expression is qualified. It always has to do with money (*pecunia*) paid back exactly in the amount that was received. Lending and borrowing are two aspects of the same transaction as the advance and repayment of a given sum, without interest. For a loan at interest there is another word, *fenus*.

The relation between the sense of *muto*, which is translated "to change," and *mutuus* is mediated by the notion of "exchange." *Muto* means "to change" something (a garment, for instance) for something equivalent. It is a substitution: instead of the thing given or "left," something identical is received. The meaning remains the same whatever noun appears as the object of the verb: *mutare vestem*, *patriam*, *regionem*, means to "replace a piece of clothing, a country, a region by another." Similarly, *mutuus* qualifies what is to be replaced by an equivalent. There is an evident link with *munus* which, although bound up with a different set of ideas, is connected with the same kind of notion. The root is Indo-European **mei-*, denoting exchange, which has produced in Indo-Iranian *Mitra*, the name of a god, besides meaning "contract." We have studied above the Avestan adjective *miθwara*, Skt. *mithuna*, exhibiting the same radical suffix *-t-* as *mūtuus*. The sense is "reciprocal, making a pair, constituting an exchange."

But the sense of *munus*, which is particularly complex, developed in two groups of terms which we had occasion to study above and which denote both "gratuity" and "official duty or function." Such notions are always of a reciprocal character, implying a favor received and the obligation to reciprocate. This explains both the sense of "administrative duty," "official function," and that of "a favor shown to somebody," because what is concerned is "public service," that is to say, an office conferred on somebody who honors it by keeping it within limits. The "favor" and the "obligation" thus find their essential unity.

"LOAN" AND "DEBT" IN GERMANIC

We shall now consider the same notions in the Germanic languages. The expressions are entirely different: Got. *leihvan* 'lend', Old High German *līhan*, Old Icel. *lān*; modern English *loan*, German *leihen*, etc. The meaning is constant and well established from ancient Germanic onwards; an indirect proof is that these terms have passed into Slavic. OSl. *Lixva* translates Gr. *tókos* 'interest on money, price', and the word is pan-Slavic. These words belong to the family of Greek *leípō* (λείπω), Lat. *linquo* 'to leave'. The early specialization of this verb, the sense "to leave" of which is general in Indo-European, poses a problem. We must try and determine the conditions in which this specialization (which is not general) took place. Thus in Indo-Iranian, *rik-* and in Armenian *lk* ᶜ *anem*, a nasal present stem, mean only "to leave" or "to remain." This curious development of sense was studied by Meillet,[1] who stressed the fact that it is not sufficient to explain "lend" as "to leave something to somebody." The problem is precisely to find out how the term has become restricted and specialized.

Meillet observed that we have in Indo-Iranian from the same root **rik-* the Sanskrit derivatives *reknas* and Avestan *raēx-nah-*, both denoting "inheritance," and they correspond exactly. These noun forms in Indo-Iranian, characterized by the suffix *-nes*, recall the Germanic noun forms, like *lehan*. It was because of the sense "loan" acquired by *lehan* that the Germanic verb became specialized in its turn in the sense of "to lend."

This root **leik* ʷ- which is translated by "leave" or "remain" according to whether the verb has an object or not in fact signifies: "to be in a deficient state," "to be wanting, absent," "to be missing from the environment where one ought to be." The Homeric perfect tense *léloipa* does not mean "I have left" like *reliqui*, the transitive perfect, but "I am in a state of deficiency," an intransitive perfect which in spite of its construction could be active: *leloipṓs* signifies "who is missing." The usual definition conforms too much to the sense of the Greek and Latin terms. Skt. *rik-* signifies "to be missing, empty, deprived"; with the verbal adjective we have the compound *rikta-pāṇi*, *rikta-hasta* (to present oneself before somebody) 'with empty hands'. We also note the phrase *riktī kr̥* (cf. Lat. *multi*, *lucri facio*) 'to empty', 'leave', and the adjective *reku-* 'empty, deserted'.

These facts are confirmed by Avestan, which offers expressions of a similar sense: a present causative in *-aya-*: *raēčaya-* 'to make to evacuate', literally "to make (the water) withdraw." The sense of *rik-* thus will be "to evacuate, to leave something empty, of one's presence," but not "to remain." The derived noun *reknas* designates "heritage," not as something which one "leaves" in general, but a property evacuated, left vacant (by the disappearance of its owner).

Meillet rightly stressed the formation in *-nas*, which characterizes *mūnus* itself and a small group of words connected with property, like Skt. *apnas* 'goods, fortune', where the *ap-* is to be compared perhaps to *ops* in Latin; derived from another root, Skt. *draviṇas* has the same sense: "movable goods, fortune." Here is the right place to cite Lat. *fēnus* 'loan at interest', the *fē-* of which evidently belongs to the group of *fēcundus*, *fēlix*, *fēmina*, words with a very different meaning, but which have in common the root *fē-* that corresponds to Gr. θη-, the original sense of which is "fecundity, prosperity." Thus *fenus* evokes the same image as Gr. *tókos*: the interest is, as it were, the offspring of the money. We

1. *Mémoires de la Société de Linguistique de Paris*, XV.

may also establish the supplementary condition which allowed this specialization. For "leave" Gothic has *letan* ('to let', German *lassen*) with a large variety of uses: to leave an orphan, to let somebody depart, to leave money. From this, given this range of meaning, *leihv-* was available for use in a special sense.

We also have in Vedic the germ of a specialized use: *rik-* 'to retire from, to abandon something', is sometimes constructed with an object noun in the accusative and an instrumental, in the meaning "to abandon the possession of something for a certain price," and in consequence "to part with for money," "to sell." Certainly this is not "to lend," but it can be seen that that *rik-* could refer to certain transactions.

The expression for "to borrow" and "to lend" in Germanic is a verb represented by the English *borrow*, German *borgen*, and the corresponding forms in the Germanic languages. It is a present denominative from *borg*, meaning "surety, guarantee"—in an ablaut relationship with the Gothic verb *bairgan* 'to guard, to preserve'. The transition can be seen in Old Saxon *borgjan* meaning "protect," then "to be a guarantor," hence "lend" and correlatively "to give a guarantee," hence "to borrow."

The parallelism "lend/borrow" is easily apprehended in Germanic because the same verb *borgen* expresses the two notions. Even in Gothic, where there are separate terms, the connection is obvious: "lend" is expressed by "leave" and "borrow" by "keep," "guard." The lexical distinction can be dispensed with; for instance, *emprunter* in Old French was used for "to lend" and for "to be made to lend."

This relationship is also observed in the Greek technical term *dános* (δάνος) 'money lent at interest' (another derivation with the suffix *-nes*), whence the present tense *daneízō* 'to lend'. By varying the voice between active and middle this verb suffices to express both "lend" and "borrow." However, there is as yet no satisfactory etymology for *dános*. If we can accept the gloss δάνας· μερίδας, the ancient sense was "part": we must then regard *dános* as a derivative in *-nes* (neuter) form of the root *datéomai* 'to share out', comparable to the Skt. verbal adjective *dina* 'shared out'. The difficulty is to explain how "to share out" could evolve to the sense of "lend, borrow." The explanation will offer itself in a different connection later on.

For "to owe, be obliged to" Gothic has a verb *skulan* in a general or specialized sense, either as a material or a moral obligation. It translates both *opheílō* in the sense of "being a debtor" and the same verb *opheílō* when it serves to express in the Greek of the Gospels "to have a duty, to impose a moral rule on oneself"; *skulan* is also used to render *méllō*, which is one of the ways of expressing the future tense "I ought" with the infinitive. The perfect participle *skulds*, when used with "to be," forms a periphrastic expression with an active infinitive to render the notion of obligation in the passive voice, because there is no infinitive of the passive voice in Gothic. It was therefore necessary to construct the infinitive with the passive voice of the auxiliary verb, "he ought to be called" is literally expressed as "he is obliged to call." There is also an impersonal use with the neuter: *skuld ist*, which translates *éxesti*, *deî* 'it is possible, it is necessary'.

The noun *skula* 'debtor' is construed either with a noun form or with the infinitive. It designates the one who "owes" money, is liable to some obligation, possibly some punishment, from which comes: culpable or accused in a criminal matter, etc. (cf. German *schuldig* 'guilty'). In the case of a monetary debt, we have a special expression: *dulgis skulans*, which translates the plural *khreopheilétai* (χρεοφειλέται). Thus in Luke VII, 41 *twai dulgis skulans wesun dulgahaitjin sumamma*: δύο χρεοφειλέται ἦσαν δανειστῇ τινι, literally "there were two debtors to one creditor." To express "those who owe a debt" the nominal derivative of *skulan* did not suffice; the notion had to be determined by *dulgis*. Furthermore, the antithetic term "creditor" is formed by means of a compound: *dulgahaitja*, which contains the same determinant. Thus the noun *dulgs*, signifying "debt," is etymologically independent of the verb *skulan* 'to owe'. This *dulgs* also enters into a compound which renders Gr. *daneistḗs* 'he who lends'.

The remarkable fact is that *dulgs* is not of Germanic origin: it is a borrowing from Celtic. The Celtic form is related to a group of important terms in Irish, *dliged* 'the law, the right which one has over somebody' and the verb *dligim* 'to have legally, to have the right over somebody, over something'. The verb can be constructed in two ways according to whether the subject is active or passive: in the passive, Old Irish *dlegair domsa* 'right, possibility of a claim against me'; or *dligim nī duit* 'I have a claim, a right over something of yours', you owe me something, I am in the position of asserting a claim on you.

The Gothic expression *dulgis skulan* is doubly significant. By itself *skulan* and its derivatives could not specify money debt; in order to specify this it was necessary to borrow the word for "debt" from Irish. It seems, then, that the Gothic vocabulary was not sufficiently evolved to express the notions of money, loan, and borrowing in their legal context.

But the problem is still more complex. We shall try to see by direct analysis of an important text how the Gothic translator managed in a particular case.

This is the parable of the pounds, Luke XIX 12-26. Faced with the constantly recurring Greek term *mnâ* ('pound', '*mina*'), Gothic seems to use several equivalents which appear to be used somewhat haphazardly. A man departs for a far-off country and entrusts ten pounds to ten servants for them to invest.

Luke XIX, 13: "he gave them ten pounds (*mnâ*)—*taihun dailos*— and he said to them: trade with (in Greek *pragmateúein* 'to carry on a financial operation') this money." Gothic uses the imperative *kaupoþ* (German *kaufen*) 'buy', also "trade in money." There is no other expression in Gothic for commerce and speculation than *kaupon*, formed from the Latin loanword *caupo*.

In verse 15, after his return, the man calls his servants "to whom he entrusted his money" until he should return: οἷς ἔδωκε τὸ ἀργύριον: "silver," *argúrion*, is translated by *silubr*.

In verse 16, "the first man presented himself: 'Lord, your pound has brought in ten pounds,'" *skatts þeins gawaurhta taihun skattans*; this time *skatts* takes the place of *dailos* for "pound."

Similarly, in verse 18, "the second came and said 'Lord, your pound has brought in five pounds.'" Again we see *skatts* and the accusative plural *skattans*.

In verse 20, the last man said to him: "here is your pound which I have kept tied up in a napkin"; here, again, *skatts*.

In verse 23, the master retorts: "why did you not put my money into a bank?" Gothic translates money by *silubr* (as earlier on) and the bank (Gr. *trápeza*) by the expression *skattja* 'changer', the agent noun derived from *skatts*.

In verse 24, the master continues, addressing those present: "take the *pound* from this man and give it to him who has the ten *pounds*."

Here, *pound* is translated by *skatt*; but the ten *pounds* by *taihun dailos*. When the number changes from singular to plural, the term also changes.

In verse 25, the others protest: "Lord, he already has ten pounds" *habaiþ taihun dailos*.

Thus, according to the context, Gothic uses one word for "money": *silubr*, but two for "pound": *skatts* and *daila*. Furthermore, Gothic possesses, to render "silver," substance (*argúrion*) or money (*khrēmata*), also the term *faihu* (cf. above, Book One, Chapter Four). We can see, therefore, four possibilities:

	→	*silubr*		→	*skatts*
silver, money	→		pound	→	
	→	*faihu*		→	*daila*

What is the cause of this strange variety in a field where it would appear that Gothic had no very developed vocabulary?

Let us first consider the words for silver: *silubr* is a foreign word, the origin of which it is impossible to trace. It is limited to Indo-European of the north and north-east: Germanic, Baltic, Slavic. The Baltic forms are not homogeneous: OPruss. *siraplis*, Lith. *sidãbras*, Lett. *sidrabs*, as against OSl. *srebro*. The forms in these languages do not correspond exactly. The variations are such and they are so irregular that they suggest borrowing from a common source unknown to us.

The word probably denotes the material rather than the coined money. In the other Indo-European languages the term for "silver" is a designation of very great antiquity, signifying "white, brilliant," as is witnessed by *argúrion* and its related terms. Gr. *argúrion* 'silver' denotes the metal as well as money. In Gothic itself, *faihu* is the correspondent of *pecus*; it does not signify "livestock," but "wealth," in particular "money": *philárguros* 'greedy for money or avaricious' is translated by *faihu-friks* 'desirous of *faihu*'," cf. *faihu-gairns* 'he who loves money', *faihu-gawaurki* 'money revenue', the second component of which links up with *gawaurkjan* 'to produce by work', the preterite of which, *gawaurhta*, occurred above (Luke XIX, 16).

We thus have two terms used for *mnâ*. One, *skatts* (German *Schatz* 'treasure'), has no correspondent outside Germanic. It translates *mnâ* '*mina*', as well as *dēnárion* (δηνάριον) in spite of the considerable difference in value between the two currencies. Further, more generally, it translates *argúria*, *argúrion* 'money'. But what emerges from this variety of terms is that *skatts* does not presuppose any precise definition of money; it translates different monetary values. From *skatts* is derived the masculine noun *skattja* 'money changer'. This is the word which was chosen by the Gothic translator to render *trápeza* 'bank'.

The second word, *daila*, is quite different: This is the only passage where it appears in this sense which, evidently, must have been usual. It belongs to common Germanic. Besides *daila* or *dails* (German *Teil* 'part') Gothic has *dailjan* 'divide' with the preverbs *af-*, *dis-*, *ga-*, the sense being specified by these preverbs; *distribute, divide, share out*. In another passage, *daila* translates Gr. *metokhḗ* 'participation' but, in the present series of examples, *mnâ*.

The master divides ten *minae* (*dailos*) among his servants. Then, one *mina* produces ten *minae* (*skatts*). Finally, he takes away the *mina* (*skatts*) to give to the one who has ten *minae* (once again *dailos*); the two terms seem to be used concurrently.

The contrast is a deliberate one: *daila*, which elsewhere is equivalent to *metokhḗ* 'participation', is here the "part" of the total sum which was evenly divided at the beginning of the story: it is also the "share" of the same sum which was given back at the end by the clever speculator. But *skatts* denotes the monetary unit itself, with its proper value. This fact dictates the choice: on the one hand the monetary symbol, counted in distinct units; on the other hand, the "part," whether it results from a division, or is something which has been increased by investment. Such considerations seem to be responsible for the choice of the terms at his disposal which the translator made.

We must here take up again an analysis left in suspense. The Gothic—and Germanic—verb for "lend" is Gothic *leihvan*, German *leihen*, Engl. *loan*, from the root of Gr. *leípō*, Lat. *linquo*. Strange to say, the verb assumes in Germanic the sense of "to lend," whereas everywhere else it signifies "to leave" or "to remain."

How has the general notion of "leave" become the expression for "to lend"? Here we must expound two facts which are interconnected and serve to explain each other.

According to the testimony of Tacitus: (*apud Germanos*) *fenus agitare et in usuras extendere ignotum* (*Germania*, 26): "(the Germans) were not acquainted with loans at interest." Certainly, Tacitus draws an idealized picture of Germany, but he has clearly not invented this particular feature: the Germans did not know the *fenus*, the loan at interest. Generally speaking, the notion "to lend" is expressed in Gothic in two ways:

1) One "leaves" to somebody the use of something belonging to one; this is *leihvan*, which is applied to any object whatsoever (Matthew 5, 42; Luke 6, 34-35) except money: herein lies the difference.
2) A loan of money consists of entrusting money on the condition that it yields. This notion may not be very old: Gothic, having no ready-made term, coined *kaupjan* 'to speculate'.

Apparently in this society one did not lend money: only professionals practiced lending.

Retrospectively, another fact may shed some light: Gr. *dános*, a technical term for "loan at interest," whence comes *daneízō* 'to lend at interest', *daneízomai* 'to borrow', *daneistḗs* 'debtor'. We have mentioned above the etymological connection of *dános* with *daíō, datéomai* 'to divide'. The Greek term is glossed *méros* 'part'; *dános* is a neuter in *-nes* of the type *fenus, pignus*, which belongs to the vocabulary of social transactions.

But how can we link "loan at interest" with "divide"? In Greek there may be some connection, as in Gothic with *daila, dails*, which translates *méros, merís, metokhḗ*, etc. In *dános* we have the designation for the "participation" or "part" which accrues to professionals from their operations in money changing or lending.

Thus the notion of "loan at interest, credit, debt," gives rise in Gothic to two different categories of terms, according to whether it concerns a professional activity or a personal transaction. Hence such different expressions as *dulgis skulan* and *daila.*

In Greek, too, we have a general verb like *opheílō* either for a monetary debt or a moral obligation. But where money is concerned, special terms are coined, these being derivatives from *khrḗ*: *khrḗmata*, cf. *khreopheilétēs*, or a term like *tókos*, interest in the proper sense. On the other hand, *dános, daneízō* denote solely the loan at interest in the varieties noted above.

"LEND" IN LATIN

It remains to consider one more verb which, originating in Latin, passed into French. This is the Latin *praestare*; the exact sense of the verb, in view of the range of its use, remains to be defined. Along with *praestare*, the adverb *praesto* (*esse alicui*) suggests a relation which finally evolved to that of French *prêter* 'lend'. But we must first make clear the links between the varied uses of *praestare.* There are two present forms *praesto* in Latin: one is *prae-sto* 'to keep oneself ahead, to be at the head of, to distinguish oneself' etc., this being one of the compounds of *sto.* The other is the one we are studying.

Whatever the etymology of the adverb *praesto, praestare* must be regarded as a derivative of it. It is a present tense based on an adverb, a curious formation. In this morphological character we find the point of departure for the sense and at the same time the reason why there are so many different constructions with this verb.

The adverb *praesto* has this peculiarity that it enters only into a predicative and intransitive construction: *praesto esse* 'to be at the disposal of, to present oneself (to view, for service)'. The problem was to convert it into the predicate of a transitive construction and to transform *praesto esse* into a **praesto facere*. Instead of this **praesto facere*, Latin coined a present derivative *praestare*, which has this function and thus signifies "to make something ready for," "to put at the disposition of." But according to the nature of the object noun, it can take on various meanings: *aliquid alicui praestare* may mean "to bring it about that somebody can count on something," hence "act as guarantor, be responsible for": *emptori damnum praestare* 'to be responsible for a loss vis-à-vis the buyer'. When the object is a personal quality, the verb means literally "to make a quality apparent (to view, for the service of somebody)," hence "to manifest" or "to offer": *virtutem praestare* 'give proof of courage', *pietatem praestare* 'to prove one's affection'; *se praestare* 'to show oneself (as such)'. These uses evidently pave the way for the expression *praestare pecuniam alicui* 'to put money at somebody's disposal, to lend (French *prêter*) it to him'.

But we can understand that in this specialized sense *praestare* at the beginning, and for a long time, was applied to a *loan without interest*, a gracious offering, a testimony of good-will, and not a financial operation. Such a "loan," which was simply an advance of money, is different from the loan called *mutuatio*, in which the notion of reciprocity appears, implying the exact restitution of what one has received, and is still further removed from *fenus* 'loan at interest'.

The history of this notion considered in the different terms and in their separate development appears as an aggregate of complex processes, each of which achieved precision in the individual history of the separate societies. The problem everywhere is to establish what was the first value of these terms and how they became specialized in use. Even if some points of detail remain obscure, we have been able to show what the respective situation of the forms which came under consideration was, and under what conditions the extension or restriction of sense of certain terms came about.

BOOK I, CHAPTER SEVENTEEN

Gratuitousness and Gratefulness

Abstract. Lat. *gratia* is a term, originally having religious value, which was applied to a mode of economic behavior: what designated "grace" and an "action of grace" came to express the notion of "gratuitousness" (*gratis*).

The terms relating to the various aspects of payment lead on to consideration of the opposite notion, namely that of "gratuitousness." This is an economic as well as a moral notion which is attached on the one hand to monetary value, and on the other to the complex idea of "grace."

We must first consider the Latin term *gratia*. The facts are abundant and have a fairly clear distribution. *Gratia* is derived from the adjective *gratus*. This is ambivalent; it is applied to both the parties concerned: "he who receives one with favor, who shows pleasure" and "he who is received with favor, who is agreeable." These are complementary senses, one or other of which comes to the fore according to the construction in which the word occurs.

The same is true of the opposite *ingratus* 'who shows no gratefulness' or "who does not attract gratefulness." We may add a noun of an archaic type *grates* (*agere*, *solvere*, *habere*), occurring only in the plural "marks of gratitude"; finally, there is the verb *grator* together with *gratulor*, a verb derived from a non-attested noun form; an abstract noun *gratia*; and the adjective *gratuitus*. It is not merely the history of these forms within the vocabulary of Latin itself which prepared the way for the religious sense of "grace." Another factor intervened: the Greek term *kháris* (χάρις) determined the evolution of the Latin term.

Gratus is an adjective which has correspondents in Italic: Oscan *brateis* '*gratiae*', genitive singular of a noun in *-i*. This links up with a lexical family which is nowhere clearly attested except in Indo-Iranian, and here it refers to a quite different semantic field: Skt. *gir* 'chant, hymn of praise', with the present tense *gr̥ṇati* 'to praise', the object being a divinity. The adjective *gūrta* 'praised, welcome' is often found with a reinforcing prefix: *ari-gūrta*, which corresponds to the old Homeric compounds in *ari-* (ἀρι-) and *eri-* (ἐρι-). It is the same form as we have in Avestan: *gar-*, nominal or verbal, "eulogy, praise."

We can recognize in the etymological relationship the point of departure for a religious development in Indo-Iranian which led to the sense of "hymn, eulogy"; it probably was a hymn of "grace" to "give thanks (to a god)."

The connection with Latin words shows that the process at the beginning consisted of giving service for nothing, without reward; and this service, which was literally "gratuitous," provokes in return the manifestation of what we call "gratefulness." The notion of service that does not demand a counter-service is at the root of the notion, which for us moderns is twofold, "favor" and "gratefulness," a sentiment which is felt by the one who gives and by the one who receives. They are reciprocal notions: the act conditions the sentiment; the sentiment inspires a certain form of behavior. This is what produced in Indo-Iranian the sense of "(words of) gratefulness, thanks, eulogy."

In Germanic there is a curious parallel. The Gothic expression for gratefulness is *awiliuþ* and the verb is *awiliudon* 'to be grateful, feel gratitude', 'to thank', which are manifestly ancient and authentic compounds which owe nothing in sense or form to the Greek words which they translate: *kharízomai, eukharisteîn, khârin ékhein*, etc.

Gothic *awi* signifies some kind of "favor" and seems to correspond well with *auja* 'favor, chance' of the ancient Runic inscriptions. This root is well known in Indo-Iranian from the Skt. *avis* 'favorable', and the verb *ū*, *avati* 'he is favorable, well disposed, disposed to help', *ūti* 'help'. In Iranian, the same root is closely linked with the preverb *adi* and yields the verb *ady-av-* 'to bring aid, to succor', which has a very long history: the agent noun *ady-āvar* 'helper' survives to the present day in the guise of Persian *jar* 'friend'.

As for Gothic *liuþ*, this is the name for a "song," of a "hymn," which is also seen in the German *Lied.* In the vocabulary of Germanic Christianity *leuđ* translates *psalmus*. The Gothic compound thus signifies "song of favor," "hymn of grace." It is with *awi-liuþ* that Gothic signifies Gr. *khári*s 'grace' and *eu-kharisteîn* 'to show one's gratefulness'. The same relationship is found between *grātus* and Skt. *gir*; the "thankfulness" is expressed by a "chant" that serves to make it manifest.

We shall now consider in their own right the Greek terms, which directly or indirectly dominate all these developments in Latin and Germanic. The large family of the words *kháris* and its relations is divided into a certain number of terms of very different signification: *kharízomai, eukharisteîn*, etc., but also *kharā́* 'joy', *khaírō* 'to rejoice'.

The cognates are securely established: the Greek root *khar-* has long been compared to Skt. *har(ya)-* 'to have pleasure', in Italic *her-* (*hor-*): Osco-Umbrian *her-* 'to wish, be willing', Latin causative *horior, hortor* 'cause to wish, urge, encourage', as well as to Germanic **ger-*: Gothic *-gairns* 'who wishes to' (German *gern*), *gairnei* 'desire' and the present tense *gairnjan* 'to have a desire, to desire strongly'.

The Greek *kháris* expresses the notion of pleasure, what is agreeable (also in a physical sense) and of "favor"; cf. in the proper sense the Greek adverbial expression *khárin* with the genitive, "for the pleasure of," and Latin *gratiā* (ablative) with a parallel development, perhaps under the influence of Greek.

Lat. *gratiosus* can mean "who feels gratitude" and "held in favor, popular" and also "what shows favor, gracious." With the same specialization, *gratiis* contracted to *gratis*, which French has borrowed from Latin, means "without paying": *gratis habitare* 'to live for nothing, without paying rent'. In this way there appears in the use of *gratia* a new sense, that of a service provided or obtained "by grace and favor, to give pleasure."

The *gratia* consists in saving expenditure. We have a witness to this development in the adjective *gratuitus* 'disinterested, gratuitous," the formation of which is parallel to that of *fortuitus* and presupposed a noun **gratu-* of the same type as *fortu-* (cf. *fortuna*). In a money-based civilization "grace" shown to a person is to "show grace" to him by suspending his obligation to pay for the service received. This is how a term of sentiment came to be used in an economic sense, without altogether severing itself from the religious context in which it arose.

It would be a serious error to believe that economic notions originate in needs of a material order which have to be satisfied, and that the terms which express these notions have merely a material sense. Everything relating to economic notions is bound up with a far wider range of ideas that concern the whole field of relationships between men and the relations of men with the gods. These are complex and difficult relations in which both parties are always implicated.

Yet the reciprocal process of supply and payment can be interrupted voluntarily: thus we have services without return, offerings "by grace and favor," pure acts of "grace," which are the starting points of a new kind of reciprocity. Above the normal circuit of exchange— where one gives in order to obtain— there is a second circuit, that of benefice and gratefulness, of what is given without thought of return, of what is offered in "thankfulness."

BOOK II

The Vocabulary of Kinship

BOOK II

Introduction

Abstract. If our knowledge of the Indo-European vocabulary of kinship has not been noticeably advanced since the study of Indo-European kinship by Delbrück (1890), ethnological research, for its part, has made great progress, and this is what today provokes the linguist to revise the traditional interpretation of certain lexical "anomalies."

The terms relating to kinship are among the most stable and securely established items of the Indo-European vocabulary, because they are represented in nearly all languages and emerge from clear correspondences. All the conditions favorable for an exhaustive study are fulfilled. In spite of this, no advance has been made in this problem since 1890, the date of publication of Delbrück's work, entitled *Indogermanische Verwandtschaftsverhältnisse*, where the two principal conclusions which can be drawn from these correspondences are set out. On the one hand, the structure of the family implicit in the vocabulary is that of a patriarchal society, resting on descent in the paternal line and representing the type of "*Grossfamilie*" (still observed in Serbia in the nineteenth century) with an ancestor, around whom are grouped the male descendants and their immediate families; on the other hand, the terms of kinship concern the man; those which relate to the woman are not very numerous, are uncertain and often variable forms.

However, the progress made in the last seven or eight decades has not merely consisted of the assembly of a greater mass of data derived from a greater number of societies, but also and more particularly of a better interpretation in the light of a progressively refined general theory of kinship.

The systems which have been studied outside the Indo-European world sometimes make use of identical terms for degrees of relationship which are distinguished in modern western societies: those, for instance, for "brother" and "cousin," or for "father" and "paternal uncle." Inversely, they distinguish relationships which we confuse, e.g. "mother's brother" and "father's brother" (for us "uncle"), "sister's son" and "brother's son" (for us "nephew"), etc.

But relationships which are strange to us nowadays sometimes have their equivalents in the ancient Indo-European world, in which we must try to discern, as with all systems of kinship, certain principles of classification.

The Indo-European vocabulary of kinship in fact presents a certain number of anomalies which can perhaps be better defined in the light of other systems. For instance, the Lycian people, according to Herodotus (I, 173) have matronymic names: "they call themselves after their mothers and not after their fathers"—and he adds: "If a female citizen marries a slave the children are considered to be of good stock; but if a citizen, even if he were the first citizen, has a foreign wife or concubine, the children are of no account." Thus in Lycia we have matrilineal descent. But Herodotus' assertion seems not to be confirmed by the personal names of Lycian inscriptions. However, Herodotus has not invented this peculiarity. He gives us other information which has since been confirmed, for instance that the indigenous name of the Lycians was *Termilai*. We can sense the importance of women in Lycia already in the legend of Bellerophon, as it is told in Homer: (*Il.* 6, 192-195). The king of Lycia gives his daughter to the Argive Bellerophon, as well as half his royal prerogatives, making him both his son-in-law and his successor. Thus Bellerophon acquired royal rank by his marriage. Now, from the inscriptions we can get an idea of the system of kinship among the Lycians. In a bilingual dedication of the fourth century BC on the base of a statue we read: Πόρπαξ Θρύψιος Πυριβάτους ἀδελφιδοῦς Τλωεὺς ἑαυτὸν καὶ τὴν γυναῖκα Τισευσέμβραν . . . Ὀρτακία θυγατέρα Πριανόβα ἀδελφιδῆν 'Porpax, *son* of Thrypsis, nephew of Pyribates, citizen of Tlos, himself and his wife Tiseusembra, *daughter* of Ortakias, *niece* of Prianobas…' The same text is given in the Lycian language. We have the name of the person with his paternal descent (assuming Thrypsis to be the name of a man, which is not certain); but it says also "nephew of…," his wife is called "daughter of…" and also "niece of..." This wording is found also in many other Lycian inscriptions and quite often the sole description is even "nephew of..." What is the sense of "nephew" in this case?

In a system which prescribes marriage between cross-cousins, a man may marry the daughter of his father's sister, or his mother's brother, but never the daughter of his father's brother or his mother's sister—and this for a classificatory reason: the brother of the father is called "father"; the sister of the mother is called "mother." Consequently, the son of the father's brother or the mother's sister is called "brother" and the daughter "sister." We understand now the impossibility of marriage with "sisters and "brothers." No less clear are, inversely, the conditions of kinship which permit a legitimate marriage: the father's sister, the mother's brother belong to other clans, as do their children. The relationship of uncle to nephew is defined as follows: the "uncle" is for the nephew his mother's brother, the "nephew" is for the uncle his sister's son. The word "nephew" in many societies means only "sister's son." In our Lycian inscription, Pyribates is the maternal uncle of Porpax, and Prianobas the maternal uncle of Tiseusembra. Thus we have here a mixed system where the paternal descendance is indicated as well as the maternal clan.

There is another fact which we have to account for. Why is the Indo-European vocabulary so poor in expressions for female kinship? This has been explained by the predominance of masculine functions in the family. This may be true, but male preponderance could have maintained itself without provoking the same lexical consequences: the legal conditions of the woman had changed little in Europe until the eighteenth century, but that does not prevent our vocabulary from being strictly reciprocal (e.g. father-in-law/mother-in-law), etc. The explanation must be rather that the wife leaves her clan to enter that of the husband and this institutes relations between her and the family of her husband which demand expression. Now, this family being a "*Grossfamilie*" of the type known from Homeric society, these relations are manifold: the newcomer enters into special relations with the father, the mother, the brothers and their wives. On the other hand, for the man, there is no necessity to distinguish relatives of his wife by specific terms since he does not co-habit with them. To characterize them he contents himself with the general term "related, allied," which refers to them indiscriminately.

A third fact must be noted: the frequent variations in the designation of certain degrees of kinship. The terms for "father" and "mother," "brother" and "sister" are clear and constant, but for "son" there is considerable variety of terms, with frequent innovations. Similarly, the term for "uncle, aunt; nephew, niece" are ambiguous and present much diversity from language to language (Latin *nepos* means both "nephew" and "grandson"). Finally it would appear that we are unable to reconstruct even partially an Indo-European designation for "cousin." These variations raise serious problems on various planes.

If we consider merely the particular systems in each separate language, some strange correlations come to light: thus *avunculus* 'uncle' in Latin is the diminutive of *avus* 'grandfather'. Here are some of the problems which arise at all levels, some of which concern the sense of the terms, others their distribution, and still others their evolution.

BOOK II, CHAPTER ONE

The Importance of the Concept of Paternity

Abstract. Father and mother, brother and sister do not constitute symmetrical couples in Indo-European. Unlike **māter* 'mother', **pəter* does not denote the physical parent, as is evidenced, for instance, by the ancient juxtaposition preserved in Latin *Iupiter*. Nor is **bhrāter* 'brother' a term of consanguinity: Greek, in *phrā́tēr*, preserves better than any other language the sense of "a member of a phratry," a classificatory term of kinship. As for **swesor* (Lat. *soror*), this word designates literally a feminine being (**sor*) of the group (**swe*)—another classificatory term of kinship, but not symmetrical with **bhrāter*.

Of all the terms of kinship the most securely established is the name for father: **pəter*, Skt. *pitar-*, Arm. *hayr*, Gr. *patḗr*, Lat. *pater*, Old Irl. *athir*, Gothic *fadar*, Tokharian A *pācar*, Tokharian B *pācar*. Only two of the forms diverge from the common model: in Irish and in Armenian, an alteration of the initial *p* took place. In Tokharian the *ā* of *pācar* does not represent an ancient long vowel; and the *c* (=*ts*) is a development of the Indo-European palatalized *t*.

The testimony of a certain number of languages reveals another term. In Hittite we find *atta*, a form corresponding to Latin *atta*, Gr. *átta* (ἄττα), Gothic *atta*, Old Slav. *otĭcĭ* (a form derived from *atta*, coming from **at*(*t*)*ikos*).

It is a piece of good fortune that we know in Hittite the form *atta* because the ideographic writing masks the phonetic form of most of the terms of kinship:

only "father," "mother," "grandfather" are written out; we do not know the words for "son," "daughter," "wife" or "brother" because they are written solely by means of ideograms.

Gothic has two nouns, *atta* and *fadar*. It is customary to quote these on one and the same plane. In reality the name for father is always *atta*. We have a single mention of *fadar*, Gal. IV, 6, where a vocative ἀββᾶ ὁ πατήρ 'Abba! Father!' (ἀββᾶ, a traditional form of invocation in Aramaic, taken up by the Greek nominative-vocative) is translated *abba fadar*. The translator, seemingly wanting to avoid **abba atta*, has recourse to the old word common in other Germanic dialects, which has given in Gothic itself the derivative *fadrein* 'lineage, parents'.

Everywhere else, Greek *patḗr* is rendered as *atta*, including the formula *atta unsar* 'Our Father'. Why is it that **pəter* does not appear either in Hittite or in Old Slavic? We do not answer the question if we are content to say that **atta* is a familiar expression for **pəter*. The real problem is much more important: does **pəter* designate properly and exclusively physical paternity?

The term **pəter* has a pregnant use in mythology. It is a permanent qualification of the supreme God of the Indo-Europeans. It figures in the vocative in the god name *Jupiter*; the Latin term *Jupiter* is taken from a formula of invocation: **dyeu pəter* 'father Heaven', which corresponds exactly with the Greek vocative *Zeû páter* (Ζεῦ πάτερ). Besides *Jupiter*, the nominative *Diēspiter* has also been preserved, which corresponds in Vedic to *dyauḥ pitā*. To the testimony of Latin, Greek and Vedic we must add that of Umbrian *Iupater* and, finally, a form less well-known, but interesting, *Deipáturos* (Δειπάτυρος), glossed in Hesychius: θεός παρὰ Στυμφαίοις 'God of the Stymphians', the inhabitants of Stymphaea, a town in Epirus. In this region occupied by an ancient Illyrian population some part of the Illyrian heritage has survived in the Dorian dialect: the form *Deipáturos* may be a vocative of Illyrian origin. The area of this divine invocation is so vast that we may be right in assigning it to the common Indo-European period as a mythological use of the name for "father."

Now, in this original usage, the relationship of physical parentage is excluded. We are outside kinship in the strict sense, and **pəter* cannot designate "father" in a personal sense. The passage from one sphere to the other is no easy matter. These are two separate ideas, and in some languages they can be mutually exclusive. To make this difference clear, we may refer to the observation of a missionary, W. G. Ivens, who has given an account of his experience in the Western Pacific. When he tried to translate the Gospels into Melanesian, the most difficult part was to express the *Pater noster*, since no Melanesian term corresponded to the collective notion of *Father*. "Paternity in these languages is only a personal and individual relationship";[1] a universal "father" is inconceivable.

The Indo-European distribution corresponds on the whole to the same principle. The personal "father" is *atta*, which alone survives in Hittite, Gothic and Slavic. If in these languages the ancient term **pəter* has been replaced by *atta*, this is because **pəter* was originally a classificatory term, a fact of which we shall find confirmation when we come to study the name for "brother." As for the word *atta* itself, a number of features serve to define it. Its phonetic form classes it among "colloquial" terms, and it is not an accident that names similar or identical with *atta* for "father" are found in very different languages which are not related, e.g. Sumerian, Basque, Turkish, etc. Furthermore, *atta* cannot be separated from *tata* which in Vedic, Greek, Latin, Rumanian, is a traditional childish way of addressing the father affectionately. Finally, as we shall see *apropos* of the Germanic adjective "noble": **atalos > edel, adel*,[2] this appellative has produced a number of derivatives which have their place in the vocabulary of institutions.

It follows that *atta* must be the "foster father" who brings up the child. This brings out the difference between *atta* and *pater*. The two terms have been able to coexist, and do in fact coexist, very widely. If *atta* has prevailed in part of the territory, this is probably due to profound changes in religious ideas and in social structure. In fact, where *atta* alone is in use, there is no longer any trace of the ancient mythology in which a "father" god reigned supreme.

For the name of the "mother" almost the same distribution of forms is to be observed: the IE term **māter* is represented in Sanskrit by *mātar-*, Av. *mātar*, Arm. *mayr*, Gr. *mḗter* (μήτηρ), Lat. *mater*, Old Irl. *mathir*, Old Slav. *mati*, Old High German *muotar*. But Hittite has *anna-*, which makes a pair with *atta* 'father', cf. Lat. *anna*, Gr. *annís* (ἀννίς) 'mother of the mother, or of the father'. The names of father and mother are of parallel formation: they have the same ending in *-ter*, which had become the characteristic suffix of kinship names, and which later was extended in a number of languages to the whole group of names designating members of the family.[3]

1. W. G. Ivens, *Dictionary and Grammar of the Language of Saea and Ulawa, Solomon Islands*, Washington, 1918, p. 166.
2. Book Four, Chapter Eight.
3. Cf. Book Two, Chapter Six.

We can no longer analyze **pəter* or **māter*, so that it is impossible to say whether from the beginning the ending was a suffix. In any case, this *-ter* is neither the morpheme of agent nouns, nor that of comparatives. We can only state that, originating in **pəter* and **māter*, it became the indicator of a lexical class, that of kinship names. This is why it has become generalized in other terms of this class.

It is probable that the two names for "mother," **māter* and **anna*, correspond to the same distinction as that between **pəter* and **atta* for "father." "Father" and "mother," under their "noble" names, express symmetrical ideas in ancient mythology: "Father Heaven" and "Mother Earth" form a couple in the Rig Veda.

Further, only the Hittite group has made *anna-* (Luvian *anni-*) into the term for "mother," like *atta* (Luvian *tati-*) for "father." Elsewhere, the sense of **anna* is rather vague; Lat. *anna*, poorly attested, seems to designate the "foster mother" and this does not accord with Gr. *annís*, given in a gloss of Hesychius as "the mother of the mother or of the father." Terms of this nature do not convey any precise placing in the system of kinship.

The name of "brother" is IE **bhrāter*, as emerged from the equation of Skt. *bhrātar*, Av. *brātar*, Arm. *ełbayr*, Gr. *phrā́tēr* (φράτηρ), Lat. *frāter*, Old Ir. *brathir*, Goth. *broþar*, Old Slav. *bratrŭ*, *bratŭ*, Old Pruss. *brati*, Tokharian *prācer*. The Hittite name is still unknown. The Armenian form can be explained phonetically by an initial metathesis: *bhr-* > *(a)rb-*, which has provoked a dissimilation of the two consecutive *r* into *l-r*.

One important fact does not appear in this picture: while Greek has, it is true, the form *phrā́tēr*, the correspondent of **bhrāter*, in the vocabulary of kinship **bhrāter* is replaced by *adelphós* (ἀδελφός) (from which comes *adelphḗ*, αδελφή 'sister'). A substitution like this could not be an accident of vocabulary; it is a response to a need which concerns the whole of the designations for kinship.

According to P. Kretschmer[4] the replacement of *phrā́ter* by *adelphós* may be due to a new way of regarding the relationship of "brother" which made *phrā́tēr* into the name for a *member of a phratry*. In fact, *phrā́tēr* does not mean the consanguineous brother; it is applied to those who are bound by a mystical relationship and consider themselves as descendants of the same father. But does this necessarily imply that this is an innovation of Greek? In reality Greek

4. *Glotta*, vol. II, 1910, pp. 201ff.

preserves here the "broad" meaning of Indo-European **bhrāter* which is still reflected in certain religious institutions of the Italic world. The "Arval Brothers" (*fratres arvales*) at Rome, the Atiedian Brothers (*fratres Atiedii*) of the Umbrians, are members of confraternities. Where these associations remained alive and their members had a special status, it was necessary to specify by an explicit term the "consanguineous brother": in Latin, for the blood brother, the expression used was *frater germanus*, or simply *germanus* (Spanish *hermano*, Portuguese *irmão*), a brother of the same stock. Similarly, in Old Persian, when Darius in his royal proclamations wanted to talk of his consanguineous brother, he adds *hamapitā, hamātā* 'of the same father, of the same mother', cf. in Greek *homo-pátrios, homo-mḗtrios*. In fact, the "brother" is defined with reference to the "father," which does not necessarily mean the "progenitor."

In the light of these facts, **bhrāter* denoted a fraternity which was not necessarily consanguineous. The two meanings are distinguished in Greek. *Phrā́tēr* was kept for the member of a phratry, and a new term *adelphós* (literally "born of the same womb") was coined for "blood brother." The difference is also reflected in a fact which has often escaped attention: *phrā́tēr* does not exist in the singular; only the plural is used. On the other hand, *adelphós*, which refers to an individual kinship, is frequently used in the singular.

Henceforward, the two kinds of relationship were not merely distinguished but actually polarized by their implicit reference: *phrā́tēr* is defined by connection with the same father, *adelphós* by connection with the same mother. Henceforth only the common maternal descent is given as a criterion of fraternity. At the same time this new designation also applies to individuals of different sex: *adelphós* 'brother' produced the feminine *adelphḗ* 'sister', a fact which completely overturned the old terminology.

There is a specific term for "sister": Indo-European **swesor* is represented in Sanskrit by *svasar*, Av. *x*ᵛ *anhar*, Arm. *k*ᶜ *oyr* (the phonetic result of **swesor*) Lat. *soror*, Got. *swistar*, Old Slavic *sestra*, Tokharian *šar*.

Greek is apparently missing from this picture although the Greek correspondent of **swesor* is preserved in the form *éor* (ἔορ). But this is only a survival preserved by the glossographers. Just as *phrā́tēr* conveys a special sense, so the word *éor*, phonetically corresponding to **swesor*, is given with divergent meanings. It is glossed as θυγάτηρ 'daughter', ἀνεψιός 'cousin', and ἔορες· προσήκοντες 'relatives'. The term, which is very vague, was applied to a degree of kinship which the commentators were unaware of. This obliteration was due to the creation of *adelphḗ* 'sister', and this in its turn was produced by the transformation of the term for "brother."

What is the proper sense of **swesor*? This form is of exceptional interest because it seems open to analysis as a compound **swe-sor*, formed from **swe*, well known as a term of social relationship,[5] and an element *-*sor*, which appears in archaic compounds where it denotes the female: the ordinal numbers for "third" and "fourth" have, alongside the masculine forms, feminines characterized by the element *-*sor*: Celtic *cethe***oir**, Vedic *cata***sra**, Av. *čata***ṅrō**, all deriving from **kʷete-sor*.

It is probable that *-*sor* is an archaic name for "woman." It can be recognized in Iranian in the guise *har-* in the root of Av. *hāirišī* 'woman, female', where it has a suffix in *-iš-i*, the morpheme which we find again in the feminine *mahiṣi* 'queen'. It is also possible that Skt. *strī* (< **srī*) 'woman', is a secondary feminization of the ancient **sor*. Thus we can identify the two elements of the compound **swe-sor*, etymologically "the feminine person of a social group *swe*." Such a designation puts "sister" on a quite different plane from "brother": there is no symmetry between the two terms. The position of the sister is defined by reference to a social unit, the *swe*, in the bosom of the "*Grossfamilie*," where the masculine members have their place. Later on, at the appropriate time, we shall study more closely the sense of *swe*.

Unlike the word for "sister" we have no means of analyzing the name for "brother," apart from isolating the final *-ter* itself, as in the case of "mother" and "father." But we can offer no explanation for the root **bhrā-*. It is useless to connect it with the root **bher-* of Lat. *ferō* because we know of no use of the forms of this root which would lead to the sense of "brother." We are not in a position to interpret **bhrāter* any more than we can **pəter* and **māter*. All three are inherited from the most ancient stock of Indo-European.

---

5. See Book Three, Chapter Three.

BOOK II, CHAPTER TWO

Status of the Mother and Matrilineal Descent

Abstract. Among other pointers to the non-existence of any legal status for the mother in Indo-European society, the absence of a word **mātrius* as a counterpart to *patrius* may be cited.

Nevertheless, the vocabulary, especially in Greek, preserves the memory of quite different social structures which are probably not Indo-European: the existence of a Zeus *Hēraîos* and of a conjugal couple *Héra-Heraklês,* the Greek names for "brother"—*adelphós*, literally "coming from the same womb" and *kasígnētos* "id."—cannot be explained by reference to a system of patrilineal filiation.

But in the historic period these are only memories: *Zeùs Hēraîos* is a hapax and in spite of their etymology, *kasígnētos*(which could for a while substitute for *phrā́ter* as a classificatory term) and *adelphós* both designate the "brother" as terms of patrilineal kinship.

All the facts adduced up till now prompt us to recognize the primacy of the concept of paternity in Indo-European. By contrast, they also help us to appreciate the deviations from this principle which can be established. This primacy is corroborated by some slight hints of a linguistic nature which are not always apparent, but which gain greater weight when traced to their origins.

One of these facts is the creation of a term in Latin, *patria* 'fatherland', from *pater*. But this derivation could not have taken place directly. It will be better appreciated if we examine the adjectives which have been coined from *pater* and *mater*.

The adjective derived from *pater* is *patrius*. Here we have an adjective which refers exclusively to the world of the "father." There is no correlative term for the "mother"; the word **matrius* does not exist. The reason for this is evidently the legal situation of the mother; Roman law did not know an institution for which the adjective would be suitable, and which would put "father" and "mother" on an equal footing: the *potestas* is exclusively *patria*. According to this law, there was no authority, no possession, which belongs to the mother in her own right. The adjective derived from *mater* is quite different; it is *maternus*, to the formation of which we shall return.

One might think that at least one common derivative of *pater* and *mater* existed, that in *-monium*, for *matrimonium* is parallel to *patrimonium*. But in fact this is no more than a quite superficial symmetry. As we shall show later on, the two formations are not correlative and do not indicate the same function.[1] Further, morphological indications betray the essential difference which separates the two concepts.

We know that one of the Indo-European societies which have longest preserved the ancient structure is that of the South Slavs, among whom the form of family called *zadruga* still exists. Vinsky[2] has subjected to close study the functioning and composition of this "*Grossfamilie*." Most often consisting of a score of members, sometimes thirty and even as many as sixty, the *zadruga* is a considerably larger unit than the nuclear family which we usually see: it unites as many of these nuclear families as there are sons living in the common home. This family is of a rigorously patriarchal type. However, a stranger may become a member by marrying a daughter: the line is continued through the heiress. The son-in-law is incorporated into his new family to the point of losing his own status. It goes so far that he takes the name of his wife, the other members calling him by a possessive adjective derived from this name. Henceforth he bears the family name of his wife, as do his children, since his own name no longer has a social function.

But there are also facts which attest the contrary, particularly in ancient Greek society. We have studied above a special peculiarity of Greek which separates it from the other Indo-European languages, the designation of "brother"

1. On *matrimonium*, see Book Two, Chapter Four.
2. Vinsky, *La grande famille des Slaves du sud. Etude ethnologique*, Zagreb, 1938.

by *adelphós*, which indicates co-uterine fraternity. This is not the only term which designated the "brother" by reference to the "mother." A parallel term of the same meaning is the adjective *homogástrios* (ὁμογάστριος) with the doublet *ogástōr* (ὀγάστωρ). It would appear that we have here an ancient pointer to a certain preponderance of the woman.

Greek mythology offers a number of confirmations of this. Let us consider for example the great divine couple, the very prototype of the couple, Zeus and Hera, united by the *hieròs gámos*, the sacred marriage, illustrating the marital powers of the husband, supreme lord of the gods. A.-B. Cook,[3] the author of a monumental work on Zeus, has studied this *hieròs gámos*. According to him, the union of Zeus and Hera is not an ancient phenomenon: it appeared towards the fifth century BC, as if to normalize a more complex state of the legend. Before this, there were two distinct couples: on the one hand Zeus and a certain partner, and on the other hand a certain god and Hera. We have a proof of this in the ritual calendar of Athens which mentions an offering to *Zeùs Hēraîos* (Ζεὺς Ἡραῖος), probably the sole case where a god is designated by the name of his wife. In this stage of the legend, Zeus is subordinated to Hera. Cook[4] has collected the evidence which shows that at Dodona, the most venerable sanctuary of Zeus, the wife of the god was not Hera, but *Diṓnē* (Διώνη). Among the Dodonians, according to Apollodorus, Hera was called Dione. *Diṓnē* is an adjective derived from *Zeùs*. The divine figure of Dione is taken from the name of Zeus and represents his emanation.

Hera, for her part, is a sovereign, particularly at Argos. Now, the person who is associated with her is Heracles, the son-in-law of Hera in the usual form of the tradition. But certain facts, the jealousy of Hera, for instance, seem to indicate a conjugal relationship and not a maternal one. We may in all probability regard Heracles as a "prince consort" of Hera at a very ancient date.

We have therefore not one single couple but two: Zeus and Dione on the one hand, and Hera and Heracles on the other.

They have been fused into a single one in which the great goddess is the wife of the great god: Zeus and Hera are henceforth united. It is therefore probable that the primitive forms of the legend preserve the memory of the major role devolving on the woman.

---

3. A.-B. Cook, *Zeus*, III (1941), pp. 1025-1065.

4. Id., *The Class. Rev.* (1st Series) XIX, 365-416.

The same trait emerges from a confrontation of the two Greek words for "brother," *adelphós* (ἀδελφός) and *kasígnētos* (κασίγνητος). The notion of *phrā́tēr*, with that of *phrātría*, is highlighted in a tradition (of Ionic origin) relating to the feast of the *Apatoúria* Ἀπατούρια; in the course of this, on the second day, a sacrifice to *Zeùs Phrátrios* (*Apatoúrios*), as well as to *Athēnaía phratría* (*Apatouría*) took place. The etymology of *Apatouría* is clear. The ancients already interpreted the word as*homopátria* (ὁμοπάτρια): it is the feast of those who have the same "father": *apátores* (ἀπάτορες), which is equal to *phrā́teres*, since the *phrā́tēr* are those who are descended from the same *patḗr*. This brings out the notion of male and paternal lineage.

Let us now consider the word *kasígnētos*. It belongs to the ancient poetic language, but it does not have the same dialect tradition as *apatoúrios*, which seems to be Ionic: *kasígnētos* is Aeolian, "Achaean" (of the Cypriot variety). The original sense is that of *adelphós*, in the light of uses like κασίγνητον καὶ ὄπατρον (*Il.* 11, 257; cf. 12, 371), which is tantamount to "from the same mother and father," and this is confirmed by *Il.* 3, 228: αὐτοκασιγνήτω τώ μοι μία γείνατο μήτηρ 'the two brothers which my mother has given me', apropos of Castor and Pollux. The formation is that of a compound in which the first term *kásis* 'brother; sister' (in Aeschylus) has been reinforced by a verbal adjective *-gnētos* 'born, of birth'.

But one use of *kasígnētos* causes difficulty: "Hector makes an appeal to all his *kasígnētoi*. And first he addresses himself to the son of Hiketaon, to the proud Melanippus" (*Il.* 15, 545-7). Thus Melanippus, the son of Hiketaon, figures among the brothers of Hector. But this person is not his brother: he is the son of Hiketaon and not of Priam. This was already noted in antiquity: the scholiasts translate *kasígnētoi* here by the vague term *sungeneîs* (συγγενεῖς) 'relatives': at this epoch in Ionian the *sungeneîs* were still called *kasígnētoi*. Today we can be more precise. According to the genealogy of the person, indicated elsewhere in the *Iliad*, Melanippus was the son of Hiketaon, the brother of Priam. He is therefore precisely the son of the brother of Hector's father. Thus *kasígnētos* does not here designate the brother issued from the same father, but the "brother" issued from the father's brother, that is to say in our terminology the "cousin."

We can draw two conclusions from this:

1) this kinship is necessarily of a classificatory type, so that *kasígnētos* joins *phrā́tēr* and *apátōr*;

2) *kasígnētos*, like *adelphós*, has probably, through synonymy, deviated from its etymological signification, which must have referred to the mother, with the result that it entered an exclusively paternal type of filiation. We now see that in spite of the persistence of local, perhaps foreign, traditions, the force of Indo-European conceptions has brought the aberrant ideas into line with the primitive norm.

We have a confirmation of this in a Laconian gloss: κάσιοι· οἱ ἐκ τῆς ἀυτῆς ἀγέλης ἀδελφοί τε καὶ ἀνεψιοί; brothers or cousins of the same ἀγέλη, the same "band," were called *kásioi*. The children called *kásioi* were organized in the same "band" because, being brothers or cousins, they acknowledged the same "father."

Such is this complex history in which we see that, when a culture is transformed, it employs new terms to take the place of traditional terms when they are found to be charged with specific values. This is what happened to the notion of "brother" in Ibero-Romance. As a term of kinship, Latin *frater* has disappeared, and it has been replaced by *hermano* in Spanish and *irmão* in Portuguese, that is to say by Latin *germanus*. The reason for this is that in the course of Christianization, *frater*, like *soror*, had taken on an exclusively religious sense, "brother and sister in religion." It was therefore necessary to coin a new term for natural kinships, *frater* and *soror* having become in some way classificatory terms, relating to a new classificatory relationship, that of religion. Similarly in Greek it was necessary to distinguish two types of kinship, and *phrā́tēr* now being used solely as a classificatory term, new terms for consanguineous "brother" and "sister" had to be forged.

These lexical creations often overturn the ancient terminology. When Greek used for "sister" the feminine form (*adelphḗ*) of the term for brother (*adelphós*), this instituted a radical change in the Indo-European state of affairs. The ancient contrast between "brother" and "sister" rested on the difference that all the brothers form a phratry mystically descended from the same father. There are no feminine "phratries." But when in a new conception of kinship the connection by consanguinity is stressed, and this is the situation we have in historical Greek, a descriptive term becomes necessary and it must be the same for brother and sister. In the new names the distinction is made only by morphological indications of gender (*adelphós*, *adelphḗ*). Apparently slight facts, like this one, throw light on the profound transformation which the Greek vocabulary of kinship has undergone.

BOOK II, CHAPTER THREE

The Principle of Exogamy and its Applications

Abstract. Only the custom of marriage between cross-cousins, which in its application means that the same person is my father's father and the brother of my mother's mother, enables us to understand that Latin *avunculus*, derived from *avus* 'paternal grandfather' signifies 'maternal uncle'.

Correlatively, *nepos* 'nephew' (indulged by his maternal uncle, but subjected to the strict *patria potestas*), beside this original sense (confirmed inter alia by Gr. *anepsíos* 'cousin', literally co-nephew), takes on the meaning "grandson" wherever the Indo-European patrilinear system was imposed with increasing rigor.

In contrast to *nepos*, the designation of "son"—generally as "offspring"— presents a considerable diversity in the Indo-European languages: we can glimpse in this traces of a structure of kinship where the relationship between father and son was eclipsed by that of maternal uncle to nephew.

A common term designates "grandfather" in most Indo-European languages: it is represented by Latin *avus* and the corresponding forms. But in certain languages the sense offers a noteworthy variant: it is no longer "grandfather" but "uncle," and in particular "maternal uncle."

We shall now enumerate these forms proceeding in the order of increasing complexity.

To Latin *avus* corresponds the Hittite term of the same sense, *huhhaš*. The relationship seems surprising considering how different the forms are. It finds its explanation in an archaic stage of Indo-European phonology. Hittite preserves an ancient laryngeal phoneme (written *h*), which has disappeared in other languages, but which is there indirectly manifested by the modifications of timbre or vocalic quantity. We shall use the notation **H*. The common prototype can be reconstructed as **HeuHos*.

Like Latin *avus* and Hittite *huhhaš*, Armenian *haw* 'grandfather' presents the word without a suffix. The initial *h* of Armenian has nothing to do with that of Hittite; it is a secondary aspiration due to a recent phenomenon: etymologically, the Armenian form pre-supposes an ancient initial vowel. The same recent aspirate has developed in the parallel Armenian word for "grandmother," *han*, which is compared with Hittite *hannaš* 'grandmother', Latin *anus* 'old woman', Greek *annís*, glossed "mother of the mother or of the father," Old High German *ana* 'grandmother,' etc.

As against Hittite *huhhaš*, Lat. *avus*, Armenian *haw* 'grandfather', the forms in the other languages fall into special groups. We have first the group of Slavic and Baltic: Old Slav. *ujĭ*, originally **auios*; in Baltic the Old Prussian *awis*, Lithuanian*avýnas*. As for the sense, we observe that the Balto-Slavic **auios* signifies "uncle." The Lithuanian *avýnas*, a secondary derivation, designates especially the mother's brother, the maternal uncle.

The Celtic forms represent two distinct developments. On the one hand there is Old Irish *aue*, Middle Irish *ōa*, which also come from **auios* but designate the "grandson." On the other hand, Welsh *ewythr*, Breton *eontr*, presuppose a derivative **awen-tro-* and signify "uncle."

In Germanic, we have a series of derivatives with a suffix in *-n* forming a new root **awen-*: in Gothic this **awen-* is by chance represented only by the feminine *awo* 'grandmother' (dative sing. *awon*); the masculine form is attested in the Icelandic *afe* 'grandfather'. This stem **awen-* is presumably represented in Old High German in the word *ōheim*, German *Oheim* 'uncle', which is reconstructed hypothetically as a compound **awun-haimaz*. We do not know how to interpret the second element: it may be a derivative of the name of the residence (*Heim*, cf. *home*) "he who has the residence of the grandfather" (?), or as a nominal form from the root $*k^{w}$ *ei-*(Gr. *timḗ*, τιμή) "he who has the esteem (?) of the grandfather"; but this root does not appear elsewhere in Germanic. Everything in this reconstruction remains uncertain and this is detrimental to the analysis of the sense. In any case, Old High German *ōheim* and the corresponding forms of Old Engl. *ēam*, Old Fris. *ēm*, likewise signify "uncle" and not "grandfather."

Such are the facts arranged according to their forms. It will, however, be noticed that not all languages figure here: Greek and Indo-Iranian are missing. These two dialect groups have new terms. In Greek, the "grandfather" is called *páppos* (πάππος), a form of address belonging to the language of children; it is not found in Homer, but it is the only one known in prose both of literature and inscriptions. In Sanskrit, the "grandfather" is called *pitāmaha-*, a descriptive compound in which the two elements are in an unusual order. It has been explained as an imitation of the compound with an intensive reduplication *mahāmaha* 'very great, all powerful'; this reveals the recent date of this designation. Moreover, Indic does not here agree with Iranian, which has a distinct word, found both in Avestan and Old Persian, *nyāka* 'grandfather', Persian *niyā*, a term with no etymological connections.

We can now see the great problem posed by the evolution of sense between Indo-European **awos* and its derivatives and compounds. The fact that these derivatives are formed with the help of suffixes in *-yo*, *-en*, explains nothing. What we have to find out is how, starting from the word for "grandfather," the same word came to be used for the "maternal uncle." The question does not arise only in the different dialect groups, but within Latin itself, since, along with *avus* 'grandfather', we have the diminutive *avunculus* as the term for 'uncle'. The problem has been recognized since ancient times and it has often been discussed. It is already found in Festus: "*avunculus, matris meae frater* (brother of my mother and not of my father) *traxit appellationem ab eo quod. . . tertius a me, ut avus... est*" (because he occupies the third degree in relation to me, like the grandfather)—or, another explanation, "*quod avi locum obtineat et proximitate tueatur sororis filiam*" (because he takes the place of the grandfather and is responsible for the supervision of his sister's daughter). It never designates anything else than the *maternal* uncle.

An idea presents itself immediately: if *avunculus* is attached to *avus*, is it not because *avus* designated the maternal grandfather? *Avunculus* could thus be explained as the son of the real *avus*. This was supposed by Delbrück, and Eduard Hermann has insisted on this explanation.[1] This idea is not acceptable either in fact or in theory. Let us take the examples of *avus* collected in the *Thesaurus*;

1. *Göttinger Nachrichten*, 1918, pp. 214f.

none has the sense of "maternal grandfather." All the definitions of the ancients connect *avus* with paternal lineage. In the *Origines* of Isidore of Seville we read: "***avus** pater patris est*; *patris mei pater avus meus est*" ("*Avus* is the father's father; my father's father is my *avus*"). If the ancestors are enumerated, a beginning is always made with the father, *pater*, and then *avus*, *proavus*, etc. are listed. For the maternal grandfather, the specific expression *avus maternus* is used. Similarly in Hittite, *huhhaš* is exclusively the paternal grandfather; we have an additional proof in the plural *huhhanteš* which designates the fathers, i.e. the ancestors, the forebears; it is in the paternal line that the ancestors are to be found.

This is a question of fact; let us now consider the theoretical reason. In a system of classificatory kinship, no special importance is attributed to the mother's father. In agnatic filiation, account is taken of the father and the father's father; on the other hand, in uterine filiation, the mother's brother is considered. But the mother's father has no special position. It follows that one could never have designated as *avunculus* such an important person as the maternal uncle with a term derived from *avus*, if *avus* indicated the mother's father, a relationship which is of no particular importance.

The difficulty which philology cannot solve unaided finds its solution in the structure of exogamic kinship. We have to envisage the situation of EGO with reference to his *avus* and his *avunculus*. We can represent the situation figuratively by a schema indicating the relationships after the lapse of two generations. We have to remember that following the principle of exogamy, the two different sexes always belong to opposed moieties: therefore marriage must always take place between members of opposed moieties.

Smith I is the *avus*, the father of EGO's father. At the same time, Smith I is the brother of the mother of EGO's mother: *avus* designates therefore, in one and the same person, the father's father and the brother of the mother's mother, that is the maternal great-uncle. The double relationship to EGO of this single person follows automatically from the marriage of cross-cousins. Starting with Jones II, the same scheme begins anew: the son of Jones I marries the daughter of his father's sister, his cross-cousin; the *avus* is always the paternal grandfather and maternal great-uncle. To sum up: Smith I is the father's father (or *avus*) of Smith III, who is EGO. But Smith I is at the same time the brother of the mother of Jones II, who in his turn is the brother of the mother of Smith III (EGO). For EGO, Smith I will be *avus* and Jones II *avunculus*.

Starting with EGO, his mother's brother, his *avunculus*, is the son of the sister of his father's father, of his *avus*. This is always the case. In this system, a relationship is established between maternal uncle and nephew, while in agnatic filiation, it is established between father and son.

Accordingly, if *avus* refers in reality to the maternal great-uncle, the maternal uncle could be called "little *avus*" or *avunculus*. This solution is a simple consequence of the necessities of the system. This suggests that we should ascribe the sense of "maternal great-uncle" to *avus* rather than "grandfather": one and the same person, the brother of the mother's mother, is at the same time the father's father. In his authoritative work on ancient Chinese society, Granet[2] draws attention to the same correspondence: the agnatic grandfather is always the maternal great-uncle. This rule applies also in other societies: it has the typical character of a necessary rule.

Latin, thus re-interpreted, offers some important evidence: but in historical times the sole meaning attested is the agnatic signification of *avus* as "grandfather," "father's father." The etymological relationship with *avunculus* implies and reveals another type of filiation, given that *avunculus* is the mother's brother.

This general structure conditions the diverse elements which it comprises. The way is open to a structural conception of Indo-European kinship and of the vocabulary of this kinship, because it contains classes and relationships between classes. This makes intelligible the variety of terms and the dissymmetry of the designations for uncles and aunts in Latin:*patruus* for the "father's brother" but *avunculus* for the "maternal uncle"; in the feminine *matertera*, the mother's sister, the "quasi-mother", but *amita* for the father's sister. The relationship of fraternity between members of the same sex puts them in the same class. As the father's brother or the mother's sister are of the same sex as the personage in virtue of whom they are defined, the terms which designate them are derivatives from the primary term. But the mother's brother, or father's sister, being of the opposite sex, have different names: this is an illustration of the principle of exogamy (see figures below).

Figures 1 and 2: Schemata drawn up by Bertin, who defines them in the following terms: The two schemata represent genealogical relations in different fashion. In both cases the information is the same, both for the individuals and their relationship.

2. *Civilisation chinoise*, 1929, p. 247.

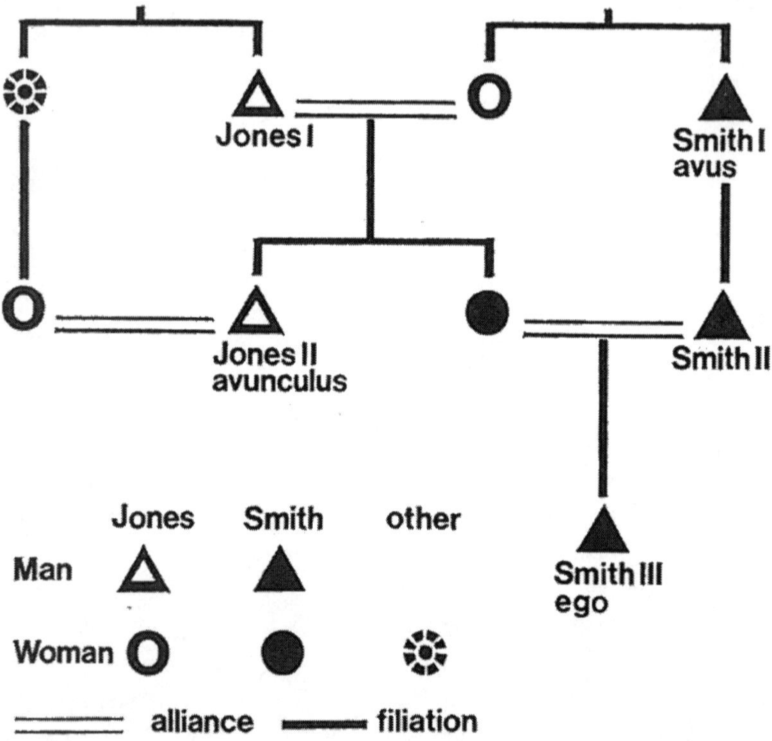

Figure 1. In this schema (a traditional genealogical tree) the individuals are represented by points (of different shape according to sex, and black or white according to family) and the relationship by lines (of different design, according to the kind of relationship: filiation or alliance).

In general, in our modern languages, this distinction has been lost. However, it is not necessary to go back very far to discover various pointers to the privileged position which the maternal uncle occupied.

For the ancient Germanic world, we refer to Tacitus, *Germania* XX, 4:

> *Sororum filiis idem apud auvnculum qui ad patrem honor; quidam sanctiorem artioremque hunc nexum sanguinis arbitrantur et in accipiendis obsidibus magis exigunt tanquam et animum firmius et domum latius teneant.*

> 'The sons of the sister are just as dear to their *avunculus* as to their father; there are even some who believe that this blood tie (that of the *avunculus*) is more

sacred and close (than that of paternity). They insist on it by preference when taking hostages, because thus they think they have a better hold on their minds and a wider hold on the family.'

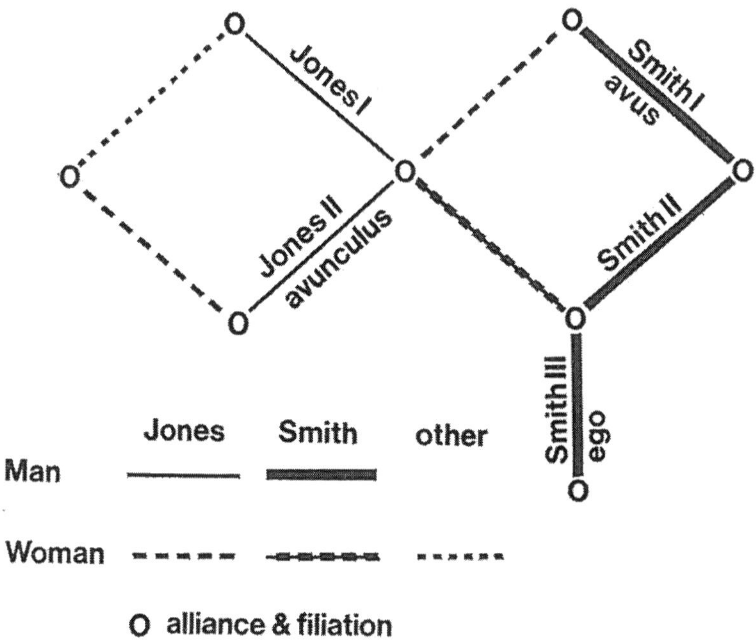

Figure 2. In this schema, less orthodox, certainly requires some effort of adaptation: the individuals are represented here by lines (different according to sex and family), their relationships by a point (representing by itself alliance and filiation). But the figure thus obtained brings out better the special relationships of cross-cousins here studied. This second system of representation has the added advantage of facilitating the recording of genealogical information that is infinitely more complex and ramified, and presenting it in easily read form (which the first type of representation does not permit).

With the Celts, too, we find concordant testimony. The great heroes of the epic call themselves after their mothers. The relationship between Cuchulainn and his mother's brother Conchobar is a good illustration of this type of relationship. In Homer, this structure remains recognizable, although the designation of the maternal uncle has been remodeled as *mḗtrōs* (μήτρως), a secondary derivative made on the model of *pátrōs* (πάτρως), which is the equivalent of Latin *patruus*. The ancient noun has disappeared, but the old idea has survived. In the *Iliad*, the only two examples of the term *mḗtrōs* are particularly significant:

1) Apollo appears in disguise to Hector to encourage him in his moment of weakness; he takes on the appearance of his maternal uncle (*mḗtrōs*) in order to have more authority (*Il.* 16, 717).
2) Tlepolemus, the bastard son of Heracles, has killed the *maternal uncle* of Heracles; he has to flee, followed by the "sons and grandsons" of Heracles; by this murder he has provoked the hostilities of the whole of his kindred (*Il.* 2, 661 ff.).

It would certainly be possible to find other examples of this kind which often pass unnoticed. Here we cite only one from Herodotus (IV, 80). At the moment when Octamasadas, the king of the Scythians, is getting ready to fight Sitalkes, the king of the Thracians, the latter makes him say: "Why should we fight since you are the son of my sister?"

Much the same is testified by a fact of the Armenian vocabulary: *kʿeri* 'maternal uncle' is a derivative of *kʿoyr* 'sister'. This morphological relationship appears clearly if we substitute the respective prototypes: *kʿoyr* goes back to **swesōr* and *kʿeri* to **swesriyos*. The maternal uncle is therefore literally designated as "he of the sister," after his sister, who is the mother of EGO. This is an explicit expression, probably a substitute for another more ancient one, which underlines the specific nature of the maternal uncle in the system of Armenian kinship. All this brings out, in a way that is all the more convincing because the facts come from languages and societies which have long become separate entities in the Indo-European world, the special position of the "maternal uncle," and it makes the formal relationship between *avus* and *avunculus* more probable.

Correlatively, the word for "nephew," a term represented in nearly all the languages, shows a parallel variation of sense: it means both "grandson" and "nephew."

First we list the forms in their etymological relationships: Skt. *napāt*, *naptṛ*, fem. *naptī*; Av. *napāt*, fem. *napti*; Old Persian*napā* (nominative); Lat. *nepōs*, feminine *neptis*; Old Lithuanian *nepuotis*, feminine *nepte*; Old Engl. *nefa*; Old High German*nefo*; Old Slavic *netĭjĭ* < **neptios*; in Celtic, Old Irl. *nia*, Welsh *nei*. We must also cite Gr. *anepsiós* (ἀνεψιός), but separately: it does not signify "nephew," but "cousin."

According to the language, **nepōt-* is sometimes "grandson," sometimes "nephew" and sometimes both.

In Vedic, *napāt* is the "grandson" or, more vaguely, the "descendant"; it is "grandson" in Iranian, too, especially in Old Persian, where it is clearly defined in the genealogy of the Achaemenid kings. The modern Iranian forms like Persian *nave*always refer to "grandson"; for "nephew" Persian employs descriptive compounds, "brother's son" and "sister's son."

In contrast to Indo-Iranian, the languages of the West, except for Latin, have **nepōt* in the sense of "nephew." If in Latin, *nepos* seems to apply at will to "nephew," to "grandson" or to "descendant," in Germanic, Slavic and Celtic, the corresponding term denotes the nephew, in fact always the son of the sister. This special expression for the descendant by reference to the mother's brother emerges even in Latin in certain uses of *nepos*.

A study by Joseph Loth[3] of the sense of *nepos* in the Latin inscriptions in Brittany has shown that it always refers to the sister's son; *nepos* therefore has the same sense as in the corresponding Celtic word *nia* in Irish and *nei* in Welsh, which designate the sister's son, while the brother's son in Irish is called *mac brathar*, a descriptive term. Apart from this, there are in Celtic legends traces of a uterine kinship; in the Ogham inscriptions, filiation is established through the mother. In Latin authors, too, we can collect important testimony. Thus in Livy (V, 34) the Gaulish king Ambigatus, wanting to rid his kingdom of surplus population, asked the two sons of his sister (*sororis filios*) to lead a portion of the tribe to new territories. This is not only a feature of the Celtic societies. According to a Lacedaemonian tradition, reported by Herodotus (IV, 147), the royal power in Sparta had been assumed by Theras, the maternal uncle of the heirs who were still too young to reign and whose guardian he was.

What are we to make of the classical use of *nepos*? Certain etymologists, confronted with the double sense of *nepos*, "nephew" and "grandson," which are distinguished in other languages, have thought that it was a vague term with no well-defined meaning.

It is nothing of the kind. What we find in all languages is that when we retrace the history of their words we meet precise meanings which later usage may have extended. This is particularly the case with terms for kinship, where words must have an exact sense, because they determine each other mutually. Insofar as it designates "nephew," *nepos* often has an emotional overtone: the nephew is a spoilt child, dissipated, spendthrift. This connotation implies a certain type of relationship between the nephew and his mother's brother. In effect,

3. *Comptes rendus de l'Acad. des Inscr*, 1932. 269ff.

ethnographers have observed that in societies where the relationship between the maternal uncle and nephew prevails, it has a sentimental value, inverse to that which unites father and son. Where relations between father and son are strict and rigorous, the other is indulgent, full of tenderness. Inversely, where the father is indulgent to his son, the relationship between nephew and uncle is more rigid; he educates the child, inculcates rules of conduct and initiates him into religious rites. The two relationships of kinship are in correlation: they are never established on the same sentimental footing.

Now we know that in Latin the relationship between father and son was characterized by its severity: the father was invested with the right over life and death over his son, and he sometimes exercised this right. In ancient Roman society, the *patria potestas* was not subject to appeal. It had to be tempered by another relationship, precisely that between uncle and nephew, in the type of filiation which this supposes.

As for the duality of the sense "nephew" and "grandson," the explanation of this is given by the homologous relationship between the name of "uncle" and that of "grandfather." Just as *avus*, in the paternal line "brother of the mother's mother," produces the diminutive *avunculus* for the "brother of the mother," similarly and correlatively, the name of the grandson may designate at the same time the nephew of the mother's brother. The two changes are symmetrical; the son of the sister's daughter receives the same name as the son of the sister. However, the increasingly rigorous patrilineal tendency of Indo-European kinship often secured the predominance of the agnatic signification: "son's son."

The related Greek term *anepsiós* (from **a-nept-iyo-*) signifies "cousin" in the sense in which we understand the term. The form itself furnishes important testimony: the literal sense is "those who are co-nephews," which supposes as the point of departure for the element *-nept-* not the sense of "grandson" but that of "nephew." Thus the "nephews" of brothers and sisters called each other by this term, which is an indirect proof of the priority of the sense "nephew." However, the sense of "grandson" was not completely abolished in proto-historic times, to judge by the gloss of Hesychius which must come from literary sources: νεόπτραι· υἱῶν θυγατέρες '*neóptrai*: daughters of the sons'. This feminine could be restored as *νεπότραι (**nepótrai*), feminine of *νεποτήρ (**nepotér*), which would have designated the son of the son.

In its historic nomenclature, Greek has a new term for "grandson" which is *huiōnós* (υἱωνός), derived from *huiós* 'son', and, correlatively, for "nephew" a descriptive term *adelphidoûs* (ἀδελφιδοῦς) 'descendant of the brother'. It may seem natural that the term for "grandson" should be related to that of "son" by way of derivation, as in Gr. *huiōnós*, or by a composition, as in Engl. *grandson*, Fr. *petit-fils*. For this reason, the cases where the "grandson" is called "little grandfather" will seem more curious and noteworthy. Such is the Irish *aue* 'grandson', which goes back to **auyos*, a derivative of **auos* 'grandfather'. Similarly, OHG *enencheli* (German *Enkel*) 'grandson' is etymologically a diminutive of *ano* 'grandfather'. Old Slav. *vŭnukŭ*, Russ. *vnuk* 'grandson' has been connected with it, and this is close to Lith. *anukas*, unless the Lithuanian word is itself a loanword from Slavic. Closer to us, in Old French, the grandson was called *avelet*, a diminutive of *ave, ève* 'grandfather'. It is the term which has been replaced by the analytical expression *petit-fils*. Thus, at least in three languages, the "grandson" is called "little grandfather." There must be a reason why such an expression has been created independently in several different societies, In fact, it is an instance of a shift for which there are parallels. Numerous systems of kinship contain reciprocal terms employed between the two members of what may be called a pair: the mother's father and the daughter's son address each other by the same term. In this peculiarity of the vocabulary there is once again a classificatory reason. In many societies we find the belief that a newly born child is always the reincarnation of an ancestor, going back a certain number of generations. They even believe that, strictly speaking, there is no birth, because the ancestor has not disappeared, he has only been hidden away. In general, the process of reappearance is from grandfather to grandson. When a son is born to somebody, it is the grandfather of the child who "reappears," and this is why they have the same name. The young child is, as it were, a diminutive representation of the ancestor which it incarnates: it is a "little grandfather," who is born again after an interval of a generation.

With the word for "son" we encounter an unexpected problem. For such a close relationship Indo-European languages present a large variety of designations. The most common one is **sūnu-*, attested in Skt. *sunu-*, Avestan *hunu-*; Got. *sunus*; Lithuanian *sunus*; Slavic *synŭ*; and, with a different suffix, Gr. *huiús* (υἱύς); Tokh. A *soyä*, Tokh. B *sä*. Hittite is isolated with its *uwa* (nominative *uwas*). Also isolated is Luvian, which has *titaimi*, Lycian *tideimi* 'son' (really "nursling"). The Latin *filius* has no immediate correspondent in this sense, and Celtic *mace* (< **makkos*) is again different. The Armenian term for "son" *ustr* has been adapted to the word for "daughter" *dustr*, which corresponds to

Gr. *thugátēr* (θυγάτηρ). The form **sūnu-* seems to be derived from **su-* 'give birth'; the word thus designates the son as being the "offspring."

The discordance between the terms for "son" have been highlighted in an article by Meillet[4] who, if he did not solve the problem, has at least made it manifest.

Starting with Latin *filius*, we can try to understand the nature of the process. *Filius* is linked in Latin itself to an etymological family represented by *felo*, *fecundus*, etc., which imply the notion of "sucking" (Umbrian *feliuf*, acc. plural, '*lactentes*, sucklings'). The real significance of the word is clear: to explain how it entered into the nomenclature of kinship, we shall have to consider *filius* as an adjective which has taken on the function of a noun. Here we have the same phenomenon as appears in *consobrinus*, *patruelis*, where the adjective, at first joined to a substantive, finally supplanted it: *patruelis*, *consobrinus* represent *frater patruelis*, *frater consobrinus*. It may be conjectured that *filius* has evolved from a group which we may hypothetically posit as **sunus filius*; the true term was eliminated from the analytical expression, the more expressive term alone survived. How is this to be explained? We observe that this instability of the term for "son" contrasts with the constancy of the word for "nephew." The fate of *filius* must be correlated with that of *nepos*: the important descendant, in a certain type of kinship, is the nephew rather than the son, because it is always from uncle to nephew that inheritance or power is transmitted. The descendant is for his father simply his *offspring*, which is expressed by the term **sunus*. We know, further, that the brothers of the father are regarded as fathers; the sons of brothers are *brothers* to one another and not cousins, cf. *frater consobrinus* distinguished from *frater germanus*. Consequently, the sons of two brothers are in their eyes equally "sons"; hence a man will also call the offspring of his brother "sons." But how can the proper son be distinguished from the son of the brother? The introduction of *filius* 'nursling' fills this gap. Then, when the relation of maternal uncle to nephew ceased to be important, and when the "*Grossfamilie*" broke up, it was *filius* alone which came to designate specifically the descendant of EGO.

Through the vicissitudes of **nepot-* and **sunu-* we discern the difficulties which societies experienced, when passing from one system to the other, in normalizing the system of agnatic kinship, which had become established, and the only one recognized in law, and in adapting or replacing the inherited terms

4. *Mémoires de la Société de linguistique de Paris*, 21, 1920, p. 45.

of previous structures. Their meaning wavers between archaic relationships and the more modern ways of regarding kinship, and it is not always easy to puzzle out the manner in which these nomenclatures have been organized or transformed in each language.[5]

5. We have not touched here on two particularly complex problems: the degrees of ancestry ("grandfather," "great-grandfather" etc.), and the relations of cousinhood (Lat. *sobrinus*, *consobrinus*). We have treated this in detail in an article in *L'Homme*, vol. V, 1965, pp. 5-10.

BOOK II, CHAPTER FOUR

The Indo-European Expression for "Marriage"

Abstract. "Marriage" has no Indo-European term. In speaking of the man it is simply said—and this in expressions which have often been remodeled in particular languages—that he "leads" (home) a woman whom another man has "given" him (Lat. *uxorem ducere* and *nuptum dare*; in speaking of the woman, that she enters into the "married state," receiving a function rather than accomplishing an act (Lat. *ire in matrimonium*).

The Indo-European vocabulary of kinship, ever since it has been the object of study, has taught us that in conjugality the situation of the man and that of the woman have nothing in common, just as the terms designating their respective relationship were completely different.[1]

That is why there is, properly speaking, no Indo-European term for "marriage." As Aristotle observed for his own language, "the union of man and woman has no name," ἀνώνυμος ἡ γυναικὸς καὶ ἀνδρὸς σύζευξις (*Polit.* I, 3, 2). In fact, the expressions encountered today are all secondary creations; this is true of Fr. *mariage*, German *Ehe* (literally "law"), Russian *brak* (derived from

1. This chapter has been already published in the *Festschrift A Pedro Bosch-Gimpera*, Mexico City, 1963, pp. 49ff.

brat'sja 'carry off'), etc. In the ancient languages the facts are more specific, and it will be of interest to consider them in all their diversity.

This diversity is not merely lexical, a testimony of independent designation in each separate language; it is also morphological, and this fact, which is less obvious, has not been noticed. We have to clarify this in order that the facts may be organized: the terms differ according to whether the man or the woman is concerned, but the important difference is that for the man the terms are *verbal*, and for the woman *nominal*.

In order to say that a man "takes a wife", Indo-European employs forms of a verbal root **wedh-* 'lead', especially "lead a woman to one's home." This particular sense emerges from close correspondence between the majority of languages: Celtic (Welsh) *dy-weddio*, Slavic *vedǫ*, Lithuanian *vedù*, Av. *vādayeiti*, with the Indo-Iranian derivatives *vadhū-* 'newly married woman', Greek *hée-dna* (ἕεδνα) 'marriage gift'.

Such was the expression in the most ancient stage and when certain languages found new words to express the notion of "to lead", the new verb also assumed the value of "marry (a woman)." This is what happened in Indo-Iranian.[2] The root **wedh-* survived in a large part of Iranian in the form of the verb *vad-*. But Indic has not preserved it: it has only kept the derived noun *vadhū-* 'newly married woman'. Instead of **vadh-* which has disappeared, it employs *nay-* for "lead" and also for "marry." The same substitution of *nay-* for *vad-* is manifested in certain dialects of Iranian from Old Persian on, so that *nay-* and *vad-* were for a long period in competition on Iranian territory. In Latin, too, we find a new verb for the sense of "lead." This is *ducere*, which also takes on the sense of "marry" in *uxorem ducere*. Another verb is peculiar to Greek, *gameîn* (γαμεῖν), which has no certain correspondences.

Besides these verbs which denote the role of the husband we must place those which indicate the function of the father of the bride. The father, or in default of this his brother, has authority to "give" the young woman to her husband: πατρὸς δόντος ἓ ἀδελπιõ, as the Law of Gortyn, chapter viii, puts it. "Give" is the verb constantly used for this formal proceeding; it is found in various languages, generally with some variation in the preverb: Greek *doûnai* (δοῦναι), *ekdoûnai* (ἐκδοῦναι), Latin *dare*, Gothic *fragiban*, Slavic *otŭdati*, Lithuanian *išduoti*, Skt. *pradā-*. Avestan uses *paradātā* and *aparadātā*

2. These lexical developments have been analyzed in detail in our study *Hittite et indo-europeén* (Paris, 1962, pp. 33 ff).

to distinguish between the girl who has been properly "given" by her father and one who has not been so given. This constancy of expression illustrates the persistence of usages inherited from a common past and of the same family structure, where the husband "led" the young woman, whom her father has "given" him, to his home.

If we now search for terms employed to designate the "marriage" from the woman's point of view, we find that there exists no verb denoting in her case the fact of marrying which is the counterpart of the expressions mentioned. The only verb which can be cited is the Latin *nubere*. But apart from being confined to Latin, *nubere* properly applies only to the taking of the veil, a rite in the ceremony of marriage, not to the marriage itself, or only by implication. In fact the verb is never used outside certain special circumstances. It serves, for instance, to stress a difference in the social condition between man and woman, as in a passage of Plautus (*Aul.* 479f.), where a character proposes "that the rich marry the daughters of the poor citizens, who have no dowry," *opulentiores pauperiorum filias ut indotatas ducant uxores domum*, but he anticipates the question: "whom will the rich and dowried daughters marry?" *Quo illae nubent divites dotatae*?; the opposition between *uxorem ducere* and *nubere* is intentional. Otherwise the verb is mainly poetical. Commonly used are only the participle *nupta* and the phrase *nuptum dare* 'give (one's daughter) in marriage', that is to say, those verbal forms which make the woman the object and not the subject. Nor can we apply the Latin verb *maritare* to the function of the woman. Even at the late date at which it appears, *maritare* as active verb signifies "to match, to join", and as an intransitive verb it is more often used of the man than of the woman.

This negative lexical situation, the absence of a special verb, indicates that the woman does not "marry", she "is married." She does not accomplish an act, she changes her condition. Now this is precisely what is shown, and this time in a positive way, by the terms which denote the change of status of the married woman. These are exclusively nominal forms which appear at two extreme points of the Indo-European territory, in Indo-Iranian and Latin.

These terms are used in a phrase which formally declares that the woman enters into the "stage of wifehood." We have in Vedic two abstract nouns of very similar form, *janitva-* and *janitvaná-* 'state of the married woman (*jani-*)', both in a formulaic context: *hastagrābhásya didhiṣós távedám pátyus janitvám abhi sám babhūtha* 'you have entered into this marriage (*janitvám*) with a husband who takes you by the hand and desires you' (to the widow, Rig Veda X,

18, 8); *janitvanā́yamāmahe* 'he has offered (two young women) for marriage' (VIII, 2, 42). We see in the first passage the connection between the set terms *janitvam* on the one hand and *hastagrābhásya patyus* on the other, the husband who, with a ritual gesture, takes his young wife by the hand; in the second, that *janitvaná* indicates the destination of the woman given to her husband in the forms required "to become a wife." An equivalent to *janitvá-* is the symmetrical term *patitvá-*, *patitvaná-* 'state of husband' (X, 40, 9) when this designates the power to which the woman is submitted, thus *patitvám … jagmúṣī* '(the young woman) who has come under the power of the husband' (I, 119, 5).

It is interesting to note a parallel fact in Old Iranian, where the same notion is expressed in an abstract derivative furnished with the same suffix, Avestan *nāiriθwana-*. The stem is here *nāiri-* = Vedic *nāri-* 'woman, wife', an Indo-Iranian feminine, which makes a pair with *nar-* in the traditional formulae: Ved. *nṛ́bhyo nā́ribhyas* (I, 43, 6; VIII, 77, 8) = Avestan *nərəbyasča nāiribyasča* (Y. 54, 1). In Avestan *nāiriθwana* formed, like Vedic *janitvaná-*, has exactly the same sense "state of wifehood", and it also appears in a formulaic passage: *xvaŋha va duγδa va … nərəbyō ašavabyō nāiriθwanāi upavādayaēta* 'a sister or woman might be led into marriage to pious men (Vd. XIV, 15); this attests a legal expression where *nāiriθwanāi vādaya-* 'to lead (a young woman) into marriage' appears with a verb *vad(aya)-*, the technical value of which was seen above.

To sum up, the term which we translate by "marriage," Ved. *janitvana*, Avestan *nāiriθwana-* is only valid for the woman and signifies the accession of a young woman to the state of legal wifehood.

This justifies us in regarding it as a trait of great antiquity, bound up with the structure of the Indo-European "*Grossfamilie*," because it recurs in Roman society. The Latin term *matrimonium* is of great significance in this respect. Taken literally, *matrimonium* signifies "legal status of the *mater*," in conformity with the sense of derivatives in *-monium*, which are all legal terms (*testimonium*, *vadimonium*, *mercimonium*, and naturally, *patrimonium*). The reason for the creation of *matrimonium* is not the analogy of *patrimonium*, which conveys a quite different notion. It emerges from set expressions from which *matrimonium* gets its full sense, that is from the point of view of the father: *dare filiam in matrimonium*; from the husband's point of view, *alicuius filiam ducere in matrimonium*; and finally from the point of view of the woman: *ire in matrimonium*. Thus *matrimonium* defines the condition to which the young woman accedes; that of *mater(familias)*. This is what marriage means for her, not an act but a destination: she is "given and led," with a view to *matrimonium*, *in matrimonium*, just as the similar terms of Indo-Iranian *janitvaná-*, *nāiriθwana-* figure in our formulae in the form of a dative of intention, designating the state to which the wife is intended. From this comes later *matrimonia* in the sense of "married women," like *servitia* 'slave women'.

The modern forms of *matrimonium* in the Romance languages, particularly in Italian *matrimonio*, have acquired the general sense of "marriage." Better still, the derivative *matrimonial* functions today in French as a corresponding adjective to *mariage*, for instance in *régime matrimonial*, so that we might easily take *matrimonial* as the Latin derivative of *mariage*, like *oculaire* from *oeil*, or *paternel* from *père*. This, it must be stressed, would be pure illusion: *mariage*, a normal derivative from *marier* (Lat. *maritare*) has nothing in common with *matrimonium*. But the fact that the two are associated so closely as to seem related shows how far we have travelled from the ancient values.

We see here a type of Indo-European correspondence which is not once treated by traditional comparative grammar. The present analysis reveals the unity of terms which are etymologically diverse but are brought together by their content and constitute parallel series. The nominal forms which finally come to designate "marriage" all denoted at first the condition of the woman who became a wife. It was necessary for this specific sense to be blurred to enable the abstract concept of "marriage" to take shape, so that the end result was a designation for the legal union of man and woman.

BOOK II, CHAPTER FIVE

Kinship Resulting from Marriage

Abstract. Except for the husband and wife, for whom no specific terms seem to have existed in Indo-European, the words in this field have a constant form and precise sense—but they are not amenable to analysis. They always designate the tie of kinship through a man—the husband's mother and father, the husband's brother, the husband's sister, the brother's wife and the husband's brother's wife. There is no linguistic fact which would permit us to affirm that **swekuros*, the husband's father, ever designated in a parallel way the wife's father, that is to say, by the rule of exogamy, the maternal uncle.

In Indo-European, nomenclature of kinship resulting from marriage is opposed to that for consanguineous kinship. This is a distinction which can be verified in modern languages as well as in ancient ones. This kinship as a result of marriage is determined by the position of the wife in the bosom of the family into which she enters: all the same, the terms designating these new ties are subject to variations. At least some modern languages employ the same basic terms as for consanguineous kinship, but they are differentiated by lexical devices. Thus, in French, *beau* is used as a classifier of kinship by alliance: on the one hand we have *père*, *mère*, *frère*, *soeur*, *fille*, *fils*, and on the other *beau-père*, *belle-mère,beau-frère*, *belle-soeur*, *belle-fille*, *beau-fils*. The nouns are identical in both series. In English, too, the same terms serve in both cases, but are differentiated by the addition of *in-law*, e.g. *father-in-law*. Each of these two devices has its historical justification. In Old French *beau-* is often a courtesy term equivalent to *gentil* 'kind'; *beau-père* is thus a polite designation which assimilates the father of the spouse to the father proper. The English *father-in-law* is more "legalistic": the "father" is defined according to the "law," that is to say, canon law. If the same terms are used, it is not because of a sentimental assimilation of the two kinships, but for reason of lexical economy and symmetry: the kinship by alliance employs the same nomenclature as the natural kinship does for connections of filiation (father, mother/son, daughter) and of fraternity (brother/sister). It is a specific classificatory kinship, which serves to define the respective connections of those who find themselves allied by the marriage of their own kin.

But these are modern developments. In ancient Indo-European, on the other hand, the two types of kinship are distinct. No less than consanguineous kinship, kinship by alliance has its own terminology.

To begin with, we find the words for "husband" and for "wife," which we will consider in their Latin expressions, *marītus* and *uxor*.

Marītus is peculiar to Latin: as a matter of fact, there is no Indo-European word signifying "husband." Sometimes the expression "master" was used, e.g. Skt. *pati*, Greek *pósis* (πόσις), without any special indication of the tie of conjugality; sometimes we find "the man," Lat. *vir*, Gr. *anḗr* (ἀνήρ), whereas *marītus* designated the husband in his legal aspect.

The etymological analysis of *marītus* raises two distinct problems: that of the formation of the derivative, and that of the sense of the word.

If we consider it only as a Latin derivative, *marītus* can be interpreted without difficulty. It belongs to a class of well-established derivatives in *-ītus* parallel to those in *-ātus*, *-ūtus*, that is, to secondary formations in which the suffix *-to-* is added to a root ending in *-ī-*, *-ā-*, *-ū-*, etc.: *armātus*, *cornūtus*, *aurītus*, etc. In virtue of this formation, *marītus* should signify "provided with the possession of *marī-*."

It remains to determine the sense of the root. This has been brought into connection with a group of terms, which from an early date were applied, with some formal variations, sometimes to the young woman, sometimes to the young man: notably Gr. *meîrax* (μεῖραξ) '(young) woman', secondarily "boy," *meirákion* (μειράκιον). Soon, from language to language, one or the other sense predominates. In Latin **mari-* seems to have designated a girl of nubile age, and *marītus* thus signified "in possession of the young woman."

The Indo-Iranian correspondent *marya* designates the young man, but with a special status: especially in his amorous relationships, as a suitor, as a gallant (Indra); in brief, a boy of nubile age. This is the usual sense in Indic. In Iranian, *marya*has taken on an unfavorable meaning: it is a young man who is too audacious, a young fiery warrior, a destroyer, and even a brigand. In fact, this sense is limited to the Avestan texts. Other texts show in Iranian itself the persistence of the ancient sense. Especially clear is the Pehlevi *mērak*, which signifies "young husband"; *mērak*, with the corresponding term for the young wife *ziyānak*, are familiar, affectionate terms. The evidence suggests that in the distant past an institutional value was attached to this term, that of the class of young warriors. That this was a very old word, is shown by the fact that *maryanni*, designating the warrior class, figures among Indo-Iranian terms which we encounter in the fifteenth century BC in the Mitanni texts, where the names of important gods like Indra, Mitra, and the Nāsatya also figure.

Latin and Greek, on the contrary, specialized the term in the sense of the "young (nubile) woman." This is what made possible the creation of *marītus* in Latin, literally "provided with **marī*-," a term without known parallels.

To *marītus* corresponds *uxor* 'spouse', an ancient word of constant sense and limited to Latin. The etymology of *uxor* is far from clear: the proposal has been made to analyze it as **uk-sor*, the second component being the name for the "feminine being," which appears in **swe-sor* "sister." It would be tempting to assign a classificatory value to this term **sor*, which would be identified in the word for "spouse" as well as in that for "sister." As for the first term **uk*-, this analysis links it with the root **euk*- 'to learn, to become used to', represented by Skt. *uc*-, Slavic *ukŭ* 'teaching', and in particular by the Armenian verb *usanim* 'I learn, I accustom myself'. Now, this verb *usanim* has been linked with the Armenian term *amusin* 'husband, wife', which, with the prefix *am*- 'together' would then literally mean "the partner with whom common life takes place." The formation *amusin* would then explain the sense of **uk*- in *uxor*. It follows from this that *uxor*, analyzed as **uk-sor*, is "the habitual woman, the female being to which one is used." It must be admitted that such a designation for the wife is far from natural. Besides, no derivative from this root **euk*- indicates a relation between individuals or a social relation. What **euk*- signifies is of an intellectual order: "to acquire by repeated use," which leads on to "to learn," and to "lesson, doctrine"; thus the Gothic *bi-ūhts* 'who has the habit', Slavic *vyknǫti* 'learn', and also Armenian *usanim* 'learn'. It is, therefore, uncertain whether we can relate *amusin* 'spouse' (husband and wife) to *usanim* 'learn'; the *-us-* 'marriage tie' which seems contained in *amusin* may be of a different origin. If we have to dissociate these two forms within Armenian itself, the parallelism with *uxor* disappears.

Another etymological interpretation of *uxor* leaves it within the vocabulary of kinship by comparing it to a term which, in Baltic, refers specially to the wife: Lith. *uošvis* 'wife's father' (cf. Lith. *uošve* 'mother-in-law', a secondary feminine form), Lett. *uôsvis*. This Baltic form is a derivative in *-vyas* of the type of Skt. *bhrātr̥-vya* 'son of the father's brother' or Latin *patruus*, Gr. *patrōós* (πατρωός); the suffix in question was, therefore, used to form terms of kinship. The prototype of the Lith. *uošvis* is **ouk*(*s*)*-vya-*. It would be natural for this term to be applied to the "wife's father," if the root **ouk*(*s*)- was already at a predialectal stage a word for the wife. The Latin form **uksor* would then only comprise a suffix *-or*, the sense of "wife" already being given in the root **uks-*. This explanation also remains hypothetical in as much as there is as yet no confirmation from a third language. The Ossetic *ūs-* 'woman, wife' cannot be adduced, though this has been proposed, because the dialect form *vosae* with its initial **w-* shows that it had a different origin.

We must thus affirm the specific character of the Latin word *uxor*, the interpretation of which remains uncertain. It will already be clear that the words denoting kinship resulting from marriage have a double peculiarity in being on the one hand constant in form and precise in sense, but on the other hand, by reason of their very antiquity, difficult to analyze.

The father and mother of the husband are designated respectively by **swekuros* and **swekrūs* (feminine). The masculine **swekuros* is represented by Skt. *śváśura*, Iranian x^{v} *asura*, Arm. *skesr-ayr*, Lat. *socer*, Gr. *hekurós* (ἑκυρός), Gothic*swaihra*, Old Slavic *svekrŭ*, and, slightly altered, Lithuanian *sesuras*, Welsh *chwegrwn*; the feminine **swekrū* is represented by Skt. *śvaśrū*, Arm. *skesur*, Lat. *socrus*, Gr. *hekurá* (ἑκυρά), Got. *svaihro*, Old Slav. *swekry*. These correspondences are perfect apart from some slight alterations. In Sanskrit, one finds irregularly *śvaś-* instead of **svaś-*, due to a secondary assimilation, the initial sibilant being guaranteed by Iranian x^{v} *a-* (< **swe*). Similar is Lithuanian *šeš-* for **seš-*. The Armenian*s kesrayr* 'husband's father' is a compound (*skesr-ayr*), which designates the man (*-ayr* = Gr. *anḗr*), that is, the husband, of the mother-in-law; *skesur* 'mother-in-law' is the primary term. On the contrary, in Greek, the terms are symmetrical: the feminine has been refashioned from the masculine. In Gothic, too, there has been remodeling: the two terms *swaihra*(masc.) and *swaihro* (fem.) have been adapted to one another.

By contrast, Latin has preserved the ancient connection between masculine and feminine: *socer/socrus* < **swekuros*/**swekrūs*, like the Sanskrit *śvaśura-*/ *śvaśrū-*.

In the light of this picture, in which all the principal languages are represented, we must conclude that a masculine **swekuros* was coupled with a feminine **swekrūs*. This is a morphological oddity of which we have no other example. We know of no other opposition masculine/feminine which takes the form of an alternation *-*kuro-*/-*krū-*, with its double anomaly. There are no feminine forms in -*ū-* which could be constituted from a masculine one in -*o-*; normally we expect a feminine in -*ā-* or in -*ī-*. Moreover, the difference of gender does not involve and cannot explain the syllabic variation between *-*kuro-* and *-*krū-*.

But let us consider this feminine form by itself: **swekrūs* would be anomalous if it was formed from the masculine, but it could be admitted as an autonomous form because there is a type of feminine in *ū*. It is seen, for instance, in Vedic *vadhū-* 'newly married woman'. This raises the possibility that the primary term was the feminine **swekrū-*, the masculine **swekuros* being secondary. This hypothesis would explain the alterations which were produced in a number of languages. We postulate that **swekrū-* is the inherited form, first because it is attested by the agreement of Indo-Iranian, Latin, Slavic and Armenian, and also because it could not have been formed from the masculine, since no similar example exists elsewhere. On the contrary, a number of indications suggest that the word for "father-in-law" has suffered refashioning. This is the case, as we have seen, in Armenian, where the "father-in-law" (of the wife) is called *skesr-ayr* 'husband of the mother-in-law'. In Slavic, the masculine *svekrŭ* 'father-in-law' is a secondary form based on the feminine. The Gothic form *swaihra* 'father-in-law' also may have been constituted from an ancient **swekr-*, that is, from the feminine stem, not from **swekur-*.

But if we now believe that we can approximate better to historical truth by posing as the primary form the feminine **swekrū-* 'husband's mother', this still does not give us an explanation of the term. We are even further from it than if we had to proceed from the masculine **swekuro-*. In effect, taken on its own, **swekuros* has the appearance of a compound: the first term could be **swe-*, the same as in the word for "sister." The second term might be regarded as related to Gr. *kúrios* (κύριος), Skt. *śūra* 'master, he who has authority'. The father-in-law would thus be considered and called master of the family. The flaw in this hypothesis is that a feminine *-*krū-* is inexplicable, the only justifiable feminine form being the -*kura* of Greek, but this is secondary. This reason alone would make the analysis improbable. Doubt is increased if we must consider **swekrū-* as original. This primacy of the term for "mother-in-law" is, as a matter of fact, quite comprehensible: the husband's mother is for the young wife more important than the husband's father: the mother-in-law is the central personage of the household. But this does not explain the interconnection of the terms. The formal relations between **swekuro*-and **swekrū-* must therefore remain obscure.

The Indo-European word for the "brother-in-law" (the husband's brother) is to be reconstructed as **daiwer* on the basis of the following terms: Skt. *devar-*, Arm. *taygr*, Gr. *dāē̄r* (δαήρ), Lat. *lēvir* (with an *l-*, perhaps dialectal, for *d-*), Old Slav. *děverŭ*, Lith. *dieverìs*, Old High German *zeihhur*. The antiquity of the term is evident, but the true sense escapes us. No analysis of the form **daiwer-* is possible; we cannot see an Indo-European root to which it could be related, although it shows a formation in *-r-*, which is close to other kinship terms.

The correlative term "sister-in-law" (husband's sister) is less well represented: Gr. *galóōs* (γαλόως), Lat. *glōs*, Old Slav. *zŭlŭva*, Phrygian *gélaros* (γέλαρος)—to be read *gélawos* (γέλαwος)—glossed: ἀδελφοῦ γυνή 'brother's wife'. According to this last testimony, this would be a reciprocal term denoting both the husband's sister and the brother's wife. We must doubtless list here the Armenian word *tal* 'husband's sister', where *t-* replaces an ancient *c-* (*ts-*) under the influence of *taygr* 'husband's brother'. Here Indo-Iranian is not represented; in spite of this there is a remarkable correspondence between Greek, Latin, Phrygian, and perhaps Armenian.

The last term defines the relationship between "brother's wives": it is the name given by the wife to the wives of her husband's brothers, who live together according to patriarchal rule. This term is everywhere a survival: Skt. *yātṛ-*; a corresponding form *yāθr-* may be restored in Iranian on the basis of the Pashto *yōr*; Phrygian *ianater-* (ιανατερ-), Gk. *einatéres* (εἰνατέρες), Lat. *ianitrīces*, Old Slav. *jętry*, Lith. *intè*.

Consequently we can reconstruct **yen°ter*, **yn̥ter-*, where the formation in *-ter* is again evident. But we have no means of interpreting this root.

Everywhere we encounter firm designations with regular correspondences, but the etymological sense escapes us. Several of these terms were replaced at an early date by analytical ones, which were more transparent: "husband's brother," "wife's sister," etc. A curious situation is revealed if we compare these terms and the notions they express with those we have considered up to now.

If we take into account the fact of classificatory kinship it should theoretically follow that one and the same connection requires a double expression. If a man marries the daughter of his mother's brother, his maternal uncle becomes his father-in-law. Is this situation attested in the terminology? It does not appear to be the case; we have no proof that **swekuros* ever meant anything else than "father-in-law," that is to say "the husband's father," and probably also the wife's father in certain languages, like Sanskrit and Latin. But Greek has *pentherós* which, with a different suffix, corresponds to Skt. *bandhu-* 'relation'; Armenian has *aner* 'wife's father' and *zok* ᶜ *anč* "wife's mother," both terms without etymology; in short, Indo-European had no term for the relations of the wife. In fact we must remind ourselves that we have no Indo-European term which specifically designated the maternal uncle. As we have seen, he is called in Latin by a derivative of the word for grandfather; elsewhere the forms are different.

We can envisage two possible explanations. Either we reason with full theoretical rigor and suppose that **swekuros* in prehistoric times did designate the maternal uncle, the mother's brother, and that **swekrū-* was the father's sister, so that the historical sense was the result of a shift. This reconstruction is completely conjectural, and has no linguistic confirmation. Or else we decide that these terms never signified anything else than what they actually denote; they were always strictly applied to the relations established by the wife on her becoming a member of her new family. We should then have to assume that the patriarchal system triumphed at an early date and eliminated, in this series of terms, all trace of the double position which all allied persons occupied in the classificatory type of kinship.

Of the two hypotheses, preference should be given to the second. In any case, there are enough proofs of this patrilineal filiation in the terminology of consanguineous kinship to make it certain that the principle of interpretation itself will not be called into question by subsequent evidence.

BOOK II, CHAPTER SIX

Formation and Suffixation of the Terms for Kinship

Abstract. From the morphological point of view, the great unity of the Indo-European vocabulary of kinship emerges from the existence of the class suffix **-ter* (or **-er*), which not only characterizes a great number of the most ancient terms (**pəter*, etc.), but still continues to figure in the most recent creations or remodeled expressions.

Even when they differ from one language to another, the terms which designate social units—clan, phratry, tribe—are often formed from roots expressing a community of birth, Greek *génos*, *phrátra*, *phulḗ*, Latin *gens*, *tribus*.

Less specific than **-ter*, and also less studied, is the suffix **-w(o)-/-wyo-*which seems to have indicated homostathmic (= 'at the same level') proximity: **pəter* father"— Greek *patrō̆(u)s*, Sanskrit *pitrvya-* "father's brother." The anomalies presented, for instance, by Gr. *patruíos* "stepfather," Skt. *bhrā́tr̥vya-* "brother's son, later "cousin" > "enemy" may lead us not to question the ancient values of the suffix, but to interpret the deviation which it has undergone by reference in each case to the particular system in which these forms occur.

After this review of the terms which permit us to reconstitute the general organization of kinship, it may be useful to examine a number of questions concerning the form of these terms together with their function. There are, in fact, special features of morphology peculiar to this group which give great unity to it. Particularly notable are certain suffixes characteristic of the kinship words, whether it is because they are found only here or because they assume a special function.

Among the suffixes we cite in the first place *-ter* or *-er*, which is the suffix of kinship *par excellence*. Not only does it serve to constitute some of the most ancient terms of this series, but it kept its proper value after the parent language split into dialects and it remained productive. The initial state of this class suffix is furnished by the common ending of four fundamental designations which cannot be further analyzed: **pəter*, **māter*, **dhugh(ə)ter*, **bhrāter*; and, further, in kinship by alliance: **yen(ə)-ter* 'wife of the husband's brother'.

These are primary words, which are unanalyzable, where this ending is constant and from which it has been extracted with its proper value. Later it was extended to new designations in at least some of the languages: **nepōt-* 'nephew', or "son-in-law," has a secondary formation **nepter*, which was introduced into the declension of *napāt-* in Indo-Iranian; e.g. the Sanskrit accusative *naptāram* and the stem of the oblique cases in Avestan, *nafəδr-*, which goes back to **naptr-*.

The "son-in-law" is in Skt. *jāmātar-*, in Avestan *zāmātar-*. The corresponding form in the other languages also exhibits final *-r*, although the stem has suffered various alterations: Lat. *gener*, Gr. *gambrós*. Whatever the particular history of these forms may be, they all come from the same root, extended by a suffix in *-er* or *-ter*, and we can see that the *-r-* is secondary, from the fact that the Avestan terminology, alongside *zāmātar-* 'son-in-law', also has *zāmaoya* (= **zāmavya*), probably "brother of the son-in-law," which is today continued by Pashto *zūm* 'son-in-law'.

There are terms connected with Latin *avus*, *avunculus* which in Celtic designate the maternal uncle: Welsh *ewythr*, Breton *eontr*, go back to **awontro-*; we recognize here, in a thematic form, the same suffix *-ter*.

Let us recall finally **daiwer* 'husband's brother', Lat. *lēvir*, etc., everywhere with *-er*.

We see that the formation in *-ter* or in *-er* is from its origin attached to many terms of kinship. It remained productive of new terms in this lexical class in the subsequent history of the languages. One of the clearest examples of this extension is observed in Middle and Modern Persian, where this suffix, eliminated by the loss of endings, has been secondarily restored. After the ancient series *pitar-* 'father', *mātar-* 'mother', *brātar-* 'brother', *duxtar-* 'daughter' developed according to phonetic laws into *pit*, *māt*, *brāt*, *duxt*, the characteristic ending *-or* was restored, resulting in the present-day Persian forms: *pidar*, *mādar*, *brādar*, *duxtar*, and, by analogy, *pusar* 'son' (for *pus*). This process of morphological repair began in Middle Persian. Few suffixes have preserved such great vitality.

There is another proof of the antiquity of this formation; it is given by one of the most ancient terms characterized by the suffix, the word for "daughter," and in a language the Indo-European character of which is now assured as a member of the Luvio-Hittite group. This is Lycian, where the word for daughter is *cbatru* (accus. sing.). The phonetic detail of the reconstruction is not completely certain. However, we may suppose that the initial Lycian group *cb-* goes back to an early **dw-*; we have a parallel development in the word or compositional element signifying "two": Lycian *cbi* < **dwi*. We can thus reconstruct a proto-Lycian **dwatr*, which corresponds to Gr. *thugátēr*, with modification of the dorsal plosive between vowels: **duga-* > **duwa-*. In any case, we can identify here the same final *-er* or *-ter* as in the other languages.

Those terms of kinship which have the suffix *-ter* are further characterized by the nature and importance of certain of their derivatives.

Above, the question of the phratry has already been discussed and particularly the connection which this term shows between "consanguineous brother" and "classificatory brother." The *phratry* is a grouping which is inserted in its proper place in the series of Greek terms which mark social divisions. We have three groups, in order of increasing size, *génos* (γένος), *phrátra* (φράτρα), *phulḗ* (φυλή), these being three concentric divisions of ancient Greek society.

Roman society similarly exhibited three divisions, but they are not exactly the same: first the *gens*, then the *cūria*, and lastly the *tribus*. In this triple organization the terms of the first rank are comparable, the others diverge; but the actual organization is much the same. These are the units which we express by the series clan, phratry, tribe.

In fact, Gr. *génos* and Latin *gens* correspond without completely coinciding. There is a difference in suffixal formation: the morphologically Lat. *genus* = Gr. *génos*, but *gens* is a feminine in *-ti*. Thus between Greek and Latin the formal connection is established as **genes-/*genti-*. By its formation Latin *genu-* corresponds to Skt. *jāti-* 'birth'. The abstract noun in *-ti-* denotes the "birth" and, at the same time, the class of persons united by the tie of their "birth"; this fact serves us a sufficient definition of a certain social group. To the same lexical family belongs the Avestan term *zantu-*, which differs from it only by the suffix *-tu* and likewise designates as "birth" an important segment of Iranian society.

If we disregard these variations of suffixes, the principal ancient languages agree in making membership of a "birth" the foundation of a social group.[1]

As for the second division, the Latin term *cūria*, equivalent to Gr. *phratría*, is quite different: *cūria* has no correspondent either in Greek or elsewhere. It is, however, possible to explain the form *cūria* in Italic itself as **co-viria* "collection of *virī*" on the evidence of Volscian *covehriu*, which has the same sense. It is at the same time both a place of reunion and an important division of the Roman people. In contrast to *phratría* in Greek, the expression *cūria* does not bring out any tie of kinship between the members of this unit. By this it reveals its more recent origin, which is also confirmed by its limitation to Italic.

It is more difficult still to establish a connection between Greek *phulḗ* and Latin *tribus*. The problem is the etymological formation of *tribus*. It is to be presumed that the two terms underwent analogous processes of development. The ancients already saw in *tribus* a unit consisting of three groups. It would thus be a compound having *tri-* as its first term. In fact, in the historical Indo-European traditions, especially among the Greeks, we know of such triple groups. We have the testimony for three Dorian tribes in a Homeric epithet: Δωριέες τριχαί (*w*)ικες 'the Dorians (divided) into three *wik-*' (cf. Gr. (*w*)*oîkos* (*w*)οῖκος). In the Greek territory which was occupied by Dorians in ancient times, a district of Elis is called *Triphulía* (Τριφυλία), clearly attesting the division into "three tribes" of the first inhabitants. We would have here the rough correspondent of the Latin *tribus*, if it signifies "a third (of the territory)." It is in fact not impossible that *tribus*, like Umbrian *trifu*, its only correspondent, contains a nominal form **bhu-*, which coincides exactly with Gr. *phu-* (in *phulḗ*). However, we do not find any historical testimony which would support this primary meaning of the term. At an early date, *tribus* gave rise to important derivatives, such as *tribunus*, then *tribunal*, and the verb *tribuo*, but they give no evidence for a connection with "three."

Among the types of formation peculiar to words of kinship other than *-ter* or *-er*, we must mention a number of secondary formations in **-w-* and **-wyo-*; they merit special attention, all the more because they have been less well studied. This type is represented in Latin by *patruus* 'father's brother', 'paternal uncle', cf. Gr. *pátrōs* (πάτρως) 'father's brother', from **patrōw-*, and the symmetrical feminine *mḗtrōs* (μήτρως) 'mother's brother'. We must compare

1. The precise sense of the terms *génos*, *gens*, *zantu-* will be studied below in Book Three, Chapter Two.

with *patruus* the words of the same sense, Sanskrit *pitṛvya-*, and Avestan *tūirya* < **(p)tṛwya-*; cf. Persian *afdar* and Pashto *trə* 'father's brother', and further in Old High German *fatureo* (German *Vetter*) < **faðurwyo*, and probably Old Slavic *stryj* 'uncle'.

This type of derivation exists in Greek with a rather different sense: *patruiós* (πατρυιός) signifies "stepfather," *mētruiá* (μητρυιά) 'stepmother'; also in Armenian *yawray* 'stepfather' and *mawru* < **mātruvyā* 'stepmother'.

On the basis of the word for brother and by the same morphological device, Skt. *bhrā́tṛvya-*, Av. *brātūirya-* was constituted. But the sense of these terms has provoked much discussion. The examples are few and not decisive. Is the meaning "the brother's son" or "the son of the father's brother"? Is he the nephew or the cousin? For the sense of Skt. *bhrā́tṛvya-* we have a formal indication in Pāṇini, who gives this brief definition: *bhrātur vyac ca*, that is to say from *bhrātṛ* 'brother', the derivative indicating descent is also formed by *-vya-*. Thus, apart from the normal derivative in *-iya-* for "descending from," there is another formation in *-vya-* with the same sense: the upshot is that *bhrātrvya-* signifies "brother's son," and not "the son of the father's brother," the translation given generally by scholars. There is no doubt that Av. *brātūirya-* (variant *brātruya-*, i.e. *brātṛvya-*, fem. *brātruyā-*) should also be interpreted as "brother's son," since for "son of the father's brother," there exists a clear analytical designation, *tūirya-puθ ra* 'son of the *tūirya*', that is, of the paternal uncle. A confirmation is also given in modern Iranian by the Pashto language of Afghanistan, where *wrārə* (from **brāθr(v)ya-*) means "nephew," that is "the brother's son."

Up till now the facts do not seem open to dispute. But for Skt. *bhrā́tṛvya-*, apart from the sense of "nephew," we have also that of "rival, enemy," which is well attested. This fact has made certain etymologists hesitate, following Wackernagel, to admit that "brother's son" was the initial sense of *bhrā́tṛvya-*, in spite of the Iranian correspondent forms. In their view, *bhrā́tṛvya-* would rather have signified "cousin" (= son of the father's brother), because it is difficult to imagine the "nephew" acting as "rival," whereas among cousins rivalry is easier to understand. In Arab society, "cousin" takes on the sense of "rival," "enemy." But the truth is that this notion appears to be alien to the Indo-European world; between the *anepsioí* of the Homeric society, the relationship of cousinhood, far from occasioning rivalries, is an amicable relation. Wackernagel thinks, however, that in the case of *bhrā́tṛvya-* a prehistorical change took place from "cousin" to "nephew," a transition which would find a parallel in Spanish *sobrino*, etymologically "cousin," which today has become the word for "nephew."

All this seems to us disputable, both for the reconstruction of the ancient state and for the chronology of the senses. If we keep to the given facts, we have to admit that Indo-Iranian *bhrātr̥vya-* designates the "brother's son" and nothing else. As for the sense of "rival, enemy," we observe that it is limited to Sanskrit. Iranian for its part explains the connection between the two notions. We find in Pashto (Afghanistan) the kinship term *tərbur* 'cousin', to be analyzed as *tər* 'paternal uncle' and **pūr* 'son', going back to **ptərvya-putra-* 'son of the father's brother'. Now this word does not only designate the "cousin" but also the "rival," "the enemy." Hence the sense of "enemy" is attached to an analytical expression "son of the paternal uncle," while the "nephew" is called *wrārə* (< **brāθr(v)ya-*) a term which does not imply rivalry, any more than the old Avestan *brāturya-* does. This is clear confirmation of the testimony of Pāṇini on the sense of Sanskrit *bhrā́tr̥vya-* as "brother's son, nephew," not "cousin." The initial relationship between *pitr̥vyà-* and *bhrā́tr̥vya-* in Sanskrit was as follows: *pitr̥vyà-* signified "father's brother" and *bhrā́tr̥vya-* 'brother's son'. This is also the situation in Iranian of the correspondent terms. The forms and their senses must therefore be attributed to Indo-Iranian. It is from this finding that we must start to reconstruct, as far as possible, the connection of these terms in the Indo-European period. This formation is certainly of Indo-European date; in fact, outside Indo-Iranian there are ancient representatives, as we have seen, in Greek, Latin and Germanic. We are here confronted with a lexical category which may be presumed to be homogeneous, but with local aberrations.

To give an explanation of it we must introduce here two theoretical considerations, one bearing on the terminology of kinship, the other on the morphology of the terms.

We believe it is necessary, in particular, in defining the changes which have come about in the course of history in the application of the words to the degree of relationship, to distinguish the relationship between members of the same generation, which we will call *homostathmic* (= at the same level), and the relationship between members of different generations, which we will call *heterostathmic* (= of different levels).[2] The relationship of fraternity is homostathmic, the relationship of ancestrality is heterostathmic.

2. These terms have been proposed and employed in an article in *L'Homme*, V, 1965, p. 15.

In the formation of the terms for kinship themselves we must pay attention to the nature of the suffix when this seems to have, as in the present case, a distinctive value. The Indo-European morpheme **-wo*, **-wyo-*, which forms the secondary derivatives in question, should indicate some kind of connection with the basic term. We can give precision to the nature of this connection by considering the function of this suffix in a class of primary nominal derivatives; these are the adjectives indicating spatial position, like Ved. *pū́rva-*, Ir. *parva-* 'previous, first'; Gr. *deksi-wós*, Got. *taihswa* 'right(side)'; Gr. *lai(w)ós*, Lat. *laevus*, Old Slav. *levŭ* 'left(side)'; Ved. *viśva-* 'all', *sarva-* 'entire, intact', Lat. *salvus* 'id.'; Ved. *ṛṣvá-* 'elevated, high', Av. *ərəšva-* 'id.', etc. By analogy, we conjecture that the derivative in *-w-* from a term of kinship will have indicated a situation of proximity to the person indicated by the basic term, a particularly close relationship which in some way is homogeneous with the basic term.

This class of derivatives for kinship in **-w-* is represented in Indic by *pitṛvya-* and *bhrā́tṛvya-*. But if they occupy almost the same lexical position in Indic, these two terms differ greatly in their Indo-European distribution: the first is widely attested over an extensive area, the second is limited to Indo-Iranian. There are reasons for thinking that the first term is the original one and that the other has been adapted to it by secondary assimilation, and only in a part of the territory.

Other indications confirm this relative chronology. The forms which in western Indo-European correspond to Skt. *pitṛvya-* show, so to speak, the foundation of the function and even of the form of the suffix. This is seen especially in ancient Greek, where several derivatives are thus made with *-w-*. There is, first, *pátrōs* (attested first in Herodotus and Pindar) "father's brother" and *mḗtros* (Homer, Herodotus, Pindar) "mother's brother," both derived by means of **-ōu-* from *patḗr* and *mḗtēr*. This formation thus indicates in general the nearest relations of the same generation (hence excluding filiation). We have here a homostathmic relation to the basic term. Consequently, "father's (or mother's) brother" is the degree of kinship to which this suffixal function is appropriate, and it is sometimes, particularly in the plural, found extended to the whole group of the nearest relations of the father or the mother. This suffix, in the thematic form **-wo-*, is that which recurs in a similar function in the Latin *patruus* 'father's brother'. Latin has no correspondent of Greek *mḗtrōs* 'mother's brother', any more than any other language has. For this relationship Latin says *avunculus*, Sanskrit *mātula-*. The variety of these designations shows that they are of different date. Whereas Lat. *avunculus* is connected with *avus* by an ancient relationship which is repeated in other languages (see above, Book Two, Chapter Three), the Greek and Indic expressions are secondary: Greek *mḗtrōs* is evidently coined after *pátrōs* and Skt. *mātula-* (for **mātura-*) is a purely Indic formation. They are recent substitutes for an Indo-European designation which disappeared when the mother's brother ceased to have a privileged position with respect to the father.

Another reason may also have contributed to its elimination. We get some idea of it in a very complex process of competition between two suffixal formations of ancient Greek which considerably modify our ideas of Indo-European. Apart from *pátrōs* 'father's brother', which corresponds exactly to the sense, but not exactly to the form of Skt. *pitr̥vyà-*, Greek has the term *patruiós*, which corresponds to the form of *pitr̥vyà-*, but does not have the same meaning: *patruiós* designates the "stepfather." Now, while *pitr̥vyà-* 'father's brother' has no Sanskrit homologue in the feminine (**mātr̥vyā* does not exist and doubtless could not have existed), Greek *patruiós* 'stepfather' was accompanied by the feminine *mētruiá* 'stepmother, second wife of the father'. In fact, in the lexical history of Greek, the primary term is *mētruiá* (attested from Homer on and in all the dialects), which is strongly characterized by its affective connotation and its metaphorical usage (the stepmother, bad mother) as compared with the *patruiós*, which is both late and rare and purely descriptive, and obviously an analogical formation based on *mētruiá*. We must conclude that the formal concordance between Skt. *pitr̥vyà-* and Gr. *patruiós* is deceptive: it is due to a simple convergence of forms created independently and at different dates. The only terms to be taken into consideration are in Indic the masculine *pitr̥vyà-* 'father's brother', and in Greek the feminine *mētruiá* 'stepmother'. The formation in *-*w*(*i*)*yo*- has been utilized in comparable, but not identical, ways in Indic and Greek: in Indic *pitr̥vyà-* denotes the nearest relation to the father, in fact his brother; in Greek, where *pátrōs* has the same sense, use was made of the suffix to form from *mḗtēr* a derivative *mētruiá*, which designates the "mother by substitution," the "stepmother."

Owing to the lack of ancient data, we know less about the fate of this formation in *-*w*(*o*)- or *-*wyo*- in other languages. It is highly probable that Old Slavic *stryjĭ* 'father's brother' (a Panslavic term, with the exception of Russian) continues, with a phonetic treatment that is somewhat obscure in detail, the same original as Skt. *pitr̥vyà-*. This type is represented in Germanic by Old High German *fetiro* 'father's brother', which is distinguished from *ōheim* 'mother's brother', just as Lat. *patruus* is from *avunculus*. In the history of

High German, *fetiro* has passed from meaning "father's brother" to "son of the father's brother," hence modern German *Vetter* 'cousin'. But this is an exceptional evolution. Everywhere else, this term, or its feminine equivalent, has kept its homostathmic value.

Let us consider now the second term of kinship exhibiting the same suffix, that is Skt. *bhrā́tr̥vya-*, Av. *brātūirya-* (cf. above). It is, as we have seen, limited to Indo-Iranian. This alone is a reason for thinking that it is less ancient than *pitr̥vyà-*. Besides this we may note that the two expressions are not homologous: *bhrā́tr̥vya-* 'brother's son' indicates a heterostathmic relationship, different from *pitr̥vyà-* 'father's brother', which is homostathmic. Thus there is morphological conformity but disparity of sense; these two features must be kept in mind; they must be explained together. We shall find the reason for it in the general structure of this terminology.

If Indo-Iranian *bhrātr̥vya-* is not applied to the same level of kinship as *pitr̥vya-*, this is because the position of the basic term required it. Given the value of the suffix, if the derivative *pitr̥vyà-* from *pitr̥-* 'father' was applied to "the father's brother," then *bhrā́tr̥vya-*, with the same formation, strictly speaking ought to designate only "the brother's brother," which is nonsense, at least in Indo-European, where all brothers have the same relationship to each other. It was, therefore, applied to another degree of proximity, "son of the brother" which, by a shift of one generation, answers a double purpose: in the first place it served to differentiate the "brother's son" from the "sister's son," who had a different designation (**nepōt-*, Indo-Iranian *napāt-*); in the second place it specified the notion more clearly than another derivative, *bhrātrīya-*, which also meant "brother's son" according to Pāṇini and which, being duplicated, was eliminated. But when *napāt-* was applied indiscriminately to the son of the brother or the son of the sister, Skt. *bhrā́tr̥vya-*, now becoming available, was reinterpreted either as "son of the *father's* brother," or as "quasi-brother," which practically comes to the same thing and designated the "cousin." The connection with EGO again became homostathmic; then, in the social conditions which seem to have been peculiar only to India, the kinship of cousins was associated with the behavior of rivals. This was the origin of the double meaning of *bhrā́tr̥vya-* in classical Sanskrit as "cousin" and "rival."

This whole evolution took place only on Indian territory. No trace is to be found in Iranian, where *brātr̥vya-* (Av. *brātūirya-*, etc.) seems never to have deviated from the initial sense of "brother's son." But this conflict between the terms for "nephew" and "cousin" was renewed in the modern phase of the

Romance languages, in Ibero-Romance, where the representatives of Latin *nepos*, *sobrinus*, *consobrinus* ended up by forming a new system.[3]

Thus, in every case, it is not one single term which must be considered in isolation, but rather the whole group of relationships: it is by this that the history of each of the terms is conditioned. Apart from the general structure of Indo-European kinship, we must recognize in each language at a given period a particular structure which must be interpreted in its own right. It is by starting from *bhrā́tṛvya-* with the sense of "brother's son," given in the Indian tradition, that we are able to reconstruct the conditions for the passage to the sense "cousin" and later "rival," which was effected in classical Sanskrit. More than with any other lexical group the terms of kinship oblige us to keep to, and to combine, the two aspects of one and the same methodological requirement, the structural study of the terminology as a whole and the consideration of the levels in each language and each society.

3. See the article already cited (Book Two, Chapter Three, n. 5) in *L'Homme*.

BOOK II, CHAPTER SEVEN

Words Derived from the Terms for Kinship

Abstract. Greek here offers a group of new designations—*huiōnós* 'grandson', *páppos* 'grandfather', *adelphidoûs* 'nephew'—which, with *adelphós* supplanting *phrátēr*, are evidence for the passage from a system of classificatory kinship to a descriptive one.

Latin has three adjectives derived from *pater*. Only one is Indo-European: this is *patrius*, which, in fact, goes back to **pəter* in its most ancient "classificatory" sense (*patria potestas*); we know that there was not, and could not have been, a corresponding **matrius*. On the other hand, *paternus* corresponds to *maternus*, and both terms are on the same personal level: *amicus paternus* is the "friend of *my* father." As for *patricius*, it exhibits the characteristic Latin suffix of derivatives denoting official functions (cf. *tribunicius*, etc.) and is thus attached not to *pater*, but to *patres* 'the Senate'. In Greek, the opposition of *pátrios* on the one hand and *patrṓïos* (Homer, Herodotus) / *patrikós* (Attic) on the other, corresponds exactly to the Latin opposition *patrius* : *paternus*—and betrays the same evolution of the notion of "father." (The form *mētrṓïos*, derived from *mḗtrōs* 'maternal uncle' and not directly from *mḗtēr*, preserves the memory of the ancient role of the mother's brother).

A complete history of Indo-European kinship must consider not only the attested terms, but also the less direct pointers, which are sometimes just as instructive, like those provided by the derivatives of certain words for kinship.

In the list given above (Book Two, Chapter Three) of the words for "grandson," we have pointed out, without going into detail, that Greek has, in opposition to **nepōt*, a new derivative *huiōnós* (υἱωνός), which does not correspond to any of the terms employed elsewhere. A derivative of *huiós* 'son', the term *huiōnós* is used by Homer and does not show any variations of sense. A derivative like this poses an *a priori* question. This secondary formation in *-ōno-* (-ωνο-) occurs in few examples and these are obscure words. It is difficult to see why this suffix, which seems quite unmotivated here, was used to form a derivative from *huiós*.

There are, however, two or three terms, the formation of which may enlighten us to some extent: principally *oiōnós* (οἰωνός) and *korṓnē* (κορώνη), two names of birds. *Oiōnós*, probably related to Latin *avis*, is the name of a bird of prey, the great bird whose flight was regarded as an omen. *Korṓnē* 'crow', compared to Latin *corvus* 'raven', shows the same formation. We may here add *khelṓnē* (χελώνη) 'tortoise', a doublet of *khélus* (χέλυς).

From these two, or perhaps three, examples we may conclude that the suffix *–ōnos* produced a doublet with an augmentative force from the basic noun. At first sight, one would, on the contrary, attribute rather a diminutive value to *huiōnós*. But the apparent contrast is due to the fact that the French generalize, quite unjustifiably, the notion familiar to us of *petit-fils* ('grandson'). There would be just as good a reason to say *grand-fils*. The designation by means of the qualifications *grand* and *petit* is traditional in French, but arbitrary. The English equivalent of *petit-fils* in French is "*grand*son," like "*grand*father," both being one degree further removed from EGO than his son and father. We should probably give a similar interpretation to *huiōnós*. In this way we could reconcile the sense of *huiōnós* with other words of the same formation. Besides, there is a separate term for "grandson" which is used in Attic, while *huiōnós* is rather Ionic. This is *huidoûs* (υἱδοῦς) (Plato, Xenophon), "son's son," coined after the model of *adelphidoûs* (ἀδελφιδοῦς) 'brother's son'.

Here we have an important fact: a new term for "grandson" in Greek. It is conditioned by the transformation of the general structure which took place in Greek.

If we consider the Greek system as a whole, one of the most notable changes is the appearance of a new term to designate "brother": *phrátēr*, which had a classificatory value, was replaced by *adelphós* (see above, Book Two, Chapter

One). At the same time, the Indo-European term **awos* 'grandfather' was eliminated: this archaic term was furthermore connected, via a derived form, with the word for "maternal uncle." Neither has left any trace in Greek. Correlatively, the word for "grandson" disappeared. Just as **awos* had a double value and represented two relationships which are differently situated according to the patrilineal or matrilineal point of view, so the term **nepōt*, which was its counterpart, oscillated between the sense of "nephew" (sister's son) and that of "grandson" (son's son).

The Greek system marks the transition from one type of designation to the other: all the terms of kinship tend to be fixed with a single signification and are exclusively *descriptive*. This is why the word for "brother" was replaced by a term meaning "co-uterine." This explains the variety of the terms for "grandfather": we have either an analytical phrase, like "the father of my father" (*Il.* 14, 118), "the father of the mother" (*Odyssey* 24, 334), or descriptive compounds like *mētropátōr* (μητροπάτωρ), *patropátōr* (πατροπάτωρ) (Homer, Pindar), or simply *páppos* (πάππος), a term of familiar and affectionate address for the grandfather without distinction of paternal or maternal descent. In the same way, the word for "nephew," *adelphidoûs*, and for "niece," *adelphidḗ*, was based on the term for "brother." But in this new terminology, "nephew" and "grandson" constitute two distinct relationships; and just as the term for "nephew" was refashioned into "son of the brother," *adelphidoûs*, similarly that for the "grandson" became "son of the son," *huidoûs*. It was the elimination of the ancient term for "grandfather" and "grandson" on the one hand and of "brother" and "sister" on the other which brought about the innovations in Greek terminology.

We thus see that despite the archaic nature of the terms for the wife's relations, the Greek vocabulary presents a recent system. Recourse to descriptive terms became necessary from the moment when classificatory kinship was abandoned.

By contrast, the Latin vocabulary reveals its great antiquity; in Roman society kinship is dominated by the preponderance of the father, which gives it its "patriarchal" character. The vocabulary has remained very stable; the form itself of the Latin terms also offers evidence of a more ancient state of affairs than that of Greek. This conservative character of Latin is also marked by the morphology as well as the vocabulary. Certainly, here as in other fields, Latin has constructed a new system with the use of archaic elements. But if we take the Latin system to pieces, we find without difficulty the elements of a much older system, which they help to reconstruct.

If we now examine the derivatives from the word for "father," we find one which exists in several languages in the same form and which therefore can be attributed to the common period of Indo-European: this is the adjective *patrius*, Skt. *pitrya-*. Gr.*pátrios* (πάτριος).

We have already pointed out that there is a corresponding adjective derived from the word for "mother." This difference is explained by the respective position of the father and mother. An adjective indicating what belongs to the father, what pertains to him, is justified by the fact that in society, the "father" alone can possess anything. The ancient laws of India say so explicitly: the mother, the spouse, the slave possess nothing. All that they hold belongs to the master, to whom they themselves belong. Such is the constant situation of the man and the woman respectively; in the light of this we can understand why **matrius* is missing everywhere.

However, there is in Latin a specific adjective derived from the word for "mother": *maternus*. The form *maternus* is instructive in itself. Attested from the most ancient texts on, and deriving phonetically from **māterinus*, it is characterized by a suffix in *-ino-*, which has a precise usage in Indo-European and Latin; it indicates the material, Gr. *phḗginos* 'of the beech', derived from *phēgós*; *láïnos* 'of stone', from *lâas*; *anthinós*, 'of the flower', from *ánthos*; Lithuanian *auksinas* 'of gold', from *auksas*'gold'; in Latin, *eburnus* 'of ivory', from *ebur*, etc.

From the beginning, *maternus* made a pair with *patrius*, which resulted in uses like: *non patrio sed materno nomine* ('not in the father's but in the mother's name'). The disparity of the formation prompted an analogical creation, and at an early date a new adjective *paternus* was made on the model of *maternus*. In the course of history, *paternus* coexisted at first with *patrius*; later, it gained territory and ended up by supplanting it: it alone survived in the Romance languages.[1]

We may ask whether analogy was the sole reason for the triumph of *paternus* for, as Wackernagel observes, *paternus* was exclusively employed from the beginning in certain combinations: in particular, as an epithet of certain words,

1. This history, with some judicious remarks on the derivation of kinship terms, has been the subject of an article by Wackernagel in the *Festgabe Kaegi*, 1916, pp. 40ff., reproduced in his *Kleine Schriften*, I, 468ff.

such as *amicus*, *hospes*, *servus*; *patrius* is never found in these cases. The reason for this usage is difficult to see, adds Wackernagel without any further explanation. We now observe that by a parallel process, to which we shall come back, Greek employs a new derivative, *patrikós* (πατρικός) which is also used exclusively with terms like "friend," "companion," etc. These combinations must have been the determining cause; we must only discover how and why.

From the moment when the inherited *patrius* and the analogical form *paternus* were used simultaneously, they tended to be distinguished to a certain extent. *Patrius* was employed exclusively in set expressions such as *patria potestas*; *paternus* is never found in these cases. But we have exclusively *paternus amicus*. The *patria potestas* is the power attaching to the father in general, which he possesses in his role as father. But the relationship is of a quite different nature in *amicus paternus*, where it means "*my* father's friend." In fact, *paternus* used with *hospes*, *amicus*, *servus* indicates a personal connection from man to man and refers to the father of a given individual. This difference between *patrius* and *paternus* may thus be defined as that between a generic adjective and a specific adjective. For instance, in Livy: *odisse plebem plusquam paterno odio* (II, 58, 5) 'he hated the plebs more than *his own* father did'.

We see here the reason for the creation of *paternus*. If *paternus* was modeled on *maternus*, it is because Indo-European **patrios* refers not to the physical father, but to the father in the classificatory kinship, to the **pəter* invoked as *dyauṣpitā* or *Iupiter*. *Maternus*, on the other hand, indicates a relationship of a physical kind: it means literally, according to its suffix, "of the same material as the mother." If *patrius* was given a doublet *paternus* on the model of *maternus*, this was to specify a relationship to the physical father, the personal ancestor of the speaker or the person spoken about.

We even have in Latin, apart from *patrius* and *paternus*, a third adjective derived from the word for father: *patricius* 'patrician', that is, a man descended from noble and free fathers. The formation in *-icius*, peculiar to Latin, forms adjectives taken from words for official functions: *aedilicius*, *tribunicius*, *praetoricius*.

Thus each adjective refers to a different notion: *patrius* is classificatory and conceptual, *paternus* is descriptive and personal, and *patricius* refers to the social hierarchy.

In Greek the adjectives "maternal" and "paternal" have a curious formation: *mētrōîos* (μητρῷος) and *patrōîos* (πατρῷος). Over and above its use as an independent word, we find *patrōîos* in the compound *patroûkhos* (πατροῦχος) from *patrōio-okhos* (παρτωιο-οχος); it designates the "heiress" who, in her legal status, is called *epíklēros* (ἐπίκληρος). If the daughter happens to be the sole descendant, since according to Greek law she cannot inherit, her status is described by a number of juridical terms, which are enumerated in the Law of Gortyn, to secure that the inheritance remains in the family: *patroûkhos* literally signifies "who possesses the paternal fortune."

In the article by Wackernagel already mentioned, he makes the observation that *mētrōîos* 'maternal' is not derived from *mḗtēr* 'mother', but from *mḗtrōs* 'mother's brother'. On the model of *mḗtrōs*, which produced the adjective *mētrōîos*, *patrōîos* was coined from *pátrōs*, 'father's brother'. Wackernagel did not elaborate any further on his remark. It is, however, strange that the adjective "maternal" in Greek should literally signify not "of the mother" but "of the mother's relation"; this was not the most natural expression of this notion, and it would be wise to check the use of the word. Homer only has *mētrṓïos* once (the reason being that the Homeric poems are more interested in the father than the mother), but the example is instructive. Autolycus addresses his daughter and son-in-law and says of their new-born child, who has just been named Odysseus: ὁππότ' ἂν ἡβήσας μητρώϊον ἐς μέγα δῶμα ἔλθῃ (*Od.* 19, 410) 'when he is grown up and comes into the great house of his mother'. From Autolycus' point of view the "house of the mother" is necessarily the house of her mother's brother and father, that of her original family. Such a use of *mētrṓïos* explains the reference to *mḗtrōs* as "relative on the mother's side," when the adjective is connected with what belongs to the mother, which in fact is what belongs to her own relations.

We must now see how *patrṓïos*, which is abundantly represented in Homer, is used alongside *pátrios*, which is not Homeric, but nevertheless ancient. The Homeric use of *patrṓïos* well illustrates its specific value. We find it in expressions such as:*skḗptron patrṓïon* (*Il.* 2, 46, etc.), *témenos patrṓïon* (*Il.* 20, 391), qualifying a scepter, an estate; with *mē̂la*, the flocks of sheep (*Od.* 12, 136); finally and frequently, with "guests" *xeînoi patrṓïoi* (*Il.* 6, 231 etc.) and "companions," *hetaîroi patrṓïoi* (*Od.* 2, 254, etc.). That is to say, on the one hand, with words for objects which are possessions (*skḗptron*, *témenos*, *mē̂la*), on the other with words indicating social relations. Particularly instructive is *patrṓïon ménos* (*Il.* 5, 125), which in its context signifies "the warrior ardor *of your father*." In Herodotus *pátrios* and *patrṓïos* coexist: *pátrioi theoi* (I, 172), *nómoi* (II, 79, cf. Thucydides IV, 118), *thesmoí* (III, 31), but *patrṓïa khrḗmata* (I, 92), *patrṓïoi doûloi* (II, 1), etc. We see that the difference exactly parallels that which exists in Latin between *patrius* and *paternus*. The qualification *pátrios* signifies "from the fathers, ancestral," and is applied to the ancestral gods, to the laws which were accepted for all times by the ancestors. But *patrṓïos* is what belongs to the personal father: wealth, slaves. By an inevitable extension, but this only occasionally, *patrṓïos* is sometimes also applied to a person of an earlier generation than the father: but it is always a personal ancestor, as in Herodotus' *patrṓïos táphos* (II, 136; IV, 127) 'family tomb'.

The third adjective, *patrikós* (πατρικός) is an Attic creation which historically replaced *patrṓïos*, an Ionic and poetical term. In fact, *phílos patrikós* (exactly like *amicus paternus*), *xénos patrikós*, *hetaîros patrikós* signify "friend (companion, guest) of*my* father."

To sum up, the adjectival couples Lat. *paternus/maternus*, Gr. *patrṓïos/ mētrṓïos* have a complex history; the two terms were not symmetrical and could not be. In Latin, the older one, *maternus*, implies physical, material relationship to the mother; the masculine *paternus* was created to differentiate the legal *pater* from the personal *pater*. In Greek, *mētrṓïos* 'maternal' was coined from *mḗtrōs* 'the mother's brother', because what belongs to the mother is not a possession, but a relationship; on the mother's side, the maternal uncle is the most important relative. It is interesting to establish thus a close connection between a derivational relationship and a characteristic form of kinship.

It seems, therefore, that *patrius* refers only to kinship of a classificatory type. When the notion of personal kinship came to prevail, it was necessary to characterize it by new adjectives, but these have been produced independently in each separate language and so there is not exact correspondence. Parallel with this, the formation of the adjective *mētrṓïos* reveals indirectly the importance of the maternal uncle. The detailed study of the history of these derivatives thus confirms some of the conclusions dictated by the terms themselves.

These terms are very instructive both because of their interrelations and their etymological meaning. The vocabulary of Indo-European kinship testifies to several successive stages and reflects to a great extent the change which Indo-European society underwent.

This society was certainly, as has always been stated, of a patriarchal type. But here, like in so many other parts of the world, different pointers reveal a superposition of systems, especially the survival of a type of kinship in which the maternal uncle was predominant.

The historical facts indicate a compromise between these two types of kinship: the patrilineal system indubitably predominated at an early date. But there remain clear traces of the role which devolved on the maternal uncle. The relationship of the sister's son to the mother's brother coexists in several societies with patrilineal line of descent.

On the level of terminology pure and simple, we must distinguish two series of terms: the one classificatory and the other descriptive.

Where the common Indo-European state of affairs has been preserved, it is characterized by terms of classificatory kinship, which tend to be eliminated in favor of descriptive terms. Depending on the society concerned, this transformation was more or less rapid and complete. The vocabulary offers us proof of this, particularly in Greek. The Greek situation is complex because, on the one hand, it has preserved archaic terms such as *dāḗr* 'brother of the husband' or *gálōs* 'sister of the husband'; on the other hand, it manifests the passage from one type of designation to another by the coexistence of the two different words for "brother," *phrátēr* and *adelphós*. In one and the same terminology, the Indo-European heritage and Greek innovations overlap, thus testifying to a transformation which culminated in terms of a descriptive type.

However, we must guard against trying to establish too-precise correlations between the changes which happened in the society and those which appear in the terminology, or, conversely, between the stability of the vocabulary and that of the society. It is not possible to conclude directly, nor in all cases, that a new term implies an innovation in an institution, or that preservation of the terminology indicates constancy in kinship relations. Three considerations must be borne in mind: (1) The word for kinship may continue to exist even when the etymological sense which determined its original structural place, has been lost: thus *avunculus*, now separated from *avus*, continues in Fr. *oncle*, Engl. *uncle*; (2) the ancient word may be replaced by a more transparent term without a change in the position of what it designates: Old French *avelet* has been replaced by *petit-fils* 'grandson', or, in our own days, *bru* has ceded its place to *belle-fille* 'daughter-in-law'; (3) the change may be due to some local cause which often eludes us; this is the case with a number of kinship terms in Armenian, which have no known correspondents. They are attributed to a "substrate language" which was spoken by the ancient peoples who later adopted an Indo-European language. The hypothesis is plausible in itself although up to the present it is incapable of proof. In the past history of languages this factor was probably responsible for many alterations and innovations. This is not surprising.

What is surprising is that, despite so many vicissitudes and after the passage of so many centuries of independent life, the Indo-European languages have preserved a vocabulary of kinship which, by itself alone, would suffice to demonstrate their genetic unity and which has retained to our own days the mark of its origins.

BOOK III

Social Status

BOOK III, CHAPTER ONE

Tripartition of Functions

Abstract. By parallel series of terms, often of revealing etymology, but which differ from language to language, Iranian, Indic, Greek and Italic testify to a common Indo-European heritage: that of an hierarchical society, structured according to three fundamental functions, those of priests, warriors and tillers of the soil.

According to Indo-Iranian traditions society is organized into three classes of activity, priests, warriors and farmers. In Vedic India these classes were called "colors," *varṇa*. In Iran, they have as their name *pištra* 'craft', the etymological sense of which is also "color." We must understand the word in its literal sense: they are indeed colors. It was by the color of their clothes that in Iran the three classes were distinguished—white for priests, red for warriors and blue for farmers, according to a profound symbolism, which is taken from ancient classifications known in many cosmologies and which associates the exercise of a fundamental activity with a certain color that is itself connected with a cardinal point.

The same classes and the members of these classes are not called by the same terms in India and Iran. Here are the respective words:

India	**Iran**
(1) *brahmán* (*brāhmaṇa-*)	(1') *āθravan*
(2) *kṣatriya* (*rājanya*)	(2') *raθaēštā*

(3) *vaiśya*	(3') *vāstrō fšuyant*
(4 *śūdrá*)	(4' *hūiti*)

These words do not correspond; however, the organization is the same and also the mode of classification rests on the same distinctions. It is in their true meanings, as in their relations within the social system, that we must examine the terms.

Here, briefly, are the lexical meanings of the two series:

India

brahmán: priest, man in charge of what is sacred in religion;
kṣatriya: who has martial power (the power of the *rāj*);
vaiśya: man of the *viś,* the clan, equivalent to "man of the people."

Iran

āθravan: priest (unclear etymology);
raθaēštā: warrior; literally: one who stands in the chariot, as a chariot fighter;
vāstryō fšuyant: provisional translation: "he of the pastures" and "he who occupies himself with live-stock."

We see that both in India and Iran these terms, although distinct, are organized in the same way and refer to the same activities. This social structure was maintained longer in Iran than in India.

This terminology is basic to the problem which dominates the whole organization of Indo-European society. The two groups of terms are different in their lexical character, but they agree in their social reference. The tripartite division of society to which they testify is the oldest to which we can attain. Its survivals in historical times have not always been recognized, especially in Indian society. It was the merit of Emile Senart to show that the Indian castes should not be explained by internal rules but are in fact the continuations of much older divisions which India has inherited and which did not originate on Indian soil. The Indian castes are the much fossilized systematization of divisions which go back certainly to the Indo-Iranian period, if not to Indo-European society itself. The problem is to examine the words which define in India and Iran this division into castes, and then to see if, in other societies of the Indo-European family, we can recognize a similar system.

If we review the various terms, we find that for the most part they can be interpreted directly and have a signification which is still accessible to us. We can show this by taking them in succession.

The Iranian term for "priest," Avestan *āθravan*, has its Vedic correspondent in *atharvan* which, to tell the truth, is not quite what one would expect, but the two words can be superimposed without great difficulty, the difference between *-θr-* in Iranian and *-thar-* in Indic not constituting any serious obstacle to the comparison. The derivatives are symmetrical in both Indic and Iranian: Av. *aθauruna-*, which denotes the function of a priest, and Vedic *ātharvaṇá* 'relating to the *atharvan*'; the detail of the structures is evidence for the concordance of the original meanings. Only the etymological analysis of the word remains uncertain.

It has long been thought that *āθravan-* and *atharvan-* can be explained by the word for "fire," which is *ātar* in Iranian. Although the connection is plausible from a formal point of view, we run into great difficulties with the meaning itself: it is by no means certain that *āθravan* is the fire-priest. In Mazdaean Iran he is responsible for religious ceremonies; in India, the *atharvan* is endowed with magical powers. This conception finds expression in the collection of magical hymns called precisely the *Atharva-Veda*. The function of this personage is divided thus: in Iran the exclusively religious side is shown, in India we see the magical aspect. But there is nothing we can see in this role which particularly relates to "fire." There never existed in Iranian any etymological relationship between *ātar* and *āθravan*; and, the second difficulty, this word for fire, Av. *ātar-*, is quite unknown in India, where fire as a material concept and as a mythological figure is called *agni-*, a term corresponding to Latin *ignis* and to Old Slav. *ognjĭ*. We cannot therefore regard the connection between *ātar-* and the word for "priest" *āθravan* as anything like certain.

Isolated as it seems to be, this term may nevertheless go back far into history. That it is confined to Indo-Iranian does not prove that it is of recent creation. In any case, to regard it as Indo-Iranian is perhaps to simplify the problem, because even within Indo-Iranian, as we have seen, the forms do not exactly coincide. Their relationship is perhaps not that of common forms which have been inherited in parallel ways by both members. A morphological detail suggests a different and more precise relationship. As against Vedic *átharvan-*, Avestan presents a root with inflectional variation, *āθravan-* in the strong cases (nominative and accusative), *athaurun-* (i.e. *aθarun-*) in the weak cases (genitive, etc.). If we posit for Iranian a primitive flexion *āθarvan-* (altered into *āθravan-* under the influence of *ātar-*), genitive *aθarunō*, etc., we get a regular structure, whereas the Vedic declension *átharvan-*, *átharvanaḥ* is not, and seems to have been recast. It would then be possible to regard the Vedic form *átharvan-* rather as a borrowing from Iranian *āθarvan-* than an authentic Indic correspondent. This would explain better the relative rarity of *átharvan-* in the Rig-Veda as compared with *brahman-*, and also its specialization in the world of charms and deprecatory rites, while the term in Iranian keeps its ancient value as a term for a social class.

To designate the functions and the class of priests in India, the hallowed term is *brahmán*. It raises a problem which is still more difficult. The exact signification and origin of the word has provoked long debates which are not yet at an end.

There are in fact two forms, differentiated by the place of the accent, by their gender, and meaning: *bráhman* (neuter), *brahmán* (masculine), the first designating a thing, the second a person. This shift of the accent from the root to the suffix is a regular procedure which, because the Indo-European tone preserved its discriminatory and phonological function, served to distinguish an action noun from an agent noun.

What is the meaning of the well-known term *bráhman*? It is almost impossible to define it precisely and in a constant fashion; in the Hymns it admits of translation in a disconcerting number of different ways. It is a mysterious fluid, a power of the soul, a magic and mystical power; but it is also a hymn, a religious practice, an incantation, etc. Consequently, how can we characterize with any exactitude the masculine *brahmán* that is "the person vested with *bráhman*," who is also designated by the derived noun *brāhmaṇa*?

There is nothing in Indian tradition to guide us in a reconstruction either of the form or the notion it designated; what we lack is a concrete sense to which we could attach the diversity of usage. India itself does not supply this firm pointer: *bráhman* is tinged with a meaning of a mystical character; it is one of the notions on which Indian speculation exercised itself at an early period and this obliterated the point of departure. The analysis of the form has fared no better: the origin of *bráhman* is one of the most controversial questions in Indo-European etymology. For a century now the most varied suggestions have succeeded one another and have been the object of dispute. Since the fluid sense of *bráhman* admits of any interpretation, the textual exegesis of the Vedic uses itself reflects in turn various tentative etymologies. Let us recall the principal ones.

It has been proposed to connect *bráhman* with a group of ritual terms in Indo-Iranian of which the principal ones are Vedic *barhiṣ-* 'sacrificial grass', Avestan *barəziš-* 'cushion' and especially Avest. *barəsman-* 'bundle of branches which the priest holds in his hand during the sacrifices'. There has in fact been a formal proposal to make the etymological equation Ved. *bráhman* = Av. *barəsman-*. However, without even insisting on the difference of the structure in the root syllable, a point which is not without importance, the gap in sense is so marked in Vedic itself between the notion of "sacrificial strewing" (*barhiṣ-*) and that of *bráhman-* that it would be vain to attempt to reconcile them. The technique of oblation to which *barhiṣ-* in Vedic and *bráhman-* in Avestan refer has never had any extensions in the abstract sense, religious or philosophical, which is the exclusive sense of *bráhman.* In fact, *barəsman* in Avestan is only a ritual term without religious implications, designating an instrument, the use of which is prescribed along with that of other cult accessories. The characteristic association of *barəsman-* with the verb *star-* 'spread', to which the Vedic phrase *barhiṣaḥ star-* 'to spread out the sacrificial grass' exactly corresponds, shows that these terms had from their origin only a material and strictly technical sense, to which they remained confined. They had nothing in common with *bráhman.*

Of quite a different kind is the ancient connection between Vedic *bráhman* and Lat. *flāmen*, which once was in considerable favor. In this concordance we were supposed to have evidence of ancient terms preserved both in Latin and Indic; an ancient neuter coined by means of the same suffix (*-man*, Lat. *-men*) is supposed to have become in both languages the word for a cult officiant. Added to this were supposedly the remarkable resemblances in the functions of *brāhmaṇa* and *flāmen* respectively. But this equation encounters numerous objections. The comparison of the essential element of the form, the root *brah-* in Indic and *flā-* in Latin, causes grave difficulties; we should have to posit for Latin **flags-men-*, a form difficult to justify, with the additional disadvantage that it does not yield any precise sense either in Italic or in Indo-European. This is why this equation has been abandoned.

We shall not linger over other attempts which have come to naught, but we think that a new fact has come to light which must put an end to this discussion. We now have at our disposal a firm foothold for the determination of the original sense of *bráhman.* It is the Iranian correspondent which supplies it, since in an inscription in Old Persian the word *brazman-* figures, which corresponds exactly to Vedic *bráhman.* The sense of the Old Persian word has been established by W.-B. Henning,[1] who has shown that *brazma*n develops to *brah*m in Middle Parthian and Middle Persian, and that *brah*m signifies "form, (decent) appearance" and is applied sometimes to clothing and sometimes to deportment and conduct

In fact *brazman* in Old Persian refers to cult and may indicate the "appropriate form," the "rite" which this cult demands. This would also be the sense of *bráhman* in Vedic; all the usages of the term have in common the notion of "ceremonial form" in the behavior of the priest who makes the offering and in the operations of the sacrifice. It is along these lines that we should define the proper sense of the term *bráhman*, which later was charged with mystical and speculative values.

Consequently, the Indic *brahmán* (or *brāhmaṇa-*) is he who ensures the performance of the rites in the prescribed forms. This is the definition which, at the conclusion of this analysis, harmonizes the functions of the cult official with the now assured sense of the fundamental Vedic term *bráhman*, Old Persian *brazman*. The conceptual basis is now established in Indo-Iranian, even if the root of the word does not recur elsewhere.

We are still too poorly informed of the Persian religion of the Achaemenids to assess the role of the *brazman* in cult. There is no proof that this abstract noun ever produced in ancient Iranian an agent noun, parallel to Vedic *brahmán*, to designate the person who knows and carries out the operations of cult. This is one reason for believing that *brahmán* is a purely Indic term which has its equivalent a different term in Iran: the *āθravan* of the Avesta.

The words for the other two classes are derivatives or compounds which are easy to interpret; they do not give rise to such complex problems as those which were raised by the term for the priest. But each is tied up with an important concept and because of this they deserve a brief comment.

The designation for the warrior class in India is Skt. *kṣatriya*, *rājanya*. The first word is a derivative form of *kṣatra* 'power', a notion which will be studied in greater detail in the Iranian world;[2] the second, *rājan*(*i*)*ya-* 'of royal stock' comes from the word for 'king' *rāj*(*an*)-. These two words are not applied to dignitaries but to the members of a class and designate them by the privilege attached to their condition. They do not refer to the profession of arms; both evoke the concept "power," "royalty." We discern in these two clear terms the

1. *Transactions of the Philological Society*, 1944, p. 108ff.
2. Book Four, Chapter Two.

manner in which the word for "warriors" was orientated in India: if there was a connection between "warriors" and "power," this is because temporal power was not the necessary attribute of the*rāj*.

We shall see in fact that, when examining the concept of *rēx* as it is defined both in ancient Rome and India, that the "king" was not endowed with the real power.[3] What we learn from the words *kṣatriya* and *rājanya* is that power, defined by *kṣatra* and *rāj*(*an*)-, was associated with the profession of arms.

In Iranian society, the equivalent term to *kṣatriya* is, in its Avestan form, *raθaēštā-*. More frequently, *raθaēštar-* is encountered, a secondary analogical form of agent nouns in *-tar* (a type corresponding to Gr. -τωρ, -τήρ and Latin *-tor*); **-star-* as an agent noun from *stā-* is impossible, as roots with an intransitive sense, like *stā-* 'to keep upright', do not supply agent nouns. The formation of the compound justifies the analysis *raθaē-štā-*, which signifies "he who stands upright in the chariot," just like the corresponding Vedic *ratheṣṭhā*, the epithet of the great warrior god Indra. This descriptive term goes back to a heroic age with its idealization of the warrior and its celebration of the young fighter who, standing upright in his chariot, hurls himself into the fray. Such is the Indo-European conception of the noble warrior. It was not on foot or on horseback that the Indo-European warrior went into battle. The horse is still a draft animal attached to the war chariot. It needed a long history and a number of inventions before the horse could become a mount and so transform the conduct of war. But long after the revolution in technique and culture represented by the appearance of the mounted warrior, the vocabulary was still to testify to the priority of the chariot as compared with equitation. Thus the Latin expression *equo vehi*, that is, "go on horseback" continued to employ the verb *vehere* 'to transport in a vehicle'. The ancient verb which was appropriate to the technique of the chariot was adapted to the new practice of horse-riding. In Homer *eph' híppōn baínō* (ἐφ' ἵππων βαίνω) signifies not "to mount a horse" but always "to get into the chariot." The sole function of the horse was to pull the chariot. To mount a horse was no more conceivable to a warrior of the Indo-European age than to ride an ox would have been for the people of the classical period. In calling the "warrior" by the term "fighter in a chariot," Iran was more faithful than India to the Indo-European ideology of the warrior class.

For the third class, the Indic term is *vaiśya*, which literally means "man of the *viś*," which is approximately "man of the people." This establishes a

3. Book Four, Chapter One.

connection between this last class and membership of a social division, called *viś*.

It is quite different in Iran, where the complex, and not always well understood, designation is composed of two associated words designating one and the same person: *vāstryō fšuyant*.

The first is a derivative from *vāstra* 'pasture', cf. *vāstar* 'herdsman'. These two terms (*vāstra*, *vāstar*) are very common in the Avesta and are endowed with great importance. We have had occasion elsewhere[4] to analyze the etymology and to study the sense which they assume in the pastoral way of life and the religious ideology of Iran; they are among the most significant words of Zoroastrian doctrine. The second, *fšuyant*, is a present participle from the root *fšu-* 'to rear stock'. The class is thus named analytically by a combination of the two words, one of which refers to "pasturing" and the other to "stock-breeding."

A double expression like this belongs to a category of compounds known under the name of *dvandva*. These are double words, the two components of which are in asyndeton, simply juxtaposed, both in the plural or, more frequently, in the dual. The two terms, closely associated, form a conceptual unit. This type is illustrated in Vedic by *Mitra Varunā*, which unites the two juxtaposed gods; *dyāvā pr̥thivī* (*dyaus*/*pr̥thivī*) 'heaven-earth'; and also *mātā-pitarā*(*u*) 'the two, mother and father'. The *dvanda* subsumes the unity of the concept in its two distinct species. It may also appear in looser forms and simply associate two qualifications. For instance in Latin the expression *Patres conscripti* only makes sense if we recognize it as two juxtaposed nouns, *patres* on the one hand, and *conscripti* on the other; that is to say, here we have two groups of persons, originally independent, who together constituted the Senate. It is an expression of the same type which we have here in Iranian: the *vāstryō* and the *fšuyant* are two different kinds of persons: one has to do with pastures, the other is in charge of livestock. Then, since each forms part of a single class, a single term serves to indicate them: *vāstryō fšuyant*. This Iranian class has an explicit functional denomination in contrast to the Indic term *vaiśya*, which simply indicates their belonging to a tribe.

For completeness' sake we must mention a fourth class which appears in the most recent lists. In India, the fourth estate is called *śūdrá*, the etymological sense of which escapes us; it is applied to people of the lowest category, ethnically mixed, people without a well-defined profession or a precise function.

---

4. *Hittite et indo-européen*, Paris, 1962, p. 98ff.

In Iran, too, after the three traditional classes, one text mentions the *hūiti*, a term which seems to signify "occupation, craft" and which is applied to artisans. We do not know the date when this new social distinction came about which lumped all the artisans together and made them into a distinct class.

To estimate the importance of this triple classification it should be noted that it did not only apply to groups of human beings. It was extended to the groups of concepts which were thus brought into relation with the several classes. This is not easy to recognize at first sight; it is indirectly revealed in expressions which appear to be of little significance, but which are understood in their full sense once they are brought into connection with what are essential social concepts. We read in an Achaemenid Persian inscription of Darius the expression for a prayer to avert three calamities from the country: *dušiyārā* 'bad harvest', *hainā* 'the enemy army', *draugā* 'the lie', that is to say, the perversion of moral and religious order. This is not a chance formulation. These three calamities correspond to a necessary order. The first, "bad harvest," ruins the farmer; the second, the attack of the enemy, affects the warrior; the third, the "lie," concerns the priest. We find here again, transposed into three kinds of misfortune, this same hierarchy of the three classes which we have found implicit in the words for their representatives. Society cannot be conceived, the universe cannot be defined, except by this triple order. Is this division, which embraces the whole people, limited to Indo-Iranian society? It might be thought to be very old, going back to the Indo-European period. In fact, it has left its traces everywhere. We recall in particular in Greek the legendary tradition about the original organization of Ionian society. A reflection of it survived in the myth concerning Ion, the eponym of the race. A legend (preserved by Strabo, 383) attributes to Ion the division of society into four classes:

(1) geōrgoí	(2) dēmiourgoí	(3) hieropoioí	(4) phýlakes
(γεωργοί)	(δημιουργοί)	(ἱεροποιοί)	(φύλακες)
"farmers"	"artisans"	"priests"	"guardians"

Plato in the Critias also alludes to it when he enumerates:

Hiereîs	dēmiourgoí	geōrgoí	mákhimoi
(ἱερεῖς)	(δημιουργοί)	(γεωργοί)	(μάχιμοι)
"priests"	"artisans"	"farmers"	"warriors"

On the other hand we know the names of the four great Ionian tribes, headed by the four sons of Ion. These four proper names may be related to the four social classes. Unfortunately they are cited in a different order in different authors, which makes the comparison difficult and prevents the direct equation of each name with one of the four functions.

Herodotus, V, 66			
Geléōn	*Aigikorées*	*Argádēs*	*Hóplēs*
(Γελέων)	(Αἰγικορέες)	(Ἀργάδης)	(Ὅπλης)

Euripides, Ion, 1579–1580			
Geléon	*Hóplētes*	*Argadē̃s*	*Aigikorês*

Plutarch, Solon, 23			
Hoplîtai	*Ergadē̃s*	*Gedéontes*	*Aigikorē̃s*

The form in which these names have been transmitted has been affected by the interpretation: it is clear, for instance, that Plutarch intends his list to designate the warriors, artisans, farmers and goatherds. All the same, this list of names may well roughly cover the four classes. We can try to establish some correlations, but we must discard Plutarch 's interpretation, which is too transparent to be anything but a late adaptation of terms which were no longer understood.

Hóplētes (*hóplēs*) is known from a number of inscriptions: e.g. from Miletus (fifth century BC) *hoplḗthōn* (ὁπλήθων), genitive plural with an orthographic variant; in Dacia, we encounter a *phylḕ hopleítōn* (φυλὴ ὁπλείτων). The name is doubtless to be connected with *hóplon*, plural *hópla*, not in the sense of "arms," which is secondary, but with the proper sense of "instruments, tools." On this interpretation the word would designate *artisans*.

Argádēs (confirmed by epigraphic reference from Cyzicus and Ephesus as a name given to a *khiliostús*, a group of one thousand men) has a resemblance to the name of *Argos*, the meaning of which we know. *Argos* signifies τὸ πεδίον 'ground', 'plain' in the language of the Macedonians and the Thessalians, according to Strabo. *Argádēs*, if it refers to the ground or soil, would then designate the *farmers*. Such is the second identification which we can make with some probability.

Geléōn and *Aigikoreús* would then correspond to the noble functions, and we should expect them to head the list, as in fact they do in Herodotus. For

Aigikoreús we are struck by the resemblance of this compound to *aigís*, the "aegis" of Athena. It is also relevant to recall that the four classes were respectively put into relation with Zeus, Athena, Poseidon and Hephaistos. We may link the last two classes to the latter two gods, *Hóplēs* as "artisans" to Hephaistos, *Argádēs* as "farmers" to Poseidon, who was patron of agriculture among his other functions. There remain the two classes attributed to Zeus and Athena. The *Aigikoreús* may be linked with the latter. As for *Geléōn*, we recall that he is under the patronage of Zeus according to an inscription (IG II^2, 1072), mentioning *Zeùs Geléōn*. This testimony associates the last term with the only divine name left at our disposal, that is, Zeus.

It is certain that we have here survivals which were no longer understood at the time when this tradition was recorded, and their interpretation remains hypothetical. However, the manner in which the different persons divided the social activities among themselves conforms with the explicit traditions of India and Iran. The fourth activity is that of the artisan, as it is in Iran. Finally, this distribution is regulated by divine order. We may therefore suppose that here, in a legendary form, the old social divisions have survived and this would in itself be a reason for considering it as Indo-European and not merely Indo-Iranian.

This analysis may also find confirmation in the Italic world, notably in the Iguvine Tablets, a ritual formulated in the Umbrian language for the use of the Atiedian priests of Iguvium (Gubbio) in Umbria.

The tablets describe the ceremony of the annual lustration performed by the priests; it consists of a circumambulation of the territory of the city. The procession is interrupted by stations at each gateway of the town, each one occasioning oblations and recitations of formulae. Now, in the prayers which are repeated in the form of litanies, certain expressions recur which are worth analyzing. They appeal for divine protection over creatures or things which are enumerated in six consecutive words, divided into three groups of two:

nerf arsmo ueiro pequo castruo frif

The first term, *ner-f* (accusative plural of *ner*) corresponds to Skt. *nar*, Gr. *anḗr* (ἀνήρ); these are the men of war, the chiefs; *arsmo* is the term designating the rites, the sacred; *uiero* = Lat. *virōs* 'the men'; *pequo* = Lat. *pecus* 'livestock'; *castruo*, which corresponds to Lat. *castra*, designates the cultivated land, the fields; *fri-f* = Lat. *fructus*. We have thus: the chiefs, the priests; the people, the herds; the fields, the products of the earth; three groups of two words or, one might say, three successive *dvandva.* One of these *dvandva, ueiro pequo* 'men-animals', recurs in Iranian in the form *pasu vīra* 'animals-men'; this correspondence, which has been long noted, illustrates the antiquity of the rite and the formulation itself of the Iguvine Tablets.

Each of the three is concerned with a department of social life: first, the priests and chiefs; then, man and the animals; finally, the earth and its fruits.

This division corresponds, although in a somewhat different manner, to the ancient scheme, with an extension. It mentions not only the society of men, but also the products of the soil. This addition apart, the principle of classification remains the same: the priests, the warriors, the farmers (men and herds).

We limit our study to an enumeration of the proofs of this social organization, where these proofs consist of specific terms or of onomastic data. The other pointers which may be gathered from a study of the religious and mythologies lie beyond the limits of our subject. In any case, it is the domain in which George Dumézil has contributed works of fundamental importance which are too well known to need citation here.[5]

5. See especially *L'Idéologie tripartite des Indo-Européens* (Brussels, 1958) and *La religion romaine archaïque* (Paris, 1966), where a recasting of earlier work is announced, such as *Jupiter, Mars, Quirinus* (Paris, 1941).

BOOK III, CHAPTER TWO

The Four Divisions of Society

Abstract. The tripartition studied in Chapter One is of a functional character and it is by no means identical with the hierarchy of the groups to which a man belongs. These are political divisions that concern societies when studied over their whole extension. Here ancient Iranian has preserved four terms, designating respectively the "family," the "clan," the "tribe" and the "country." But the comparatist often has great difficulty in determining precisely the ancient Indo-European value of these terms.

A close study of the root **dem-*, which furnishes the name of a small unit (Iranian *dam-*), of the "house" as a social entity (Lat. *domus*, Homeric Greek *dṓ̄*), shows that it must be distinguished from the roots **dem(ə)* 'to construct' and **dom(ə)* 'to tame', with which the dictionaries usually associate it. As for the change of sense, observed in several languages, from "house as family" to "house as construction," this reflects a social change: the breakup of the "*Grossfamilie*," which led to the gradual substitution of a society structured according to genealogy by a society subdivided geographically.

We must therefore separate Gr. *dómos* 'building, house' and Lat. *domus*, which designates not an edifice, but the "home" as a social entity, whose incarnation is the *dominus*. Consequently, *domus* entered into contrasting pairs, the second term of which designates what is outside the circle of the home: *domi militiaeque*, *domi* : *peregre*, *domesticus* : *rusticus*; the couple *domi* : *foris* 'home-outside' shows that the word **dhwer-* 'door' designated the frontier, seen from inside, between the inside and the outside world. As contrasted with Iranian terms, the Homeric words for "family," "clan," "tribe"—*génos*, *phrḗtrē*, *phûlon*—attest both lexical innovations and political conservatism.

Finally, if to the Iranian word for "country"—*dahyu*—there corresponds the Skt. word for "foreign slave," *dasyu*, this is because the Iranians naturally called their people, seen from inside, by a derivative of *daha* 'man', whereas for the Indians the same *dahyu*, seen from the outside, appeared necessarily as a "slave-stranger": here we find once again another illustration of the importance of the opposition inside: outside.

The tripartite organization which has just been described establishes functional classes within society. This division is not of a political nature, except for the fact that the priestly class, being the first, determined the hierarchy of powers. The social organization proper rests on a quite different classification: society is considered not in the light of the nature and hierarchy of its classes, but as what may be called its national extension, a man being regarded as belonging to circles of increasing magnitude. This structure is clearest in ancient Iran. It comprises four concentric circles, four social and territorial divisions which, proceeding from the smallest unit, increase in size until they comprise the whole of the community. The terms which designate them are:

1. *dam-*, *dəmāna-*, *nmāna-* (equivalent forms which are distributed according to the date of the texts), "family" and "house." The second form, *dəmāna-*, is derived from the first, *dam-*, by suffixation, and *dəmāna-* evolved by sound change to *nmāna-*.
2. Above this, *vīs* 'clan', a group of several families.
3. Above this, *zantu* 'tribe', properly "the whole of those of the same birth."
4. Finally, *dahyu*, which may be rendered as "country."

Alongside each of these Iranian terms we can put the Sanskrit correspondent: *dam* 'house' (Av. *dam-*); *viś-* 'community, people' (Av. *vīs-*); *jantu-* 'creature' (Av. *zantu-*). To the fourth term, Avestan *dahyu-* 'country', corresponds Vedic *dasyu* which, in circumstances which we shall try to determine, has taken on the sense of "barbarian enemy population." But in India we do not find an organic connection between these four terms. They no longer form a whole. The ancient schema is already altered. Iranian society has been more conservative.

The same observation is true of the classical languages. We find words that are the congeners of the first three terms: Gr. *démos* (δέμος), Lat. *domus*; Gr. *woîkos* (ϝοῖκος); Lat. *metis*; and Gr. *génos* (γένος) (a neuter in *-s*), Lat. *gens* (a feminine in *-ti*, hence Lat. **genti-* as compared with **gentu-*, the prototype of the Iranian term). But in the classical world they do not constitute a series any more than they do in India. The correspondence is simply etymological. In Greek and Latin, these inherited words are not arranged as they are in Iranian. There is not even parallelism between Latin and Greek. Far from constituting two distinct social units, Gr. *dómos* and (*w*)*oîkos* signify practically the same thing, "house." Date, dialect and style govern the choice of one or the other. Nor does Latin present the Iranian structure: *vīcus* is not the superior grade to *domus*; it differs from *vīs* in Iranian and also from (*w*)*oîkos* in Greek.

Furthermore, in Greece and Rome, new words unknown to Indo-Iranian joined this ancient series; e.g. Gr. *phulḗ* (φυλή) and Lat. *tribus*.

We may nevertheless take it as certain that the Iranian terminology for the social divisions goes back to the Indo-European period. The four terms cited from ancient Iranian reappear in the compound words designating the "chief" (*pati*) of each division: *dmāna-paiti*, *vis-paiti*, *zantu-paiti*, *dahyu-paiti*. This hierarchy (because it is one, with deep roots) persisted in the same order into Middle Iranian, in spite of the evolution of the vocabulary and of the language: *mānbed*, *visbed*, *zandbed*, *dehbed*. The fact is that this structure goes back far in time. We discover it, for two of the terms, in a state previous to Iranian and in the same composite form: Av. *dəmāna-pati* has parallels, (1) in Vedic *dam-pati-* 'master of the house', and (2) in Greek *despótēs* (δεσπότης), while Av. *vīs-pati* 'chief of the clan' has correspondents in (1) Vedic *viś-pati-* and (2) in Lithuanian *vẽš-pats* 'chief of the clan', which developed the sense "lord."

The grouping of these terms shows how they were organized. We must now consider them successively and define each of them individually.

The word for "house," which comes first, is one of the best known elements of the Indo-European vocabulary. Moreover, it is connected with a verbal root in a manner which seems immediately comprehensible and satisfying. The Iranian form *dam-* can be linked with the word family of the Latin *domus*. If in Latin *domus* (fem.) is a stem in *-u-*, we know from indirect evidence of Latin itself that it coexisted with a masculine stem in *-o-*, for **domo-* is presupposed by the derivative *dominus*. The Greek form *dómos* confirms this. In Greek, side by side with *dómos* 'house', we have the feminine *domḗ* (δομή) 'building' and the agent noun **domós* (*δομός) with the accent on the suffix, which enters into the compound *oiko-dómos* (οἰκο-δόμος) 'he who builds the house'. The thematic form is also known in the Ved. *dama-* 'house'. The stem in *-u-*, attested by the Latin *domu-* and the Old Slav. *domŭ*, is also seen in the derived

Vedic adjective *damū-naḥ* 'domestic (protector) of the house', and further in the Armenian compound *tanu-(tēr)* '(master of) the house'.

Both **domo-* and **domu-* come from an ancient root noun which may have the forms **dem-*, **dom-*, **dm*, **dm̥-*. It appears both as a free form or in compounds; e.g. the Skt. expression *patir dan* and *dam-patiḥ*, Av. *dəng paitiš* (where *dəng* represents **dams*) "master of the house," the Greek correspondent of which is *despótēs* or *déspoina* (δέσποινα). These two Greek compounds were no longer analyzable in historical times, but the elements are easily recognizable, and their combinations also occur elsewhere: *-pótēs* (-πότης) and *-poina* (-ποινα) represent respectively the ancient masculine form **poti* 'master' and the ancient, archaic feminine **potnya* 'mistress'; the compound *des-poina* has as its Vedic counterpart *dam-patnī* 'mistress of the house'.

There is further evidence for the root-noun **dem* in Greek, e.g. the Homeric expression *hēméteron dō̃* (ἡμέτερον δῶ) 'our house', originally **dōm* (like Armenian *tun* 'house'), which was later on extended to *dō̂ma*. It is generally accepted that*dámar* (δάμαρ) 'legitimate wife' belongs to the same word-family and is analyzed into *dam-* 'house' and *-ar* from the root of ἀραρίσκω 'to order, to arrange'; the meaning is thus "she who administers the house." The zero grade of **dem-*, that is, **dm-*, appears in the Homeric *mesó-dmē* (μεσόδμη), in Attic *mesómnē* (μεσόμνη), which designates the central beam that joins together two uprights, two pillars in the interior of the house. Apart from this we have **dm-ōu-* in *dmṓs* (δμώς) 'servant', genitive *dmōós* (δμωός), feminine *dmōḗ* (δμωή) 'female servant', the term meaning "he (or she) who belongs to the house."

This whole group of noun forms is traditionally attached to a verbal root **dem-* 'to construct'. The forms of **dem-* testify to what is called a disyllabic root: **dem-ə-* and **dmā*, Gr. *démō* (δέμω), perfect passive *dédmētai* (δέδμηται) cf. *neódmātos* (νεόδματος) 'recently constructed', *démas* (δέμας) 'form, physical appearance', properly "structure."

From different stems of this root a number of noun forms are made. Particularly noteworthy are those Indo-Iranian derivatives with the suffix *-ana-*, Avestan *dəmāna-*, Old Persian **māna-*, Vedic *māna-* (from **dmānā-*), and those with the suffix *-ro-*, the Germanic **dem-ro-*, Old and Modern English *timber* 'wood for construction', German *Zimmer* 'wood-work', then "room," as well as the ancient Gothic denominative verb *timrjan* 'to carpenter.'

Finally, scholars consider that this root **dem-* 'construct' has yielded, apart from the word for "house," a derived verb from this noun, signifying "to tame," a verb represented in Latin by *domare*, in Greek by *damáō*, etc. The basic sense is posited as "to attach (an animal) to the house, to domesticate."

The whole of this etymological group is listed in recent dictionaries under the same heading **dem-*, and in their arrangements the entries start from the basic notion "construct." However, Meillet expressed some reservations about the morphological connection between **dem-* 'construct' and **dem-* 'house'.

At first sight, this great etymological reconstruction, comprising a large number of forms culled from all the languages of the family, raises no major difficulty. The proposed connections between the notions are at least plausible. It seems quite natural that words designating "house" and common to almost all languages should be derived from a verbal root no less ancient signifying "construct." It would follow that the first social unit, the "house" or "family," owed its name to the technique of carpentry.

But a demonstration cannot be regarded as certain simply because it is not improbable. Each of these lexical groups thus brought into relationship reveals, on closer examination, peculiarities of form and sense which seem original and irreducible; these must be brought out before we can collate them. Only this preliminary analysis will enable us to pass judgment on the genetic relationship of the forms. The comparative method is here put to the test over the whole extent of our investigation. We must start with the data basic to this comparison and attempt their description with all proper precision.

If we examine the word for "house," we shall soon notice that *domus* in Latin and *dómos* in Greek, although they appear, apart from the morphological difference of stem (Lat. *-u-*, Gr. *-o-*), to tally completely, differ in many respects in their lexical usages. In Homer, *dómos* is accompanied by descriptive epithets; the house is "great, high, well constructed, wide," etc. That is to say, it has the characteristics of a construction; the *dómos* includes a vestibule, which is called *pródomos*, 'the front part of the *dómos*'. In Latin we find nothing comparable: *domus* always signifies "house" in the sense of "family," which is quite foreign to *dómos*. Moreover, certain case forms of Lat. *domus* are fixed in an adverbial function: *domi*, *domum*, *domo*. In Greek, these adverbial uses are impossible with *dómos* and *dõma*; they certainly exist, but the word concerned is*oîkos*. We have, corresponding to Lat. *domi*, *domum*, *domo*, Gr. *oíkoi* (οἴκοι), *oíkade* or *oîkonde* (οἴκαδε, οἶκονδε), *oíkothen* (οἴκοθεν).

In the same order of ideas, we observe that *domi*, *domum*, *domo*, signify only "the home," with or without movement, as the point of arrival or departure. These adverbs oppose the "home" to that which is outside it (*foras*, *foris*), or to foreign parts (*peregre*); or they contrast everyday occupations, the works of peace, *domi*, to war, *militiae*. Such ideas could hardly be reconcilable with the word for "house" if we had to take it in a constructional sense. It is clear that these adverbial uses imply a moral rather than a material connotation for *domus*. Let us consider for the present the accepted connection between *domus* and a root **dem-* 'construct'. If the "house" was simply the "construction," we would expect to find a verb **dem-* in Latin. But the verb corresponding to Greek *démo* 'construct' is absent from Latin vocabulary, which removes *domus* still further from Gr. *dómos*. The divergence between the two languages and the distance between the two notions is clearly brought out if we examine the expressions for "to construct (a house)." Greek has a verb *oikodomeîn*, the denominative of the composite expression *oiko-dómos* 'house builder', where we note that the agent noun from **dem-* has as its object *oîkos* and not *dómos*. What is the Latin equivalent of *oikodomeîn*? It is a compound verb: *aedificare*. Thus to Gr. *-domeîn* corresponds Latin *facio* and not a verb from the same root; to *oiko-* corresponds not *domus*, but *aedes*. The formation of *aedificare* is thus a clear proof that the true value of *domus* has nothing in common with that of *aedes*, and consequently that *domus* cannot have been an architectural term. If further confirmation were needed, it will be found outside Greek or Latin in a third compound verb of the same sense: in Oscan "construct" is *tríbarakavúm* (infinitive in *-um*). This verb is formed from *tríib-* (= *treb-*) 'house' and *ark-* 'to enclose, to entrench' (cf. Lat. *arceo*). This may be an Oscan calque on the Greek *oikodomeîn*, the result, like a number of other Oscan borrowings, of the influence of Greek civilization. But in Oscan also, the material "house" has a special word, **trēb*.

We therefore have in each of these three languages a verb indicating the material construction which is a compound including the name for "house"; now, this noun is never made from **dem-* 'construct'. This is a new indication which marks the difference between the sense which had been reconstructed for *domus* and the sense actually found.

This clarifies the problem in Latin. Two nouns, *aedes* and *domus*, can equally be translated by "house"; but they are not equivalent, and they differ greatly in their derivation. *Aedes*, meaning "house," "temple," viewed as a construction, gave rise to a derivative *aedilis*, the magistrate in charge of the construction of houses and more especially temples. From *domus* we have no comparable derivative: **domilis* does not exist. Conversely, two derivatives are peculiar to *domus*: (1) *domicilium*, the second term of which is itself derived from ancient

-cola which figures in *agricola*; now *domicilium* 'seat of the *domus*' indicates the house as a residence and not as a construction; (2) *dominus*, a social term. For us, *domus* and *dominus* are different words, but the Romans felt them as closely linked. For instance, in one of those etymological verbal games favored by the early Latin poets, we find: "***O domus*** *antiqua, heu quam dispari dominare* ***domino***"; in Cicero: "***domus*** *erat non* ***domino*** *magis ornamento quam civitati*"; finally in St. Jerome: "*in navi unus gubernator,* ***in domo*** *unus* ***dominus***." So the *dominus* is in no way responsible for the construction of the house.

Finally, the usages of *domus* in Latin exclude all allusion to construction: frequently used with possessive pronouns, *domus mea, apud me domi*, it always means "home." From this comes the turn of phrase *aliquid est mihi domi* 'I have something at home', equivalent to "I possess." Thus in Plautus, *cui argentum domi est* 'he who has money (at home)'. All these features characterize *domus* as a family, social and moral notion, but never as a material one.

In Cato we read an ancient prayer, addressed to Mars on the occasion of the lustration of the fields. It consists of archaic formulae, transmitted from generation to generation and reproduced literally. The person making the offering, after having performed the rite, calls for the protection of the divinity *mihi, domo familiaeque nostrae*. Thus *domus* takes its place between the person of the celebrant and his *familia*.

When in Virgil Aeneas calls out as he disembarks: *Hic domus, hic patria est* he joins *domus* and *patria* in their common membership of the sphere of social and moral notions.

But the term which it is most important to define, because it itself defines *domus*, is the derivative *dominus*. Its peculiar formation by itself arrests our attention. The stem is *domo-*, not *domu-*; the formation is peculiar, with *-no-* as a secondary suffix, that is to say, applied to a noun already existing in the language. This type of derivation is not very common. The suffix occurs in a small series of words, the meaning of which is instructive: first, *tribunus*, which stands to *tribus* as *dominus* (stemming from **domo-no-*) does to *domus*. Apart from this, the formation is found in some proper names, all names of gods. *Portunus* is the god charged with protection of the ports and the wealth accumulated there; he has in his service a *flamen portunalis*, and festivals are devoted to him—the *Portunalia*. From this name it is clear that he is the god of the *portus*, meaning strictly the mouth, but also the crossing of a river. *Neptunus* is not analyzable in Latin itself; but by means of the comparative method we can restore a noun **neptu-* (stem in *-u*) which would signify "humidity, aqueous element."

The formation of *Fortuna* demands an explanation. In the traditional, but not altogether clear, expression *forte fortuna* 'by chance', we can see that *fors* and *fortuna* constitute a single phrase, but it is not immediately evident how the two words are coordinated. *Fors* is ancient **forti-*, going back to **bhr̥-ti-*, an action noun from the root of *fero*; we must remember that the root **bhr̥-* does not simply signify "to bear," but rather "to bring" and also "to take away," so that *fors* is "the action of bringing," "what fate brings." *Fortuna*, for its part, is not a simple doublet of *Fors*; it is an adjective which qualifies *Fors* and gives it greater precision. The *Fors Fortuna* is the divinized *Fors* of **Fortu-*; the existence of the form **fortu* is confirmed by the adjective *fortuitus*. As a female personage *Fortuna* stands to **fortu* as *Portunus* does to *portus*.

Finally, we have *Tiberinus*, a figure of ancient Roman mythology. Ancient prayers invoke *Pater Tiberinus*, the god whose name is derived from *Tiberis*, the Tiber. This secondary formation in *-nus* thus comprises a certain number of divine names for divinities who preside over an element or a force, and two terms designating a social function, *dominus* and *tribunus*.

This lexical peculiarity is revealed in its full significance when we find that the same suffix is employed outside Latin with the same function. In ancient Germanic, we have a group of words with this suffix which comprise, just as in Latin, on the one hand words for social functions, and on the other proper names: *þiudans*, the word for the king in Gothic, goes back to an ancient **teu-ta-nos*, which signifies the "chief of the **teutā*," of the tribe, the community; Gothic *kindins* 'chief of the clan', from **genti-nos*, chief of the *gens*. By combining the evidence from other Germanic dialects, we get also **druxti-nos*, Old Icel. *drottinn* 'chief of the troop', cf. Old English *dryhten*; the basic term is *drott-* 'troop' in Old Icelandic. This type of formation reappears in Old Icelandic *Herjan*, the second name of Odin, which is coined from *herr* 'army'. The prototype is **koryo-nos*, which recalls Gr. *koíranos* 'chief'. Certain of these terms feature in personal names, even outside Germanic, e.g. Gaulish *Toutonos*, Illyrian *Teutana* and Gaulish *Coriono-totae*.

But there is a far more famous name which belongs to this series; that of the great god of Germanic mythology, *Wodan* (*Wotan*, *Odin*): *Wōda-naz* (a derivative in *-*nos*) made from a term **wōδa-*, an ancient form of German *Wut* 'fury'. The problem is only how to interpret the name. In these secondary suffixations in *-nos*, the root term designates generally a group of men, a social division. For an abstract notion like *wōδa* to find its place in this series, we must transpose the abstract into a collective noun and understand **wōδa* as "the people possessed by fury." This interpretation is not without support, if not in the language, at least in the conceptions of ancient mythology. This notion is that of the *Wild Hunt* known from the literatures of the Middle Ages; a band of the dead who once a year, led by their chief, return to the land of the living, and after devastating everything in their path vanish into the underworld. *Wotan-Odin* would then be their chief. This is a plausible hypothesis. We note also that it accords with the surname of *Wotan*, Old Icel. *Herjan*, literally "chief of the army," cf. Gothic *harjis* 'army', German *Heer*.[1]

We thus possess, to illustrate the function of the derivative in *-no-*, a considerable body of facts which give us a good deal of help, but we do not find in them in all cases the notion of "chief." For some of them, this translation is well suited: Lat. *Portunus* is effectively the master of the ports, and Gothic *þiudans* that of the people. It is difficult to interpret the name of *Neptu-nus* in the same way. The connection between *Neptunus* and the element of water cannot be transposed as such into the social domain. In fact here we have an incarnation, not the exercise of authority: *Neptunus* personifies the watery element, he represents it. We can therefore say that *þiudans* in the same way personifies his people. This must be understood in the light of the nature of the institution itself. We use the term "personifies" here, bearing in mind the manner in which the king was appointed by the Indo-European peoples of Central and Western Europe.

There was no hereditary king, but only a king by election; he was chosen from among the people, says Tacitus. Similarly, in India, the assembly had to choose from among a certain class the one who was to represent it. Seen from this angle of "representation," "personification" or "incarnation" of the basic notion, the two series of words formed by the suffix *-nos* can be brought together. The list can in fact be increased. There are secondary derivatives in *–no* elsewhere; thus the Greek word for "moon," *Selḗnē* (Σελήνη < *σελασ-νᾱ), derived from *sélas* '(lunar) radiance', is a noun formed in the same way as Lat. *tribunus* or Gothic *þiudans*. We see in *Selḗnē* the personification of the particular luminosity of the moon. In this way we can find a single principle in this mode of derivation which later became specialized so that it formed the names for heads of social sections.

This brings us back to the formation of *dominus*. The personage called *dominus* has authority over the *domus*; he represents and incarnates it. This leads

1. Cf. Book One, Chapter Eight.

once again to the same conclusion regarding the meaning of *domus*. This word does not signify the material construction. It is within an exclusively social and moral conception of *domus* as a human group that *domus* and *dominus* find their respective explanations, and this illuminates their relations.

This is supported by the meaning of another derivative, *domesticus*, the formation of which is parallel to that of **rowesticus* (> *rūsticus*), if it is not coined on the basis of the latter. The adjective *domesticus* qualifies what belongs to the house, as against what is foreign to it; it does not imply any connection with the material aspect of the house.

Do we have to suppose that Latin has transformed into a social notion a word which originally had a material significance, which was inherited, and which was the basis of Latin *domus*? Such a transformation, if it took place, could not have been a total one; it would have left traces in the Roman world itself. But there appears to be no reason at all to suppose this. We are of the opinion that there was an unbroken continuity between the Indo-European sense of the word and that of Latin *domus*. We can project back into the Indo-European period the correspondence of Skt. *dam patiḥ* with Gr. *despótēs* 'master of the house'. It is true that the sense of "master of the house" has been effaced, or at least weakened, in Greek, where *despótēs* signified at an early date "master" in general, and not only of the house, so much so that in the New Testament it was felt necessary to create *oiko-despótēs* to express "master of the house."

This was because in *despótēs* the word for "house" was not felt any more. As early as Attic prose we find phrases like οἴκου, or οἰκίας δεσπότης '*despótēs* of the *oîkos*, the *oikía*', when he exercises his authority within the house. Now this archaic compound **dem*(*s*)*-poti-* 'master of the house' refers in the first component to "the house *qua* family" and not to the "house *qua* construction." We find this confirmed in a parallel expression to *dam-patiḥ* (or *patir dan*), that is, in Vedic *śiśur dan* 'son of the house', with a term of kinship, *śiśus*, which implies the "house" as a family and social entity.

Now that we have completed this examination, it appears that **dem-* (**domo-*) 'house', in Indo-European as in Latin, had an exclusively social value. Many other indications can confirm that there is no connection between the notion of "house" and that of "building." Even in a language which has abolished many traces of its Indo-European past, in Armenian, the term *tanu-tēr* 'master of the house' applies to the head of the family. Similarly, the adjective Skt. *damū-na* qualifies the divinities particularly honored by the family.

We can also bring out this relationship of *domus* with the family by a comparison with the term immediately superior to *domus* in the social hierarchy. This is the Avestan expression *vīsō puθra*, which designates the heir of a noble family, literally "the son of the *vīs*." He is, according to this appellation, the son of the **weik-*, the social unit corresponding to *vīcus* in Latin and *(w)oîkos* in Greek. This word can only be understood if we regard *vīs* as a social and family group (in the wider sense of Gr. *oîkos*) and not as a collection of houses. His designation by *vīsō puθra-* is thus, at the next higher level, parallel to that of Vedic *śiśur dan* 'son of the house'. The two expressions provide mutual support.

After having established the agreement of these testimonies, we must now examine the Greek facts, some of which bring striking confirmation of our conclusions. Not only *despótēs* but also *dámar* is no longer analyzable in Greek itself, a word which denotes "she who administers the house"; *dmṓs* 'the servant, the slave', *dmoḗ* 'the female servant', that is as a whole, "those who form part of the household," like the *famuli* of Latin. Finally, the Homeric form *dô̄* in ἡμέτερον, sometimes ὑμέτερον δῶ 'in my house, at my home', 'at your home', parallel with Latin *domi*, *domum*, conveys the notion of the house as "inside." Here is a lexical series which has clearly carried on in ancient Greek the sense of **dem-*, **dom-* which we have already recognized as Indo-European.

But against this group we have to posit a group of forms which in Greek must be recognized as distinct and belonging to another family. First the noun *dómos*, which applies to buildings: "house," "temple" and also "a room," and sometimes "nest." Herodotus takes it in the sense of "an arrangement of stones or bricks" serving for the construction of a wall, or of a house. It is exclusively to construction that *mesódmē* 'the large transverse beam' of a building refers. An essential term of architecture is *oikodómos*, with the derived verb *oikodomeîn* 'construct', which was the model for Latin *aedificare*. We also cite the Homeric expression *busso-domeúein* (βυσσο-δομεύειν) 'to build in depth, to intrigue, to plot secretly'. Latin offers a parallel expression, which may be a literal translation, in the shape of *endo-struos*, Classical Latin *industrius*, literally "constructing inside, in a secret manner." The parallelism of the formation reveals the equivalence of Gr. *-domeúein* and Lat. *struere*. Finally, there is a primary verb *démō* 'construct', which governs objects such as *teîkhos* 'wall' and *oîkos* 'house', this combination being seen in the compound *oikodómos*; or, furthermore, *(h)amaxitós* 'way': ἀμαξιτός … δέδμηται in Herodotus (VII, 200). We add here the noun *démas* 'physical shape, stature, appearance' which was used adverbially as "in the manner of, literally "according to the appearance, the form of …"

These forms grouped around the verb *démō* are not a creation of Greek alone. They also have exact correspondents in Germanic: Got. *ga-timan*, German *geziemen* 'to be in accord, to agree', literally "to be constructed in the same manner"; there is a derived noun **dem-ro-*, Old and Modern English *timber* 'wood for construction'. From this noun stem **dem-ro-* Gothic formed a verb *timrjan* 'to work in wood' (German *zimmern*) and an abstract word *ga-timrjo* 'construction'. If we compare these terms, we see that they require us to posit a root **dem-* which, according to the technique involved, had the sense of "construct in tiers" for masonry, and "construct by joinery" for timber construction.

We must recognize another and quite different group. These are the noun forms or verbal forms of a root signifying "to tame," Lat. *domāre*, Gr. *damáō*, *a - dámatos* 'untamable', etc. The sense has no connection with the idea of "house," but to quite a different notion by a much more satisfactory link. Hittite presents a present tense *damaš-* 'to do violence, to oppress, to subject'. It is from this sense that the meaning "to tame" develops by specialization, and we know that the Gr. verb *damáō*at first referred to taming of horses as practiced by equestrian people, a technical development of sense at first limited to a dialectal area, which cannot be attributed to the Indo-European period.

To sum up, we must carve up the lexical conglomeration which figures in our etymological dictionaries under **dem-* 'construct; house' into three distinct and irreducible units.

1. **domā-* 'to do violence; to tame' (Lat. *domāre*, Gr. *damáō*, Skt. *damayati*, Got. *gatamjan*, etc.);
2. **dem(ə)* 'construct' (Gr. *démō* and its derivatives, Got. *timrjan*);
3. **dem-* 'house, family'.

We dissociate, therefore, in the common Indo-European period, the term **dem-* 'family' from all verbal connections. There is nothing more than homophony between **dem-* 'family' and **dem(ə)-* 'construct'. But it cannot be denied that contaminations came about between the forms issuing from these two roots, as for instance in Homeric Greek between *dô(m)* 'house *qua* family' and *dómos* 'house *qua* construction'. This is due to a tendency in all the terms of the series to identity social groups with material habitat.[2]

***

The same fact recurs at a higher level of society, in the forms of the nominal stem **weik*-, **woiko*-, denoting the unit formed from several families. They appear everywhere in the Indo-European area, except in Celtic. The social sense is well established by the concordance between Indo-Iranian *viś*- 'clan' (cf. Vedic *viś-pati* above) and the Lithuanian *vẽš-pats* 'lord'. But it has evolved to the material sense of "group of houses," "village," "town," in Latin *vīcus* 'town, quarter of a town', Old Slavic *vĭsĭ* 'village', Gothic *weihs* 'village, domain'. Gr. (*w*)*oîkos* occupies an intermediate position: first "(large) house," in which all the descendants of the head of the family lived, then a word substituted for *dómos*, as we have seen above, and finally "house, building" in *oiko-dómos* 'builder, architect' with its numerous derivatives and compounds. Thus the word for a social unit has been transferred to the material sphere which delimits that unit. A new relationship then becomes established between those grouped together in the same habitat: this relationship is illustrated in Latin by the connection of the sense of between *vicus* and the derivative *vicinus* 'who belongs to the (same) *vicus*', hence "neighbor." In separate languages, the representation of ancient **weik*- enters into a given specific series and so in each language takes on the sense assigned to it by its place in the series. But it is still clearly apparent in historical times that in the period of Indo-European unity this word was one of the terms referring to a division of society.

It is thus clear that the Indo-European terms have been subjected to profound changes of sense. Through these changes we can detect an important fact of civilization, a transformation of the institutions themselves, to which the vocabulary gives indirect witness.

What **dem*- and **weik*- once signified in the Indo-European organization, namely the divisions at different levels of society, are in languages of the historical period designated by new terms, such as **genti*- or **teutā*-, in a part of

2. On the homophonous roots for "tame," "construct," "house-family," see our article "Homophonies radicales en indo-européen," *Bull. de la Soc. de Linguistique de Paris*, vol. 51 (1955), pp. 14-41.

Western Indo-European. In Latin, once *vicus* had become the term for a "quarter" of a "village," new designations had to be devised: *tribus* and *civitas*.

This change is just as far reaching in Greek, but it takes on a different aspect. The largest unit is that of the *génos*, which was much more extensive than the Roman *gens*, and is not to be confused with the *phratría*, a division which is also purely Hellenic. The *phratríai*, in their turn, are grouped into *phulaí*.

Two important transformations have come about:

1) the break-up of the "*Grossfamilie*" into separate families. The ancient period was characterized by the "*Grossfamilie*" in which, after marriage, all the sons continued to live together, bringing up their own families, while sometimes even the daughters brought their husbands. At this stage, there was no individual property; the whole family domain was an undivided property. We cannot properly speak of inheritance because the "*Grossfamilie*" itself remained the proprietor, and its rights over its possessions never lapsed. Then the "*Grossfamilie*" broke up. For economic reasons, the sons left at an early age. The terms which applied to this "*Grossfamilie*" were more and more rarely used, for the notion itself no longer corresponded with any real institution; the "*Grossfamilie*" was divided up into much smaller units when the descendants in their turn went off to found new homes.

2) The second transformation was the establishment of the Achaean warriors in a *pólis* (πόλις), a common township. This evolution slowly abolished the earlier social framework in favor of new territorial divisions. The old social divisions founded on genealogical line of descent were progressively replaced by groupings determined by a common habitat.

This habitat is no longer the privilege of those with a common origin. In the *pólis* or the *kṓmē* (κώμη) it was chance or war which brought together those who lived in it. Aristotle, at the beginning of his *Politics*, does no more than codify an established situation when he characterizes the elements of the society *qua* "community" (*koinōnía*). The ultimate unit he describes as the *oîkos* (the Romans would say *domus*); for him it is the smallest division and the first form of society which existed, and he defines it as a community of husband and wife, of master and slaves: this is the notion of the Roman *familia*. The *oîkos* is, in fact, constituted by the daily participation in food and worship. After this, Aristotle posited a progress upwards to the village (*kṓmē*) and the city (*pólis*).

Today we see things differently; such a reconstruction, which starts from a social cell and proceeds by successive accretions, is false. What existed from the start was the society as a whole and not the family, then the clan, then the city. Society *from its origin* was divided into units which it comprised. The families are necessarily grouped within a unit, and so on. But Aristotle makes into a universal phenomenon and a philosophic necessity what was represented in his own society: he makes an absolute of a particular social state of affairs.

It is this great process of transformation which is reflected in the vocabulary: like *dómos*, the term *oîkos* from then on became a word for a habitat. In Greek prehistory, as we have seen, the "house" was not a building; similarly, the Homeric expression designating the Dorians as *trikhaí-wikes* 'those divided into three *tribus*' preserves *wik-*, related to (*w*)*oîkos*, in its first sense of a social grouping. But soon *oîkos* took the place of the ancient **dem-* 'house' and so came to mean "house" as building. The change which came about in society produced (1) the new reference of the terms to the material sphere; (2) the "hierarchical" transfer of the term to the place of another: the sense of **dem-* passed to *oîkos* in Greek; hence the locative *oîkoi*, etc., which corresponds to Lat. *domi*, etc. and signifies "at my home," "at your home." Thus *oîkos* has taken over the whole of the ancient semantic domain of **dem-*. In general, we observe the abolition of the Indo-European structure and the advance of new terms. The old genealogical words become emptied of their institutional and social meanings and become a terminology of territorial divisions. Each language proceeds to a new adaptation of its terminology. The very way in which this transformation takes place in different languages is highly instructive, because the languages are not Indo-European in the same way. Latin is Indo-European in its fidelity to ancient usage, to the vocabulary of institutions, even when this vocabulary relates to new realities: Greek, conversely, is Indo-European in the persistence of the primitive model, around which it organized a new series of terms.

The category of meaning in which the word for "house" finds its Indo-European value determines also the same notion in its other aspects. Among the uses of *domus* we must now consider the adverbial form *domi* and the opposition which Latin usage has established from the beginning between *domi* 'at home' and *foris* 'outside', or, with reference to movement, between *domum* and *foras*.

We have here, on closer examination, an opposition which could not have been foreseen, and which contrasts two terms that are not by nature antithetical, because one is the word for "house" and the other the word for "door" (*fores*). Here a new notion came into play with lexical consequences, that of "door."

There are in the Indo-European languages several words for "door": the distribution is haphazard. The word may even be restricted to a single family of languages. Thus in the Italic dialects, Oscan *ueru* '*portam*', Umbrian *uerofe* '*in portas*' with a postposition *-e*. The word goes back to an ancient neuter form **werom* 'closure', derived from the root **wer-* (Skt. *vr̥ṇóti*, 'it closes, it encloses', German *Wehr*), a localized term which apart from Oscan and Umbrian has a correspondent form only in Slavic and Baltic. In other languages, on the contrary, a multiplicity of terms invites our attention. In Latin, we have four: *fores, porta, ianua, ostium*. Even if some authors seem to use them indiscriminately, we know that at an ancient date they did not have the same signification.

Of all the words the one represented in Latin by *fores* has the widest distribution; it is attested in nearly all the other languages. The Indo-European form is **dhwer-*, in the reduced grade **dhur*, Gr. *thúra* (θύρα), generally in the plural, because it seems that the door was conceived of as having various elements.

**dhwer-* is an unanalyzable term by itself, which cannot be attached to any verbal root, and its etymological signification escapes us; but is it possible that we have here a term for a material object which owes its name to the functions which it fulfills?

What is important to stress is the concordance of the adverbial usages of **dhwer-* in Latin and in other languages. Some of them, in fact, present uses exactly comparable to that of Latin *fores* 'door' and *foras* 'outside': Gr. *thúra* 'door' and *thúra-ze* (θύρα-ζε) 'outside'; Armenian *durkᶜ* 'door' and *durs* (acc. plur.) 'outside'. We also have in Gothic a compound *faura-dauri*, literally "out-of-doors," which translates *plateía* (πλατεία) 'street'.

We have here an adverbial form which was fixed at a very early date and became independent, so much so that *thúraze*, having lost in Homeric times its connection with *thúra* 'door' (of the house), it was possible to say ἁλὸς θύραζε 'out from the sea' in the *Odyssey* (5, 510; cf. *Il.* 16, 408). In the Slavic languages, the connection between the two terms continues; on the one hand *dvĭrĭ* 'door', but also, in all modern Slavic languages: Russ. *na dvorě*, Serbian *nadvor*, etc. "outside," literally "at the door." Such correlations, the antiquity of which is evident, explain the nature of the idea. The "door," **dhwer-*, is seen from the inside of the house: it is only for the person inside the house that "at the door" can signify "outside." The whole of the phenomenology of the "door" proceeds from this formal relation. For the person who lives inside, **dhwer-* marks the limit of the house conceived as an interior and which protects the inside from the menacing outside. This notion is so deeply and enduringly inscribed in the Indo-European languages that, for us too Fr. *mettre quelqu'un à la porte*, lit. "to put someone at the door," is "to put him outside"; "open or close one's door to somebody" is "to admit or not admit him into one's home."

We can understand why in Latin *foris* is the opposite of *domi*: the "outside" begins at the door, and is called *foris* for the one who is "at home," *domi*. This door, according to whether it is open or shut, becomes the symbol for separation from, or communication between, one world and the other. It is through the door that the secure and enclosed space which delimits the power of the *dominus* opens on an extraneous and often hostile world; cf. the opposition *domi/militiae*. The rites of passage through the door, the mythology of the door, give a religious symbolism to this idea.

It is significant that the adjective made from the word for door does not designate what concerns the door itself, but what is outside, the extraneous world. This is also the meaning of the adjective *thuraîos* (θυραῖος) 'extraneous, from abroad', from *thúra* 'door', in Greek. Similarly, late Latin has coined from *foris*, *foras* the derivatives *foranus*, *foresticus*, *forestis*, all of them referring to the outside, the extraneous world. This sense remained alive; it continued to be productive even after the ancient name of the "door" was replaced by new terms, e.g. in the Romance languages, where it has produced adjectival derivatives such as Italian *forestiere* 'foreign'; in Old French, specially Norman French, *horsain* means 'stranger', 'he who is outside, who does not inhabit the locality'—and also in modern French, *forain* 'who arrives from outside' (Lat. *foranus*). Even the French adverb *hors* necessarily implies a subject who is inside; to put somebody "***hors** la loi*" implies that the subject is *inside* the law. Thus, although the notion of the "door" is no longer expressed in the Romance languages by forms of ancient *fores*, it continues to act like an invisible boundary separating the interior space from what is outside. On the other hand, the material sense of **dhwer-* is reflected in certain ancient derivatives connected with architecture, like Gr. *pró-thuron* (πρό-θυρον) 'vestibule' (literally what is in front of the door) or Old Slavic *dvorŭ* 'courtyard (of the house)'.

The opposition *domi/foris* has a variant where *foris* is replaced by a quite different adjective. The opposite term to *domi* is here taken from *ager* 'field' (< **agros*), in the shape of the adverb *peregri*, *peregre*, from which comes the derivative *peregrinus* 'stranger'. Here again we have two notions which seem difficult to reconcile with the historical meaning of the terms.

Now, this feature of Latin is not isolated. Other Indo-European languages associate the word for "field," in an adverbial form, with the idea of "outside."

Whereas in Greek *agrõi* usually means "in the country" in contrast to "in town," elsewhere we find "in the field" means no more than "outside." Thus Armenian *artak*ᶜ*s* 'outside' is derived from *art* 'field'. In the Baltic languages, Lith. *laũkas* 'field' (Latin *lūcus*) has an adverbial for *lauke* 'outside'. Irish has *immach* 'outside' from **in mag* 'in the fields'.

These different but parallel terms conjure up the image of an ancient relationship: the uncultivated ground, the waste land, as opposed to the inhabited area. Outside this physical community, which constitutes the family or tribal habitat, stretches the waste land. This is where the extraneous world begins, and what is strange is necessarily hostile. The Greek adjective derived from *agrós* 'field' is *ágrios*, which means "wild," "savage," and so gives us more or less the counterpart of what is called in Latin *domesticus*, which brings us back to *domus*. Whether we start from an opposition like *domi/foris* or from the wider one in which it is opposed to the "field" (*domi/peregre*), we always come to the same conclusion, namely that *domus* denotes the "house" in its social and moral aspects and not as a construction.

In the light of *domus* and the related forms we can assess the richness and specificity of a terminology which must be counted among the most ancient of the Indo-European world. The other terms relating to the political structure of society are less well attested, according as they apply to larger entities. We might say that the dialectal extension of terms is inversely proportional to the generality of concepts.

We started, we may remind ourselves, with the Avestan series *dam-*, *vīs-*, *zantu*, (*dahyu*). Now the data are more abundant for the first than for the second division. Both have in common a tendency to assume the meaning of physical habitat.

The third, *zantu*, belongs to the same etymological family as Lat. *gens* and Gr. *génos*, but it differs from these two in its formation. It differs from Lat. *gens* in that it contains a suffix *-tu* against Lat. *-ti*. The study of the two suffixes and their relationship would involve a long discussion, which we have presented elsewhere.[3] Both have the capacity of forming abstract nouns; *-ti* has developed more especially in compounds, *-tu* in simple words. Nevertheless there are simple words in *-ti*, and *gens* is one of them.

From a morphological point of view, Latin *gens* has a correspondent in the Avestan derivative *fra-zanti-* 'line of descent', as well as in Gothic *kindins*

3. *Noms d'agent et noms d'action en indo-européen*, Paris, 1948, 2nd part.

(from **gentinos*) '*hēgemṓn*, governor', a word which has been analyzed above. But the Avestan word *zantu-* is limited to Indo-Iranian; moreover, Ved. *jantu-* 'living creature; a collection of human beings, race', which corresponds to it, does not have the institutional meaning which attaches to Avestan *zantu-*. We can see here that the situation of *zantu* is different from that of *gens*, and in spite of the resemblance of the terms, there is nothing to prove that they are of the same date.

The important fact is that, as compared with the neuter *génos* in Greek, we have here words of what is called the "animate" gender, masculine-feminine. The sense of these terms remains close to that of the root **gen-*, which does not indicate only physical birth, but birth as a social fact. A number of nominal derivatives make this clear. In a social organization defined by its classes, the birth is the condition of personal status. Terms are required which by the names themselves characterize the birth as legitimate, because of the rights conferred on those whose legitimacy is acknowledged. Besides, such legitimacy is valid first for the men; it is to the men that the collective nouns derived from the root **gen-* are applied, and they designate the group which recognizes a common ancestor in the male line. The following conditions express the essential feature of the notion: free, legitimate birth and male descent. They help us to define better these parallel terms from the same linguistic stock, Av. *zantu*, Lat. *gens*, Gr. *génos*.

But the size of the group which each of these terms designates may vary from society to society; they do not occupy the same place in the vocabulary of social and territorial divisions. If in the Iranian series, *zantu* is the third largest social group, *génos* on the contrary is the starting point of the Greek series. We come back to the great transformation which in Greece culminated in a new organization of the ancient structure. In Athens, in the ancient form of society, above the *génos* was the *phratría*, and above the *phratría* the *phulḗ*. According to the Athenian constitution, thirty *génē* (plural of *génos*) were necessary to form a *phratría*, and three *phratríai* constituted a *phulḗ*. Here, then, we have specific words which were applied to new entities. But the words themselves are old Indo-European formations, and the notions which they convey formed part of those which informed the ancient Indo-European societies.

This transformation of the ancient structure which finally resulted in the *kṓmē* and the *pólis* cannot be connected with any external event, except perhaps the establishment of the Greeks in their historical home and the new circumstances of this habitat. We cannot discern any foreign influence. Everything seems to proceed from native Greek sources—the structure, as well as the vocabulary, of these institutions.

As we proceed from *génos* to *phratría*, we pass from a group founded on common descent to a group formed by the totality of "brothers." These are not blood brothers, but brothers only insofar as they recognize themselves as descended from a common ancestor. This mythical relationship is a profoundly Indo-European notion; and Greek has preserved, better than any other language, the original sense of *phrátēr*. This is also the case for the correlative term *patḗr* in Greek (and partially in Latin, too).[4]

This conservatism is still apparent in many social usages described in the epic. The Heroic Age of which it tells was an historical age. We have in certain respects, in the Homeric usage of certain words, in the connection between the different human groups, the image of what common Indo-European society must have been—in civil life and in war. The manner in which the family, the clan assemble, what their chiefs speak about and how they act, must reflect quite closely the behavior of the warrior class in the Indo-European world. We quote only two passages:

> ἀφρήτωρ ἀθέμιστος ἀνέστιός ἐστιν ἐκεῖνος
> ὃς πολέμου ἔραται ἐπιδημίου...
>
> – *Iliad* 9, 63f.

This condemns the man who wages a "civil" war, πόλεμος ἐπιδήμιος, against his fellow citizens within the same *dêmos*.[5] Such a man is without phratry, without *thémis*, without a hearth (*hestía*). The notions of phratry and *hestía* are correlative, and between the two, *thémis* is the customary law which holds good in the family.[6] The nature of these notions, and especially their interconnection, reproduce those which we have studied from a different angle above.

We thus have, in inverse order, the series: *hestía*, the "hearth," that is to say *domus*; then *thémis*, the customs which constitute the law, and lastly the phratry. Only the two first divisions of society are mentioned or implied here, because what is concerned is a personal crime. But in war, it is the large social units which are involved, and this is what tests their solidarity. When battle is joined,

4. Cf. Book Two, Chapter One.
5. On *dêmos* see Book Four, Chapter Nine.
6. On *thémis* cf. Book Five, Chapter One.

it is this solidarity which must be maintained among the members of the same clan and the same tribe. This condition governs the disposition of the troops and the plan of battle.

Nestor says as much to Agamemnon:

> κρῖν' ἄνδρας κατὰ φῦλα κατὰ φρήτρας, Ἀγάμεμνον,
> ὡς φρήτρη φρήτρηφιν ἀρήγῃ, φῦλα δὲ φύλοις.
> – *Iliad* 2, 362–63.

"Position the men by *phûlon* and by *phrḗtrē* so that *phrḗtrē* may aid *phrḗtrē* and *phûla phûla*." To be victorious in the great trial of strength which battle represents is everybody's affair; the organization of the army must conform to the structure of society. In this way it will have the greatest effectiveness.

We find in the ancient texts of India and Iran similar recommendations. "Friend" fights with "friend": each social group must maintain or reconstitute its unity in all circumstances in which the whole of the society is engaged. This principle is not always stated in so explicit a manner as in Homer, but it is no less inherent in the functioning of the institutions of each class.

It remains to consider the last term of the series. This is, in contrast to the two others, limited to Iranian. The Avestan word for "country," *dahyu* (ancient *dasyu*) has as its Sanskrit correspondent *dasyu*. In spite of the complete identity of form, some scholars doubt the connection because of the difference in sense. In Avestan and Old Persian, *dahyu* signifies "country"; in Vedic, *dasyu* is a foreign slave. But the difference can be explained in the light of the older stage of these notions.

In Indic, *dasyu* may be taken as an ethnic. The *dasyu* are a foreign people which the Aryans had to fight; they are barbarians, slaves.

But in Iranian, *dahyu* is part of the traditional and official vocabulary. Darius proclaims himself as "King of Countries (*dahyu*)." This is a reference to each of the "countries" Persia, Media, Armenia, Egypt, etc., the union of which constituted the Achaemenid Empire. This term must have had a long history in Iranian. It even originated in Iranian society. Today we have some possibility of analyzing its formation. An eastern Iranian dialect, Khotanese, possesses the word *daha* 'man'. We know from other sources that in the Iranian world there were a people, the *Dahae*, as they are called by Latin authors. This people, like many others, simply called themselves "the men." Thanks to this connection, the sense of *dahyu* becomes clear: it is a derivative based on the root **das-*, of which we have little evidence, signifying a group of men, the most extensive in the tribal order, and hence also the territory they occupy.

We can now understand the strange sense of Skt. *dasyu*. If the word referred at first to Iranian society, the name by which this enemy people called themselves collectively took on a hostile connotation and became for the Aryas of India the term for an inferior and barbarous people. Thus the connection between the senses of *dahyu*/*dasyu* reflects conflicts between the Indian and Iranian peoples.[7]

7. Cf. Book Three, Chapter Five.

BOOK III, CHAPTER THREE

The Free Man

Abstract. Although the opposition "free/slave" is common to all Indo-European peoples, a common designation of the notion of "liberty" is unknown. The fact that this designation evolved along parallel lines in two groups of languages merely serves to bring out better the specific content of the notion.

In Latin and Greek the free man, *(*e*)*leudheros*, is positively defined by his membership of a "breed," of a "stock"; proof of this, in Latin, is the designation of (well-born) children as *liberi*; to be born of good stock is to be free; it comes to the same thing.

In Germanic, the connection which is still felt, for instance, between German *frei* 'free' and *Freund* allows us to reconstitute a primitive notion of liberty as the belonging to a closed group of those who call one another "friends." To his membership of this group—of breed or of friends—the individual owes not only his free status but also "his own self": the derivatives of the term **swe*, Gr. *idiṓtēs* 'individual', Latin *suus* 'his', but also Greek *étēs*, *hetaîros* 'ally, companion', Latin *sodalis* 'companion, colleague', show that the primitive **swe* was the word for a social entity, each member of which realizes his "self" only in the "inter-self."

The general framework of Indo-European society and the great divisions it comprises are already "institutions." To bring greater precision to our study, we shall now investigate the fundamental notions which inform the structure of these institutions.

Each of the Indo-European societies is pervaded by a distinction founded on free or servile condition. One is born free or born a slave. In Rome we have the division between *liberi* and *servi*. In Greece, the free man, *eleútheros* (ἐλεύθερος), is opposed to *doúlos* (δοῦλος).

In Germany, according to Tacitus, society comprised *nobiles*, *ingenui*, *liberti* and *servi*. It is clear that *nobiles* and *ingenui*, with the distinction of nobility and birth, are the equivalent of the *liberi*; on the other hand, the *servi* form a group with the *liberti*, former *servi*. Thus the division of society, evidenced by these four terms, is much the same. In India, the *ārya* (the name by which the Indo-Iranians called themselves) are opposed to *dāsa* (slaves and foreigners).

Despite innovations of terminology the same institution is maintained. But we have at least one term common to two or more languages: Lat. *līber*/Gr. *eleútheros*. There is a perfect correspondence; the two terms can be superimposed and traced back to an ancient form *(*e*)*leudheros*, which is found in a third language, in Venetic.

There is in fact a Venetic goddess *Louzera*, the Latin equivalent of which would be *Libera*, the feminine consort of the god *Liber*, who is identified with Bacchus. Furthermore, we have a case form *louzeroφos*, interpreted as *liberibus*, with a root diphthong -*ou*-, which is accounted for by the ablaut alternation *e*/*o*, as in Faliscan *loferta* (= *liberta*) and Oscan *Luvfreis* (gen. sing.) (= *Līberī*), as contrasted with *(*e*)*leud-heros*, Lat. *līber*.

The etymological analysis brings to light in *liber* a complex of relationships. First and foremost, we must decide whether there is one word *liber* or several. For are the adjective *liber* and *Liber*, the name of a divinity, one and the same words? There are also *liberi* 'children', which is apparently something different again. What complicates the question in another way is that the root from which *liber* and *eleútheros* are made, that is, **leudh*-, produces in Old Slav. *ljudŭ*, 'the people', *ljudĭje* '*gens*'; in Germanic, in OHG *liut*, OE *leod*, modern German *Leute* 'people'. Finally, apart from these adjectives and nouns, the verbal root supplies in Gothic *liudan* 'grow'; in Indo-Iranian, Skt. *rudh*-, Av. *rud*- 'grow, develop'.

The relationship between these forms is easy to establish, but what are we to make of the variety of meanings? These are so peculiar that at first sight they seem irreconcilable. How can we explain by a root **leudh*- 'to grow, develop' a collective term for "the people," then the adjective "free," and, locally in Latin, a divine name *Liber* and a noun *liberi* 'children'?

We have here a fairly frequent model of the relationships to be studied: at one extremity of the chain (in the case of Rome), the term refers to institutions, whereas elsewhere it forms part of other structures and designates different things.

Let us begin with the simplest forms, the verbal ones: Gothic *liudan* means "increase, grow" and it is used of a plant which reaches fullness of growth. In fact this verb *liudan* also gives rise to *laudi* 'figure', and *-lauþs* in the compound *jugga-lauþs*, literally "of young stature"; *sama-lauþs* 'of the same growth, equal'. Similarly, in Indo-Iranian we have Skt. *rudh-*, Av. *rud-*, *raod-* 'grow', and the Av. noun *raodah-* 'growth, stature, figure'.

We now see how the image of accomplished growth, culminating in "stature" and the human figure, has produced elsewhere a collective notion such as "stock, breed," or "growth group" to designate an ethnic group, the totality of those who have been born and grown up together. The social sense of a noun such as **leudho-* favored the transition to the sense of "people" (as in Old Slavic *ljudĭje* 'people' and in Germanic *leod* 'people'). From this noun **leudho-* (or **leudhes-*) it was easy to form the adjective *(*e*)*leudhero-* to designate those who belong to the same ethnic stock and enjoy the status of "free men."

It thus appears that the notion of "liberty" was constituted from a socialized notion of "growth," the growth of a social category, the development of a community. All those who issued from that "stock" are endowed with the quality of * (*e*)*leudheros*.

We can now return to *liber* and recognize the connection between the several different notions it designated. The god *Liber* and the adjective *liber* may coexist without the name of the god being an application of the adjective. *Liber*, like the Venetic *Louzera*, is the god of growth of vegetation, later specialized in the domain of viniculture.

Eleútheros, *liber*: the pair of words now illuminates the origin of the notion of "liberty." In Latin, as in Greek, all the ideas which we connect with the word "free" appear from the earliest texts on: the word is used with reference to the *free* man in the city, and the man who is *free* of illness, of suffering (with the genitive). In Homer, *eleútheron ễmar* (ἐλεύθερον ἦμαρ) 'the free day' designates the day which is that of the free man, the state of being free, and it is opposed to *doúlion ễmar* (δούλιον ἦμαρ) 'the day of slavery'.

We grasp the social origins of the concept of "free." The first sense is not, as one would be tempted to imagine, "to be free of, rid of something"; it is that of belonging to an ethnic stock designated by a metaphor taken from vegetable growth. Such membership confers a privilege which a stranger and a slave will never possess.

Let us consider finally the term *liberi* 'children'. It shows a double peculiarity: first, it is only used in the plural; further, and this is particularly important, it designates the children by age only, not by social condition. Nevertheless, *liberi* 'children' is nothing more than the plural of the adjective *liber*. It is explained by a very ancient formula which accompanied the celebration of marriage and which we find in legal texts and in Plautus. It describes the purpose of marriage. The man who gave his daughter in marriage addressed the future husband with the words *liber(or)um quaesundum causa* (or *gratia*) 'to obtain legitimate children'. This formula recurs in Greece, where it is well established through the allusions of Attic orators, by a quotation of Menander, and various legal texts. The pronouncement is literally the same: *epì paídōn gnēsíōn sporā̂i* (ἐπὶ παίδων γνησίων σπορᾷ) 'to generate *legitimate* children'. If we keep to the proper sense of *liber*, we can translate the Latin formula literally as "to obtain free (beings)"; the aim of marriage is precisely to give to those who will be born the status of free persons by legalizing their birth. It is in this phrase, and only by implication, as an object of *quaerere* 'to obtain', that *liberi* has taken on the sense of "children"; by itself, the plural *liberi* is equivalent to *paîdes gnḗsioi* (παῖδες γνήσιοι) of the Greek formula. It was in the legal language that this development of meaning originated. There are numerous legal terms which passed into the common vocabulary of Latin. Thus *liber*, which corresponds to *gnḗsios* 'of free birth', ended up by forming an independent term, *liberi* 'children'. Such is the formation of the notion of "liberty," which we have been able to reconstruct by combining facts which at first sight seemed irreconcilable and by resuscitating a deep-lying conceptual image, that of "the stock."[1]

The history of this term throws light on the formation of the concept of the "free man" in those languages where it is expressed by a derivative of **leudh-*, such as the Gr. *eleútheros*, by showing the primary notion from which the concept evolved.

But the genesis of the corresponding term was different in other parts of the Indo-European world, where different terms have prevailed and remain in use today. What especially deserves our attention is the Germanic *frei* (German *frei*, English *free*). Thanks to favorable conditions for comparison, here, too, we can describe the genesis of a word which has become synonymous with Gr. *eleútheros* but which evolved, along quite different lines, notions relating to the individual and not to the society.

1. Cf. our article "*Liber* et *liberi*," *Revue des Etudes Latines*, XIV, 1936, pp. 51-58.

The dialect distribution of the forms in the present case seems complementary to that of *(*e*)*leudheros* in the sense that neither Greek nor Latin possess the etymological correspondent. Conversely, the languages which share with Germanic the word *frei* did not use derivatives of **leudh-* to express the notion of "free." In this way a lexical distribution came about between the dialects which permits us to compare two distinct processes which started from different points and finally converged.

The evolution which has produced *frei* 'free' in Germanic starts not from a verbal root, but from an Indo-European adjective which can be reconstructed as **priyos*. This alone is worth noting: everything has evolved, from common Indo-European times onwards, from a nominal form, from an adjective, attested as such in Indo-Iranian, Slavic, Germanic and Celtic, which has remained productive. The second fact worth noting is the sense of **priyos*. This term indicates a notion of an emotional character which appears clearly in Indo-Iranian, where Sanskrit *priya*, Av. *frya-* means "dear." The adjective is in fact charged with the sentimental overtones which we attach to the word "dear," i.e. it qualifies those for whom we feel affection. But in certain idiomatic usages it refers to personal possessions and even to parts of the body. It can be shown that this was the original sense: **priyos* is the adjective for personal belongings, implying not a legal but an emotional connection with the "self" and always prone to take on a sentimental coloring. The result is that, according to the context, it can be translated sometimes by "his own" and sometimes by "dear, beloved." This aspect of the notion is the one most apparent and which becomes most frequent: thus *priya-* in Vedic qualifies the beings most closely associated with the person and which are "close" to him in affection: the feminine *priyā* 'dear' was substantivized and became the name for "wife." The personal sphere also occasionally comprises the relations between man and the gods, thus expressing a sort of "mutual belonging." Vedic *priya-*, Av. *frya-* thus enter into the religious terminology.

On the basis of this ancient adjective, Slavic has coined a present denominative *prijaję* (Russ. *prijaju*) 'to show oneself favorable, to show affection', from which comes the agent noun *prijatel'* 'friend', known in all Slavic languages.

In Germanic, too, the sentimental value is apparent from Gothic onwards in the verb *frijon* 'to love' (translating Gr. *agapân, phileîn*) and in the abstract noun *friaþwa* 'love'. The participle *frijonds* 'friend', OHG *friunt* 'friend' survives in this sense to our own days (German *Freund*, English *friend*).

But Gothic also possesses the adjective *freis* 'free, *eleútheros*' with the abstract noun *frijei* 'liberty, *eleuthería*', that is to say, the literal correspondent of the ancient **priyos*, but with quite a different sense, that of "free." It shares this function with Welsh *rhydd* 'free', which also goes back to **priyos*. There is thus in Gothic a division between *frijon* 'to love' and *freis* 'free'. This peculiar lexical situation suggests that the passage of *freis* to the sense of "free" was due in Gothic to Celtic influences, where **priyos* signifies only "free." Perhaps it is even a direct borrowing in Gothic from Celtic. This specialization is not attested anywhere except Celtic and Germanic.

The evolution from the Indo-European sense of "personal, dear" to that of "free" which appears in Celtic and Gothic may be explained by the exclusiveness of a social class. What was a personal qualification of a sentimental kind became a sign of mutual recognition which was exchanged between members of the class of the "well-born." It is a tendency of closed sections of society to develop among those who belong to it the sense of closely belonging to the same group, and to evolve a distinctive vocabulary. The term which in its first form expressed an affectionate relationship between persons, **priyos*, took on an institutional sense when it became the name for the members of a kind of class "friendly society" and later the denomination for a social status, that of "free" men.[2]

Finally, a last word for "free" is the ancient Iranian *āzāta-* (Persian *āzād*). It properly signifies "born of the stock," the preverb *ā-* marking the descent towards and up to a present moment. It is always birth in a succession of generations which guarantees the condition of a "free man."

The history of these terms imposes the conclusion that words for individual social status and class status are often connected with individual notions such as that of "birth," or with terms for friendship, like those which are applied to each other by members of closed groups. These names mark them off from strangers, slaves and, in general, from those who are not "well-born."

We must draw attention to a fact which is rarely commented upon: how closely connected with certain forms of society some of the terms are which define the individual in his personal status.

A whole group of words with different interconnections will serve to illustrate these relations, some of them directly, others in a more distant way. We

2. A recent bibliography of the problem is given, with a different interpretation, by F. Metzger, *Zeitschrift für vergleichende Sprachforschung*, 79 (1965), p. 36ff.

shall first consider the Gr. adjective *ídios* (ἴδιος), which is connected with the notion of "private, what belongs to somebody," as opposed to what is public or common to all. The origin of the term has been much discussed. It could not be solved until an Argive inscription was found (on Dorian territory) with the word *whediestas* (*wh*εδιεστας), which was recognized as the local form of the classical term *idiṓtēs* (ἰδιώτης). This form *whediestas* is of great interest because of its orthography with *wh-* (going back to an original initial **sw-*), as well as the vocalism *e* of the first syllable. It shows that the initial *i-* of *ídios* is an ancient *e-* that has been assimilated to the following *-i-*. In addition to this, the formation of *whediestas* does not accord exactly with that of *idiṓtes*. The Argive word belongs to a category of social terms in *-estās*, Ionic-Attic *-estēs*, like Gr. *penéstēs* 'mercenary, domestic' (in Thessaly). But the root is identical in the Argive *whediestas* and in Gr. *idiótēs*, and this is now reconstructed as **swed-*. In two slightly different forms, we have here the Greek designation for "the individual, the private citizen," as opposed to the public personage, the one who holds power or fulfils a public function. As so often, each of the Indo-European languages has used in its own way an inherited root and each has made its own specific derivatives. This is the case with the Greek term in question, for which no other languages offer a correspondent.

However, there exists a related form in the Latin adjective *sodālis*, a derivative in *-ālis* from a stem *sod-*, which can be traced back to **swed-*. Between *sodālis* 'companion, colleague', especially "member of a religious college," and the Greek *whediestas*, in spite of the difference in institution, there appears a common trait, that of a closed circle around the "private person," or a closed professional group. This trait specifies it and separates it from the rest of society by conferring a special status. The characterization remains a social one; it takes its place among the words for classes and functions, as is shown respectively by the Greek formation in *-estās* and the Latin one in *-ālis*.

Let us now consider the radical element itself, **swed-*, an enlarged form of the basic term **swe*. This **swe*, which is attested in a long series of different words, is a very important term of the Indo-European vocabulary. Its intrinsic meaning can be seen in isolation in a definite morphological category (see below on the pronoun). Its final *e* is fixed, constant, without vocalic alternation; it is therefore not the ending of an inflected term. We have here a vestige of an archaic state: **swe* remains fixed also in compounds or derivatives.

Its final *-e* is found in a small group of other words which likewise testify to a very ancient linguistic stage and which survived as such in various parts of the vocabulary: e.g. *k^w *e*, an enclitic meaning "and," Gr. *te* (τε), Lat. *que*, Skt. *-ca*; the root, with another vocalic grade, is found in the stem of the relative interrogative *k^w *o-*, Gr. *po-* (πο-: πότερος, πόσος) and in *k^w *i*, Gr. *ti, tis* (τι, τις). But *k^w *e*, with the fixed final ending *e*, has the form and function of a particle, and it is not susceptible to inflexion or alternation.

Another word which presents this final *-e* is the numeral **penk*^{w} *e* 'five', Gr. *pénte* (πέντε), Lat. *quinque*, Skt. *panca*, the endings of which, *-te*, *-que*, *-ca*, exactly reproduce the forms of the connective particle: Gr. *-te*, Lat. *-que*, Skt. *-ca*.

This word **swe* has given rise to an adjective indicating "personal belonging": Skt. *sva-*, Lat. *suus*, Gr. **swós* (*σwός). We must note that **swos* is not in Indo-European the pronoun of the third person singular, as might be supposed by the relation of Lat. *suus* to *meus* and *tuus*. We instinctively make *suus* the third term of the series. Just as we put *I*, *you*, *he* in the verbal inflexion, it seems normal to us to have the pronominal series *my*, *your*, *his*. The relationship of these forms was quite different in Indo-European: **swos* is the reflexive and possessive pronoun equally applicable to all persons.

This is what we still see today in the Slavic languages: Russian has *svoj* for "(my, your, his, our, your, their) own." Similarly, Gothic *swes* 'own, personal' was used with reference to any person whatsoever. Again, in Sanskrit *sva-* was used without distinction where, with us, the insertion of *mine* or *yours* would be necessary. This neutrality as regards the person reveals the fundamental sense of the word.[3]

It has already been noted above (Book Two, Chapter One) that **swe* appears in the ancient compound **swe-sor* 'sister' as well as in **swekrū-* 'mother-in-law', **swekuro-* 'father-in-law'.

In this connection we may note a peculiar feature of the terms for kinship formed from **swe* in Slavic, Baltic, and particularly in Germanic; in this group the terms derived from **swe* refer to kinship by alliance and not to consanguineous kinship. This is a common feature of a whole group of terms: Russian *svat* 'suitor' and also "related by marriage" (for instance for the relationship between the husband's father and the wife's father); *svojak* (a derivative from *svoj* 'own') 'brother-in-law', *svest'* (feminine) 'wife's sister'; Lithuanian *sváinis*,

3. We have no occasion here to study the formal relationship between the alternating stems **swe* and **se*. For a reconstruction of an older state of affairs we refer to *Bulletin de la Société de Linguistique de Paris* 50, 1954, p. 36ff. The stem **sw-* is also relevant to the formations of the derivatives that figure in the present study.

'wife's brother, sister's husband', fem. *svainé* 'wife's sister, brother's wife'; Old High German *swîo*, *geswîo* 'brother-in-law, sister's husband'. If we have in these derivatives survivals of an ancient lexical state of affairs, we can see how interesting they are for the interpretation of those fundamental words common to all Indo-European languages which seem to be composed with **swe*, that is, "sister" (**swesor-*) and "parents-in-law" (**swekrū-*, etc.). It would mean that these terms connect those so designated with the other exogamic "moiety." In fact, the sister belongs there potentially, and the mother-in-law does so in fact. Theoreticians, who might be prompted by the present study to reconsider the analysis of kinship in Indo-European societies, will be better able to assess the significance which is to be attached to this observation.

This **swe* is likewise the stem of the Gr. word *étēs* (ἔτης) 'kinsman, relation' and *hetaîros* (ἑταῖρος) 'companion'. These two words, which are used together in Homer and in competition with one another, are closely related in sense, although they differ in their suffixation. It would be necessary to study the passages in which the two words occur if we wanted to make an exact distinction between them. It seems, however, that *hetaîros* has a more precise signification: "companion," "friend" in the exercise of some activity, in battle, but it is not properly speaking a term of kinship, while *étēs* designates "kinsmen" in general.

In *étēs* 'kinsman' and also, dialectally, "fellow citizen," "private person," the root **swe* points to a connection with *whediestas* 'private person'. In the two words the same fundamental notion is evident, a notion which we also detect in another semantic family in Greek, the perfect *eíōtha* (εἴωθα) 'to be accustomed to' and the noun *éthos* (ἔθος) 'habit'. The verbal form and the nominal form particularize the notion of "habit" as a distinctive mark and manner of being individual.

We may thus identify **swe* in several groups of Greek forms where it is specialized by distinctive affixes:

**swe-d-*	in	*ídios*
**swe-t-*	in	*étēs*
**swe-dh-*	in	*éthos*

These few examples illuminate the relationships which connect the concept signified by the root **swe* with a group of derivatives, all implying a bond of a social character of kinship or sentiment, such as companionship, alliance (by marriage) and friendship.

If we now take a comprehensive view of all the derivations based on the stem **swe*, we observe that they divide along two conceptual lines. On the one hand **swe* implies the membership of a group of "own people"; on the other it specializes the "self" in its individuality. The interest of such a notion is evident, both for general linguistics and for philosophy. The notion of "self," of the *reflexive*, is crystallized here. It is this expression which a person uses to delimit himself as an individual and to refer to "himself." But at the same time the subjectivity is expressed as a "belonging." The notion of **swe* is not limited to the person itself; from the beginning it implies a tight and closed group which encompasses the "self."

All that is ascribable to **swe* becomes **swos*, Lat. *suus* 'his' (in the sense indicated above), and ownership proper is defined only within the group included within the limits of **swe*. Thus, to return to the Greek terms, **swe* explains at the same time *ídios* 'peculiar to oneself' and *hetaîros*, which implies a bond with an age group or a profession. The situation which has been reconstituted by this connection reproduces the proper sense of Indo-European **swe*, which implies both distinctiveness from all else, the isolation of the "self," the effort to separate oneself from everything which is not **swe*, and also, within the exclusive circle thus marked off, the close relationship with those who form part of it. From this comes the double heritage, both *idiṓtēs*, the isolated member of society, and also the *sodālis*, the member of a closed fraternity.

This duality survived, as is revealed by the etymology, in the two forms *se* of Latin, which have become independent; the reflexive *se*, indicating "self," and the separative *se-*, *sed* 'but', marking distinction and opposition.

We see here again (as in the case of *liberty*) that it is society and social institutions which furnish concepts which are apparently the most personal. In this great lexical complex made up of numerous subdivisions which has evolved from the term **swe*, institutional values consort with those of personal self-reference, and these prepare the way, at a higher degree of abstraction, for the grammatical categories of "person."

This double relationship is apparent in the historical facts; Sanskrit *sva-* signifies "his," but in a technical sense which goes beyond mere personal possession. *Sva-* is applied to the person who forms part of the same tight group; this term plays an important role in legal provisions affecting property, inheritance or the succession to titles and honors. The corresponding term exists with the same technical meaning in Latin. In the Law of the Twelve Tables, there is a clause relating to inheritance: "if a man dies intestate, *heres suus nec escit*

(= *non sit*), and if he has no heir who is a *suus*." The expression *heres suus* is also an archaism, for *suus*, if it had only a possessive sense, would not be necessary. A *heres* who is a *suus*, this is what the provision intends: there is no transmission of property outside the *sui*, that is to say the closed group of immediate descendants; it remains within the group of collaterals.

We observe all kinds of developments which start from these connections. Gradually legal kinship, and the consciousness of self, the connections of confraternity and individuality, are constituted as autonomous concepts and develop groups of new terms. But the comparison and analysis of these lexical families reveal their initial unity and lay bare the social foundations of the "self" and the "inter-self."

BOOK III, CHAPTER FOUR

Phílos

Abstract. The specific values of Lat. *cīvis* 'fellow citizen', Got. *heiwa-* 'family group', Skt. *śeva* 'friendly' lead us to postulate for the Indo-European word **keiwo-*, which these words enable us to reconstruct, a meaning with both a social reference and sentimental overtones.

The uses, especially the Homeric ones, of Gr. *phílos* and its derivatives point in the same direction, however unsure we may be about the full sense. The social meaning is prior and connected in particular with hospitality—the guest is *phílos* and benefits from the specific treatment designated by *phileîn* 'to be hospitable'—but also with other forms of attachment and of mutual gratitude: *phileîn, philótēs* may imply the exchange of oaths and *phílēma* denotes the "kiss," the regular form of greeting or welcome among *phíloi*. Emotional values appear when the term is used with reference to relations within a family group: *phílos* 'dear', *philótēs* 'love'.

Such are the constant values of *phílos*, and meticulous analysis of the passages where *phílos* qualifies objects and enables us to dispel the illusion, as old as Homeric philology itself, that *phílos* could be equivalent to a simple possessive word.

A connection between the terms signifying "friend" and others which denote in various ways "possession" is a fact of far-reaching importance. The use of these terms throws light on the close connection between social notions and sentimental values in Indo-European. But this connection is not apparent at first sight.

Let us consider the Latin term *cīvis* 'citizen', from which the abstract noun *cīvitās* is derived, designating properly the quality of a citizen and, collectively, the totality of the citizens, the city itself. *Cīvis* is peculiar to Latin vocabulary and it is hardly represented in Italic. So far as it designates the "citizen" it has no correspondent elsewhere. We can, however, link it together with terms found in Sanskrit and Germanic which can be equated formally, but which present a very different sense: Skt. *śeva-* 'friendly', Goth. *heiwafrauja*, which translates Gr. *oikodespótēs* 'head of the family'. The Gothic form *heiwa-* exactly coincides with those of Sanskrit and Latin. All three presuppose an ancient **keiwo-s*, which in Latin became an *i*-stem.

We are here confronted with a term common to a group of languages which is certainly ancient, but which had a different semantic evolution in each of them. Faced with these divergences some etymologists have doubted the correctness of this connection. But the objections do not take into consideration the relationships revealed by a closer examination of these forms, considered in their proper context.

In Germanic, the notion can be defined as familial and conjugal. The Gothic compound *heiwa-frauja* (with *frauja* 'master') translates Gr. *oikodespótēs* in Mark 14, 14, where the sense is "head of the family (who performs his duties of hospitality)." In other passages where Gr. *oikodespótēs* designates the "master of the house" with reference to his slaves, Gothic uses a different term, *garda-waldans*. The choice is instructive. To render the same Greek title, the translator distinguishes two notions; the "master of the house" is, according to the context, rendered either as *garda-waldans* 'he who has the power (*waldan*) in the precincts of the house (*gards*)', i.e. the one who commands the servants, or *heiwa-frauja* 'he who is master (*frauja*) of the family', i.e. the one who welcomes the passing guest under his roof. Gothic separates the "house" as a place of habitation and an enclosed domain (*gards*) from the "house" as a family grouping and a circle of personal relations, which is called *heiwa-*. In other Germanic languages this sense is clearly confirmed by Old High German *hīwo* 'husband', *hiwa* 'wife', *hīun* (Old Icel. *hjōn, hjū*) 'conjugal couple', *hīrat* (German *Heirat*) 'marriage', Old Icel. *hy-ske* 'family', etc. All these show that **keiwo-* (**kiwo-*) referred in ancient Germanic to the situation of persons united by the marriage bond and comprised in the family circle. This institutional notion also appears in the Skt. words *śeva-*, *śiva*-which are translated as "propitious, friendly, dear." They reflect the sentimental aspect of a relation between groups. This is seen especially in the very frequent association in the

Vedic hymns between *śeva-*, *śiva-* and *sakhā-* 'companion' (cf. Latin *socius*), implying a certain type of friendly behavior towards partners in the alliance.

Finally, Latin *cīvis* is also a term of companionship implying a community of habitat and political rights. The authentic sense of *cīvis* is not "citizen," as it is traditionally translated, but "fellow-citizen." A number of ancient uses show the sense of reciprocity which is inherent in *cīvis*, and which alone accounts for *cīvitās* as a collective notion. We must look upon *cīvis* as the designation by which the members of a group, who enjoy indigenous rights, originally addressed each other, as contrasted with the different varieties of "strangers," *hostes*, *peregrini*, *advenae*. It is in Latin that Indo-European **keiwos* (in the form of **keiwis*) acquired its strongest institutional sense. From the ancient relationship of "friendship," which Vedic *śeva-* denotes, to the better attested sense "group by matrimonial alliance," which appears in Germanic *heiwa-* and, finally, to the concept of "co-partners in political rights," which Latin *cīvis* expresses, there is a progression in three stages from the "closed group" to "the city."

In this way we can restore the connection between "the house" as the family circle (Gothic *heiwa*), and the group within which the man who is a member of it is called *cīvis*. This close association engenders friendly relations: Skt. *śeva-* 'dear' is one of these terms which transpose what once expressed membership into a term of affection.

Not only is this connection irreproachable but it also illustrates the real nature of "friendship" at an ancient stage of the societies which are called Indo-European, where sentiment was inseparable from a lively awareness of group and class membership.

To this same category belongs another term of greater complexity, the history of which is played out in only one language—Greek. It appears to have an exclusively sentimental value and at first sight does not imply any truly social notions: this is the Gr. adjective *phílos* (φίλος) 'friend'.

To all appearances nothing looks simpler than the connection between *phílos* 'friend' and *philótēs*, *philía* 'friendship'. But what gives us pause is the well-known fact that in Homer *phílos* has two meanings: besides that of "friend," *phílos* also has a possessive sense: *phíla goúnata*, *phílos huiós* (φίλα γούνατα, φίλος υἱός) do not indicate friendship, but possession: "his knees," "his son." Inasmuch as it expresses a possessive, *phílos* is used without reference to grammatical person, and may refer, according to context, to the first, second, or third person. It is a mark of possession which does not imply any friendly relation. Such is the difference between the two senses of *phílos*.

This has been much discussed; it suffices to recall the latest proposed attempts at an explanation. There is in fact no immediate satisfactory etymological connection for *phílos*. In 1923, Loewe[1] suggested that *phílos* might be connected with the first term in certain Germanic personal names: Old High German *Bil(i)-frid*, *Bil-trud*, *Bili-gard* etc. and further, with an Old English adjective *bilewit* 'compassionate'. He traces all these terms back to the original sense of "well-meaning, friendly," and then compares the stem of the Old English adjective with that of Gr. *phílos*. To this one can object that, first, the interpretation is made *ad hoc* from proper names which do not even belong to common Germanic; further, the Old English term does not actually signify "friendly"; finally, we have no ancient Germanic form for which we can posit with certainty an adjectival use.

In our case we are still left with the problem of explaining the possessive sense of *phílos*. This was felt by Kretschmer, who proposed a solution along quite different lines.[2] Like some other linguists he starts from the possessive sense, reversing the connection between the two *phílos*. He thinks that the original sense of *phílos* was "his"; this developed to "friend," and this evolution of sense is supported by the analogy of Lat. *suus*. From the fact that *suus*, a possessive pronoun, gave rise to such expressions as *sui* 'his own people' and *aliquem suum reddere* 'to make somebody his friend', Kretschmer concludes that it is easy to pass from a possessive relationship to one of friendship. This would impel us to seek the etymology of *phílos* no longer as meaning "dear," but as an ancient possessive. Now, neither the root nor the formation in *-l-* has correspondents among possessive pronouns within the classical limits of Indo-European. So Kretschmer adduced a Lydian word *bilis*, which in all probability signifies "his own," and connects it with *phílos*.

The demonstration is hazardous in the extreme: both the original sense and the form are equally arbitrary, to say nothing of the legitimacy of a comparison with a language still as little known as Lydian. The point must be made that the whole construction rests on the exclusively possessive meaning from which Kretschmer started. But this sense is itself questionable. In fact, the sense is not that of a simple straightforward possessive, as we have a right to expect from this etymology. Examples of Indo-European possessives are not lacking in Homer, notably the forms of *hós* (ὅς) < **swos*. Moreover, and this is the

1. *Zeitschrift für vergleichende Sprachforschung* 51, p. 187ff.
2. In *Indogermanische Forschungen* 45, 1927, p. 267.

essential point, *phílos* marks the possession in a particular way and with restrictions which we must take into consideration.

Given that the notion of possession which *phílos* expresses is specific and limited we should, as a sound methodological principle, try to find as a point of departure a relation which would also cover the other sense of *phílos* as "friend." We see now that Kretschmer did not pose the problem in the proper terms.[3]

Finally, there is a third fact to be taken into account: the verb *phileîn* (φιλεῖν), which does not only signify "love, feel friendship," but also, from the earliest texts on, "to kiss"; the derivative *phílēma* (φίλημα) signifies nothing else but "kiss." Now neither *amor*, nor *amicus* on the one hand, nor *suus* on the other, ever developed this precise sense. Thus any explanation, to be valid, must account for all three senses.

To understand this complex history we must remember that in Homer the whole vocabulary of moral terms is strongly permeated by values which are not personal but relational. What we take for a psychological terminology, an effective and moral one, refers in fact to the relations of an individual with the members of his group; and the close associations of certain of these moral terms with each other is such as to throw light on the initial sense.

For instance, there is a constant connection in Homer between *phílos* and the concept of *aidṓs* (αἰδώς), a very interesting term, and one which we must treat on its own. Expressions like: *phílos te aidoîós te* (φίλος τε αἰδοῖός τε), *aidṑs kaì philótēs* (αἰδὼς καὶ φιλότης), *aideîsthai kaì phileîn* (αἰδεῖσθαι καὶ φιλεῖν) indubitably show a close connection. Even if we keep to the accepted definitions, *aidṓs* 'respect, reverence', both as regards one's own conscience and towards members of the same family, shows by its association with *phílos* that the two notions were both institutional and that they denote sentiments proper to the members of a closed group.

Thus, if a member of a given group is attacked or insulted, *aidṓs* will bring one of his kinsmen to act in his defense; more generally, within a given group one may assume the obligations of another because of *aidṓs*; the word also denotes the feeling of deference towards a person with whom one has ties. If a

3. The same may be said of a recent study of the same problem, that of H. B. Rosén, *Strukturalgrammatische Beiträge zum Verständnis Homers*, Amsterdam, 1967, p. 12ff., which traces all the examples of *phílos* back to a possessive sense without regard for the variety of contexts, or the precise meaning of *phileîn*, *philótēs*, *phílēma*.

warrior spurs on his faltering comrades with the cry of *aidṓs*! he recalls them to a sense of that collective conscience, the self-respect, which will restore their solidarity.

Within a much larger community, *aidṓs* defines the sentiment felt by superiors towards their inferiors (regard, pity, mercy, sympathy in misfortune, etc.), as well as honor, loyalty, collective propriety, the prohibition of certain acts, of certain modes of behavior—and it develops finally to the several senses of "modesty" and "shame."

Aidṓs throws light on the proper sense of *phílos*. Both are employed with reference to the same person; both designate on the whole the same type of relationship. Relatives, in-laws, servants, friends, all those who are united by reciprocal duties of*aidṓs* are called *phíloi*.

It now remains to determine what properly characterizes *phílos*, or the relationship of *philótēs*. The abstract word is more informative than the adjective. What is *philótēs*?

In order to define this notion we can use a valuable pointer provided by Homeric phraseology: this is the connection between *phílos* and *xénos*, between *phileîn* and *xenízein*. We may state straight away what this combination tells us in a number of uses: the notion of *phílos* expresses the behavior incumbent on a member of the community towards a *xénos*, the "guest-stranger." This is the definition which we propose.

This relationship is fundamental both in the Homeric picture of society and in the terms which refer to it. In order to understand it clearly, we must envisage the situation of a *xénos*, of a "guest," who is visiting a country where, as a stranger, he is deprived of all rights, of all protection, of all means of existence. He finds no welcome, no lodging and no guarantee except in the house of the man with whom he is connected by *philótēs*. This bond is given visible expression in the*súmbolon*, the sign of recognition, which has the form of a broken ring, the matching halves of which were kept by the parties to the relationship. The pact concluded in the name of *philótēs* makes the contracting parties *phíloi*: they are henceforth committed to a reciprocity of services which constitute "hospitality."

This is why the verb *phileîn* expresses the prescribed conduct of the person who welcomes a *xénos* to his hearth and whom he treats according to ancestral custom. The heroes in Homer on many occasions insist on these ties: "it is I," says Antenor, recalling a visit which Odysseus and Menelaus paid him, "it is I who entertained them (*exeínissa*) and welcomed (*phílēsa*) them in my house" (*Il.* 3, 207). The sense of "welcome (a guest)" comes out clearly in an example like the following: "There was a rich man but he was *phílos* to men, because he welcomed (*philéesken*) everybody, his house being on the roadside" (*Il.* 6, 15). The relation of sentiment to behavior, of *phílos* to *phileîn*, comes out clearly in this passage. In the *Odyssey*, Odysseus, welcomed as a guest (*xeînos*) in Laodamas's house, is invited to show his talents in a competition. He accepts: I do not reject any competitor, he says, with the exception of Laodamas, "because he is my *xénos*. Who could compete against his host, the one who welcomes him (*philéonti*)?" (*Od.* 8, 208). Elsewhere a messenger comes to warn Menelaus that two foreign visitors (*xeínō*) are outside the house: "Shall we unharness their horses or shall we conduct them to somebody else who will make them welcome (*hós ke philḗsēi*)?" (*Od.* 4, 29). In yet another passage Calypso tells how a survivor from a shipwreck had been cast ashore on her island. "I made him welcome (*phíleon*), I fed him and promised to make him immortal" (*Od.* 5, 135). This close relationship between *xénos* and *phílos* is also evidenced by the Homeric compound *philóxenos* 'he for whom the *xénos* is a *phílos*' (a quality associated with *theoudḗs* 'who reveres the gods', *Od.* 6, 121), the only compound with *phílo-* where the second term applies to a person.

The gods are said to *phileîn* mortals, that is to say, they show them the regards and favors due to *phíloi*. This is why it is said that a man is *phílos theoísin* '*phílos* to the gods' and, more specifically, *diíphilos*, *arēíphilos* '*phílos* to Zeus, to Ares'. Here we find the institutional basis of the notion of *phílos* in society, with all the implications with which this personal relationship is fraught. *Philótēs* in particular can come about in exceptional circumstances, even between combatants, as a solemn covenant in which the sentiment of "friendship," in the ordinary sense, is not involved.

We have an instructive example in the *Iliad* (3, 94). Hector proposes that Menelaus and Paris should fight by themselves for the possession of Helen; they shall meet in single combat and the victor shall take her with all her possessions … *hoi d'álloi philótēta kaì hórkia pistà támōmen* (οἱ δ'ἄλλοι φιλότητα καὶ ὅρκια πιστὰ τάμωμεν), 'The rest of us shall conclude a *philótēs* and bind ourselves by a solemn oath'. The *philótēs* is put on the same level with *hórkia* 'oaths'; it is a group relationship sealed by a solemn oath. This terminology is what is employed to conclude pacts which are sealed by a sacrifice. The *philótēs* appears as a "friendship" of a very definite type which is binding and involves reciprocal pledges, accompanied by solemn oaths and sacrifices.

In another passage of the *Iliad* (7, 302), the duel between Ajax and Hector is drawn out; they have fought each other for a long time and night falls. They pledge themselves to separate. Let us exchange gifts, says Hector, so that it may be said among the Achaeans and Trojans: "they have met in single combat," *ēd' aût' en philótēti diétmagen arthmḗsante* (ἠδ' αὖτ' ἐν φιλότητι διέτμαγεν ἀρθμήσαντε) 'and then they separated, having bound themselves in *philótēs*'. As witness of the *philótēs* thus concluded the two champions exchange their most precious arms. Hector gives his finest bow and Ajax a magnificent belt. This behavior, as well as the formula used in the pledge, shows the compelling force of *philótēs*, which intervenes between combatants who are enemies and remain so. In these circumstances, it comes to an agreement to break off the combat for the time being by mutual consent in order to resume it at a more favorable moment. It is agreement which is expressed by the word *philótēs*: a precise action which binds (ἀρθμήσαντε) the two partners. But we see also that the pledge follows a set form. It comprises the exchange of arms and gifts. We have here an example of a well-known type of exchange, which solemnizes a pact.

A further example follows. When Hector and Achilles are going to face each other in a final duel, Hector proposes an agreement that the corpse of the loser should not be thrown to the beasts. Achilles replies: "Do not propose an agreement. There are no pledges (*hórkia pistá*) between lions and men. The hearts of wolves and sheep do not beat in unison, but constantly do they devise evil for each other; even so is it not possible for you and me to be in *philótēs*, and there will be no *hórkia* between us": *emè kaì sè philḗmenai oudé ti nō̂in hórkia ésson-tai* (ἐμὲ καὶ σὲ φιλήμεναι, οὐδέ τι νῶιν ὅρκια ἔσσονται), (until one or the other is killed), (*Il.* 22, 261-266). Here, too, we have a mutual pledge of a binding nature. Thus we have three examples which show how far the use of *phileîn* may extend. The behavior expressed by *phileîn* always has an obligatory character and always implies reciprocity; it is the accomplishment of positive actions which are implied in the pact of mutual hospitality.

The institutional context also illuminates the special meaning of the verb *phileîn* in the sense of "to kiss" (modern Greek *philô* 'to kiss'), which gave rise to the exclusive sense of the derivative *phílēma* 'the kiss'. Here, again, we must go back to the original meaning of the term, which seems to us merely to denote affection. The act of "kissing" has its place in the comportment of "friendship" as a mark of recognition between *phíloi*. This usage was not exclusively Greek. Herodotus remarks on it among the Persians, and he uses the verb *phileîn* as the natural expression to describe it. We quote this very instructive text:

> When the Persians meet on the street, we can tell by this sign whether they belong to the same rank: instead of greeting each other with words, they kiss each other (*philéousi*) on the mouth. If one of the two is slightly inferior in status, they kiss (*philéousi*) each other on the cheek. If one of them is of very inferior rank, he throws himself on his knees and prostrates himself before the other. (I, 134)

The same custom is reported by Xenophon:

> At the moment of the departure of Cyrus, his relations (*sungeneîs*) took leave of him by kissing him (*philoûntas*) on the mouth, following a custom which still exists today among the Persians. (*Cyropaedia* I, 4, 27)

We might also recall here, in the Christian period, the "kiss" (*phílēma*, Lat. *osculum*), as the sign of recognition which Christ and his disciples, and later the members of the first communities, exchanged. In more recent times, the kiss is the gesture which dedicates the knight in the ceremony of accolade, and even today it marks the reception of a dignitary into an order of chivalry, at the time of the delivery of the insignia.

In these different forms we find the same ancient relationship of favor from the host to the guest, from god to man, from master to his inferiors, from the head of the house towards the members of his family. It is a close tie which is established between persons and which subsequently turns this "friendship" into something personal.

This mutual relationship entails a certain form of affection which becomes obligatory between the partners of the *philótēs*. The manifestation of this relationship is the welcome of the *phílos* to the hearth of his *phílos*, the exchange of presents, the reminder of the similar ties established between the ancestors of the partners and sometimes of matrimonial alliances concluded on the occasion of visits made or returned.

All this gives an emotional color to the relationship between *phíloi* and, as tends to happen, the sentimental attitude goes beyond the bounds of the institution; the name of *phílos* is extended to relations living in the same house as the master of the house, especially to her whom he has introduced as his wife. This is why we frequently have the qualification of *phílē* in apposition with *álokhos*, *ákoitis* 'spouse' in Homer. Certain uses still show the nature of this relationship and how it is attached to the ancient norm; for instance, the following passage of the *Iliad*:

> I possess, says Agamemnon, three daughters in my manor. Let Achilles take away the one whom he would like as *phílē* in the house of Peleus, and this without offering me gifts. (9, 146–47)

From the fact that she is taken away in the required form, the young girl given by her father whom the young husband introduces into his own home is bound to this family group by conventions as well as by ties of affection: the conditions under which her father has given her make her in some way into a pledge of a *philótēs* concluded between two men, at the same time as she acquires, once installed in her new home, the status of *phílē ákoitis*, a wife (cf. *Il.* 9, 397).

Once an emotional value was attached to *phílos* it became an epithet or form of address used towards those who live in the home, whether as relations, father, mother, wife, children, or even as domestics, such as the old nurse (*maîa*) Eurycleia. The term is affectionate and this quality finds, after Homer, its proper expression in the abstract *philía* 'friendship', which is distinguished from *philótēs*, as well as from the verb *phileîn*, which in current use, from Homer on, had the meaning "to love" (with sensual love).

Here we find the most curious development in this semantic history. It is especially characteristic of the language and style of Homer. The use of *phílos*, going beyond the sphere of human relations, is extended to objects of various kinds to which the common and constant meaning of "dear" could hardly apply. Apparently *phílos* denotes nothing more than possession; it becomes the equivalent to a simple possession and is generally translated as such. But there is no agreement about the explanation of this development.

We begin by delimiting it into three groups of usage. In the first place, *phílos* appears often with things which are most closely linked with the person: soul, heart, life, breath; with parts of the body: limbs, knees, chest and eyelids; to these we add the more general reflexive function. Then it is used with the terms designating places which are presumably "dear," notably the "homeland" (*phílēn es patrída gaîan* is a frequent formula), or the "return" (*nóstos*). Finally, we have a short list of terms which do not seem to involve any emotional coloring: gifts, house, clothes, bed; and the function here must be one of possession pure and simple.

How can we classify these notions by relating them to the persons who habitually receive the epithet *phílos*, that is, those who, as we have seen, are united by the bond of *xenía*, as well as the members of the family, father, mother, spouse, children? And how can we establish the transition between these uses, some of which are of frequent occurrence, and those which are connected with institutions?

Some scholars have thought that the possessive sense of *phílos*, for instance when it qualifies *ễtor* 'heart', resulted from the use of *phílos* with kinship terms. As in French *les miens*, *les siens* 'my people, his people' are said for the members of the family, similarly *phílos* would have become restricted to a possessive function. But this argument is false from the start: in the expression *les miens* for "my parents" the contrary development has taken place, i.e. the possession has come to be used with reference to relatives.

Still others think on the contrary that the first sense attributable to *phílos* should be "his," as illustrated by the possessive uses, and that this gave rise to the notion of "dear." In this way the problem would be most simply and easily solved. But this solution would merely replace one difficulty by another, and a still greater one: how can a simple possessive adjective have produced such a wealth of conceptions? This fact would be unparalleled. Finally, as has been shown above, *phílos* is deeply rooted in the most ancient institutions of society and denotes a specific type of human relationship. This alone would be a sufficient reason to reject so fine-spun and flimsy a semantic thread.

We find ourselves finally left with two equally unsatisfactory solutions. We should be deluding ourselves if we believed that there is any easy transition from "dear" or "friend" to "personal" and finally to "(his) own." Such an evolution, where the primary sense was supposedly so quickly attenuated, is hardly conceivable. But it goes against all the evidence to reverse the relationships and to posit a possessive "his" as the original sense, which gradually developed the meaning "friend" or "dear."

Such is the present state of the problem. We find ourselves faced with a choice of roads which lead nowhere. This state of affairs, because of its very peculiarity, suggests that the dilemma may be due to inexact interpretation. We must therefore take up the problem again from the beginning. The crucial point lies in the relation of the "emotional" sense to the "possessive" sense. We have already seen that one of the two fundamental facts, the notion of "friend," must be reinterpreted within the framework of "hospitality." What of the other datum, that of *phílos* as a possessive? A new examination is necessary here, too. We shall therefore run through the Homeric examples which are everywhere registered as simply indicating possession, where *phílos* qualifies objects rather than persons. We list these combinations one after the other and comment briefly on the principal passages quoted. The contexts are always important in such material.

Phílos with *dôron* 'gift'. The context of *phíla dôra* (*Odyssey* 8, 545) is as clear as one would wish: the situation is that of the host (*xeinodókos*) vis-à-vis his guest (*xeînos*). Alkinoos recalls the duties incumbent on him: the guest is escorted (*pompḗ*), he is offered the *phíla dôra* which are the "gifts of hospitality," because of the above mentioned relation between the *phílos* and the *xénos*. The expression recurs in Odysseus' speech of thanks to Alkinoos, who has given him shelter: *pompḕ kaì phíla dôra* (13, 41). Further (*Il.* 24,68), the *phíla dôra* of Hector are the gifts offered to Zeus, and he in return regards Hector as *phíltatos* because of his devotion to him and towards all the gods. The term in this example illustrates the relationship between men and gods, who are mutually *phíloi*. In all these examples, therefore, the epithet applied to the "gifts" is that which is appropriate to those who offer it as a mark of hospitality, so that *phílos* is in no way a simple possessive.

Phílos with *dō̃ma* 'house' (*Od.* 18, 421) introduces us to the same situation: "let us, says Amphinomos, leave this guest (*xeînos*) to the good offices of Telemachus, since he has come under his hospitable roof (*toû gàr* ***phílon*** *híketo* ***dō̃ma***)." Here, too, we must evidently focus on the connection *phílos-xénos*: *phílon dō̃ma* is the home of the one who conducts himself as a *phílos*.

Phílos with *démnion* 'bed' (*Od.* 8, 277): *phíla démnia* designates the "marriage bed" in the episode when Hephaistos is deceived by his wife. We have seen above that *phílos* is the frequent epithet of *ákoitis*, *álokhos*, of the wife and the hearth. The misfortune of Hephaistos highlights the value of the adjective: the bed, called *phílos* because it is the marriage bed, has been the place of the infidelity; it will also be the place of revenge.

This brings us to the uses where *phílos* is applied to terms for habitation.

With *oikíon* 'house, nest': *phíla oikía* is the nest where the bird finds its young (*Il.* 12, 221). Very frequent is the formula *phílē gaîa* for the homeland, the dream of wanderers, and those away at the wars, the earth which contains his hearth and home. It is especially when they express their desire to return home that the phrase *phílēn es patrída gaîan* 'to their *phílē* native land' becomes charged with emotional force. Consequently it is not surprising to find *phílos* used with *nóstos* 'the return home' (*Il.* 16, 82). All that *phílos* suggests when it evokes the persons living in the same home is transferred here to the "land" where this home is situated and to the "return" which is longed for. If we reduce all this to a simple possessive use, it would empty *phílos* of its true sense.

We must restore all its components to the adjective in order to interpret *phílos* with *heímata* 'clothes':

> (Take care, Odysseus shouts at Thersites, if you continue your insults) I will take away the *phíla heímata*, the mantle and tunic which cover your secret parts (*aidô̄*) and I will beat you black and blue before chasing you away ignominiously. (*Il.* 2, 261)

Here we have an allusion to the relationship which unites *phílos* and *aidō̂s* (see above) in a particular application: the clothes have at one and the same time an intimate relation with the user (they are the clothes which protect his modesty) and also with respect to society. "These clothes which are *phíla* to you" is here, too, a transposition to things of *phílos* which is properly applied to persons.

We now pass on to another group of notions, the limbs and other parts of the body qualified by *phílos*. In some examples the use of *phílos* in its full sense is beyond any doubt. When Priam appeals to Hector not to expose his life, which is *phílē*, in combat (*Il.* 22, 58), it is a father who is speaking, trembling with emotion. When Achilles announces that he will go to confront Hector "the destroyer of the *phílē* head" (*Il.* 18, 114), we must understand that the head of Patroclus was *phílē* to him, being that of a *phílos*. A little more subtle, but still fully comprehensible provided that we put it in its context, is the use, at first surprising, with *laimós* 'throat' (*Il.* 19, 209). But we must read the whole passage: Achilles refuses to stop fighting until he has avenged Patroclus:

> No food nor drink shall pass my *phílos* throat, now that my companion (*hetaîros*) is dead and lies surrounded by his weeping companions.

The sorrow of Achilles is that of a *phílos*, and the feeling of having lost his *hetaîros* makes him put aside all desire for food. Later, when the elders again press him to take food, Achilles exclaims again, with a significant repetition of the epithet, but this time replacing the "throat" by the "heart."

> No, do not ask me to satisfy my *phílon ē̂tor*, when a terrible anguish afflicts me. (*Il.* 19, 305–7)

Used with *ē̂tor* 'heart' or with *laimós* 'throat', in the circumstances where everything reminds Achilles of his lost friend, *phílos* retains its full sense, both institutional and sentimental. There is simply a transference of the epithet, a bold use with *laimós* (of which it is the only example), but quite frequent with *ȇtor*, which applies to a part of the body the expression appropriate to a person.

With *kheîres* 'hands', *phílos* preserves in several passages its proper function: to lift towards the gods *phílas kheîras* (*Il.* 7, 130) is certainly the gesture appropriate to those bound to the gods by the relationship of *philótēs*. When Ino gathers *khersí phílēsi* Odysseus, who is exhausted after the shipwreck (*Od.* 5,462), the epithet is a good expression of the intention to welcome and protect. Similarly the sailors stranded on the Island of the Sun, in search of food, try to catch birds and fishes, *phílas hó ti kheîras híkoito* 'everything which came to their *phílas* hands' (*Od.* 12, 331): here, again, the gesture of the extended hands, ready to receive, is that of the *phíloi* to whom the gifts are offered; the epithet denotes a gesture which imitates that of welcome.

This is also the sense of a passage of the *Iliad* (18, 2) where Achilles, grieved by the death of Patroclus, rends his own face *philēsi khersí*: the pain of a *phílos* is transferred to the hands which manifest it.

With *goúnata* 'knees' *phílos* can also be restored to its proper function. What does the gesture of Eurycleia signify, when she puts on the knees, *phíla goúnata*, of Autolycus the newly-born grandson which his daughter has presented him with (*Od.*19, 401)? Here we have a ritual of recognition, an acknowledgement, the *phíla goúnata* of the father or grandfather who receive the newborn child and thus legitimize it as a member of the family. The same connection between the bond of kinship and the expression *phíla goúnata* explains another passage in the *Odyssey* (21, 55), when Penelope takes on her *phíla goúnata* the bow of Odysseus, who is still absent, and bursts into tears. Significant also, but in a different way, is *phílos* for the knees of a warrior (*phíla goúnata*) in the heat of battle: Hector's shield knocking against his *phíla goúnata* (*Il.* 7, 271); or in facing one's fate: Achilles (9, 610) says and Agamemnon repeats (10, 90) "as long as the breath stays in my chest and my *phíla goúnata* move." It is at the moment when, chosen by the fate of Zeus, the hero faces his supreme test and must fight to the limit of his strength, that he speaks of his *phíla goúnata*: his knees will carry him until the end, they will not fail him, and in so doing they will show themselves *phíla*. The context shows what this quality represents in such circumstances.

Very close in sense is the connection of *phílos* with *guîa* 'limbs': the *phíla guîa* of a warrior are "loosened," "become tired" in combat. We must see in the *phíla guîa* an expression as significant as *phaídima guîa* 'shining, glistening limbs'.

We finally come to the examples—and they are very numerous—where *phílos* accompanies the word for "heart": *phílon ê̄tor* (or *kē̃r*) is so frequent a phrase that it passes for the typical example of the "possessive" use of *phílos*. We believe, on the contrary, that the adjective here keeps its full force and that it often suffices to refer to the context to see this. We must of necessity limit ourselves to a few examples.

In the first book of the *Odyssey* there are no less than six of them. Athena wants to influence her father Zeus in favor of Odysseus: "Cannot your *phílon* heart be softened?" (1, 60), and she reminds him that formerly he took pleasure in the offerings of Odysseus. Her wish is then that Zeus again become a *phílos* to Odysseus and she repeats (1, 82): "if it is *phílon* to the gods that Odysseus should return to his home…" Next we have examples of *phílos* in family relationships: Telemachus is sad in his heart (*phílon*) when he recalls the memory of his father (114), and the heart (*phílon kē̃r*) of Penelope is anguished when the song of the bard recalls her loss (341). *Phílos* occurs also in connection with hospitality: Telemachus welcomes the *xénos*, wants to detain him and assures him he will return bathed, heaped with gifts and glad in his (*phílon*) heart. But the *xénos* (in fact it is Athena in disguise) excuses himself for not being able to stay: he will return to accept the gift which his *phílon* heart prompts Telemachus to give (316). This is the terminology of the *philótēs*, and the epithet is simply transferred from the host to his heart.

The following passages should also be read: the *phílon* heart of Menelaus breaks when he learns that his brother has been assassinated (*Od.* 4, 538); the *phílon* heart of Penelope is afflicted in her fear for her son (804), and it is relieved when a dream reassures her (840). Sometimes there is a play on the senses of the same expression. Menelaus learns from Proteus that he must return to the shores of the Egyptus before he comes back home and joins his *phíloi*, his family (375), and this his *phílon* heart laments (481). But when Menelaus recalls the valor of Odysseus and says that he has never seen a hero who had a *phílon* heart like his (270), he evokes an echo of the lament of Telemachus: of what use was it to him to have a heart of iron (*kradíē sidērée̅*) in his breast? (293) Here, as with *phíla goúnata*, the quality indicated is "not to weaken," "to remain constant and firm."

It would take many chapters to list and analyze with the necessary care all the examples of *phílos* where it is said to be "possessive." We believe, however, that we have interpreted the most important. This re-examination was necessary to expose a long-standing error, which is probably as old as Homeric exegesis, and has been handed down from generation to generation of scholars. The whole problem of *phílos* deserves a full examination. We must start from uses and contexts which reveal in this term a complex network of associations, some with institutions of hospitality, others with usages of the home, still others with emotional behavior; we must do this in order to understand plainly the metaphorical applications to which the term lent itself. All this wealth of concepts was smothered and lost to view once *phílos* was reduced to a vague notion of friendship or wrongly interpreted as a possessive adjective. It is high time we learned again how to read Homer.

As to the etymology of *phílos*, it is now clear that nothing which has been proposed on this subject holds good any longer.[4] We now know that the protohistory of the word belongs to the most ancient form of Greek: Mycenean already had proper names composed with *phílo-*: *pi-ro-pa-ta-ra* (= *Philopatra*), *pi-ro-we-ko* (= *Philowergos*), etc. The discussion about its origins is thus not yet finished. It is more important to begin to see what it signifies.

4. The interpretation of *phílos* given here goes beyond and greatly adds to what was proposed in December 1936 to a meeting of the Société de Linguistique; a resumé of the paper appeared in *Bulletin de la Société de Linguistique de Paris* 38 (1937), Procès-verbaux, p. x.

BOOK III, CHAPTER FIVE

The Slave and the Stranger

Abstract. The free man, born into a group, is opposed to the stranger (Gr. *xénos*), that is to say, the enemy (Lat. *hostis*), who is liable to become my guest (Gr. *xénos*, Lat. *hospes*) or my slave if I capture him in war (Gr. *aikhmálōtos*, Lat. *captivus*).

A stranger by necessity, the slave is designated in the Indo-European languages, even modern ones, either by a foreign word (Gr. *doûlos*, Lat. *servus*), or by the name of a foreign people (*slave* < Slav).

The notion of slave is not designated by a single word, and this is true both of the Indo-European languages as a whole and for quite a number of dialects.

In the ancient civilizations, the status of a slave puts him outside the community. The word for the slave has this negative aspect.

There are no slaves who are citizens. They are always introduced into the city from outside, in the first instance as prisoners of war. In the primitive Indo-European society, as in the ancient non-European societies (Sumero-Akkadian, for instance), the slave is a man without rights, reduced to this condition because of the laws of war.

A little later, a slave may be acquired by purchase. To the great markets of Asia Minor slaves flowed in abundance, coming from all regions, but their state was due after all to their being prisoners of war or people carried off in raids. Asia Minor supplied large contingents of them, to judge by the nicknames of slaves which are often *ethnics*: Phrygian, Lycian, Lydian, Samian, etc.

Given the conditions, we can understand why the slave was identified with the stranger, and why they were called by specific names of places. Apart from this, certain qualifications define them as captured or bought. There are two series of designations which can sometimes coincide; that of "prisoner of war" and that of "slave" properly called as such.

Let us consider, in the first instance, the "prisoner of war." His condition is often expressed by various words denoting "taken" (e.g. French *prisonnier* < *pris*); this is the case in Latin with *captus*, *captivus*, with Gr. *aikhmálōtos* (αἰχμάλωτος), Homeric *douríktētos* (δουρίκτητος), Gothic *frahunþans*, Old Slavic *plěnĭnikŭ* (Russ. *plennyj*). Greek *aikhmálōtos* must be looked at a little more closely, not because the sense of "taken at the point of the spear" is obscure; the composition of the word was clear to the Greeks themselves, a proof of this being the doublet—*douríktētos* which was formed with the word *dóru* 'lance' as first element. But the interpretation of *aikhmálōtos* is not as obvious as it seems: -*alōtos* does not simply mean "taken"; this is rather a rough translation. The root of *halískomai* (ἁλίσκομαι) conveys the idea of being suddenly seized, being taken unawares, without any possibility of defense, whether it is applied to a city or a person: from this comes the sense of the perfect *hḗlōka* (ἥλωκα) 'I am lost', which is one of the rather irregular forms attached to *halískomai*. This notion of surprise, which eliminates the power of resistance, makes *aikhmálōtos* a quite different expression from *captus*, *captivus*, which is derived from *capio* 'to take with the hand'.

The substantive *aikhmḗ* (αἰχμή) must also be considered. It designates the "point of the spear"; then, by extension, the whole of the weapon, a spear, pike or javelin, etc. What we must note is that *aikhmḗ* is the weapon *par excellence* of the Homeric warrior, so much so that the derivative *aikhmētḗs* (αἰχμητής) is the poetical term for warrior; and, further, that in Homer it has always an elevated value. Thus, to put an end to the fight between Ajax and Hector, Talthybius says to them: "Zeus loves you both… you are both valiant warriors," *amphotérō gàr sphōï phileî … Zeus, / ámphō d'aikhmētá* (ἀμφοτέρω γὰρ σφῶϊ φιλεῖ … Ζεύς, / ἄμφω δ' αἰχμητά), (*Il.* 7, 280-281). The weapon called *aikhmḗ* is therefore that which specifies the warrior, without which he loses his status and, as a consequence, his power in battle.

In Iranian, the designation for "prisoner of war" reflects a different image: Middle Iranian *dast-grab*, literally "taken with the hand." This time it is the hand which is the instrument of capture, which is also suggested by *captivus* and High German *hafta*, taken from a root corresponding to Lat. *capio*. The

Iranian verb *grab-* 'to take' is used in the Persian Achaemenid inscriptions of Darius in the sense "to take prisoners of war." *Dasta* 'hand' relates to the same notion: "he put him in my hand," says Darius of Ahura Mazdā, with reference to an enemy. Thus *dasta* and *grab-* pool their respective senses in the expression for a prize of war. Similarly, one sees in Armenian *jerb-a-kal* 'prisoner of war' (literally "taken with the hand"), a calque on the Middle-Iranian *dast-grab*; this is further evidence of the Iranian influence on Armenian.

All these compounds depict the prisoner of war according to the manner of his capture. But these are not the only terms. We must mention also Old Iranian *banda(ka)*, Skt. *bandhin*, which define the prisoner as he who is "bound." We find in Gothic *frahunþans*, a participle of *frahinþan* 'to make a prisoner, Gr. *aikhmalōtízein*', cf. *hunþs* 'capture in war, *aikhmalōsía*', Old English *hunta* 'hunter', *huntian* 'to hunt' derivatives from a root not attested elsewhere which have become specialized in the terminology of the hunt and of war. The same notion inspired Old Slavic *plěnŭ* 'booty' (Russ. *polón*), whence *plěniti* 'take prisoner' and *plěnĭnikŭ* 'prisoner', to which the Lithuanian *pel̃nas* 'advantage, gain' and Skt. *paṇa* '(gambling) stake' correspond; these words can be linked up with the root **pel-* of Gr. *pōleîn* 'to put up for sale' (cf. Book One, Chapter Ten) and this would associate the idea of "spoils, prize of war" with that of "economic profit."

We must now turn to the word for the "slave."

The best-known Greek term, *doûlos* (δοῦλος) is the usual one in the Homeric period. Although it does not appear in Homer, some derivatives are already Homeric, such as the feminine *doúlē* and the adjective *doúlios* (δούλιος) in expressions like *doúlion ē̂mar* (δούλιον ἦμαρ) 'day of servitude, condition of a slave' (see especially *Il.* 6, 463).

There are in Homer other words, such as *dmṓs* (δμώς) and also to some extent *oikétēs* (οἰκέτης), although with the latter word it is difficult to draw the line between "servant" and "slave." We leave these two terms aside; they are derivatives from the word for "house" (cf. Book Three, Chapter Two). Virtually equivalent is Lat. *famulus*, although the idea behind it is different. From *famulus* the collective noun *familia* was coined. What constitutes the *familia* is, etymologically speaking, the whole of the *famuli*, the servants who live in the same house. The notion does not coincide with what we understand by "family," which is restricted to those connected by kinship.

It seems that we can associate the term *doûlos* with this notion of "house"; the specific word for slave, if we accept the testimony of Hesychius, who glosses *doûlos* as *oikía* 'house', while a compound *dōlodomeîs* is glossed *oikogeneîs* 'born in the house'. Consequently, *doûlos* would be close in sense to *oikétēs*, whatever Greek dialect it may first have belonged to.

But now *doûlos* has appeared in Mycenaean in the form of *do-e-ro* (*do-e-lo*), which presupposes a prototype **dowelo*- or **doselo*-. This greatly complicates the origin of this term, which has thus been in use in the Hellenic world at least since the twelfth century BC. Only two hypotheses compatible with this situation shall be discussed. An ancient **doselo*- could be compared, for its root, to the Indo-Iranian term *dāsa*- which, as we have seen, has taken on in Indic the sense of "barbarian, slave." But we have also seen that *dāsa*-, in the Indo-Iranian period, was probably merely the name for "man" (cf. Book Three, Chapter Two). It is difficult to see how the correspondent could have acquired from the most ancient Greek onwards, under the form of **doselo*-, the sense of "slave." Thus we can only suppose, as scholars have done before, that *doûlos* was taken from a non-Indo-European language of the Aegean basin. But the borrowing must have taken place much earlier than was thought, and must have entered Greek in the form represented by Mycenaean *doelo*. The chances of finding the origin diminish the further back in time the term in Greek recedes. There are other pointers which suggest that *doûlos* is a foreign word. First, we have the geographical distribution of proper names in *doulo*-, which indicates an Asiatic origin, although we are unable to specify the language of Asia Minor that acted as the source. Lambertz has collected the ancient examples of *doûlos* and the numerous proper names composed with *doûlos*.[1] Most of these names are attested in Asia Minor, so much so that it seems probable that *doûlos* comes from Asia Minor.

Besides, it would not be surprising if Greek employed a foreign term to designate the slave, because—and this is frequently the case with this term in Indo-European—the slave is necessarily a stranger: the Indo-European peoples only knew what we may call "exodouly."

The same is true of the Latin word *servus*.[2] It is impossible to consider *servus* as a derivative of the verb *servare* and to imagine that it was the function of the *servus* to "guard." The verb *servare* has a clear Indo-European etymology: Avest. *harva* 'who watches', Gr. *horân* (ὁρᾶν) 'to observe, consider'. But

1. *Glotta* V, 1914, p. 146, n. 1.
2. The demonstration has been published in volume X of the *Revue des Etudes Latines* (1932), pp. 429ff.

servus indicates the legal and social condition of a slave and not a specific domestic function. Surely the *servus* was not obliged to *servare*.

Since no citizen could be a slave in Rome, it is probably outside Rome and the Latin vocabulary that we must look for the origin of the word *servus*. Now there is considerable evidence from proper names to show that the root existed in Etruscan in the form *serui-*, *serue-*. We find also among Latin proper names some of Etruscan formation, such as *Servenius*, *Servena*, *Servoleni*, with the suffixes which characterize Latin names of Etruscan origin. It is therefore probable that *servus* is an Etruscan term, although it has not yet been found in any Etruscan inscriptions which we are in a position to interpret. Thus, in very different historical circumstances, we find for *servus* the same initial situation which is very probable in the case of *doûlos*.

We can also recall the modern French word *esclave* 'slave': it is properly the name for the Slavs in the South Slavic form (Serbian or a related dialect), an ethnic *Slověninŭ.* From *Slověninŭ* is derived the Byzantine Greek form *Sklavēnoí* (Σκλαβηνοί) (Italian *Schiavoni*) which, being regarded as a derivative, produced the ethnic *Sklávoi* (Σκλάβοι). This was the source in the whole western world of the word *esclave* and its related forms. We find another parallel in the Anglo-Saxon world, where *wealh* 'slave' properly means "the Celt," the subject people.

We can point to yet another parallel, this time a medieval one; it concerns not the slave, but the vassal, who has an inferior and subject status: *vassus* (from which comes *vassalis*) is in the Latin of the period a borrowing from the Celtic form represented in Irish by *foss*, Welsh *guas*, both meaning "servant, slave." Thus, each language borrows from another its designation for "slave." A people even designates the slave by the name of its neighbors, if they have been subjected by it. Here we see the emergence of a profound semantic correlation between the expression "free man" and its opposite "slave." The free man designates himself as *ingenuus*, as "born in" the society in question, hence endowed with full rights; correlatively, the one who is not free is necessarily someone who does not belong to this society; he is a stranger without rights. A slave is something more: a stranger captured or sold as prize of war.

The notion of stranger is not defined in the ancient civilizations by fixed criteria, as he is in modern societies. Someone born elsewhere, provided that he has certain conventional links, enjoys some specific rights, which cannot be granted even to citizens of the country: this is shown by the Greek *xénos* 'stranger' and 'guest', that is to say, the stranger who benefits by the laws of hospitality. Other definitions are at hand: the stranger is "he who comes from outside," Lat. *advena*, or simply "he who is outside the limits of the community," Lat. *peregrinus*. There is no "stranger" as such: given the diversity of notions, the stranger is always a particular stranger, who carries a distinct status. In short, the notions of enemy, stranger, guest, which for us form three distinct entities—semantically and legally—in the Indo-European languages show close connections.

We have studied above (Book One, Chapter Seven) the relations between *hostis* 'enemy' and *hospes* 'guest'; Latin *hostis* 'enemy' has a correspondent elsewhere in the Gothic *gasts* 'guests'. In Greek *xénos* designates the "stranger" and the verb *xeinízō* refers to "hospitable behavior."

This cannot be understood except by starting from the idea that the stranger is of necessity an enemy and correlatively that the enemy is necessarily a stranger. It is always because a man born elsewhere is *a priori* an enemy that a mutual bond is necessary to establish between him and the EGO relations of hospitality, which would be inconceivable within the community itself. This dialectic "friend-foe," as we have seen, is already operative in the notion of *phílos*: an enemy, even one's adversary in battle, may become temporarily a *phílos*, as the result of a pact concluded according to the rites and customary pledges. In the same way, in the early history of Rome, the stranger who becomes a *hostis* enjoys *pari iure cum populo Romano*, legal rights equal to those of the Roman citizen. Rites, agreements and treaties thus interrupted this permanent situation of mutual hostility which existed between peoples or cities. Under the protection of solemn conventions and by means of exchange arrangements, human relationships could develop, and as a result the words for agreements or legal status came to denote sentiments.

BOOK III, CHAPTER SIX

Cities and Communities

Abstract. The Western dialects of Indo-European (Celtic, Italic, Germanic, Baltic) have preserved the word **teutā*, derived from a root **tew-* 'to be swollen, powerful', to designate "the people" as a full development of the social body. Quite naturally, this term, which supplied national ethnics among the Germans (*Teutoni*, *deutsch*) acquired the opposite meaning when Slavic borrowed it from German: Old Slav. *tŭždĭ* means "stranger."

The Greek *pólis* and the Latin *civitas*, which were closely linked in the development of Western civilization, provide a good illustration of the phenomenon of convergence in institutional expressions: nothing could be more different at the outset than the old Indo-European word for "citadel" (cf. Gr. *akró-polis*) and the Latin derivative *civitas* 'the whole body of citizens'. *Arya*, which signifies "people" (= my people) in Indic and was the source of the name of Iran (< *aryānām*) is the common ancient designation of the "Indo-Iranians." Isolated in Iranian, *arya* can be analyzed in Sanskrit as a derivative from *arí*; the latter seems to designate, in contrast to the stranger, the man of my people; perhaps more precisely, the relation by marriage, the member of the other exogamic moiety.

We have analyzed, by means of the terms which express it, the condition of the free man, born and integrated within a society and enjoying full rights that belong to him by birth.

But how does this man imagine the society to which he belongs and how can we form a picture of it ourselves? Do we know of a "nation," dating from the time of the Indo-European community, which is designated by a single and constant term? To what extent could an aggregate of tribes conceive of itself as a political entity and call itself a "nation"?

Let us state straight away that there is no term, from one end of the Indo-European world to the other, which designates an organized society. That is not to say that the Indo-European peoples did not evolve this concept; we must guard against concluding that a deficiency in the common vocabulary implies the absence of the corresponding notion in the dialectal prehistory.

In fact there are a whole series of terms which encompass the whole extent of territorial and social units of varying dimensions. From the beginning these territorial organizations appear to be of great complexity, and each people presents a distinct variety.

There is nevertheless a term which is attested in the western Indo-European world over a considerable area. In Italic, excluding Latin, this term is represented by the Umbrian word *tota*, which means "*urbs*" or "*civitas*," "town" or "city." In the great lustration ritual called the Iguvine Tablets, which contain a detailed list of sacrificial rites, processions, and prayers, carried out in order to secure the favors of the gods for the city and territory of Iguvium, the formulae *totaper iiouina, tutaper ikuvina* 'for the city of Iguvium' often recur. No distinction is made between the town and the society: it is one and the same notion. The limits of the habitation of a given group mark the boundaries of the society itself. Oscan has the same word in the form *touto* 'city' and Livy (xxiii, 35, 13) tells us that the supreme magistrate in Campania was called *meddix tūticus* '*iudex publicus*'.

We find **teutā* also in Celtic, in Old Irl. *tuath* 'people, country', in Welsh *tud* 'country' (Breton *tud* 'people') and in the Gaulish proper names *Teutates*, *Teutomatus*, etc.

The corresponding term in Germanic is Gothic *þiuda* 'Gr. *éthnos* (ἔθνος), people, nation', an important term because of its date and because it is constant from the oldest Germanic text onwards, important also because of its extent and persistence. We have seen above (Book Three, Chapter Two) its important derivative *þiudans* 'chief'. From the Old High German form *deot* 'Ger. *Volk*', there was formed by means of the very frequent suffix *-isc-* the adjective *diutisc* (transcribed in Middle Latin as *theodiscus*), which developed to German *deutsch*. This derivative at first designated the language of the country, the popular language as opposed to the learned language, Latin; then it became the ethnic for a part of the German people—those who called themselves "those of the people," to be understood as "those of the same people as we, those of our community." Another ethnic formed from the same root is *Teutoni*. It is as well to note that, in the evolution which has produced the ethnic *deutsch*, it was the language to which this description first applied. A curious testimony to the peculiarity of use survives in the shape of the German word *deuten*, which is traced to the same origin as *deutsch*. In fact *deuten*, Old High German *diuten*, comes from a Germanic **þeudjan*, a verb derived from *þeudō-* 'people'; its meaning would then have been "to popularize, to make accessible to the people" (the message of the Gospels), then generally "to explain, interpret."

In this dialectal area Baltic is also included; Lith. *tautà* 'people, race', Old Prussian *tauto* 'country'. Here Old Slavic shows an interesting divergence vis-à-vis Baltic, both in the form and the sense of the adjectives *tŭždĭ* and *štŭždŭ*, which signify "foreign" (Russian *čužoj*). In reality the Slavic forms which represent **tudjo-* and **tjudjo-* do not come from an inherited root; they are derivatives from a Germanic loanword, and this explains the sense of "foreign."

It is easy to understand, says Meillet, that an adjective coined from a foreign word signifying "nation" should become the word for "stranger"; the Germanic nation was for the Slavs the foreign nation *par excellence*: the *němĭcĭ*, that is the dumb, the βάρβαρος, is the German. It is incidentally curious that Lettish *tauta* at an early date meant mainly a foreign people.[1] Thus the form and sense of Slavic *tŭždĭ* confirms that the term **teuta* characterized the Germanic peoples, in particular in the eyes of the neighboring Slavs.

Apart from Italic, Celtic, Germanic and Baltic, it seems that we must include Thracian and Illyrian among the languages which possessed the word **teutā*, to judge by the Illyrian proper names *Teutana*, *Teuticus*, Thracian *Tautomedes*, a fact which extends this lexical area towards Central and Eastern Europe. But contrary to a widely held view, we must exclude the Hittite *tuzzi-*, which signifies "camp," and refers only to the army. Some scholars proposed a different solution and traced back to **teutā-* the Latin adjective *tōtus* 'entire, all'. This connection has a certain appeal, for it would relate the notion of "totality" to that of "society"; it is all the more attractive because another adjective meaning "all," Skt. *viśva-*, Av. *vispa-*, has been adapted to *viś-* 'tribe'. But this origin for *tōtus* is not admissible except at the cost of a number of indemonstrable hypotheses: (1) that the *ō* of *tōtus*, instead of the expected **tūtus*, is to be explained as a

1. Meillet, *Etudes sur l'étymologie et le vocabulaire du vieux-slave*, Paris, 1902-1905, p. 175.

dialect form; (2) that the feminine **teutā* directly produced in Latin an adjective **teutus*, which later disappeared without a trace, whereas in the languages in which **teutā* remained alive, it never produced a derivative indicating totality. Thus this affiliation is hardly probable. It seems that *tōtus* must be connected in Latin itself with *tōmentum* 'stuffing' and that the first sense of *tōtus* was, more vulgarly, "stuffed full, compact," which developed to "complete, entire."

The formation of the social term **teutā* is clear. It is a primary abstract in *-*tā* made from the root **teu-* 'to be swollen, mighty'. This root was very productive. Notably, it has given rise in Indo-Iranian to the verb "to be able," Av. *tav-*, and numerous nominal forms with the same sense: Sanskrit *tavas-* 'strength', *taviṣī-* 'might', Old Persian *tunuvant-* 'mighty', etc. **teutā* may therefore be explained roughly as "plenitude," indicating the full development of the social body. An analogous expression is found in Old Slavic *plemę* 'tribe' (Russ. *plemja* 'tribe, people'), which is derived from the root **plē-* 'to be full', like Gr. *plêthos* 'crowd', and perhaps Latin *plebs*.

The group of dialects which have **teutā* (Celtic, Germanic, Baltic, Italic) form a continuous zone in Europe, from which Latin and Greek are excluded to the south and Slavic, Armenian and Indo-Iranian to the east. This dialect distribution apparently implies that certain ethnic groups, those which were to become the Indo-Iranians, Latins and Hellenes, had become separated from the community before the term **teutā* came into use among a certain number of peoples who became established in the center and west of Europe. In fact in Latin, Greek and Indo-Iranian different terms are in use to denote the respective societies.

We must take the Greek term *pólis* (πόλις) and Latin *civitas* together. Intrinsically they have nothing in common, but history has associated them first in the formation of Roman civilization, in which Greek influence was paramount, and then in the development of modern Western civilization. They are both the concern of a comparative study —which has not yet been attempted—of the terminology and political phenomenology of Greece and Rome. For our purposes two points must be stressed: the Greek *pólis*, even in historical times, still shows the sense of "fortress, citadel," as Thucydides said: "the *akrópolis* (citadel) is still today called *polis* by the Athenians" (II, 15). This was the prehistoric sense of the word, to judge by its Vedic correspondent *pūr* 'citadel' and Lithuanian *pilìs* 'castle, stronghold'. We thus have here an old Indo-European term, which in Greek, and only in Greek, has taken on the sense of "town, city," then "state." In Latin things are quite different. The word for "town," *urbs*, is of unknown origin; it has been conjectured—but without proof—that it may come from Etruscan. But it is a fact that *urbs*, in the sense of "town," is not correlative with the Greek *pólis*, but with *ástu* (ἄστυ); its derivatives came to have senses which were calques of the corresponding Greek word, e.g. *urbanus* 'of the town' (as opposed to *rusticus* 'of the country'), which came to mean "fine, polished" after the Greek *asteîos*. To correspond to Gr. *pólis*, Latin has a secondary term *civitas*, which literally indicates the entire body of *cives* 'fellow-citizens'. It follows that the connection established in Latin between *civis* and *civitas* is the exact reverse of that shown in Greek between *pólis* 'city' and *polítēs* 'citizen.'[2]

***

In the principal eastern group of Indo-European, in Indo-Iranian, a term of quite a different kind may represent the notion studied here, but in the ethnic aspect rather than the political one: this is *ārya-*, which was at first a social qualification before becoming the designation of the community; it was in use both in India and in Iran from the earliest records.

All terms of an ethnic character were in ancient times differential and oppositional. The names which a people gives itself expresses, either clearly or otherwise, the intention of setting itself off from neighboring peoples; it affirms that superiority inherent in the possession of a common, intelligible language. This is why the ethnic often forms an antithetic pair with the opposed ethnic. This state of affairs is due to the little noticed difference between modern and ancient societies with regard to the notions of war and peace. The relation between peace and war was once exactly the reverse of what it is today. For us peace is the normal condition, which is interrupted by a state of war; for the ancients, the normal state was war, to which peace puts an end. We have little understanding of anything about the notion of peace and of the vocabulary which designates it in ancient society if we do not grasp that peace intervenes as a sometimes accidental and often temporary solution to a quasi-permanent state of hostility between towns and states.

The problem of the word *ārya* is of interest because, in the region defined as Indo-Iranian, it is a designation which free men apply to themselves as opposed

2. This point is developed in an article contributed to a collection of *Mélanges* offered to C. Lévi-Strauss.

to slaves, and also because it is the only word which comprises a common nationality, that of those whom we must call "Indo-Iranians."

For us, there are two distinct entities, India and Iran. But seen in the light of evolution from the Indo-European parent language, the distinction between "India" and "Iran" is inadequate. The word "India" has never been used by the inhabitants of the country; whereas the Iranians do call themselves "Iranians."

This difference is due precisely to the uneven survival, between one region and the other, of the ancient word *ārya*. The Greeks, to whom we owe our knowledge of India, themselves first knew India through the mediation of Persia. An evident proof of this is the form of the root *India* (Ἰνδία), generally *Indikḗ* (Ἰνδική), which in fact corresponds to the name of the river and of the province called "Indus," Skt. *Sindhu*. The discordance between the Greek and the Sanskrit is such that a direct borrowing of the indigenous form is out of the question. On the contrary, everything is explained if the Persian *Hindu* was the intermediary, since the initial *h*- corresponds regularly to *s*- in Sanskrit, while the Ionian psilosis accounts for the root *ind*- (ἰνδ-) with loss of the initial aspirate. In the Persian inscriptions of Darius, the term *Hindu* only applies to the province which is today called *Sindh*. Greek usage has extended this name to the whole country.

The Indians, at an early date, gave themselves the name of *ārya*. This form *ārya* is used in Iranian territory as an ethnic term. When Darius lists his ancestry, "son of Vištāspa, grandson of Aršāma," he adds to characterize himself *arya ariyačissa* 'Aryan of Aryan stock'. He thus defines himself by a term which we would now express as "Iranian." In fact it is *arya*- which, in the genitive plural form *aryānām*, evolved in a more recent phase of Persian to the form *ērān*, later *īrān*. "Iranian" is thus the continuation of ancient *ārya* in Persian territory proper.

Very far away, towards the northwest, encircled by peoples of Caucasian speech, there is an Iranian enclave in the shape of a people called Ossetes, descendants of the ancient *Alani*, who were of Sarmatian stock. They represent the survival of the ancient Scythian peoples (Scythians and Sarmatians) whose territory once comprised the whole of south Russia as far as Thrace and the Balkans. The name of *Alani* goes back to **Aryana*-, which is yet another form of the ancient *ārya*. We thus have a proof that this word is an ethnic description preserved by several peoples belonging to the "Iranian" family.

In Iranian, *arya* is opposed to *anarya* "non-*arya*"; in Indic *ārya* serves as the antithetic form to *dāsa*- 'stranger, slave, enemy'. Thus the term confirms the observation made above that there is a fundamental difference between the indigenous, or the "self," and the stranger.

What does *ārya* mean? This is a very difficult problem which is seen in all its complexity if it is given its place in the Vedic vocabulary; for *Arya* is not isolated in Sanskrit, as it is in Iranian (where it appears as a word not amenable to analysis, serving only to describe those who belong to the same ethnic group). We have in Vedic a coherent series of words, proceeding from the form which is at once the most simple and the most ancient one, *arí*; the group comprises no fewer than four terms: *arí*, with its thematic derivatives *árya* and *aryá*, and fourthly, with lengthening of the root vowel, *ārya*. The difficulty is to distinguish these forms by their sense and to recognize their relationship. The basic term, *arí*, presents itself in so confused and contradictory a way that it admits flatly opposed translations. It is applied to a category of persons, sometimes only to one, designated sometimes in a friendly and sometimes in a hostile way. Often the author of the hymn decries the *arí*, from which we may conclude that he regards him as his rival. However, the *arí* as the singer offers sacrifice and distributes wealth; his cult is addressed to the same gods with the same ritual gestures. This is why we find *arí*translated in the dictionaries by "friend" and by "enemy" concurrently.

The German Indologist P. Thieme devoted a detailed study to this problem in 1938; it is entitled *Der Fremdling im Ṛgveda*, because at the end of a long analysis, the author believes he can translate the root *arí-* as "stranger." The two contradictory senses "friend" and "enemy" may be compared, he suggests, to the two senses of **ghosti-*: on the one hand Lat. *Hostis* 'guest', Got. *gasts* 'guest', on the other Lat. *hostis* 'enemy'. Similarly, *arí* is "the stranger, friend or enemy." Based on *arí*, the derivative *arya* would signify "he who has a connection with a stranger," hence "protector of the stranger, German *gastlich*'hospitable'," and also "master of the household." Finally, from *arya-* the secondary derivative *ārya* would literally mean "belonging to the guests"; hence "hospitable." The *ārya* called themselves "the hospitable ones," thus contrasting their humanity with the barbarism of the people who surrounded them.

Following this study, there appeared from 1941 on a number of works by M. Dumézil, who proposed other interpretations which tend to establish the social sense and then the ethnic sense of this family.[3]

---

3. Theses and antagonistic interpretations: on the one hand, P. Thieme, *Der Fremdling im Ṛgveda*, 1938; *Mitra und Aryaman*, 1958; on the other, G. Dumézil, *Le troisième souverain*, 1949; *L'idéologie tripartite des Indo-Européens*, 1958, p. 108ff.

On the whole our views are close to those of Dumézil. But it will not be possible to justify them here in detail. The examples involve, for the most part, detailed questions of Vedic exegesis, and the discussion would require a whole book of its own. We shall limit ourselves to a few observations and a summary definition.

In such matters, philological criteria must not run counter to intrinsic probabilities. To define the Aryans as "the hospitable ones" is a thesis remote from all historic reality; at no time has any people whatsoever called itself "the hospitable ones."

When peoples give themselves names, these are divided, as far as we can understand them, into two categories; if we exclude names of a geographical character, they are either (1) an ethnic consisting of a complimentary epithet, e.g. "the valiant," "the strong," "the excellent," "the eminent" or (2) most often they simply call themselves "the men." If we start with the Germanic *Alamanni* and follow the chain of peoples, whatever their origin or their language, to Kamchatka or the southern tip of South America, we encounter peoples by the dozen who call themselves "the men"; each of them thus presents itself as a community of the same language and the same descent, and implicitly contrast themselves with neighboring peoples. In a number of connections we have occasion to insist on this character which is native to many societies.

In these circumstances, to imagine that a people, in this case the Aryas, called themselves "the hospitable ones" would run counter to all historical probability. It is not in this way that a people affirms its individuality vis-à-vis its neighbors, who are always presumed to be hostile. We have already seen (Book One, Chapter Seven) that the relationship of hospitality is not established either between individuals or between groups except after the conclusion of a pact under special circumstances. Each time a specific relation is established. It is thus inconceivable that a people should proclaim itself as "the hospitable ones" in general and towards everybody without distinction. We must always determine by precise contexts the original sense of institutional terms such as "hospitality," which for us has only a moral or sentimental sense.

Without going into the details of the very numerous examples, the exegesis of which is sometimes difficult, we may stress certain features which help us to define the status of the *arí* or the *arya*.

The connotations of the word *arí*, which are sometimes favorable and sometimes unfavorable, do not affect the true sense of the word. It designates a man of the same people as the one who speaks about him. This man is never considered as the member of an enemy people, even if the singer is enraged with him. He is never confused with a barbarian. He takes part in all the cults, he receives gifts which the singer may envy him, but which put him on the same footing. He may be generous or avaricious, friendly or hostile—but it is always a personal hostility. At no time can we perceive that the *arí* belongs to a different ethnic group from the author of the hymn.

Further, the *arí* are often associated with the *vaiśya*, that is to say the members of the third social class, which confirms that the *arí* is not a stranger. There is more precise testimony to the social position of the *arí* in the complaint of the daughter-in-law of Indra (Rig Veda X, 28, 1): "All the other *arí* have come (to the sacrifice); only my father-in-law has not come." Indra is thus counted among the *arí* of his daughter-in-law. If we took the expression in the most literal sense, we should conclude that the *arí* formed the other moiety in an exogamic society. Nothing contradicts this inference, and some facts seem to confirm it. In this way we could understand why the *arí* are sometimes in a relationship of friendship, sometimes of rivalry, and that they together form a social unit: the expression "all the *arí* (or *ā̆rya*)" often recurs in the Rig Veda; it is also known in the Avesta, so that it is an inherited item of Indo-Iranian phraseology.

We must also pay attention to the name and role of the god *Aryaman*, who belongs to the Indo-Iranian pantheon. This name is a compound of *arya-man-* 'of the spirit of *arya*'. Now the god Aryaman in Vedic mythology establishes friendship and, more particularly, he is the god of marriages. For the Iranians, too, Aryaman is a friendly god, but in the different guise of a healer. As a noun, *aryaman-* in the Zoroastrian Gāthās designates the members of a religious confraternity. In the Persian proper name *Aryarāmna* 'who gives peace to the *arya*', we again find the communal sense of *arya*.

In summary, we can disentangle from the brief mentions and often fleeting allusions in the Vedic texts some constant features which enable us to form a probable idea of what the word meant: the *arí* or *arya* (we cannot always distinguish the two forms) form what was doubtless a privileged class of society, probably entering into the relation of exogamic moieties, and maintaining relationships of exchange and rivalry. The derivative *ārya*, which at first designated the descendants of the*arí* (or the *arya*), indicated that they belonged to the *arí*, and it soon came to serve as a common denominator for the tribes who recognized the same ancestors and practiced the same cults. These comprise at least some of the components of the notion of *ārya*, which among both the Indic people and the Iranians, marks the awakening of a national conscience.

It remains to determine what the stem of *ari*, *arya-* properly signifies, and to decide whether the form *ari-* belongs to the Indo-European vocabulary or whether it is limited to Indo-Iranian. Scholars have often suggested that *ari* may be connected with the prefix *ari-*, which in Sanskrit denotes a degree of excellence and may correspond to the Greek prefix *ari-* (ἀρι-), which also indicates excellence; and since this Greek prefix *ari-* probably connects up with the group of *áristos* 'excellent, supreme' this would suggest for *ari-*, *arya-* some such sense as "eminent, superior." But these etymological connections are far from certain. In any case, to return to our point of departure, the idea of mutual behavior (whether friendly or hostile) is more strongly felt in the uses of *ari-*, *arya-* than any suggestion of eulogy. Only a more profound analysis based on new facts would permit us to make any pronouncement on the etymology.

BOOK IV

Royalty and its Privileges

BOOK IV, CHAPTER ONE

Rex

Abstract. *Rex*, which is attested only in Italic, Celtic, and Indic—that is, at the western and eastern extremities of the Indo-European world—belongs to a very ancient group of terms relating to religion and law.

The connection of Lat. *rego* with Gr. *orégō* 'extend in a straight line' (the *o*- being phonologically explicable), the examination of the old uses of *reg*- in Latin (e.g. in *regere fines*, *e regione*, *rectus*, *rex sacrorum*) suggests that the *rex*, properly more of a priest than a king in the modern sense, was the man who had authority to trace out the sites of towns and to determine the rules of law.

There are certain notions which we can attribute to the Indo-Europeans only by indirect means because while they refer to social realities, they are not manifested by facts of vocabulary common to the whole group of languages. Such is the concept of *society*. In western Indo-European it is designated by a common term. But this seems to be lacking in the other groups. In fact, it is expressed in a different way. It may be recognized under the name of *kingdom*: the limits of society coincide with the extent of a given power, which is the power of the king. This poses the problem of the words for "king," a problem which involves both the study of society and the divisions which characterize it and the study of the hierarchies which, within society, define its groupings.

When we approach this notion of "king" in its lexical expression, we are struck by the fact that the word represented by *rex* appears only at the two extremities of the Indo-European world and is missing in the central part. We find on the one side *rex* in Latin, while Celtic is represented by Irl. *ri* and Gaulish *-rix*; at the other extremity we have Sanskrit *rāj-(an)*. There is nothing in between, not in another Italic language, nor in Germanic, Baltic, Slavic or Greek, or even in Hittite. This correlation is extremely important for appreciating the distribution of the common vocabulary among the different languages. We must regard the case of *rex* as an instance—probably the most notable—of a wider phenomenon studied by J. Vendryes:[1] that of the survival of terms relating to religion and law at the two extremities of the Indo-European world, in the Indo-Iranian and Italo-Celtic societies.

This fact is bound up with the very structure of the societies in question. It is not a simple accident of history if in the "intermediate" languages, we find no trace of this word for "king." In the case of both Indo-Iranian and Italo-Celtic we are concerned with societies of the same archaic structure, of an extremely conservative nature, where institutions and their vocabulary persisted long after they had been abolished elsewhere. The essential fact which explains these survivals that are common to the Indo-Iranian and Italo-Celtic societies is the existence of powerful colleges of priests who were the repositories of sacred traditions which they maintained with a formalist rigor.

It will suffice to cite, among the Romans, the colleges of the Arval Brothers, among the Umbrians the *fratres Atiedii* of Iguvium, among the Celts, the Druids, and in the Orient priestly corporations like the Brahmans or the Atharvans of India, the *āθravans* or the "Magi" in Iran.

It is thanks to the persistence of these institutions that a large part of the religious ideas of the Indo-Europeans have survived and are known to us, inasmuch as they were regulated by complex rituals which remain our best sources of information.

However we should guard against believing that it was only because of the archaism of society that these facts have been preserved in these cases and not elsewhere. The changes made in the very structure of institutions have brought it about that the specific notion of *rex* was unknown to other peoples. There are certainly words both in Greek and in Germanic which may be translated as "king." But the Greek *basileús* has nothing in common with the *rāj*, and the

1. *Mémoires de la Société de Linguistique de Paris*, XX, 1918, 265ff.

numerous words in Greek which mean "king" or rather "chief" go to show that the institution had been remodeled.

The nominal stem **rēg-* of the Latin *rēx*, *rēgis* is exactly that of the Irish *ri* and the Gaulish *-rix*, which is found as a component of compound personal names such as *Dumno-rix*, *Ver-cingeto-rix*. The form presupposed by Sanskrit *rāj-* is exactly the same; it goes back to an ancient **rēg-*. This root is probably also found in the royal Thracian name *Rhēsos*.

What is the meaning of this term? What is the semantic basis of the concept? In Latin *rex* produced a whole family of words, among which is the derived verb *rego*, *regere*, the derived neuter noun *reg-no-m*, the feminine *rēgīna*, with a very characteristic formation seen also in Skt. *rājñī* 'queen', both formations making use of a suffix *-n*-to mark the "motion," that is, the feminization of an ancient masculine. *Regio* and *rectus* form a group of their own. There is no longer any connection in Latin itself between *rex* and *rectus*. However, morphological relationships which are clear and of a well known type attach*regio* and *rectus* to the root of *rex*. Both these derivatives have a correspondent elsewhere. Thus Latin *rectus* is paralleled by Gothic *raihts* (Germ. *recht*); yet Germanic does not exhibit the nominal term **rēg-*.

The first question we must pose is therefore whether other Indo-European languages have not preserved, in some vestigial way, related forms. Greek has a verb which it is tempting to connect with *rego* and the family of *rex*; but it is so different in sense that one is reluctant to do so in a formal way. This is the verb *orégō* (ὀρέγω), which is translated as "stretch, stretch out." It is difficult to see how this connection can be established, and so it is usually put forward with some doubt and merely as a possibility. If we were able either to refute this relationship or to make it acceptable we should have made an important contribution towards the definition of the notion of "royalty."

The problem is in the first place a phonetic one: since the correspondence between the roots **reg-* of Latin *rego* and *reg-* of Gr. *o-rég-ō* is self-evident, can we explain the initial *o-* of the Greek word? This is not an insignificant detail. It concerns the most ancient morphology of Indo-European. In Greek we find under similar conditions, especially before *r*, a prothesis consisting of one of the vowels *a*, *e*, *o*, in a position where no initial vowel appears in the other languages. An example is *eruthrós* (ἐρυθρός) with a prothetic *e-* as compared with Latin *ruber*. We see in this particular instance the same phenomenon as in *orégō*. It will not be possible to discuss this peculiarity in detail here and we content ourselves with noting that it forms part of a general linguistic phenomenon. The languages of the world do not all necessarily possess both the liquid consonants *r* and *l*. We must not believe that it is absolutely necessary to distinguish these two liquids and we should look in vain for them in all languages. In fact languages may use either *r* or *l* or both. There is a striking contrast between Chinese which uses *l* but not *r*, and Japanese, which uses *r* but not *l*. In other cases both *r* and *l* actually are heard in the language, but they do not correspond to distinct phonemes. In French it is not permissible to confuse *roi* and *loi* ("king" and "law"), for *r* and *l* are certainly two different phonemes, each of which has its place within the phonemic system. But there exist languages of very different type which use *r* and *l* without distinction (Polynesian is a case in point), that is to say, as a liquid with a variable mode of articulation.

How does it stand with Indo-European? The common system certainly possesses two phonemes *r* and *l*, though they have different functional values: *r* is used more frequently and in more different ways than *l*. But both existed at the earliest period, although they came to be confused to a great extent in Indo-Iranian.

However it is not sufficient to establish the presence of the two liquids in Indo-European. It is known that not all the phonemes of a language appear in every conceivable position. For each phoneme certain positions are permitted while in others it is excluded. In Greek a word may end only with one of the consonants *-n*, *-r*, or *-s*, the sole exception being the negation *ou*(*k*). It follows that there is in each language a register of possibilities and impossibilities which characterize the use of its phonological system.

Now it is a fact that in many languages there is no initial *r*. In Finno-Ugrian, Basque, and other languages no word may begin with *r*. If a borrowed word begins with an *r*, it is given a preceding vowel, which puts the *r* in a medial position. Such is also the situation in common Indo-European: an *r* is not permitted in the initial position. In Hittite, for instance, there is no initial *r* although we find words with initial *l*. Similarly with Armenian: in order to accommodate borrowed words beginning with an *r* Armenian prefixes them with an *e* or, more recently, replaces the original *r*- by a strongly rolled *r* distinct from the normal *r*. This is also the case in Greek where a "prothetic vowel" appears before *r*, so that the words begin with *er*-, *ar*-, *or*-.

The fact must be stressed. If Greek, Armenian and Hittite have no initial *r*-, this is because they have continued the absence of initial *r*- in Indo-European. These languages have preserved the ancient state of affairs. It is by virtue of a phonetic transformation that Latin on the one hand and Indo-Iranian on the other present *r* at the beginning of a word. On the other hand initial *l*- existed in Indo-European and is preserved as such: cf. the root **leik* ʷ- and Gr. *leípō* (λείπω), Lat. *linquo*, without prothesis. When Greek presents an initial *r*-, it always carries a rough breathing, i.e. ῥ (= *rh*-), which indicates an original **sr*- or an original **wr*-. Apart from this, the original initial **r*- is always preceded by a prothesis.

Thus in theory there is nothing against the connection of *rex* with Greek *orégō*: the *o*- offers no obstacle to the equation, for it attests an original word beginning which has not been preserved in Latin. It remains to determine the sense of the Greek forms. The present *orégō* or *orégnumi* (ὀρέγνυμι) with its derivative *órguia* (ὄργυια) (feminine form of the substantivized perfect participle with the sense "fathom") does not simply mean "stretch"; this is also the sense of another verb, *petánnumi* (πετάννυμι). But *petánnumi* means "spread out sideways," while *orégō*, *orégnumi* mean "stretch out in a straight line," or more explicitly, "to draw forward from the point where one stands in a straight line," or "to betake oneself forwards in a straight line." In Homer *orōrékhatai* (ὀρωρέχαται) describes the movement of horses which stretch themselves out at full length as they run.

This sense is also present in Latin. The important word *regio* did not originally mean "region" but "the point reached in a straight line." This explains the phrase *e regione* 'opposite', that is, "at the straight point, opposite." In the language of augury *regio* indicates "the point reached by a straight line traced out on the ground or in the sky," and "the space enclosed between such straight lines drawn in different directions."

The adjective *rectus* can be interpreted in a similar way: "straight as this line which one draws." This is a concept at once concrete and moral: the "straight line" represents the norm, while the *regula* is "the instrument used to trace the straight line," which fixes the "rule" (*règle*). Opposed to the "straight" (*droit*) in the moral order is what is *twisted, bent*. Hence "straight" (*droit*) is equivalent to "just," "honest," while its antonyms "twisted, bent" (*tordu, courbé*) is identified with "perfidious," "mendacious," etc. This set of ideas is already Indo-European. To Lat. *rectus* corresponds the Gothic adjective *raihts*, which translates Gr. *euthús* 'straight'; further the Old Persian *rāsta*, which qualifies the noun "the way" in this injunction: "Do not desert the straight way."

In order to understand the formation of *rex* and the verb *regere* we must start with this notion, which was wholly material to begin with but was susceptible to development in a moral sense. This dual notion is present in the important expression*regere fines*, a religious act which was a preliminary to building. *Regere fines* means literally "trace out the limits by straight lines." This is the operation carried out by the high priest before a temple or a town is built, and it consists in the delimitation on a given terrain of a sacred plot of ground. The magical character of this operation is evident: what is involved is the delimitation of the interior and the exterior, the realm of the sacred and the realm of the profane, the national territory and foreign territory. The tracing of these limits is carried out by the person invested with the highest powers, the *rex*.

Thus in *rex* we must see not so much the "sovereign" as the one who traces out the line, the way which must be followed, which also represents what is right. The concrete idea expressed by the root **reg-* was much more alive than we imagined in *rex* at the outset. This concept of the nature and power of the *rex* also agrees with the form of the word. It is an athematic form without suffix and it has the aspect of words which are used especially as the second term of compounds; e.g. *-dex* in *iū-dex*, an agent noun based on **deik-*. This is supported by examples in other languages than Latin: e.g. in the compound Gaulish names containing *–rix* such as *Dumno-rix*, *Ver-cingeto-rix*. In Sanskrit *rāj-* occurs less frequently as an independent word than in composition: *sam-rāj-* 'king common to all', *sva-rāj-* 'self-ruler, he who is king of himself'. In fact in Latin itself *rex* appears with specific determinants, notably in the ancient phrase *rex sacrorum*. The *rex* was charged with the task *regere sacra*, in the sense in which the expression *regere fines* is taken.

In this way we can give definition to the concept of the Indo-European kingship. The Indo-European *rex* was much more a religious than a political figure. His mission was not to command, to exercise power, but to draw up rules, to determine what was in the proper sense "right" ("straight," *droit*). It follows that the *rex*, as thus defined, was more akin to a priest than a sovereign. It is this type of kingship which was preserved by the Celts and the Italic peoples on the one hand and the Indic on the other.

This notion was bound up with the existence of great colleges of priests whose function it was to perpetuate the observance of certain rites. It needed a long process of evolution and a radical transformation to reach the kingship of the classical type, which was founded exclusively on power, political authority becoming progressively independent of religious power, which in the end devolved on the priests.

BOOK IV, CHAPTER TWO

xšay- and Iranian Kingship

Abstract. Iran is an empire and the notion of the sovereign has nothing in common with that of *rex*. It is expressed by the Persian title *xšāyaθiya xšāyaθiyānam* (Gr. *basileús basiléōn*, Pers. *šāhān šāh*), the King of Kings; this title designates the sovereign as he who is invested with the royal power, the *xšāy*-.

Now an epithet of the Achaemenid king, *vazraka*, which may also be applied to the god Ahuramazda and the earth, reveals that the power of the king is essentially mystical.

The terms which we have just examined form only one of the expressions for this notion of kingship, the one which is common only to the two extremities of the Indo-European world, to the Italo-Celtic and the Indic domains. It is noteworthy that on this fundamental notion Iranian differs from Indo-Aryan. The term *rāj*-, characteristic of the latter, is missing from the ancient Iranian vocabulary. The sole trace of a corresponding term in Iranian occurs in the dialect of the region of Khotan (in the extreme southeast of Iran bordering on India), where it is attested from the eighth century of our era in a literature of Buddhistic inspiration composed chiefly of translations. This Khotanese dialect contains the terms *rri* 'king', *rris-pur* 'king's son', which correspond to Sanskrit *rāja* and *rāja-putra*. But it is not absolutely certain that these are not borrowings from Indic, given the numerous borrowings evinced by this language and the late date at which it is attested.

If in Iranian the term **rāz-* is not current as the name for "the king," this is because, properly speaking, there was neither king nor kingdom, but rather a Persian empire. This is the reason for the lexical innovation.

In the Indo-European world, particularly as seen through the eyes of the Greeks and the Romans, it was Iran which created the notion of "empire." Certainly a Hittite empire had existed previously, but this had not constituted an historical model for neighboring peoples. The original organization is that created by the Iranians, and it was the Iranian terms which constituted the new vocabulary referring to it.

There is, in the vocabulary common to India and Iran, a term represented in Sanskrit by *kṣatra* and in Iranian by *xšaθra* which indicated in both cases the royal power. It is a derivative of *kṣā-* (*xšāy-*) 'be master of, have at one's disposal', a root which provided in Iranian numerous derivatives of the highest importance. A derivative of this root is used in Old Persian (but not in the Avesta) to designate the king: *xšāyaθiya*. It is from this Old Persian word, which has persisted for twenty-five centuries, that the modern Persian *šāh* comes by regular processes of development.

The form of the word admits of a more precise analysis: *xšāyaθiya-* is an adjective derived by a suffix *-ya* from an abstract noun **xšayaθa-*, which is itself a derivative in *-θa* from the verbal stem *xšaya-*. The "king" is designated as "he who is invested with royalty." It will be noted that the abstract notion is here the primary one. In exactly the same way it was the abstract *kṣatra* which was the base of *kṣatriya* 'member of the warrior class', literally "he who is invested with the *kṣatra-*."

It may be noted further that the form *xṣayaθ(i)ya* is not consistent with the phonetic laws of Persian, according to which the cluster *-θ(i)y-* develops to *-šy-*:- for instance the Iranian *haθya* 'true' yields *hašiya* in Old Persian. It follows that *xšāyaθiya-* is not a form of the Persian dialect in the strict sense. It did not evolve in the language in which it played so notable a part, but in an Iranian language in which this change of *-θiy-* to *-šy-* did not take place. For linguistic and historical reasons this must have been the language of the Medes, who occupied the northwest of Iran. Thus the Persian name for the "king" was borrowed by the Persians from the Medes, an important conclusion from the historical point of view.

This term enters into a formula which is characteristic of the Achaemenid titulature, *xšāyaθiya xšāyaθiyānām* 'Kings of Kings'. This formula was first coined in Persia and in the translation *basileùs basiléōn* (βασιλεὺς βασιλέων) it immediately became the designation of the Persian king among the Greeks. This is a curious expression, which does not mean "king among kings" but "he who reigns over other kings." It is a suzerainty, a kingship of the second degree which is exercised over those considered by the rest of the world as kings. However, the expression reveals an anomaly: the order of words is not what one would expect. In the modern form *šāhān šāh* it has been reversed: as such it corresponds to the syntax of nominal groups in Iranian with the qualifying term first. In this we may see a second indication of a foreign, non-Persian origin. The expression must have been taken over ready made and not coined together with the kingdom of the Achaemenids. It was probably invented by the Medes.

From this same root Iranian has derived a number of other terms. First we have the Avestan *xšaθra*, (which corresponds to Sanskrit *kṣatra*), the Persian form of which is *xšas͜sa*. This word denoted both power and the domain within which it is exercised, both royalty and kingdom. When Darius, in his eulogies, says "Ahuramazda has granted me this *xšas͜sa*" this implies both power and kingdom. This word forms part of an important compound which in Old Persian is *xšas͜sapāvan* 'satrap'. In the form of a neighboring dialect, which is more faithfully reproduced in Ionian by ἐξαιθραπεύω 'exercise the power of a satrap', it is the title which became in Greek *satrápēs*, whence "satrap." This title signifies "he who guards the kingdom." The high dignitaries thus designated had the task of administering the great provinces ("satrapies") and thus ensuring the safety of the Empire.

This notion, which crystallized in Iran, of a world constituted as an empire is not only political but also religious. It might be said that a certain terrestrial and celestial organization took as its model the kingdom of the Persian sovereigns. In the spiritual universe of the Iranians, outside Persia itself, and particularly in Mazdaean eschatology, the realm to which the faithful will attain is called *xšaθra* 'kingdom' or *xšaθra vairya* 'the desirable kingdom (or royalty)'. In its personified form *Xšaθravairya* (in Middle Iranian *šāhrēvar*) designates one of the divinities called "Immortal Saints," each of whom, symbolizing an element of the world, plays a double part, both eschatological and material.

Here we have the prototypes of what became in the eschatology of prophetic Judaism and of Christianity the Kingdom of Heaven, an image which reflects an Iranian conception.

The Iranian vocabulary of royalty utilized still other forms made from this root *xšā-*: the strictly Achaemenid terms are not the only ones. New titles were devised which show the importance of the notion of *xšā-* and the unity of the

Iranian world. The most notable of these, *xšāvan*, was used in Khotanese in the sense "sovereign." We encounter it again in the titulature of the petty Indo-Scythian kingdoms the coins of which bear, along with the names of the kings, the title of *ÞAONANO ÞAO*, which is to be transcribed phonetically as *ṣaunanu ṣau*. This is not the correspondent of *šahān šāh*, but an expression constructed on the same model, with *šau* coming from *xšāvan*.

There were, however, other local titulatures. In the Middle Iranian dialect of the northeast, Sogdian, which occupied the region of Samarkand, we know a different name for the king in the form *xwt'w*, that is to say *xwatāw*, which represents an ancient *xwa-tāw-*(*ya*) 'he who is powerful by himself, he who holds power only from himself'. This is a very remarkable formation and (Meillet was the first to point this out) it is the exact counterpart of the Greek *autokrátōr* (ἀυτοκράτωρ). It is not possible to decide whether the Iranian form was translated from the Greek, for on the one hand the Sogdian compound could be much more ancient, as is evidenced by the Vedic epithet *sva-tava* 'powerful by himself'; on the other hand, the Greek title *autokrátōr* does not appear before the fifth century BC.

Whether or not it was created in Iran itself, this title *xwatāw* is also notable from another point of view. It passed into Middle Persian, where it assumed the form *xudā*, which is in modern Persian the name of "God," who is thus conceived as the holder of absolute sovereignty.

This gives us some idea of the gap between this concept and the notion of royalty which is implicit in the Latin term *rex* and the Sanskrit *rāj*. This is no longer a kingship of a "ruling" (in the literal sense) kind; the role of the sovereign is not "to trace out the straight road" according to Indo-European ideology. In Iran we see the development of an absolute power which in the eyes of the Occidental world of classical times was incarnated in the Achaemenid Persian kingdom.

It is not merely in the name for the king but also in certain of its epithets that the tradition of Achaemenid Persia shows its originality. Persian is the only Iranian language which possesses certain terms relating to royalty. Among them is the adjective of Old Persian *vazraka* 'great' which has become *buzurg* in modern Persian. This is exclusively a Persian adjective; it is not known from any other Iranian dialect, and Indic offers no exact correspondent. In the Achaemenid texts, which are royal proclamations, this adjective appears as an epithet of specific notions.

(a) *baga vazraka* 'the great God' is the designation of Ahuramazda and of him alone. Certain texts begin with this eulogy: *baga vazraka ahuramazdā* 'the great God is Ahuramazda'.

(b) *vazraka* is applied to the king: *xšāyaθiya vazraka*, the royal protocol, repeated immutably after the name of the sovereign, in his three titles: "Great King," *xšāyaθiya vazraka*, "King of Kings," *xšāyaθiya xšāyaθiyānām*, "King of the Countries," *xšāyaθiya dahyunām*. This is a triple definition of his status. The qualification "Great" added to the title "King" was a novelty to the Greeks. Hence the use of *basileùs mégas* (βασιλεὺς μέγας) to designate the King of Persia. The second title, "King of Kings," makes him into the supreme sovereign, master of an empire which comprises the other kingdoms. Finally, "King of the Countries" establishes his authority over the provinces of the Achaemenid empire: Persia, Media, Babylonia, Egypt, etc., which are so many "countries."

(c) *vazraka* is also applied to the "earth," *bumi*, understood in the widest sense as the domain of the royal sovereignty.

The analysis of the adjective remains hypothetical in part. In all probability it is a derivative in *-ka* of a stem in *r-* which is not attested, **vazar* or **vazra-*, from a root **vaz-* 'be strong, full of vigor' (cf. Lat. *vegeo*), which corresponds to that of the Vedic substantive *vāja-*'strength, combat'. In the "heroic" terminology of the Veda *vāja*, with its derivatives, has an important place and has a variety of senses which mask the original sense. It appears that *vāja* indicates a force proper to gods, heroes, horses, which assures them the victory. It is likewise the mystical virtue of the sacrifice together with what this procures: well-being, contentment, power. It is also the power which is manifested in the gift, whence the sense "generosity," "wealth."

We glimpse a reflection of this notion in the Persian uses of *vazraka*. If the god Ahuramazda is defined as *vazraka*, this is because he is animated with this mystical force (the Indian *vāja-*). The king is also endowed with this power and likewise the earth, the natural element which supports and nourishes everything.

This qualification by *vazraka* is perhaps distributed according to the schema of the three classes: god as the source of religious power; the king as master of warrior power; the earth, the prototype of fertility. A simple adjective may express a rich conceptual content.

BOOK IV, CHAPTER THREE

Hellenic Kingship

Abstract. As compared with the Indo-Iranian and the Italic concept of the king the Greek names *basileús* and *wánaks* suggest a more evolved and differentiated notion close in several respects to the Germanic conception.

Of unknown etymology, but both attested in the Mycenaean texts, these terms are in distinctive opposition, in that only the second designates the holder of power.

As for *basileús*, although he is not a god like the Indian *rāj-*, he exercises functions of a magico-religious type which were doubtless structured originally along the tripartite lines already studied. The scepter, the symbol (of Hellenic origin) of his authority, is nothing more in its origin than the staff of the messenger who bears an authorized message.

There is no better measure of the transformation of the political structures of the Indo-Europeans than the vocabulary of primitive Greek institutions. From the dawn of history, royalty and everything pertaining to it has in Greek new designations which are unknown elsewhere and remain quite inexplicable.

Greek possesses two names for the king, *basileús* (βασιλεύς) and *wánaks* (*wάναξ*). These two terms do not exist on the same level, but they both defy any etymological analysis. They have no correspondent in other languages, and we cannot even detect any connections, even partial ones, within Greek itself.

There has been much fruitless discussion over the origin of *basileús*. If the identification of the root is impossible, we may at least suggest a probable analysis of its morphology: *basileús* is derived by means of the suffix *-eus*, which is preceded by the morpheme *-il-*, this being an element characteristic of the personal names of Asia Minor: e.g. *Trō̆il-os*, *Murs-íl-os*, to which the Hittite *Muršiliš* corresponds. This is all that can be said.

As for the root element *bas-*, none of the numerous hypotheses recorded in the etymological dictionaries can even be discussed today. The term *basileús* has in fact been detected in the Mycenaean tablets, where it has the form *qa-si-re-u*, with the derivative *qa-si-re-wi-ya*, which is probably equivalent to *basileía*. If the phonetic value of the sign *qa-* is secure, the initial *b-* of *basileus* must go back to an original labiovelar g^{w}-. The Mycenaean form may be posited as g^{w}*asileús*. It is from this basis that we must proceed in the future if some chance of a connection should present itself. For the moment we have merely advanced a stage along the road of reconstruction.

The case of *wánaks* is comparable but different. Like *basileús* it is Homeric and Mycenaean. But it has a wider dialectal extension and it is encountered once outside Greek.

In a number of old inscriptions this title is given both to divinities like Poseidon and the Dioscuri and to men invested with supreme power. Thus in a bilingual Greco-Phoenician inscription of Cyprus *wánaks* translates the Phoenician *ádon* 'Lord'. It is interesting to note that in a dedication in Old Phrygian dating from about 600 BC the king Midas is qualified as *wánaks* although we cannot tell whether the word is native to Phrygian or whether it comes from Greek.

But the most important data are provided by Mycenaean where the term appears in a number of forms: *wa-na-ka* (*wánaks*), *wa-na-ke-te*, *wa-na-ka-te* (=*wanáktei*, dative singular), *wa-na-ka-te-ro* (=*wanák-teros*, with a comparative suffix), *wa-na-sa-wi-ja*, *wa-na-so-i* or *wa-no-so-i*, of less clear interpretation.

Further, the contexts in which the terms are used in Mycenaean throw light on the relation between the words *basileús* (in fact g^{w}*asileús*) and the *wánaks*. It seems that the *basileús* was merely a local chieftain, a man of rank but far from being a king. He does not seem to have possessed any political authority. On the contrary the *wánaks* is regarded as the holder of royal power, even if we cannot define the extent of his territory. Is the title also bestowed on divinities and priests? We are not in a position to assert this, but it remains a possibility.

The respective positions of the *basileús* and the *wánaks* in the Homeric epic correspond well with what characterizes these two persons in Mycenaean society. Only it should be noted that *wánaks* is also a divine qualification reserved for the highest gods. Apollo, the god of the Trojans, is the *wánaks par excellence*. Zeus is also dignified with this title but less frequently. The Dioscuri are also specifically called *wánake* (a dual form which contrasts with the declension which is based on the stem *wanakt-*).

It would be of interest to make precise the relation of sense between *basileús* and *wánaks*, at least in its main features. According to Aristotle, the brothers and the sons of the king bore the title of *wánaks*. It would thus seem that the relation between *basileús* and *wánaks* was that which exists between "king" and "prince." This would be the justification of the title *wanake* bestowed on the Dioscuri, Διόσ-κουροι, royal princes. We cannot, however, accept the limitation of the term *wánaks* to the son or the brother of the king; for in Homer a person can be at one and the same time *basileús* and *wánaks*. One title does not contradict the other, as we can see from *Odyssey* 20, 194. Moreover, *wánaks* by itself serves as a divine qualification: the invocation to Zeus Dodonaios, one of the most solemn texts of the *Iliad*, begins thus: Ζεῦ ἄνα ... (16, 233). A god is never called *basileús*. On the contrary the title *basileús* is widespread in human society: besides Agamemnon it is bestowed on a whole crowd of people. There are even degrees and a kind of hierarchy among *basileîs*, to judge by the comparative *basileúteros* and the superlative *basileútatos*, whereas there is no such variation on *wánaks* in Homer. Apart from the Mycenaean *wanaktero-*, the sense of which remains uncertain, the title of *wánaks* denotes an absolute quality. Further, it should be noted that in almost every case *basileús* has no qualification: a man is simply a *basileús*. There are only two or three examples of *basileús* with a genitive. On the other hand *wánaks* usually has a qualification, the name of a community: *wánaks andrȭn* '*wánaks* of men' or else the name of a country: *wánaks Lukíēs* '*wánaks* of Lycia'. Similarly the verb *wanássō* 'to be *wánaks*' is constructed with a place name.

This implies that *wánaks* alone designates the reality of royal power; *basileús* is no more than a traditional title held by the chief of the *génos*, but which does not correspond to a territorial sovereignty and which a number of persons may hold in the same place. There are a large number of *basilē̂es* living in Ithaca (*Od.* 1, 394). One single town, that of the Phaeacians, counted no fewer than thirteen *basilē̂es* (8, 390). A respected person, the *basileús* had certain privileges in the assembly, but the exercise of power was the prerogative of the *wánaks* alone, and this is what is indicated also by the verb *wanássō*. Similarly testimony is also afforded by expression preserved as proper names:

Iphi-anassa 'who rules with power', the name of the daughter of Agamemnon. The feminine *(w)ánassa* is the epithet of goddesses like Demeter and Athena. Further, when Odysseus sees Nausicaa for the first time he addresses her thus, believing her to be a goddess.

***

In the Homeric conception of kingship there survive certain ideas which recur in some guise in other Indo-European societies. Of special importance is the idea of the king as the author and guarantor of the prosperity of his people, if he follows the rules of justice and divine commandments. We read in the *Odyssey* (19, 110ff.) the following eulogy of the king: "a good king (*basileús*) who respects the gods, who lives according to justice, who reigns (*anássōn*) over numerous and valiant men, for him the black earth bears wheat and barley, the trees are laden with fruit, the flocks increase unceasingly, the sea yields fish, thanks to his good government; the people prosper beneath his rule."

This passage was frequently echoed in later literature; writers took pleasure in contrasting the happiness of peoples governed according to justice with the calamities born of deceit and crime. But this is not simply a moral commonplace. In fact, the poet exalts the mystical and productive virtue of the king, whose proper function it was to promote fertility about him, both in animals and vegetables.

This conception is found, at a much later date, of course, in Germanic society, but attested in much the same terms. Among the Scandinavians the king ensures prosperity on land and sea; his reign is characterized by an abundance of fruits and the fecundity of women. He is asked, according to a consecrated formula, for *ár ok friðr* 'abundance and peace', just as sacrifice was made at Athens at the Bouphoniae "for peace and prosperity."

These are not mere empty formulas. Ammianus Marcellinus reports that the Burgundians, after a defeat or a calamity, inflicted a ritual death on their king because he had not brought prosperity and success to his people. We find here, in a different form, the idea which animates a prayer of the Achaemenid Persian king, which Darius formulates thus: "May Ahuramazda bring me help along with all the other gods and protect this land from the army of the enemy, from bad harvests, from the lie."

Above (Book Three, Chapter One) we have commented on this prayer. It lists the evils proper to the three divisions of society and their respective activities:

religious spirit (*drauga* 'falsehood'), the cultivation of the soil (*dušiyāra* 'bad harvest'), martial activity (*hainā* 'hostile army'). This sum total of misfortunes which Darius begs the god to ward off from his kingdom is the counterpart of the benefits which he himself should procure for the people. It is only insofar as he enjoys the favor of Ahuramazda that he will ensure the prosperity of his country, the defeat of his enemies, and the triumph of the spirit of truth.

This image of the king as provider created in Old English the name of the "lord." The English term *lord* goes back to an ancient compound *hlāford*, the first element of which is *hlāf* 'loaf'. *Hlāford* is traced to an original form **hlāf-weard* 'guardian of the loaf'. He is an "alimentary" lord, one who provides sustenance, "the master of the loaf." Similarly *lady* in Old English is *hlæf-dīge* 'the loaf kneader'. The subjects of the *lord*, those who are under his authority, are called "the eaters of bread." In the medieval economy the petty English "lord" played within his domain the same role as the Homeric "king" according to Indo-European conceptions.

However, not all these peoples have the same ideas of the royal function. Between the Vedic kingship and that of the Greeks there is a manifest difference which may be brought out by the two definitions we propose to contrast.

In the Laws of Manu the king is characterized in a single phrase: "the king is a great divinity (*mahatī devatāhi*) in human shape (*nararūpena*)." This definition is confirmed by other formulations: "There are eight sacred things, objects of reverence, of cult and circumambulation: the brahman, the (sacred) cow, fire, gold, *ghṛta* (melted butter), the sun, the waters, and the king" (he being the eighth).

With this we may contrast the definition of Aristotle (*Politics* I, p. 1259): "The king has the same relation to his subjects as the head of the family has to his children." In brief, he is a *despótēs* in the etymological sense of the word, the master of the house, certainly an absolute master but not a god.

It is true that in Homeric phraseology the *basileús* is *diogenḗs*, *diotrephḗs*, 'born of Zeus', 'nurtured by Zeus'; he has some attributes which come to him from Zeus, such as his scepter. Everything that he is and everything that he possesses, his insignia and his powers, have been conferred on him by the gods, but he does not hold them in virtue of divine descent. This essential change, which is peculiar both to the Greek and the Germanic worlds, brings into being a type of kingship which is opposed to the Indian and Roman conception of the king: the Roman *rex* is in effect on the same plane as the Indian *rāj*: the two personages have a common role and the same name.

The more "modern" conception, which is also more "democratic," manifested in the Greek and Germanic societies must have evolved independently of each other. It is not accompanied by common terminology, whereas India and Rome are in this respect profoundly conservative. The coincidence of terms is instructive: the term **rēg-* survived in the Italic languages and in Indic, at the two extremities of the Indo-European world. It is here that the most traditional institutions and the most archaic concepts survived, thanks to a religious organization which was maintained by colleges of priests (cf. above, Book Four, Chapter One).

On the contrary, in the center of Europe, great movements of peoples have overthrown the ancient structures. We must not think merely of the Greeks and Germanic peoples but also of other peoples, far less well known, who seem to have participated in the same social organization, such as the Illyrians and the Veneti, of whom we possess only scanty and indirect testimony.

***

In the series of terms relating to the king and kingship it appears to be legitimate to include the name of one of the insignia proper to the royal function, the scepter, the Greek word for which is *skêptron* (σκῆπτρον). This is not an Indo-European term; in fact it is confined to Greek. Here we see something rather peculiar, for the institution of the scepter soon spread to a number of European peoples. In fact the term passed from Greek to Latin and Slavic, and then from Latin to Germanic, thus covering a great part of Europe. This makes even more noteworthy the absence of the notion in Indo-Iranian.

No designation for the scepter exists either in India or in Mazdaean Iran. No word of this sense is found in the lexicon of the Rig Veda or the Avesta; this is a negative fact, yet one of considerable significance. Some scholars have sought to find a scepter on an Achaemenid bas-relief in an object carried by a follower of the king, and its bearer is designated on this monument as *vassa-bara* 'the bearer of *vassa*'. Was he the scepter-bearer of the king? Today there is general agreement that the object in question is a bow; thus the term presumably designates the bow-bearer or archer of the king. Thus the result of the enquiry is negative for Achaemenid Persia, as it is for India.

We know the importance of the scepter for the Homeric kingship, since the kings are defined as "scepter-bearers": σκηπτοῦχοι βασιλῆες.

The name itself, in Homer and in everyday language, is *skêptron*, which became *sceptrum* in Latin, but we also have the form *skâpton* (σκᾶπτον) in Doric, in Pindar. Besides there exists a form with a different grade of the vowel, Latin *scipio* which is paralleled by Greek *skípōn* (σκίπων).

In Homer this *skêptron* is the attribute of the king, of heralds, messengers, judges, and all persons who, whether of their own nature or because of a particular occasion, are invested with authority. The *skêptron* is passed to the orator before he begins his speech so that he may speak with authority. The "scepter" in itself is a staff, the staff of the traveler or the beggar. It takes on an august aspect when it is in the hands of a royal person, such as the scepter of Agamemnon, apropos of which the poet enumerates all those who have transmitted it, going right back to Zeus himself. This divine scepter was preserved with great reverence at Chaeronea, where it was kept under the guard of a priest to whom it was entrusted annually in the course of a ceremony, according to Pausanias. However, the name given to this was not *skêptron* but *dóru*, literally "wood" (Pausanias IX, 40, 11). It was therefore a long staff, the shaft of a spear. Now, in the earliest history of Rome the scepter of the king was called *hasta*, according to Justinus 43, 3: "*hastas quas Graeci sceptra dicere ...*" *Hasta* is thus certainly the Latin equivalent of the "scepter" as the shaft of a spear. As for the scepter of the Germanic peoples, the Latin historians call it "pike," *contus*. The Germanic word in OHG *chunin-gerta*, OE *cyne-gerd* 'king's staff'; now OHG *gerta* 'wand' (Goth. *gazds* 'goad') corresponds to Latin *hasta*.

It would be of interest to try and establish the original meaning of *skêptron* in order to see if we can infer in what form this emblem was imagined. We may start from the concept of royalty itself, for the insignia of royalty are of a different order from mere ornaments. The scepter and the crown are royalty in themselves. It is not the king who reigns but the crown, because it makes the king. It is the crown which through all time is the foundation of royalty. Today we still speak of the "possessions of the crown"; the son of the king is "the crown prince" (German *Kronprinz*). Thus the king derives his power from the crown, of which he is merely the trustee. This mystical notion also attaches to the Homeric *skêptron*: a person can reign, judge, harangue only when he has the *skêptron* in his hands.

There is nothing mysterious about the formation and the sense of the Greek term: *skêptron* is the instrument noun formed from the verb *skḗptō* 'lean on'; it is an object on which one supports oneself, a staff. But this etymological sense tells us nothing about the origin of the powers which were attached to this emblem. This translation is itself too bald. "Support oneself" can be expressed in other ways, e.g. by *klínō*. The proper sense of *skḗptō* is "to lean with all one's weight on something which gives support." The poet in order to describe the attitude of a wounded man sustained by his companions says that "he leans with all his weight" on those who are helping him to get away. The beggar of the *Odyssey* "supports himself on his staff." From this comes the secondary sense of the verb *skḗptō* 'to put forward as a pretext, give as an excuse', that is, to justify oneself by "supporting oneself" on an established fact.

This verb is sometimes translated as "fly, speed" on the basis of as few passages from the tragedians. This translation needs revision. In a passage of the *Agamemnon* of Aeschylus four examples of this verb are used in succession (ll. 302, 308, 310) in the description of a fire which is used as a beacon transmitted from one station to the next. Along the chain of stations the fire illuminates the hearths. The torch covers a certain distance and the light shoots down (*éskēpsen*) over Lake Gorgopis, in this place, and urges the following fire not to tarry but to take flame in its turn: "Lo! it shot down (*éskēpsen*) and reached the Arachnaean peak." Then "Lo! it shoots down (*skḗptei*) on the roof of the Atreidai." The flame leaves one summit and "supports itself" on the different summits that it must inflame. It is always the same movement which is pictured.

Speaking of the god who brings a calamity, Sophocles (*Oed. Rex*, 28) says that the god descends (*skḗpsas*), swoops down on the town. Finally, in an inscription (IG II^2, 1629) the subject is some triremes on which a storm has "swooped down."

The sense of the verb is everywhere to "weigh down on, press with all one's weight." It follows that the *skêptron* is the staff which one presses down on and which prevents one from falling. Now there is only one type of staff that meets this purpose and this is the *walking stick* or *staff*.

The question is how an instrument so defined by its descriptive term can invest its bearer with such high dignity. We may discount the various explanations which have been proposed; it is not in itself the emblem of power, the symbol of authority, the staff of the orator. Nor is it a magic wand; this is called in Greek *rhábdos*, and the *skêptron* is never the attribute of the magician. Since *skêptron* designates the staff, the walking stick, we have to ask ourselves how we can unify the different functions of this *skêptron* in the hands of the different persons who are authorized to hold it.

Originally the *skêptron* seems to have been the staff of the *messenger*. It is the attribute of a traveler who advances with authority not to perform some act but to speak. These three conditions, the man on the march, the man with authority, the man with something to tell, imply a single function, that of the messenger who combines them all and who alone can explain them. From the fact that it is necessary to the bringer of a message the *skêptron* becomes a symbol of his function and a mystic sign of his credentials. Henceforward it is an attribute of the person who brings a message, a sacred personage whose mission it is to transmit the message of authority. This is why the *skêptron* starts with Zeus from whom, by a succession of holders, it descends to Agamemnon. Zeus gives it as a kind of credential to those whom he designates to speak in his name.

The uneven distribution of the scepter in the Indo-European world thus reflects the variable conception of royalty. For the Indo-Iranians the king is a god; he does not need any such symbolic credential as the scepter. But the Homeric king is merely a man who holds from Zeus his qualification and the attributes which manifest it. Among the Germans, too, the king exercises an authority which is purely human, whereas at Rome the *rex* is of the same essence and invested with the same divine powers as the Indian *rāj*.

It was only in the first beginnings of Rome that, under Greek influence, the king adopted the scepter as his attribute. Both the word and the idea came to the Romans from the Greek civilization. This whole process shows how a secondary phenomenon of historical diffusion may conceal and mask profound differences of origin.

BOOK IV, CHAPTER FOUR

The Authority of the King

Abstract. The Greek *kraínō* is used of the divinity who sanctions (by a nod, *kraínō* being a derivative of *kára* 'head') and, by imitation of the divine authority, also of the king who gives executive sanction to a project or a proposal but without carrying it out himself. *Kraínō* thus appears as the specific expression for the act of authority—divine in origin and subsequently also royal and even susceptible of other extensions in given contexts—which allows a word to be realized in action.

If we study the vocabulary of royalty in Greek, we observe that there is a unilateral relationship between the verbs and nouns relating to the concept of "ruling." The principal verbs are derived from nouns and not vice versa. Thus *basileúein* is a denominative verb from the noun *basileús*, just as *anássein* is based on *ánaks*. It follows that by themselves these verbs add no new element to what is already known from the basic noun.

However, we have an important verb which does not appear as a derivative from a living substantive. At least from a synchronic point of view, in Homeric Greek it is a primary verb. In the epic language it has the form *kraiaínō*, which is contracted to *kraínō*.

This verb, which is exclusively poetical, is frequent in Homer; it is widely attested in tragedy in the sense "to reign." But in the majority of Homeric examples *kraínō* means "execute, accomplish." At least this is how it is everywhere translated. Let us compare two Homeric formulas to measure the range of sense of which this verb is capable in the same language: *krḗēnon eéldōr* 'fulfill this desire'; but also *basilêes kraínousi* 'kings reign'. How can we reconcile these two senses? We do not know. It would, however, be relevant to see what was the basic idea which gave rise to a certain concept of (royal) power.

From the morphological point of view, *kraínō* is a denominative derived from the name of the "head." The Homeric present tense *kraiaínō* goes back to **krās ° n-yō*, which is based on the Indo-European stem represented in Gr. *kára*, Skt. *śīrṣan*, etc., "head." What is the relation of sense between the basic noun and the derived verb? It will be the same as that between French *chef* and *achever*. We can cite a parallel from Greek itself: *kephalaióō*. The ancients themselves had the same idea when they said that *kraínein* is "to put the head on something."

But these connections solve nothing. The relation in French is of quite a different order: *achever* is "to bring to a head." The *chef* is certainly the "head," but understood as the final stage of a movement, whence the sense "to bring to the limit, extremity." Now the word for head in Greek, whether it is *kephalḗ* or *kára*, evokes quite different images, those of the initial point, the source and origin. So we cannot group it with *caput* in Late Latin or with *chef* in French, where it designated the "ultimate point, the extremity." As for *kephalaióō*, it means not "to finish" but "to sum up, bring under one head" (*kephalḗ*) or, as we say, to give the heads of the chapters (*donner des* ***têtes*** *de chapitre*).

Thus these parallels do not illuminate the formation of *kraínō* and the explanation given by the ancients falls to the ground. Only a complete study of the Homeric usages can enlighten us. We propose to review them in order to site the verb in each instance in its context. Nearly all the Homeric examples of *kraiaínō* and of *epikraiaínō* will be contained in our list.

In the *Iliad* (1, 41 = 504, cf. *Od.* 20, 115), *tóde moi krḗēnon eéldōr* is a prayer formula addressed to a god which is translated "fulfill my wish."

If we now read *Il.* 2, 419 *hṑs éphat', oud' ára pṓ hoi epekraíaine Kroníōn* (ὥς ἔφατ', οὐδ' ἄρα πώ οἱ ἐπεκραίαινε Κρονίων), we see that the god has not strictly to "fulfill" this wish; he does not execute it himself. He may accept the vow, and only this divine sanction enables this wish to be realized. The action designated by the verb is always exercised as an act of authority, applied downward. Only the god has the capability of *kraínein*, which indicates not the actual execution but (1) the acceptance by the god of the wish formulated by the man, and (2) the divine authorization accorded to the wish to reach accomplishment.

These are the two components of the sense. The process referred to by the verb always has a god as its agent or a royal personage or some supernatural power. And this process consists in a "sanction" and in an act of approval, which alone makes a measure capable of execution.

The god in the passage cited (*Il.* 2, 419) has therefore refused this sanction, without which the wish remains nothing more than a form of words, something empty and of no effect. In *Il.* 5, 508 *toû d' ekraíainen ephetmàs Phoíbou Apóllōnos* (τοῦ δ' ἐκραίαινεν ἐφετμὰς Φοίβου Ἀπόλλωνος) can we understand that the commands of Apollo are "accomplished" by Ares? But the verb, we repeat, is only used of a god. In fact, and this is shown by the context, Ares does not here carry out an order. He sheds a cloud over the combatants; he acts in such a way that the wish of Phoebus can be fulfilled. But the execution falls to the combatants themselves. They could do nothing if this sanction had not been granted to them, which comes by divine authority. Here we may give precision to the explanation simply by considering the circumstances and the persons concerned.

Another passage (9, 100ff.) had already attracted the attention of the ancient commentators:

> τῶ σε χρὴ περὶ μεν φάσθαι ἔπος, ἠδ' ἐπακοῦσαι,
> κρηῆναι δὲ καὶ ἄλλῳ, ὅτ' ἄν τινα θυμὸς ἀνώγηι
> εἰπεῖν εἰς αγαθόν.

This is a speech by Nestor addressed to Agamemnon with the purpose of urging him not to disregard the opinions expressed to him. Responsible for numerous men by virtue of his royal authority, he ought to listen to the wise counsels that can be given to him. "You more than others it behooves to speak and listen and at need act according to the opinion of another when his heart has impelled him to speak for the good of all." This translation is in need of some revision. We must first elucidate the construction *krēênai dè kaì állōi*. It is to be explained by the ellipsis of the direct object, which is *épos* and is to be understood from the preceding line: "pronounce and listen to the word (*épos*)" and from *eipeîn* in the following line. The construction is therefore to be understood as follows: *krēênai* (*épos*) *állōi* and so is exactly symmetrical with *krênon kaì emoì épos* (*Od.* 20, 115). We may thus translate "You more than anyone should speak, lend your ears to, and ratify (*krēênai*) the word of another if his spirit prompts him to speak to good purpose."

In Achilles' reply (9, 310) ᾗπερ δὴ κρανέω τε καὶ τετελεσμένον ἔσται, two verbs are coordinated: *kraínein* and *teleîn.* The translation "I must tell you bluntly how I intend to act and how it will come to pass" does not bring out the logical relation between *kraínein* 'to sanction' and *teleîn* 'to accomplish'. We translate "I must make plain my intention, how I shall confirm it and how it will be accomplished."

After the refusal of Achilles to lend aid to the Achaeans, Ajax says "Let us go, it does not seem that the accomplishment of our plan is sanctioned (*kranée-sthai*) by this journey" (9, 626). The embassy to Achilles will thus not be followed by any success. It has failed.

We can go a step further in this analysis if we consider the opposition between *noêsai* and *kraínein* in the *Odyssey* (5, 169). Calypso undertakes to do everything in her power to help Odysseus return home "if that is pleasing to the gods, who are superior to me both in planning (*noêsai*) and in execution (*krênai*)." Here the notable fact is the absolute use of *kraínein* and that the act of *kraínein* is also credited to the gods. These "accomplish," but always in their proper sphere: *kraínein* is never used of accomplishment by a human individual. From this moment we observe an evolution of meaning which produces different senses according to the construction of the verb. We have the transitive construction (notably with *eéldōr*), of which we have seen some examples above; and the intransitive construction which must now be illustrated by means of a few examples.

It already appears in the *Odyssey* and gives to *kraínein* the sense of "to decide by supreme authority." In this way it comes about that Alkinoos can say: "twelve kings *kraínousi*" (8, 390) among the Phaeacians. This is equivalent to "rule," but without implying that this verb is necessarily bound up with the exercise of the royal function. It always signifies the capacity to give effect to an authoritative decision. After Homer the intransitive construction of *kraínein* retains this sense; e.g. in Aeschylus *épraksan hōs ékranen* 'They fared as Zeus in his authority had decided' (*Ag.* 369). Furthermore we have an epigraphic passage of particular interest, because it is unique among its kind, in the oath formula of the ephebes[1] "I shall obey those who exercise authority (*tôn krainóntōn*) with wisdom," with reference to the supreme magistrates of the city.

1. A text discovered and published by Louis Robert, *Etudes épigraphiques et philologiques*, 1938, p. 302.

The transitive construction of *kraínein* in tragedy usually is found in the passive; it serves to announce the things effected by great sovereign powers: "More than once my mother predicted to me how the future would be accomplished" (*kraínoito*) (Aeschylus *Prom.* 211); "It is not fated that Moira should accomplish (*krânai*) these things in this way" (ibid. 512); "The curse of his father Kronos will be accomplished then entirely" (*kranthḗsetai*, ibid. 911); "In such a way is a unanimous vote accomplished (*kékrantai*), decided by the people" (*Suppl.* 943).

It is also invariably the case that the negative Homeric adjective *akráantos* 'not effected' (*Il.* 2, 138), classical *ákrantos*, later "vain," refers to the action of a supra-individual power. It has this full sense in two passages of the *Odyssey*; in one it applies to a prophecy which is not fulfilled (2, 202). The other is the celebrated passage on dreams (19, 564). Here we must recall the Homeric distinction between the *ónar*, the dream which may be merely an illusion and the "good *húpar*, which shall be accomplished" (ibid. 547). Dreams have a reality of their own order independent of human reality. It is within the framework of this dream world that we must place the relationship between the two varieties of dream: some (we disregard the play of assonance in the Greek text) come by the ivory gates and deceive, "bringing words not to be fulfilled (*akráanta*)"; others come by the horn gates, those which give the sanction of fulfillment (*kraínousi*) to true things (*étuma*). The sovereign power of dreams is the condition of their truth, already established, which is perceptible only to the seer and will be confirmed by events. Thus the two adjectives correspond: *akráanta* denotes the things which will not come to pass as opposed to the *étuma*, the things which will be revealed as true.

Finally, to complete this review, we cite some more difficult uses of *kraínein*: the three examples in the *Homeric Hymn to Hermes* which we take in their order of occurrence. "Hermes raises his voice as he plays the cithara harmoniously, the lovely song of which accompanies him as he 'celebrates' (*kraínōn*) the immortal gods as well as the dark earth" (l. 427). The proposed translation of *kraínō* as "celebrate" is taken from the ancient commentators. The use of the verb seemed so different from those of Homer and even those encountered in later texts that the usual translation was regarded as inadmissible. So scholars have fallen back on a gloss of Hesychius, who translates *kraínōn* as "honoring, celebrating" (*timôn, geraírōn*). It is highly probable that the gloss applies to the passage in question; it simply indicates the embarrassment felt by ancient commentators in the face of a usage apparently so aberrant. Others have suggested translating *kraínōn* by *apotelôn* 'performing the song until the end', which is certainly extremely artificial. In our opinion*kraínō* is to be interpreted here in the same way as in the *Odyssey*. The god is singing of the origin of things and by his song the gods "are brought into existence." A bold metaphor, but one which is consistent with the role of a poet who is himself a god. A poet causes to exist; things come to birth in his song. Far from disrupting the history of the word, this example illustrates its continuity.

The state of the text in l. 559 makes the problem somewhat more complex but this does not alter its character. The poet alludes to the *Moîrai* 'Fates', who are invested with prophetic powers and give instruction in the art of divination. They are the *Thriaí*, "bee-women." Apollo refuses to divulge to Hermes the secrets of his mantic art but offers him the *Thriaí*, who taught him a part of this art while he was still a child: " … three virgin sisters taught me the arts of divination, which I exercised while still a child tending my cattle; my father made no objection. Thence they take flight hither and thither to feed on wax, bringing all things to pass (*kraínousin*)."

These bee-women who, taking flight, go and feed on wax and then *kraínousin hékasta* could hardly "bring all things to pass." They do not possess the more than divine power which this would require, but simply the gift of prophecy, which is their sole capacity. It follows that the meaning of *kraínein* is here the same as in the preceding passage. It is the power of making effective, but within the field of prophecy. The meaning is not "cause to be realized" but "to predict" the things or, as is said later in the passage (561), *alētheíēn agoreúein* 'tell the truth', in explanation of *kraínein*. Prophetic pronouncement calls things into existence.

Finally we come to the most difficult example, in line 529 of the hymn. Apollo refuses this prophetic gift to Hermes, which is the exclusive privilege of Zeus and has been conceded to Apollo alone. But to console Hermes Apollo grants him certain minor powers and an attribute described in these terms: "a wand marvelously rich and opulent, made of gold, three-leafed: it will protect you against all manner of dangers by bringing to pass (*epikraínousa*) favorable decrees, words and deeds, which I declare that I know from the lips of Zeus."

There are textual difficulties, to be sure: the manuscripts give the accusative *theoús* 'gods' as the complement of *epikraínousa*, which makes no sense and this has been corrected to *themoús* 'decrees'. If this emendation is accepted, the line becomes intelligible and *epikraínein* recovers the sense which it has in the epic. The wand "gives the sanction of accomplishment" to the counsels of

Apollo which he knows from the lips of Zeus, that is, to his oracles. In this passage, too, there is nothing which obliges us to translate *kraínein* in a different way from what we have done elsewhere.

We can now review the meaning of *kraínō* as a whole. The first idea is that of sanctioning with authority the accomplishment of a human project and so according it existence. From this proceed the other usages which we have reviewed: to reach in an authoritative way a political decision, exercise an authority which sanctions and ratifies decisions already taken, and in general to be invested with executive authority.

Given this single and constant meaning, if we now look for the connection between *kraínein* and *kára* 'head', we can see it in a different light from previous proposals. The act of sanctioning is indicated by a movement of the head. Approbation is declared by a sign of the god's head (Gr. *neúō*, Lat. *ad-, in-nuo, nutus*). In the *Homeric Hymn to Aphrodite* we read in line 222: "Zeus gave a sign with his head (*epéneuse*) and ratified (*ekrḗēnen*) his wish."

Whether this was the intention of the poet or not, this passage may well serve to illuminate what could be the proper sense of *kraínō*. And if at a later date Sophocles uses *kraínein* to denote power over a country (*kraínein gâs, khō̂ras*), we see that this human power is defined by the gesture which indicates divine assent.

It is this divine sanction, the sign from the head of the god, which transfers a word into the order of reality. This is why the royal power indicated by the verb *kraínein* proceeds from the gesture by which the god gives existence to what would otherwise be nothing more than words.

BOOK IV, CHAPTER FIVE

Honor and Honors

Abstract. In Greek *géras*—the connection of which with *gérōn* 'old man' is no more than a popular etymology—is the honorific supplementary share occasionally granted to a king by his subjects which is a mark of his rank. If the *timḗ*, like the *géras*, enters into the apanage of the king, if it likewise entails honorific material prestations, it is distinguished in being a permanent dignity of divine origin. Since it designates the honorific royal portion which the gods receive from destiny and men from Zeus, *timḗ* is to be separated from the group of Gr. *Tínō* 'pay', *poinḗ* 'ransom, punishment', the constant sense of which is of a juridical character.

The special privileges of Homeric royalty are conveyed by a number of terms relating to *honor* and *honors*. They form part of a vocabulary the specific meanings of which are linked with archaic institutions. These meanings must be elucidated by textual analysis. We begin this study with a word which occupies an important place in epic: this is the word *géras* (γέρας), usually translated as "honor," "sign of honor," a translation which seems to fit everywhere.

The particular interest of this word, quite independently of what it tells us about social conditions, is that it is illuminated by an etymological connection which has won general assent. *Géras* is said to be related to *gérōn* 'old man'. This notion is, therefore, defined as a privilege attached to age, as an honor paid to old men; a right peculiar to a certain age class rather than to a social rank or a political function.

From a morphological point of view, *géras* is a neuter, the very structure of which is indicative of a high antiquity. The formation in *-as* is in fact ranked among the most ancient categories of the neuter, examples being *sélas*, *kréas*, *téras*, which are specified in their function by the vowel grade *e* (which is proper to ancient Indo-European neuters) and by the suffix *-as* with its variations. The word *géras* has been identified in the Mycenaean *ke-ra*.

From *géras* is derived an adjective *gerarós* (γεραρός) whence in its turn the denominative verb *geraírō* (γεραίρω) comes, and this presupposes an ancient form **gerar* alongside *géras*, a stem in *-s* which is confirmed by the negative form *agérastos* (αγέραστος). Thus this neuter in *-as* is flanked by a stem in *-ar*, thus conforming to the ancient type of Indo-European neuters.

The sense of *géras* emerges from certain uses, especially in the first book of the *Iliad*, and particularly in the middle part of this book. The *géras* is precisely the center of a dispute involving Agamemnon and Achilles. The situation is familiar. The divine oracle requires Agamemnon to restore his captive Chryseis to her father. He consents to do so on one condition. "But in that case, without delay, prepare for me another honorific portion (*géras*) so that I alone of the Argives shall not be deprived of such a portion (*agérastos*); that would be unseemly. For you all see that my own *géras* (*hó moi géras*) goes elsewhere" (118-120). Here the *géras* is naturally represented by the captive girl. She was certainly his honorific portion. But in virtue of what quality did Agamemnon receive her?

Achilles makes a spirited reply: "How shall the great-souled Achaeans give you a *géras*? We have, so far as I know, no common treasure laid in store. All that we have got from the sack of cities has been distributed; it would be unseemly to gather these things back from the people" (123–126).

The *géras* is thus a privilege in kind bestowed by the members of a social group on the occasion of a sharing out, after a haul of booty (e.g. the sack of a town), all the said booty being first put into a common pool on which the *géras*, the portion of the chief, is levied.

Achilles continues: "Give back this woman to the god and we, the Achaeans, will recompense you threefold and fourfold if Zeus one day should grant us to sack Troy," that is to say, if conditions are favorable for the allocation of a new *géras*.

Then the discussion continues and Agamemnon gets angry: he will come and get his share from Achilles, Ajax or Odysseus. These are the heroes who have a right to a *géras*. They are all *basilêes*, men of the royal class.

This motif recurs often: *géras* is the key word in the whole of the first book of the *Iliad*. On it will depend the course of events which follow. From the moment when Agamemnon takes Briseis from him, Achilles, deprived of his *géras*, deems himself dishonored, *átimos* (ἄτιμος): "For behold the son of Atreus, the powerful prince Agamemnon, has dishonored me, for he has taken and holds my prize of honor (*géras*); by his own hand he has taken it away" (355–56). This is the origin of Achilles' resentment and later Agamemnon will say that he must have been struck with madness the day he deprived Achilles of his *géras*.

In Book 9, line 334, the precise conditions of this allocation are defined. It is always Agamemnon who distributes to the *aristēessi* (ἀριστήεσσι) and the *basile û si* (βασιλεῦσι), to the lords and kings, their *géras*, their portions of honor.

In another passage Achilles asks the Trojan Aeneas, who advances against him: "What reason impels you to oppose me? Do you hope to rule over the Trojans and win the rank which Priam holds? Even if you killed me, Priam would not entrust his *géras* to you. He has children, and he is not so foolish. Unless the Trojans have already granted you a *témenos* if you succeeded in killing me" (*Il.* 20, 178ff.).

Thus the *géras* can be bestowed as reward for some exploit. It may take the form of a kingdom like the one which, according to Achilles, Aeneas hopes will be conferred on him by the ruling sovereign Priam. This prerogative is, or can be, hereditary, if we may judge by the reference to Priam's sons. The grant of this *géras* may be accompanied by an allocation of land (*témenos*), but these are independent things.

After the capture of Troy Neoptolemos distinguished himself by his valor. As a consequence he receives his portion (*moîra*)—to which all the warriors have a right—and over and above this a fine *géras*. The nature of the *géras* is not specified; it may have been a woman, like Chryseis in the first book of the *Iliad*, or like Eurymedousa, who was given as a *géras* to King Alcinous and was made his waiting-maid in his palace in Phaeacia (*Od.* 7, 10-11).

In the fourth book of the *Odyssey* we see Menelaus, who is a king, offering to his guests, besides the meat which has already been served to them, (ll. 57-59) his own *géras*, the chine (*nôta*) of an ox, a supplementary portion of the meat (ll. 65-66).

When Odysseus, in the underworld, enquires about his possessions and the present fate of his family, he asks what has become of his *géras*: "Tell me, what has become of my father and my son, do they still hold my *géras*?" (*Od.* 11, 174f.). He receives the reply: "No one possesses your *géras*, but Telemachus looks after your *teménea*." The two notions are not linked: the *témenos* is distinct from the *géras*, the privilege of royal dignity. This is why each of the suitors desires, by marrying Penelope, to obtain *géras*, the royal apanage of Odysseus.

Those examples show what the *géras* represents. It consists of extraordinary prestations reserved as the right of the king, in particular a special portion of the booty, and certain material advantages bestowed by the people; a place of honor, allocation of the best pieces of meat, cups of wine. Let us listen to Sarpedon, king of Lycia, as he enumerates his royal privileges (*Il.* 12, 310ff.): Why are we honored with so many privileges, the place of honor, meat, cups of wine? Why do all honor us as gods? Why do we enjoy a large allocation of land (*témenos méga*)? . . . Is it not our duty, in view of this, to fight in the first rank so that it will be said of us 'Our kings are not men without glory. . ., but valiant men who fight in the first rank'?"

These are not merely poetic imaginings. Here we touch on real institutions, the memory of which is preserved by the historians. Thucydides (I, 13) in speaking of primitive Greece says in a lapidary formula: "hereditary monarchies comprising fixed *géra*." Thus the *géra* form part of the definition of *basileía*, of royalty.

Herodotus (VI, 56ff.) gives a detailed account of the privileges of the kings in ancient Sparta. They have two priests, the right to wage war wherever they please; on the land, as many cattle as they wish, and the skins and the chines (*nôta*, cf. above *Od.* 4, 65) of the animals offered in sacrifice.

Even longer is the enumeration of the rights in time of peace: the first place at public banquets, the first fruits of every kind, at banquets portions twice as big as that of others (each term seems contrived to illustrate a Homeric text); they have the right to an allowance of victims for a sacrifice. At the games, they occupy the seat of honor (cf. above, *Il.* 12, 311); when they do not appear at the public meal, their portion is brought to them, but this portion is double if they attend in person; they preserve the oracles which are given, etc.

These historical testimonies may in their turn throw some light on a passage from the *Homeric Hymn to Hermes* (lines 128-129). The subject is a sacrifice made by Hermes while he was still a child. He has taken the cows from the herd and sacrifices two of them; he pierces them with spits, roasts them and spreads them out. Then he divides the flesh into twelve portions, which he draws by lot, and then he "adds to each *moîra* a *géras*."

Previously Hermes has prepared the meat: σάρκας … καὶ νῶτα γεράσμια (l. 122); we pick out this expression *nôta gerásmia*'the chine which constitutes the royal portion'; it is always the chine which is offered as a *géras* at festivities.

Thus to each of the twelve parts Hermes adds a piece of the *nôta*, which by definition serve as *géras*. Since he does not wish to make a mistake, he does this twelve times; he offers to each of the gods the *géras* which belongs properly only to one. The term is here very concrete; it is a "privilege consisting of meat."

The definition at which we have arrived appears to be uniform and it exhibits everywhere the features which we have culled successively from the texts. We are now in a position to take up again the problem of the etymology and of the connection of *géras* with *gérōn* 'old man'.

This connection was proposed by Osthoff in 1906[1] and it has won general acceptance. Osthoff started from the Homeric formula: *tò gàr géras estì geróntōn*, which appears twice in the *Iliad* (4, 323; 9, 422), from which it appears to emerge that the *géras* properly belongs to old men (*gérontes*). This serves to illustrate an etymology which the very form of the words seems to impose. But what is the precise meaning of this expression? Let us read it in its context.

In 4, 323, Nestor declares: "I am too old to fight, but all the same I remain among the warriors to guide them with my counsel and my voice: that is the privilege (*géras*) of old men."

In the other example (9, 422), Achilles dismisses in similar terms the venerable envoys of Agamemnon: "Go, declare my message to the chiefs of the Achaeans, since that is the privilege (*géras*) of elders."

This expression, regarded by Osthoff as so revealing, in fact boils down to the simple metaphorical use in which *géras* goes beyond its specific meaning: to give counsel, to intervene to reconcile men of power—such is the *géras* of old men, the privilege of those whom age excludes from combat. From this nothing of value can be extracted for the etymology. We can convince ourselves of this by another formula of the same structure which recurs six times and not merely two, which Osthoff has ignored: *tò gàr géras estì thanóntōn* 'such is the privilege of the dead': if we make offerings to the dead, this is the privilege which accrues to them. No one would think of drawing the conclusion from this use that the *géras* has any connection with death.

Thus there is nothing which relates *géras* 'privilege' to *gérōn* 'old man'. The formula in which these two words occur side by side does not imply any etymological connection between them. Besides, nowhere do we see that the

1. *Indogermanische Forschungen*, XIX, 1906, pp. 217ff.

géras is the perquisite of old men. Certainly, old age is surrounded with respect; the old men formed the council of elders, the senate; but royal honors are never accorded to them and an old man never receives a royal privilege, a *géras* in the strict sense of the term. Osthoff has been the victim of a popular etymology which was suggested by the ancient commentators in their anxiety to explain everything: "*geraiós* (γεραιός) 'old' comes from *géras* because the old men (*gérontes*) are *geraioí*, worthy of honor and respect."

These fantasies of the scholiasts are refuted by the forms in question. For besides *géras* (γέρας) 'privilege' there is another word in *-as*: *gễras* (γῆρας) 'old age', which has the vocalic grade of the aorist *égēra* (ἔγηρα). Thus we have two alternatives: either *gễras* 'old age' is a form with an original long grade and it would be impossible that *géras* 'privilege' came from the same root, or the long grade of *gễras* 'old age' is borrowed from the aorist of the verb "to grow old" and this is a proof that by this means *gễras* 'old age' was distinguished from *géras* 'privilege'. Everything goes to confirm the view that these two terms must be kept apart and no connection between them was felt.

We know further that *gérōn* 'old man' and *gễras* 'old age' are etymologically connected with Skt. *jarati* 'make decrepit', *jarant-* 'old man', Avestan *zarvan* 'old age'. The forms derived from this root never indicate anything else than physical decrepitude and are never linked with the notion of honor. We can judge the force of the word from the Homeric expression *sákos géron* (*Od.* 22, 184) which designates an old shield, worn out and decrepit.

The connection between *géras* and *gérōn* must, therefore, be rejected. Released from an etymological relationship which falsified it, the term *géras* is restored to its real meaning and antiquity. It designates one of the royal prerogatives, a prestation due to the *basileús* and constitutive of his dignity. Achilles is no longer himself—he loses his rank—if his *géras* is taken away.

This is what characterizes this notion in Homeric society. Even if we are not in a position to recover the Indo-European pre-history of the notion, at least we can be assured that the institution belongs to the most ancient form of royalty in Greece.

In the vocabulary which we are studying a good many words do not look as though they referred to institutions. They seem to have only a general meaning. Only certain modes of employment can reveal their institutional character.

While *géras* is found especially in poetry and remains confined to the most ancient phase of the language, the word *timḗ* (τιμή) occurs at every period and in all kinds of text. The place which it occupied in the language can be gauged by the number of forms which belong to the same family. Further, it is a word so clear, so constantly employed, that it might seem sufficient to recall that *timḗ* 'honor, dignity' (with the derived verb *timáō*) is the abstract noun from the old verb *tíō* (τίω) 'honor'.

In fact, *timḗ* is one of the most specific terms of certain social conditions. It remains to analyze it, and in order to give the problem its full scope we shall first consider the etymological group with which *timḗ* is connected. It constitutes a vast family of words, so extensive and diversified that the connections between the forms sometimes create difficulty. We list the chief members: besides *tíō, timáō, átimos* 'deprived of *timḗ*', we must cite the group of *tínō* (τίνω) 'pay', *tínumai* (τίνυμαι) 'cause to pay, cause to expiate', *tísis* (τίσις) 'punishment, vengeance', *átitos* (ἄτιτος) 'not paid, unpunished', etc. As we see, the terms refer to the payment of a debt, compensation for some misdeed. Further relatives are *poinḗ* (ποινή), debt which must be paid to atone for a crime, and in Latin *poena, pūnīre*.

Outside Greek, we can list Skt. *cāyate* 'pay, cause to pay, punish, chastise'; *cayati* 'respect', *cāyu* 'respectful'; Av. *kay-, čikay-* 'punish'; *kaēθā, kaēnā* 'vengeance, hatred', this last corresponding to Gr. *poinḗ*.

Such are the forms which present themselves in Greek and Indo-Iranian; they can all be derived from a root **k ʷ ei-*.

But the disparity of sense creates a difficulty; which is predominant, the sense "punish" or the sense "honor"? Is it possible to begin with the sense "obtain punishment, take vengeance" and derive from this the idea "honor, pay honor to"? It is only by positing a somewhat vague transition that we can unify the two senses. This is why, long ago, W. Schulze in his *Quaestiones epicae* (1892) proposed to separate the two etymological families. He posited two forms, one in *ē*, **k ʷ ēi-*, whence *tíō, timḗ* and the Sanskrit forms having the meaning of "respect," and another in *e*, **k ʷ ei-*, whence *tínō, tínumai, tísis* and the Sanskrit forms with the sense "to punish," etc.

In general, scholars have not made up their minds firmly on this question. Schulze has the merit of having underlined the difficulty of ascribing a single origin to the two sets of forms and meanings, and he has provided the means of solving it. The question is to decide whether the sense of *timḗ* and the words related to it support or exclude a connection with the family of *poinḗ*. It will not be sufficient to translate *timḗ* as "honor, esteem." We must give precision to the definition by reference to terms of similar sense. We shall choose some of the most explicit examples.

In the first place we consider again the passage in which *géras* and *tīmḗ* are associated as two connected concepts. This is in the passage about the quarrel between Achilles and Agamemnon in the first book of the *Iliad.* Achilles, when Agamemnon is proposing to take away his share of the booty, reproaches him in these words: "I never had any personal interest in coming here. It is you whom we followed, to please you, to win a *tīmḗ* for you (τιμὴν ἀρνύμενοι, l. 159), for you and Menelaus from the Trojans."

The translation of *tīmḗ* as "recompense" is incorrect, for we cannot see by what Agamemnon could be recompensed and how he would receive recompense from the very people whom he will defeat. What is involved here is the honorific portion and material advantages which men accord to a person in virtue of his dignity and rank. Agamemnon replies: "Be off with you, if your heart bids you. There are many others besides you who will accord me the *tīmḗ* (*tīmḗsousi*), above all wise Zeus" (174ff.). Here we have an important feature: the consideration which men—and gods—will accord to him; this *tīmḗ* is thus the apanage of royal status. Conferred by gods and men, it comprises consideration, manifestations of respect and also material advantages.

This definition may be supplemented by other testimony. In his effort to allay the quarrel Nestor says to Agamemnon: "Leave to Achilles the *géras* that the Achaeans have awarded to him" and to Achilles "Do not dispute with a king. The king to whom Zeus has granted *kûdos* 'glory' (cf. below, Chapter 6) has not the same *tīmḗ* in the division. You are strong and a goddess was your mother; but he is superior because he commands more men" (276ff). Here appears an important difference between *géras* and *tīmḗ*; the former is granted by men whereas *tīmḗ* is conferred by destiny: it forms part of one's personal lot. A text like *Il.* 15, 189 brings confirmation. The three sons of Kronos, Zeus, Poseidon, and Hades, divided all things among themselves; the world was divided into three parts and each one got his *tīmḗ* by drawing lots (*ḗlakhen*). Thus among both gods and men it is chance which decides the attribution of *tīmḗ*, and the key terms *moîra* and *lakheîn* serve to underline this fact. Thus no one can challenge the legitimacy of this apanage.

If there remained any doubt about the connection between *tīmḗ* and the royal power, it would be dispelled by *Il.* 6, 193. The King of Lycia, wishing to retain Bellerophon, gives him his daughter in marriage and "half of his royal *tīmḗ* (*tīmês basilēḯdos hḗmisu pásēs*)." In a passage already quoted (apropos of *géras*), Achilles upbraids Aeneas, who marches towards him with the words: "do you hope that this combat will give you the right to rule over the Trojans with the *timḗ* of Priam?" (*Il.* 20, 180f.); the expression associates the *timḗ* with the exercise of royal power. And there is a large number of kings (*basilêes*) who count these *timaí* among their privileges: places of honor, seats of honor, meat in abundance and full cups (*Il.* 12, 310). Not simply honor, but substantial advantages are linked with the status of *basileús* and are accorded by fate. What is therefore the origin of *timḗ*? The poet tells us in express terms: "the *timḗ* (of the king) comes from Zeus, and Zeus has taken him into friendship" (*Il.* 2, 197). The *timḗ* is of divine origin. This statement will be found elsewhere. We must also take note of the fact that the verbs which govern *timḗ* are verbs of giving: *didónai* 'give', *opázein* 'accord', *phérein* 'confer' or of deprival: Achilles was deprived of his *timḗ* when his captive girl was taken away. This notion of *timḗ* may be defined as a dignity of divine origin, conferred by fate on a royal person, which comprises not merely power but privileges of respect and material advantages. Thus *timḗ* is distinct from *géras*, which is an occasional prestation of a material kind which men accord to a sovereign or a hero.

Does *timḗ* also have a religious significance? This is often asserted, with citation of the passage from the *Homeric Hymn to Hermes* (l. 172) where *timḗ* is linked with *hosíē* (ὁσίη). This is the sole example, in Homeric poetry, which might seem to suggest this value for *timḗ*. Hermes replies to his mother's reprimand by saying that he has no desire to remain obscure and despised. It would be better to live with the immortals than to be cooped up in a dark cave all by himself. He adds "Then, in point of honors (*timês*), I shall have—I shall see to it—the same holy privileges (*tês hosíēs*) as Apollo."

Does this mean that there is a connection between *timḗ* and *hosíē* as sacred privileges, which would make the *timḗ* the privilege of a god? In this case the sense of the word would go beyond everything that has been read into it hitherto. It would no longer designate merely the regard shown to a powerful personage.

But is this the meaning of *hosíē*? In another passage of the hymn, Hermes, who desires that the wishes he has formulated should be fulfilled, sees in Apollo all that he has wished for himself: "You are the first, you dwell among the immortals, Zeus holds you in affection *ek pásēs hosíēs* (470)—this is only *justice*—and has bestowed on you wondrous gifts."

The translation of *hosíēs* as "justice," a term devoid of any religious value, might cause surprise. We shall see below (Book Six, Chapter One) in a study devoted to *hósios*, that this adjective is not the equivalent of *hierós*: it is opposed to *hierós* as the "profane" to the "sacred."

Thus the first passage from the *Hymn to Hermes* (173f.) must be understood as follows: "As regards *timḗ*, I also wish to have a right to this *hosíē* which Apollo enjoys." This concerns profane advantages and not a sacred privilege. The best proof of this lies in what follows: "...if my father does not grant me them, I will make myself the Prince of Brigands. If they punish me, I shall go to Pytho and take away the tripods, the gold and the cauldrons." Such are the advantages which a god enjoys outside the domain of the sacred. There is no need in this passage to give *timḗ* a special sense. The word is to be taken in its usual sense and does not denote a religious notion.

We may now proceed to an examination of the other half of the problem. What here concerns us is the notion expressed by *tínumai*, *tísis*, and *poinḗ*, with the corresponding forms in other languages. This notion could be described as "cause to pay a premium, claim the price of a fine, especially for a capital offence." Has this any connection with *timḗ*?

In the first place, let us consider the forms themselves and the difference in the root vowel. We have on the one hand *tīmḗ*, *tíō*, and on the other *tī́numai* (= *teinu-*, cf. *apoteinútō* from a fifth-century Cretan inscription). The formal difference brings out the difference which separates the two notions.

It has often been maintained that in one passage of Homer *timḗ* is the equivalent of *poinḗ*. This text forms the basis for those who argue for the connection of the two lexical families. Let us therefore reread it. Agamemnon announces the solemn pact which will bind the Trojans and Achaeans and asks the gods to serve as witnesses: "If Alexander should kill Menelaus, let him have for himself Helen and all the treasure; we ourselves shall depart on our ships. But if on the contrary it should be Menelaus who kills Alexander, it will be for the Trojans to give back Helen and all the treasure to us and to pay to the Argives an appropriate recompense (*timḕn apotínemen*), from which future generations shall profit. And if Priam and Priam's sons refuse to pay (*timḕn tínein*), seeing that, it is I who will fight to obtain satisfaction (*poinḗ*) and I shall not depart until I have brought the war to its end" (*Il.* 3, 275ff.).

It has been proposed to read into this passage an etymological link between *tínō*, *apotínō* 'pay' and *timḗ* on the one hand, and an equivalence between *timḗ* and *poinḗ* on the other. In fact neither relation stands up to examination. The pact envisages in the case of a victory by Menelaus that the Trojans will give back Helen and all the treasures and that they will pay in addition the *timḗ* to Agamemnon and to the Argives. This is a tribute which goes beyond the simple restitution of the property: it implies a recognition of royal power and the accordance of the honor which accompanies such recognition. This being so, under the conditions in which the pact is concluded, the *timḗ* takes the form of a payment which the Trojans will make over and above the property which they are to return. It is only by chance and in this single example that *timḗ* comes to be associated with the verb "pay in return." It follows that the poet did not conceive of *timḗ* as a morphological correlative of *apotínō*. On the contrary, this text clearly brings out the gap separating *timḗ* and *poinḗ*. If the Trojans refuse the *timḗ*, then Agamemnon will have the right to fight to obtain a *poinḗ*. That is quite a different matter: *poinḗ* is the punishment and the reparation due for violation of an oath.

The comparable forms outside Greek are no less foreign to the notion of consideration or honor and they all refer to punishment: this is the case with the Latin *poena*, a term of criminal law, an old borrowing from the Greek form *poinḗ*. It is clear that *poena* and *pūnīre* have nothing in common with the idea of *honos*. In Avestan, the verb *kāy-* and the derivatives *kaēnā-*, *kaēθa-* are connected with the idea of exacting vengeance, obtaining reparation for a crime or an injury. No term in the Avestan group corresponds to the Sanskrit *cāyati* 'respect'.

In sum, outside Greek, nothing can be found to compare with the sense "to honor" except a few Indic forms, the verb *cāya-*, and the adjective *cāyu* 'respectful'.

There are, however, secondary contacts in Greek between the two families; as a result of this we have notably the form *timōreîn* 'bring aid, help, chastise', *timōrós* 'protector, avenger'; literally "he who watches over the *timḗ* (*tima-oros*)." This is a mixture of the two notions. Similarly, the most ancient forms *tínō*, *tinúō*, seem to have borrowed their vowel *i* from *timḗ*, as is shown by the alternation between *i* and *ei* attested in the dialects.[2]

2. For a detailed treatment of these problems of the vowels and their quantity see Schwyzer, *Griechische Grammatik*, I, 697 and n. 4.

BOOK IV, CHAPTER SIX

Magic Power

Abstract. *Kûdos*, a term almost exclusively confined to the epic, which has been regarded by ancient and modern scholars as a synonym of *kléos* 'glory', 'renown', has in fact a quite specific sense: it designates a magic power that is irresistible and is the apanage of the gods, who occasionally grant it to a hero of their choice and thus ensure his triumph. *Kûdos arésthai*, used of a warrior, properly means "to seize (from the gods) the *kûdos*," and consequently, strengthened by this talisman, to cover oneself with glory.

The formal correspondence between *kûdos* thus understood and O.Slav *čudo* 'miracle, marvel' is thus not surprising: the notion of "supernatural force" common to the two terms makes it fully intelligible.

When we study this vocabulary, we must pay close attention to the connections which are established between the words. Each of them taken separately does not always appear to be significant but its force is made clear in the light of its connections. Then we shall notice certain qualifications which reveal their full sense and bring to light a new value. In Homer it is sometimes necessary to read a long continuous passage in order to grasp the subtle play of values; an important term, by the connections into which it enters, may throw light on terms which attract less attention.

After *géras* and *timḗ* we can turn our attention to another notion which belongs to the same sphere and is equally notable: this is the word *kûdos* (κῦδος). We have several hundred examples in Homer of this neuter, which is uniformly translated "glory," and its derivatives, both nominal and verbal: *kudrós*, *kudálimos*, *kudánō*, *kudaínō*, *kudiáneira*, etc.

This traditional sense of "glory," which seems demanded by the context in certain passages, was already given to us by the ancient commentators. The meaning has been fixed since ancient times: it forms part of the humanist tradition.

It must be said, however, that our understanding of the Homeric vocabulary is still in its infancy. We have received from antiquity a system of interpretation to which we continue to cling and which is enshrined in our lexica and translations. While great efforts have been made to restore a reliable text and to define the dialectal characteristics of the epic language, our interpretations are those of an epoch in which aesthetic conventions took precedence over exactitude. The more one studies the Homeric texts, the more clearly we see the gap between the real nature of its concepts and the picture of them given in traditional scholarship.

From this point of view certain recent studies do not mark any real progress. For instance the dissertation by Greindl devoted to the study of five Greek words, *kléos*, *kûdos*, *timḗ*, *phátis*, *dóxa* (Munich, 1938) is a convenient assemblage of facts, but it is essentially a literary and psychological study. The author comes to the conclusion that *kûdos* designated majestic appearance and also an advantage in combat which is equivalent to victory: the sense was thus "*Ruhm*, glory, authority" which is more or less the meaning given everywhere in translations.

There is, however, a reason why *kûdos* should not mean "glory": namely that Homer uses another word meaning "glory"—*kléos*. We know with certainty that the concept of *kléos* is one of the most ancient and constant of the Indo-European world: Vedic *śravas*, Avestan *sravah-* are the exact correspondents of the Greek word and they have exactly the same sense. Moreover, the poetic language preserves in Greek and in Vedic one and the same formulaic expression: Hom. *kléwos áphthiton*, Ved. *śravas akṣitam* 'imperishable glory', designating the supreme recompense of the warrior, this "imperishable glory" which the Indo-European hero desires above all else and for which he will lay down his life. Here we have one of the rare pieces of evidence from which we can infer the existence, if not of an epic language, at least of stock poetic expressions from the time of common Indo-European onwards.

This alone makes it improbable that *kûdos* has the sense of "glory." In the epic terminology, we may be sure, the major terms are all specific and synonymy is unknown. *A priori* we can assert that *kléos* 'glory' and *kûdos* are not equivalent terms, and in fact, as we shall see, *kûdos* never signifies "glory." This translation, which is generally accepted, is to be rejected. There is not even any special relation between these two notions. Their respective qualifications differ in number and in kind. First, *kléos* is qualified as *esthlón* 'good', *méga* 'great' (with the degrees of comparison *meîzon* and *mégiston* 'greater, greatest'), *eurú* 'wide', *ásbeston* 'inextinguishable', *áphthiton* 'imperishable', *hupouránion* 'sub-celestial'; it is used in the plural *kléa* and with certain determinants ("glory of men," etc.); and it lends itself to hyperbole ("his fame was raised to the skies"). With *kûdos* we find only two epithets: *méga* 'great' and *hupérteron* 'superior', and one example of *áspeton* 'immense'; it has no plural, it never appears in a syntagm formed with a determinative and it never admits any description. Such differences suggest that *kûdos* is a distinct concept which has to be defined separately.

The sense of *kûdos* is thus not "glory," as is given in our dictionaries and commentaries. We must determine the meaning exclusively by study of its contexts and by extracting the elements of the definition solely from its uses. Once again, the traditional exegesis of Homer must be fundamentally revised.

The constructions of *kûdos* do not show any great variety. With the exception of the formula *kúdeï gaíōn* in which the dative-locative *kúdeï* is joined in a unique syntagm with an equally unique participial form *gaíōn*, the only case of *kûdos* used is the nominative-accusative. But the uses, amounting to more than sixty, fall into two groups. In one, *kûdos* is the object of a verb "to give," the subject being a divinity; in the other *kûdos* is the object of a verb meaning "to gain," the grammatical subject of which is the name of a man. The two groups must be analyzed separately.

In the first category of uses, *kûdos* designates something that the god "gives" (*dídōsi*, *opázei*), "offers" (*orégei*), or on the contrary "takes away" (*apēúra*). The gift of *kûdos* ensures the triumph of the man who receives it: in combat the holder of *kûdos* is invariably victorious. Here we see the fundamental character of *kûdos*: it acts like a talisman of supremacy. We use the term talisman advisedly, for the bestowal of *kûdos* by the god procures an instantaneous and irresistible advantage, rather like a magic power, and the god grants it now to one and now to another at his good will and always in order to give the advantage at a decisive moment of a combat or some competitive activity.

The goddess Athena, in order to favor Diomedes in the chariot race, breaks the harness of his rival Eumelos, who rolls on the ground, and in this way

Diomedes passes him, for "Athena filled his horses with spirit and she put in him the *kûdos* (*ep' autôi kûdos éthēke*)." The others immediately understood the source of Diomedes' advantage which they were unable to question. Behind him, Antilochos, while urging on his horses, shouts to them: "I ask you not to compete with those of Diomedes, to whom Athena has just given speed and she has put *kûdos* in him" (the same formula, *Il.* 23, 400-406). The position is clear to all: when a god has given *kûdos* to a man, he is assured of victory, and his adversaries or his rivals know that it is vain to oppose him (cf. 5, 225). This is why Achilles, at the moment when Patroclus goes to confront Hector in his stead, beseeches Zeus: "Send him *kûdos* and fortify his heart" (16, 241). This is also why Nestor pleads with Achilles: he should not persist in his opposition to Agamemnon "since the *timḗ* has never been equal for a scepter-bearing king to whom Zeus has given *kûdos*" (1, 279). When Hector is pursued and is pressed hard by the chariot of Diomedes and Nestor, Zeus thunders violently in front of them. Nestor takes fright and warns his companion: "the only thing for us to do is to turn tail and flee. Do you not see that today Zeus grants *kûdos* to our adversary? Tomorrow he will give it to us, if that is his pleasure." However Diomedes retorts: will he not run the risk of a reproach of cowardice? So he persists, against the advice of Nestor. Then Zeus thunders three times "giving the Trojans presage of their revenge" and Hector exults: "I see that Zeus promises me the victory and a great *kûdos*, but ruin to the Danaans" (8, 140-160). He hurls himself into the fray and presses irresistibly on the Danaans "since Zeus has given *kûdos*" (ibid. 216). In the face of this danger Agamemnon stimulates the courage of his warriors by appeals and sarcastic remarks and addresses Zeus: "Have you never blinded in this way one of the all-powerful kings by taking away from him the great *kûdos*?" (ibid. 237).

In this long episode, marked out by characteristic uses, a new refinement is added to the definition of *kûdos*. We already know that this attribute emanates from a god, that it is bestowed on a king or a hero and that it confers the victory on him. But how does the man so favored know, in the heat of the fray, that the god has just granted him *kûdos*, and how does his adversary also perceive this? They are both informed by a prodigious sign, which makes manifest the divine choice. It is the thunder that bursts out and rolls in the middle of the battle; it is the chariot of the rival which breaks in full course; it is the string of the bow which breaks in the hands of Teucer while he is aiming at Hector and the arrow that goes far astray of its target; and Hector is not mistaken, Zeus is on his side: "Yes, I have seen with my own eyes the shafts of a hero going far amiss of their target. Easy to see is the aid that Zeus gives to men, whether he grants them a superior *kûdos* or he weakens others by refusing to help them. Now behold, he weakens the ardor of the Argives and comes to support us" (15, 488ff.). From this there emerges the sense of *kûdos hupérteron.* While Zeus refrains from intervening, the two sides are equally matched: "The Trojans and the Achaeans strive to see to whom father Zeus will offer the *kûdos*" (5, 33); it is at the moment of the greatest danger for Hector that Zeus inclines his balance in his favor, giving him a "superior *kûdos*" (12, 437). This imagery expresses the relation between the forces engaged: when Zeus has given the *kûdos* to the one whom he favors, his adversary is immediately doomed to defeat and he knows it: the Trojans hurl themselves into the fray "carrying out the orders of Zeus"; the lord of the gods "roused a great *ménos* in them, but on the Argives he cast a spell and took away the *kûdos*, while he spurred on their adversaries. For it was to Hector that he desired to offer the *kûdos*" (15, 593ff.).

The effect of the *kûdos* is temporary. Zeus or Athena grant it so that a hero can triumph at a given moment of the combat or can press his advantage up to a given point: they give him "the *kûdos* of killing" (5, 260; 17, 453), an expression comparable with "*krátos* of killing" (11, 192; 207). It is always at a moment's notice and according to the fluctuations of the battle that one or other of the adversaries receives this advantage which restores his chances at the moment of peril. The gods thus give play to their preferences and settle their own personal rivalries by granting the *kûdos* in their turn to Achaeans and Trojans. We see how Zeus uses it to pacify the dispute which breaks out among the gods after the victory of Achilles. Some of them, outraged by the treatment that Achilles inflicts on the corpse of Hector, want to send Argeiphontes to steal him away. Others oppose this: Hector and Achilles do not have equal *timḗ*; Hector is only a mortal, whereas Achilles is the son of a goddess. Zeus then intervenes; no, the *timḗ* will not be equal between them, but let us not try to steal away the body. He summons Thetis, Achilles' mother, and says to her: "Certain of the gods are urging Argeiphontes to steal the body of Hector. But I grant this *kûdos* to Achilles, just as in the future I shall preserve your *aidṓs* and *philótēs*" (cf. above, Book Three, Chapter Four). This is the plan of Zeus: Achilles will give back the body of Hector, but only if Priam comes in person to ransom it and brings splendid presents (24, 109ff.). Thus Achilles will not be deprived of his triumph even though he gives back the corpse of Hector.

In some examples *kûdos* is given to a hero, not by a god, but by his own adversary. In such a case it is a simple stylistic figure. The warrior who by mischance or recklessness exposes himself dangerously and lays himself open to the blows of the enemy himself puts *kûdos* into the hands of his adversary. In this way Periphetes "puts *kûdos* into the hands (*enguálikse*)" of Hector when, stumbling over his shield, he falls on the ground before him (15, 644). Hecuba begs her son Hector to stay inside the walls of Troy "so as not to give Achilles a great *kûdos*" by going to confront him (22, 57). In the same way we say of an incautious man that he seeks his own downfall.

We now pass to the second group of examples, in which the expression *kûdos arésthai* predominates, this being applied to a warrior in battle (never to a god). The fact that this occurs so often (a score of times) suggests that it had a precise value, and alone the fact that in this usage *kûdos* is never conferred by a god, but is "seized" by a man is an indication of a new sense which is worthy of attention. How could it be possible for a man to "take away" *kûdos* without the consent of a god when, as we have seen, the gods alone confer it on men? This privilege is presented in one example as a divine gift: "Zeus has granted (*édōke*) me to carry off *kûdos* at the ships and to pen the Achaeans by the sea," Hector proclaims in the assembly of the Trojans (*Il.* 18, 293). However, apart from a few very rare examples, no mention is made of a god on the occasions when a warrior "carries off *kûdos*." Besides, the expression is often accompanied by a dative indicating the beneficiary: "carry off the *kûdos* for someone."

Here we have a specific phrase which must be studied both in the circumstances in which it appears and in the syntactical forms in which it is embedded. If we examine it from these points of view we shall discover that there are two types of use.

In the first it is an offer made to a warrior to undertake some extraordinary exploit alone. If he succeeds, "he will win *kûdos*" for his king, for his people or for himself, and a great reward is promised him.

The phrase is situated in a prospective context and it is used in the future tense, often accompanied by the word for the beneficiary in the dative.

We find this schema in a whole series of episodes. Athena in disguise incites Pandarus to a deed of daring: to let fly an arrow at Menelaus. "In this way," says Athena, "you will win *kháris* and *kûdos* for the Trojans, and above all for King Alexander. You will obtain from him splendid presents if he sees valiant Menelaus subdued by your arrow" (4, 95). When he is sent as an ambassador to Achilles, Odysseus presses him to return to the combat: "The Achaeans will honor you like a god. For you will certainly win for them a great *kûdos*, for this time you will triumph over Hector" (9, 303). Hector in his camp appeals for a volunteer to carry out a nocturnal reconnaissance among the Achaeans. The man who is bold enough to do this will have a great reward and "he will win *kûdos* for himself (10, 307). Poseidon exhorts the Danaans in these words: "Are we again going to yield victory to Hector, so that he may take our ships and win *kûdos*?" (14, 365). Achilles instructs Patroclus as he sends him out to fight against Hector: "Follow faithfully the plan which I put in your mind, so that you will win for me a great *timḗ* and *kûdos* at the hands of all the Danaans. . . . But once the enemy is repulsed from the ships, return. Even if Zeus grants you to win *kûdos* again, guard against the desire to fight against the warlike Trojans without me" (16, 84-88). The phalanxes of the Trojans "had taken their stand around the body of Patroclus and were strongly minded to drag him to the city and win *kûdos*" (17, 286f.). "Zeus," says Hector, "has granted me to win *kûdos* at the ships and to pen the Achaeans by the sea" (18, 293). Achilles rushes into the fray and crushes his enemies "hotly desiring to win *kûdos*" (20, 502; cf. 12, 407; 21, 596), but "Apollo does not allow him to win *kûdos* (21, 596). Disguised as Agenor, Apollo gets Achilles to pursue him; then having removed him from the battle, he reassumes his divine shape. Achilles, infuriated, shouts at him: "You have foiled me, most destructive of all the gods, by diverting me hither far from the walls. ... Now you have deprived me of great *kûdos*, and you have saved the Trojans" (22, 18). Achilles, as he pursued Hector, makes a sign to his men not to shoot any arrows "lest some other should win *kûdos* by striking Hector and he should come second" (22, 207). The balance of Zeus has marked Hector's day of doom. Then Athena says to Achilles: "This time I am confident that we two shall win great *kûdos* for the Achaeans at their ships by slaying Hector" (ibid. 217).

It is exceptional for the expression to be used in the past tense indicating the accomplished act. Only one example is found of this, and it has the additional peculiarity that the subject is in the plural. This occurs in the paean which the victorious Argives intone: "We have won great *kûdos*; we have slain the divine Hector" (22, 393).

The second type of use of *kûdos arésthai* puts the verb in the past conditional: the hero would have won *kûdos* had not a god intervened to save his adversary. The examples are much less numerous. In his single combat against Alexander, Menelaus chokes him with the strap of his helmet: "He would have dragged him off and thus won great *kûdos* had not Aphrodite seen him"; the goddess breaks the strap and takes Alexander away (3, 373). "The Argives by their might and strength would have won *kûdos*, even beyond the fate apportioned by Zeus, had not Apollo himself aroused Aeneas" (17, 321). Hector would have dragged off the corpse of Patroclus and won immense *kûdos* had not Iris, dispatched by Hera, warned Achilles (18, 165).

Under these two aspects, prospective (future) or retrospective (conditional) "to carry off, win *kûdos*" is generally the act of a man, sometimes but very rarely, of a people, whereas, as we have seen, "to give *kûdos*" is always the act of a god. There is this further difference in that "to give *kûdos*" is a condition which precedes victory, whereas "to win *kûdos*" appears as the consequence of an exploit: "provided that Zeus grants to us to slay Odysseus and win *kûdos*" (*Od.* 22, 253). We may conclude from this that *kûdos*, which was properly the talisman of victory, came to have the sense of "triumph" by a natural shift of sense: the hero, having accomplished some remarkable exploit, wins by his valor this *kûdos* which only a god can grant; in a certain sense he wrests it from a god. Thus the formula *kûdos arésthai* enters into the repertory of heroic eulogy on a par with *kléos arésthai* 'win glory' (*Il.* 5, 3). Besides, it will have been noticed that the *kûdos* thus won by the hero often rebounds to the credit of a king. "I shall not reproach Agamemnon," says Diomedes, "for urging the Achaeans to battle, for it is to him that the *kûdos* will accrue if the Achaeans slay the Trojans and take holy Ilion; his, too, will be the great grief if the Achaeans are slain" (14, 415). Thus a resemblance is established between *kûdos* and *timḗ*, both being prerogatives of the king, and both substantives being constructed with the same verb: "We followed you to please you, and to win (*arnúmenoi*) for you and Menelaus a *timḗ* at the hands of the Trojans" (1, 159). The *kûdos* may also accrue to the whole community of a people (*Il.* 13, 676).

By another extension of sense *kûdos* comes to denote an attribute of a man. Of certain heroes it is said that they are "the great *kûdos*" of the Achaeans (Agamemnon, Nestor, Odysseus) or of the Trojans (Hector). By themselves each is a talisman of victory.

In the light of the definition which we have proposed for *kûdos*, for its nature and what it represents in the relations between gods and men and for the chances of battle, we can get a better appreciation of the sense of the derivatives based on *kûdos*: the adjective *kudrós*, especially in the superlative *kúdistos*, which is applied to the highest of the gods, particularly Zeus, or, among men, Agamemnon alone; and further of *kudálimos*, bestowed on heroes or peoples. Of the verbs formed from *kûdos* we may note particularly *kudaínō* or *kudánō*, which means literally "fill with *kûdos*," whether in the physical sense to express "endow with *kûdos*, with the talisman of victory" (13, 348; 14, 73), whence "to infuse a wounded body with the power to overcome the injury" as Leto and Artemis do to Aeneas when they are tending him (5, 448), or metaphorically "to honor by a mark of distinction" (10, 69; *Od.* 14, 438). So strong was the force of *kûdos* that it lent itself to many metaphorical usages in which its essential value is always visible. And this value was certainly, at the beginning, of a magical nature, as emerges from the oppositions into which it enters. *Kûdos* acts like a charm: it ensures the triumph of the warrior or of the side to which Zeus grants it, whereas the arms and the hearts of his adversaries are "benumbed" or "bound" as if by an enchantment. This motif runs through some episodes, and it brings out the power of this attribute. "I now know," says Agamemnon before the rout of his army, "that Zeus endows certain men with *kûdos* (*toùs mèn kudánei*) to make them like the blessed gods whereas for us he has bound (*édēsen*) our hearts and arms" (14, 73). "Zeus casts a spell (*thélge*) on the mind of the Achaeans, but to the Trojans and to Hector he grants *kûdos*" (12, 225). "The Trojans like ravening lions hurled themselves towards the ships, carrying out the order of Zeus, and he ever roused great might in them, whereas he cast a spell (*thélge*) on the spirit of the Argives and took away *kûdos*, while he spurred on the others. For his spirit was set on giving *kûdos* to Hector, son of Priam, that he might cast a fierce fire on the curved ships" (15, 595-6). Apollo, shaking his aegis before the Danaans and uttering loud cries, "cast a spell (*éthelxe*) on their hearts and they forgot their zest for the fight. . . . Deprived of their valor the Achaeans fled in panic. For Apollo had sent panic on them but to the Trojans and to Hector he gave *kûdos*" (15, 327).

It was necessary to go through the uses of *kûdos* in some detail, to establish its collocations, its oppositions, and its derivatives in order to reach the authentic sense of this sadly misunderstood term. The royal or heroic *kûdos* forms part of the powerful charms which the gods grant and withhold instantaneously at their own whim to one or other of the parties in war, to restore the equilibrium in battle, to save a chief who has honored them with sacrifices or as a move in their own rivalries. These changing favors reflect the play of factions in the camp of the gods, over which Zeus is arbiter. The *kûdos* thus passes from one to another, from the Achaeans to the Trojans, then from Hector to Achilles, as an invisible and magical attribute, surrounded by prodigies and as a prodigy itself, an instrument of triumph, which Zeus alone holds forever and which he concedes for a day to kings or heroes.

This description of the sense opens up new possibilities for the etymology. The formal resemblance of Gr. *kûdos* to Slavic *čudo* 'miracle, marvel' has long been noted, but the sense of "glory" traditionally attributed to *kûdos* was not favorable to the connection. Now the question can be posed in new terms: *kûdos* never means "glory" but designates an attribute of a magical nature which ensures triumph. The prodigious character of *kûdos*, its immense and instantaneous effects, the confusion which it spreads among the enemy, all this brings it close to Slavic *čudo* and the etymological connection is completely acceptable. Incidentally both words are connected with one and the same verbal root, which is that of *čuti* 'feel' in Slavic and of *koeîn* 'perceive, notice' in Greek. Its proper sense must have been "notice something unusual, perceive as new or strange." This agrees with the focal sense which seems to be common to Gr. *kûdos* and Slavic *čudo*.

We have taken all or nearly all our examples from the *Iliad*, and these constitute in fact virtually the whole evidence for the word. There are few in the *Odyssey*, especially if the passages regarded as interpolated are excluded. Some simply reproduce the uses already studied (*Od.* 4, 275; 22, 253), while others relate to the authority of the king or the head of a house (3, 57; 19, 161).

In all the examples *kûdos* is always the condition leading to success, whatever this may be, to superiority in some domain in which it is manifested. There are grounds for defining it as an advantage of supremacy which is manifested by a triumph of a magical character, an advantage which is permanent when it is in the hands of Zeus, and temporary when the gods grant it to men. This talisman, which devolves by divine favor on a king or a valiant warrior, in all circumstances ensures preeminence to them and on occasion confers victory on them. But if there is no victory without *kûdos*, *kûdos* is not necessarily linked with the triumph of the warrior. Although it is never described, it can be represented in a material guise: it seems to confer a kind of brilliance on those who are endowed with it. In the epithet *kudrós*, applied to divinities, there is the idea of a certain majesty, of a radiance which is the external manifestation of *kûdos*.

To return to the notions which were our starting point, we now see how they are to be distinguished. *Géras* denotes exclusively material goods; it forms part of the portion belonging to men, the prestation due to the sovereign person, recognition by means of offerings of his rank and of his supremacy. *Timḗ* is an honor, paid to the gods and also accorded by the gods to men as a reward for merit in the form of respect and also of gifts. Finally, *kûdos* does not depend on men but is the exclusive possession of the gods and forms part of the apanage of these gods. It is a magic power the possession of which confers superiority in certain circumstances, often in battle, where it is a guarantee of victory.

The analysis of the term *kûdos* opens up a domain into which we are rarely introduced by Greek terms, that of the magical powers of royalty. In the most ancient world of Indo-European concepts the king had a role which was both political and magical. He assumes complete power, ruling over the relations of men among themselves and also their relations with the gods. Because of this he is possessed of a formidable power that consists of law and magic.

It is remarkable that a notion like *kûdos* should have survived in a world so bereft of magic as that of the Homeric poems. This is perhaps due to the fact that it is used for the most part in formulaic expressions. This term had ceased to be understood even in ancient times, so that it was assimilated to *kléos* 'glory' or *níkē* 'victory'. It is necessary to transcend these rationalistic interpretations in order to recover the full and true sense of the word.

BOOK IV, CHAPTER SEVEN

Krátos

Abstract. *Krátos* does not mean "physical force" (*iskhús*, *sthénos*) or "spiritual force" (*alkḗ*) but "superiority," whether in battle or in the assembly. This sense, which is constant for *krátos*, is confirmed by some of the uses of the derivative *kraterós* which means "without equal," especially in combat. But in other uses *kraterós* comes close in sense to *krataiós* 'hard, cruel', *kratús* 'hard'.

The etymology gives the reason for this peculiar state of affairs: *krátos* is to be connected with the Indo-Iranian *kratu-*, which designates "the (magical) power of the warrior"; *kratús* is to be connected with a quite different group, that of Gothic *hardus*, which means exclusively "hard." In Greek there was some overlap of the two word families and this is particularly well illustrated by the two-fold use of the word *kraterós*.

The terms which have been studied up to now enable us to define certain ideological concepts of Homeric society. They help us to define the status of the king and to determine the attributes of *basileía* 'kingship'. We have analyzed three of these terms: *kûdos*, *timḗ*, *géras*.

There is a further attribute that we must now study, which the texts associate closely with those just listed, and which because of its meaning is of central importance for the understanding of this kingship. This is the word *krátos* (κράτος), a well-known term of great generality, which because of the simplicity of its sense would appear to be easy to analyze. From the outset it is supposed to have meant nothing more than "force, power." Its form is both *krátos* and *kártos* without distinction of meaning. This ancient neuter has a long series of derivatives which are based on the stem *krat-* or *kart-*.

We have: *kraterós* or *karterós* with the comparative form *kreíssōn* and the superlative *krátistos* or *kártistos*; and the verb *krateîn*. Further, on the stem in *-u-*, we have the adjective *kratús* and the verb *kratûnein*, and finally, some derivatives in *-ai-*, *krataiós* and the compounds *krataípous*, *krataigúalos*.

The translation which is everywhere accepted as "force, power" is in our view unsatisfactory. We shall attempt to give precision to its meaning by analysis of its uses, which are often formulaic, and try to circumscribe the original concept.

That *krátos* cannot simply signify "strength" emerges from the fact that at least six other Homeric terms have this sense: *bía*, *ís*, *iskhús*, *sthénos*, *alkḗ*, *dúnamis*. This profusion creates many difficulties for translators. But the choice of equivalents can only be guided by exact definitions, that is, an exact idea of the *differences* between these seven ways of designating "strength." Here the arbitrary and uncertain hold sway. Translators proceed as they think fit and translate each example differently.

To start with we take a particularly challenging example, an instance of *krátos* associated with *alkḗ*, in the stinging address of Diomedes to Agamemnon: "Zeus has given you contrary gifts: he has granted you to be honored above all with the scepter, but he has not given you *alkḗ*, which is the greatest *krátos*" (*Il.* 9, 39). What does Diomedes mean, and what is the meaning of a translation like "Valor, he has refused to you. Yet it is supreme power" (tr. P. Mazon)? Everything is interconnected in these problems and, as soon as the attempt is made to fix the sense of a word, its synonyms present themselves in all their abundance and intricate interrelationships. Let us therefore make the attempt to delimit *krátos* and *alkḗ*, and in the first place to determine what *alkḗ* is.

It is some kind of "force" to be sure, but not physical force, the word for which is *sthénos*. To understand its nature we must take note of the utterance itself in which the absence of this quality is made the subject of reproach. Why does Diomedes reproach Agamemnon with lacking *alkḗ*? It is because Agamemnon, under the impact of the reverses suffered, believing that the game is lost since Zeus has betrayed him, advises the assembly to raise the siege and depart: "Let us flee in our ships to our native land; we shall no longer take Troy with its broad streets" (9, 27). Diomedes then challenges him: "Zeus has not given you *alkḗ*. . . . If you have so great a desire to return home, depart! Others will remain until we have laid waste Troy. Nay, let them also in their turn flee with their ships to their native land. We two, I and Sthenelus, shall fight alone until we win the goal of Ilion, for we have come here with the god" (ibid. 39ff.).

To give up the fight, this is to have no *alkḗ*, just like those who, wearied of running, stop, "having no *alkḗ* in their hearts" (4, 245). At the moment of the decisive combat in his house Odysseus finds himself alone with three companions faced with the "numerous and valiant" suitors. Athena comes to him in the guise of Mentor and Odysseus implores him: "Mentor, save me from misfortune! " Athena, scolds him with the words: "Odysseus, have you no courage or *alkḗ*? . . . How is it, now that you have come to your house and possessions, in the face of the suitors you wail at having to be *álkimos*?" (*Od.* 22, 226; 231f.).

From this passage we may deduce—*a contrario*—the definition of *alkḗ*; to face up to danger without flinching, not to yield under attack, to stand firm in the fray, this is *alkḗ*. These features characterize the notion in all the examples.

Poseidon, in the guise of Calchas, addresses the two Ajaxes when the Achaeans are giving way under the assault of the Trojans: "You two go and save the Achaean army, having *alkḗ* in your hearts and not chilly rout" (*Il.* 13, 48). These are always the alternatives: *alkḗ* or rout. Menelaus, when he is defending the corpse of Patroclus against Euphorbus, threatens him: "I shall break your spirit if you confront me. I bid you get back into the throng." But Euphorbus retorts: "The combat will decide: either *alkḗ* or flight" (17, 42). Between Achilles and Aeneas there is a long exchange of challenges, which the latter concludes thus: "You will not with words deter me, burning with *alkḗ*, before we battle, face to face, with the bronze" (20, 256). On many occasions when the troops are giving way, the chief exhorts them to "remember *alkḗ*," to stand fast without fear and not to retreat. The two Ajaxes make a rampart before the corpse of Patroclus; "clothed in *alkḗ*" they thrice repulse the assaults of Hector. This hero, too, "confident in his *alkḗ*" now hurls himself forward, now comes to a halt, but "without retiring one step." Like a lion that the shepherds cannot drive away from his prey "even so can the two Ajaxes not frighten Hector and hurl him back from the corpse" (18, 157f.). The comparison is no empty one: the great beasts of prey in their hour of danger also give evidence of *alkḗ*. "Like a panther, plunging forth from a deep thicket and coming face to face with a hunter, is unafraid at heart and does not take flight. If the hunter strikes or wounds her first, even though pierced with the spear she does not cease from *alkḗ*, until she has come to grips or is killed" (21, 573ff.). The antithetic terms *alkḗ* and *phóbos* reappear in the derivatives *álkimos* 'endowed with *alkḗ*' and *phobeîn* 'affright, put to flight', for instance in the words of Hector: "Zeus is always superior, he puts to flight (*phobeî*) even the *álkimos* warrior" (17, 177). But when *alkḗ*, manifested by portents, comes from Zeus, it is indestructible. When an unexpected thunderbolt strikes in front of the chariot of Diomedes, who faces Hector unafraid, his companion Nestor is seized with fear: "Turn back the horses! Do you not understand that *alkḗ* that comes from Zeus does not accompany you?" (8, 140). And when Zeus turns aside the shaft launched by Teucer at Hector and breaks the string of his bow, Hector is not deceived: "The *alkḗ* of Zeus is easy to recognize" (15, 490).

It is the same virtue which is named by Hesiod in his description of the winds which lash the sea, shatter the ships and drown the sailors: "Against this evil there is no *alkḗ*" (*Theog.* 876). The formula recurs at the end of a vision of an age to come when all will be overturned: "Against the evil there will be no *alkḗ*" (*Works*, 201). The investigation could continue with the works of Pindar and Herodotus; everywhere *alkḗ* shows the same sense: it is spiritual strength, *fortitude*, which does not yield in the face of danger and remains resolute whatever fate brings.

***

Now that the nature of *alkḗ* has been determined, we can approach the definition of *krátos*. Above we have seen that a passage of the *Iliad* assimilates these two qualities. However, this would not justify our equating the two terms. Another example would also deter us: "Come to my aid, friends, I am alone," shouts Idomeneus, "I am sorely afraid of swift-footed Aeneas, who is coming against me; he is very *karterós* to slay men in battle and he is in the flower of youth, which is the greatest *krátos*" (*Il.* 13, 481ff.). This time it is physical strength, the flower of youth, which is *krátos*. We may conclude that in this logical formula "the *x* which is *krátos*," in which *x* stands for different things, the predicate "which is . . ." does not imply identity but the necessary condition. There are therefore, according to circumstances, different conditions of *krátos*, some pertaining to age and physical condition, and others to qualities such as *alkḗ*. We may immediately add another condition, a fundamental one, the goodwill of the gods, which shows that in *krátos* there is a relationship of forces which may vary: "Let us now leave this bow and entrust ourselves to the gods. Tomorrow the god will give *krátos* to whom he wishes," says Odysseus to his young rivals (*Od.* 21, 280). Here *krátos* is the capacity to win in a trial of strength. Now if we survey the circumstances in which *krátos* appears, we see that they always amount to such a trial, and that everywhere *krátos* indicates the superiority of a man, whether he manifests his strength over those of his own camp or the enemy. This "superiority" is said to be "great" (*méga*) or "greatest" (*mégiston*). It has no other qualifications.

Being of a temporary character, it is always being put to the test. It can consist in superiority of physical strength. When Idomeneus sees Aeneas coming against him he calls on his friends: "I am afraid: he has the flower of youth, this greatest superiority (*krátos mégiston*). For if we were of like age in this our ardor, swiftly would he win great advantage (*méga krátos*) or else I would" (*Il.* 13, 486). To Athena, who in the guise of Phoenix is urging Menelaus to defend at all costs the corpse of Patroclus, Menelaus replies: "If only Athena would give me *krátos* and deflect from me the onrush of the shafts." Then Athena, delighted that he has invoked her first of all the gods, puts strength in his shoulders and his knees, and in his breast the daring of the fly" (17, 561ff.). Glaucus, when he is wounded, implores Apollo: "Lord, tend this my wound; put to sleep my pains, grant me *krátos* so that I may call and urge my Lycian comrades into battle and that I myself may do battle over the corpse of my dead friend" (16, 524). Apollo has just launched Aeneas against Achilles. Hera is roused and convokes the gods: "Now let one of us stand beside Achilles and give him great *krátos* so that his heart does not fail him" (20, 121). "I shall give to Hector the *krátos* of killing," Zeus proclaims (11, 191; cf. 17, 205). Peleus, when sending his son Achilles to Agamemnon, gave him this advice: "*Krátos* will be given you by Athena and Hera if they so wish. Do you restrain your proud heart in your breast" (9, 254).

Zeus may confer *krátos* on one of the two armies engaged. In this case the beneficiary of this superiority is a people, not an individual. Thetis appeals to Zeus in support of her injured son: "Give *krátos* to the Trojans until the Achaeans do honor to my son and increase him in honor" (1, 509). This "superiority" shifts from camp to camp according to the whim of the gods. Diomedes says to Odysseus under the onslaught of the Trojans: "Truly I shall remain and stand fast: but short will be the advantage for us since Zeus likes better to give *krátos* to the Trojans rather than to us" (11, 319). "She (Andromache) has heard that the Trojans were weakening, that a great *krátos* was with the Achaeans" (6, 387). "Use the lash now until you come to our swift ships; you will see that the Achaeans no longer have *krátos*" (17, 623). "Shall we fall upon the many-benched ships in case the god shall grant us *krátos*?" (13, 743). "That day Zeus granted *krátos* to the Pylians" (11, 753). "If Zeus intends to spare steep Ilion and refuses to destroy it and to give great *krátos* to the Argives, let him know that there will be between us bitter wrath without remedy" (15, 216).

But this "superiority" is manifested not only in combat, as might appear to be implied by the numerous passages which have been quoted and which all come from the *Iliad.* It is also displayed in the other activity of the hero, in the assembly (cf. 12, 214) and it amounts to a "power" exercised by the king or chief. Achilles is indignant that a man, Agamemnon, wants to deprive a peer of his legitimate portion "because he is superior to him in *krátos*." The girl whom the Achaeans had given him as his portion, "Lord Agamemnon has taken her from me" (16, 54ff.). Here we see that *krátos* is the "power" of the king, a personal and permanent advantage, like the *krátos mégiston* which Polyphemus has over the other Cyclops (*Od.* 1, 70), like that of Alcinous in his deme (11, 353) or that of Telemachus in his house (21, 353)·

These two values of *krátos*, "superiority" in a trial of strength or skill and, more particularly, "power (of authority)," recur in the Homeric uses of the verb *krateîn*. First "to have the advantage, triumph" (*Il.* 5, 175; 21, 315); secondly, "exercise power," often with a determinant in the genitive, the name of a country or people: "over the Argives" (1, 79), "over all" (1, 288), or in the dative in the *Odyssey*, "over the dead" (11, 485), "over men and gods" (16, 265).

It now remains to examine the sense of the derived adjective *karterós*. Here an unexpected complication arises. In principle, *karterós*, formed with the same suffix *-r-* as in other adjectives, belongs to the same sense group such as*iskhurós*, *sthenarós* 'strong' and means "provided with *krátos*." In a number of its uses it gives clear confirmation of the definition advanced above of the term *krátos* and it qualifies either, as a conventional epithet, certain heroes, especially Diomedes, or, as an occasional attribute, various persons. "You are very *karterós*, a goddess gave you birth" says Nestor to Achilles (*Il.* 1, 280), that is to say, "you will be superior to other men (in strength or in valor)"; *aikhmētḗs kraterós* 'a spearsman who triumphs (over his adversary)', *amúmōn kaì kraterós*, which could be rendered "blameless and without equal." The superlative *kártistos* magnifies this quality to its greatest extent: "I am the *kártistos* of all the gods," proclaims Zeus (8, 17), he who holds supreme power. All this, once the relation between the sense of *kraterós* and that of *krátos* has been confirmed, needs neither commentary nor laborious verification. The examples of *kraterós* in this sense can be found easily.

However, there is another sense, perhaps even more frequent, which the dictionaries record but without indicating how far it is different; it is in fact different in several respects.

When we pass from *krátos* to *kraterós*, we expect to find in the adjective a notion of the same character as the substantive: since *krátos* always denotes a heroic quality, one pertaining to brave men or chiefs, it should follow (and this is actually the case) that the adjective *kraterós* is of a eulogistic character. So it is all the more surprising to find that in its other uses it is far from complimentary and in fact implies blame or reproach. When Hecuba, the wife of Priam, addresses Achilles, who has just killed her son Hector, she calls him *anḕr kraterós* (24, 212), and this is certainly not meant as a tribute to his warlike qualities; it is translated as "*brutal* hero." In order to understand the meaning of *kraterós* when applied to Ares we must recall other epithets bestowed on this god: "homicidal" (*miaiphónos*), "man-slayer" (*androphónos*), "plague of the mortals" (*brotoloigós*), "destructive" (*aídēlos*), etc. None of these presents him in a favorable light.

The discordance goes further, and is shown in another relationship. Whereas *krátos* is used exclusively of gods and men, *kraterós* can also be applied to animals and things, and the sense is always "hard, cruel, violent." The poet calls the lion *kraterós*, not because of its courage, but because it brings on the hind and her young an "outrageous fate" (*Od.* 4, 335). Entering the hind's lair, it seizes her young "with its *krateroí* teeth" (*Il.* 11, 114, cf. 175). Battle (*husmínē*), and discord (*éris*) also receive this epithet and in the most illuminating contexts: *éris kraterḗ* linked with *homoíios ptólemos* 'cruel(?) combat' (13, 358), and *kraterḕ husminē* with the adjectives *argaléē polúdakrus* 'grievous (battle), which causes so many tears' (17, 543). Of great significance is, further, the use of *kraterós* with the names of sufferings or maladies. The sense of the adjective is unmistakable when it is applied to *hélkos* 'wound' (*hélkos karterón, Il.* 16, 517; 523), if we note that the other epithets are "painful" (*argaléos*), "mournful" (*lugrós*), "evil" (*kakós*). The same is true of the combination with *álgea* 'sufferings' in the expression which had become a cliché *kratér' álgea páskhōn* 'suffering *grievous* pains' (2, 721); with *pénthos* 'grief' in *krateròn pénthos* '*violent* grief' (11, 249); with *anágkē* 'necessity' in *kraterḕ anágkē* 'brutal destiny' (6, 458); with *desmós* 'bond': *dê̄san kraterô̄i enì desmô̄i* 'they bound him with a *brutal* bond' (5, 386). We may note, further, the phrase *karterà érga* 'painful things' in the complaint of the wounded Ares to Zeus: "*Zeû páter, ou nemesízēi horô̂n táde karterà érga*, which may be translated "Father Zeus, are you not indignant when you see *all these horrors*?" (5, 782, cf. 757). We are indeed far from the laudatory use of *kraterós*. Further, *kraterós* has the sense "hard" when it enters into the compound *kraterônux* '(wolf, lion, horse) with hard claws or hoofs': the same sense can be seen figuratively in the phrase *krateròs mûthos* 'a hard, wounding saying', where it was observed in ancient times that here *kraterós* was equivalent to *sklērós* 'hard'.

The two senses of *kraterós* thus distinguished in Homer can be found also in Hesiod, sometimes in the same expressions: the sense is favorable when it accompanies *amúmōn* 'without flaw' (*Theog.* 1013), and unfavorable when it is applied to Ares, slayer of men (*Shield* 98; 101), a serpent (*Th.* 322), the Erinyes (*Th.* 185), Echidna "of the violent heart" (*karteróphrōn*, *Th.* 297), etc. Here, too, we find the material sense of "hard" for *kraterós* when it is applied to iron (*sídēros kraterṓtatos*, *Th.*864) and to steel (*Works* 147).

We now consider the nominal forms based on the stem *kratai*-. The adjective *krataiós* is the epithet of a number of persons, and also of Destiny (*moîra krataiḗ*), and of the lion. Here it could be taken in either sense. But the choice is restricted in the compounds: *krataípedos* certainly means "with a *hard* ground," *krataigúalos* '(a cuirass) with a *solid* plate'; and *kartaípous* (*krataípous*), which is mainly post-Homeric, is an epithet of mules "with *hard* hoofs" and resembles in sense the epithet *khalkópous* '(horses) with hoofs of bronze' (*Il.* 8, 41).

Finally we have the adjective *kratús*, which is constant in the formula *kratùs Argeïphóntēs*, and is to be understood in the sense "hard." This sense is supported by the denominative verb *kratúnein* 'make hard', which in Homer describes the maneuvers of the phalanx. The order of battle forms "in serried ranks, dark and bristling with shields and spears" (4, 282). It presents a continuous and compact front. From this comes the choice of figures, which are all material, depicting the phalanx as a solid and metallic body: the phalanx is "broken," "cut into" (16, 394); one "knocks" against the compact phalanxes (13, 45) or "makes them hard" (*ekartúnanto phalággas* 11, 215). This is also the sense of *kartúnein* in Classical Greek, for instance in Hippocrates, for the "hardening" of the bones, or in Xenophon in the following passage: whereas the other Greeks "soften" (*hapalúnousi*) the feet of their children by giving them shoes, the Spartans "harden" (*kratúnousi*) the feet of their own children by making them walk barefoot (*The Republic of the Lacedaemonians*, II, 3). It is worth stressing the gap between this use of *kratúnein* 'to harden', based on *kratús*, and *kratúnein* 'to govern' (found in tragedy), which was a secondary formation based on *krateîn* 'exercise power'.

We must, therefore, take note of a peculiar semantic situation which has been brought out by our investigations and has hitherto passed unnoticed: the lexical family with *krátos* as its focus is not homogeneous. It is divided into two distinct groups which can be characterized separately.

(1) The first is distinguished by the physical or moral notion of "superiority," of "advantage" in battle or in the assembly:*krátos*. From this there develops a whole series of terms with a moral or political reference, which contain the idea of "power" as an individual attribute (*egkratḗs*, *akratḗs*, 'who is' or 'who is not master of himself') or "power" in a territorial or political sense: *krateîn* 'be master, have authority', with numerous derivatives and compounds in *-krátēs*, *-krátōr*, *-kráteia*etc., as well as the comparative and superlative *kreíssōn*, *krátistos*. What gives unity to this development is the idea of political "authority," both individual and collective.

(2) The second group proceeds from the physical notion of "hard" (as opposed to "soft"): *kratús*, *kartúnein* 'harden'; *kratai-* 'hard'. This is the only sense which it has, either literally or figuratively: "brutal, cruel, painful." It never acquires a social or political value and it has unfavorable connotations.

These are two different semantic domains. Between them lies the field of the adjective *kraterós*, which, as we saw, has uses which belong to both fields. Some belong with *krátos* and indicate possession of authority; others are attached to *kratús* 'hard' and qualify things such as wounds, maladies or discord as "painful, hard, brutal." We should not blur this distinction by translating *kraterós* as "strong." Such tricks of translation simply obscure the problem. It has already been shown that *kraterós* does not mean "strong." A supplementary proof is that this adjective may, without pleonasm, qualify *ís* "physical strength": *kraterḕ ìs Oduseos* 'the rude vigor of Odysseus' (*Il.* 23, 720). For the time being we rest content with the conclusion that in these uses of *kraterós* there coexist without confusion the two notions which the other terms in *krat-* enable us to distinguish: on the one hand the abstract notion of "superiority, domination" and on the other the physical quality "hard."

Now it so happens that this distinction which we have elicited by the analysis of its uses and confrontations of senses within Greek itself finds outside Greek its justification in etymological correspondences. Hitherto comparatists have sought the correspondents of the family of *krátos* in two directions: on the one hand in Got. *hardus* and on the other in I-Ir. *kratu-*. But the majority of scholars feel bound to opt for one or the other of these alternatives. They hesitate to accept both because of the great disparity of sense. No one has ventured to question the interpretation of Greek *krátos* as "force, strength." Herein lies the error. It now appears that by restoring to the Greek forms their authentic sense we can give a new slant to the etymological problem.

The Gothic adjective *hardus* means "hard" just like German *hart*, English *hard*. It translates the Greek *sklērós* 'hard', and *austērós* 'severe, rough'. From it comes the adverb *harduba* 'in a hard way', the compound *hardu-hairtei* 'hardness of heart', Gr. '*sklērokardía*' and the verb *gahardjan* 'harden', Gr. '*sklērúnein*'. We can see now that in every respect Gothic *hardus* 'hard' from **kartu-* corresponds exactly to Gr. *kratús* 'hard', *kartúnein* (from **kartu-* or **kr̥tu-*). It is the same adjectival form with the same meaning, since Gr. *kratús* and *kratúnein* mean "hard" in a physical sense.

Quite different is the semantic sphere of Vedic *krátu-*, Avestan *xratu-*. This substantive designates an intellectual and spiritual quality, the "power" of the spirit, of ardor, inspiration, which animates the warrior, the poet, or the believer. It is a complex notion[1] which was enriched and refined by later speculation.

Here it will suffice to note the evident connection of the Indo-Iranian *kratu-*, restored to its original meaning, with the Homeric *krátos*, which always indicates the notion of "superiority." In both areas it is a substantive and no longer an adjective. Only in its formation is there a slight difference (masculine in *-u* in I-Ir., neuter in *-es* in Greek). But the conceptual nucleus is the same.

We do not believe that it is possible to combine these two groups into a single whole. They must come from two distinct roots, though they were very similar in form, if not actually identical, in Indo-European. We distinguish therefore: (1) an adjective meaning "hard" represented by Gr. *kratús*, etc., and Got. *hardus*; (2) a substantive denoting "power," "superiority" which is represented by I-Ir. *kratu-* and by the Greek *krátos*. It will be noted that in Germanic the forms Germ. *hart* and Engl. *hard* never developed a moral or political sense and, further, that in Indo-Iranian the forms of *kratu-* never show the slightest connection with the idea of "hard." This fact alone brings out the disparity noted above within Greek between *kratús* 'hard' and *krátos*, *krateîn* 'dominate'. But

1. Analyzed in detail by K. Rönnow, *Le Monde Oriental*, XXVI, 1932, 1-90. The studies that have appeared since are reviewed by L. Renou, *Etudes védiques et paninéennes*, III, 1957, p. 59; IV, 1958, p. 18.

the adjective *kraterós* brought about a contamination between the two families. On the one hand it provided a doublet (on the model of *iskhurós*, *sthenarós*) to *kratús*, with the sense "hard, cruel, painful," and on the other hand it provided *krátos* with an adjective signifying "provided with authority."

The notion of *krátos* thus finds its proper definition and, at the same time, its Indo-European correspondence. In this way we lay the foundations for a study of this concept in the epic. It will fall to Hellenists to follow the evolution of the term in the political vocabulary of post-Homeric Greek, in which it so richly proliferated.

BOOK IV, CHAPTER EIGHT

Royalty and Nobility

Abstract. The king in Germanic (Engl. *king*, Germ. *König*, etc.) is the one who is born, that is "well born," "noble" (from the root **gen-* 'be born'). But the noble has another name, which is extremely instructive, e.g. Germ. *edel*, originally **atalo-*, derived from **atta* 'foster-father': this designation for the nobleman implies that the great Indo-European families practiced fosterage. In fact, the use in Homeric poetry of the terms *átta*, *atalós*, *atitállō* seems to confirm this hypothesis.

To pursue this description in the western part of the Indo-European world, we now consider the name of the "king" and the "noble" in the Germanic world.

The designation of the king, exemplified in English *king*, German *König*, etc. goes back to **kun-ing-az*. This is a derivative in *-ing* from the root *kun-*, cf. Got. *kuni* 'race, family', a nominal form derived from the root **gen-* 'be born', which belongs to the same group as Lat. *gens* and Greek *génos*. The "king" is so named in virtue of his birth as "he of the lineage," he who represents it and is its head. In fact every time that his birth is specified it turns out to be noble. *Reges ex nobilitate . . . sumunt*, as Tacitus remarks of the Germans (*Germ.* VII, 1). In this conception the "king" is considered as the representative of the members of his tribe.

Quite different is the Germanic conception of the "noble," which is expressed by the German *edel*, and it poses a much more difficult problem. The word appears in Old English, in Middle English, and in Old High German in forms which do not show great differences from those in use today. They all go back to an ancient **atalo-*, cf. Old Norse *edal*, which alternates with *uodal*, corresponding to German *Adel* 'the nobility'. This reconstructed Germanic form **atalo-* has no etymological connections and appears to be quite isolated. However, there is a form which corresponds to it but has an entirely different sense: this is the Greek *atalós* (ἀταλός) 'childish, infantile, puerile'. This adjective may be linked with the verb *atállō* (ἀτάλλω) the translation of which would be "play like a child, jump, amuse oneself." Finally we have a reduplicated present *atitállō* (ἀτιτάλλω) 'feed a child, rear it'. All this is not very precise in Greek itself; but the main point is that it is difficult to see any point of contact with the notion designated by the Germanic group. Because of this disparity of meaning, the etymological dictionaries dismiss this connection.

All the same it is worth while giving close scrutiny to the sense of the Greek words. Our research will lead to another realm of the vocabulary, but we shall still be dealing with institutions.

While the verb *atállō* is hardly attested at all, we have numerous examples of *atitállō*, and it has a much more precise sense than "rear, feed." Certainly it is used together with *tréphō* 'feed, bring up': e.g. *Il.* 24, 60 "I fed him and reared him"; but we may also quote *Odyssey* 18, 323: "she had brought him up like a child." These two passages contain the essential significance: "rear *like* a child," that is, as if he were a member of the family, which was not actually the case. In all the examples the verb is exclusively applied to a child who is not one's own child, like Hera for Achilles' mother (*Il.* 24, 60). It was never used in speaking of one's own child. Hesiod also takes it in this sense (*Theog.* 480).

We now see what this verb refers to. It denotes an institution which is known under the scientific term of "fosterage," the use of a foster-parent. This is a very important custom, particularly in Celtic and Scandinavian society, and it was the rule in the case of royal children. Noble families had the custom of entrusting their children to another family to be reared until a certain age. This was a real relationship, often stronger than the blood tie, which was established between the two families. In the ancient Scandinavian law codes there are laws, called *gragas*, which define the status of the child so entrusted and the conduct of the parents who are to rear it. Among the Celts the fact is well known from historic traditions and the legends. Normally the royal children are entrusted to another family, generally that of the mother, that is, to the maternal grandfather of the child. There is a special term to designate the foster-father: this is *aite*, which corresponds to the Latin *atta*, the Greek *átta*, and the verb which designates this custom is in Scandinavian *fostra*. Hubert, in his book on the Celts, cites many witnesses to this institution. Fosterage is also well attested among the Caucasian nobility, especially in Georgia.

We may now posit the existence of this institution in Greece itself, where it is to be recognized in the verb *atitállō*. There must have been other terms relating to this notion, but they have been preserved only by chance. Thus we have an inscription from Gortyn in Crete which presents the word *atitáltas* (ἀτιτάλτας), which certainly designates the *tropheús* 'foster-father'.

Now that we have determined the institutional sense of this verb, we find traditions which may be connected with it. We recall how Achilles was brought up by Phoenix (*Il.* 9,485-495) or, according to a different tradition, by Chiron. If we explored mythical and legendary traditions, we would be sure to discover other confirmations: the essential point is to be able to identify and designate this custom. We may be sure that *atitállō* was applied solely to children reared outside their own family, whatever the reason may have been, whether to escape from some danger or to be brought up in a certain tradition.

We may now proceed to an examination of this root **atalo-* of the Greek adjective. It has a striking resemblance to the Tocharian *ātäl*, but this word simply means "man" and it is not possible to tell whether this is not a simple coincidence. The formation itself of *atalós* suggests that it is a derivative in *-lo-* from the word which is represented by *átta,* a word denoting "father," which is known all over the Indo-European world: e.g. Got. *atta*, Lat. *atta* 'father'; Gr. *átta*, Skt. *attī*, feminine, a familiar term for the elder sister, Irl. *aite*, Hittite *attaš* 'father' (the word *pater* does not appear in Hittite).

The form *atta* is always regarded, because of its geminated consonant, as a word of the child's language (cf. *pappa, mamma*).[1]

However the Irish form *aite* takes on a special significance because the institution of fosterage still existed in Ireland in historical times: *aite* is the term for the foster-father and not for the natural father. It is perhaps not an accident that Telemachus addresses Eumaeus by the term *átta*, if *átta* was the specific name for foster-father in Greek.

At the conclusion of this study we return to the Germanic *Edel*. If it was the tradition of great families, particularly royal families, to entrust their children to foster-fathers, it might follow that the very fact of being so brought up would

1. On *atta* see Book Two, Chapter One.

imply a degree of nobility. *Edel* in that case would simply have meant the "nursling," with the implication that children brought up by foster-parents could only be of noble birth. This would give precision to the relationship indicated by OHG *adal* 'race' and OE *adelu* 'noble origin', etc. In this way some scattered fragments of a prehistoric tradition would, on this hypothesis, find their original unity and the correspondence of form would agree with the sense posited.

BOOK IV, CHAPTER NINE

The King and His People

Abstract. The two Homeric words for "the people," *dễmos* and *laós*, are distinguished in sense and in origin.

Dễmos designated both a division of land and the people who inhabit it; it is a term of Dorian origin.

Laós is the community of men, a warrior group which is defined by its relationship to the chief, the "shepherd" (*poimḗn*), or the "leader" (*órkhamos*) of the *laoí*. In Homer it is principally heroes from Thessaly and Phrygia who are dignified with the title of *poimèn laôn*. Other testimony, both literary and epigraphic, confirms this distribution of the term *laós*, which, from the Greek point of view, seems to belong to the Achaean stratum. But it attests also the existence of some degree of community which we may call Aeolo-Phrygian, which does not go back much further than the beginning of the Greek literary tradition, so that it would not be surprising to find reflections of it in the Homeric epic.

In defining the position and the characteristics of the king we should also envisage those persons over whom he exercises royalty, in other words the terms which designate in different ways the "people" of whom he is sometimes the master, and sometimes the most immediate representative.

In Homer there are two different words for "people," both of which deserve close scrutiny: *dễmos* (δῆμος) and *laós* (λαός). We also have the metaphorical expression for the king as "the shepherd of the people": *poimèn laôn.* What is the exact meaning of this phrase? It is to be noted that *poimḗn*, like other titles with a more political sense, *órkhamos*, *koiranós*, *kosmḗtōr*, is never constructed with *dêmos*, but exclusively with *laós*; while *ánaks*, *agós* and sometimes *órkhamos* take solely *andrôn* 'of the men'.

Because of the limitations of our language we translate both *dêmos* and *laós* as "people," but it would be of interest to distinguish between these two notions. For there is a distinction and it is a considerable one.

Dêmos is a territorial and political concept, and it designates both a division of land and the people who inhabit it. By "people" we must understand in this connection something other than *éthnos* (ἔθνος), which is in any case clear from the fact that *éthnos* is not solely used of men but also of animals, such as bees, whereas *dêmos* is never used in such applications. Besides, *éthnos* enters into such expressions as *éthnos laôn*, *éthnos hetaírōn* to designate groups of comrades in battle. It emerges finally also from Homeric examples that *dêmos* designates a grouping of men who are united solely by their social status and not by any bond of kinship or attachment to a political community.

The peculiarity of *laós* (the term is used both in the singular and the plural) is that it expresses the personal relationship of a group of men to a chief. It is an organization peculiar to ancient warrior societies such as those we have established among the Germans and which, in the term *laós*, comes to life in ancient Hellenic society. The *laoí* form part of the retinue of the chief; they are often under his orders; they owe him fidelity and obedience; they would not be *laoí* unless they were attached to him by mutual consent. They may be engaged in his cause in battle, which is the situation most familiar to us, but this is probably due to the epic character of the *Iliad.* In any case *laós* is the name of the people insofar as they are capable of bearing arms. Thus the term does not comprise the old men or the children, but only the men in their prime. Thus the *laós* is the warrior community, and so is different from the *dêmos*. The use of the plural *laoí* suggests that this community was made up of different sections.

We must now study more closely the conditions in which the expression *poimḕn laôn* is used. To whom is this description applied, and in what circumstances does it occur in the *Iliad* and the *Odyssey*? This, curiously enough, is a question which, so it seems, has never been posed.

The expression is very ancient, and what gives some idea of its antiquity is that we have forty-four examples of it in the *Iliad*as against only twelve in the *Odyssey*, and these are mainly in passages of a formulaic character, so that they would appear to be no more than a survival for the poet of the *Odyssey.*

If we attempt to classify the examples and to draw up a list of the persons to whom it is applied, we arrive at a peculiar result which should prompt reflection. We find it attached most often to Agamemnon, and also to Achilles, Machaon, Jason, a Lapith (Dryas), and finally Nestor. This list is not exhaustive, but, as we shall see, it constitutes a distinct group within the Achaean world.

Is there something in common between these persons? They are all men whose ancestry and origin are known. The poet tells us where they come from. Achilles comes from Phthia, from the Phthiotis, a region of Thessaly; Machaon is from Ithoma, a place in Thessaly, Jason from Iolkos, a place in Thessaly, which was the point of departure for the expedition of the Argonauts. Dryas the Lapith, like all the Lapiths, comes from the north of Thessaly. Finally, Nestor is king of Pylos, but (this has already been observed) different features of his legend and the expression *hippóta Néstōr* link him likewise with Thessaly.

Here we reach down to the most ancient stratum of the epic. It is not a simple accident that some of the most notable *poiménes laôn* should come from Thessaly. The title, which had become a cliché, was later extended to all the kings of the Achaeans, among whom was Agamemnon.

There are several others dignified by this title in the opposing camp: Hector, Bienor, Hyperenor, Hypeiron, Agenor. We are less well informed about these. They belong to the Trojan camp, some being Trojans and other Phrygians.

This, then, is the distribution of the expression *poimèn laôn* in the two Homeric groups: the first is specifically Thessalian and the second Ilio-Phrygian.

This point established, we may return to the word *laós* to carry the investigation further. It is a word which has no correspondent outside Greek. We cannot therefore ascribe it to the Indo-European vocabulary or illuminate it by its prehistory. But it has enough connections inside Greek itself to make possible a more penetrating study which will bring out some new aspects of the word.

An important historical piece of information, though it bears only indirectly on *laós*, has been preserved by Herodotus (VII, 197) apropos of the expedition of Xerxes into Thessaly. When Xerxes arrived in this region, at Alos in Achaia, his guides told him about a local legend concerning Zeus Laphystios. Athamas had plotted with Ino against Phryxus, and to punish them the Achaeans laid down a rule which was to be applied to their descendants. The eldest son was forbidden to enter the prytaneum. If he does so enter, he will leave it only to be sacrificed. This is a curious story and it seems to imply the sacrifice of the eldest son to Zeus Laphystius.

In relating the story of this interdiction Herodotus uses the expression *érg-esthai toû lē̆ïtou* 'to forbid access to the *lḗïton'* and he adds this gloss: *lḗïton dè kaléousi tò prutanḗion hoi Akhaioí* 'The Achaeans call the prytaneum the *lḗïton'*.

We recall that this scene occurred in Achaea Phthiotis. This word *lḗïton* (the Ionic form of *lā́ïton*) is connected with a whole series of forms preserved in the glossators and particularly in Hesychius: *lā́ïton· tò arkheîon* 'the residence of the magistrates'; *laḯtōn· tôn dēmosíōn tópōn*, that is to say, "of public places"; *lēḯtē, lḗtē· hiéreia* 'public priestess'; finally *leitoárkhai*, the title of those concerned with sacrifices and who have public posts, magistrates.

Another gloss—an important one because it gives us its source— provides an agent noun: *lētêres· hieroì stephanophóroi Athamā̂nes*. Now the legend reported by Herodotus concerned the descendants of Athamas, and the word *lētḗr* comes precisely from the language of the Athamanes, from the people who had as their eponym the hero Athamas. Another agent noun **leítōr* is attested by the denominative verb *leitoreúō* 'to exercise a magistracy, a public office', which is found exclusively in Thessalian inscriptions.

What information is provided by this testimony? The basic term *lḗïton*, which goes back to *lā́(w)iton*, a derivative of *lā(w)os*, among the Achaean people designated the prytaneum, the "people's" house. The distribution of the terms quoted shows that it was in Thessaly and Arcadia that these traditions were localized and nowhere else. We are justified in concluding that *laós* was an Achaean word. Those who vouch for the legend reported by Herodotus are Achaeans originating in the region which in Greece itself preserves the name of Achaea Phthiotis. This region is considered as Aeolic along with Thessaly, a part of Boeotia, certain islands, and part of Asia Minor. There is a further connection, loose though it is, between Aeolic and the language of Homer, in the sense that it exhibits a number of features found in the epic language. Now here this term, which is defined as Achaean, is applied to Athamas, the son of Aeolus, the ancestor of the Aeolians. There is thus concordance between the historical traditions and the dialect distribution. The term *laós* may therefore be attributed to the Achaean stratum of Greek. This seems to find confirmation in the study of proper names. *Laós* enters into a large number of personal names whether as the first or the second component: we have *Lao-medon, Lao-koon*, and, on the other hand, *Mene-laos*, and all the names in *-las*. Their number is considerable. Among the most ancient persons bearing these names we find a large number who come from the Aeolic regions. We go still farther.

The word *laós*, or more precisely the derivative *lā*(*w*)*ito*-, occurs, though this is not generally realized, in a well-known compound of common Greek: this is *lĕ̄itourgós* (ληι-, λειτουργός) with the abstract *leitourgía* (λειτουργία) 'liturgy', which is to be analyzed as **lēito-werg*-. Thus this word *lḗïton*, which in Herodotus is still given as a local word and provided with a translation, served as the base for the name of an institution which became part of the common language. The "liturgy" was in fact a *public* service, a public due paid by a citizen to the state. The compound must, therefore, also be of Aeolo-Achaean origin. It could have only been formed in a dialect in which the usual term for "public" was *lḗïtos*.

In another part of Hellenic territory, in the domain of Doric, this notion of "liturgy" was expressed on Cnidus by *dāmoûrgos* (δᾱμοῦργος). The two words *lēitourgós* and *dāmoûrgos* correspond exactly in sense, but their difference is instructive: we see that *dâmos* is the Dorian form which corresponds to the Aeolo-Achaean form *lā*(*w*)*ós* (and *lā́*(*w*)*iton*). The analysis provides us with a kind of stratigraphy within the Greek vocabulary.

There are thus as early as Homer two distinct sources for the concept of "people." We must attribute *laós* to the Achaean period, whereas *dêmos* must be ascribed to the Dorian invasion, that is, to a later date.

But up till now we have considered only half the available facts. The title *poimḕn laôn* is also bestowed in the *Iliad* on heroes who are neither Achaean nor Greek, but Trojan. Further, among those who bear proper names in *-laos* there are found persons of Asiatic origin, Phrygians. We have in fact the word in Phrygian itself in two forms. Ancient Phrygian inscriptions present the proper name *Akenano-lawos* and also the word *lawaltaei*, which is interpreted as meaning "he who nourishes (cf. Latin *alo*) the people." In any case we cannot doubt that the first element is to be identified as *lāwós* 'people'.

We should not be surprised that elements of vocabulary seem common to Greek and Phrygian. We distinguish between Greeks and Phrygians for historical and linguistic reasons. But it is probable that the Greeks themselves were more conscious of their similarities than their differences. The Phrygian and Trojan world is exactly similar to the Greek world in Homer. The language presented no obstacle to their communications. The heroes address each other and understand each other perfectly. They invoke the same gods on both sides. They have the same institutions, the same relations of hospitality, the same type of family. There is intermarriage between the two sides, and they travel freely to each other. For Homer the Trojan War is not a dispute between Greeks and barbarians, it is a quarrel within one and the same world, even though the Carians are called "barbarophones."

In ancient tradition the Phrygian world is closely associated with that of Thessaly and the Aeolis. The Phrygians, Φρύγες, Βρύγες, were regarded as originally from Thrace. Thus located in the region in which the abode of the Athamanes lies, the Phrygians are simply an offshoot of the same ethnic group as the Thracians. It is not surprising that evidence of their community or of their proximity should be preserved in the epic.

The title *órkhamos laỗn* belongs to the same repertory of terms. The form *órkhamos* is connected with *árkhō* 'command', but the initial *o-* represents a specifically Aeolic treatment like that of ὀν for the preposition *aná*.

It is in the light of this overall survey, which is both ethnic and social, that we must judge the title *poimền laỗn*. It goes back to an age when, in a social structure founded on animal husbandry, the profession of war was in the hands of "bands" subjected to a chief. It is doubtless not an accident that one of the oldest pieces of evidence for the existence of the word *lāwos* is represented by the Mycenaean word *ra-wa-ke-ta* = *Lāwāgetās* 'chief of the *lāwos*' (cf. Dor. *lāgétās* 'chief of the people' in Pindar). But "royalty" introduces a conception of power which is different: the authority of the king is that of the guide, of the "shepherd"[1] and we find it in Iranian, in Hittite, as well as in Homeric Greek.

1. Cf. *Hittite et indo-européen*, Paris, 1962, p. 100.

BOOK FIVE

Law

BOOK V, CHAPTER ONE

Thémis

Abstract. The root common to Skt. *ṛta*, Iran. *arta*, Lat. *ars*, *artus*, *ritus*, which designates "order" as a harmonious arrangement of the parts of a whole, did not provide any juridical term in Indo-European.

"Law" is in Skt. *dhāman* and in Gr. *thémis*, and the term means literally the rule established (root **dhē-* 'to bring into existence') by the gods. This rule defines family law: thus *thémis* is opposed to *díkē* 'interfamily law'.

The general structure of society, defined in its broad divisions by a certain number of concepts, rests on an assemblage of norms which add up to "law." All societies, even the most primitive, and *a fortiori* Indo-European society (we have seen that it had a rich material civilization and a no less rich culture), are governed by principles of law relating both to persons and goods. These rules and these norms are traceable in the vocabulary.

By what means can we gain knowledge of the juridical organization of Indo-European society? Is there a term which goes back to the original common period and denotes "law"? To a question posed in these terms which imply both the generality of the notion and all the languages concerned the answer must be in the negative. There are numerous terms for "law," but they are all confined to one of the separate languages. However, the chief terms concerned are connected with elements of the common vocabulary and may be evidence for special legal terms going back to Indo-European times.

It will be necessary to study both the origin of the terms attested in historical times and their evolution, which, starting from common terms, has specialized their sense so that in the end they developed into names for institutions.

We can in the first place posit for common Indo-European an extremely important concept, that of "order." It is represented by Vedic *ṛta*, Iranian *arta* (Avestan *aša*, by a special phonetic development). We have here one of the cardinal notions of the legal world of the Indo-European, to say nothing of their religious and moral ideas: this is the concept of "Order," which governs also the orderliness of the universe, the movement of the stars, the regularity of the seasons and the years; further, the relations of gods and men; and finally, the relations of men to one another. Nothing which concerns man or the world falls outside the realm of "Order." It is thus the foundation, both religious and moral, of every society. Without this principle everything would revert to chaos.

The importance of this notion is shown by the considerable number of lexical forms drawn from it. It would be pointless to enumerate in full all the Indic and Iranian derivatives of *ṛta* and *arta*, both in the vocabulary and proper names. That the term belongs to an ancient stratum of Indo-Iranian is shown by certain archaisms of morphology: the one "who is faithful to *arta*, who is morally accomplished" is called in Sanskrit *ṛta-van*, feminine *ṛta-varī*; similarly we have in Iranian *artavan, artavarī*. This remarkable difference between the masculine and the feminine of the suffixal form *-van*, *-varī* is explained by the ancient mode of declension which is called "heteroclitic," which has left traces in the declension of Greek *húdōr*, *húdatos* and Latin *iter*, *itineris*.

Moreover in the Avesta this notion is personified: we find a god *Arta*. With the aid of an abstract suffix *-tu-*, Indo-Iranian formed the stem Vedic *ṛtu-*, Avestan *ratu-*, which designated "order," particularly in the seasons and periods of time, and also "rule" and "norm" in a general sense.

All these forms are referable to a root *ar-*, which is well-known because of numerous formations outside Indo-Iranian which belong to several of the formal categories just mentioned. The root is that of Greek *araríškō* 'fit, adapt, harmonize' (Arm. *aṙnel* 'make'), which is connected with a number of nominal derivatives. Some are formed with the suffix *-ti-*, e.g. Lat. *ars*, *artis*, 'natural disposition, qualification, talent'; others with *-tu-*, e.g. Lat. *artus* 'joint' and also, with a different form of the root, *ritus* 'rite'; Gr. *artús* (Arm. *ard*, genitive *ardu* 'order'), as well as the present tense *artúnō* 'arrange, equip'; with **-dhmo-*, Gr. *arthmós* 'bond, league, friendship'; and finally with **-dhro-*, Gr. *árthron* 'joint, limb'.

Everywhere the same notion is still perceptible: order, arrangement, the close mutual adaptation of the parts of a whole to one another, even though the derivatives have undergone different semantic specialization in the different languages. We thus have for Indo-European a general concept which embraces, by numerous lexical variants, the religious, legal, and technical aspects of "order." But within each domain distinctive terms were found necessary. This is why "law" was given more precise expressions which must be studied each in their proper sphere. We limit our study to some of the most important.

In Vedic Sanskrit we find first the term *dharma-*, neuter *dharman*, which is equivalent to "law," but the proper sense is "what is maintained, held fast" (from *dhar-* 'to hold'), and, according to the context, "custom, rule, usage." It is a term of great importance in religion, philosophy, and also in law, but it is confined to India.

This Indo-Iranian root *dhar-* 'hold firmly' corresponds probably to that of Latin *firmus*, which has a formation in *-m-* like *dharman*. The "law" as thus named is "what holds firmly, what is solidly established."

Another way of looking at it is reflected in Skt. *dhāman* 'law',and also "seat," "place." The formation of *dhāman* is parallel with that of *dharman*, but it comes from the root *dhā-* 'place', 'put', Indo-European **dhē-* 'put, place, establish', to which Latin *facio* and Greek *títhēmi* are also traced. It should be noted that the strict sense of **dhē* is "to put (in a creative way), establish in existence," and not simply to leave an object on the ground. The derivative *dhāman* thus designates "the establishment," both what is placed and created, and the place of the "putting" or "establishing"; in other words it designates the domain, the site and also the thing put or created in the world. Given this basic meaning, we see how the meaning of "law" is also defined by *dhāman*: law is in the first place an "establishment," an institution that is founded and so takes on existence.

This conception is not confined to Indo-Iranian. We also find in other languages terms derived from the same root which are connected with the vocabulary of law. We have several of the greatest importance in Greek. First, *thesmós* (Doric *thethmós*, *tethmós*, an old reduplicated form **dhedhmo-*) 'that which is laid down, law, ordinance'. But the most notable term is *thémis*.

The formation of *thémis* is close to that of *thémethla* (in Homer *themeília*) which is a building term meaning "base, foundation." *Thémis* presents an archaic type of declension: in Homer the genitive is *thémistos* and the plural *thémista*, but later we have the normalized forms genitive *thémitos*, accusative *thémin*. The word was probably an ancient neuter. At the moment the Mycenaean form *ti-mi-to* can contribute nothing, either morphological or semantic, to our problem, though it has been compared with *thémis*.

Apart from the quantity of the root vowel, *thémis* is exactly comparable to the Avestan *dāmi-* as regards its formation, and this equation is remarkable because suffixation with *-mis*, like that seen in *dúnamis*, is extremely rare. This makes it probable that *thémis* is a word of great antiquity and that it has undergone morphological modifications which tended to normalize an archaic mode of declension.

The Avestan *dāmi-*, on the other hand, has become an agent noun and means "creator." If we look for a word corresponding to *thémis* which has the same sense, we find it in the derived neuter in *-man* made from the same root in Indo-Iranian: this is *dhāman* 'law', the precise sense of which is, within the order prescribed by Mithra and Varuna, an ordinance relating to the house and to the family. This is an important specification, because it shows the sphere of application of this law. Now, what does *thémis* mean? Here we have a striking correlation: *thémis* designates family law as opposed to *díkē*, which is law that holds good among the families that make up a tribe.[1]

This point must be stressed, for the dictionaries take no account of this distinction. Further, *thémis* is of divine origin. Only this sense enables us to understand and unify uses which look very different. In the epic, what is understood under *thémis* is the prescription which lays down the rights and duties of each person under the authority of the chief of the *génos*, whether in everyday life or in exceptional circumstances: alliance, marriage, war.

Thémis is the prerogative of the *basileús*; it is of heavenly origin, and the plural *thémistes* stands for the sum total of these ordinances, which is a code inspired by the gods, a set of unwritten laws, a collection of dicta, of oracular responses, which determine, in the conscience of the judge (in actual fact the head of the family), how to proceed every time the order of the *génos* is at stake.

The specific characteristics of this notion can be found in the most stereotyped expressions. Let us consider the stock phrase *hḕ thémis estín*, which is usually translated "as is meet and right." An example is *Il.* 2, 72-73: "First I will make trial of them with words, *hḕ thémis estín*." Here Agamemnon is speaking

1. The history of these two terms, their exact meaning and their relationship have been studied in an excellent work by Gustave Glotz, *La solidarité de la famille dans le droit criminel grec*, Paris, 1904 (see especially p. 21).

in his capacity as *basileús* responsible for his army; he is their chief, and he exercises the *thémis*, which prescribes the way he has to proceed and the usages to be observed. This *thémis* is manifested by *thémistes*, which are decrees, or ordinances. In Book 16 of the *Iliad*, l. 387, we see "the anger of Zeus towards men who in the assembly judge crooked *thémistes* through violence," that is, those who deliver, by the use of violence, unjust decrees.

Sometimes the context is indispensable for the understanding of the sense. Patroclus rushes into the fray and lays low a succession of opponents; but his death is being prepared, although he does not know it, for Phoebus Apollo himself comes to meet him in disguise.

> From his head Phoebus Apollo smote the helmet and as it rolled it rang loud beneath the feet of the horses . . . and the plumes were befouled with blood and dust. . . . Not until then had it been *thémis* (*ou thémis ễen*) for the helmet with the plume of horse-hair to be befouled with dust, but it guarded the head and comely brow of a godlike man, of Achilles; but then Zeus granted it to Hector to wear on his head. (16, 796)

It is expressly stated: it was in virtue of a divine order that this helmet which belonged to Achilles must never be sullied with dust. This is because Achilles is a "godlike man" (*anễr theîos*, l. 798); he is a member of the divine family and even his arms enjoy this divine privilege.

This social organization and the *thémis* which is operative within it is better brought out by the inverse picture which the poet sketches in his description of the land of the Cyclops. These, he says, are *athémistes*; among them there are neither deliberative assemblies nor *thémistes*; each one lays down his own law (*themisteúei*) to his wife and children and none has regard for the others (*Od.* 9, 106-115). This provides an illuminating definition of the concept of *thémis*. Where there is no *génos* and no king there can be no *thémis* or assembly. Each family lives according to its own law. These Cyclops are certainly savages.

We now turn to a text which presents a correlation between the two terms *thémis* and *díkē* so that the study of one leads on to that of the other. Odysseus has been received by Eumaeus without being recognized by him and he thanks him for his hospitality: "May Zeus and the other gods grant you all you desire." Eumaeus replies: "*Thémis* does not allow me (*oú moi thémis ést*') to do outrage to a guest even if one came to me even more wretched than you. For all guests come from Zeus and beggars too" (*Od.* 14, 53ff.).

Thus a stranger is received within the family because of *thémis*, because he comes from Zeus. Eumaeus continues: "I can give you only a paltry gift but I give it gladly; for that is the *díkē* of slaves, always in fear when new masters have power . . ." He is thinking of the tyrannical, capricious and brutal domination of the suitors. This time the use of *díkē* shows clearly that it goes beyond the confines of the family and concerns relations with other groups. Justice and law are strictly defined by the limits of the domain within which they apply.

Everything reminds us that this *thémis*, these *thémistes* were not invented or arbitrarily laid down by those who have to apply them: they are of divine origin. As Nestor says to Agamemnon, son of Atreus: "You rule over numerous *laoí*, to you Zeus has entrusted the scepter and the *thémistes*, so that you can guide their deliberations" (*Il.* 9, 97). The king, designated by Zeus, is invested with these two attributes: one, the scepter, is material; the other is knowledge of the *thémistes*.

At the other social extremity, the swineherd Eumaeus, a man of the humblest status, also invokes *thémis* to do better honor to his guest who comes from Zeus. Everywhere we find proof of this relation between the order within the *génos* and divine decisions. Outside Homeric civilization we find in Indic *dhāman* a precise correspondent of *thémis*: it is the order within the house and the family established by divine will, that of Mitra and Varuṇa.

BOOK V, CHAPTER TWO

Díkē

Abstract. Latin *dico* and Greek *díkē* together imply the idea of a formulaic law which lays down what is to be done in every particular situation. The judge—Hom. *dikaspólos*—is the one who keeps the formulary and pronounces (*dicit*) authoritatively the appropriate sentence.

The counterpart of *thémis* is the notion of *díkē*. The first, as we have said, relates to justice as it is exercised within a family group, whereas the second is that which regulates relations between families.

Straight away we perceive two significant differences between these two notions. The first relates to the formation of the terms. We saw above that *thémis* is a derivative from **dhē-* by means of a suffix the equivalent of which is found in Indo-Iranian. It is quite different with *díkē*, which is made from the root **deik-* with the addition of the feminine *-ā*. Its nominal correspondents simply reproduce the root without a suffix. These are the so-called root nouns like Skt. *diś-* 'direction, region', Lat. **dix*, which survives in the phrase *dicis causā* 'for form's sake'.

Another difference between *thémis* and *díkē* lies in the way in which they are conceived. The basis of *thémis* is a root meaning "put, place, establish." The basic meaning of the term is thus plain, and its institutional value is derived from the same conception as is present in the verbal forms of this root. With *díkē*, on the other hand, we have a root which does not immediately explain the sense assumed by the noun and which in Greek itself has a different development in its verbal and its nominal derivatives.

The root in question is **deik-*, which appears in Sanskrit as *diś-*, as *dis-* in Iranian, as *dic-* in Latin and *deík(numi)* in Greek. But these forms, though in perfect formal correspondence, do not agree in meaning, for Greek *deíknumi* means "show" and Latin *dico* 'say'. It will be necessary, therefore, to undertake an analysis to elicit the sense which will explain why *díkē* in Greek has the sense of "justice."

If the agreement of Indo-Iranian and Greek makes it plausible that the sense "show" is primary as against "say," this does not make the transition from one sense to the other any easier. Here we have the first problem.

Let us try and reconstruct this ancient idea of "showing."

(1) "To show" in what way? With the finger? This is rarely the case. In general the sense is "show verbally," by speech. This first determination is confirmed by a number of Indo-Iranian uses in the sense "teach," which amounts to the same thing as "showing" by words and not by gesture. Besides, there is in Latin a compound to which we shall have to come back, in which **deik-* is joined with *ius*: this is *iu-dex*, in which **deik-* stands for an act of speech.

(2) "To show" in what way? Incidentally, by way of example? And can simply anyone "show"?

The Latin compound *iu-dex* implies the notion of showing with authority. If this is not the constant sense of Gr. *deíknumi*, this fact is due to the weakening of the force of the root in Greek. The whole history of Lat. *dicere* highlights a mechanism of authority: only the judge can *dicere ius*. This combination is also found in an Italic language, with *med-* substituted for *ius* in Oscan *med-diss*, which was Latinized as *meddix*, where *med-* is related to Lat. *medeor*. In this Oscan equivalent of *iudex*, the term for "law" is a different one, but *dicere* remains constant.

We should also bear in mind the Latin formula in which the praetor summed up the three functions which he had the right to exercise only on certain days prescribed by the calendar: *do*, *dico*, *addico*. He has the right to "give," to "announce certain rules" and to "adjudge." This same concept leads to the frequent use of *dicere* in the language of the law courts: *diem dicere* 'fix a day for the hearing of a case', or *multam dicere* 'pronounce a fine'.

(3) "Show," but what? A visible thing, an existing object? Here we have the last feature in the meaning of **deik-*: it means to show what must be, a pronouncement which may take the form of a court judgment.

These indications allow us to state with greater precision the original sense of Gr. *díkē*, insofar as it is an institutional term. By comparing the forms Skt. *diś* and Latin *dicis causā*, we see that **dix* insists on the normative implications: *dicis causā* really means "according to a formal pronouncement," or as we should say, "for form's sake." We might therefore define **dix* literally as 'the fact of showing verbally and with authority what must be'; in other words, it is the imperative pronouncement of justice.

This imperative value of *díkē* appears in a number of examples. In the description of the Shield of Achilles a court scene is described in detail (*Il.* 18, 497ff.). Two parties are pleading their case before the court: the assembly, in great excitement, is divided, some favoring one side and others the other. What is at stake is a *poinḗ*, blood money for manslaughter. In the center of the assembly are the elders sitting in a sacred circle on polished stones. Each of them rises in turn and gives his judgment. In their midst are two talents of gold reserved for the judge who will have given "the straightest judgment," *díkēnithúntata eípoi* (l. 508).

A *poinḗ* is the typical instance of a case involving *díkē*, that is, inter-familial justice. The terms of the Homeric expression attest one and the same construction both in Greek and in Latin: we have *díkēn eipeîn* 'say the *díkē*' just like Latin *dicere*. We now see how this "showing" became an act of speech: in Greek the substantive *díkē* attracts a verb "to say" (*eipeîn*); in Latin it is the verb "to show" (**deik-*) which took on the sense "to say."

We now turn to the adjective *ithús* (*ithúntata*) 'straight' (in the sense of a straight line). This figurative expression fills in what is implied by **deik-*: 'to show what must be done, prescribe a norm'. For we should not forget that *díkē* is a formula. To give justice is not an intellectual operation which requires meditation or discussion. Formulas have been transmitted which are appropriate to given cases, and the role of the judge is to possess and apply them. In this way we can explain one of the ancient and rare names for the "judge," the Homeric *dikas-pólos*. This is a curious term, formed like *ai-pólos* 'goatherd', *bou-kólos* (with *-kolos* alternating with *-polos*, both going back to *k^w *ólos*) 'cowherd', *oiōno-pólos* 'he who observes the flight of birds' (and interprets it to foretell the future). In his capacity as *dikas-pólos*, the judge is "he who watches over the *díkai*." Here we have an archaic type of juxtaposition with an accusative plural as the first term. The *díkai* are certainly the formulas of law which are handed down and which the judge is responsible for keeping and applying.

This idea corresponds to what we know of codes of law among peoples of a traditional civilization, collections of oral pronouncements, which are centered around the relations of kinship, of the clan and the tribe.

Such is the point of departure for the sense which is usually assigned to *díkē*: 'custom, usage, the way of being', in which the institutional value is apparent. When Odysseus in his descent to the underworld meets his mother, he asks her why he cannot embrace her: such, she replies, is the *díkē* of mortals, *all' haútē díkē estì brotȏn* (ἀλλ' ἅυτη δίκη ἐστὶ βροτῶν, *Od.* 11, 218). It is not "the way of being," but rather "the imperative rule," the "formula which regulates one's fate." In this way we can understand the adverbial use of *díkēn* 'in the manner of', that is to say, "according to the norm of a certain category of beings." The "habitual" manner is in reality an obligation of nature or convention.

Hence this formula which determines one's lot and allocation became in Greek the word for "justice" itself. But the ethical notion of justice, such as we understand it, is not included in *díkē*. This has gradually evolved from the circumstances in which *díkē* was invoked to put an end to abuses. This traditional legal formula becomes the expression for justice itself when *díkē* intervenes to put an end to the power of *bía*, 'violence'. Then *díkē* is identified with the virtue of justice—and he who has *díkē* towards this is *díkaios* 'just'.

BOOK V, CHAPTER THREE

Ius and the Oath in Rome

Abstract. Parallel with *díkē*, the Latin *ius*, which is translated as "law," has a derived verb *iurare* which means "to swear." Strange though this seems from a semantic point of view, this derivation is illuminated by two complementary pieces of research:

(1) When brought into connection with Avestan *yaoš-* and considered in the light of its particular affinity with the verb *dico (ius dicere, iudex)*, *ius* may be defined as "the formula of conformity."

(2) A number of texts show that in Rome "to swear" (*iurare*) is to pronounce a formula, the *ius iurandum* 'oath', literally "a formula to be formulated," an expression in which the very repetition brings out what is essential in the act of swearing. In fact the person swearing must repeat word by word the formula imposed on him: *adiurat in quae adactus est verba.*

Another Latin term connected with jurisdictional practice, *arbiter*, denotes, curiously enough, both the "witness" and the "arbiter." In fact the texts show that the *arbiter* is always the invisible witness, who has the capacity to become, in certain determined judicial actions, impartial and sovereign *iudex.*

The analysis of the uses of *díkē* has brought out the frequency of the correlations between the Greek *díkē* and the Latin *ius*. These two terms, although different in origin, enter into parallel series: *díkēn eipeîn* corresponds to *ius dicere*; *díkaios* to *iustus*, and finally, *dikaspólos* corresponds more or less to *iudex*. A further point which may be noted is that just as *díkē* contrasts with *thémis* in referring to human as opposed to divine law, so *ius* is opposed to that which the Romans called *fas*.

What is then the real significance of this word *ius*? On this point we are still in the dark. We know that *ius* denotes "law," but this lexical meaning does not give us the true significance of the word. And if we search for it in the relation between *ius* and its derivatives, we encounter a fresh problem: the verb derived from *ius* is *iuro*, but this means "to swear." How did this verb come to diverge semantically from the basic noun in this strange way? At first sight there is an inexplicable gap between the notions of "law" and "swearing." And yet the formal relation between *ius* and *iurare* is certain since the "oath" is called *ius iurandum*. What is the meaning of this expression and why do we have a future passive participle *iurandum*? Finally, what is the relation of *ius* to *iuro*?

The dictionary of Ernout-Meillet cites an expression *ius iurare* in the sense "pronounce the sacred formula which binds," but unfortunately without giving the reference. To our knowledge such a phrase is not found. We only have the residual form *ius iurandum*, which leaves the gap between *ius* and *iuro*. The relation of the substantive to the verb can thus be elucidated only by appeal to a prehistoric phase, and this requires the aid of etymology. It is true that correspondents of *ius* have been identified, but they present a different sense. Certainly in Celtic the Irish adjective *huisse* < **yustiyos* means "just"; apart from the final suffix this form is identical with Latin *iustus*. But because this gives us only a derivative and we do not know the basic noun in Celtic, this comparison tells us nothing. It is in Indo-Iranian that we find the correspondents of Lat. *ius*: Ved. *yoḥ*, Av. *yaoš*, which have exactly the same form.

But Ved. *yoḥ* means "prosperity" and Av. *yaoš* 'purification'. Despite the exact correspondence of the forms the meanings expressed are different and perplexing. Nevertheless we have here one of the important correlations of vocabulary between Indo-Iranian and Italo-Celtic, one of those terms which have survived only at the extremities of the Indo-European world. The sense of *yoḥ* must be "happiness, health." The word occurs only in phrases where it is coupled with *śam*; either *śamyoḥ* as a single word, or *śamca yośca* with the sense "happiness and health" in wish formulas such as "The happiness and prosperity which Manu has acquired by his offering, may we attain to them under your guidance, O Rudra" (R.V. 1, 114, 2).

Iranian, too, has preserved *yaoš* only in formulaic expressions in which *yaoš* is combined with the verb *dā-* 'place', to form the new verb *yaoždā-* 'purify'.

This is an old compound comparable to the Latin *crēdō*. This Avestan verb *yaoždā-* gave rise to numerous derivatives: an agent noun *yaoždātar-* 'whose function it is to purify'; the abstract *yaoždāti-* 'purification', etc. To recover by means of these derivatives the proper sense of *yaoš*, which is not found in independent usage, we must assign to *yaošdā-*, literally "to make *yaoš*," the sense "to make in accordance with prescriptions, put into the state required by the cult." This is a condition of sacrifice: the person making the offering must make the object of oblation ritually appropriate. We have here a fundamental expression of the religious code. Each act must be ritually carried out and the object which is at the center of this operation must itself be without defect or flaw. This ritual integrity is what *yaoždā-* is intended to secure. In this way we can better understand the Vedic *yoḥ*; it is not happiness as enjoyment, but the state of "integrity," i.e. of physical perfection as yet unaffected by misfortune or disease.

We must now pay attention to a difference of usage of **yaus* between India and Iran. In Vedic *yoḥ* is an expression of wish: it is a term pronounced to someone to express the wish that prosperity and "integrity" may be granted him. From this it follows that *yoḥ* is effective in that it is a word to be pronounced. The situation of Avestan *yaoš* is different: here the connection of *yaoš* with *dā-* 'put, make' shows that *yaoš* denoted a state to be realized and not merely a word to be pronounced. Thus on the one hand the notion of **yaus* is something "to be done" and on the other something "to be said." This difference has considerable consequences in the sphere of law and ritual, where the "acts" often consist of "words."

Thanks to Iranian and Indic we are in a position to penetrate into the prehistory of the Latin word *ius*. The Indo-European word **yous* meant "the state of regularity, of the normality required by the rules of ritual." In Latin this state assumes the double aspect which we have just distinguished in Indo-Iranian. The idea of *ius* admits of these two conditions. One is the factual situation which is denoted by the derived adjective *iustus* in the legal expressions *iustae nuptiae* 'lawful marriage', *iusta uxor* 'legitimate wife', that is, "conforming to the state of *ius*." The other is implied in the expression *ius dicere*. Here *ius* denotes "the formula of normality," prescribing what must be conformed to. Such is the foundation of the idea of "law" in Rome.

We thus have grounds for believing that *ius*, in general, is a *formula* and not an abstract concept; *iura* is the collection of legal judgments. Cf. Plautus: *omnium legum atque iurum fictor* (*Epidicus* 522-523). These *iura*, like the *díkai* or the *thémistes*, are formulas which embody an authoritative decision.

And wherever these terms are taken in their strict sense, we find, for *thémistes* and *díkai* as for *ius* and *iura*, the idea of fixed texts, of established formulas, the possession of which is the privilege of certain individuals and of certain corporations.

Typical of these *iura* is the most ancient code known from Rome, the Law of the Twelve Tables, which is composed originally of judgments formulating the state of *ius* and using the formula *ius ita esto*. We find ourselves in the domain of the word, manifested by terms that agree in sense: in Latin *iu-dex*, in Oscan *med-diss*, in Greek *dikas-pólos* (and *díkas eipeîn*) and in Germanic *eo-sago* 'he who says the rule, the judge'.

What is constitutive of "law" is not doing it, but always *pronouncing* it: *ius* and *iu-dex* bring us back to this constant combination. Along with *ius* the verb *dicere* looms large in juridical formulas, such as *multam* (*dicere*) 'fine', *diem* (*dicere*) 'day for a hearing'. All this stems from the same authority and is expressed by the same turns of phrase. It was from this act of speech, *ius dicere*, that the whole of court terminology developed: *iudex*, *iudicare*, *indicium*, *iuris-dictio*, etc.

The sense of *ius* is thus defined as an expression of "law." But we cannot yet see the direct connection between this notion and the sense taken by the verb immediately derived from it, that is, *iurare*. This constitutes a challenge to the interpretation of *ius* which has just been proposed. If it is valid, it ought to account for the relation of *ius* to *iurare*. This strange derivation points in a different direction and opens a new chapter in law. Do we find elsewhere than in Latin a connection between the notion of "law" and that of "the oath"? An investigation into this point in other languages of the Indo-European family will be necessary. The result will be negative—we may say this straight away—but it will at least serve to bring out the originality of Latin.

We have barely one example which establishes the existence of an Indo-European verb meaning "to swear": this is the Sanskrit *am-* 'swear' which appears particularly in the imperative *amī-ṣva* 'swear' and is connected with the Greek *ómnumi* of the same sense. The correspondence embraces only these two terms but at least the equation is exact as regards the form and the meaning. We do not know whether this Indic verb ever existed in Iranian, but this isolated survivor suffices to attest a common term.

In Greek there is an asymmetry between the noun and the verb: "the oath" is expressed by a different word: *hórkos*. This word has been connected, within Greek itself, with *hérkos* 'fence', but this explanation, to say the least, is vague and unsatisfactory: the oath is conceived as a prohibition or a constraint which one determines for oneself. In any case, this is not an Indo-European equivalent but simply the result of a secondary development (cf. Book Five, Chapter Eight).

For the verbal expression "to swear" we find, apart from this, only forms limited to two languages, sometimes confined to a single language. Persian uses *sōgand xurdan*, literally "consume, eat the *sōgand*", in Middle Persian *sōkand* x^{v} *ar-*. This word *sōkand* goes back to the old Avestan *saokənta* 'sulfur'. Thus "to swear" is "to swallow sulfur." The expression is to be understood literally. The oath consisted of a veritable ordeal: it was the ingestion of sulfur which was supposed to test the sincerity of the person swearing the oath.

In Oscan the verb for "to swear" is known to us in the verbal form *deiuatuns* 'may they swear'; the verbal root *deiua-* in Latin would appear as **divare*, the proper meaning of which would be "take the gods to witness," a clear expression, but one not actually found in Latin.

In other Indo-European languages the expression for the oath reflects the way in which one swears: Irish *tong* corresponds to the Latin *tango* 'touch'; similarly in Old Slavonic *prisegati* and *prisegnoti* mean etymologically "to touch." The primary sense of Skt. *am-* is "seize." This correlation is explained by the custom of touching the object or the living thing by which one swears. For to swear by someone or something is to bring a divine curse on this person or thing if he should be false to his oath.

A final expression is common to Celtic and Germanic: Irish *ōeth*, Got. *aiþs*, which is connected with German *Eid* and English *oath*. This form is literally a verbal substantive from the root "to go." We still have a memory of this in the German expression *Eidegang*, literally "the fact of going to the oath," that is, the place of oathtaking, a survival of an ancient practice. The solemn oath comprised a number of acts, one of which was to proceed towards the place where the oath was given. One "betook oneself to the oath": Latin *ire in sacramentum*, ORuss. *iti na rotu* 'to go to the oath' (cf. Book Five, Chapter Eight).

Thus we have almost as many expressions as there are languages. Only Greek and Sanskrit have an expression of Indo-European date. Thus there is outside Latin no parallel which might help us to understand the relation of *ius* to *iurare*. We must have recourse to the language itself to elucidate the origin of this expression. How was the oath taken in the Roman world? A whole series of explicit testimonies inform us about the way in which an oath was taken and enable us to understand how *iurare* in its given sense can be a derivative from *ius*.

We must first read a scene from the *Rudens* of Plautus (ll. 1331ff.). Gripus and Labrax, who are trying to deceive each other, enter into a pact. Gripus wants to bind Labrax by an oath:

> Gr. *tange aram hanc Veneris* 'Lay your hand on this altar of Venus'. 1333
> La. *tango* 'I touch it'.
> Gr. "You must now swear by Venus."
> La. "What shall I swear?"
> Gr. "What I am going to dictate to you."
> La. *Praei verbis quidvis* 'Dictate to me anything you like in words . . .' 1335
> Gr. "Take hold of this altar."
> La. "I do so."

Then comes the text of the oath, which is formulated by Gripus in the form in which it has to be repeated by Labrax.

Here we have, transposed into the comic vein, the hallowed mode of oath taking among the Romans. The initiator who induces the other to swear an oath must *praeire verbis*, he recites the text which the one who binds himself must repeat word for word while touching a sacred object; this is the essential part of the ceremony.

The solemnity of the usage is confirmed by Gellius (*N.A.* 11 24): the chief men of the city receive the order to swear "*apud consules, verbis conceptis*," they swear between the hands of the consuls "in fixed terms," according to a formula which they will repeat word for word.

In his *Panegyric of Trajan*, ch. 64, Pliny praises the scrupulous observation by Trajan of all the constitutional forms. Trajan goes to take an oath before the consul, although he could have easily been content to make others take the oath: "After all the ceremonies of the *comitia* were performed, see now how at the end you approach the seat of the consul; *adigendum tepraebes in verba . . .* you offer yourself to be led to the words which the chiefs (*principes*) generally ignore except to lead others to (them) . . ."—and the merit of the emperor is that he goes there himself. Then the consul, seated while Trajan stood before him, dictated the oath formula, *praeivit iusiurandum*, and Trajan swore, expressed, pronounced the words clearly by which he devoted his own head and his house to the anger of the gods if he should be false to his oath. And he swore in the presence of the gods, *attendentibus diis*, in the presence of all those who must swear the same thing, *observantibus his quibus idem iurandum est*.

The expression recurs a number of times in Livy: *Brutus . . . populum . . . **iureiurando adegit** neminem Romae passuros regnare*, he led the people to this oath (II, 1, 9). T. Manlius threatens to kill the tribune if he does not take the oath in the terms which he is going to dictate to him: *nisi, in quae ipse concepisset verba, iuraret*. The tribune, seized with fear, swears in the terms imposed on him: *adiurat, in quae adactus est verba* (VII, 5). We now recall the well-known passage in which Hannibal, while still a child, is led to an altar, touches it and takes the oath that as soon as he can he will become the enemy of the Roman people: *tactis sacris, iureiurando adactum* (XXI 1,4). The verb *adigere* is standard for saying "to lead someone to the oath," since the one swearing does nothing but repeat the words dictated to him. Tacitus *Hist.* 1,37, when speaking of a general who administers an oath to his troops, uses the expression *sacramento adigit*. Here, then, are the ritual expressions of the *ius iurandum*: *praeire verbis*; *verbis conceptis*; *adigere in iusiurandum*.

Thus *iurare* does not designate what we understand by "swearing," that is, the act of engaging oneself in a solemn way by invoking a god. The oath itself, the "commitment," is called *sacramentum*, a term which is preserved in the Romance languages and which yields French *serment*. At Rome the *sacramentum* became at an early date the word for the military oath. Here we must therefore distinguish two notions, the *sacramentum* which is the act of consecrating oneself to the gods, to call on their vengeance if one is false to one's word; and *iurare* which is the act of repeating a certain form of words. The taking of an oath requires two persons: the one who *praeit verbis*, who "precedes with words," who pronounces the *ius*, and the one who really *iurat*, who repeats this formula, which is called *ius iurandum* 'the formula to be formulated', that which must be repeated after the person "*qui praeit*" has pronounced it, the formula fixing in stereotyped and time-honored terms the text of the engagement.

We thus come back to the literal analysis of *iurare*. If we start with *ius*, defined as the formula which lays down the norm, the model, we can define *iurare* as "to pronounce the *ius*," and the *ius* must be pronounced *in verba alicuius qui praeit*, 'in the terms indicated by the one who precedes'. It is the obligatory relation which secures the imperative character of *iusiurandum*. The expressions "*adigere in verba*," "*iurare in verba magistri*" are a clear indication of the binding nature of the words which the man swearing the oath must reproduce.

Now that we have come to the end of this analysis we find in *iurare* a confirmation of what the examination of *ius* itself taught us, namely that *ius* designates a formula, in the present case the formula which declares what course of conduct the swearer of the oath will take, the rule to which he will conform. But the *ius iurandum* indicates the nature of the procedure and the solemn character of the declaration, not the text of the oath itself.

By restoring to *ius* its full value, which is indicated both by its etymological correspondences and the Latin derivation, we reach back beyond "law." The word derives its value from a concept which is not merely moral but primarily religious: this is the Indo-European notion of conformity to a rule, of conditions which have to be fulfilled before the object (whether thing or person) can be approved, can perform the duties of his office, and be fully effective: *yoḥ* in Vedic, *yaoždā-* in Avestan are impregnated with this value. A further result of this investigation has been to establish the connection between *ius* and *sacramentum* in Latin vocabulary, the intermediary being the derived verb *iurare*. Thus the religious and oral origins of law are clearly marked in its fundamental terms.

With the semantic family of *iudex* we can link a term of an entirely different form, which appears only in Latin, with a correspondent in Umbrian. This is *arbiter* (Umbr. *arputrati* '*arbitratu*'), which also designates a judge. *Iudex* and *arbiter* are closely associated and often taken for one another, the second being only a specification of the first. He is, therefore, a particular form of judge, the "arbiter." What concerns us is not so much the etymology as the proper sense of the word. *Arbiter* has two different senses: (1) the witness, the man who was present on a given occasion, and (2) the "arbiter," the man who decides between two parties in virtue of some legal power.

How did the "witness" come to be the "judge-arbiter," "he who decides" between two parties? The dictionary of Ernout-Meillet gives the two senses in succession, without making any attempt to reconcile them. According to the dictionary of Walde-Hofmann, the first sense was "the one who, in his character of disinterested witness, decides between two disputants." But it is an arbitrary proceeding to agglomerate two distinct meanings in order to achieve a definition.

Here again we are obliged to make a study of the uses of the word. This shows in the first place that by translating *arbiter* as "witness" we are not giving a complete account of its meaning. We quote a few examples from Plautus which illustrate the oldest and most significant meanings.

> *Secede huc nunciam si videtur, procul,*
> *ne **arbitri** dicta nostra **arbitrari** queant*
>
> Come over here, please, a way off, so that *arbitri* cannot *arbitrari* our words.
>
> – *Captivi* 219

This already makes it plain that the sense of "witness" does not adequately render the force of the word.

> *eamus intro, non utibilest hic locus factis tuis*
> *dum memoramus,* ***arbitri*** *ut sint, qui praetereant per vias*
>
> Let us go into the house; this is not a suitable place for us to talk about your conduct, the passers-by may be *arbitri.*
>
> – *Mercator* 1005
>
> *mihi quidem iam* ***arbitri*** *vicini sunt, meae quid fiat domi*
> *ita per impluvium intro spectant.*
>
> The neighbors are *arbitri* of everything that goes on in my house: they look through the *impluvium.*
>
> – *Miles* 158
>
> *Sequimini; simul circumspicite ne quis adsit* ***arbiter****.*
>
> Follow me and at the same time look around to see that there is no *arbiter* present.
>
> – *Miles* 1137

These passages show clearly the difference between *testis* and *arbiter*: the *testis* is in full view of, and known to, the parties in question; the *arbiter* sees and hears without being seen himself. The character in *Miles* 1137 expressly states this: if he does not take precautions, everything will take place in the sight of an *arbiter* without the parties knowing it. In law the evidence of an *arbiter* is never invoked as testimony, for it is always the idea of seeing without being seen that the term implies.

The verb *arbitrari* 'to be a witness' has the same implication: a character in the *Aulularia* of Plautus has been "sent to reconnoiter" (*speculatum misit me*) to find out what would happen. "I shall go and sit here without anyone suspecting it,"*hinc ego et huc et illuc potero quid agant arbitrarier* 'from here, in this direction and in that, I shall be able to *arbitrari* what they are doing' (l. 607), that is to say, to see what is going on on both sides without being seen.

How then can we explain the sense "judge" for *arbiter*? How can the "clandestine witness" evolve into a judge? We must recall that in the most ancient sense of the word the name *iudex* was given to every authoritative person charged with passing judgment in a disputed case. In principle it was the king, the consul, the holder of all powers. But for practical reasons this power was delegated to a private judge who, according to the nature of the cases, was called *iudex* or *iudex privatus* or *iudex selectus* or *arbiter*. The last was empowered to decide in all cases which were not foreseen by the law. There was in fact a *legis actio* for those cases not provided for by the law, and the parties presented the following request "*iudicem arbitrumve postulo uti des*." The ancient character of the *arbiter* in this sense is also attested by the law of the Twelve Tables where we read: *praetor arbitres tres dato* 'the praetor shall give three *arbitri*'. What characterizes the *arbiter* is the extent of his power, which Festus defines: . . . *pontifex maximus, quod iudex et arbiter habetur rerum divinarum humanarumque* and elsewhere: *arbiter dicitur iudex quod totius rei habeat arbitrium* "the *iudex* is called *arbiter* because he has the decision in the whole matter." In effect, the *arbiter* makes his decision not according to formulas and the laws but by a personal assessment and in the name of equity. The *arbiter* is in fact a *iudex* who acts as an *arbiter*; he judges by coming between the two parties from outside like someone who has been present at the affair without being seen, who can therefore give judgment on the facts freely and with authority, regardless of all precedent and in the light of the circumstances. This connection with the primary sense of "witness who did not form a third party" makes comprehensible the specialization of the sense of *arbiter* in legal language.

This was the starting point for the extension of the meaning of the verb *arbitrari* to the sense of *aestimare*, to fix in a decisive way the price of something. This particular sense again comes from a specialized use connected with the function of the *arbiter*: this was the *arbitrium litis aestimandae*, the indisputable power to assess the price of a disputed object; hence arose the wider sense "to fix the price of something."

Every time we find technical applications of a term it is advisable to look for the explanation within the sphere to which it belongs, but only after having defined its primary meaning. The same principle and procedure applies on a larger scale when we are trying to determine the proper sense of notions in the vocabulary of institutions.

BOOK V, CHAPTER FOUR

***med- and the Concept of Measure**

Abstract. In historical times the root **med*- designated a great variety of different things: "govern," "think," "care for," "measure." The primary meaning cannot be determined simply by reducing all these to a vague common denominator nor by a confused agglomeration of the historically attested senses. It can be defined as "measure"—not "measurement," but "moderation" (Lat. *modus*, *modestus*)—designed to restore order in a sick body (Lat. *medeor* 'care for', *medicus*), in the universe (Hom. *Zeùs* (*Idēthen*) *medéōn* 'Zeus the moderator'), in human affairs, including the most serious like war, or everyday things like a meal. Finally, the man who knows the *mḗdea* (Hom. *mḗdea eidṓs*) is not a thinker, a philosopher, he is one of those "chiefs and moderators" (Hom. *hēgḗtores ēdè médontes*) who in every circumstance know how to take the tried and tested measures which are necessary. **Med*-, therefore, belongs to the same register of terms as *ius* and *díkē*: it is the established rule, not of justice but of order, which it is the function of the magistrate to formulate: Osc. *med-díss* (cf. *iu-dex*).

As has been observed several times in the course of our previous discussions, neighboring dialects may have different expressions for essential ideas. This is the case, once again, for the term *iudex*, which was coined by Latin.

We do not find elsewhere a comparable term: not only is *ius* as a term of law unknown among the Indo-European languages apart from Latin, but even within the Italic group the idea is designated by a different root. As a correspondent of the Latin *iudex* we have already cited the Latinized Oscan term *med-dix*. The sense is the same: he is the supreme magistrate who, besides the function of judge, holds authority over the community. Oscan resorts to a different stem, *med-*, to form a compound analogous to Latin *iu-dex*. The original form *meddíss* is incidentally not isolated in Oscan. In spite of the scantiness of our information about this language we possess a series of derivatives. We have *meddikíai* '*in iudicio*', *medicatinom* (accusative singular) '*iudicationem*', *medicim* '*iudicium*', and finally, built directly upon *meddix*, *meddixud* (ablative) '*iudicio*'.

Meddix is also used in certain other dialects of the Italic group of which only rare and short inscriptions survive (Paelignian, Volscian). The substantive *med-*, which is the first element of the Oscan compound, appears in Umbrian as *mers*, which is translated as *"ius"* or *"fas"*, while the derived adjective *mersto-* is equated with "*iustus*."

The root **med-*, which here takes the place of the Latin *ius*, is not unknown in Latin, where it is represented by the family of *medeor* (*medeo*), which also comprises the frequentative present *meditor*. It provided in Italic a new expression for the notion of law which we propose to examine and try to determine in its exact sense.

At first sight it is difficult to see, if we take Latin *medeor* 'heal' as our starting point, how we can arrive at a term which designates the exercise of a magistracy. But the variety of the senses of **med-* is still wider and must be considered as a whole. We must begin by listing the various forms together with the senses attached to each in order to see how all these senses diverged and the origin which can be recognized in them all.

Latin *medeo* (*medeor*) 'heal' has as a derived noun the word *medicus* 'doctor', and this was the basis for a numerous group of derivatives such as *medicare*, (*medicari*), *medicatio*, *medicina*, *medicamentum*, and *remedium*. Here the sense of *med-* is narrowly specialized. This medical sense, oddly enough, coincides with what we observe in Iranian: Avestan *vi-mad* 'doctor' (with the preverb *vi-* underlining the idea of separation). In Irish, on the contrary, *midiur* (with a middle inflection like the Latin *medeor*) means "I judge" and, with the preverb *con-*, *con-midathar* 'he exercises authority, he possesses power, he dominates'; this Celtic **med-* also gives rise to a derived abstract *mess* (**med-tu*) '*iudicium*'. This approximates to the sense found in Oscan.

On the other hand we are far from this sense with the Greek forms, which are numerous and constitute a unitary group: *médomai* (μέδομαι) 'take care of', which in the form of the present active is hardly attested except in the participial form *médōn*, Homeric *medéōn*, 'the chief'. We must also include in the group the name of a measure, *médimnos*.

Another series, closely connected, hardly differs from the preceding except by the length of the radical vowel: *mḗdomai* (μήδομαι), 'meditate, reflect, invent' and the neuter noun **mêdos*, which is attested only in the plural, Hom. *mḗdea* 'designs, thoughts'; to *mḗdomai* corresponds an old agent noun *mḗstōr* 'counselor'. The feminine counterpart of this agent noun is *–mḗstra* which appears in a famous name, *Klutai-mḗstra* 'she who takes decisions in a celebrated way', which was remodeled to *Klutaimnēstra.*

The root is also represented in Germanic by well-known verbs which have persisted down to the present day: Got. *mitan* 'to measure', OHG *mezzan*, Germ. *messen*, with the same sense; and, with a derived form of the present stem, **medā-*, Got. *miton*, OHG. *mezzōn* 'reflect, make plans', cf. Germ. *ermessen.* A substantive is evidence for an ancient ablaut form: OHG *māz*, Germ. *Mass*, 'measure'. We find a correspondent in Armenian in *mit*, genitive *mti* (a stem in *-i*) 'thought', a substantive with the root vowel *ē*, corresponding in form to the Greek **mêdos* (*mḗdea*).

We must list in a category by itself the Latin present tense *meditor*, which has diverged so far from the sense of *medeor* that it has become a distinct verb, the primary sense of which is "meditate, reflect" but which soon took on the sense "practice, exercise oneself in, study." Scholars agree in attributing this development to the influence of the Greek word *meletân* 'to exercise oneself': the Romans in certain words of their vocabulary were used to an alternation of *d*/*l*, which had originated within Latin phonology or was of dialect origin, examples being *oleo*/*odor*, *dingua*/*lingua*. Because of this, *meditor* was formally equated with the Greek *meletân* and rapidly acquired the senses of the Greek verb.

Latin presents a final series of forms characterized by a stem **med-* but with the *o*-grade of the ablaut alternations with **med-*. First *modus*, a derivative of the same type as Greek *lóg-os* as contrasted with *lég-ō*. From *modus* we get the adjective *modestus* and the verb *moderor*, *moderari*. *Modestus* actually presupposes a neuter noun **modus*, gen. **moderis*, in the same relation as *scelestus* is to *scelus*. This substantive subsequently passed into the thematic declension in *-o* with the animate gender.

We now have surveyed the whole group of forms. The types of formation are all clear: they do not call for any particular comment, and they correspond satisfactorily. Only the sense is something of a problem. The very fact that the root has produced in neighboring languages terms of different meanings makes us hesitate to decide which of these meanings should predominate in our reconstruction. Shall we choose "to heal," as might be suggested by the agreement of Latin and Iranian; or is it "to measure," as in Germanic, or "to attend to, to reflect," as in Greek?

In general **med-* is translated as "think, reflect." And from this a number of technical meanings are derived: "weigh, measure, judge" or "care for a sick person" or again "to govern."

Once again with the problem which interests us now, we are faced with the questions encountered every time it is necessary to define the sense of an Indo-European root.

(1) Generally the meaning given to the root is the vaguest sense, the one which is most general, in order that this may be capable of divergence into a variety of special meanings.

But the fact is that "to care for" is one notion, and "to govern" is another. In the Indo-European vocabulary "to reflect," or "to measure," or "to govern," or "to care for" are so many distinct concepts which can neither coexist in the same forms nor be derived from one another. Besides, for a notion of such general scope as "to think" there are traditional terms: in particular we have the root **men-*. Now it is obvious that the sense of the terms which have been cited does not permit us to merge **med-* with **men-*, for **med-* does not indicate simply a mental activity, a process of reflection, as **men-* does.

(2) Often the attempt is made to reach back to the original sense of a root simply by a summation of the different senses which it comes to designate in historical times. But is it permissible to operate with such a conglomeration of ideas, each of which is distinct and presents itself in the history of each language fixed in a particular sense?

Comparatists thus practice two operations—(1) and (2)—the first of which is an *abstraction* which consists of emptying the meanings historically attested of all real content, the vague residue being elevated as the "primary meaning," while the second is a *juxtaposition* which simply adds together all the later senses: this is no more than a figment of the mind, which has no basis in real usage. In fact a meaning such as the one we are looking for cannot be reached except by an analysis in depth of each of the historically attested meanings. Simple and distinct notions like "to judge," "to cure," and "to govern" simply transfer into our language a semantic system which was differently structured. They are all components of a global sense which it is our business to reconstruct in order to restore the fundamental unity of meaning.

Should we take as our starting point "to care for the sick," a sense attested in two separate languages, Latin and Iranian? We cannot trace the sense "to measure" back to so precise a meaning. And yet it does seem that *a priori* (and in a confused way) it is the notion of "to measure" which predominates. This is limited in Greek to *médimnos*, but is more amply represented by Latin *modus* and in Germanic by Got. *mitan*, Germ. *messen*, etc. At the same time the notion of "reflection" crystallizes out, as we see in Gr. *mḗdomai, mḗdea.*

Let us begin with Latin *modus*. This means "measure," but not a measure in the sense of material dimension. For the notion of "to measure" Latin uses a distinct verb, *metior*. *Modus* signifies a measure imposed on things, a measure of which one is master and which implies reflection and choice, and also presupposes a decision. In short, it is not something to do with *measurement* but with *moderation*, that is to say, a measure applied to something to which measure is unknown, a measure of limitation and constraint. This is why *modus* has a moral rather than a material sense. The word *modestus* means "he who is provided with measure, who observes measure"; *moderari* means "to submit to measure (what escapes it)."

Latin makes it clear to us that if **med-* meant "measure," it was quite different from **mē-*, the root from which IE **mens* 'moon', Latin *mensis* 'month' are derived, which is a measure of dimensions, a fixed and as it were passive quality—the symbol of which is the moon which measures the months. *Modus* appears to us in quite a different guise: a measure of constraint, presupposing reflection, premeditation, which is applied to a disorderly situation. Here we have our starting point.

Now, with the help of Greek, but giving precision to the evidence it provides, we may carry our analysis a stage further. The usual translation of the Greek **médō*, considered in the light of its present participle *médōn*, is "protect, govern," while the substantive use of the participle is rendered as "lord, master." The present middle *médomai* is translated as "to watch over, devote oneself to something." It is however the same verb, and it ought to admit of the same translation.

We must study on the one hand the Homeric uses of *medéōn* in fixed phrases, with Zeus and a place name: *Idēthen medéōn*, literally "who rules from Ida" (*Il.* 3, 276; 7, 202), cf. *Dōdṓnēs medéōn* (18, 234); and on the other hand the frequent expression *hēgḗtores ēdè médontes* (*Il.* 2, 79). Is it sufficient to translate the verb or its participle in these examples as "protect" or "govern"? It is clear that scholars, seeing that *medéōn* was applied to a personage such as Zeus, have contented themselves with a vague translation implying authority: 'governing, ruling over'. But in the nominal group *hēgḗtores ēdè médontes* we must distinguish two separate notions. In the verb *hēgéomai* we have the notion of the conduct of operations, implying calculation and planning; in *médōn* we feel primarily the notion of authority and secondly—in the same way as in Latin—the notion of a directing "measure."

Let us give further precision to this result by study of the middle *médomai*. This verb takes a number of objects in greater variety than in the case of *médōn*. Some of the terms relate to battle: *polémoio medésthō* (*Il.* 2, 384) 'let them bethink themselves of war'; or again *medṓmetha alkē̂s* 'let us think of stout resistance' (5, 718; cf. 4, 418). But we also find *médomai* applied to "food": *sítou, dórpoio* (24, 2), or to "return," *nóstou* (*Od.* 11, 110; 12, 137), or more vaguely to objects of thought: e.g. in *Il.* 4, 21 two goddesses, Athena and Hera, "pondered evil things (*kakà … medésthēn*) for the Trojans."

In this last use, *médomai* coincides with *mḗdomai*, which means fairly frequently "prepare, premeditate" (an evil fate), with reference to a god: "The whole night wise Zeus pondered evil things" (*kakà … mḗdeto*, 7, 478) or again "Zeus pondered their destruction" (*mḗdet' ólethron, Od.* 14, 300).

Let us now consider the substantive *mḗdea*. It is constantly used with *boulaí* 'counsel, designs' (e.g. *Il.* 2, 340), or else it refers to one who knows, who is wise and inspired: *pepnuména mḗdea eidṓs* (*Il.* 7, 278; *Od.* 2, 38).

These are the principal uses from which scholars have extracted the sense of the verb as "premeditate, advise, dominate, busy oneself with . . ." and "to govern." All these activities comprise a notion of authority, and, in the case of the substantive, the idea of sovereign decision.

We are now in a position to give a more precise definition to this notion of a "measure" applied to things. What is involved is a measure of a technical character, of something tried and tested by long use. There is no suggestion of a procedure invented on the spur of the moment or of reflection on the part of one who has to devise his plans. This "measure" is supposed to be applicable always in certain given circumstances to solve a particular problem. Thus we are far from the notion of "reflection" in general, and no less far away from the notion "to protect" or "to govern." To give a rough definition of **med-*, we might say that it is "to take with authority measures appropriate to a present difficulty; to bring back to normal—by a tried and tested means—some particular trouble or disturbance"; and the substantive **medes*- or **modo*- will probably mean "the tried and tested measure which brings order into a confused situation." The notion is not preserved everywhere in the identical form. It differs from language to language, but there is no difficulty about recognizing the original sense. We can now see that the Latin *medeor* and the Avestan *vi-mad-* do not properly mean "to heal" but rather "to treat a malady according to the rules." This is not a simple tautology: the idea conveyed is not "to give health to a sick man" but "to submit a disturbed organism to given rules, to bring order into a state of confusion."

In Greek we find much the same sense. The word always involves measures, ordered authoritatively, to face a particular problem by tried and tested means. Whatever the subject—war, an embarkation, or even a meal—all these require a given technique. When Zeus is called *médōn,* this traditional epithet relates to the power possessed by the lord of the gods to apply the "measure" in given circumstances, on the occasion of a solemn oath or when help is required. We wish to secure his intervention in the resolution of a specific difficulty, since he has the power implied by the verb *médō*.

Finally we come to the legal sense which is found in Oscan *meddix*. All the constituents of meaning can be found here, and they serve to bring out the equivalence observed between *med-* and *ius*: first we have the notion of authority, which is included in the use of *dico*. The central idea is that of a "measure" chosen from a traditional repertoire to be applied in a given case.

One striking fact should be pointed out: neither *med-* nor *ius* give rise to any real derivatives; this means that they were no longer living forms. What have we in Latin by way of derivatives from *ius*? The verb *iuro* no longer has the sense of *ius* and can be attached to it only by appeal to a prehistoric meaning. The synchronic relation is broken. Apart from this verb, all that *ius* yields is the adjective *iustus*, which is paralleled by the couple *modus*/*modestus*. All the derivatives are, in fact, drawn from *iudex*: *iudicium*, *iudicari*, *iudicatio*, etc. Similarly in Oscan we have *medicatinom* from *meddix*. The derivatives are thus made from the agent noun. We must, therefore, conclude that these two legal terms, *ius* and *med-*, represent dead and not living forms. We can buttress this observation with another fact. There does not exist in Latin any derivative of *ius*, either adjective or substantive, with the meaning: 'he who is a jurist, who is learned in the law and practices the law'. There is no term **iuricus* to match *medicus*. We have, to be sure, complex expressions, but these are mere juxtapositions: *iuris prudens* (and *prudentia*), *iuris consultus*, *iuris peritus*. We can take this fact, too, as another proof that *ius* was incapable of providing any derivative whatsoever.

The reason for this is probably that the law was considered exclusively as a body of formulas and the practice of law as a technique. It was not a science, and it did not give scope to invention. It was fixed in a code, in a collection of sayings, of prescriptions which had to be known and applied.

Thus the role of the supreme magistrate will have been to show the "measure" which is to be imposed in such and such a dispute. We have established that the law is a thing which has to be shown, said, or pronounced, which is expressed in parallel formations—Gr. *dikaspólos*, Latin *iudex*, Oscan *meddíss*, and Germanic *eosago*. This gives us a means of measuring one of the great changes which occurred in the languages and institutions of the Indo-European peoples when law, going beyond its technical apparatus, was constituted of moral ideas, when *díkē* gave rise to the adjective *díkaios*, when *ius* and *iustus* finally developed into the notion of *iustitia*.

It is necessary for law itself to be renewed and to become identified in the last resort with what is just. But it took a long time for this convergence of the notions of law and justice to come about. It was in virtue of their increasing approximation that the very designation of law was transformed so that *ius* has been replaced in the Romance languages by *directum* (*derectum*). The "law" (*droit*) is what is "straight" (*droit*) as opposed to what is "crooked" or "perverse" (*pervers*). It is in this way that *directum*, like the German *Recht*, has taken the place of *ius* as an institutional term, whereas in English the "right" is identified with the "law." In English we do not study "right" (German *Recht studieren*); we study "law."

All this hangs together: this historical process whereby *ius* evolved to *iustitia* and a differentiation was made between *iustitia* and *directum* is connected by obscure paths which are difficult to trace with the very way in which law was conceived in the minds of the Indo-European peoples. The study of the vocabulary of institutions gives us a glimpse of how these notions of a formal character evolved and achieved new precision, concurrently with the growing refinement of conscience, finally to engender moral notions with which in some cases they become identified.

BOOK V, CHAPTER FIVE

Fas

Abstract. The existence of two derivatives in *-*to*-, Lat. *fastus* and *festus*, of diametrically opposite meaning, is sufficient to demolish the connection often proposed between *fas* and the group of *fanum*, *feriae*.

It is perfectly evident that *fas* must be brought into connection with the Lat. *fari* (Gr. *phēmi*, IE **bhā*-). Irreproachable from a formal point of view, this etymology requires semantic justification: how can a connection be established between "to speak" (**bhā*-) and "divine law" (*fas*)? It is shown that in fact the root **bhā*- designates speech as something independent of the person uttering it, not in virtue of what it means but in virtue of its very existence. Thus what has been said, Lat. *fatum*, or what is being said, *fama*, Gr. *phḗmē*, Hom. *dêmou phêmis*, '*vox populi*', is charged, as impersonal speech, with a positive religious value: *phḗmē* is itself a god (*theós ... tis*) (Hesiod, *Works* 764).

In Latin the conditions in which *fas* is used—*fas est* + infinitive 'the *fas* exists that . . .'—explain why (divine) speech provided the expression for (divine) law.

In the pair Gr. *thésphatos*: *athésphatos* 'limited (by destiny)': 'not limited' the verbal adjective of *phēmi*, *-phatos* clearly reflects the specific value which has been recognized in the root **bhā*-.

The legal expressions considered up till now are all related to human law, which regulates social relations in general and applies between definite groups either within the family or between families.

But there is, in at least one Indo-European language, a specific term which designates divine law: this is *fas*, which is distinct from *ius*. The relation of these two terms raises a problem which is in the first place a problem of sense. It does not look as though this opposition *ius*: *fas* can be projected into the Indo-European common period. It is however worthwhile seeing whether it was really a Latin creation.

It cannot be asserted that this opposition did not exist at least in common Italic. We still know so little about the Italic dialects that no argument could be drawn from their silence: only Umbrian is attested in a continuous text of any length. But this ritual couched in a formulaic style is far from providing us with the whole vocabulary. There are certainly important notions for which the Umbrian expression escapes us.

Thus in Latin, since we must confine ourselves to this language, we have *ius*: *fas*, and this opposition is reflected in their derivatives *iustus*: *fastus* as well as the parallel expressions *ius est*: *fas est* 'it is permitted by human law, divine law' respectively. From a morphological point of view, *fas* is an indeclinable neuter noun; it is a stem in *-s*, of the same formation as *ius*. But to go beyond this we must enquire into the etymology. Some scholars have proposed to connect *fas* with a group of words represented by the word *fanum* 'temple' because of the religious value which would be confirmed for *fas* by this connection.

This interpretation must certainly be rejected for a number of formal reasons: *fānum* comes from an original **fasnom* with a short *a*; the lengthening, which is a secondary development, is normal when the group *-asn-* is reduced to *-ān-*. **Fasnom* in its turn goes back to **dhəs-nom* which is connected, with a different vocalic grade, with the name of the temple known from Oscan and Umbrian: Osc. *fíísna*, Umbrian *fesna*. We thus have the alternation **fēsna* (Oscan and Umbrian)/**fasnom* (with reduced vocalic grade in Latin). This contrast, carried back a stage further, would appear as **dhēs-na*/ **dhəs-nom*. Besides we have other words which belong to the same group: e.g. the Latin *fesiae* (*feriae*) 'festivals' and the adjective *festus* 'festive, solemn'. It is probable that the stem **dhəs-*/*dhēs-* designated some religious object or rite, the precise nature of which we can no longer determine. In any case it certainly belonged to the religious sphere.

This stem **dhēs-* recurs elsewhere: in the Armenian plural *dik*[c] 'the gods', which goes back to **dhēs-es* (the *-k*[c] being the mark of the plural) and in the ancient Greek compounds *thésphatos*, *thespésios*, *théskelos*, where *thes-* corresponds to the **dhēs-* of *dik*[c]. The sense of *thes-* attaches these poetic adjectives to the notion of the divine: *thésphatos* 'fixed by divine decree'; *thespésios* 'marvelous', applied to the song of the Sirens, an expression of divine origin, *théskelos* of less clear formation, "prodigious," perhaps "divine."

Finally, it is quite possible—this is a hypothesis advanced long since—that we must also include here *theós* 'god', the original form of which was probably **thesós*. The existence of the Armenian *dik* ᶜ 'gods' would then enable us to set up a Greco-Armenian lexical pair.

Are we justified in bringing *fas* into connection with this word family? If we consider the sense of *feriae*, the most marked representative of this group in Latin, we shall see the difference. *Feriae* are "the festivals, holidays"; *festus* means "appointed as a holiday." How could *fastus* be cited here? It would be difficult to understand, if they had a common origin, how two distinct adjectives in *-to-* could be made from the same root. Moreover, what is the meaning of *fastus*? *Dies fastus*is the name given to the day on which the law courts could be in session, when the praetor had the right to pronounce the words which sum up his functions: *do, dico, addico.* This is what Macrobius writes: *Fasti* (*dies*) *sunt quibus licet fari praetori tria verba solemnia*: *do, dico, addico. His contrarii nefasti.* The *fasti* are "working" days, on which magistrates and citizens can go about their business. It is because of this that *fasti dies* was able to take on the sense of "calendar." Thus *fastus* 'working day' is the exact opposite of *festus* 'day appointed for a holiday'. This would suffice to demolish the connection proposed between *fas* and *feriae*, which, it may be said, has not won general approval.

We must therefore reject this explanation and look for a different origin for *fas*. The explanation which seems most plausible has already been proposed. It has in its favor, though this is not always a guarantee of correctness, the *Sprachgefühl* of the ancients who never separated *fas* from *fari*, **for* 'to speak'.

This is far from being a self-evident explanation which it would be sufficient merely to quote. In fact no immediate connection is apparent between the notion of "to speak" and that of "specifically divine law," as these words are defined in the dictionaries. Scholars who reproduce this etymology, which is certainly correct, do not attempt to demonstrate it. The sole means of justifying it would be to study more closely the proper sense of *fari*.

Along with *fas* we must include also its contrary *nefas* 'a sin against religion', which exhibits the negation *ne-*, which is older than *non*. For *nefas* in fact has emerged from the expression *nefas est*, where *ne* must be regarded as a sentence negation and not as a prefix; the negative prefix is not usually *ne-* but *in-*. A similar syntactic turn of phrase also gave rise to the word *negotium* which has been extracted from the expression *nec otium est* (cf. Book One, Chapter Eleven).

The formation of *fas* is like that of ancient indeclinable neuter nouns: *ius*, *mos*, the latter having at a later linguistic stage been provided with a declension.

The connection of *fas* with **for, fari, fatus sum* is in any case suggested by a form of this verb which deserves emphasis because of its religious value. This is the participle of **for*, the neuter *fatum* 'destiny', often "evil destiny" (cf. *fatalis* 'fatal'), which appears as an independent substantive from the earliest texts.

The verb **for* itself was obsolete from the beginning of the historical period; it is used only in poetry in the sense "to speak." But it produced a number of old derivatives: *facundus* 'eloquent, glib', *fabula* 'conversation, piece of dialogue, fable, legend'; and finally, *fama* 'fame', especially in a good sense, whence *famosus* 'of good repute' and its counterpart *infamis* 'who does not enjoy good repute, of ill fame'. Behind each of these there is a long series of derivatives (e.g. from *fabula*: *fabulari, fabulatio*, etc.). This Latin verb corresponds to Gk. *phēmi, pháto*, the conjugation of which is partly active and partly middle; then *phḗmē* 'fame'; *phê̄mis*, which has virtually the same sense "rumor, conversation, gossip," and also *phátis*. This root is completely absent from Indo-Iranian. It is restricted to the central part of Indo-European; in addition to Latin and Greek it is also attested for Armenian in the word *bay* 'speech' which goes back to **bati-* and so corresponds exactly to Greek *phátis*, *ban* 'word, rumor, report' and in the interpolated verbal form *bay* 'says he'. It is also represented in some Germanic forms, e.g. OE *bōian* 'boast', and finally also in Slavic *baju, bajati* 'narrate, pronounce charms', and, with a more complex suffixation, *baliji* 'doctor, sorcerer'.

The initial sense is given in the etymological dictionaries as "to speak," with a number of specializations, as for instance in Old Slavic. But they give no indication which would explain how the general meaning "to speak" came to be specialized in the sense "divine law."

What is the precise sense of "to speak" with this verb? What particular features distinguish it from all the other expressions relating to speech? There is a Latin form which is important in this connection: this is the present participle *infans* 'the child of tender years, which does not speak'. Varro, to explain the connection with *fatur*, tells us (*L. L.* VI, 52): "***Fatur*** *is qui primum homo significabilem ore mittit vocem. Ab eo ante quam id faciant, pueri dicuntu* ***infantes****, cum id faciant, iam fari . . .*" 'A man speaks (*fatur*) who for the first time utters a sound endowed with sense. This is why children are called "infants" until they can do this; but when they do it we say that they now speak (*iam fari*)'.

We also say that a child "can speak" or "cannot speak." By this we mean articulated speech, the act of speech as a manifestation of language, as an emanation of the human personality. In much the same way, underlying the different senses of "conversation," "stage play," etc. of *fabula* we can see its meaning as "putting into words," much as we say "to set to music." The term *fabula* is applied to a legend, an action, or anything which is put into words. Whether it is a narrative, a fable, or a play, the only relevant aspect is this transposition into words. This explains why *fabula* denotes what is nothing but words, what has no basis in reality. This is the way in which we must understand the other derivatives of the root: *facundus* 'who is talented in speaking', a verbal manifestation considered independently of its content; not one who is eloquent, but one who has a great abundance of words at his disposal. In *fama* 'reputation, rumor' we observe a new feature: the act of speech which is impersonal and not individualized. Even when a child "speaks," *iam fatur*, the point of the remark is not what it says but that it manifests an impersonal faculty, common to all human beings, the fact that they are capable of speech. Similarly *fama* is speech as a human phenomenon, impersonal, collective, rumor, renown: in the French expression *le bruit court que* 'a rumor is current', *bruit* 'noise' is a vocal phenomenon, speech considered purely in its acoustic aspect, because it is depersonalized. This is also the meaning of the Greek *phátis* 'fame, rumor', not connected speech or discourse.

The same sense emerges also from *phêmis*. In the *Iliad* (10, 207), a character goes among the Trojans to see if he can learn any *phêmis*. What is meant here is things which "are said" impersonally, not remarks made by this person or that. In the *Odyssey* there is frequent mention of the *dḗmou phêmis* 'the rumor of the people, the voice of the people'. Some person or other does not dare to act in a certain way because of the *dḗmou phêmis*, because of what people may say (6, 273–274). The word does not denote individual speech.

We now turn to *phḗmē*. First a particularly significant example. Odysseus asks Zeus to confirm that it is his will to bring him safely back to his home after having made him suffer so much. "Let one of those awake in the house utter a *phḗmē* and from outside may another sign from Zeus appear" (*Od.* 20, 100). Odysseus expects the *phḗmē* as an utterance of divine character, as a manifestation of the will of Zeus, equivalent to a sign; and in fact, a woman is the first, while a thunder clap is heard, to utter a *phḗmē* and this *phḗmē* is a *sêma*, a portent for Odysseus (11, 100 and 111). In Herodotus, too, we find (III, 153) *phḗmē* accompanying *téras* 'portent'. Sophocles (*Oed. Rex* 86ff.) offers *phḗmē theō̃n* '*phḗmē* of the gods', referring to an "oracle."

All this hangs together: *phḗmē* is an emanation of words, whether it refers to rumor, reputation, fame, or an oracle. We now see why the root of *phḗmē* and of Latin **for* came to indicate the manifestation of a divine saying: this is because it is always impersonal, because there is always something confused about it, always something mysterious, just as the first beginnings of speech on the lips of a child are mysterious.

This sense of *phḗmē* is especially highlighted in a passage from Hesiod (*Works* 763–764): "*phḗmē* cannot perish completely when many people repeat it; for it is in some way divine." This is why the *dḗmou phêmis* is so important and can make a man hesitate at a moment of action: it is a divine warning. *Vox populi, vox dei* 'the voice of the people is the voice of god'. This is also why *fatum* is an enunciation which has no personal source, which is not connected with a man, which derives from this supra-human origin its mysterious, fatal, and decisive character.

Finally, the verb *phásthai*, which is so common, conveys more than it seems. We do not take sufficient note of the strong sense of *phasi* 'it is said, rumor will have it'; *pháto* is to be taken literally not simply as "he said" but "this utterance emanated from him."

This power of speech, cut off from its human source, and often of divine origin, can easily become a magic power. This is why in Slavic *baliji* denotes the man, whether doctor or sorcerer, who has at his disposition this inspired power of speech, of incantation, and who understands how to use it and direct it.

We can now return to *fas*. We now see how the notion is steeped in the general meaning of "the spoken word," and now *fas* derives from this its religious sense. But we still do not see why *fas* should be applied particularly to "law." This sense may have developed from the phrase in which *fas* is actually used at an early date: *fas est*, with an infinitive proposition, literally "there is *fas*, the *fas* exists that . . ." By this was understood the enunciation in divine and imperative words. By means of this impersonal speech the will of the gods is made manifest, the gods say what it is permissible to do. It is via this expression *fas est* 'what is willed by the gods' that we arrive at the idea of *divine law*.

In *fas* there is nothing which indicates the real nature of this law, but because of its origin the word has this value of a solemn enunciation, of a positive prescription: *fas* or *nefas*. It is one of the functions of the priest to know and to codify divine enunciations which lay down what may be done and what is prohibited.

It is for the same reason, although in a different sphere, that Gr. *phēmi* has the sense "say yes, affirm, give an affirmative reply," *oú phēmi* that of "say no, refuse," primarily in reference to oracles or collective bodies.

Although it is not particularly connected with *fatum*, *fas* belongs to the same general signification, which did not arise in Latin itself. It was already present in the whole family of forms clustering round this root **bhā*-, which in the vocabulary of Indo-European expressed this strange, extra-human power of the word, from its first awakening in the human infant to its collective manifestations, which were non-human in virtue of their being depersonalized and were regarded as the expression of a divine voice.

***

We must now examine a very important Greek derivative, the sense of which is extremely difficult: the verbal adjective -*phatos* from *phēmi*. It enters into compounds: *palaí-phatos* 'what has been said long ago'; *thés-phatos*, an adjective used in the old poetical language along with its counterpart *a-théspha-tos*. *Thésphatos* is interpreted as "uttered by a god" (*thes*- being the root which may underlie the word for "god," *theós*), and hence "marvelous, prodigious," as an epithet describing certain phenomena. But in that case what would be the meaning of *athésphatos*? Practically the same sense is given to it: "prodigious, marvelous," literally "what not even a god could express." This reduction of both the positive and the negative adjective to the same sense has been used, or allowed, in order to explain certain uses which look as though they were equivalent. But their interpretation poses for the linguist a strange problem: how can an adjective have the same sense both in its positive and its negative forms? Certainly, *thésphatos* is used of unheard of, divine, and oracular things. It refers to destiny (this is the predominating use): *tà thésphata* denotes divine decrees or ordinances. But the expression *thésphatón estí* (*moi*, *soi*, etc.) has a special sense: it is applied to an event which is fated, not simply an event which will come about, which is prepared or foreseen by the gods, but the foreseeing of a fate that is marked out by the gods. We have an example in *Iliad* 5, 64: *oú ti theō̃n ek thésphata ḗidē* (οὔ τι θεῶν ἐκ θέσφατα ἤιδη) 'he did not know that the gods had set a limit to his life (that he was advancing to his death)'.

In Sappho and Pindar *thésphatos* is used of what is going to destroy something and not of every divine prediction. We shall, therefore, give to *thésphatos* the sense "that to which a limit has been set by divine pronouncement."

In expressions such as *thésphatos*, *palaíphatos*, the divine character is expressed by the verbal adjective. But the first term is not to be understood as "god" but as "limit."

We now consider *athésphatos*. We can infer from its negative form that the sense ought to be "that to which no limit has been set." This is the literal sense suggested by the formal analysis. We now examine the examples. We have *athésphatos ómbros* (*Il.* 3, 4): is this marvelous, divine, prodigious rain? Not at all; it is rather "unlimited, infinite rain, rain to which no limit has been set." Take *athésphatos thálassa* (*Od.* 7, 273): the idea is the same, "boundless sea" with a poetical exaggeration; or again *athésphatoi bóes* (*Od.* 20, 211), not marvelous oxen but of unlimited number; the same is true of the use with *sîtos* (*Od.* 13, 244), which denotes an unlimited amount of corn.

In the *Odyssey* Alcinous invites his guest (who is Odysseus) to speak and tell of his adventures: he should take advantage of the night: "We have the whole night before us, without limit (*athésphatos*)" (*Od.* 11, 373). The same sense can be found in the *Theogony* of Hesiod (830), in an interesting usage which has not been well understood. This is the passage referring to Typhoeus, son of the Earth, a monster from whose shoulders grow a hundred serpents' heads, from which terrible heads voices are heard uttering speech of every kind (*pantoíēn*), *athésphaton*. Sometimes the utterance was a sound which only the gods can understand, sometimes it was the voice of a bull, at other times the voice of a lion, at others cries like those of young dogs, at still others a hissing noise. In this passage *pantoíēn* is combined with *athésphaton*. By this we must understand "of every kind and *in unlimited number*."

We have a second example in Hesiod (*Works* 662) in which the poet says of himself: "The Muses have taught me to sing this *athésphaton* song." The context helps us here: "I shall sing of the sea, of ships, of navigation, the laws of the sea, although I understand nothing either of ships or navigation. Never have I embarked on the vast sea." It needed great daring on the part of the poet to give advice on things of which he had no experience. "But all the same I shall tell of the purpose of Zeus, for the Muses have taught me to sing a *song which has no limits*," that is in practice any kind of song; cf. *pantoíēn*. This is why, knowing nothing of the sea, I venture to sing even of navigation. This is the interpretation which the analysis of the term itself suggests: "without fixed limits" for *athésphatos*, "with fixed limits" for *thésphatos*.

In conclusion we may say that in the compounds in *-phatos* there appears the idea of an enunciation which is divine both in its character and its authority. We could hardly wish for a better proof of the true and profound sense of the verb *phēmi*, and it is all the more necessary to stress this because *phēmi* is in widespread use in ordinary conversation and reduced to being used of any human utterance whatsoever. We must get behind this ordinary everyday use and work back to the original sense which is better preserved in the verbal adjective and in the terms like *phḗmē*, *phêmis*, *phátis*.

BOOK V, CHAPTER SIX

The *Censor* and *Auctoritas*

Abstract. If the Roman magistrate with specifically normative functions is called *censor* and if the senators whom he enrolls formally register their authoritative opinion by saying "*censeo*," this is because the IE **kens*- strictly meant "to affirm a truth (which becomes law) with authority."

This authority—*auctoritas*—with which a man must be invested for his utterances to have the force of law is not, as is often stated, the power of promoting growth (*augere*), but the force (Skt. *ojaḥ*), divine in principle (cf. *augur*), of "causing to exist."

We have established a frequent relation between terms used with reference to institutions and verbs which denote in one way or another the idea of "to say." There is often a close connection between the act of speech and law or rule insofar as they serve to organize certain social functions. In particular, political institutions are sometimes called by terms which involve some specialization of the notion of "speech" in the direction of authoritative pronouncement. Thus the diversity of the notion of "speech" is illuminated by a study of the words used with reference to it. We see that the terminology of speech proceeds from a variety of origins and concerns very different semantic spheres. The work of the comparatist can be instructive in determining the point of departure for the terms which denote "to say" that have become words denoting institutions and names for authority.

We may take a new example, peculiar to Italo-Celtic and Indo-Iranian, one of those words which throw light on inter-dialectal relationships and attest survivals of a cultural nature: the Latin *censeo*, *censor*, *census*.

The *censor* is a magistrate, but the verb *censeo* means no more than "estimate, judge, pronounce an opinion"; whereas *census* is a technical operation, the assessment of the wealth and classification of the citizens. The same verb is known elsewhere than in Latin, in one of the Italic languages. In Oscan we have the infinitive *censaum* '*censere*' and also a noun *kenzstur*, *kenzsur* '*censor*', probably imitated from Latin. On the other hand the corresponding stem in Indo-Iranian has given rise to a considerable number of verbal and nominal forms with a marked difference of meaning. This is the root seen in Skt. *śams*- 'praise, pronounce a eulogy of' and of the abstract *śasti* 'praise, eulogy, recitation of hymns'. Parallel with Sanskrit *śams*- we have in Iranian: (1) Avestan *saŋh*- 'proclaim solemnly, pronounce', (2) Old Persian *θanh*- and *θah*-, which is usually translated as "to proclaim." On this basis we can posit an Indo-European verbal stem **kens*- the sense of which, according to all the dictionaries, was "proclaim solemnly."

However, the very precise sense of the Latin terms can hardly be reconciled with so vague a definition, which incidentally would also suit equally well a number of other verbs. The magistrate called the *censor* had as his primary function the duty of making a roll of the citizens. It was the *census*, the assessment, which gave the term *censor* its whole meaning. To evaluate the private fortune of each person and assign each to his appropriate class is a hierarchizing function which must be derived from a root with an already specialized sense.

The *censor* was also concerned with the recruitment of the senate (*lectio senatus*). He also had the task of supervising the morals of the citizens and repressing excess of every kind: the breaking of moral rules and the correction of excessive luxury and extravagance. It was from this that *censura* got its moral sense. Finally the *censor* was charged with placing the contracts for farming the taxes, with public works, and with regulating the relations between the contractors and the state. All these different functions are in some way connected with the essential function of the *censor*, which was the *census*, the classification of the citizens.

The verb *censeo* is used in a formula which is often quoted (Livy 1, 32, 11-12). In the procedure for the declaration of war established by Numa, the *rex* consulted each of the Fathers of the Senate: *dic quid censes*—and the other would reply: *puro pioque duello quaerendas* (with *res* understood) *censeo*. 'I am of the opinion that we should seek what is our due by a just and holy war'. By this formula the Father in question pronounced in favor of the war and underlined its necessity. This same verb also figures in the rule laid down by the *senatus consulta* 'the decrees of the senate'.

In describing these uses we could content ourselves with translating *censeo* by "judge, think, estimate." But the nouns from the same root, *censor* and *census*, require a more precise sense which must reflect the real sense of the Indo-European root. G. Dumézil[1] has applied himself to the task of giving a precise sense to the root. He has sociologized the notion of *śams-* in a definition, which is also valid for Indo-European and which already contains in essence the Roman *census*:

> The technical sense of *censor* and *census* must not be a secondary sense but must preserve what is essential in the primary meaning. At the outset we must doubtless posit a politico-religious concept such as: to site (a man or an act or an opinion, etc.) in its correct place in the hierarchy, with all the practical consequences of this situation, and to do so by a just public assessment, by a solemn act of praising or blaming. (p. 188)

Unlike the usual translation, we have here a definition of great precision, the result of which is to take back to the Indo-European common period the sense of the Latin *census*, *censor*. It seems to us that this definition, if we posit it as Indo-European, includes some elements which owe their inclusion to perhaps too close a reliance on the sense of the Latin words.

A study of other words of the same root, particularly in Iranian, leads us to a rather different view, which takes more account of the different senses which are attested. It will be useful to analyze the evidence offered by Old Persian:

(1) In the inscriptions the king uses the verb corresponding to the Skt. *śams-*, Lat. *cens-* in the form of the third person of the present stem *θātiy* to introduce his own speech. He introduces each section of the text by the formula: *θātiy dārayavahuš xšāyaθiya* 'thus speaks (proclaims, pronounces) Darius the King'. There follows a text of variable length and then the formula recurs to introduce a new topic, and so on until the end of the next. This

1. In his book *Servius et la Fortune*, "Essai sur la fonction sociale de Lounge et de Blâme et sur les éléments indo-européens du cens romain," Paris, 1943.

is the set way of composition in use during the whole of the Achaemenid period.

(2) Darius enumerates his ancestors back to the eponymous *Haxāmaniš* (Achaemenes) and says: "this is why we call ourselves (*θahyāmahiy*) Achaemenids."

(3) Darius boasts of the submission of the peoples who have remained faithful to him and of the solidity of his power: "Everything which was commanded to them and prescribed (*aθahiya*) by me, this they carried out whether by day or by night."

(4) Darius comes to the subject of the Magus Gaumāta, the false Smerdis of Herodotus. This magus falsely usurped the kingship by deceiving his subjects. He was greatly feared because of the massacres which he had ordered "and no one dared to say (*θastanaiy*) anything against him."

(5) Then comes the list of all the rebels who have usurped royal authority. Each one is evoked in the same terms "such and such rebelled; he usurped power saying (*aθaha*): I am so and so, the sole legitimate king."

(6) At the end of the inscription, after telling of his accession to the throne and expounding his political acts, Darius addresses the future reader: "If you read this inscription and you get others to read it and you tell (*θāhy*) what it contains, Ahura Mazda will protect you and your lineage will be long. If you conceal the contents of this inscription, Ahura Mazda will strike you and you will have no descendants."

(7) Finally in an inscription called the "Testament of Darius," the king proclaims the rule which he will follow with regard to what a man says (*θātiy*) against another man.

We have now gone through all the forms and uses of the verb. Certainly, on a cursory reading, we could make do with equivalents, according to the passage in question, such as "say, proclaim, prescribe" and elsewhere, "call oneself." But we should try and give a closer definition of the sense. The most frequent use (1) is not the most instructive. Light will be thrown on this formula by other uses. Let us take rather (4): No one dared to "say" anything against Gaumāta, because they feared him. There is another verb for "to say" in Old Persian (*gaub-*). In the above passage what is meant is that no one dared "to tell the truth" (many people were aware of the identity of the usurper and Gaumāta had put numerous persons to death for fear of being recognized); thus "to say" in this connection is analytically "to say who he was *in reality*." Similarly, with

(5): the rebel chieftains falsely assumed the title of king. They "spoke" (untruthfully); however, they claimed to be telling the truth, and their assertion was an emanation of authority.

Next we have (6): if you make this proclamation known to the people, if you "say (what it contains)," that is, if you report its true content.

(7) concerns what a man "says" against another; such an utterance claims to be true, and it may entail legal consequences.

We now return to usage (2): after having enumerated his ancestors back to the eponymous *Haxāmaniš* (Achaemenes), Darius concludes: "this is why we call ourselves Achaemenids"; this is a statement of dynastic legitimacy; we proclaim the fact of being Achaemenids as our true and authentic status.

We now come to the last, the most usual use of the verb, the use to introduce each section of the text. The king *θātiy*; he "proclaims" what is the case: Darius maintains what is true, both in the reality of the facts which he relates and in the reality of duties towards Ahura Mazda and towards the king. It is both a factual and a normative truth.

Thus at the conclusion of this review of the evidence we reach a definition of the verb which we might put thus: "to assert with authority as being the truth; to say what corresponds to the nature of things; to proclaim the norm of behavior." He who "speaks" is thus in a position of supreme authority; by declaring what is, he fixes it; he proclaims solemnly what is imposed, the "truth of fact or duty."

Such is the witness of one of the Indo-European languages, Old Iranian. The evidence of Old Persian is confirmed by the uses of *saŋh-* in the Avesta, whereas in Vedic the semantic development is directed towards religious proclamation: *śams-* 'proclaim, praise'.

We may now return to *censeo*. Our definition makes intelligible the specialization of sense undergone by *censeo*, *census*, *censor* in Roman institutions. In that he establishes with authority a factual truth, the *censor* proclaims the situation of each citizen and his rank in society. This is what is called the *census*, the assessment which establishes a hierarchy of status and wealth. More generally, *censeo* means "to assess" everything according to its true value, hence both "to appraise" and "to appreciate." To perform this function the requisite authority is needed: hence the question *quid censes*? which was ritually put to the senators by the king.

Censor has a complementary notion which is constantly associated with it in the uses of the word in Latin and which is implied by our definition, that of "authority": *censeo* is often collocated with *auctor* and *auctoritas*.

What is the significance of these words and what is its etymological foundation? It is clear that *auctor* is the agent noun from *augeo*, which is usually translated "grow, increase." To *augeo* corresponds the Greek present tense *auxánō* and, on the other hand, the alternative form **weg-*, represented in German *wachsen* and English *wax* (opposite of *wane*). In the guise of these two alternating forms of the root the Indo-European stem means "to augment, grow, increase." But the Indo-Iranian correspondents are exclusively nominal: Skt. *ojaḥ*, a neuter in *-s*, 'might, power', in Avestan *aogar-*, *aoǰah-* 'might', and the adjective Skt. *ugra-*, Av. *ugra-* 'strong'.

In Latin, besides *auctor*, we have an old neuter which has become masculine in the shape of *augur*, with its derivative *augustus*; these words form a group apart.

We now see the double importance of this group of words. They belong to the spheres of politics and religion and they fall into a number of sub-groups: that of *augeo*, that of *auctor*, and that of *augur*. It would be of interest to find out how the notion of "authority" came to be derived from a root which simply means "grow, increase." Our dictionaries, which translate the verb with this meaning, also define *auctor* as "he who causes to grow, the author."

This definition may appear strange and in any case it is inadequate. We are invited to believe that the profound meaning of *auctor* could be simply traced back to the notion of "growth." This is hardly satisfactory. The notion expressed by *auctor* and its abstract *auctoritas* is difficult to reconcile with the sense "to increase," which of course is indubitably that of the verb *augeo*. But is this the primary sense of the verb *augere*? We leave *augur* for the moment, to come back to it later on. The fact that in Indo-Iranian the root *aug-* means "might" is noteworthy. Further, Skt. *ojas-*, like Av. *aoǰah-* and their derivatives, refers in particular to the "might" of the gods; the Avestan adjective *aoǰahvant-* 'endowed with might' is almost exclusively used of gods. This implies a power of a particular nature and effectiveness, an attribute which belongs to the gods. But we disregard the sense peculiar to Indo-Iranian and confine ourselves to Latin. The problem here, as it so often is, is to give an exact definition of the real sense of the basic term, in such a way that the derivatives find herein their own explanation. Now the sense of *auctor* in its different uses cannot be derived from that of "increasing" which is assigned to *augeo*. A large proportion of the senses of *augeo* remain in the dark, and this is precisely the essential part, that from which the special applications have developed so that they have in the last resort ended up by splitting off into distinct units.

Scholars persist in translating *augeo* as "increase." This is accurate for the classical period but not for the earliest texts. For us "to augment" is equivalent to "increase, make something *which existed before* bigger." Herein lies the unnoticed difference from *augeo*. In its oldest uses *augeo* denotes not the increase in something which already exists but the act of producing from within itself; a creative act which causes something to arise from a nutrient medium and which is the privilege of the gods or the great natural forces, but not of men. Lucretius often makes use of this verb when he is retracing the genesis of beings in the universal rhythm of birth and death: *quodcumque alias ex se res auget alitque* 'whatever thing gives rise to other things from itself and nurtures them' (V 322); *morigera ad fruges augendas atque animantis* 'prone to engender plants and living creatures' (V 80). In the archaic prayer formulas the Romans also used *augere* of the benefits they expected from the gods, namely of "promoting" all their enterprises: *Divi divaeque . . . vos precor quaesoque uti quae in meo imperio gesta sunt, geruntur, postque gerentur, . . . ea vos omnia bene iuvetis, bonis auctibus auxitis* 'Ye gods and goddesses, I pray and beseech you, that whatever has been done, is being done, and shall be done hereafter under my *imperium*, you shall aid all those things and increase them with good increases', that is, cause them to prosper (Livy 29, 27).

Much the same sense is evident in the uses of the agent noun *auctor*. The term *auctor* is applied to the person who in all walks of life "promotes," takes an initiative, who is the first to start some activity, who founds, who guarantees, and finally who is the "author." The notion expressed by *auctor* is diversified according to the different contexts in which it is used, but they all go clearly back to the primary sense "cause to appear, promote." This is how the abstract *auctoritas* acquired its full force: it is the act of production or the quality with which a high magistrate is endowed, or the validity of a testimony or the power of initiative, etc., each of these special applications being connected with one of the semantic functions of *auctor*.

The religious term *augur* may also be linked to *augeo*. This was already the opinion of the Latins. *Augur* would have been an ancient neuter which designated at first the "promotion" granted by the gods to an undertaking and made manifest in an omen. This confirms that the action of *augere* is of divine origin. From **augus*, a doublet of *augur*, is derived the adjective *augustus*, literally "provided with **augus*," that is to say, "endowed with such (growth)-promoting power."

From an early date this single semantic unit broke up into five independent groups: (1) *augeo* with *augmen*, *augmentum*, *auctus*; (2) *auctor* with *auctoritas*, *auctoro*; (3) *augur* with *augurium*, *auguro*; (4) *augustus*, a title which became a proper name and then produced *augustalis*, *augusteum*, etc.; (5) *auxilium* with *auxilior*, *auxiliaris*.

The primary sense of *augeo* is discovered in *auctoritas* with the help of the basic term *auctor*. Every word pronounced with *authority* determines a change in the world; it creates something. This mysterious quality is what *augeo* expresses, the power which causes plants to grow and brings a law into existence. That one is the *auctor* who promotes, and he alone is endowed with the quality which in Indic is called *ojaḥ*.

We can now see that "to increase" is a secondary and weakened sense of *augeo*. Obscure and potent values reside in this *auctoritas*, this gift which is reserved to a handful of men who can cause something to come into being and can literally 'bring into existence'.

BOOK V, CHAPTER SEVEN

The *Quaestor* and the **Prex*

Abstract. Lat. *quaero* 'seek, ask' (whence *quaestor, quaestus*), a word without an etymology, has close connections with *precor*, **prex* 'to pray, prayer' which must be pinned down: in fact it is not only in Latin that the two terms seem to form a redundant combination, as in the old formula "*Mars pater, te precor quaesoque*," but in other languages too, derivatives from **prek-* (Iran. *frasa*, OHG *forscōn*) have exactly the same sense as the Latin *quaero*. In the absence of decisive pointers in the languages in which only **prek-* is represented, it is only in Latin that a distinction appears: as opposed to **prek-*, which denotes a verbal request (*precor, procus*), the group of *quaero, quaestus* 'means of gaining, gain', *quaestio*, 'question, torture', *quaestor* 'examining magistrate' and 'tax collector' is defined by the material and non-verbal character of the methods used to obtain what is being sought.

In the terms studied up till now it has been etymology which helped us to determine the primary sense which is the source of the others. But there are instances where etymology fails us; in such cases our sole recourse is to traditional stock uses. It is in such conditions that oppositions of vocabulary can operate, those differentiations which, by establishing a connection between two terms, enable us to distinguish and illuminate the terms involved.

Now in the lexical series under examination, in the Latin vocabulary in particular, two words present themselves: one is the verb *quaero*, the other is the agent noun from this verb *quaestor*. The sense of the verb is a general one, whereas that of the noun is specialized. *Quaero* is translated as "to seek," the *quaestor* is a magistrate who had the dual function of "examining magistrate" and "warden of the treasury." In the judicial language *quaero* meant "to make an enquiry, investigation," and in this sense it was the equivalent of the Greek *zēteîn*. However the accepted meaning of the verb does not account for the sense which the noun *quaestor* has.

Further there is a verb which in other languages conveys the same sense as the Latin *quaero*: this is the verb whose root appears in the Latin *precor*, **prex*. In Latin there is a difference between the verbs *quaero* and *precor*, but elsewhere we find forms of the root corresponding to *precor* to designate the kind of activity in which the *quaestor* specialized. Here we have one of those problems when two verbs of similar sense have been specialized in different ways in different languages. Only the conditions of their use can enlighten us in the absence of any etymology.

Let us first consider *quaero* by itself and in its relation to *quaestor*. The *quaestor* was properly the magistrate whose full title was *quaestor paricidi et aerari*. The function of the *quaestor* as the guardian of the finances of the state (*aerarium*) was secondary to his first function, cf. Festus (247, 19): *parricidi quaestores appellabantur qui solebant creari causa rerum capitalium quaerendarum* 'The name *parricidi quaestores* was given to those who were appointed to investigate capital offences'.

It will be noticed that *quaero* is expressly used in the formula which explains the noun *quaestor*. Here we already see a technical use which invites us to interpret with greater precision the sense of the verb: we have to start with a special use of *quaero* in order to find the sense of *quaestor*, especially in the title *quaestor paricidi*.

Here we shall have to make a digression on the subject of *paricidium* and *paricida*. In the last few years a series of different interpretations have been put forward in explanation of this very ancient word on which the Romans themselves have no very clear opinion. In the first place we have the etymology which identifies the first component with *pater*. This is certainly to be rejected. Today a number of comparatists would see in the first term of *paricida* a word signifying "man" in general. This is the thesis of Wackernagel[1] who starts from the idea that *paricida* is a general term for the murderer of a man. *Pari-*,

1. *Gnomon* VI, 1930, p. 449 ff. (= Kleine Schriften II, 1302 ff.)

according to him, is a word for "man," unknown elsewhere in the western vocabulary, but corresponding to Skt. *puruṣa* 'man'. There is no great formal difficulty about this equation, if we admit that *puruṣa* goes back to **purṣa*. But what constitutes an obstacle to the acceptance of this equation is the sense of the Latin compound and its use in the legislation of the Romans.

In our view we should retain the old etymology which equates *pāri-* with the Greek *pēós* (originally **pāso-*): it has been taken up again and justified on a number of occasions, most recently by L. Gernet,[2] who by means of juridical arguments shows that we must adhere to this interpretation.

The Greek term *pēós* properly designates "the kinsman by alliance, by marriage." Thus in the *Iliad* (3, 163) we see it associated with *phílos*, which has the full sense studied above.[3] In the *Odyssey* (8, 581ff.) we find it used with other kinship terms which explain it: "Have you a *pēós* who died before Troy, a son-in-law or a father-in-law, those who are dearest to us after those of our own blood and our own race? Or was he a dear companion? For it is better to have a companion full of wisdom than a brother . . ." Thus *pēós* is, linked on the one hand with *gambrós* 'brother-in-law' and *pentherós* 'father-in-law', and on the other with *hetaîros* 'companion' or *phílos*: it is therefore someone with whom one has contracted an alliance. This is the category of kinship which *pēós* defines: it is kinship by alliance, within a tribe. This kinship imposes certain precise obligations, notably in the case of violence done to one of the parties concerned.

We may now examine the famous text of Numa Pompilius on the parricide (Festus, *loc. cit.*): "*Si quis hominem liberum dolo sciens morti duit, parricidas esto.*" In this text, as in all the codes and rituals at Rome, the words must be taken in their full sense. The man who puts to death with malice aforethought a man of free birth must be a *parricida*, must be considered as "the murderer of a kinsman by alliance."

There are, as we have seen, certain legal provisions which concern simply the family, and there is on the other hand inter-family law which regulates the relations between different families. One might say that *thémis* and *díkē* are involved in the semantic context of this provision. We see that one who kills a *liber* man is treated as a *parricidas*; the notion of a murderer within a family is extended to the case of a murderer within society itself. Homicide in general is

2. *Revue de Philologie* 63, 1937, pp. 13-29.

3. Book Three, Chapter Four.

not punished as such in the ancient law codes. In order to be punishable it was necessary for the murder to affect a man of the group: morality stopped at the frontier of the natural group.

Thus the *quaestor paricidi* exercised his functions within the social group which was considered as being the family group in its full extension including its connections by alliance. With the help of this closer definition of the sense we can now attempt to give precision to the meaning of *quaero*. The meaning "to make an investigation" is evidently too closely linked with *quaestor* and its derivatives to be posited as the primary sense. It will be better to start from an example which has every mark of antiquity and authenticity.

This is an old prayer (Cato *Agr.* 141), an invocation to *Mars pater* on the occasion of the lustration of the fields. This text, which is important in itself, is full of archaisms and has been preserved to us in its original state.

In it we find a reference to the sacrifice called "*su-ove-taurilia*," a term which has been analyzed above[4] and which reveals a profound social symbolism. Neither the order nor the nature of the animals is accidental. We have here three symbolic animals: the *pig* is sacred to the divinities of the earth, to Ceres: it is associated with the fertility of the soil; the *bull* is traditionally sacred to Jupiter and to Zeus; it is the animal offered in the most sacred and solemn sacrifices, those which are in the charge of the priests of the highest divinities. Coming between these two we find often if not always, the *sheep*, the *ram* which is the animal of the warriors. We have here precisely the three social classes, represented by symbolic animals. This is what gives the key to the sacrifice of the lustration. The sacrifice called "*suovetaurilia*" united symbolically the three orders of society in this solemn communion for the protection of the great god who is invoked, Mars: and the society as a whole which makes the sacrifice is represented at the ceremony.

This symbolism reveals the archaism of a prayer like this. It begins with this invocation: *Mars pater, te* ***precor quaesoque*** *uti sies volens propitius . . .* "I beg and beseech you": is this a simple duplication? Some scholars have reproached the religious language with redundancy: the terms look as if they were duplicated and even triplicated, as though the authors had the purpose of accumulating equivalents. But this is not the case. On closer examination we see that these juxtapositions do not in fact associate terms of identical, or even

4. Book One, Chapter Two.

closely related sense; each one keeps its full sense and this is a condition for the effectiveness of the prayer.

A second example is provided by Lucretius: *prece quaesit* (V 1229) 'he asked with prayer'. Such examples in which **prex* and *quaero* are collocated are most instructive for our analysis.

Finally, and this is especially important, we must ask how the verb *quaero* and its frequentative form *quaeso* 'ask persistently' are employed. We have had occasion to examine from a different point of view the formula which in ancient Roman law summed up the purpose of marriage: *liberum(-orum) quaesundum(-orum) causa (gratia)* 'to obtain (legitimate) children';[5] we can hardly translate the verb otherwise than as "obtain." In any case the sense is certainly not "ask insistently, to pray repeatedly."

Finally the nominal derivative *quaestus*, in its usual application, denotes "gain, profit" and also "the way one earns one's living, profession." This term falls completely outside the legal series which begins with *quaestor* and continues with *quaestio* '(judicial) investigation' and also "torture" (whence *quaestiono* 'investigate by means of torture, to torture'). Here then is the list of the principal terms of the semantic group of *quaero*, with the variety of meanings which they present.

To achieve further precision we must now turn to the verb with which it is associated: *precor*. This present tense is derived from a well-known root **perk-/*prek-*, which is widely represented in both stem forms without difference of meaning. In Latin we have **prex, precor, posco* (the inchoative present of *preco*), *postulo*. The Romans remained conscious of the connections between these forms as well as of the difference of sense which each one specifies.

Outside Latin we have (1) the verbal stem Skt. *pṛccha-* 'ask', Iranian *pṛs-* (< **perk-*) and *fras-* (< **prek-*); OSl. *prositi*, Lith. *prašýti* and (2) a noun Skt. *prāt- (vivāka)* 'judge', literally "he who decides a *prāt*". The sense is restricted in an instructive way, for *prāt* is a "question" in the legal sense; it is the "case," that is, the semantic equivalent of the *quaestio* of the *quaestor*. To Skt. *Prāt* corresponds also the OHG *frāga* 'question (Germ. *Frage*)', a term which differs from **prex* only in the root vowel *ā*.

(3) In a different semantic sphere we have Lat. *procus*, 'he who demands' in marriage, the suitor. This specialization of sense recurs in the Lithuanian *piršti* 'ask in marriage'.

5. Book Three, Chapter Three.

(4) With the present morpheme -*ske*-, known from Latin *posco*, we have the Avestan and Persian *frasa* 'make an investigation, ask' and also "punish, chastise": *avam hufraštam aprsam* (where *hufraštam* contains the participle *frašta*- of the same verb) '(he who has disobeyed me, says Darius), him I questioned (in such a way that he was) well questioned', which means "I punished him severely." Finally we have OHG *forscōn* 'seek, make an investigation' in speaking of a judge.

We see, then, that in a number of languages particular forms and uses of **prex*- coincide with those of *quaero*, but always outside Latin: in Sanskrit, Iranian, and Old High German.

Table. Table of the various forms and uses of **prek*-. (The words which, outside Latin, coincide in sense with words of the family of *quaero* are in bold.)

Latin ****prex***	Skt. ***prāt-vivāka*** OHG *frāga*	Lat. *Procus* Lith. *piršti*
precor	Skt. *pṛcch*- (cf. Skt. *pṛs*-, Iran. *fras*) OSl. *prositi* Lith. *prašýti*	
posco	OHG ***forscōn*** Iran. ***frasa***	

In Latin itself, however, as we have seen, the two verbs are associated in such a way that their meanings seem to be closely akin. We can see how far they coincide and how they differ. In two cases the context was the formulation of a request, but in two different ways: *precor*, **prex* must be taken together with the agent noun *procus* 'he who asks in marriage'; **prex* is the request which is exclusively verbal and is especially addressed to gods to obtain what one hopes for from them. Such is the distinctive character of *prek*-: it is an oral request, addressed to a superior authority and which does not comprise any other means than speech.

On the other hand, *quaero*, with the derived nouns *quaestio* and especially *quaestus*, denotes a different procedure: *quaestus* 'way of making a profit,

profit', *quaestio* 'interrogatory torture', and the verb *quaero* itself involves not the attempt to get information or other things by oral request but to obtain something by the appropriate material means.

It is not precisely some information that is solicited or a favor that is requested but rather some material object, often some advantage, but always something concrete, which is considered necessary to life or activity.

This is confirmed by an expression like *liberum quaesundum causa*: seek to obtain (and not to know). The *quaestus* and the *quaestio* show this no less clearly and it is also apparent in *quaerere victum* 'get one's living, earn one's living', and *quaerere rem* 'to get rich'. We also read in Terence: *hunc abduce, vinci, quaere rem* (*Ad.* 482): 'take him away, bind him and get something from him', that is to say, "extract the truth from him by appropriate means." They seek to gain by some material means something which is vaguely referred to as *res*. What is relevant here is only the means employed for obtaining it; it is not simply a matter of asking.

Thus the formula *precor quaesoque* is by no means a tautology or a rhetorical duplication. *Precor* is to ask by means of **prex*. Here speech is the intermediary between the one who asks and the one who is asked. Speech is by itself the effective means. But *quaeso* differs from *precor* in that it implies the use of means appropriate to getting what is desired, like the sacrifice of the three animals and the association of the formula with the offerings.

To achieve this reconstruction we have had to use the forms of **prek-* which occur in languages other than Latin, especially Iranian. We have stressed above that Iran. *fras*, *frašta* take on the sense of "punishment" and generally "torture."

We can now return to our point of departure, which was the Latin title *quaestor*. It is now clear that the *quaestor* was not merely charged with "making an enquiry"; his role was rather *quaerere*, to try and obtain by material means, either, in a criminal case, the person of the guilty party, or (and the word is associated with *quaestus*) money for the treasury, for the incomings and outgoings of which he was responsible.

Such is the meaning which we propose (based on the uses of the verb) for the agent noun *quaestor*. In the example from Lucretius, *prece quaesit*, there is also no tautology: the object of *quaerere* is *pacem*, and this is the material object which he seeks to gain: by what means? By **prex*, by an oral request. In other circumstances other means would have been employed.

Thus we have established a duality of function which betrays an ancient functioning. For us "to request" is "to seek to obtain." This notion is specified in different ways according to the context. But in Old Latin two different notions of asking were distinguished: in ancient societies they had a precise and concrete form and only the vocabulary can reveal this to us. The verbs or certain of their derivatives preserve for us, or yield by the application of the comparative method, the evidence of more complex semantic distinctions: such is the gap between *procus* and *precor* because of their early specialization. If we did not know the senses which justify us in bringing *procus* into relationship with Lith. *piȓšti*, it would be difficult for us to give the root **prek-* its exact sense, and to see that **prek-* denotes a purely verbal activity, not employing any material means and consisting of a request generally addressed by an inferior to a superior. It is thus that **prek-* 'ask a favor' differs from the root, not attested elsewhere, which is represented by the Latin verb *quaero* and the agent noun *quaestor*.

BOOK V, CHAPTER EIGHT

The Oath in Greece

Abstract. The oath, a solemn declaration placed under the guarantee of a superhuman power that is charged with the punishment of perjury, has no Indo-European expression any more than the notion of "swearing" has. Different languages have coined expressions which relate to the particular forms assumed by the ordeal which the taking of an oath involves. Notably in Greek, thanks to the Homeric expression *hórkon omnúnai*, meaning "to swear an oath," we can grasp its concrete origin: "to take hold of the *hórkos*," an object charged with malevolent powers which will be unleashed in case the oath is broken. The old sacramental formula *ístō Zeús* is an appeal to the divinities as eyewitnesses and consequently as irrefutable judges (cf. Lat. *iudex arbiter*). Latin *sacramentum* 'oath', and perhaps Hittite *lingāis* (cf. Gr. *élenkhos*?), underline the potential malediction which specifically defines the binding declaration of the oath.

Of the religious expressions in which speech has a particular force and its own procedures none is more solemn than that of the oath and none would seem more necessary for the functioning of social life. Yet it is a remarkable fact that we look in vain for a common Indo-European expression. There is no Indo-European term of which one can say that it is found in all the ancient languages and that it properly refers to this notion. Each language has its own expression, and for the most part the terms used have no etymology. The obscurity of the terms seems to conflict with the importance and the ubiquity of the institution which they denote. On reflection one sees the reason for this discordance between the extent of the institution and the rarity of common forms. It is because the oath is not an autonomous institution; it is not an act which has its significance in itself and is self-sufficient. It is a rite which guarantees and makes sacred a declaration. The purpose of the oath is always the same in all civilizations. But the institution may appear in different guises. There are in fact two components which characterize it:

1. The nature of the declaration, which assumes from this fact a special solemnity;
2. The sanctifying power which receives and solemnizes the declaration.

These are the two constant and necessary elements of the oath. This may take two forms, according to circumstances: it will be an oath relating to truth, a declaratory oath, when it pertains to facts under dispute in a law case; or it will be a binding or promissory oath when it is used to support a promise.

One could define an oath as an anticipated ordeal. The one taking the oath stakes something that is essential to him, some material possession, his kin, even his own life, in order to guarantee the veracity of his affirmation. There is no necessary correspondence between the gestures and the various expressions of the oath; each time the oral or formulaic rite and the accompanying practices may differ. When we find that the oath is referred to by a specific term, this may apply to the actual procedure by which the oath is taken rather than to the oath itself. If we always knew the circumstances in which the swearing of the oath took place, we should be better placed to understand the proper sense of the term. But very often these conditions are unknown and the expression remains obscure.

In Germanic we have Got. *aiþs*, which has cognates in all the Germanic languages: OIcel. *eiðr*, OHG *eid*, OE *āþ*, Engl. *oath*, and this corresponds exactly to OIr. *ōeth*. The correspondence between Celtic and Germanic is so close that one wonders whether borrowing has not taken place—as happens so often with cultural terms between these two groups—and if so, in what direction. Got. *aiþs* and OIr. *ōeth* go back to **oito-*, which can be interpreted as a form derived from the root meaning "to go", and therefore as "the march." The difficulty is to see what a "march" has to do with an "oath." We might accept the view of the historian K. von Amira, who regarded this "march" as the act of "*going solemnly to the oath*", cf. Lat. *in ius ire*. This is possible, but one can imagine other explanations, especially if we recall a rite which is known in a number of ancient civilizations. The swearing of an oath occasioned a sacrifice: an animal was cut in two and then the man or men who were swearing the oath had to walk between the two halves of the animal so sacrificed. This rite is already attested in Hittite, and survivals of it are found in Lithuania in the fourteenth century. At the conclusion of an oath sworn by the Grand Duke of Lithuania to the king of Hungary, the juror walked between the two halves of an ox which was sacrificed and he proclaimed that such would be his own fate if he did not keep his promise, *sic sibi contingi si promissa non servaret.* However, since this rite is not attested in the Germanic world, such an interpretation of **oito-* remains hypothetical.

In Germanic, as in a number of other languages, but not everywhere, the noun and the verb are different. The verb is Got. *swaran* (Germ. *schwören*, Engl. *swear*) which translates Gr. *omósai*; *ufarswaran* is a calque of Gr. *epi-orkeîn* 'to commit perjury, swear a false oath'. This verb has correspondents outside Germanic: in Italic, Osc. *sverrunei*, the dative singular of the nominal form, which means "to the orator, to the guarantor." But *sermo*, which has also been brought into connection with it, must rather be related to *serere*. This same Germanic verb also yields the Icelandic *svara* 'reply', OHG *andsvara* 'reply' (Engl. *answer*); for the formation we may compare the Lat. *re-spondeo*, from which we might conclude that the sense of *swaran* is close to that of *spondeo*, that is "to guarantee, be responsible for something." Thus the Germanic **swer-* 'to act as a guarantor' is well suited to the notion of the "oath" which is expressed by the substantive which acts as the object of the verb.

In Greek too the verb *ómnumi* and the substantive *hórkos* are different. The verb by itself can mean "to swear," but neither term is used in any other context than the swearing of an oath. Thus within Greek itself we find nothing at our disposal which would throw light on its real significance. Now the comparatist finds material for his reconstructions only if he can observe variations and here the sense is fixed and immobile. But the etymology of the Greek verb permits certain deductions. The root *om-* of the present stem *ómnumi* can be connected, as has been proposed long ago, with the Sanskrit verb *am-*, of the same sense, which is ancient and attested irreproachably in Vedic and Brahmanic texts. This correspondent is the only one which can throw light on the origin of *ómnumi*. In Vedic *am-* is found both as a simple verb and with the preverb *sam-*, just as we have in Greek *sun-ómnumi* along with *ómnumi*. We also have the imperative form in a legendary tale: a character is invited to swear that he will do what he says; the god says "*ṛtam amīṣva*", "swear by the *ṛta*" (that is, taking the *ṛta* as guarantor); and the character in question *ṛtam āmīt* 'swore by the *ṛta*'. In the Śatapatha-Brāhmaṇa: *etad dha devāḥ . . . samāmire* 'and that the gods swore conjointly, they swore it to one another'; and again, *samam-yate* 'he binds himself vis-à-vis another for a certain length of time'.

By virtue of the specific nature of the use we have the opportunity of delimiting the proper meaning of the term: *am-* properly means "to take, seize," with or without a preverb; *tam abhyamīti Varuṇaḥ* is equivalent to the expression, with a different verb, *taṃ gṛhṇāti Varuṇaḥ* 'Varuna seizes him'. The man who is "taken, seized" by an attack of some illness is called *abhyānta*, the participle of the same verb *am-*. This is a particularly valuable pointer to the prehistory of the notion: our starting point must be the sense "seize." Although no trace of this is left in Greek, this idea must find its place in the total explanation of the expression. For we can justify it indirectly. When Hypnos makes Hera swear that she will give him as a wife one of the young Graces, Pasithea, he asks her for a solemn oath: "Swear to me by the inviolable waters of Styx, touching with one hand the nurturing earth and with the other the sparkling sea, so that all the nether gods who surround Kronos may bear witness" (*Il.* 14, 271).

Let us now consider *hórkos*, the noun which usually functions as the object of the verb in the expression *hórkon omósai*. The sense of *hórkos* shows no variation. In the poetical language, from the time of Homer onwards, *hórkos* with *ómnumi* is the expression pure and simple of the "oath." We may also cite the important derivative *epíorkos* 'perjury' and *epiorkeîn* 'commit perjury', a term which requires a separate examination.

We have no etymological connections which would help to explain *hórkos*. All that we have is the link with *hérkos* 'fence' which was suggested by the ancients and taken up again in more recent times. At first sight we have here an example of a familiar type of alternation: since *hérkos* is a neuter *i*-stem, we should expect the alternation to be *hérkes-/hórko-*. But the meaning of *hérkos* is exclusively "wall, fence, enclosure, etc."; we have the familiar Homeric expression *hérkos odóntōn* 'the barrier of the teeth'. We should in that case have to imagine that the form with the *o*-grade of the root vowel meaning "oath" had something to do with the notion of "barrier." But however we exercise our imagination, there is nothing in Greek ideas that favors this interpretation, which in any case is far from satisfying. This is a reason for not neglecting the task of clarifying the sense as far as possible within Greek itself.

In the Homeric language *hórkos* designates every kind of oath: the type which gives a guarantee of what one is going to do, a pact; or else the type which supports a statement relating to the past, the so-called judiciary oath. Thus the sense of *hórkos* does not depend on the nature of the oath.

But it is important to note that the Homeric *hórkos* is not an act of speech. Let us read the formula of the "great oath" of the gods: "May Earth and the vast Sky above and the waters of the Styx which go down (to the lower world), which is the strongest oath for the blessed gods, be witnesses" (*Il.* 15, 36ff.).

Cf. *The Homeric Hymn to Demeter* 259: "May the *hórkos* of the gods, the implacable waters of the Styx, be witness." Here the "*hórkos* of the gods" is put in apposition with *húdōr* 'water': it is the water of the Styx which is the *hórkos*.

Hesiod, in fact, in the *Theogony* (l. 400) makes the Styx into a nymph whom Zeus wished to honor by making her "the great *hórkos* of the gods." This is why Zeus, when he wants to find out which of the gods has lied (l. 784f.), sends Iris far away to bring back the "great *hórkos* of the gods" in an ewer. This is the famous water which flows cold from a steep and precipitous rock, the water of Styx. We see, then, that the water of Styx by itself constitutes the *hórkos* of the gods, being a material invested with baneful powers.

There are other types of *hórkos*: Achilles desires to give to Agamemnon a solemn promise; he gives him his scepter, which guarantees the *thémistes* of Zeus. He adds: "This scepter will be for you a *mégas hórkos*" (*Il.* 1, 239).

This is not merely a turn of phrase: the literal interpretation leads to the identification of the *hórkos* with a material object: some sacred substance, the wand of authority, what is essential is always the object itself and not the act of affirmation. We can now see a possibility of harmonizing, in their primary significance, the verb and the substantive: just as *ómnumi* goes back to a prehistoric meaning "grasp firmly", so *hórkos*, in Greek itself, suggests some material substance, hence the expression "to grasp the *hórkos*." Whether it is an object or some substance, this *hórkos* is a sanctifying object, one which has a potency which punishes every breach of the pledged word.

This is presumably how the Greeks imagined the personification of *hórkos*; it is sinister. Let us quote Hesiod again: "*Hórkos* is the worst of the scourges for every terrestrial man who knowingly shall have violated his oath" (*Theog.* 231-32); cf. *Works* 804, where it is said that *hórkos* was created only to be the scourge of perjured men. "He keeps pace with crooked judgments" (ibid. 219).

The mythical imagination has done no more than personalize the notion implicit in the sense of the word, by representing *hórkos* as a destructive force which is unleashed in case of breach of oath, for the substantive *hórkos* designates a substance charged with bane, a divine, autonomous power which punishes perjury.

Behind this concept we can guess at the idea present in other terms for the oath. In Latin we have apart from *ius iurandum*, studied above, the term *sacramentum* (from which French *serment* 'oath' comes); this implies the notion of making "*sacer*." One associates with the oath the quality of the sacred, the most formidable thing which can affect a man: here the "oath" appears as an operation designed to make oneself *sacer* on certain conditions. We recall that a man who is declared *sacer* may be killed by anyone whatsoever.

This "consecration" recurs also in the same term of Sanskrit *śapatha* 'swearing', derived from *śap-* 'to curse' and also in Slavic in the OSl. *klęti* 'to curse', whereas *klęti sę* means "to swear," just like Russian *kljast'* 'to curse' and *kljast' sja* 'to swear'. The expression reveals the phenomenology of the oath. The person taking the oath vows himself to malediction if he commits perjury, and he solemnizes his act by touching the object or substance invested with this terrible potency.

We must now test the validity of this interpretation for the compound of *hórkos* which designates the "perjurer"; this is *epíorkos*, a term so fraught with difficulty in spite of its transparent formation that it remains the subject of discussion among scholars.

The word enters into two different constructions, the oldest having the attribute in the nominative: *epíorkos omnúnai* 'to swear in such a way as to be *epíorkos*'; the other has an object in the accusative: *epíorkon omnúnai*. The first construction is found in Hesiod *Works*, 804, the second in Homer, e.g. *Il.* 3, 279.

The literal sense of this compound term has been discussed a number of times. A recent interpretation is that by Schwyzer.[1] To explain why *epi* + *hórkos* means "to swear a false oath» Schwyzer starts from a verse of Archilochus (Diehl, *Anthol. Lyr.* I, 265): "He who was once a companion has trampled on the oath" *làx ébē eph' horkíois*.

This would be the literal explanation of the compound, from the fact that *epí* 'on' figures in an expression which formulates the notion analytically. This would imply that we must understand *epíorkos* as *ho epì hórkōi* < *bás* >, i.e. "he < who walks > on the *hórkos*." But the flaw in the explanation is obvious: the essential term is lacking, for it is precisely the verb *baínō* which is missing

1. *Indogermanische Forschungen*, 45, 1927, 255ff.

from the compound. We certainly have the nominal construction of *epí*, but without the idea of "walking on", trampling on." This is why we must reject the explanation of Schwyzer.

The explanation of *epíorkos* 'perjurer' and of the verb *epiorkeîn* 'perjure oneself' must start with the observation that the form *epíorkos* cannot be ancient: if it were we should expect **ephorkos*. It must therefore be an adjective (or a verb, according to whether we posit one or the other as the primary term) which was based on an expression in which both *epí* and *hórkos* occurred together. This expression is attested and we find it in Hesiod (*Works* 194) in a description of the Age of Iron. In this age, he says, no one will care about good and evil, traditional conventions will no longer be respected: "the base man will do mischief to the better, speaking in crooked words, and he will add an oath, *epì d' hórkon omeîtai*." We find here, still as distinct elements, the members of the compound *epí-orkos*, and we can see how they add up to the idea of perjury: there is an implicit connection between the oath which is taken and the lie (the crooked words) which it supports. The idea, therefore, is the "addition" (*epì*) of an oath (*hórkon*) to a statement or a promise which one knows is false. This is confirmed by a second example from Hesiod (*Works* 282): "the man who deliberately bears false witness by swearing a false oath, *hòs dé ke marturíēisi hekȭn epíorkos omóssas pseúsetai* . . ." In the *Homeric Hymn to Hermes*, Hermes himself gives the example of the great oath offered in support of an entirely false statement (ll. 274 and 383). Thus the fact of "adding a *hórkos*" (*epí-orkos*) always supposes, whether explicitly or not, that the person swearing will not keep his word, that he will be *epíorkos*. It is by implicit reference to the use of a false oath which must have become habitual (and proverbial) that the expression "to add (to one's statement) an oath" soon came to signify "to swear a false oath," "to perjure oneself." Thus the term *epíorkos* throws light on a fact of morals; it shows that all too lightly support was given by an oath to a promise which one had no intention of keeping or a statement which one knew to be false. The evidence of language finds support, curiously enough, in a historian, the first of the Greek historians, Herodotus. He tells a story about an episode in the struggle between the Medes and the Greeks. The Lacedaemonians having warned Cyrus not to do harm to any Greek city because they would not tolerate it, the latter replied to the herald who brought this message: "I have no fear of these men who have at the center of their city a place where they assemble to deceive one another by (false) oaths" (I, 153: *allḗlous omnúntes exāpatôsi*). The expression which is literally "deceive one another by oaths" evidently implies that the oaths are false. Here we see clearly how the intention to deceive turns the oath into a stratagem. Herodotus relates many other examples of this. Glaucus calmly goes to ask the oracle whether he can use an oath to gain possession of a deposit entrusted to him which he does not wish to give back. The Pythia makes this crushing reply: "There is certainly profit in thus winning by an oath and in acquiring riches. Swear, then, if you will, since death also awaits the man who keeps his word. But there is a son of the oath, nameless and without hands or feet. Yet swiftly he pursues (the perjurer) until he seizes him and destroys all his progeny and his whole house; whereas the descendants of the man who keeps his word will have the better fate hereafter" (VI, 86). Elsewhere we read how Etearchus made his guest swear to agree to all his demands and profited by it to make him kill his own daughter: the other outraged by the "deceit of the oath" (*têi hapátēi toû hórkou*) ingeniously gets out of his obligations (IV, 154). It was also by the device of false oaths (*tôi hórkōi kaì têi hapátēi*) that Ariston procured the wife of a friend (VI, 62).

The analysis of the compound *epíorkos* thus links up with the description of morals: in the expression which was coined at an early date for "perjury" we can find confirmation of the deceitful use of the oath in the social life of the Greeks. The only curious thing is to find that this feature is so old, since *epíorkos* and *epiorkeîn* are already in use in the *Iliad*.[2]

We have now explored, etymologically and conceptually, the interpretation of the notions connected with *hórkos* and *ómnumi*. We can now turn to the Hittite term for "to swear": *ling*- 'swear' with the substantive *lingāi*- (genitive -*iyas*) 'oath', and the denominative verb *linganu*- 'cause to swear an oath, bind by an oath', notably for the taking of a military oath imposed by a chief on his troops. Sturtevant was of the opinion that the Hittite *ling*- corresponded to Greek *élegkhos*. Now *élegkhos* means "inculpation, a proof of guilt," whence in the vocabulary of philosophy it came to mean "refutation." Consequently it would follow that "to swear" in Hittite meant "to inculpate," which would correspond fairly well with Greek and Roman ideas. The person swearing

2. In an earlier article on the expression of the oath in ancient Greece (*Rev. Hist. Relig.* 1947-48, pp. 81-94) we gave a different explanation of the term *epíorkos*. The interpretation offered here is close to that given by M. Leumann, *Homerische Wörter*, 1950, p. 79. The term *hórkos* has been the subject of articles by J. Bollack, *Rev. ét gr.*, 1958, 1ff., and by R. Hiersche, ibid. 35ff. Other studies are cited in the etymological dictionary of Frisk, under *epíorkos* and *hórkos*.

inculpates himself in advance and conditionally, and this inculpation takes effect in case of perjury.

This is an idea which recurs in the Latin expression *sacramentum*, and this poses a problem of law rather than one of etymology or philology. We know different senses of *sacramentum*: the *legis actio sacramenti* is a particular form of proceeding bound up with archaic practices in making a claim before the *pontifex*. If the proof should not have been established in the regular way, a *poena* would afflict the one who instituted the action. Another formula defines the soldier's oath, which is of a special kind: *consulibus sacramento dicere*, 'to bind oneself to the consuls by the *sacramentum*'.

Sacramentum is a derivative, not of *sacer*, but of *sacrare* 'to declare *sacer*, to pronounce anathema', the man who commits a certain offense. The *sacramentum* is properly the action or object by which one anathematizes one's own person in advance (the military *sacramentum*) or the pledge deposited (in the judiciary oath). Once the words are spoken in the set forms, one is potentially in the state of being *sacer*. This state becomes effective and invites divine vengeance if the undertaking is transgressed. In all circumstances the process of engagement is ordered in the same way, and to some extent this is apparent in the terms themselves.

We now consider the formulas and the particular ways in which the oath is sworn. There is one aspect which seems to us particularly striking but which usually escapes comment. This is the formula which in Homer recurs every time the text of the oath is reproduced. Appeal is made to Zeus and to a series of gods: "*ístō nûn Zeùs prôta . . . Gê te kaì Ēélios* (*Il.* 19, 258f.) "May Zeus, the Earth and the Sun *know* it . . ." The purpose is not merely to acquaint the gods with the text of the undertaking by which one binds oneself. We must give to *ístō* its full etymological force: not simply "May he know", but more accurately "May he see." The root **wid-* in this use preserves its original meaning. It calls upon the gods to be eyewitnesses of the oath. The witness at an early period is a witness insofar as he "knows" but primarily in virtue of what he has *seen*.

This interpretation is not a simple etymological conjecture. When the other Indo-European languages offer ancient and explicit evidence for the sense of **weid-*, they agree with Greek. Thus *vettar* in Sanskrit, which has the same sense of "witness" is, apart from the vocalic grade of the root, the form corresponding to the Greek *ístōr* 'witness' and certainly means "the one who sees"; Got. *weitwōþs*, the perfect participle (cf. Skt. *vidvas-*, *viduṣ-*) is "he who knows because he has seen"; similarly the Irish *fiadu* (< **weidōn*) 'witness'. The Greek *ístōr* takes its place in the same series and the proper meaning of this root **wid-* is illuminated by the rule enunciated in the Śatapatha Brāhmaṇa: *yad idānīm dvau vivadamānām eyātām aham adarśam aham aśrauṣam iti ya eva brāyād aham adarśam iti tasmā eva śraddadhyāmā* 'If now two men dispute (have a law suit), one of them saying, "I have seen," and the other "I have heard," the one who says "I have seen" is the one whom we must believe'.

As between the one who has seen and the one who has heard, it is always to the one who has seen that we should give credence. The fundamental value of eyewitness emerges clearly from the name of the witness—*ístōr*. This is why the gods are taken to witness by inviting them to *see*. The evidence of sight is irrefutable: it stands alone.

In Latin, too, the oath is accompanied by an appeal to the gods, but the formula is different. We read it in "the first covenant" (thus Livy I, 24, 7), that between Rome and Alba. After the conclusion of the pact, the *fetial* pronounces the words: "***Audi*** . . . *Juppiter* ***audi***, *pater patrate populi Albani*; ***audi***, *tu populus Albanus*." Thus Jupiter, the *pater patratus*, and the Alban people are requested to *hear*. It is necessary to *hear* to be a witness of the oath at Rome. For the Roman, who attaches such importance to the pronouncement of solemn formulas, to see is less important than to hear.

There remains some obscurity, however, about a particular (Homeric) use of *ístōr* in an important passage (*Il.* 18, 498ff.), which we have studied from a different point of view[3] —does *ístōr* here mean "witness" or "judge"? In a scene which figures on the shield of Achilles two men appear in a dispute, which concerns the *poinḗ* to be paid for the killing of a man. Both of them resort to an *ístōr* for a decision in the case (501).

It is difficult to see how he can be a witness, since his presence would have obviated the debate; he must be an "arbiter." For us the judge is not a witness; this variation prejudices the analysis of the passage. But it is precisely because the *ístōr* is the eyewitness, the only one who can settle the dispute, that made it possible for *ístōr* to acquire the sense of "one who decides by a final judgment on a question of good faith."

At the same time we also grasp the proper meaning of the Latin term *arbiter*, which is the source of our own term. As has been expounded above,[4] *arbiter* in fact designates two functions: (1) first the "witness" (the older sense), this

3. Cf. Book Five, Chapter Two.

4. On *arbiter*, see Book Five, Chapter Three.

being the sole sense in Plautus, and even in the classical period *remotis arbitris* means "without witnesses." And later (2) "arbiter." As a matter of fact, this sense is explained by the proper function of the *iudex arbiter*. As we have seen, *arbiter* is etymologically "the one who supervenes," as a third person, in an action in which he is a witness without having been seen, and consequently the one whose evidence settles the dispute. In virtue of the law, the *iudex arbiter* has the power of deciding as though he were the *arbiter-witness*, as though he had been present at the scene.

All this is evoked by the oath formula in Homer. Why were the gods invoked? This is because the punishment of perjury is not a human concern. No ancient Indo-European code provides a sanction for the perjurer. The punishment is regarded as coming from the gods since they are guarantors of the oath. Perjury is an offence against the gods. To bind oneself by an oath always means devoting oneself in advance to divine vengeance, since the gods are implored to "see" or to "hear", to be present in every case at the action which binds and commits.

BOOK VI

Religion

BOOK VI, CHAPTER ONE

The “Sacred”

Abstract. The study of the designation of the “sacred” confronts us with a strange linguistic situation: the absence of any specific term in common Indo-European on the one hand, and a two-fold designation in many languages (Iranian, Latin, and Greek) on the other. The investigation, by throwing light on the connotations of the historical terms, has the aim of clarifying the structure of a notion, the expression of which seems to demand not one but two terms. The study of each of the pairs attested—Av. *spənta* : *yaoždāta* (cf. also Got. *hails*: *weihs*); Lat. *sacer*: *sanctus*; Gr. *hierós*: *hágios*—lead us to posit, for the prehistorical period, a notion with a double aspect: positive “what is charged with divine presence,” and negative “what is forbidden for men to contact.” (The Greek *hósios* does not enter into the designation of the sacred; a double opposition, to*hierós* and to *díkaios*, determines its value: “what is permitted to men by the gods.”)

The chapters which follow are devoted mainly to the study of the religious vocabulary of Indo-European, at least the expressions for the fundamental notions. Here we encounter the same difficulties of method which made themselves felt in our study of the other institutions. The problem is, through an analysis of the lexicon, to reach back to the realities of the Indo-European world. If in fact we limit ourselves to a consideration of that portion of the vocabulary which can be immediately and completely defined by regular correspondences, we find ourselves condemned to see the object of our study gradually dissolving before our eyes.

What comparative grammar enables us to achieve has been expounded in an article by Meillet.[1] He shows that we cannot determine in any fullness Indo-European conceptions concerning religion because comparison only provides us with general terms, whereas the study of the real world shows us that each people had its own beliefs and its own rites and cult.

Comparative grammar, because of its very method, tends to eliminate special developments so as to reconstruct the common fund of words. This mode of proceeding leaves only a handful of Indo-European words: thus there would be no common term to designate religion itself, or cult, or the priest, not even one of the personal gods. The only thing which could be credited to the original community would be the idea of "god." This is well attested in the form **deiwos*, the sense of which is 'luminous' and 'celestial'; this is the quality which marks the god off from human beings, who are "terrestrial" (such is the meaning of the Latin word for "man," *homo*).

All the same we can inform ourselves about the religious vocabulary of Indo-European without looking for correspondences attested in all the languages of the family. We shall try to analyze the essential terms of the religious vocabulary, even when the religious value of the terms examined appears in only one language, provided that they are open to interpretation by the etymologist.

AVESTAN—*SPƎNTA* : *YAOŽDĀTA*

We shall in fact discover that the religious value of a term is often perceptible only in one language. Our task will then be to try and find out how far it is a survival or how far it constitutes a new development. The interest of this branch of research lies precisely in such differentiation and delicate distinction of sense.

It will be advisable to take as our starting point this first notion which is so important, namely that of the "sacred," in relation to which so many other concepts and terms of religion find their due place. For this notion of the "sacred" we have a rich vocabulary which differs considerably from language to language. Rare are those which present a common term; but when we have this good fortune, we must utilize it to the utmost and try to give all precision possible to the meaning of the term. Now there is a term of the greatest significance

1. *Linguistique historique et linguistique générale*, I, Paris, 1921, 323ff.

which is found in a group of contiguous languages: in Slavic, in Baltic, and in Iranian. This is the word represented by OSl. *svętŭ* (Russ. *svjatój*), Lith. *šventas*, Av. *spənta.*

This correspondence defines an adjective which has kept its strongly religious value in beliefs of different character: in Slavic and Baltic it belongs to the Christian vocabulary and signifies "holy, *sanctus*"; in Iranian, in its Avestan form, it is, in Mazdaean beliefs, the best equivalent of what we call the "sacred."

This term has in each of the languages a certain number of etymological relationships either with other survivals or with secondary derivatives. In Baltic, the Lithuanian *šventas* forms a group with OPr. *swints*, Lettish *svēts*, which have the same form and meaning and so contribute nothing new. But in Iranian *spənta-* is connected with a numerous group of distinct terms. From a formal point of view, *spənta* is a verbal adjective in *-ta-*, made from a root *spən-* which appears in the comparative *spən-yah-* and the superlative *spən-išta-*. In conformity with the ancient rule, the comparative and superlative are formed not on the stem of the positive but from the root. The same root *spən-* provides a neuter substantive *spān-ah-*, *span-ah-* 'the quality of *spənta*'; and from this substantive comes a derived adjective *spanah-vant-*.

The adjective *spənta* which is translated by "*sanctus*" has a fundamental importance in the religious vocabulary of the Avesta. With another adjective *amərəta* (> *aməša*) 'immortal', it constitutes the title *aməša-spənta*, the group of seven divinities who preside over the material and moral life of man, and who—although they bear abstract names—were at an early date incarnated each in an element: water, earth, plants, metals, etc. Each of them is both the symbol of a virtue and the guardian deity of an element of the world. They are grouped round the supreme god, Ahura-Mazda and they are constantly invoked in the hymns called the *Gāthās*, which contain the teaching of Zoroaster himself, as well as in the mythological and epic texts in the collection of the *Yašts* of the Avesta. Their collective name can be translated "the Immortal Saints."

Apart from this *spənta* is often used to specify the most important concepts of the religious universe. It is associated with *mąθra* 'effective word'; with *mainyu* '(divine) spirit'; with *xratu* 'mental force, spiritual vigor'; with *gāθā* 'chant, hymn'. We also find it with the names of individual beings: it is the epithet of the god of the beverage *haoma* (Vedic *soma*), it is the epithet of an animal so important as the bovine in cosmology: *gao-spənta*. It became an element of the name of *Aramati*, a divinity of the earth: *spəntā-ārmaiti* became in Middle Iranian *Spandarmat*, with the two elements closely joined, the name no longer being felt as a compound. In the vocabulary of Armenian, which owed so much to Iranian loan words, and which preserves an abundance of terms of the Iranian tradition, the name *Spandaramet* survives as the equivalent of Dionysus, while the substantive *sandarametk* ᶜ 'subterranean world' has as its first element *sand-*, which may represent a dialect form of the ancient *spənta-*. Along with *sandaramet-* we have derivatives created in Armenian itself: *sandaramet-ayin*, translating Greek *khthónios* 'of the earth' and *sandaramet-akan*, translating Greek *kata-khthónios* 'of the lower world'. It was therefore in virtue of his being an ancient divinity of the earth that *Spandaramet* was transferred in Armenian to the rôle of Dionysus as a god of fertility. But the details of the evolution are not clear. With *spənta* we must group various adjectives and substantives drawn from the same root which have in some cases become dissociated from it. First, apart from the comparative and superlative, which at least show that the quality denoted by *spənta* was capable of degrees, we have the substantive *spānah* '*sanctitas'*, associated with *masti*, which denotes knowledge or the understanding of religious truths.

The other members of the same etymological family are less immediately recognizable. In order to identify them we must try and reconstruct the Indo-European prototype, which offers no difficulty. In the three languages, Iranian, Slavic, and Baltic it takes the form **k'wen-to*; the root appears in the form of the comparative in **-yos* (Av. *spm-yah*); we thus have a root **k'wen.* But * *k'wen-* in fact represents an infixed form of the root, which must be posited as **k'eu-*. This is what appears in the Avestan verb *sav-* 'to be useful, advantageous', with its derivatives *sava-*, *savā-*, *savah*, substantives meaning "profit, advantage"; *sūra*, an adjective "strong, powerful."

The sense of *sav-* in Avestan "to be advantageous, to profit" emerges from a formula which has three symmetrical compounds: *frādat-gaēθā*, *varədat-gaēθā*, *savo-gaēθā*. The common term *gaēθā-* denotes the totality of creatures and in particular possessions of live-stock. These three compounds each have as their first element a present participle; *frādat-gaēθā-* means "what causes creatures to grow"; *varədat-gaēθā-* "what increases the creatures," and the third *savō- gaēθā-* "what *benefits* creatures." But such increase does not depend on the ordinary methods and means of man; it is of a divine nature. The three epithets are always divine attributes. Thus they sum up a property of a supernatural character, that of producing increase in the world of creatures.

The adjective *sūra* does not mean simply "strong"; it is also a quality of a number of gods, of certain heroes one of whom is *Zaraθuštra*, and of certain notions such as the "dawn." Comparison with related forms of the same root shows the primary sense. The Vedic verb *śū-* (*śvā-*) means "to swell, to grow," implying "strength" and "prosperity"; hence *śūra-* 'strong, brave'. The same conceptual relationship recurs in Greek where we have the present *kueîn* 'be pregnant, carry in the womb', and the substantive *kûma* 'swelling (of the waves), wave' on the one hand and *kûros* 'strength, sovereignty', *kúrios* 'having power' on the other.

This comparison brings out the identical primary sense "to swell," and in each of the three languages a specific evolution. All three coincide in having a derivative in *-ro*, **k'ū-ro-*, a noun or an adjective, which has taken on the meaning of "power" and "authority." But Iranian has developed the implications of this sense, given it special values and used it for the religious notion which we have just studied.

Both in Indo-Iranian and in Greek there is an evolution of sense from "swelling" to "strength" and "prosperity." Thus "strength," defined by the adjective Av. *sūra*, is the strength of fullness, of swelling. Finally, *spənta* characterizes the notion or the being endowed with this virtue, which is internal development, growth and power. In this way we can restore the connections between Gr. *kuéō* 'be pregnant' and *kúrios* 'sovereign', and between Av. *Sūra* 'strong' and *spənta*; and the relations between these words enable us to determine the peculiar origin of the notions of "the sacred." The being or object which is *spənta* is swollen with an abundant and supernatural force. It is invested with a power of authority and effectiveness which has the property of increasing, augmenting, both in the intransitive and transitive senses. This value long remained alive in the Iranian world; the translation and the commentary of the Avesta in Pehlevi translates *spənta* by *aβzōnīk* 'exuberant, swollen with power'.

Although the corresponding Slavic term is known only as a translation of a Christian concept (*hágios* 'holy'), we may presume that the original idea behind the OSl. *svętŭ* was charged with notions of natural religion. The Slavs preserved after their conversion many traces of pagan ideas. In popular songs impregnated with prehistoric folklore *svętŭ* refers to words or beings endowed with supernatural power.

The Iranian forms of the group of *spənta*, which are the most numerous, assumed considerable importance once they had taken on a religious value; they designate both supernatural power and the "sanctity" of certain mythological figures.

Thus the character of the holy and sacred is defined as a notion of exuberant and fertilizing force, capable of bringing to life, of bringing into being the products of nature.

We now turn to another expression of the same idea, the notion of the sacred in Germanic. The Germanic term corresponding to *svętŭ* in Slavic is, in Gothic, the adjective *weihs*, which translated Gr. *hágios* and yields the verb *weihan* (Germ. *weihen*) 'consecrate, Gr. *hagiázein'*, and *weihnan* 'to be consecrated, Gr. *hagiázesthai*'. The abstract noun *weihiþa* translates Gr. *hagiasmós* 'consecration' and *weiha* denotes "the priest."

The word is represented in Germanic as a whole: OE *wīh-dag* 'holy day', OHG *wih* 'holy', OIcel. *vē* 'temple, consecrated place', etc. On the other hand, we do not find outside Germanic anything which corresponds beyond certain limited, uncertain items which are difficult to define. The only form which can be compared with any degree of probability is the Latin *victima* 'animal offered to the gods', but the formation of the Latin word is obscure. It would be practically the only example of a suffix *-ima*, except perhaps another adjective of the same semantic group, *sacrima*, which is known only from an old gloss in Festus, with the sense 'sweet wine' offered as first fruits to Bacchus. Thus the comparison is satisfying and plausible only as regards the root element.

We might perhaps be justified (and this is a hypothesis often advanced) to find a third correspondent in Umbrian, granted a variation in the final consonant of the stem; here we have the imperative *eveietu*, which may mean "let him consecrate" or something of the kind. The context favors this interpretation, which, it must be admitted, is partly etymological. The form *eveie-tu* (cf. the Latin imperative in *-to*) is traced to **e-weig-e-tod*; if we accept this interpretation, this would give us an identical meaning in the two groups of languages. In this way we should have a confirmation that the notion of the "sacred" in Gothic was defined by the nature of the "consecrated" object, which was offered to the god as his exclusive possession.

We see how different this notion is from that current in Iranian, Baltic, and Slavic. For the moment there is no conclusion to be drawn from this difference: it will suffice simply to note it. It is only at the end of our study that we shall be able to see, once we have reviewed the different terms in use in each language, how to define the profound significance of a notion which appears to us to be unitary, but which found such different modes of expression among the Indo-European peoples.

One striking fact is that, nearly everywhere, we have for the notion of the "sacred" not one but two distinct terms. In Iranian, besides the word *spənta* we may recall the verb *yaoždā-* quoted in connection with *ius*.[2] This duality recurs in Germanic: Gothic *weihs* 'consecrated' and Runic *hailag*, Germ. *heilig* 'holy'; in Latin *sacer* and *sanctus*; in Greek *hágios* and *hierós*. It poses a problem which must be considered in the terms peculiar to each language.

Let us first consider the Germanic facts. The starting point for the notion represented today by German *heilig* 'holy' is the Gothic adjective *hails*, which expresses a quite different idea, that of "safety, health, physical and corporal integrity"; *hails* translates *hugiḗs*, *hugiaínōn* 'in good health, sound'; *ga-hails* translates *holóklēros* 'entire; intact', the negative adjective *un-hails* is the equivalent of *árrōstos*, *kakôs ékhōn* 'unwell', and the substantive *un-haili* means "sickness." From the nominal stem come the verbs *(ga)hailjan* 'to make healthy, cure' and *gahailnan* 'become healthy, be cured'.

The meaning changes slightly when we turn from Gothic to Old Icelandic: OIcel. *heil* means 'good omen'; similar is OE *hael* 'good omen, happiness, omen'; and the derived verb in Icelandic is *heilsa* 'salute, wish good health'. On the other hand we find a form made with the help of a suffix common to the whole of Germanic, the adjective **hailaga-*. We find the neuter form in an old Runic inscription inscribed on the gold ring from Petrossa: *Gutan Iowi hailag*, which appears to mean "sacred to the god of the Goths." Another inscription, also in runes, reads *Wodini hailag* which is translated as "endowed by Wotan with good fortune." The adjective is attested in the other Germanic languages: OIcel. *heilagr* '*sanctus*', OHG *heilag* '*heilig*'. In English, it appears as *holy*, and this is related to the word *whole*, which corresponds to the Got. *hails*: thus the two notions, though differentiated today, were closely connected in early times.

It is only in Germanic that this group of words underwent this development. But it is not isolated etymologically; it is connected with the OSl. *cělŭ*, 'hale, entire, *salvus*', with the derived present *cěljǫ* 'to cure'. In Baltic there corresponds OPr.*kails* 'whole, safe' and the abstract (feminine accusative in *-un*) *kailūstiskun* 'good health'. Finally, the word is also known from Celtic, if we may compare Welsh *coel* 'omen', Old Breton *coel* 'interpreter of omens'.

All these forms may be traced to a prototype, the adjectival form **kailos*, which is completely unknown to Indo-Iranian and Greek and which, even in

2. Cf. Book Five, Chapter Three.

the western group of languages, is confined to the group formed by Slavic, Germanic, and Celtic. It is not certain whether Baltic has not borrowed it from Germanic in the ancient form with initial *k-*.

From Gothic onwards, *hails* 'in good health, who enjoys physical integrity', is also used as a wish to translate the Greek *khaîre* 'hail'. This is explained by supposing that physical integrity has a pronounced religious value. The one who is possessed of "health," that is who is physically intact, is also capable of conferring this state on others. "To be intact" is the good fortune one wishes for, the omen which one expects. It was natural that such perfect "integrity" was regarded as a sign of divine grace, with a sacred significance. By its very nature divinity possesses this gift which is integrity, well-being, good fortune, and it can bestow this on men in the form of physical health and by omens of good fortune. The notion of *heilig*, though not present in Gothic, was latent in that language even though the nature of our texts do not bring it to light. In the course of time the primitive Gothic term *weihs* was replaced by *hails*, *hailigs*.

LATIN—*SACER* : *SANCTUS*

We now turn to the study of an important group, that of the words which still today in their modern form denote the idea of the "sacred."

Latin has two words, *sacer* and *sanctus*; their relation from a morphological point of view is perfectly clear, but the problem lies in the meaning of the terms.

The Latin word *sacer* includes the idea of what is most precise and specific about the "sacred." It is in Latin that we find the clearest distinction between the sacred and the profane; it is also in Latin that we discover the ambiguous character of the "sacred": consecrated to god and affected with an ineradicable pollution, august and accursed, worthy of veneration and evoking horror. This double value is peculiar to *sacer* and it serves to distinguish *sacer* and *sanctus*, for it does not appear in any way in the related adjective *sanctus*.

Further, the relation established between *sacer* and *sacrificium* opens the way to a better understanding of the mechanism of the "sacred" and its connection with sacrifice. This term "sacrifice" which is familiar to us associates a conception and an operation which seem to have nothing in common. How does it come about that "to sacrifice" although it properly means "to make sacred" (cf. *sacrificium*) actually means "to put to death"? Why does a sacrifice entail a death?

On this fundamental implication the study of Hubert and Mauss has thrown a vivid light.[3] It shows that the sacrifice takes place so that the profane world can communicate with the divine world through the priest and by means of the rites. To make the animal "sacred," it must be cut off from the world of the living, it has to cross the threshold which separates these two universes; this is the point of putting it to death. From this comes the value, which we feel so profoundly, of the term *sacerdos*, which goes back to **sakro-dhot-s*, the second component being derived from the root **dhē-* 'make, put', whence "to make effective, accomplish" (cf. *facio*). The *sacerdos* is the agent of the *sacrificium*, the one who is invested with powers which authorize him "to sacrifice."

The adjective *sacer* goes back to an ancient **sakros*, which has a variant form in the Italic *sakri-*, which recurs in Old Latin in the plural form *sacres*. This form **sakros* is a derivative in *-ro-* from a root **sak-*. Now *sanctus* is properly the participle of the verb *sancio*, which is derived from the same root **sak-* by means of a nasal infix. This Latin present tense in *-io-* with a nasal infix stands to **sak-* as *jungiu* 'to join' in Lithuanian does to *jug-*. The morphological procedure is familiar.

But this morphological relationship does not explain the sense, which is different. It is not sufficient to attach both *sancio* and *sanctus* to the root **sak-*, since *sacer* for its part has produced the verb *sacrare*. This is because *sancio* does not mean "to make *sacer*." We must define the difference between *sacrare* and *sancire*.

We have an instructive and explicit definition in Festus: *homo sacer is est quem populus iudicavit ob maleficium; neque fas est eum immolari, sed qui occidit parricidi non damnatur*. A man who is called *sacer* is stained with a real pollution which puts him outside human society: contact with him must be shunned. If someone kills him, this does not count as homicide. The *homo sacer* is for men what the *sacer* animal is for the gods: neither has anything in common with the world of men.

For *sanctus*[4] we have a definition in the *Digest* I, 8, 8: *sanctum est quod ab iniuria hominum defensum atque munitum est*: 'a thing is *sanctum* which is

3. Hubert and Mauss, "Essai sur la nature et les fonctions du sacrifice" in M. Mauss, *Oeuvres*, vol. I, Paris, Ed. de Minuit, 1968, 193–307.

4. For *sanctus*, reference may be made to a study which is still valuable for its documentation: the dissertation by Link, *De vocis sanctus usu pagano*, Königsberg, 1910.

defended and protected from damage by men'; cf. *Digest* I, 8, 9§3: *proprie dicimus sancta quae neque sacra, neque profana sunt, sed sanctione quadam confirmata, ut leges sanctae sunt*...; *quod enim sanctione quadam subnixum est, id sanctum est, et si deo non sit consecratum*: 'the term *sancta* is properly applied to those things which are neither sacred nor profane, but which are confirmed by a kind of sanction, in the way that the laws are *sanctae*: what is submitted to a sanction is *sanctum*, even though it is not consecrated to a god'. These are circular definitions: a thing is *sanctum* if it is supported by a *sanctio*, an abstract formed from the word *sanctum*. However, what emerges is that *sanctum* is neither what is "consecrated to the gods," the word for which is *sacer*, nor is it what is "profane," that is what is opposed to *sacer*. It is something which, while being neither of these two things, is affirmed by a *sanctio*, which is protected against every kind of assault, like the *leges sanctae*. We must understand that in the phrase *lex sancta* the adjective still has its full force as a passive participle.

If the old divine name *Ampsanctus* in Virgil (*Ampsancti valles*) is really to be understood as *undique sancti* (so Servius), that is, "*sancti* everywhere," the meaning of *amb-* being "on both sides," this would confirm the use of *sanctus* in the sense "surrounded by a defense, defended (by a limit or an obstacle)."

In the expression *legem sancire*, the *sanctio* is properly that part of the law which lays down the penalty which will be inflicted on the person who transgresses it; *sanctio* is often associated with *poena*. Consequently *sancire* is equivalent to *poena afficere*. Now in ancient Roman legislation the penalty was inflicted by the gods themselves who intervened as avengers. The principle applied in such a case may be formulated as *qui legem violavit, sacer esto*, 'may he who has violated the law be *sacer*'. Laws having this character were called *leges sacrae*. In this way the law became inviolable, and this "sanction" put the law into force. Hence came the use of the verb *sancire* to indicate that clause which permitted the promulgation of the law. The expression used was not only *legem sancire, lex sancta* but also *lege sancire*, that is to say to make something inviolable by means of a law, by some legal disposition.

In all these uses it emerges that the use of *sancire* is to delimit the field of application of a measure and to make this measure inviolable by putting it under the protection of the gods, by calling down on the violator divine punishment.

The difference between *sacer* and *sanctus* comes out clearly in a number of circumstances. There is not only the difference between *sacer* as a natural state and *sanctus* as the result of some operation. One said: *via sacra*, *mons sacer*, *dies sacra*, but always *murus sanctus*, *lex sancta*. What is *sanctus* is the wall and not the domain enclosed by it, which is said to be *sacer*. What is *sanctus* is what is defended by certain sanctions. But the fact of making contact with the "sacred" does not bring about the state of being *sanctus*. There is no sanction for the man who by touching the *sacer* himself becomes *sacer*. He is banished from the community, but he is not punished any more than the man who kills him is. One might say of the *sanctum* that it is what is found on the periphery of the *sacrum*, what serves to isolate it from all contact.

But this difference is gradually effaced, as the old sense of the sacred is transferred to the sanction: it is no longer the *murus* which is *sanctus*, but the whole of the field and everything which is in contact with the divine world. Now we no longer have a definition of a negative kind ("neither sacred nor profane") but a positive concept: a person becomes *sanctus* who is invested with divine favor and so receives a quality which raises him above the generality of men. His power makes him into an intermediary between man and god. *Sanctus* is applied to those who are dead (the heroes), to poets (*vates*), to priests and to the places they inhabit. The epithet is even applied to the god himself, *deus sanctus*, to the oracles, and to men endowed with authority. This is how gradually *sanctus* came to be little more than the equivalent of *venerandus*. This is the final stage of the evolution: *sanctus* is the term denoting a superhuman virtue.

Thus if we attempt a definition of what distinguishes *sacer* from *sanctus*, we can say that it is the difference between implicit sacredness (*sacer*) and explicit sacredness (*sanctus*). By itself *sacer* has its own proper value, one of mystery. *Sanctus* is a state resulting from a prohibition for which men are responsible, from an injunction supported by law. The difference between the two words appears in a compound which associated them: *sacrosanctus*, what is *sanctus* by a *sacrum*: what is defended by a veritable sacrament.

It is not superfluous to insist on this difference, seeing the errors committed by those who neglect it. A comparatist[5] cites the following passage from Varro, *De re rustica* 3,17: "*Proinde ut sacri sint ac sanctiores quam illi in Lydia . . .*" and draws the conclusion that the comparative of *sacer* is *sanctior*. Seeing that the comparative suffix of Indo-European is added to the bare root, *sanctior* stands for **sacior*; the superlative *sacerrimus* offers no obstacle because this Latin form does not go back to an Indo-European form. Such a line of reasoning misapprehends the facts. If we had to take *sanctior* as the comparative of

5. Specht, *Zeitschrift für vergleichende Sprachforschung*, 65, 1938, 137.

sacer, the two adjectives would be wholly interchangeable, since *sacer* was able to borrow the form of *sanctus* to make its comparative. Must we therefore translate: "as if they (the fish) were *sacred* and *more sacred* here than in Lydia"? Evidently not: these fish are on the one hand "sacred" and on the other "more *sancti*" than those of Lydia. *Sacer* is an absolute quality and does not admit of degrees. At the most a supreme state is conceivable; *sacerrimus* 'sacred above all else'. But *sanctus* is in the domain of the relative: something may be more or less *sanctum*.

We find confirmation of this in another work by Varro, *L. L.* VIII, 77. This time we have a grammatical text, which is concerned with the formation of comparatives and superlatives. Varro draws attention to the differences presented in this respect by adjectives which have the same form in the positive. He takes the three adjectives *macer*, *sacer*, and *tener*: the superlatives are the same: *macerrimus*, *sacerrimus*, *tenerrimus*. But he cites only two words in the comparative, *macrior* and *tenerior*. If he was not in a position to cite **sacrior* (although he quotes *sacer* and *sacerrimus*) this is because *sacer* had no comparative, because the sense of the word did not admit of degrees, and this is confirmed by what we can gather from the passage just quoted.

GREEK—*HIERÓS*

The Greek facts demand a detailed study. Here we have to deal with two terms: *hierós* and *hágios*. Both raise many problems within Greek and outside Greek as regards their etymology and the exact sense to be attributed to them.

The general opinion is that it is possible to propose an Indo-European etymology for *hierós*, but this produces a sense which is not reflected in the actual use of the term. Here Sanskrit plays a decisive part. *Hierós*, with another phonetic variant *hiarós* (Aeolic), corresponds to Vedic *iṣiraḥ*, and such is the exactness of the correspondence that it has never been contested despite the difficulties of sense.

The Vedic adjective *iṣiraḥ* expresses a quality which is predicated of certain divinities, of mythological characters, and of religious notions. The translation varies, but they all connect up in one way or another with the idea of "vigor" and "vivacity." The equivalents proposed rest on the derivation of *iṣiraḥ* from the root *iṣ*(*i*)- 'to be lively, ardent, vigorous'. Such is the presumable sense, rather a vague one it must be admitted, like many of the epithets of gods in the Vedic hymns. The consequence is that the equation of *iṣira-* with *hierós*, although it is formally irreproachable, cannot form the base for the analysis of *hierós* in Greek. On the contrary, the sense established by the internal analysis of *hierós* might well enable us to give a better definition of *iṣiraḥ*.[6] The epithet *iṣiraḥ* is added to the word for "wind": *iṣiro vātaḥ* 'the swift' or 'gusty wind'. The sense is not very different when *iṣiraḥ* is applied to *aśva-* 'horse': *áśvaiḥ mánojavebhir iṣiraíḥ* 'with swift horses as impetuous as thought', or to Indra in his quality as a dancer: *nṛtav iṣiro babhūtha* 'O dancer, you have been impetuous, agile'; it could be also said of *ketu-* 'flag, standard': *iṣiram ketum*, probably "waving flag."

But it also qualifies other notions, e.g. the voice: *vācam anamīvām iṣirām* 'a voice without flaw, powerful'; beverages such as soma or the milk of the heavenly cows; the sense is then "which refreshes" and "which makes vigorous."

Still other categories can be qualified by this epithet: e.g. the spirit or mind and its modalities in the person making the sacrifice. We find the expression *iṣiram manaḥ*, a phrase all the more striking because it corresponds exactly to the Greek *hieròn ménos*: *iṣirṇéa te manasā sutasya bhakṣīmahi* Rig Veda VIII, 48, 7, "May we partake of you, O soma, with an inspired, ardent spirit."[7]

From the morphological point of view the formation of *iṣira-* is clear. It is an adjective derived from *iṣayati* 'he makes lively, strong', a denominative verb from the feminine *iṣ-* 'a beverage used in offering which strengthens and refreshes'. Despite the difficulty of finding satisfactory equivalents, we may conclude that *iṣira-* had some general sense like "lively, vigorous, alert" when applied to gods. It quite frequently happens that similar notions develop into that of the "sacred." To cite only one example, the Irish *noib* '*sacer*, *sanctus*' from **noibo-*, is in ablaut relationship with **neibo-* which has yielded the substantive *nīab* 'vital force'.[8]

Such are the preliminary data provided by a comparative study for the examination of the word *hierós*. What is the meaning of *hierós*? If we take

---

6. A study by J. Duchesne-Guillemin, *Mélanges Boisacq*, I, 325ff. contributes some new points apropos of *iṣiraḥ* in relation to *hierós*; cf. L. Renou, *Etudes védiques et paninéennes*, IV, p. 40 and A. Pagliaro, *Saggi di critica semantica*, 1953. p. 89ff.

7. L. Renou, *Etudes Védiques*, IX, 1961, p. 69 translates: "D'une âme fervente nous souhaitons avoir part à toi, (soma) pressé" with a note justifying this rendering of *iṣira-*, p. 123.

8. This connection was established by Meillet, *Zeitschrift für celtische Philologie*, X, 309ff.

immediately the sense which is imposed by each passage we find such a diversity of meaning that some scholars have proposed distinguishing three different words *hierós* in Homer. In the epic language *hierós* is in fact applied to things and beings which do not appear to have anything to do with the sacred. This opinion is found in Boisacq's etymological dictionary: he lists *hierós* (1) meaning "holy," (2) meaning "strong" and (3) meaning "lively." Today this distinction is regarded as artificial, and everyone is agreed on the unity of the sense. But how has it evolved? As the point of departure the sense of "strong" is posited, then "filled with strength by some divine influence" and then, secondarily, "holy, sacred." Is it necessary to accept this evolutionary chain? It would be as well to make sure. Let us therefore undertake a review of the uses of the word.

In the first place *hierós* accompanies designations of cult such as *bōmós* 'altar', *hekatómbē* 'sacrifice'. It is also used with names of towns such as Troy, with place names such as citadel (*ptolíethron*, *Od.* 1,2), the walls of Troy (*krḗdemna*, *Il.* 16, 100), Thebes and its walls, Pergamum, Euboia, and the course of the Alpheus. We must conclude that *hierós* is an epithet of veneration.

Let us now look at some of the more peculiar combinations, which are also the most instructive. The judges sit *hierôi enì kúklōi*, *Il.* 18,504, "in the *hierós* circle." Even if they are not "sacred" in themselves, the judges are regarded as inspired by Zeus. When Hera, in a solemn oath, invokes the *hierḕ kephalḗ* of Zeus, which she calls to witness, the word can be interpreted immediately.

But why should a chariot be called *hierós* (*Il.* 17,464)? The passage must be read as a whole. The translation by "strong, powerful" is inappropriate. What is concerned is a chariot which was immobilized, since the horses refused to advance (cf. 441, 451, 456): then Zeus inspires the horses and impels them to take away the chariot of Automedon. This is why the chariot is called *hierós*. It is so in these particular circumstances; it is not the natural epithet for a chariot.

It is for the same reason, and here it is still clearer, that the scales in which Zeus weighs the chances of the two countries engaged in the struggle is called *hirá* (*Il.* 16, 658). The same epithet is bestowed on the threshing floor (*Il.* 5, 499), but here too the context is instructive: "Just as the wind carries the chaff about the *hieraí* threshing floors . . . when fair-haired Demeter separates the grain from the chaff . . ." It is the association of the threshing floor and the operation of winnowing with the divinity which protects them which here prompts the use of *hierós*.

What is the meaning of *hieròn êmar* in a formula which is often repeated: "When it was dawn and the sacred day" (*Il.* 8, 66); why "sacred"? Again the whole passage must be read. It is a significant day, the day when Zeus contemplates from the summit of Ida the preparations for the battle at the approaches to Troy, after he has forbidden the gods to intervene. In all the examples of *hieròn ễmar*, we find that it is in relation to some such circumstance.

Hierós is also the qualification of an army (*Od.* 24,81): is it a "sacred" or a "strong" army? Once again we examine the context: the subject is the honors rendered to Achilles: "we have put your bones with those of Patroclus and the *hierós* army has raised a great and noble mound," Here again what we have is a circumstantial, and not a natural epithet, one which qualifies the army as it performs the pious rite.

These uses are not prompted by an effort at variety but by the context in which they are embedded.

In *hierề elaíē* 'the *hierós* olive tree' (*Od.* 13, 372), we could easily have a traditional epithet for a tree which was consecrated by many legends. However, the context is not irrelevant: under this olive tree Athena and Odysseus are sitting and, apart from this particular circumstance, we do not find a repetition of this expression.

When a valley is qualified by *hierós* (*Od.* 10, 275), this is because we are near the abode of Circe where Odysseus meets with a god in disguise. If the epithet is applied to *Sunion*, to "the sacred cape of Athens" (*Od.* 3, 278), this is because it is already considered as such, since the temple of Athena is found there.

There remains a strange and unique use in which *hierós* is applied to a fish (*Il.* 16, 407): Patroclus lifts an enemy warrior with the point of his spear just like a man who sitting on a rock pulls a *hierós* fish out of the sea. A sacred fish? A lively fish? The adjective appears rather to mean "leaping, thrashing": it describes the movements of the fish struggling at the end of the line. This is only passage in which *hierós* preserves something of the meaning which comparison would lead us to posit.

The expression *hieròn ménos* with a personal name, e.g. *Od.* 8, 421 *hieròn ménos Alkinóoio*, is not more than a bit of padding, a metrical convenience. We could not read into it the value *hierós* once had when it was still in living use.

In this survey we do not think that any important use of *hierós* has been omitted, and everywhere, whether with names of places or rivers (the rivers are divine), with names of persons or objects, with names of divine or human things or names of elements, we have found the same value: everywhere *hierós* belongs to the domain of the "sacred," whether this quality is attached to the notion by a natural connection or is associated with it by circumstance. Without this meaning the term *tà hierá* would not have been used to denote the sacrificial act.

In geographical proximity to Greek, but outside Greek and even outside Indo-European itself, we find a series of words which are close in form to *hierós* and to the prototype which is reconstructed for it and also belong to the same semantic sphere. These are the adjectives which, in the Italic languages and in Etruscan, relate to the gods and to the divine.

Aesar is an Etrusco-Latin word cited by Suetonius to explain the name *Caesar*; he says that it is the Etruscan word meaning "god." We find it in various forms in some Italic languages which are Indo-European and which had close contacts with Etruscan, such as the Oscan *aisusis* '*sacrificiis*', the Volscian *esaristrom* '*sacrificium*', and the Umbrian *esono* '*divinus*' or '*sacrificalis*'.

On the other hand, in Etruscan itself, the adjective *aisuna, aisna, eisna* (according to place and date) means "divine" or has reference to the sacrifice. Obviously, this Italic root has a certain resemblance to that of *hierós* and *iṣiraḥ*, and some linguists have been inclined to interpret this as the proof of a (largely prehistoric) relationship between Etruscan and Indo-European. Kretschmer regarded it as a relic of a proto-Indo-European stratum in the Mediterranean basin.

Here, in connection with our limited theme, there is no call to discuss a thesis of such breadth. However, one difference between the two series of forms should be pointed out. The root **ais*- appears to mean "god,"[9] and this fact alone suggests that it can have nothing in common with that of *hierós* 'sacred' and Skt. *iṣiraḥ*, the primary sense of which is entirely different, as we have seen. There is no term for "god" which, whether in Greek or elsewhere, can be attached to the family of *hierós*. These are two distinct ideas. The adjective meaning "divine" in Greek is *theîos*, which is never confused with *hierós* 'sacred'; nor in Latin is *divinus* ever confused with *sacer*.

We are now in a position to discern that in Greek the "sacred" had a special value which did not coincide with that of the Latin *sacer*. The sense of *sacer* is brought out by its opposition to *profanus* 'outside the *fanum*'.[10] The domain

9. From the stem *aisar* we may derive the Celto-Germanic **isarno*- 'iron' (Germ. *Eisen*), which designates this metal as "divine" (see *Celtica* III, 1955, 279ff.).

10. On the sense of *profanus* and *profanare* see *Hommages à G. Dumézil* (Collection *Latomus*, 45, 1960, 468ff).

of the *sacer* is a domain separated by the very arrangement of the places. Making *sacer* consisted in making a kind of entrenchment, of putting something outside the human domain by attribution to the divine. In *hierós*, on the other hand, on the evidence of the Homeric examples analyzed above, we find a property, which is sometimes permanent and sometimes incidental, which can result from an infusion of the divine, from some divine circumstance or intervention.

In Greek we do not find this contamination with the "sacred" which is equivalent to a pollution and can expose the *sacer* man to death.

GREEK—*HÓSIOS, HOSÍĒ*

Very close in sense to *hierós* is the adjective *hósios*, which also related to the "sacred," but with quite different senses. The dictionary of Liddell and Scott states that *hósios* first means "hallowed, i.e. *sanctioned* or *allowed by the law of God or of nature*." "The sense of *hósios* often depends on its relation on the one hand to *díkaios* (sanctioned by *human* law), on the other to *hierós* (*sacred* to the gods)."

Here we have a term of paradoxical meaning. *Hósios* could thus be applied just as well to what is sacred as to what is profane. We can escape from this apparent contradiction by an exact delimitation of the field of application of this adjective: the term *hósios* is applied to what is prescribed and permitted by divine law, but with reference to human relations. Consequently, an expression like *díkaios kaì hósios, díkaia kaì hósia* signifies "what is fixed as a rule in human relations by men and by gods." The duties called *hósia*, like those designated by *díkaia*, are duties towards men; some are prescribed by a human law and others by a divine law.

We may now turn to the second series of uses of the expression *hierà kaì hósia*. Despite appearances, the sense of *hósios* does not change. The opposition bears on another point: on the one hand *tà hierá*, sacred things, what properly belongs to the gods, on the other *tà hósia*, what is permitted to men. The domain of *hierós*, reserved to the gods, is opposed to the domain of *hósios* which is conceded to man by the gods. Thus the proper sense of *hósios* always stays the same: what is prescribed or permitted to men by the gods. But this opposition of *hieros* 'forbidden to men', and *hósios* 'permitted to men' is later reduced to an opposition *hierós* 'sacred': *hósios* 'profane' which permits a usage such as the following: *kosmeîn tẽn pólin kaì toîs hieroîs kaì toîs hosíos* 'to adorn the city with both *sacred* and *profane* monuments' (Isocrates VII, 66).

This interpretation of *hósios* is imposed by an examination of the examples from the classical period, but it is also implicit in the oldest uses. However, the latter concern not the adjective *hósios*, but the Ionic substantive *hosíē*, which presents the word in the feminine form. In fact *hosíē* is the only form which occurs in Homer: twice in the *Odyssey* and five times in the Hymns. Each of these examples helps to determine the definition of *hósios*.

The two examples from the *Odyssey* consist of the negative formula *oukh' hosíē*: e.g. 16, 423 *oukh' hosíē kakà rháptein allḗloisin.* The sense is "It is not permitted by divine law to weave evil designs against one another." All the same, at the moment when the female slave is preparing to utter a cry of triumph over the slaughtered suitors, Odysseus reprimands her and commands her to observe discretion; it is wrong to show jubilation at the sight of slain men: "that is not permitted by divine law (*oukh' hosíē*)" (22, 412). Thus the term *hosíē* is applied to the law imposed on the society of men by the gods. The sense of *hosíē* thus conforms with what we have attributed to *hósios*: what is prescribed or permitted by the gods to men.

Apparently quite different are the five examples of *hosíē* in the Homeric Hymns. Here classical scholars regard *hosíē* as "the service or worship owed by man to God, rites, offerings, etc." This would be the exact opposite of what emerged everywhere else. We must check therefore to see if this sense is necessary here.

(1) Hermes, after having roasted two cows, "divides the flesh into twelve parts, which he distributes by lot, while giving to each the value of a perfect offering. Then the glorious Hermes felt a desire to partake of the sacred meats" (*Hymn to Hermes*, I, 130). The expression translated by the last two words is *hosíē kreáōn*, the literal meaning of which is "the *rite* of the flesh-offering" (Liddell-Scott). But what follows makes this translation suspect: "their sweet fragrance provoked him immortal though he was. But even so his valiant heart did not persuade him, despite his sore longing, to pass them down his sacred throat (*hierȇs katà deirȇs*)." Here the poet clearly contrasts *hosíē* with *hierós*. The young god feels the desire to make a *hosíē* of the meats, but it is impossible to "pass them down his sacred throat." The text leaves no room for doubt: a god cannot do something that is a *hosíē* because the operation so named would do violence to the quality of *hierós* which is inherent in his divine status. We must conclude from this that *hosíē* is the strict opposite of *hierós*. It does not mean "offering" or

"rite" but rather the contrary: *it is the act which makes the "sacred" accessible*, which transforms flesh consecrated to the gods into food which men may consume (but this is something which Hermes, being a god, cannot allow himself), in other words it is an act of deconsecration. In the context cited *hosíē kreáōn* is to be understood as "the deconsecrated consumption of the meats," and it cannot be understood in any other way. We find here in *hosíē* the same sense which has been posited for *hósios* 'granted by the gods to men', but adapted to the special circumstances of the offering of food.

(2) In line 173 of the same Hymn Hermes says to his mother: "As regards honor (*timḗ*), I want to enter into the same *hosíē* as Apollo. If my father (Zeus) does not grant me this, well, I shall try—and I can do it—and be the Prince of Brigands." Here too *hosíē* is translated as "sacred privilege, worship": "I will enter into (enjoyment of) the same *worship* as A." (Liddell-Scott). But this does not fit into the situation. We must recall how Hermes, while still an infant, became aware of his vocation. He is the son of Zeus and the nymph Maia. His mother lives a life of seclusion in a cave, avoiding the society of the Immortals (l. 5), to which evidently she is not admitted. Zeus comes to see her secretly at night, unknown to his wife Hera and the other gods. This semi-clandestine situation deprives Hermes of his divine privileges. Hermes revolts against this; he wants to be fully a god, and does not accept the situation in which he and his mother alone of the Immortals receive neither gifts nor food[11] and they squat in a dark cave instead of lording it in opulence like the other gods (ll. 167ff.). It is not "worship" that he desires but the enjoyment of the same honors (*timḗ*) and the same privileges in the way of food (*hosíē*) as Apollo. In this he will find the revenge of the base-born, the compensation for a life of humiliation and frustration. The choice of *timḗ* and *hosíē* for the good things he aspires to reveals the condition in which Hermes sees himself as compared with the other gods: inferior in privileges, reduced to the position of humans who consume the meat offered to the gods after it has been deconsecrated.

11. We adopt the reading *ápastoi* 'deprived of food' which is that of a number of manuscripts and which agrees with*adṓretoi* 'deprived of gifts', rejecting *álistoi* 'not prayed to', which is given by one manuscript and is a hapax. The whole Hymn shows Hermes as a claimant of material privileges; he is eager for roast meats, he steals cows, he threatens to plunder the rich treasury of Apollo (l. 178). He shows no interest in prayers.

(3) Hermes uses the word *hosíē* on another occasion in the flattering words which he addresses to Apollo: "You have a seat of honor among the Immortals, son of Zeus, you are valiant and strong, the wise Zeus holds you dear, this is only right, and has granted you wondrous gifts" (469ff.). The expression *ek pásēs hosíēs* "in all justice" (translated above as "as is only right") also defines this *hosíē* as a concession by a higher god to one who is necessarily his inferior in rank.

(4) Two other examples are found in the Hymns. One unfortunately occurs adjacent to a textual lacuna. Demeter, sorely afflicted by the death of her daughter, remains inconsolable. Her follower Metaneira offers her a cup of wine, which she refuses because wine is forbidden to her; she asks only for a certain beverage. The servant prepares it and offers it to her. Demeter accepts it *hosíēs héneken*, which has been translated "to found the rite" (*Hymn to Demeter*, 211). It would be better understood as "in conformity with what is permitted by divine law." The following line is missing.

(5) We find a last example in the *Hymn to Apollo*, l. 237: *hỗs hosíē egéneto* "the rites were established" (Liddell-Scott). Here, too, the translation must be revised. The subject is a custom practiced at Onchestos, in a sacred wood dedicated to Poseidon. A chariot is taken there harnessed to horses that the driver allows to proceed of their free will while he follows on foot. If the horses run away and break the chariot against the trees, he takes charge of the horses but leaves the chariot propped up (against the temple). The god is then invoked and the chariot is left in his care. Insofar as this old custom can be interpreted, the clause "thus in the beginning was the *hosíē*" refers to something permitted or granted by the god. We should compare a provision of the sacred law of Cyrene: *tỗn hiarỗn hosía pantí* 'everybody shall have free access (*hosía*) to the sacred places'. The *hosía* of Onchestos apparently consists in the fact that the driver is authorized to take away the horses while leaving only the chariot on the ground sacred to Poseidon.

Such seems to be the interpretation required by the Homeric examples of *hosíē*. It squares with the uses of the adjective *hósios*, which always has the meaning '"permitted by divine law (to men)." There was all the more need for reaching this precise definition from analysis of the texts because we have no etymology which could guide us in our search for the original sense.

GREEK—*HÁGIOS*

We now turn to *hágios*.[12] The family comprises a verb and two adjectives: *házomai*, *hágios*, and *hagnós*. These are the three terms which we must consider. There is a marked difference between the use of these terms as regards both style and date. The verb *házomai* is Homeric and remains poetical, whereas *hágios* is not and first appears in Ionic, in Herodotus. On the other hand, *hagnós*, an Homeric epithet, is primarily a poetical word.

The verb *házomai* in Homer is constructed like a verb of fearing: *házeto . . . mḕ Nuktì . . . apothúmia érdoi* 'he was afraid lest he should do things displeasing to Night' (*Il.* 14, 261). We may compare two successive passages, in one of which the verb of fearing is *deídō*: "Have confidence in me, do not fear (*mḗte … deídithi*) Ares" (*Il.* 5,827) and, a few lines further on, *házomai*: "do not fear (*mēd' házeo*) Ares" (l. 830).

It is also in this relation to a divinity that we must interpret the oldest example (*Il.* 1, 21). Chryses comes to beg the Atreidae to give back his daughter, and he offers them a ransom in exchange. He adjures them to "fear (*hazómenoi*)" Apollo, the son of Zeus. His intention is to evoke in them the respectful fear of the god. Similarly, it is said (*Od.* 9, 200) that the priest of Apollo, his son, and his wife were spared because of "respectful fear" (*hazómenoi*). The verb denotes the respect felt towards a god or a divine personage; but it is a negative respect which consists in not giving offense. As Williger has pointed out, there is a striking analogy between *házomai* and *sébomai* which is also to be observed in the parallelism of the derived adjectives *hagnós* and *semnós* (**seb-nos*).

To these examples from Homer it would be possible to add many others from tragedy which would confirm them. It seemed better to start with the verb to determine a first definition of the sense because the adjective *hagnós* by itself yields nothing of any great precision. It is used with names of goddesses, Artemis and Persephone, and once with *heortḗ* 'feast' (*Od.* 21, 258-59). In tragedy *hagnós* is applied to the domain of a god, and to the *áduton* 'shrine' of the god. It is also the epithet for the Earth (*hagnḕ ároura*, Aesch. *Septem*, 753), but in a bold metaphor where what is meant is the mother's womb. Everywhere *hagnós*

12. We have used the extremely detailed study by Williger, *Hagios. Untersuchungen zur Terminologie des Heiligen*, 1922. See also P. Chantraine and O. Masson, *Festschrift A. Debrunner*, 1954, pp. 85ff., who connect *hágios* with *ágos* 'pollution' and refer to the ambivalence of the "sacred."

evokes the idea of a "forbidden" territory or a place which is defended by respect for a god. From this comes the use in tragedy to denote a person who is "ritually pure, in a state required for a ceremony." This is a new sense, for *hagnós* is the quality not merely of a construction, a domain, a sacrificial animal, but also a pure virgin, and this accords with the sense of *házomai*.

There remains the third term, *hágios*. It is first found in Ionic prose, in Herodotus, as an epithet for a "temple" in general, but also of a particular temple, that of Heracles. It is not found in the tragedians. Aristophanes applies it to the mysteries. The historians, following Herodotus, make *hágios* the constant epithet of temples. In Pausanias *hágios* implies that the temple is defended against every kind of pollution by the threat of divine punishment. But Pausanias also imitates Herodotus. Finally, in Strabo *hágios* remains the frequent epithet of a place or an object considered sacred. Thus the uses are of great consistency, and they show that from the beginning it was differentiated from *hagnós*. We must now approach the difficult question of the etymology of *hágios* and *házomai*.

The traditional etymology connects *házomai* with Skt. *yaj-* 'sacrifice'. This is given in all the etymological dictionaries. It was however contested by Kretschmer and, more fully, by Meillet,[13] who proposed to connect it instead with the Latin *sacer*. If this were so, we should have a Greek stem **sag-* alternating with **sak-* of Latin *sacer*.

Even if we accepted the proposal to posit the double form **sak-/ *sag-*, it would be necessary to point out that the Greek word which corresponds in sense to *sacer* is not *hágios* but *hierós*. Thus *sacerdos* is equivalent to *hiereús*; *sacra via* to *hierà hodós*; *sacrilegus* (*sacrilegium*) to *hierósulos*; *Sacriportus* to *Hieròs Limḗn*. The facts of translation, whether from Latin into Greek or vice versa, attest the same sense: the expression *sacrosanctus* is rendered as *hieròs kaì ásulos*; corresponding to *sacer morbus* we have *hierà nósos*; *sacra . . . publica . . . et privata* is translated in Dionysius of Halicarnassus as *tà hierà . . . koinà . . . kaì ídia*; *os sacrum* corresponds to *hieròn ostéon* and *hieròn pneûma* to *sacer spiritus* (Seneca).

We thus encounter a major difficulty in establishing *hágios* as the correspondent of *sacer*. These convey two entirely different religious notions. The relationship between *hierós* and *hágios* in Greek seems to be roughly equivalent to that between *sacer* and *sanctus* in Latin. *Sacer* and *hierós* 'sacred' or

---

13. Kretschmer, *Glotta*, 10, 155ff.; Meillet, *Bull. de la Soc. de Linguistique de Paris*, 21, 126ff., and *Dict. Etym. de la langue latine* s.v. *sacer*, *sanctus*.

'divine', are used of a person or a thing consecrated to the gods, whereas *há-gios*, like *sanctus*, indicates that the object is defended against all violation, a negative concept, and not, positively, what it is charged with the divine presence, which is the specific sense of *hierós*.

This brings us back to the classical comparison of *hágios* with the Skt. *yaj-*. Phonetically there is no difficulty, the two forms going back to an ancient **yeg-*. But the sense calls for some comment. *Yaj-* in Vedic refers to the act of sacrifice, the operation whereby an element is transferred from the world of men to the world of the gods. In this way communication is established between the human and the divine world; it is by this act that the gods are fed. The very fact that the Sanskrit verb denotes a specific and positive act makes it very different in sense from the negative notion conveyed by the Greek *házomai*, which consists in the abstention from all intrusion, from all offence.

In fact the semantic gap is rather less than might appear. The Avestan correspondent of Skt. *yaj-*, *yaz-*, does not mean simply "to sacrifice" but "to revere the gods," which is also the meaning of OPers. *yad-*; it is applied to worship in general and not simply to sacrifice. Among the derivatives there is one of particular importance which in the Veda became a constant epithet of the gods and in the Avesta the name itself for "god": Skt. *yajata*, Av. *yazata*, literally "he who is worthy of worship." There are grounds for believing that Vedic has specialized in the ritual sense of "sacrifice" a verb of wider meaning, "*colere*" rather than "*sacrificare*." This may explain why *yaj-* is constructed with the name of the god in the accusative and the name of the offering in the instrumental: "to worship a god *with* something." If the verb meant "to sacrifice" we should rather expect the construction with the dative of the name of the deity.

If we now reread the speech of Chryses to Agamemnon (*Il.* I, 20-21): "release my daughter and accept the ransom, *thus giving evidence of your respect for Apollo* (*hazómenoin … Apóllōna*)," which would not be forcing the sense of the passage too much, this would not be so very different from the uses found in the Veda and Avesta. It is not a negative attitude which is required towards the god but a positive act of worship and reverence. Thus nothing compels us to abandon the traditional etymology, even if the sense is not as close as could be desired in view of the importance of the notion.

The review of these terms has brought out both their antiquity and the etymological disparity between them. Each of them has its own history and makes its own contribution to our knowledge. But we do not attain to a common term for the notion of the sacred.

Moreover, we establish that a number of languages possess two expressions, which are distinct in each language, which are complementary and reveal two aspects of the sacred. In Greek *hierós* and *hágios*, in Latin *sacer* and *sanctus*, in Avestan *spənta* and *yaoždāta*.[14]

But we are not in a position to construct a single model on the basis of these coupled terms. They function only within a given language, and the relations established between the members of the pairs are not on the same plane; or else the notions expressed are the same but the terms are different. In Av. *spənta* and Gr. *hierós*, under etymologically different expressions we can discern the same idea, that of a power which is full of ardor and swollen with fecundity. To this there corresponds in Gothic *hails*, the notion of integrity, of perfect accomplishment: a force which protects the object or being from all diminution and makes it invulnerable. Latin *sacer*, on the contrary, conveys simply a sense of something set apart and hedged round, an august and awful quality of divine origin, which separates it from all human relations.

There is a difference of quite another kind between the natural quality indicated by the Avestan *spənta* and the state of *yaoždāta*. In the neuter *yaoš*, bound up with the Iranian form of the Indo-European **dhē-*, we find the idea of rigid conformity to a norm: "to make suitable for a religious operation, to put an object in a position to satisfy all the rites." This is the result of an operation which confers ritual purity.

We have seen the etymological relationship between Latin *sacer* and *sanctus*, but the formation of *sanctus*, which is new, underlines the secondary character of this creation. It would seem that this Indo-European notion has undergone innovation in Latin, precisely because, in the Indo-European period, there was no single term denoting both aspects of the sacred. But even at that early date there existed the two notions which each language expressed in its own way.

Finally *hierós* and *hágios* show clearly the positive and negative aspects of the notion: on the one hand, what is animated by a sacred power and force; on the other hand, what is forbidden and placed out of bounds to human beings.

This is how these two qualities are distributed in the vocabulary of each language and illustrate the two aspects of the same notion: what is filled with divine power and what is forbidden to human contact.

---

14. For the interpretation of *yaoždā-*, see above in Book Five, Chapter Three.

BOOK VI, CHAPTER TWO

The Libation

Abstract. The liquid offering, such as is denoted in Greek by the verb *spéndō*, *spéndomai* and the noun *spondḗ*, is defined specifically as the "offering of security." Every enterprise that involves a risk, such as a voyage, a warlike expedition, but also a pact or a peace treaty, is thus preceded by a *spondḗ*. The notion of an insurance against risk, of a guarantee, is also basic to the sense, which is solely juridical, of the Latin *spondeo*. Here the liquid offering has disappeared, but its function persists: *filiam spondere* is to give one's daughter to wife (*sponsa*) by offering oneself as a guarantor of the union. As for*respondere*, this means "to reply that . . ." by "answering for . . ."

What is the "libation" which is defined once and for all by the correspondence of Gr. *leíbō* with Latin *lībō*, for it is neither*khoḗ* nor *spondḗ*? The group of Gr. *leíbō* expresses the notion of "oozing, trickling" and of "dripping": *leíbō* 'to sprinkle a few drops' is thus opposed to *khéo* 'to pour (in abundance)'. From a functional point of view, *loibḗ* seems to be in opposition to*spondḗ* in that it denotes an apotropaic rite as opposed to a propitiatory rite.

The baffling polysemy of Lat. *lībāre* 'to make a libation, to taste, sip, take a portion of, . . . wear away, impair', becomes intelligible if from the ancient sense "to pour a few drops" we posit the meaning "to deduct a very small part."

I. *SPONSIO*

A number of terms are associated with the "oath" and it seems logical to examine those which are attached to it by the nature of the institution. One rite accompanies the swearing of an oath or the conclusion of a pact: it is denoted by the Gr. *spéndō* 'to make a libation', Hittite *šipant* and *išpant*, i.e. *spand-*, of the same sense, and Latin *spondere*.

The three forms, which are evidently related, refer to notions which are not characterized in the same way. In Latin *sponderes* a legal term; in Hittite *spand-* designates a particular way of sacrificing; thus the idea of sacrifice is completely absent from the Latin word. The Greek *spéndō* associates the two meanings which Hittite and Latin give separately; it means both "to make a liquid offering" and "to conclude a pact." The nominal derivative *spondḗ*, with the *o*-grade of the root, means "liquid offering," but in the plural it means "agreement, truce, armistice." In Greek we can best see the connection with the oath, when a *spondḗ* accompanies the swearing of the oath. This association explains how the verb in Greek was specialized, both in the active and in the middle, in the sense "to conclude a pact." We may presume therefore that the primitive sense was that of a liquid offering which consecrated a pact.

Here we have a linguistic problem, for the fact that in both Greek and Latin *spend-* developed a political and juridical sense suggests that something prepared the way for this particular semantic development.

Now Greek *spéndō* is confined exclusively to the "libation," although there is nothing which enables us to circumscribe the meaning more closely. If the verb implied that the libation was always made on the occasion of some agreement, the specialization of the sense would be a matter of course. But often there is no obvious implication of such an association. In the *Odyssey* the libation can be carried out without any relation to a pact. The suitors make a libation in the evening and there is nothing to suggest that it had anything to do with a pact or any ritual act. On many occasions Odysseus and his companions pour libations without any kind of agreement being involved. In general the mention of a *spondḗ* is not followed by any collective covenant. And yet Herodotus already frequently uses *spéndomai* and *spondḗ* in the sense "to conclude peace." This contrast in usage is rather odd. The only way to solve the puzzle is to undertake a careful analysis of the oldest uses and, in the first place, the most significant Homeric examples.

In *Iliad* 2, 341; 4, 159 *spondaì ákrētoi* are mentioned in connection with the oath, while the parties to the proceedings grasp each other by the right hand.

This is certainly of a ceremonial character; now these are the only Homeric examples of *spondḗ* and the use of the term implies precisely the conclusion of a pact.

In several examples *spéndō* accompanies a speech. In *Il.* 16, 227 Achilles addresses *Zeùs Dōdōnaîos Pelasgikós*: he washes his hands, and utters a prayer while making a libation of wine and looking up to heaven. It should be noted that he asks Zeus for the safe return of the companion whom he is sending into battle.

In 24, 287 it is the eve of a dangerous enterprise: Priam is going to ask the Achaeans for the return of his dead son. On the advice of his wife, he then makes a libation; he presents himself before the gods and addresses Zeus. His wife previously says to him: "Ask Zeus to send a favorable sign in the shape of an eagle which will appear on our right hand so that you can go in full certainty; then I will not oppose your going." Then Priam in his turn says: "Grant me, O Zeus, the power to go to Achilles and give me a favorable sign in the form of an eagle which will show that I can go in all confidence among the Achaeans."

Thus the libation accompanies a prayer which aims at obtaining security. It is at the moment of beginning a dangerous enterprise for oneself or for others that a liquid offering is poured to Zeus, an offering which should guarantee the interested party that he will return safe and sound. A confirmation of this is found in Herodotus (VII, 54). Xerxes makes a libation at the moment of invading Greece and asks the god that no misfortune should prevent him from invading Europe as a whole and from reaching its furthest confines. The idea is to forearm oneself against a danger with the aid of the gods.

These are exactly the conditions we observe in Homer, *Od.* 18, 151. Odysseus, still in disguise, is among the suitors. He is offered dinner. He pours a libation, and since Odysseus has just been mentioned, he warns the suitors: "It will be a misfortune for the man who stands in Odysseus' way the day he returns; let us wish that this may happen to no one." He prepares himself for the decisive combat to regain his home.

The aim is always to protect the one who is engaged in a difficult enterprise. The context often illuminates the use: thus in *Od.* 3, 334, at the moment of undertaking or continuing a dangerous voyage by sea, a libation is poured to Poseidon.

In the episode of the oxen of the Sun (12, 363) the companions of Odysseus, who are famished, come upon a herd which is protected by an interdiction: no man may slay these oxen. Now they have cut the throat of one and have roasted it; but before eating the flesh they pour a libation, with water in default of wine. They know that they have committed sacrilege; they try to appease the interested god. Elsewhere this purpose is stated in express terms as when Pisistratus welcomes Telemachus to his feast together with Athena in disguise:

> Stranger, first pray to Poseidon, our king, for this is his festival at which you have just arrived. Pour libations; pray as is customary; afterwards you will give the cup to your friend so that he in his turn can offer some of this honey-sweet wine; he too must pray to the immortal gods, I think; have not all men the same need of the gods? (*Od.* 3, 43ff.)

There follows the prayer of Athena to Poseidon, listing the favors desired. The same procedure vis-à-vis Poseidon is followed at the time when the guests prepare to go to bed (ibid. 3, 333; cf. 18, 425, etc.).

When Pindar says figuratively: (*Olumpíōi*) *spéndein aoidaîs* (*Isthm.* 6,9) 'to make libations (to the Olympian) with songs', it should be noted that the *spondḗ* is directed towards Zeus the Savior, *Sōtêri Olumpíōi*: it is therefore made to assure the victory of a great champion who is facing an ordeal.

The same conditions are found throughout literature, whether in prose or verse. The Greeks pour a libation and say prayers to Poseidon the Savior at the time when, after the naval disaster of the Persians, they want to return to Artemisium with all speed (Herodotus VII, 192). In the *Orestes* of Euripides (l. 1688) Apollo promises to Helen that she will have splendid future honors among men and "she will always receive libations": she will share with the Dioscuri the function of protecting men from the perils of the sea, *naútais medéousa thalássēs*; it is to them that mariners return thanks when they escape from danger: henceforth Helen shall have this privilege which will bring her the *spondaí* of sailors.

It is therefore not probable that the verb *spéndō* in one passage of Herodotus has the sense of "to sprinkle" (IV, 187), as is generally supposed. The Libyans, says the historian, have a remedy when their children have convulsions: they save them by "sprinkling," (*epi*)-*speísantes*,[1] them with the urine of a ram. It is difficult to see why the verb in this one use should not have the sense which it shows in all the other examples. This could also quite well be a rite performed to save someone from danger. Herodotus did not have to use the verb *spéndō* if

1. The manuscripts give *speísantes* which Herwerden corrects into *epispeísantes*.

he wanted to say "sprinkle." More probably what we have here is a real "libation" performed to help the child through a difficult crisis.

In the Attic orators and in the subsequent history of the verb it no longer refers simply to a religious act but takes on a political significance. The middle *spéndomai* becomes the predominant form. If the active *spéndō* denotes the fact of using a libation to make the gods guarantors of something, the middle expresses the fact that the process affects the one who makes the libation or those between whom it is made. This is tantamount to saying "to take each other as mutual guarantors," whence "to enter into a mutual engagement." Herodotus thus could say: *triḗkonta étea eirḗnēn spéndesthai* 'to conclude a peace for thirty years' (VII, 148). This is a pact of mutual security which the contracting parties pledge themselves to respect: the sailor assures himself against the perils of the sea, and, in the case of a treaty, the parties assure themselves against the bad faith of the other, against possible violations. In the same way the Greeks could say *spéndesthai têi presbeíāi* 'to give an embassy an assurance of safe conduct' (Aeschines, *Against Ctesiphon* 63).

We can see how the political and legal sense develops from the religious sense. The play of the active and middle is also observable, but in a slightly different form, in the great law text of Gortyn (Crete), on the subject of the status of the woman: in the active *epispéndein* 'to guarantee money' to a woman; it is the father or the wife's brother who guarantees her this sum against the risks of a divorce or a repudiation; in the middle *epispéndesthai* has the sense "to accept a guarantee."

Many other texts could be found to support these indications. We have chosen those which bring out the proper sense of the verb and give an insight both into the religious sense and the political sense which is derived from it. Our conclusion will be that the etymological and religious sense of *spondḗ* is "an offering made to ensure security."

Now in the same line of development we encounter the Latin word *spondeo*. This verb was specialized in legal terminology with the sense "to act as a guarantor in a legal case, to give a personal pledge on someone's behalf, to post bail for." It has become fixed in the terminology of marriage; this is what is implicit in the terms *sponsus, sponsa* 'husband', 'wife'. We also know the formulas used in asking and giving in marriage. Plautus reproduces them (*Trinummus* 1157,1162): *sponden* (=*spondesne*) . . . *tuam gnatam uxorem mihi*? 'do you pledge your daughter to me as wife?' asks the suitor of the father of the girl. The latter replies: *spondeo* 'I do so pledge', and again: *filiam tuam sponden mihi uxorem dari?—spondeo*. Conversely, the father may ask of the young man "do you take this young woman in marriage?" and the reply is *spondeo*, "I pledge myself" (Aulus Gellius IV 4, 2). These notions continue in the legal developments of the *sponsio*. How does this specifically Roman idea fit in with what we have just learnt from a study of the Greek correspondents? The idea of a guarantee, a security is present in both languages. Just as in the Hellenic world the libation served to assure the security of the one who offered it, so in Rome security is involved, but it is of a legal kind which the *sponsor* guarantees in law. He is there to guarantee the judge, the opposing party, and the law against a possible loss: e.g. default by the defendant, etc. In marriage the *sponsio* is the security given by the father to the suitor, in respect of his daughter; it is what we still call an "engagement."

Along with *spondeo* we must consider *re-spondeo*. The proper sense of *respondeo* and its relation to *spondeo* emerge clearly from a dialogue in Plautus (*Captivi* 899). The parasite Ergasilus brings Hegion a piece of good news: his son, who has disappeared for a long time, is about to return. Hegion promises Ergasilus to feed him his whole life long, if what he says is true. And the latter pledges himself in his turn:

> . . . *sponden tu istud?—Spondeo.*
> *At ego tuum tibi advenisse filium respondeo.*

> "Is this a promise?"—"It is a promise."/ "And I for my part promise you back that your son has arrived."

This dialogue is constructed on a legal formula: a *sponsio* by one party and a *re-sponsio* by the other, forms of a guarantee which is henceforward mutual: "I guarantee you, in return, that your son has arrived."

This exchange of guarantees (cf. the French expression *répondre de* 'answer for . . .') gives rise to the sense, already well established in Latin, "to reply." *Respondeo*, *responsum* are used with reference to interpreters of the gods, priests, especially the *haruspices*, when in return for the offering a promise is given and security in return for a gift; this is the "response" of an oracle and a priest. This explains a legal use of the verb: *respondere de iure* 'to give a legal consultation'. The jurist with his competence guarantees the value of the opinion which he gives.

We may adduce a parallel expression from Germanic: OE *and-swaru* 'answer', with which we may compare Gothic *swaran* 'to swear, pronounce a solemn formula'; the Old English (and modern English) word is almost literally *re-spondere*.

In this way we can delimit, in the prehistory of Greek and Latin, the meaning of a highly important term of the religious vocabulary and the sense acquired by the root **spend-* vis-à-vis other verbs which denoted the offering in general.

In Latin a large part of the primitive meaning has disappeared, but the essential core remains, and this is what determines on the one hand the legal concept of the *sponsio* and on the other its connection with the Greek concept of *spondḗ*.

II. *LIBATIO*

In the vocabulary of religious institutions there is a verb meaning "to offer a libation." Like the Gr. *spéndō* and the Lat. *spondeo* it is confined to the two classical languages: Gr. *leíbō*, Lat. *lībō*.

The sense is perfectly clear, the uses constant, and the expressions themselves correspond exactly in Greek and Latin. The usual translation for the Greek verb *leíbein* is "to pour" in general, and, in Homer, exclusively of wine: *leíbein oînon*, cf. Latin *libare vinum*. Connected with the verb *leíbō* is the noun *loibḗ* 'libation', which stands in exactly the same relation to the verb as *spondḗ* does to *spéndō*.

The sense "to pour" is generally accepted because of certain non-religious uses: *dákrua leíbein* 'shed tears', an expression which is attested from Homer on, as well as *leíbein oînon Dií* 'to make a libation of wine to Zeus'.

But on closer examination the sense does not appear quite as simple as this. Difficulties are encountered in the interpretation of the rite designated by the verb. If *leíbein* simply meant "to pour," we should have to ask what is its relation to another verb which also has this meaning and also has a religious sense: *khéō*, with a corresponding noun *khoḗ*. We know the importance of this operation, especially in the funeral rite of pouring a *khoḗ* on the tomb. This verb **g'heu-* is one of the best established items of the Indo-European vocabulary. It is represented in Indo-Iranian by Skt. *hav-* (*ho-*) 'to make a liquid offering', a central rite in Vedic ritual; the neuter *hotra* is the name for this offering, and the agent noun *hotṛ-* designates the person who offers it. In Iranian the terms correspond exactly: *zav-* 'make an offering', *zaotar-* 'the person offering' *zaoθra-* 'the offering'. Armenian *jawnem* has the same meaning "make an offering, consecrate."

This same root **g'heu-*, with enlargement by a dental suffix, provides the Latin word *fundo* 'pour' and in Gothic *giutan*, German *giessen* 'pour'. To judge by the wide dialectal spread and the constancy of meaning, we should also attribute to the Greek *khéō* the primary sense "to pour." This means that *leíbō* cannot express the same idea, at least not in the same way and in the same circumstances.

Moreover Lat. *libare* has a number of other senses. It also means: to touch lightly; to taste (*libare* or *delibare* is used of bees gathering honey from flowers); to take a little from (a common use); to do harm to something (an object or a living creature). From among these different senses that we observe with the Latin *libare* it is difficult to see at first glance wherein its unity lies. But it is clear that they do not derive from the primary sense "to pour." The pre-Latin history of the word is less simple than it seems. This is true even if, with the German etymologist Walde, we posit two different roots, one meaning "to pour" and the other "to tear (out), remove." Without going so far, the recent etymological dictionaries underline the difficulty of positing a single meaning.

We must reconsider the comparison of the Greek and Latin uses, since there is no third language to which we can appeal in case of difficulty.

Besides *leíbō* there are in Greek some simple forms, used in a non-religious sense, the meaning of which is sufficiently clear to provide an assured basic meaning. This evidence has not been used.

First we have the root noun **lips*, gen. *libós*, acc. *líba* 'drop', the isolated case forms of a noun which has become obsolete:*mélitos líba* 'drop of honey' (Apollonius Rhodius); *eks ommátōn leíbousi líba* (Aeschylus *Eumenides* 54), with an etymological figure: the tear is conceived of as a drop. Then we have a derived noun in *-ad-*, *libás* 'dripping, pouring drop by drop', whence 'a spring', 'small stream', 'standing water that wells up'. From *libás* comes the diminutive *libádion* and a present tense *libázesthai* 'run out in drops, trickle'. Finally we have the adverb *leíbdēn* 'drop by drop'; and *leíbēthron* 'a water conduit'.

We are therefore in a position to give a closer definition of *leíbō*: *kómai leíbousi élaia* (Callimachus) 'the hair drips olive oil'; *aphròs perì stóma leíbetai* (Hesiod *Shield* 390) 'the foam falls drop by drop from his mouth'; *tḗkein kaì leíbein* (Plato *Republic* 411b) 'to melt and liquefy'.

We can now see that *leíbō* does not denote the continuous pouring of a liquid in large quantities, which is the precise sense of *khéō*. On the contrary, *leíbō* denotes "to pour out drop by drop"; a liquid *drips* from a container which can no longer hold it. The hidden spring does not "pour"; it allows the water to trickle out drop by drop. Similarly *dákrua leíbein* (frequent at the end of the verse in Homer) does not mean "to pour tears"; the tears escape "drop by drop." Thus there is no need of any kind of sense transference to understand the expressions we have cited. The sense is apparent in Homer himself in an example which has escaped attention: *Od.* 7, 107 . . . *othonéōn apoleíbetai hugròn élaion* (to prevent the fragile threads of a cloth from breaking oil is applied to them and) "from the linen cloth the oil drips."

In all the examples we have examined the sense of the verb is plain and obvious. It must also be applied to the religious expression *oînon leíbein*: here it means not "to pour" a wine that comes in large quantities from a cup but to allow the wine to drip.

The noun *loibḗ* must be interpreted in the same way. It figures only in the double expression: "to honor the god with the *loibḗ* and the *knísē*" (*Il.* 9, 500). *Knísē* denotes the fat which surrounds certain parts of the body of the victim as well as the burning of this fat and the odor which it gives off. The *loibḗ* will thus be the offering of the liquid, drop by drop.

The conclusion to be drawn from this evidence is that the operation denoted by *leíbein* was to pour, drop by drop. This is quite different from the lavish effusion (*khoaí*) made over tombs.

In Latin, if we only had the verb *libare*, it would not be easy to find the connection between the different senses which it presents. They are difficult to reconcile and they point in different directions. Fortunately there are two related forms which help to establish a connection with the Greek forms.

First we have the neuter substantive *libum* 'sacrificial cake offered on the occasion of certain anniversaries and in certain ritual ceremonies'. Ovid *Fasti* III, 761 shows how *libum* could be connected with *libare*, in the circumstances of an offering to the Father, to the god Liber who loves honey: *liboque infusa calenti . . . candida mella damus* 'we give (to the father who has given us honey) honey poured over the hot *libum*'. This is the point we must seize on: the cake called *libum* is offered soaked in honey. We can therefore define the *libum* in a more precise way: it is "a cake, in so far as it is soaked with a liquid (such as honey)."

This is confirmed by the nominal form *delibutus*, the verbal adjective from *delibuo* (which is not attested), which is preserved in certain old phrases: *delibuto capillo* 'with hair dripping with perfume'; *delibutus gaudio* (Terence *Phormio*, 856) 'inundated with joy', literally 'streaming with joy'. The basic sense is therefore "steeped in a liquid which drips."

If we keep within Latin and draw no conclusions for Latin on the basis of Greek, we find in this way a means of interpreting directly certain religious uses: *libare melle, vino* with a construction in the ablative, comparable to *facere vino, victima* 'to perform the rite *by means of* wine, a victim'. Finally, in *libare melle, vino,* we have the exact equivalent of the Greek *leíbein oînon.* The sense is "to make by means of wine, honey, a libation which consists in pouring out the liquid drop by drop."

Such is the point of departure for the strictly Latin history of the terms of this family. In order to follow the evolution in the various senses in which *libare* comes to be used, we must first establish correctly the primary meaning, which is not "to pour" but "to cause to drip," that is "to offer a small quantity of the liquid which is allowed to drip from its container."

This notion of the liquid offering, which was essential in the religious application of *libare, libatio,* etc., evolved in ordinary usage to that of "to take a small quantity of": in Lucretius *libare aequor* 'to take some sea water' or with a metaphorical turn of phrase, *delibata deum numina* 'divine power from which something has been taken away, which is diminished'. This is presumably the same as in the phrase *truncum delibare*: a yoke of oxen "tear away as they pass a part" of the bark of a tree. The verb can also be used with reference to food, according to a definition by a Latin grammarian: *libare est aliquid leviter contingere ut si quis invitatus ad convivium vel potum perexiguum quiddam de esca vel potione sumat* '*libare* is to touch something lightly, for example when someone who is invited to a meal or drinking party takes a small quantity of the food or drink'.

Such is the change which endowed *libare* with a new sense. At the beginning this meant to take a small quantity of a liquid offered to a divinity. Then it came to mean to take a portion (of food, for instance) and to "loot, plunder" just as the bees despoil the flowers.

The senses in which the Latin verb is used find their unity in relation to a primary sense which we can determine in Latin itself, in *libum* and *delibuo.* Now this is the same as that which emerges from the Greek uses of the corresponding verb. Thus an examination of the Latin evidence, after that provided by Greek, leads to precise results which bring the two traditions closer together.

A final point may be made even though it is not strictly linguistic. What was the purpose of the "libation"? What was the significance of this rite? This boils down to seeing in what circumstances *leíbein* is used. This verb does not alternate with *spéndein.* Let us consider in its context a Homeric use (*Il.* 7,

481). While the Achaeans were feasting in their camp, "Zeus pondered baneful designs against them and thundered dreadfully. Green fear seized them and they poured the wine from their cups upon the ground and no one dared to drink until he had poured a libation (*leîpsai*) to Zeus."

The intention is clear: before drinking, a few drops poured as a libation may appease the angry god. What is concerned here is not an agreement to be reached, as we have seen in the case of *spéndō*, but wrath, the effect of which it is hoped to avert. The same idea comes out, as it were in parody, in the episode where Odysseus outwits Polyphemus (*Od.* 9,349). The Cyclops has devoured two of Odysseus' companions; in order to disarm him Odysseus brings a skin of old wine: "Cyclops, drink this wine since you have partaken of human flesh, so that you may know the quality of the wine which our ship carried. I have brought you a *loibḗ* in case you should take pity and allow me to return to my home, but your fury knows no limits." Odysseus by this *loibḗ* is trying to appease the fury of Polyphemus, in much the same way as the Greeks, in the above passage, were trying to soothe the anger of Zeus. The word *loibḗ* has its authentic and apt use.

BOOK VI, CHAPTER THREE

The Sacrifice

Abstract. The absence of any common term to designate the "sacrifice" is contrasted, in the separate languages and often within one and the same language, by a great diversity of expressions corresponding to the various forms which the sacrificial act may take: libation (Skt. *juhoti*, Gr. *spéndō*), a solemn verbal undertaking (Lat. *voveo*, Gr. *eúkhomai*), a sumptuous banquet (*daps*), fumigation (Gr. *thúō*), a rite of illumination (Lat. *lustro*).

In so far as *hágios* may be related to Skt. *yaj*-, this implies a connection between the "sacrifice" and the notion of the "sacred." In Vedic *yaj*- is strictly "to sacrifice," but first (and this is implied by the construction of the verb, accusative of the name of the god and instrumental of the object sacrificed), it meant "to honor the god, to solicit his favor, to recognize his power by means of offerings" (see above).

With this we are introduced to the study of the positive acts and the ceremonies by which the sacred is defined and maintained: these are the offerings, which are certainly "sacrifices," means of making sacred, of transferring what is human to the divine.

These offerings take various forms and they are denoted by different terms according to whether they designate *things* or *prayers*. For the prayer is itself a kind of offering, and it acts by its effective power; in the shape of fixed formulas which accompany the rites it puts man and god in relationship to one another through the agency of the king or the priest.

The material offering may be solid or liquid: either a *libation* or what might be called "mactation." It appears that the most generally attested of all the terms referring to sacrifice is that which denotes the libation. It is derived from the root which is represented in Sanskrit by *hav-*, *juhoti* 'to offer sacrifice', *hotar-* 'sacrificial priest', *hotra-* 'sacrifice'. The corresponding Iranian form *zav-* also provides *zaotar* 'priest' and *zaoθra-* 'sacrifice'. Here we have terms of great importance each of which is the source of numerous and frequent derivatives.

The root is also attested in Armenian by *jawnem* 'offer, consecrate' with a religious application. Finally we have the Greek *khéō* 'to pour' discussed in the previous chapter. All these forms, as we have already said, go back to the Indo-European **g'heu-*, as do the present stems with enlargement, Latin *fundo*, Gothic *giutan*, 'to pour'. This root has, therefore, in the majority of the Indo-European languages taken on a religious sense which is also shown by certain derivatives of *khéō*.

With reference to the "libation," the proper sense of **g'heu-* is "to pour in the fire." In Vedic it is the liquid offering, consisting of melted butter, fat which feeds the fire and nourishes the divinity.

In this connection we may briefly recall what has been discussed above, namely a more limited correspondence which also concerns the "libation" with an interesting dialectal distribution: Gr. *spéndō*, *spondḗ*, 'libation', Latin *spondeo*, which preserves only the purpose of the act which the libation supports, namely the "engagement," Hittite *šipant-* (*išpant-*) 'offer a libation' (cf. Book Six, Chapter Two, of this work).

In the Latin terminology of the sacrifice there is one word which is confined to Latin but which may be the relic of a pre-dialectal form: this is the verb *mactare*, the most frequent sense of which in the classical period was "to sacrifice an animal." This cannot be separated from the nominal form *mactus*. This is known only in the vocative form *macte*, especially in the expression *macte* (*animo*) 'courage!', a sense which is difficult to fit in with the meaning of the verb *mactare*. The connection between these forms is so obscure that scholars have supposed that there are two verbs *mactare*, one meaning "to kill" and the other "to exalt" or something of the sort. This is an idea which is certainly to be rejected.

Mactare is to be regarded as the denominative verb from *mactus*, but the relation of meaning can only be elucidated by a close study of the uses. The Romans explained *mactus* as "*magis auctus*." The literal form of this proposal cannot of course be maintained but it may be right in its basic idea, namely that of an enhancement, a reinforcement of the god, achieved by means of the sacrifice which nourishes him. It is beyond doubt that this "popular etymology" affected the use of the word*macte*; *macte* (*animo*) 'be of good courage', where *macte* may be explained by the sense attributed to *mactus*. This adjective may simply be a verbal adjective **mag-to-* parallel with **mag-no-* (Lat. *magnus*). It would not be surprising if we had two forms of the verbal adjective, one in *-to-* and the other in *-no-*; this is the case with the root **plē-* from which we have both *plē-nus* and *-plē-tus*; one of these, the one in *-no-* indicates the natural state and the other in *-to-*, the state into which a thing has been changed. Thus the present denominative *mactare* would denote "to make big, to increase"; this is the operation which puts something in the state *mactus*. The oldest use *mactare deum extis* shows the name of the god in the accusative and the name of the sacrifice in the instrumental. It is, therefore, to make the god bigger, to exalt him, and at the same time to increase his strength by the offering. Then, by a change of construction analogous to that known from *sacrare*, the expression *mactare victimam* was coined "to offer a victim in sacrifice." By a further development we have *mactare* 'put to death, slaughter' which is preserved in the Spanish *matar* 'to kill'.

Each of these terms adds something to the idea of the sacrifice, of the offering, and the libation by the connection it establishes between the fundamental notion and the varied implications of the terms used.

Here is another example: Lat. *voveo*, *votum* certainly means "to vow, consecrate by a sacrifice," but the correspondents of the Latin verb throw more light on the original meaning. First we have the verbal adjective in Vedic *vāghat* 'making a vow of sacrifice' and 'sacrificing'; then Greek *eúkhomai*, *eukhḗ*. In these Greek words at first sight we seem to have a very different notion: "to pray," "to promise" and also "to boast," "to affirm in a solemn manner." Finally a fourth important term of the same series is the Avestan verbal form *aogədā* 'he said' (3rd pers. sing, of the preterite).

We thus have a great variety of senses, one which is very precise in the Latin *voveo* 'to vow' and rather vague in the Avestan *aogədā* 'he said'. Greek introduces a notion which is neither "to say" nor "to offer" nor "to sacrifice" but "to make a vow," "to make a public announcement of an obligation," "to affirm the quality of something" and consequently "to give oneself out as." It is a solemn declaration that one pledges something or pledges oneself to do or to be something. This delimitation of sense evokes another. The verbal form of the Avestan *aogədā* is more instructive than it appears. If we take note of its uses, we see that it appears in solemn circumstances, with reference to important persons and divinities. It is a declaration which has the appearance of a promise, an undertaking, and has its authority from those who enunciate it.

We thus see that the senses have an unequal distribution in the correspondences which comprise several forms from the same root. It is not a rare occurrence that the properly religious sense is established in only one language, while elsewhere the word becomes part of the common vocabulary, or else is specialized in a different way. This remark may be illustrated by a new example, a word which has a religious sense in only one language although it enters into the lexicon of several others. This is a name for the offering which is peculiar to Latin: *daps* or more commonly the plural *dapes*, which denotes the ritual meal offered after the sacrifice. This was a term which soon was drained of its religious sense and came to denote no more than "meal."

Here, too, although there are certain congeners, the sense to be deduced from the comparisons is still not clearly established. Along with *daps* we must list certain forms which deviate from it in meaning. Festus (P.F. 59, 21) defines *daps* as follows: "*Apud antiques dicebatur res divina, quae fiebat aut hiberna sementi, aut verna.*" The offering thus took place at sowing time either in the winter or the spring. Besides *daps* we have *dapatice*, adds Festus, the sense of which is "*magnifiée*"; *dapaticum negotium*, that is "*amplum ac magnificum.*" How can we reconcile the notion of "ample, magnificent, liberal" with that of "ritual meal"?

According to the dictionary of Ernout-Meillet the primary sense of *daps* was "sacrifice." This opinion is supported by Gaius *Inst.* 4, 28: *pecuniam acceptant in dapem, id est in sacrificium impendere* 'to spend money received for a *daps*, that is, for a sacrifice'. Hence comes the sense, according to E-M., "ritual meal which follows the sacrifice," then, in the secular sense "meal, food."

Outside Latin we have a group of words consisting of Armenian *tawn* 'feast', OIcel. *tafn* 'sacrificial animal', 'animal destined for sacrifice' and Greek *dapánē* 'expenditure', which is connected with *dáptō* 'to divide, rend'.

This correspondence leads on to another Latin word belonging to a family and a meaning which are apparently very different: this is *damnum* 'damage', an essential term in ancient Roman law. The form *damnum* goes back via an ancient **dap-nom* to the same type of formation as Gr. *dapánē* and presents the root with the same suffix *-n-*. But "meal," "offering," "expenditure," "damage" lack any obvious unity and even seem contradictory. Consequently the Latin etymological dictionary is hesitant about admitting a connection of *daps* with *damnum*.

In our opinion the formal resemblance is sufficiently precise to warrant a search for the conditions which will make a semantic equation possible. For this it will be necessary to delimit the senses. Why should *daps* be a "meal" in particular and not an offering or a sacrifice; why does the derivative, the adjective *dapaticus*, imply lavishness and sumptuousness? Finally, how can we justify a connection, which is suggested by the form, with *dapánē* and also with *damnum*?

In our opinion it would seem that *daps* is not properly an offering in general to the gods but the meal offered after a consecration, a lavish and sumptuous meal. We know this type of meal in very different societies in which the point is to make an ostentatious expenditure of money. It is a "sacrifice" in the sense in which the word is used today in a spirit of parsimony: to spend money as an ostentatious act without regard for what it costs and in the knowledge that it will never be seen again. It is this attitude which is properly signified by "expenditure," the money which is poured out for a "sacrifice" without reckoning on any return whatsoever. In much the same way in commerce the expression to sell "at a sacrificial price" is used.

Nor is it an accident that we say today (in French) "***offrir** un repas, un banquet*" just as "***offrir** un sacrifice*." *Daps* would thus be the feast dedicated in someone's honor without there being any benefit or return, and the sense of *dapaticus*, *dapatice* evokes the idea of profusion, of what one "sacrifices" to make a display of generosity in the treatment of a guest. The Latin *daps* and the Greek *dapánē* thus have in common the feature of a lavish expenditure on the occasion of a religious feast, of a "sacrifice." The notion of "expenditure" is by no means a simple one (cf. above on the "gift," in Book One, Chapter Five).

Given the clear connection of form between *dapánē* and *damnum*, it remains to see how the connection of sense can be explained. *Damnum* is primarily "expenditure," as emerges clearly from Plautus (*Miles* 699): a character complains of financial embarrassment brought on him by marriage, of the expenses occasioned by his wife, *haec atque eius modi damna*: these "expenses" which are really a "loss of money," a *damnum*. This sense persists in the adjective *damnosus*, which means nothing more than "extravagant"; and finally in *damnare* itself, again in Plautus. Here is one example of many (*Trinummus*, 829, a prayer to Neptune): "Haven't you heard it said that people say in your honor" *pauperibus te par cere solitum* 'that you have of the custom of sparing the poor but' *divites damnare atque domare* 'you hit the rich in their pocket? *Damnare* here must be understood as "to compel to spend," expenditure always being regarded as a "sacrifice" of money.

Here we have the origin of the sense of *damnum* as "damage": it is properly money given without any return. *Damnare* does not primarily mean to condemn in general, but to compel someone to spend money for nothing.

Daps, which has a religious sense, like the words connected with it in Armenian and Icelandic, throws light on the meaning of the terms related to it and also receives some illumination in return: it means "sacrifice" but also "a ceremony on the occasion of a festival." According to an ancient rite, after the conclusion of a ceremony, by way of pure ostentation, a meal was offered which involved a great deal of expense, which diminished the fortune of the person offering it but gave him the satisfaction of honoring his guests and being honored himself by his generosity.

In this way we can account for the relation between notions which became specialized either in law, like the Latin *damnum*, or in economic life, like the Gr. *dapánē*.

This review of the terms relating to sacrifice may also include the Greek *thúō* 'sacrifice', with the numerous derivatives made from it. Its origin is certain: *thúō* goes back to a present tense **dhu-yō* the root of which properly means "to produce smoke," and it is directly related to the Latin *suf-fiō* 'to expose to smoke, to fumigate'. A confirmation of the etymology is brought by a Greek derivative, the relation of which to **dhu-* is, however, not obvious: this is the word for "sulphur," the Homeric *théeion* or *theîon*, which naturally has nothing to do with the adjective *theîos* 'divine', as is clearly shown by the Homeric form. It is derived from the root by means of the suffix *-s* and goes back to an ancient form **dhwes-ion*, cf. the Lithuanian present stem *dvesiu* 'breath, pant'.

The word for "sacrifice" in Greek thus goes back to the idea of "fumigation," the fat which is burnt, the exhalation of the flesh which is roasted, the smoke which rises and ascends as an offering to the gods: a conception of which the Vedic and Homeric texts offer numerous examples.

If this etymology throws some light on the notion of "sacrifice" in Greek, it may also illuminate a family of Latin words which are probably related to it. Starting with a form with a suffix *-ro*, **dhwes-ro*, we get in Latin the stem *febro-*, *februum* and *februare*, together with the noun *februarius*. The whole group relates to "purification," a function which is illustrated by specific rites: *februarius*, the month of purifications, is the last month of the old Roman year.

This "purification" is etymologically a "fumigation," the intermediary being the Greek term for "sulphur," for sulphur was used to purify by fumigation.

The prehistory of these two important lexical groups may thus be illuminated by a comparison which strives after the highest degree of rigor. Nevertheless it must be insisted that certainty has not been reached. For the derivation of *febro-*, for instance, a Latin f- may have a number of origins, and the internal *-br-* could also be interpreted differently. Hence it cannot be proved that *febro-* may not have a different origin than **dhwes-ro-*. It is sufficient that this provides a probable explanation.

If we examine the terms which denote "purification" in Latin, we may single out another because it raises a problem which has been much discussed: this is *lustrum, lustrare.* This was the term given to a ceremony which every five years served to purify the people assembled on the Campus Martius and gave rise to solemn rites accompanied by a military review. Under *lustrum* we distinguish three lexical units: *lustrum*, a period of time, the five-year interval between successive performances of this ceremony; *lustrare* 'to review' (e.g. *perlustrare oculis* 'to survey an object', 'to allow one's eyes to rove over'); and *lustratio*, 'purification'.

There has been much discussion of the proper meaning, the etymological meaning, of these words. Two explanations have been advanced which we must briefly discuss. One suggests that *lustrum* has a connection with the root that means "to shine," that of *lux*, which produces the verb *illustrare* with the adjective *illustris*, which is probably a derivative of it. Now *lustrare* and *illustrare* cannot be dissociated, in point of form, nor associated in point of meaning. *Illustrare* can be explained directly from *lux* but does not show any of the technical senses of *lustrare*. Similarly the neuter *lustrum* could go back to **loukstrom*, just as *luna* does to **louksna*. But since for semantic reasons there appears to be no connection between *illustrare* and *lustrare*, efforts have been made to find a different explanation for *lustrum*. The proposal has been made to connect it with the root which means "to wash," *loúō* in Greek. But *lustrum* shows no trace of the proper sense of *loúō* 'to wash': to wash is not to purify, and the *lustrum* is not characterized by the kind of purification which is brought about by the use of water either in the form of aspersion or immersion. There is also a phonetic difficulty. If we trace the word back to the root of *loúō* we should posit an ancient **lowestrom* and this would give **lōstrum* as a regular development. In that case we should have to regard *lustrum* as a dialect form.

In default of a definitive explanation we may try to delimit the exact sense of the term.

The most explicit text is very short (Livy I, 44). It relates to the foundation of the ceremony of the *lustrum*, at the time of the first operation of the *census*. The rite is said to have been instituted on the occasion of the census proclaimed by Servius Tullius. After the census had been taken, Tullius commanded all the citizens to present themselves on the Campus Martius drawn up in their centuries:

Ibi instructum exercitum omnem suovetaurilibus lustravit, idque ***conditum lustrum*** *appellatum, quia is censendo finis/actus est*. 'Once all the troops had been lined up, he purified them by the *suovetaurilia*; and that was called the *conditum lustrum* because it was the end of the taking of the *census*.' *Conditum lustrum* is translated as the "conclusion of the *lustrum*." But the preceding sentence contains an indication which ought not to be neglected: "*edixit ut omnes cives Romani . . . in Campo Martio* ***prima luce*** *adessent*." The citizens had to present themselves *at dawn*, on the Campus Martius, formed up in centuries, both infantry and cavalry. It is, therefore, probable that *prima luce* was a ritual condition of the ceremony and not a fortuitous circumstance. We know how the *lustratio* was performed. The purifiers, priests or kings, made a circuit round the group of people or the building which was to be purified, always proceeding towards the right. Thus the purification occasioned a circumambulation: consequently *lustrare* denoted "to traverse, to review" as well as "to purify." If we could connect *lustrare* with the *prima luce* of the preceding sentence, an explanation would emerge: *lustrare* would be literally "to illuminate." The procession would then be the imitation of the sun which with its rays illuminates in a circular way. There would be a correspondence between the circumambulation of the priest and the circular motion of the star.

Such an explanation, which is the simplest from the etymological point of view, would be founded on the facts and would agree most simply with the tradition. Once the circumambulation was finished and all the people reviewed, the census was taken: *is censendo finis /actus est.*

BOOK VI, CHAPTER FOUR

The Vow

Abstract. The root of Gr. *eúkhesthai*, Latin *voveo*, recurs in Indo-Iranian. Latin *voveo*, *votum* means specifically "the vow," while Iran. *aog-* and Skt. *oh-* means "to pronounce solemnly or with pride"; but Homeric *eúkhesthai* is usually translated either as "to pray" or "to boast."

This polysemy becomes less surprising if we assign to the root **wegh*^{w}- the double meaning of "vow": a thing solemnly vowed, an assurance demanded in return for devotion. The first sense would be the source of Greek *eúkhesthai* in the sense "to boast," or rather "to give a solemn guarantee of the truth of what one asserts"; the second sense is the source of "to pray" or rather "to ask for divine protection by means of vows." This semantic unity also extends to *eûkhos*, *eukhōlḗ*, Homeric substantives derived from the root of *eúkhomai*. If *eûkhos* may, in a warrior context, mean "glory" or "victory," its meaning is nonetheless "vow" (in the sense of the favor granted by a god in return for a human *eúkhesthai*).

Thus **wegh*^{w}- denotes in the domain of speech what **spend-* does in the realm of act: a solemn pledge with the purpose of ensuring security, a real oath when a man's own person is pledged (*devotio*).

In our special study of the terminology of the oath in Greek we met with a number of terms which denoted the various modes of swearing it and others which described the rites involved, such as *spéndō*. There is another verb often associated with *spéndō*, whether on the occasion of an oath or in either circumstances: this is *eúkhesthai*, for instance in this command (Homer, *Iliad* 24, 287): *speîson … kaì eúkheo*. This association between the two verbs is thus an established fact.

There are numerous passages in which the two verbs occur together; evidently the two acts are linked. As in the case of *spéndō* we must undertake the task of determining the proper meaning of this verb by an examination of its uses and by comparison with other languages. The verb *eúkhesthai*, invariably in the middle, is found throughout Greek literature in two senses: (1) "to pray" and (2) "to boast, to brag." This double meaning is also found in the nominal derivatives, *eukhḗ* (once in Homer, *Od.* 10, 526), *eûkhos*, and *eukhōlḗ*, "prayer" and "boast."

These two senses were already recognized in antiquity but it is difficult to see how to interconnect them. One refers to a religious act and the other to an arrogant mode of speech. They seem to have nothing in common.

If we turn to the other languages we find that the root is attested in Indo-Iranian and Italic. In Sanskrit it appears in the form*oh-*, *ohati* 'to make an announcement in an oratorical way', and it is used in the religious vocabulary. Avestan has the corresponding form *aog-*, which simply means "to say, speak": e.g. Ahura Mazda "said" (*aogədā*) to Zarathuštra. There is nothing here which suggests the idea of "prayer." For this notion Avestan and Sanskrit have several other terms.

In Latin the corresponding verb is *voveo*, with the derivatives *votum*, *votivus* and *de-voveo*, *de-votio*. This time the sense is "to vow, consecrate to a god," but not "to pray." The same meaning must no doubt be attributed to the Umbrian term *vufru* '*votivus*'. We find therefore that in Italic at least this root was confined to the expression of "vow."

We may add an isolated form in Armenian, *gog*, 'said', from a verb which has not survived.

All these forms go back to the root **wegh* ^{w}-, but the meaning differs from one language to another and gives no hint how they can be brought under one head. The Latin sense "vow" is a special one, and this is unknown in Indo-Iranian. Greek, while it gives emphasis to the notion of "prayer," also uses the words with reference to "boasting," which is difficult to reconcile with the first sense.

Let us now try by analyzing the uses to establish the interconnections. One hint which we may use to detect the meaning of Gr. *eúkhesthai* is given in the fact that the verb is linked with *spéndein*. We may then use the proper meaning of *spéndein* to discover what intention is involved in the act denoted by *eúkhesthai*.

Let us consider a Homeric example: *Il.* 24, 287 . . . *speîson Diî patrì kaì eúkheo oíkad' hikésthai*. We might content ourselves with the translation "pour a libation to father Zeus and pray to him to come back to your native land." But it would be more precise to observe that here we have the expression of a wish addressed to Zeus and accompanying the *spondḗ*. Now, as we have seen, the *spondḗ* in Homer and in other ancient uses is an offering intended to guarantee security (cf. Book Six, Chapter Two). Here the act of *spéndein* is accompanied by a certain form of words indicated by *eúkhesthai*. The operation and the act of speech are complementary; they serve the same purpose. What is involved is an entreaty to Zeus for the favor of a safe return home in a case where the person making the offering of a *spondḗ*, Priam, is venturing among the enemy and is not certain of his return. One might therefore translate *eúkhesthai* by "express a vow."

But it should be realized that this term "vow" has an ambiguous meaning. There are two different senses, as we can see in the use of the Latin terms *votum, voveo*. On the one hand a vow is *made* to perform some action; on the other a vow is *expressed*. In the first case the vow is something that one binds oneself to perform; e.g. one makes a vow to build a temple; this is a promise made to a god. But at the same time the "vow" is the substance of what one hopes to gain from the god in return for what is promised; *hoc erat in votis*, says Horace, *Sat.* II, 6, 1, "This is what I wished for." Latin has two different expressions to make this distinction: *votum solvere* 'to discharge a vow'; the person who has made a vow to consecrate a statue to a divinity if he escapes the perils of war must discharge it; but we also have *voti potiri* 'to obtain one's vow' (in speaking of the man); that is "to obtain from the god the fulfillment of the wish which was formulated."

We must stress this double sense: sometimes the wish which the person making the vow asks the god to fulfill, at others what he promises the god to accomplish. We must keep these two senses in mind in interpreting the forms of other languages. We first turn to Indo-Iranian: *oh-* 'to pronounce' in Sanskrit and *aog-* in Avestan correspond not only in form but also in characteristic collocations: Rig Veda VIII, 5, 3: *vacām dūto yathohiṣe* 'The word I pronounce like a messenger'. Avesta *Yt* XIII, 90: *yō paoiryō vāčim aoχta* 'he who has first pronounced the word'.

What this verb expresses is more than a simple "enunciation"; it is a certain activity of the *hotar* (who is making the offering and announces the offering to the gods and invites them to partake of it), with the same connection between *oh-* and the offering as we have observed in Greek between *eúkhesthai* and *spéndein.* Furthermore, this Vedic verb *oh-* means "to boast, to take pride in something, to assert something with pride." This links up with one of the senses of the Greek verb.

Finally the nominal form *vāghat* is connected with the verb *oh-*, and this denotes the "person sacrificing," the one who organizes the sacrifice, who declares its consecration. He enunciates with authority (on the occasion of a sacrifice destined for the gods) what is expected from them *dūto yatha* 'like a messenger'.

In Iranian the verb *aog-* means "to say"; but it is not used with reference to just anyone; those concerned are the highest personalities, the gods, Zarathuštra their spokesman, whose words are introduced by *aog-*. They bring forth a decisive utterance, one which is pronounced with authority. The sense is rather wider in Avestan than in Vedic, but they have closely related meanings: "to announce with authority an utterance which binds, to give a solemn assurance (the sense of which is made precise in the course of the operation itself)." This permits the utterance of a vow on the occasion of an offering from which some return is hoped for.

If we now turn to Italic, we have to consider in Latin *voveo, votum* and in Umbrian *vufetes* '*votis* (*consecratis*)' and perhaps also *vufru*, which is translated as "*votivum*."

At first sight the precise sense of Latin *vovere* does not coincide with that of the Greek *eúkhesthai* 'to pray' nor with *eukhḗ* 'prayer'. They are, however, concerned with the same institution, the foundations of which must be laid bare. The only way we can do this is to give precision in both languages to the sense of the terms.

The sense of "to vow" in Latin may be illustrated from an episode of Roman history which highlights the notion of *vovere* (Livy VIII, 10, 11). The subject is Decius Mus, who in 340 BC "devoted" his own person to nether deities that they might grant victory to the Romans. This anticipated consecration of his own person to the nether deities is the pledge offered by Decius Mus in exchange for the support he expected from them.

An anticipatory offering, this act is founded on the principle of a constantly increased reciprocity which we know from other institutions. What one offers provokes a superior gift. Thus the person "vowed," although he still remains in the land of the living, is acquired in advance by the divinity: "to vow" is a consecration and one in the most stringent form. It is as well to recall that in Roman religious law the "vow" was the subject of strict rules. First there had to be a *nuncupatio*, the solemn enunciation of the vows for the "devotion" to be accepted by the representatives of the State and religion in the proper set terms. Then the vow had to be formulated, *votum concipere*, which meant conforming to a given model. This formula, in which the priest took the initiative, had to be repeated exactly by the person making the vow. Finally, it was necessary for the authorities to receive this vow, and to sanction it by an official authorization: this was *votum suscipere*. Once the vow was accepted, the moment came when the interested party had to put his promise into execution in return for what he had asked for: *votum solvere*. Finally, as with every operation of this kind, sanctions were provided in case that the obligation was not carried out. The man who did not fulfill what he had promised was *voti reus* and prosecuted as such and condemned: *voti damnatus*. These rules are fully in the spirit of Roman law.

If we now turn our attention to Greek, we see that in spite of the variety and richness of the testimony, the terms appear to be of quite a different character. The precise notion of the "vow" is foreign to them. We must take up the whole problem again and examine a large number of examples. The first question we must face is one which concerns the whole domain of *eûkhos* in the Homeric vocabulary. This is the two senses of *eúkhomai* 'to pray' and 'to boast'. If we look at the examples, which are of great number (the verb occurs more than a hundred times), it seems that the usual translation is inescapable. According to context *eúkhetai* means variously "he asserts emphatically (that he is braver, the son of so and so)" or "he prays."

The question is how a verb which preserved a religious sense throughout the history of Greek could also be used in Homer for "to assert emphatically." Could it perhaps be that the true sense is "to proclaim in a loud voice, to announce solemnly," as is stated in the etymological dictionaries? In this case the whole development to the special meaning of "vow" must have taken place in Latin. Thus we have no resource but to examine some characteristic examples of the verb and the noun in Homer.

In *Il.* 4, 101 the translation cannot give rise to any doubt: "Make a vow (*eúkheo*) to offer, on your return, a hecatomb to Apollo." This example will throw light on *eúkhomai* in other passages, where, according to the translations, we have to do with "prayer," but the act of "praying" occurs in the description of a ceremony. Such is the great prayer of the priest Chryses when his daughter has been given back to him and he consecrates a hecatomb round the altar:

> And Chryses, in a loud voice, prayed (*megál' eúkheto*) for them, with his hands stretched out to heaven: Listen to me, O God of the silver bow . . . you have just fulfilled my vows . . . this time too fulfill my wish and avert the plague from the Danaans. Thus he speaks making a *eukhḗ* (*eukhómenos*) and Phoebus heard him; and the others *eúksanto*, casting the barley grain before them. (*Il.* 1, 450ff.)

This whole scene is structured by the verb of "prayer," *eúkhesthai*. Formerly we have seen "you have heard me *euksámenos*" (453). We may introduce the essential notion by translating "you have formerly listened to *my vows*." The "prayer" is not distinguished from the "vow"; it is one and the same operation, for here the "prayer" announces a "vow" in favor of the Danaans and it is accompanied by a sacrifice. The god is bound by this consecration, which anticipates the support expected from him, along the lines of the request "avert this plague."

In a second example (*Il.* 2, 410ff.) the formulas are the same; the context deserves examination. Agamemnon is making a sacrifice: "When they had all surrounded the ox and taken the barley grains, king Agamemnon in their midst pronounced (*eúkhomenos metéphē*) the words 'O Zeus . . . do not allow the sun to set . . . until I have first overthrown . . . the palace of Priam . . > and until I have torn from his breast Hector's coat of mail and seen at his side a crowd of his followers fall with their brow in the dust . . .'" He speaks, but the son of Kronos "was not disposed to fulfill his vows . . ." The person making the offering consecrates the sacrifice to the divinity *on condition*: this is the vow which he announces, the object of his "prayer." This passage provides in a textual correlation the verb which indicates the vow (*eúkhomai*) and the verb which indicates the acceptance of the vow by the god (*epi-kraiaínō*).

Finally, as if there were a serial development, we find in *Il.* 6, 302ff. new facts which give further details of the development of the ceremony. The women go up to the temple of Athena: "all stretch out their arms to Athena with the ritual cry"; Theano takes the veil and puts it on the knees of the fair-haired Athena; then praying (*eukhoménē*) she addresses this vow to the daughter of Zeus. . . . The following details are given in succession: the veil which is deposited in the temple, then an invocation to Athena, with the arms stretched out to heaven, and finally the request: "break the spear of Diomedes and immediately in your temple we shall offer up to you twelve heifers one year old."

Here we have a complete "vow," including both the thing vowed and the form of words which vows it.

This complex is found in all the examples of the Homeric formula *hỗs éphat' eukhómenos*: an actual offering, which is anticipated, but always as a *quid pro quo* for something which is expected. Thus the sense "prayer" is too vague, and in all cases it should be defined more precisely as a "vow."

We now come to the second category of uses, where *eúkhomai* is constructed with an infinitive proposition or with a nominal predicate. "Agamemnon who today 'flatters himself' with being (*eúkhetai eînai*) far the foremost in this camp" (*Il.* 1, 91); "march to the battle and show what you have long 'flattered yourself' with being, *eúkheai eînai*" (4, 264).

We propose to explain this sense as a development of the religious use of which it is properly only a variety. It is the same mechanism as the declaration before the gods. This time the gods are committed to guaranteeing an affirmation of existence; in support of this affirmation the man's own person is, figuratively, what is offered: "I consecrate myself to the gods, as being the son of so and so, or, the bravest of all."

It is from this metaphorical consecration that the emphatic value of *eúkhomai* developed: *eúkhomai* remains a verb of commitment: "pledge myself that I am . . ." and, if it can be said, "I make a vow that I am (the bravest, or, the son of so and so)."

The consecration, in the religious sense, of the offering, which we have seen either actually performed (the first sense in Homer) or promised (the Latin sense), here supports the affirmation of existence, which is itself a consecration: there is a real "devotion" in support of an affirmation. An English parallel may be adduced: it is usual to say "I *promise you* (for "I assure you") that such and such is the case." This is a way of binding oneself to the truth of the proposition which is enunciated.

Only one variety of use seems to elude this explanation, because of its grammatical construction. It is represented by a single example, but it is one of great interest. Whereas *eúkhomai* is everywhere used with reference to the future or the present, in this example it looks as though it referred to the past. This is the oddity of a passage in the description of the shield (*Il.* 18, 499-500). A crowd is assembled on the square. "A dispute has arisen and two men are arguing about the '*wer-geld*' (*poinḗ*) for a man who has been killed. The one claims (*eúkheto*) that he has paid in full and he makes this declaration to the people; the other denies (*anaíneto*) having received anything. The people are divided into two camps. The heralds restrain the crowd; in a sacred enclosure the Elders are seated, etc." This translation of *eúkhesthai* and the interpretation of the scene seems to be generally accepted, but we do not believe that it is possible. The sense and interest of a scene described in these terms is incomprehensible. One party claims to have paid the *poinḗ* and the other denies having received it. But how could such a dispute rouse the passions of the crowd? Why should the Elders be assembled to decide a question of fact, if it were simply a case of verifying whether the payment had been made? What is the connection, therefore, between the *poinḗ* of a man who has been killed and this fierce debate? Still worse, we cannot see how such a debate could be translated into images, nor how the artist of the Shield would have represented what was at stake in such a quarrel.

The grammatical construction is also open to objection. Can one say *eúkheto apodoûnai* 'he claims *to have paid*', where the notion of priority is expressed by the simple aorist? Can one interpret *anaíneto helésthai* as "He denied having received anything," seeing that *anaínesthai* never means "to deny" but only and always "to refuse"?

Let us be guided by the second phrase: "the other *refuses* to receive anything." Then by induction we immediately apprehend the meaning of the first: "the one promises (binds himself) to pay the full sum, the other refuses to accept anything."

Now the scene has quite different implications. It is a very serious debate. A man who has committed manslaughter can redeem himself by a payment to the family of the victim; but this is a relaxation of the primitive rule of *lex talionis*, and according to ancient law the murderer had to pay for his crime with his own blood.

Here the murderer binds himself to make full payment but the opposing party refuses to accept any payment; this means that he is demanding the blood of the murderer and he has the strict law on his side. What is at stake is the life of the man who offers to pay this *poinḗ*. Now we can understand the passions of the crowd and why they are divided into two camps. The Council of Elders assembles, the heralds go round, etc. We can imagine what the artist could make of this; the offer of the one, the refusal of the other, before the corpse of the victim: the scene can be vividly imagined. Thus *eúkhesthai* does not mean here "to affirm that one has done something"; it does not refer to a past event but "to commit oneself to doing something, to make a vow with a divine sanction" as it does everywhere else.

This interpretation is not given in any translation or in any dictionary. It is simply alluded to as a possibility in the grammatical commentary of the edition of the *Iliad* by Leaf. In our opinion this interpretation is obviously right. We conclude that *eúkhomai* never involves a reference to the past nor to an accomplished fact but always to a present or future situation.

We now turn briefly to the substantive *eûkhos*. This is constant in Homer although later the feminine *eukhḗ* becomes predominant. We shall now consider *eûkhos* in its relation to *eukhōlḗ*. The usual translation of *eûkhos* is "victory, triumph." A number of different equivalents were accepted by the ancient Greek scholars: *eukhōlḗ* is glossed in Hesychius by *eukhḗ* (prayer), *kaúkhēsis* (boasting), *thusía* (sacrifice), *níkē* (victory), *térpsis* (pleasure), *khará* (joy). In its ordinary construction *eûkhos* is always the complement of a verb of giving: "to give, grant, refuse." Here is an example (*Il.* 5,285): "You are wounded right through the belly. I imagine you will not last very long; and you will give me great glory, *még' eûkhos*." Is *eûkhos* 'glory' or 'victory'? It is neither: in battle a warrior makes one "vow" and only one: that is to win a victory. For a warrior, to grant him his "vow" is to give him victory. The conditions of its use thus make plain the apparent change of sense. We may thus restore to *eûkhos* the meaning of "vow" and *eukhōlḗ* denotes, more concretely, the motive for the vowing, for the *devotio*.

In cult *eúkhesthai* indicates a promise to a god to consecrate something to him in return for a favor that is asked of him. Here the two senses divide: at some times it means to give a solemn assurance of an advantage promised to the god, *eúkhesthai hiereîon* (Lat. *vovere templum*), at others to announce expressly the favor expected, *eúkhesthai thánaton phugeîn*, to ask as a favor from the god, avoidance of death. The evolution of *eukhōlḗ* is parallel to that of the verb: it is an affirmation of truth, publicly and solemnly announced, in circumstances where it might pass for a boast; thus it may be an affirmation of being the bravest of all: *eukhōlḕ áriston eînai*, the emphatic affirmation of a superiority for which a man offers himself as a guarantee.

Thus the religious sense of *eúkhomai* is: "to pronounce some binding undertaking towards the god, a pledge which one hopes will be paid by a favor." There is nothing which justifies the translation "prayer"; this translation does not suit a single example, to say nothing of the examples as a whole.

To return finally to our point of departure, we can see how *eúkhesthai* consorts with *spéndein*: the "rite" and the "myth" are closely associated. The act of speech has the same significance as the act of offering: the two together accompany the taking of the oath which binds two peoples or two armies. The *spondḗ*, a rite of security, guarantees the contracting parties against a possible misfortune, against a violation of the given word; *eukhḗ* is the same action enunciated in words. It is a public declaration, solemn and even emphatic, which is appropriate to the circumstances since the two parties are swearing an oath. For the oath is a kind of *devotio*: as we have seen, the Greek *hórkos* signifies an act of self-consecration by anticipation to the power of an avenging deity if the given word is transgressed.

This consecration to a deity is proclaimed as an assured thing in exchange for an explicit favor: one so engaged is delivered in advance into the power of the divinity. Similarly, once the oath is formulated, the man taking it is by anticipation a "devoted" person. Everything fits together and it is no accident that in its fundamental uses (and here Homer is an important witness) these verbs are collocated together and recall each other. Through these turns of phrase we recover the traces of an institution which is really Indo-European and is common to a number of Indo-European societies.

BOOK VI, CHAPTER FIVE

Prayer and Supplication

Abstract. Apart from **prek-*, studied above, several terms meaning "to pray" have limited sets of correspondences within the Indo-European family. One dialect group consisting of Hittite, Slavic, Baltic, Armenian (and perhaps Germanic) present forms related to Hitt. *maltāi-* 'to pray'; another group, Iranian-Celtic-Greek, all present terms made from the root **gh*^{w} *edh-* 'to pray, desire'. Etymologists have been embarrassed by the divergence of sense between Greek *litḗ*, *líssomai* 'prayer, to pray' and Lat. *litare* 'to obtain a favorable omen, to appease the divinity'. However, the formal identity of the roots makes the equation irresistible. The difficulty is resolved if it is observed that the translation of *litḗ* in Homer is too vague; the terms means properly 'a prayer to obtain restitution, or an agreement on compensation' and as such is distinct from *eukhōlḗ* 'a prayer of "devotion"'. The etymological link between Gr. *litḗ* and Latin *litare* lies in their common denominator, the idea of propitiation. In Latin and Greek the words for "to supplicate," "suppliant" are made from a root of concrete meaning: it denotes the gesture which is characteristic of supplication. Lat. *supplex* means etymologically "bent at the feet of (sub)" from the root **plek-*; *supplicium*, which was doubtless originally the material offering of supplication, took the sense of "punishment, execution" when the offering of reparation consisted of corporal punishment. As for Gr. *hikétēs*, a number of Homeric examples (e.g. *Od.* 5, 445-450; 9, 266-260) make certain the connection with *hikánō* 'reach, touch'; the gesture of supplication in fact consists of touching the person who is supplicated.

All these ceremonies serve the purpose, by offerings and invocations, of bringing man and god into mutual relationships. But the act is opposed to, or is added to, the act of speech. The terms considered up till now have involved consideration of the "practical" part of this relationship between man and god. Everywhere "to sacrifice" is presented as "doing something," whether it is Lat. *sacrificare*, *sacrumfacere* and also, with the ablative, *tauro facere*, or Greek *rhézein*, or Indo-Iranian *kar-* 'to do'. But every religious "action" is accompanied by a "prayer." These are the two halves of the complete rite; the two ways of communicating with the divine world.

For "prayer" there are few words which are common to more than one language. One of these has been studied above; it comes from the root **prek-*, the derivatives of which are found in various departments of the vocabulary: Lat. *precor*, **prex*, *preces*. We allude to this only to recall the proper sense of *precor*, 'seek to obtain, to ask in appropriate terms for what is regarded as justified', a procedure which implies the use of words. The verb *precor* is often associated in ancient Roman formulas with *quaeso* (*quaero*), the combination indicating the wish to procure or to acquire something.

With the identification of the Hittite verb *maltāi-* 'to recite invocations, to pray', with its derivative the neuter noun *maldeššar* 'prayer, invocation',[1] an Indo-European term common to a number of languages came to light. This Hittite verb links up with forms previously known only from Baltic and Slavic, and this established a peculiar connection between dialects which otherwise have no special interconnections. Hittite *maltāi-* may be compared with Lithuanian *meldžiù melsti* 'to pray', *maldà* 'prayer'; OSl. *moljǫ* with the middle form *moliti* (*sę*) translating respectively *déomai*, *parakalô* of the Gospel and *proséukhomai*; Polish *modlić się* 'to pray', *modla* 'prayer', Czech *modla* 'idol, temple'. Baltic and Slavic thus attest the present tense **meld-yō*. With a phonetic difference in the final consonant of the root, we could also compare Armenian *maltᶜ em* 'I pray, I implore', where the *t* ᶜ goes back either to **t* or **th*. There would thus be an alternation *d*/*t*(*h*) which we should perhaps accept in view of the close semantic relation. The sense which appears everywhere of "to pray, recite a prayer, implore" reveals a group consisting of Hittite, Baltic, Slavic, and Armenian with perhaps the addition, though with a weakened sense, of the family of the German *melden*, OHG *meldōn*, *meldjan* 'to say, announce, report'.

1. *Bull, de la Soc. de Ling, de Paris*, 33, 1932, 133ff.

We have here one of the rare cases where Hittite provides evidence which is of immediate use for the reconstruction of an institutional term relating to religion.

Another lexical unit can be posited in the form **gh* ^{w} *edh-* with the sense 'to pray, desire'. It includes in Iranian the Old Persian *ǰadiya-*, Av. *ǰadya-* 'to ask by means of prayer (to the divinity)', Sogdian *ā-gad-ak* 'vow'; at the other end of the Indo-European world the Irish *guidim* 'ask, pray', *guide* 'prayer'. Between these two extremes we have the Greek forms which present two different forms: *pothéo* 'desire, miss' and *thêssasthai* 'to implore'.

Germanic has its own terminology for "prayer": Got. *bidjan* 'ask, pray', *bida* 'demand, prayer'. But the intra-Germanic relations as well as the relations of Germanic to the rest of Indo-European are complicated by the appearance of two groups, represented by German *bitten* and *beten.* Two etymological possibilities have been envisaged: (1) a connection with the family of Latin *fido*, Gr. *peithō* (see Book One, Chapter Eight) and (2) a root **bhedh-* 'to bend', this being prompted by comparison of Old Saxon *knio-beda* 'prayer (on one's knees)' with the Skt. *jñu-bādh-* 'one who bends the knees'.

The main problem in this field is presented by a nominal form peculiar to Greek, where "prayer" or "supplication" is expressed by *litḗ*, which is the basis of the denominative verb *líssomai* 'to pray, supplicate'. There is only one form which can be compared and this is very close, in fact virtually identical, and this is the Latin *litare.* But this verb has a very different sense: *litare* does not mean 'to supplicate' but 'to obtain a favorable omen', as a consequence of a sacrifice, this when speaking of the person making the offering, or 'to present a favorable omen' when speaking of the sacrificial animal. The sense of *litare* is extended to 'to propitiate a divinity', 'to obtain one's desire', 'to appease'. This semantic difference is enough to cause hesitation about equating the Greek and Latin forms. The Romans themselves felt that there was a relationship between the Latin and the Greek terms and some of them explained it by assuming borrowing from Greek: "*. . . alii ex Graeco, a precibus quas illi* λιτάς, *dicunt*" (Festus 103,13). This notice of Festus implies that *litare* is a denominative verb from **lita*, which was presumably taken over from Greek.

Opinions are still divided on this point: the dictionary of Ernout-Meillet envisages a borrowing but expresses doubt and says nothing about the meaning; J. B. Hofmann takes *litare* as a borrowing from Greek and explains the sense by supposing that *litare* first meant "to supplicate," whence, in connection with, and in opposition to *sacrificare*, it came to mean "to accomplish favorably an offering of supplication." But this is far from convincing.

We also think that *litare* is the denominative from **lita* and that this noun was borrowed from Greek *litḗ*. But the gap between Gr. *litḗ* 'prayer, supplication' and Lat. *litare* 'to obtain favorable omens' is insurmountable if we keep to the traditional translations. The problem is to give precision to the sense of Gr. *litḗ*, *líssomai*, for "supplicate" is too vague an equivalent. What was the purpose of this "supplication"? And from what attitude does it proceed?

In order to reach a closer definition of *litḗ* we must re-examine the celebrated passage of the *Iliad* (9, 500ff.) where, on the occasion of the embassy to Achilles, the "Prayers" (*Litai*) are invoked as divine persons. Phoenix implores Achilles to forget his wrath and to take up his arms again:

> You need not have a pitiless heart; the gods themselves can bend. And their merit, glory and strength is greater than yours. Yet men can sway them . . . by imploring them (*lissómenoi*), whenever one has transgressed and has done wrong. For there are the Prayers (*Litai*), the daughters of mighty Zeus. . . . They are mindful to follow after *Atē* (blind folly, delusion) . . . *Atē* is strong and fleet of foot and she far outruns them all and comes first in doing harm to men over the whole earth. But they (the Prayers) come after and heal the hurt. To the man who respects the daughters of Zeus when they approach him they bring much help and hearken to his vows. He who refuses them and roughly rejects them, they go to ask Zeus, son of Kronos, to attach *Atē* to him that he may suffer and pay the penalty.

From this passage two hints may be derived regarding the sense of *líssomai*. Men "supplicate" (*lissómenoi*) the gods when they have sinned by transgression or error (1. 501). This supplication (*litḗ*) has the purpose of obtaining pardon for a wrong done to the gods. We interpret in the same way the role of the Prayers. The point of the allegory is that the one who suffers from having sinned through blindness or distraction will be cured and achieve the fulfillment of his vows by means of Prayer (*Litḗ*). But if he rejects Prayer she will bring on him the punishment of Zeus. The purpose of a *litḗ* is to do reparation for an offence given to the gods—and not only to the gods. When Chryses presents himself with the fillets of Apollo on a scepter, in an elaborate and solemn approach, he supplicates (*elísseto*) all the Achaeans (*Il.* 1,15): "May the gods grant you to take the city of Priam and to return safe and sound to your homes; but for my part, may you also give me back my daughter and accept a ransom, showing thereby that you revere the son of Zeus, Apollo . . ." This is because the Achaeans have affronted the priest of Apollo and for this the god exacts payment. This *litḗ* of Chryses is a demand for reparation; see also Thetis when she supplicates (*lissoménē*) Zeus for the affront to her son Achilles (1, 502ff.). Another example is the supplications addressed to Meleager by the elders, by his parents, and by his wife to make him forget his anger (9, 553ff.); or Antilochus supplicating Menelaos to disarm his anger (23, 608ff). There are many other passages which lead to the same conception. Thus *litḗ* is very different from *eûkhos* or *eukhōlḗ*.

To sum up, the *litḗ* is a prayer to offer reparation to the person, god or man, who has been outraged, or with a view to obtaining from the god for oneself reparation for an outrage.

We now see that the relation between Latin *litare* and Greek *líssomai* can be restored. The intermediate form Latin **lītā* will have meant "prayer to offer reparation to a god whom one has offended," just like the Greek *litḗ*. In the denominative *litare*we shall see the idea "to make the god accept the offering of reparation," which in fact corresponds to the normal use of the word. The god signals his acceptance by a favorable sign, after an expiatory sacrifice (cf. Plautus *Poen.* 489; Livy 27, 23).

We always have the tendency to transpose into other languages the precise meanings which terms of the same general sense connote in our own language. To pray and to supplicate for us are words of almost identical meaning and differ only in emotional intensity. By translating them in this way we deprive the ancient terms of their specific value so that the difference which was originally proper to the words is blurred by a spurious uniformity. To correct these distorting translations we always need contact with, and the inspiration of, living usages.

The expression of supplication is different in the two classical languages, but more precise in the ancient world than it is today, because it was charged with a material sense which the terms no longer convey but which we can still bring to light.

The Latin verb *supplicare* 'to supplicate' is made from the adjective *supplex*, from which the substantive *supplicium* is derived, a word which has a curious development.[2]

For *supplex*, from *sub* + *plex*, there are two possible explanations. The first is the one given by the Romans themselves, who connected *-plex* with the verb

2. The Latin facts as a whole have been clarified in a study by Heinze, *Archiv für lateinische Lexicographie* XV, 89ff.

placare, which appears with tmesis in the phrase *sub vos placo*, in a Latin poet cited by Festus p. 309, for *vos supplicio*. But this runs into a phonetic difficulty: *plāco* has a long root vowel *a*, and this could not have yielded the short *a* implied by *-plex*. In fact, *plācō* is a causative verb with root lengthening from the verb expressing a state *plăceo*, 'I please', whence *plācō* 'I make pleasing', 'calm, appease, reconcile'. Nor could one posit a relation between *placeo* and *-plex* to bring the etymology into conformity with Roman *Sprachgefühl*.

The true explanation of *supplex* is provided by the series of adjectives in *-plex* with which it must be associated: *sim-plex*, *du-plex*, etc., corresponding to Greek *ha-ploûs*, *di-ploûs*, etc. We recognize in this *-plex* the nominal form of **plek-*, which is attested by *(im)plicare* and, with a present stem form with the suffix *-t-*, by *plecto*, *amplector*, etc. The idea is clearly "to fold or bend"; thus *simplex* is "what makes only one fold," *plecto* 'to fold' for the purpose of plaiting, rolling up, knotting together plaited threads; *amplector* literally "to curve oneself round," hence "to embrace." This same *-plex* is also found in *com-plex* 'plaited with', that is "closely bound up with"; such is the primary sense of *complex*. Later, in Christian Latin, *complex* is limited to the meaning "bound to an evil action," hence "accountable," "accomplice."

When it is integrated into this series of words, *supplex* is seen to be a term descriptive of the posture of the suppliant, "the one who is bent at the feet of, . . ." and the present *supplice* means "to adopt the posture of the suppliant."

With the substantive *supplicium* the perspective changes. From early Latin, from Plautus onwards, *supplicium* only means "punishment, execution." Between *supplicium* and *supplicare* there was already the difference of sense that is still found today between French *supplice* 'punishment' and *supplier* 'to supplicate'.

Supplicium has a very peculiar history the beginnings of which may be imagined as follows. We start with a literal sense "the fact of being *supplex,*" "to behave as a *supplex*," then "the proof of the state of *supplex*." From this *supplicium* was used to denote first the object, in practice an offering, by which the *supplex* manifests his submission to the god. With this initial sense of *supplicium* there went also that of *supplicare* 'to offer the god an oblation in order to appease him' and of *supplicatio* 'an offering, prayer or ceremony to appease the anger of a god'.

This enables us to see how *supplex* came to have connotations which are not revealed by its etymology and which are due to the particular circumstances of "supplication," that is the intention to appease the wrath of a divinity. Very early on, in conditions which we do not know precisely, all the terms of this family came to be restricted to the idea of appeasement of a divinity.

Later, in metaphorical uses, the terms were employed in the same sense for human relations: Plautus *Merc.* 991, *supplici sibi sumat quid volt ipse ob hanc iniuriam* 'let him take what he wants by way of *supplicium* because of this injury'. The person wronged "takes" (*sumat*!) a certain *supplicium*. This example explains why *supplicium* assumed the construction with *dare*, and *sumere*, which was to become the usual one, as in Terence *Heaut.* 138 . . . *illi de me supplicium dabo*. Here *de me* suggests that what he is offering is corporal punishment, a physical compensation inflicted on his own person. The construction of *supplicium* is, in fact, the same as with *poena* in the phrase *poenas dare*. In these conditions *supplicium* from now on acquired a specific sense; this is the "compensation" *par excellence* in circumstances where only personal chastisement is an adequate recompense for a wrong done; what is suffered is a "*supplice*," to use the French word derived from *supplicium*, meaning "severe corporal punishment, torture."

The conditions in which the word was used in religious contexts thus show how the legal sense came to be established. The *supplicium* becomes a mode of *placare*, of "appeasing," and this is how the gap in sense between *supplicium* and *supplicatio* came about. We see how particular conditions can break up a family of words and install some members in different semantic groups.

Having now briefly analyzed the Latin facts, we can turn to the Greek concept. This is expressed by the agent noun *hikétēs* 'suppliant'. Such is the classical form which has survived in the tradition, whereas the variants *híktōr*, *hiktḗr* are limited to tragedy. Its derivatives are the epithet *hiketḗrios* 'pertaining to the *hikétēs*', 'he who has the function of protecting the suppliant', and the denominative *hiketeúō* 'to be a *hikétēs*', the equivalent of the Latin *supplico*.

The noun *hikétēs* is derived from the verb *híkō* 'to come, arrive', which furnishes the present stems *hikánō*, *hiknéomai*. From a morphological point of view this derivation is regular; but these different present tenses convey no more than the simple notion of "arriving."

Is it possible to conceive of a relation between "to arrive" and so precise a notion as "suppliant"? One comparatist, Wilhelm Schulze,[3] suggested that *hikétēs* had nothing to do with these verbs, but should be connected with another root, *ik- (without an initial aspirate), that of the Gothic *aihtron* 'to beg,

3. *Quaestiones epicae*, 1892, 493.

beseech', which translates *aiteîsthai, proseúkhesthai.* This approximates to the sense of *hikétēs*, but at the price of a difficulty: Schulze had to suppose that the initial aspirate of *hikétēs* was due to a secondary connection with *híkō*. We should have to resign ourselves to this explanation only if there were no other possibility in Greek. Now the formal relation between *hikétēs* and *híkō* is as satisfying, both phonetically and morphologically, as one could wish; the external unity of the forms is evident. The problem is one of sense.

Híkō is everywhere translated as "to arrive": we have the Homeric cliché *dómon hikésthai* 'to arrive home'. But the most frequent use is not necessarily the most revealing. It may well be that the use which eventually became general for various reasons obliterated an essential element of the primary sense.

The verb in fact presents a variety of senses to which it is worth drawing attention. Thus in Homer (*Il.* 4, 303) we read: "Let no one go alone, in front of the others, to do battle with the Trojans. . . . But whoever from his own chariot reaches (*híkētai*) another chariot, let him thrust with his spear." Similarly, "the smoke of the sacrifice *reaches* (*hîke*) the sky" (1, 317); or again with *kléos* (cf. *Il.* 8, 192; *Od.* 9, 20), fame "reaches" the sky. Here is another thing which specifies *híkō*, as it does *hiknéomai* and *hikánō*: it can take as its subject a noun denoting some strong emotion like anger (*Il.* 9, 525), anguish (*ákhos*) (23, 47; 2, 171, etc.): the anguish "touches" the heart of the hero; a physical sensation, fatigue (13, 711) "attains" the knees.

Seen from this angle, the trite expression *dómon hikésthai* acquires its full force: "attain to, touch one's home (at the end of a movement or effort)."

Some examples imply a more precise notion: "This is why I now 'arrive' at your knees (*tà sà gounath' hikánomai*) to find out if you are disposed to give my son a shield and a helmet" (*Il.* 18,457). The verb certainly has the sense "to arrive, to reach," but at the same time it leads on to that of *hikétēs*: "I contact your knees in order to supplicate you." In a long passage of the *Odyssey* the notion that we have dissociated are clearly brought together. This is the prayer of Odysseus to the god of the river on the banks of which the storm has just cast him: "I come to (*hikáno*) you, sought with many prayers (*polúlliston*); and worthy of respect (*aidoîos*) also to the immortal gods is the man who arrives (*híkētai*) after long wandering, as I now do at your stream and your knees after much suffering." And the last line completes the relation between the verb *hikáno* and *hikétēs*: "Take pity on me, O Lord, I declare that I am your suppliant (*hikétēs*)" (*Od.* 5, 445).

It suffices to read this passage as a whole to grasp its clear implications. The concatenation of the terms itself shows how the two notions of *hikánō* and *hikétēs* were felt to be associated. The formation of *hikétēs* is regular: it is certainly the agent noun from *híkō*. In any case we are not forced to rely on a single example. Here is another which is equally clear (*Od.* 9, 267-9) "We finally reach your knees . . . but have respect for the gods. We are your *hikétai*."

We may conclude that *hikétēs* may after all be regarded as an agent noun from the root of which *híkō* is the thematic present.

One situational fact has prepared the way for this curious development. The meaning "suppliant" is explained by a custom of war known from the epic: a man who is hard pressed by the enemy and wishes to be spared must, in order to save his life, touch the knees of his adversary before the other in the heat of the battle can wound him. Thus, in *Iliad* 21, 65, Achilles lifts his long spear, intent on striking Lycaon, "but he stooped and darted underneath it and grasped his knees, crying 'I beseech you (*gounoûmai*), Achilles, have respect for me and have mercy on me. I am in the position of a *hikétēs* to you' . . ." Here we have the link of the verb *hikésthai* with *goúnata* 'to arrive at the knees of' which gave the agent noun the meaning of "suppliant."

BOOK VI, CHAPTER SIX

The Latin Vocabulary of Signs and Omens

Abstract. Latin is remarkable for the abundance of terms which in literary usage are employed indifferently to denote the divine sign, the omen. But etymology enables us to restore the preliterary distinctions between:

omen 'a veracious presage'.

monstrum 'a creature whose abnormality constitutes a warning' (*moneo* 'to warn').

ostentum 'a phenomenon which extends (**ten-*) opposite (*obs-*) the observer in his field of vision'.

portentum 'a vast perspective presented (*por-*) to one's gaze which reveals the future'.

prodigium 'an utterance invested with divine authority (*aio*, cf. *Aius*) pronounced in public (*prod-*) which functions as a presage'.

Our examination of the terms referring to signs and presages[1] will be confined to Latin for a very good reason: this is the relative abundance of these terms in Latin. In this respect Latin contrasts with Greek and still more with the other Indo-European languages. In Greek we find only *téras* 'divine sign, prodigy,

1. For a comprehensive view of the historical and religious problem see Raymond Bloch, *Les prodiges dans l'antiquité classique*, Paris, 1963, which also touches on (pp. 79-80, 84-5) the Latin terminology.

miracle', which has no clear etymology. The other languages have no specific term at all.

In Latin we have at our disposal a whole series of terms each with a precise sense and of clear formation. The chief ones are: *miraculum*, *omen*, *monstrum*, *ostentum*, *portentum*, *prodigium*. To match these six terms Greek can muster only *téras* and this has to cover the whole of the field divided up between the six Latin terms. We take no account of *sēmeîon*, *sêma*, the meaning of which is simply "sign" in general, corresponding to Latin *signum*, even when it is applied to a natural phenomenon.

The first task will be to delimit each of these terms in Latin itself, according to their precise sense. In general use they can admittedly be interchanged. On this subject Servius *ad Aen.* III, 366 writes: *confusa plerumque ponuntur* 'they are for the most part used without distinction'. Modern historians follow the same practice: in their works the terms are used haphazardly with reference to one and the same phenomenon. We leave it to philologists to pass judgment.

Our own purpose will be to assign to each its etymological meaning and to see what can be learned from it, even if the Romans themselves had no very clear idea what the differences were. They are all of Latin morphology, and that means of secondary lexical creation, except for *ōmen*.

The formation of *ōmen* presents the difficulty that if the suffix *–men* is stripped off, this leaves us with the vowel *ō-* as the root. This naturally leaves open a number of possible etymological connections, and these have in fact been explored by etymologists without any certain proof being established. There is however a connection which enables us to explain both the sense and the formation of *ōmen*. The Latin root *ō-* can be directly compared with the Hittite verbal stem *hā-* 'to believe, to regard as true'. Consequently *ōmen* will be interpreted as 'declaration of truth'. A chance word, pronounced in a decisive circumstance, may be accepted as an *ōmen*, as a true presage, as a sign of destiny. This will be a word of good "augury," one that announces fate.[2] Several examples are quoted by Cicero, *De divinatione* I, ch. 46.

The neuter *monstrum* clearly connects up with the present *monstrare*, but there is a marked difference of sense. We cannot decide *a priori* which sense comes first. However, it is probable that *monstrare* is the denominative of *monstrum*, for a morphological reason, namely the nominal formation in *-strum*. But from the time of the earliest texts, the two terms have nothing in common:

2. See our book *Hittite et indo-européen*, 1962, 10ff.

monstrare means more or less "to show"; *monstrum* denotes "something which is out of the ordinary" and sometimes "something hideous, which violates in a repulsive way the order of nature, a monster": e.g. Virgil's *monstrum horrendum*.

The Romans were aware of the formation of the word: *monstrum*, they said, stands for *monestrum* from *moneo*. Whether *monestrum* ever existed or not, it is certain that *monstrum* and *monstrare* are connected with *moneo*. If we start with *moneo*, what would *monstrum* mean? To find the connection we could have recourse to the denominative *monstrare* which has not been diverted from its proper sense by religious considerations. It is generally translated as "to show," but that is only a rough equivalent. Moreover, there is another verb which is commoner in the sense "to show": *ostendo*. The difference is this: *monstrare* means not so much "to show" an object as "to teach a way of behaving, to prescribe the way to be followed" as a preceptor does: *qui tibi nequiquam saepe monstravi bene* 'I who have often, to no purpose, given you good lessons' (Plautus *Bacch.* 133); *quotiens monstravi tibi . . .* 'how often have I advised you to . . .' (*Men.* 788); *non periclumst ne quid recte monstres . . .* 'there is no danger of your not giving good advice' (*Pseud.* 289). If then we may work back from *monstrare* to *monstrum*, to find the original sense, we see that *monstrum* must be understood as "a piece of advice," "a warning" given by the gods. Now the gods express themselves by prodigies, signs which confuse human understanding. A divine "warning" may take the aspect of a supernatural object or being; as Festus says "the term *monstra* is applied to what goes beyond the natural world, a serpent with feet, a bird with four wings, a man with two heads." It is only the divine power which can manifest its "warning" in this way. This is why *monstrum* ceased to have its original meaning. There was nothing in the form of *monstrum* which suggested anything "monstrous" except the fact that in the doctrine of presages a "monster" represented a divine instruction, a "warning."

This first delimitation of sense may help us in its turn to distinguish *monstrum* from *ostentum* and *portentum* since the notion of "showing" still survives, in a vague way, in the last two terms. There is no clear distinction in the use of *ostentum* and *portentum*. The same facts may be designated indifferently by one or the other term, whether they refer to favorable or unfavorable events. Let us consider the two present tenses *ostendo* and *portendo*. Their frequency of use is quite different: *ostendo* is widely used, whereas *portendo* is restricted to the vocabulary of presages, just like *portentum*, while the gap between *ostendo* and *ostentum* is like that between *monstrare* and *monstrum*, though less marked.

The simple verb *tendo* 'to stretch', related to Indo-Iranian *tan-*, Gr. *teínō*, goes back to an Indo-European root **ten-* 'to stretch'. Its use in so specific a meaning is given precision by the use of the preverb: *ob-/obs-* generally indicates that the action is carried out "towards something, in the opposite direction so as to block the way" (cf. *obviam*). The prefix still has its full force in an ancient example such as that of Cato in his treatise on agriculture: *ager qui soli ostentus erit* 'a field which is exposed to the sun'. The literal sense of *ostentus* here is "stretched out towards." This provides a good explanation of the literal sense of *ostendo* and of the religious use which covers only a part of its semantic range: an *ostentum*, as a presage, will have been something "stretched out towards, offered to the eyes," not something merely "shown" but "presented to view" (as a sign which must be interpreted). Tacitus in writing of a presage, associates *obtendo* and *ostentum* (*Hist*. 3, 56).

We now consider *portendo*; what is essential here is the prefix *por-*, only a few examples of which occur, but they are all instructive: *porrigo* 'to stretch out, offer', *polluo* 'pollute', *polliceo*(*r*) 'promise'; *polluceo* and *porricio*, two verbs relating to offerings. Such, with *portendo*, are the examples of the prefix *por-*, and remarkably enough, they all belong to the sphere of religion. The only exception, at least in its usual sense, is *polliceo*(*r*): *liceo* means "to be put up for bidding," *liceor* 'to acquire by bidding'. Thus the preverb *por-* gives to *polliceor* the etymological meaning of "to make a higher bid at a sale, to offer more than the price asked for" (cf. Plautus *Mercator* 439), whence the ordinary meaning "to promise."

In the dictionaries *por-* is given much the same sense as *pro-* and *prae-*, because of their common origin. But these preverbs are not synonymous, since they have distinct Latin forms and they cannot be freely interchanged. We may, therefore, suppose that *pro-*, *prae-* and *por-* each has some distinctive traits of its own which delimit them. The difference between *pro-* and *prae-* has already been the subject of a detailed study.[3] It now remains to try and define *por-* in its turn.

It can already be seen in *porrigo*, the proper sense of which is "to extend lengthways, to develop, to prolong." The preverb *por-* implies the idea of "to draw out, spread out to its whole extent." If *porricio* (from **por-iacio*) has

3. "Le système sublogique des prépositions en latin," *Travaux du Cercle linguistique de Copenhague*, V, 1949, 177–185 = *Problèmes de linguistique générale*, Paris, 1966, 132–139.

acquired the sense of a verb of offering, this is because "to throw" (*iacio*) has been further defined by the preverb *por-* 'over the whole width (of the altar)'. This is what was done with the entrails of the victim (*exta*), which were spread out (*porricere*) on the altar: *si sacruficem summo Iovi atque in manibus exta teneam ut poriciam* . . . 'Even if I were sacrificing and I held the entrails in my hands to arrange them on the altar . . .' (Plautus *Pseud.* 265); *inter caesa et porrecta*, a phrase meaning "between the cutting and the arranging on the altar" that is "at the last moment" (Cic. *Att.* 5, 18, 1). The same idea emerges from *polluceo*, a verb of the ancient religious language, "to offer a rich feast by way of sacrifice" (with *daps*, Cato *Agr.* 132), and also "to serve up at table the remains of the sacrifice." There is no example of this verb *luceo*, but the prefix *por-* clearly indicates that the dishes are placed over the whole width of the altar or the host's table. This is why *pollucere*, *polluctura* always evoke the idea of a sumptuous feast. This is doubtless the same image that we must see in the preverb of *polluo* (we do not know the verb **luo*, but only the derivative *lutum* 'mud'), which means more or less "soil completely, to pollute."

The special sense of *portendo* among the other verbs denoting presages and in particular what distinguished it from *ostendo* now emerges. *Portendere*, *portentum* were terms denoting a series of presages which were spread over a period of time. This is what emerges from the following examples all taken from Livy: *dii immortales* . . . *auguriis auspiciisque et pernocturnes etiam visus omnia laeta ac prospera portendunt* 'the immortal gods, by auguries and auspices and by nocturnal visions announce to us that all will turn out well' (26,41,18); *ominatur, quibus quondam auspiciis patres eorum ad Aegates pugnaverint insulas, ea illis exeuntibus in aciem portendisse deos* 'he prognosticates by way of omen that the gods have portended the same auspices at the moment of battle as they gave to our forefathers when they fought at the Aegatian islands' (30, 32, 9); *di immortales mihi sacrificanti precantique ut hoc bellum mihi, senatui vobisque feliciter eveniret, laeta omnia prosperaque portendere* 'the immortal gods, when I was sacrificing and praying that this war would have a successful outcome for me, for the senate and for you, gave portents that all would be favorable and successful' (31, 7). Let us note this formula of the augural language: "*omnia laeta prosperaque portendere.*" The examples of *portenta* in fact announce what is tantamount to a whole survey; *portentum*, as distinguished from *ostentum*, prognosticates not a single event but a whole panorama and a continuous prospect, revealing a large part of the future.

The term *prodigium* is easier to study in the sense that it can be analyzed in Latin itself, but it is more difficult in that the formal components themselves require interpretation.

The word can be analyzed into the components **prod-* (a doublet of *pro-* before a vowel) and *-agium*, a nominal derivative from *ag-*. But which root *ag-* is concerned here? All are agreed in eliminating the root *ag-* 'drive' and favor *ag-* which appears in the noun *adagio* with its doublet *adagium* 'adage, proverb'. Its formation in Latin must be of recent date since the internal *-a-* has been preserved as contrasted with the treatment in *prodigium*. Thus both *prodigium* and *adagium* are connected with the root of the Latin verb *aio* 'to say'.

Given this derivation, how are we to interpret literally *prodigium*? It must be conceded that this root **ag-* has no certain representatives outside Latin. Greek *ê* 'said he' is explained as coming from **ēg-t*, but the reconstruction of a root which presents itself as a simple vowel leaves room for much uncertainty. One possible congener is the Armenian *aṙ-ac* 'a proverbial saying', but Meillet himself, who proposed it, insists on the phonetic irregularity of *-ac* as contrasted with the verb *asem* 'I say'.

According to the Latin glossators, *adagium* (*adagio*) corresponds in sense to the Greek *prooímion* 'introduction, prelude, preamble'. This is difficult to check in the absence of literary examples. It is only attested in Varro in the phrase *vetus adagio est*.

The change of *adagio* to *adagium* seems to be due to the analogy of *proverbium*, which is synonymous with *adagium*. But this sense does not agree with that of the Greek *prooímion* 'prelude', whether musical or oratorical (exordium); it occurs in the figurative sense in tragedy as "prelude" to an event: *phroímia pónōn* 'a prelude to sufferings' (Aeschylus), what announces them. We should then have to interpret *adagio* as a proverb which is quoted by way of introduction, to set the tone for the speech. But this remains uncertain.

Let us now consider the relation of *prodigium* to *aio*. The dictionaries give only the sense "say" to *aio*. Our task must be to specify *aio* and to distinguish it from other verbs meaning "to say." We may note a curious observation of Donatus: *aio* is applied to *invisa*, *vana*, *contemnenda*, *falsa*, to unpleasant, vain, contemptible, and false things.

Let us now run through the chief uses of the verb. One of the functions of *aio* is as the opposite of *nego*, "to say yes" as opposed "to say no." Also frequent is the use of the expression *ut aiunt* 'as they say', whether to refer to a rumor, a report, or to introduce a colloquial or vulgar saying, or to introduce the actual words used as in *ut ait Cicero*. Further, *ait* is inserted in reporting verbatim statement.

In the legal language *aio* often occurs in the first person in set phrases. According to Gaius, the formula used in making a claim of possession was: *hunc ego hominem ex iure Quiritium meum esse aio* 'I declare that this man is mine according to the law of the Quirites'. This formula is reproduced on a number of occasions in Plautus as well as in Cicero (with variants such as *fundum* instead of *hominem*) when two men claim possession of the same thing: *et ego idem esse aio meum*. The subject of *aio* may be the law itself: *uti lex ait* 'as the law says' or in Ulpian *lex Iulia ait* or *uti mos ait*.

Here we have, grouped under a general meaning which seems to be adequate, the main categories of the use of *aio*. Besides this, we have a derivative from the verb in the shape of a noun *Aius*, which is used as the name of a god. This god is familiar to us, either under the name *Aius* or *Aius Locutius*, as the god who in the silence of the night announced to the Romans the arrival of the Gauls. Varro tells us the reason for so naming him: *Aius deus appellatus araque ei statuta quod eo in loco divinitus vox edita est* 'the god Aius was so called and an altar erected to him because on this spot a voice coming from a divinity was heard' (Cf. Livy 5, 50 and 52).

Now that we have seen the characteristic functions of the verb *aio*, and taken into account the nominal derivative *Aius*, which is explained by Locutius, we may say that *aio* refers primarily to the verbatim quotation of an utterance and that this quotation carries a certain authority.

That *aio* implies an authoritative enunciation is clear from the most trite uses. This is the reason why *aio* is necessary in legal, expressions, and not *dico*; it announces not an opinion, a belief, but an authoritative saying, which has a binding force. Hence the expression *lex ait* whereas we do not find *lex dicit*. Similarly the expression *Livius ait* is used when his actual words are quoted, in a case where the presumption is that they will carry authority.

We have seen that *aio* is opposed to *nego* in meaning to "say yes." It has the value of a categorical and positive affirmation. The speaker who uses *aio* lays claim to an assertion of truth. The god *Aius* is so called *quod divinitus vox edita est*, because a voice of a divine character was heard. His name was not **Dicius*, but *Aius*, that is a voice invested with authority. Everywhere *aio* refers to an impersonal utterance which gets its authority from the fact that it can be attributed to a supra-personal agency, like a law or a divinity. It will be noted that there is a certain resemblance between the connotations of *aio* and the Greek *phēmi*.

Once *ag-* has been thus defined, what is the meaning of *prodigium*? It will be useful to refer to the description of a *prodigium*, which took place in the reign of Tullus, according to Livy (1, 31). After the defeat of the Sabines it was announced to the king and the senators that there had been a rain of stones on the Alban Mount. Men were sent to verify the prodigy (*ad id visendum prodigium*). They in fact saw a heavy rain of stones resembling hailstones. They also believed that they heard a loud voice (*visi etiam audire vocem ingentem*) coming from the wood which crowns the summit and prescribing to the Albans sacrifices according to their national rites. Following on this prodigy (*ab eodem prodigio*), the Romans also celebrated a rite, whether because of the heavenly voice (*voce caelesti*) from the Alban Mount or on the advice of the *haruspices*.

This text would appear to contain an etymological explanation of *prodigium*.

We have seen the connection of *Aius* with a divine voice; similarly the *prodigium* is characterized by the emission (*prod-*) of a divine voice (*-agium*), if we may judge by the circumstances which accompanied the *prodigium* just quoted. Thus originally the *prodigium* would have been the "prodigy" of a divine voice which made itself heard along with other signs. This is the factual justification which could be offered in support of an interpretation founded on the proper sense of *aio*.

BOOK VI, CHAPTER SEVEN

Religion and Superstition

Abstract. Since the Indo-Europeans did not conceive of that omnipresent reality which religion represents as a separate institution, they had no term to designate it. In those languages which do present such a term it is of great interest to trace the process by which it was constituted.

In Ionic Greek, in Herodotus, the term *thrēskeíē* properly refers to the observances of cult prescriptions. The term is unknown in Attic Greek and it does not appear until a late date (first cent. BC) to designate "religion," as a complex of beliefs and practices.

Nothing has been the subject of a greater or longer dispute than the origin of the Latin word *religio*. Here it is shown, for both semantic and morphological reasons, that the word must be attached to *relegere* 'to collect again, to take up again for a new choice, to return to a previous synthesis in order to recompose it': thus *religio* 'religious scruple' was originally a subjective attitude, an act of reflection bound up with some fear of a religious kind. While it is false historically, the interpretation of the word by "*religare*" 'to tie, bind', which was invented by the Christians, is significant for the renewal of the notion: *religio* becomes "obligation", an objective bond between the believer and his God. No less disconcerting is the term for superstition: as between *superstes* 'survivor', 'witness' and *superstitiosus* 'diviner' how can we define *superstitio*? Originally it was the faculty of testifying retrospectively to what has been obliterated, of revealing the invisible. The evolution of the term towards an exclusively pejorative sense is explained by the discredit which attached at Rome to soothsayers, magicians and "seers" of every kind. We can see by what roundabout and unforeseeable processes the fundamental pair of terms *religion-superstition* was constituted.

All the lexical terms studied in the immediately preceding chapters have been concerned with a central notion—that of *religion*. How can we define, by means of the Indo-European vocabulary, what we understand by "religion"?

One fact can be established immediately: there is no term of common Indo-European for "religion." Even in the historical period there are a number of Indo-European languages which lack such a term, which is not surprising. For it lies in the nature of this notion not to lend itself to a single and lasting expression.

If it is true that religion is an institution, this institution is nevertheless not separated from other institutions or outside them. It was not possible to evolve a clear conception of what religion is or to devise a term for it until it was clearly delimited and had a distinct domain, so that it was possible to know what belonged to it and what was foreign to it. Now in the civilizations which we are studying everything is imbued with religion, everything is a sign of, a factor in, or the reflection of, divine forces. Thus outside special confraternities no need was felt for a specific term to designate the complex of cults and beliefs, and this is why to denote "religion" we find only terms which appear as separate and independent creations. It is not even certain that we understand them in their true and proper meaning. When we translate as "religion" the Sanskrit word *dharma* 'rule' or the Old Slavic *věra* 'belief', are we not committing the error of extrapolation? We shall examine only two terms, one from Greek and the other from Latin, which can pass for equivalents of our word "religion."

The Greek word *thrēskeía* denotes properly both cult and piety. It has a curious history in Greek itself. According to Van Herten[1] *thrēskeía* was applied only to foreign cults; whereas in fact, in the Augustan period, the word may designate every cult, whether indigenous or foreign. The word is ancient. It appears for the first time in Herodotus and then disappears completely from the tradition to reappear in the time of Strabo. From then on examples multiply both in texts and in inscriptions. The word is properly Ionic, and it did not find its way into

1. J. Van Herten, *Thrēskeía, eulábeia, hikétēs*, diss. Utrecht, 1934. Documentation has been enriched and the history of the word given new precision by Louis Robert, *Etudes épigraphiques et philologiques*, 1938, 226ff.

Attic, but it later became popular because it was the most convenient term to designate a complex of beliefs and cult practices.

The first uses, two of *thrēskeíē* and two of the verb *thrēskeúein*, all in Herodotus in his second book, relate to observances: "The Egyptians, the neighbors of the Libyans, did not tolerate the *regulation* of the sacrifice and especially the prohibition of the flesh of the cow" (II, 18).

Elsewhere Herodotus refers to the rules of physical purity to which the Egyptian priests subject themselves. Then he adds: "They observe a thousand other *thrēskeías*" (II, 37): these are practices imposed on priests. Such is also the meaning of the verb *thrēskeúō* (II, 64; 65) "to follow minutely religious prescriptions," and always with reference to the Egyptians. The idea is thus that of "observance," a notion of practice rather than belief. Thanks to scattered testimony we can reach further back into the history of the word. The substantive *thrēskeía* derives, curiously enough, from a present tense in *-skō* which we have in the form of a gloss in Hesychius: *thrḗsko*: *noô* and also *thráskein*: *anamimnḗskein* "cause to recollect." *Thrḗskō* in its turn is susceptible of analysis: it goes back to a verb **thréō* which is attested by *enthreîn*: *phulássein* 'guard, observe'. We can add a further link to this chain of words: **thréō* presupposes a root **ther-*, and this enables us to attach to it the adjective *atherés* which is glossed *anóēton* 'senseless' and, what is more interesting, *anósion* 'impious'. Finally, *atherés* lies at the base of the Homeric present tense *atherízō* 'to neglect, make light of'.

All these data link up and are complementary to the notion which the word *thrēskeía* itself evokes: that of "observance," "rule of religious practice." It links up with a verbal stem denoting attentiveness to a rite, preoccupation with being faithful to rule. It is not "religion" as a whole but the observance of the obligations of cult.

We now come to the second term, which is infinitely more important in every respect: this is the Latin *religio*, which remains, in all western languages, the sole and constant word, for which no equivalent or substitute has been able to establish itself.

What does *religio* mean? The question has been discussed since ancient times and even then scholars were unable to agree. Modern scholars remain no less divided. Opinions waver between two alternatives each of which is favored from time to time and finds new supporters, but no final decision has been reached. One of these alternatives is represented by Cicero, who, in a text quoted later on attaches *religio* to *legere* 'gather, collect', and the other by

Lactantius and Tertullian, who explain *religio* by *ligare* 'to bind'. Modern writers are still divided between *legere* and *ligare.*

We can do no more than cite the principal studies. Cicero's solution has been supported by W. Otto,[2] and he has been followed by J. B. Hofmann.[3] By contrast the dictionary of Ernout-Meillet opts firmly for *religare,* and this is also true of the article on *religio* in Pauly-Wissowa.[4] Other scholars remain undecided: W. Fowler[5] provides a good descriptive study of the meaning of *religio*, but for the etymology he cites the opinion of Conway that "either opinion can be defended."

This is the text of Cicero which was destined to dominate the whole discussion (*De natura deorum* II, 28, 72*): Qui autem omnia quae ad cultum deorum pertinerent diligenter retractarent et tamquam relegerent, sunt dicti religiosi ex relegendo ut elegantes ex eligendo, ex diligendo diligentes. His enim in verbis omnibus inest vis legendi eadem quae in religioso.* 'Those who rehandled (*retractarent*) diligently and so to speak *relegerent* all the things which relate to the worship of the gods, were called *religiosi* from *relegere*, like *elegantes* from *eligere* and *diligentes* from *diligere*. All these words have in fact the same sense of *legere* as *religiosus*.'

For Lactantius, on the contrary, *religio* is a "bond" of piety which "binds" us to god, *vinculo pietatis obstricti et religati sumus*. The opinion of Lactantius was followed by Kobbert, who defines *religio* "as a force external to man, a tabu attached at certain epochs to certain places, to certain things and whereby man, deprived of his will, is bound, attached."

What we must first ask ourselves is what *religio* denotes in actual fact and what the proper and constant uses of the word are. It will suffice to recall a few examples from among the most striking. Originally *religio* did not mean "religion"; that at least is sure.

An old fragment of a lost tragedy by L. Accius has preserved these two verses:

Nunc, Calcas, finem religionum fac: desiste exercitum
morari meque ab domuitione, tuo obsceno omine

– (Non. 357, 6 = *Astyanax* fr. V. Ribbeck)

2. In the study of *religio* and *superstitio* published in *Archiv für Religionswissenschaft* XII, 533; XIV, 406.
3. *Lat. etym. Wb.*, I, 35a.
4. The author, M. Kobbert, gives a resumé of his dissertation on the subject (1910).
5. *Transactions* of the 3rd International Congress of the History of religions, Vol. II.

"Put an end, Calchas, to your *religiones*; cease to delay the army and so preventing me from returning home by your unfavorable omen."

The *religiones* of the seer Calchas, arising from an unfavorable omen, compel the army to stay where it is and the hero from returning home. We see that *religio*, a term of the augural language, denotes a "scruple relating to the *omina*," that is to say a subjective frame of mind.

Such is also the dominant feature that attaches to *religio* in its more "secular" uses.

Plautus Curculio 350: *vocat me ad cenam; religio fuit, denegare volui* "He invites me to dinner; *I had a scruple about it* and I wanted to refuse." In Terence (*Andria* 941) Chremes finds himself in the presence of a young girl, his own daughter whom he believes lost. He hesitates to recognize her: *At mihi unus scrupulus restat, qui me male habet* "I still have a scruple which troubles me," he says. The other replies: *dignus es cum tua religione, odio*: *nodum in scirpo quaeris* "You with your *religio*, you deserve to be hated: you want to find difficulties where there are none (literally, you try to find a knot on a reed)." The word *religio* takes up *scrupulus*. Hence comes the expression *religio est* 'to have a scruple', and also *religioni est* or *religio tenet* with an infinitive proposition: *religioni est quibusdam porta Carmentali egredi* (Festus 285 M.) "some people feel a scruple about going out by the Carmental gate."

This use is constant in the classical period. For instance, in the course of an election the first teller of the votes dies and the whole proceedings have to be suspended. Despite this Gracchus decides to continue although *rem illam in religionem populo venisse* 'although the affair had awakened scruples in the hearts of the people' (Cicero *Nat. deorum* II, 4,10). The word is frequent in Livy, often in connection with religious phenomena: *quod demovendis statu suo sacris religionem facere posset* 'a fact which might cause misgivings about changing the site of certain cults' (IX, 29, 10). This is an allusion to the punishment of the Potitii who had abandoned the cult of Hercules: *adeo minimis etiam rebus prava religio inserit deos* 'so true is it that a misguided scruple involves the gods in the most trivial matters' (XXVII, 23, 2).

The cult of Ceres, says Cicero, must be carried out with the most meticulous care for the rites, according to the vows of our ancestors: *sacra Cereris summa maiores nostri religione confici caerimoniaque voluerunt* (*Balb.* 24, 55).

The sense of *religio*, which recurs in a large number of other examples, is confirmed by the derivative *religiosus* 'scrupulous with regard to cult, having a case of conscience in a matter involving rites'. A number of Roman learned men tell us that *religiosus* could be used with reference to the cult itself: *religiosum quod propter sanctitatem aliquam remotum ac sepositum a nobis sit* 'a thing is said to be *religiosum* which, because of some sanctity, is remote and set apart from us' (Masurius Sabinus *apud* Aulus Gellius N.A. 4, 9); *religiosum esse Gallus Aelius ait quod homini facere non liceat, ut si id faciat contra deorum voluntatem videatur facere* 'a thing is said to be *religiosus* which a man is not permitted to do, if in so doing he seemed to be acting against the will of the gods' (Festus p. 278, Mull.).

In sum, *religio* is a hesitation, a misgiving which holds back, a scruple which prevents and not a sentiment which impels to action or incites to ritual practice. It seems to us that this sense, which is demonstrated by ancient usage without the slightest ambiguity, imposes as the only possible interpretation of *religio* the one given by Cicero, who attached it to *legere*.

Let us consider more closely the form of *religio*. Is it even possible to explain *religio* by *ligare*? Our reply will be in the negative for a number of reasons:

(1) There was never an abstract **ligio* corresponding to *ligare*; the abstract from *religare* is *relegatio*; on the other hand we have the conclusive evidence of the word *legio* in favor of *legere*.

(2) It is a little noticed fact that the abstracts in *-io* are generally based on verbs of the third conjugation and not the first: e.g. *ex-cidio, regio, dicio, usu-capio, legi-rupio* (*rumpere*), *de-liquio* (*linquere*), *oblivio* (**oblivere, oblivisci*), and *legio*.

(3) A quotation by an ancient author would alone suffice to decide the question: *religentem esse opportet, religiosus nefas* (*ne fuas*?) 'One ought to be *religens*, not *religiosus*' (Nigidius Figulus *apud* Aulus Gellius *N.A.* 4, 9, 11). It makes no difference that there is a textual corruption in the last word. The form *religentem* from *lego, legere*, points clearly to the origin of *religiosus*.

All these reasons would have been clearly apparent long ago if the verb **religere* had left other proofs of its existence than the participle *religens* so as to provide a firmer foundation for the connection between *legere* and *religio*. But we can reason from verbs of the same formation, such as *diligo* and *intelligo*, which Cicero had already cited, in the passage quoted above: *his enim verbis omnibus inest vis legendi eadem quae in religiose* 'in all these words (*diligo, intelligo*) there is the same sense of *legere* that we have in *religious*'.

In fact *legere* 'gather, collect, recognize' had a number of concrete applications and, with various prefixes, it was used to denote different intellectual processes and emotions. The opposite of *lego* is *neg-ligo* 'not to trouble oneself about'; *diligo* is "to gather by isolating, with preference, esteem, love"; *intelligo* is "gather by choosing, discern by reflection, understand"; and is not "intelligence" the capacity for choice and synthesis?

From these connections we can infer that the sense of *religere* was "to re-collect": its meaning was 'to take again for a new choice, to reconsider a previous approach'. Here we have a good definition of the religious "scruple." While it is a good thing to be *religens*, said Nigidius Figulus, "to be careful of religious things," it is bad to the *religiosus* "to have constant scruples" about them. To take up again a choice already made (*retractare* is the word Cicero uses), to revise the decision which results from it, this is the proper sense of *religio*. It indicates a subjective attitude not an objective property of certain things or a complex of beliefs and practices. Roman *religio* was, at the beginning, essentially subjective. It is no accident that it is only in Christian writers that we find the explanation of *religio* by *religare*. Lactantius insists on it: *nomen religionis a vinculo pietatis esse deductum, quod hominem sibi Deus religaverit et pietate constrinxerit* "the term *religio* has been taken from the bond of piety, because God has bound man to him and attached him by piety." This is because the content of religion itself has changed. For a Christian, what characterizes the new faith in opposition to the pagan religions was the bond of piety, this dependence of the faithful on God, this *obligation* in the true sense of the word. The concept of *religio*was remodeled on the idea that man made for himself about his relation to God, an idea that was totally different from that of the old Roman *religio* and prepared the way for the modern sense of the term. This broad outline is what is essential in the history and origin of the word *religio*, what emerges from the uses and the morphology of the word.

This analysis of the sense of *religio* also contributes to our understanding of the term which was regarded by the Romans themselves as its contrary: *superstitio*. In fact the notion of "religion" requires, so to speak, by opposition that of "superstition."

This is a curious notion which could only have arisen in a civilization and at an epoch in which the mind could detach itself so far from the practice of religion that it could appreciate both the normal forms as well as the exaggerated forms of belief and cult. There are barely two societies in which we can observe such a detachment and where, along independent lines, terms were created to express the distinction.

In Greek the notion is expressed by the compound *deisidaimonía*, an abstract noun derived from *deisidaímōn*, literally "he who fears the *daímones*." This compound, in the course of history, came to have two different senses: first, "he who fears the gods (*daímones*)" as they ought to be feared, who is respectful of religion and devout in its practices; later, as the result of a double semantic process, "superstitious." On the one hand *daímōn* acquired the sense of "demon"; secondly religious practice was complicated by observances of growing complexity and minuteness thanks to the influence of magic and foreign cults. Parallel with this we have the growth of philosophical schools which, detached from the practice of religion, distinguished between true worship and purely formalistic practices. This evolution is interesting to follow within the history of Greek, but it results from a rather late and limited attitude of awareness.

The word *superstitio*, on the other hand, with its derived adjective *superstitiosus* was in use as long as *religio*, to which it stands in opposition. This is the term which, for us moderns, has fixed the concept. The formal structure of the word appears to be perfectly clear, but the same cannot be said for the meaning.

In the first place, the word was used in a number of senses in Latin, but none of these agrees with the sense of the elements of the compound. One fails to see how the sense of "superstition" could emerge from the combination of super and stare.

To judge by its form, *superstitio* ought to be the abstract corresponding to *superstes* "surviving." But how can these words be connected for their sense? For *superstes* itself does not mean only "surviving," but in certain well-attested uses it denotes "witness." The same difficulty arises for *superstitio* in its connection with *superstitiosus*. If we accept that somehow or other *superstitio* came to mean "superstition," how is it that *superstitiosus* meant not "superstitious" but "having prophetic gifts, a seer"?

We see the complexity of the problem, which is limited in so far as it concerns formation, but is of great consequence for the history of beliefs. This is why the word has been so often studied, discussed, and explained in very different ways. We may briefly review these varied interpretations in order to appreciate all the elements of the discussion.

(a) The literal interpretation by *superstes* 'surviving' leads to the notion of *superstitio* as "survival." *Superstitio* would then mean a "remainder" of an old belief which would appear superfluous at the time implied by the term. In our opinion this explanation involves an historical misconception. It would mean attributing to the ancient people, before the beginning of history proper, the attitude of mind and the critical sense of the nineteenth century or modern ethnographers, who are in a position to pick out in religion "survivals" of an earlier epoch which do not harmonize with the rest. In any case this explanation takes no account of the special sense of *superstitiosus*.

(b) In Otto's study of the word *religio*, cited above, the word *superstitio* is also considered. The author defines the sense which it has in the ancient writers but he makes no attempt to explain it from the resources of the Latin language: for him *superstitio* is simply the translation of a Greek word: it is the Latin calque of *ékstasis* 'ecstasy'. This is a surprising conclusion, for *ékstasis* has nothing whatever to do with *superstitio* either as regards form or meaning. The prefix *ek-* does not correspond with *super-* and magic and sorcery are absent from the sense of *ékstasis*. Finally, the very date at which the word *superstitio* appears in Latin excludes all philosophical influence on its formation. In fact, this proposal has not found acceptance.

(c) According to Müller-Graupa,[6] *superstes* is a euphemism for "the spirits of the dead": the dead are always alive; they may appear at any time; hence their name *superstes* 'the survivor', and *superstitio* in the sense "*Dämonenwesen*, demoniac being," and also "belief in demons." The meaning of *superstitiosus* is thus "full of demoniac elements, possessed by evil spirits"; then, in an age of reason, the word would have denoted belief in phantoms. The author realized that his explanation had already been proposed by Schopenhauer, for whom the dead "survived" (*superstites*) their destiny; *superstitio* would thus be the quality of the *superstites*.

This whole conception is gratuitous. *Superstes* did not have this connection with death, and it is difficult to see how a dead person "survives" in this way or how he was ever described as *superstes*. In Roman religion, if the dead have a life, it is not a life of survival but a life of quite a different kind. Finally, *superstitio* does not designate the belief in a demon; this

6. *Glotta*, XIX, 1930, 63ff.

intrusion of the demoniac and the demons into the concept of *superstitio* is pure invention.

(d) Other explanations have been sought along different lines. Margadant[7] for his part starts with the sense of "witness," which *superstes* has, and attributes to *superstitiosus* the primary meaning of "seer, prophet." The given sense of *superstes* 'witness' developed in *superstitiosus* to that of "*wahrsagend*, prophetic," the transition being the sense "*qui divinitustestatur*," that is, "he who is a witness of the divinity." This is a very odd idea: it is not permissible to introduce the notion of "testimony" into the divine sphere or to connect a legal term with second sight. The person endowed with divinatory powers was not, in the eyes of the Romans, a "witness" to the divinity as later the Christian martyr was to become. In any case we still are not given an explanation of the proper sense of *superstitio.*

(e) Finally, an explanation has been proposed by Flinck-Linkomies,[8] "*superstitio* developed from the sense of 'superiority' (*Überlegen-heit, super-stare,* to be above) via 'divinatory power, sorcery' to that of 'superstition'." It is difficult to see how "superiority" leads to "sorcery" or how we get from "sorcery" to "superstition."

Such is the state of the problem. Here, as in all similar cases, an explanation can be accepted only if it is applicable to all the senses, by harmonizing them in a reasonable way, and if it is founded on the exact sense of the elements of the compound.

Let us take the first and last terms, *superstes* and *superstitiosus*, since the intermediary *superstitio* yields us no more than a substantive already fixed in the sense which has to be explained. In fact there are differences between the basic term*superstes* and the derivative *superstitiosus* which are instructive for the proper meaning.

How does *superstes*, the adjective from *superstare*, come to mean "surviving"? This has to do with the sense of *super*, which does not solely or properly mean "above" but "beyond" in such a way as to cover and to constitute an advance, according to the context: *satis superque* 'enough and beyond, enough and more than enough'; the *supercilium* is not only "what is above the eyelash," it protects it by overhanging. The very notion of "superiority" does not denote

7. *Indogermanische Forschungen*, 48, 1930, 284.

8. *Arctos*, 2, 73ff.

simply what is "above" but something more, some measure of progress over what is "beneath." Similarly, *superstare* means "to stand beyond," in fact, beyond an event which has destroyed the rest. Death has come upon a family: the *superstites* exist beyond this event. A man who has passed through danger, or a test, a difficult period, who has survived it, is *superstes*. A character in Plautus says "I require of a woman that you should always *survive* your husband" *ut viro tuo semper sis superstes* (*Cas*. 817-818).

This is not the only use of *superstes*: "To continue existence beyond" implies not only "to have survived a misfortune, or death" but also "to have come through any event whatsoever and to exist *beyond* this event," that is to have been a "witness" of it. Or again, it can mean "he who stands (*stat*) over the thing, who is present at it." Such would be the relation, with respect to the event, of the witness. We can now see the explanation of the sense 'witness' for *superstes*, which is attested several times, for instance in a fragment of a lost play of Plautus. *Nunc mihi licet quidvis loqui*: *nemo hic adest superstes* "Now I can say whatever I want to: there is no *witness* present" (Plautus *in Artemone apud* Festus 394, 37). This is not an isolated use, and there is other testimony which gives us the assurance that it is of great antiquity. In Festus *loc. cit. superstites* means "the witnesses, those present": *superstites*, *testes*, *praesentes significat*; *cuius rei testimonium est quod superstitibus praesentibus ii inter quos controversia est vindicias sumere iubentur*, '*superstites* means *testes*, *praesentes*; the proof of this is that those who are involved in a dispute receive the order to formulate their claims in the presence of witnesses', *superstitibus praesentibus*. Cicero (*Pro Murena*, 12) reproduces an old formula which was in use at the time when roads were consecrated: *utrisque superstitibus istam viam dico*; this is confirmed by Servius (*ad Aen*. III 339): *superstes praesentem significat*.

We can now see the difference between *superstes* and *testis*. Etymologically *testis* means the one who attends as the "third" person (**ter-stis*) at an affair in which two persons are interested; and this conception goes back to the Indo-European community. A Sanskrit text has it: "every time two persons are together, Mitra is there as the third person"; thus Mitra is by nature the "witness." But *superstes* describes the witness as the one "who has his being beyond," a witness in virtue of his surviving, or as "the one who stands over the matter," who was present at it.

We can now see what *superstitio* can and must theoretically signify, namely the quality of being a *superstes*. This would be the "property of being present" as a "witness." It now remains to explain the relation between the postulated sense and that which we actually find in the texts. *Superstitio*, in fact, is often associated with *hariolus* 'seer'. This is well illustrated by Plautus. A one-eyed parasite explains his infirmity: "I lost my eye in a fight"; the other retorts: "I don't care whether you had your eye gouged out in a fight or by a pot that someone threw at you." "What," exclaims the parasite, "this man is a seer, he has guessed aright": *superstitiosus hic quidem est*; *vera praedicat* (*Curc.* 397). The "truth" consists in the fact of "divining" what one has not been present at. Similar is *illic homo superstitiosus* (*Amph.* 322). In the *Rudens* 1139ff. the subject is a woman and one of the characters says:

> —*Quid si ista aut superstitiosa aut hariolast atque*
> *omnia quidquid inerit vera dicet*?
> "And suppose this woman is *superstitiosa* or *ariola* and she tells truly everything that is (in this casket)?"
>
> —*non feret, nisi vera dicet: nequiquam hariolabitur*
> "She won't get it unless she speaks the truth; sorcery will be no use."

We can now see the solution: *superstitiosus* is the one who is "endowed with the power of *superstitio*," that is, "*qui vera praedicat*", the seer who speaks of past events *as if he had actually been present*: the "divination" in these examples did not refer to the future but to the past. *Superstitio* is the gift of second sight which enables a person to know the past as if he or she had been present, *superstes*. This is how *superstitiosus* denotes the gift of second sight, which is attributed to "seers," that of being a "witness" of events at which he has not been present.

The word is constantly associated in common use with *hariolus*, but it was in the language of divination that it must have acquired the sense of (magic) "presence." In fact, it is always in special vocabularies that words take on their technical sense. We have an example of it in the French word *voyant* 'who is endowed with sight', but not of normal sight but something that goes beyond it, "second sight."

In this way the terms can be seen to have a natural relationship: *superstes* 'the one who can pass as a "witness"' because he has been present at some event; *superstitio* 'the gift of "presence"', the faculty of giving testimony as if one had actually been there; *superstitiosus*, the one who is endowed with this "gift of presence," which permits him to have been present at past events. This is the sense which we find in Plautus.[9]

But how are we to explain the modern sense? The fact is that this is the last to appear in the semantic history of the word. The evolution from the sense which has just been described—which must have arisen in the language of seers—to that which is familiar to us can be traced. The Romans had an abhorrence for divinatory practices: they regarded them as charlatanism. Sorcerers and seers were despised, and all the more so because the majority of them came from foreign parts. *Superstitio*, associated with disapproved practices, took on a pejorative coloring. At an early date it denoted the practices of a false religion which were considered base and vain, unworthy of a reasonable mind. The Romans, faithful to their official augurs, always condemned any recourse to magic, to divination, to these practices which were regarded as puerile. It was then, on the basis of the sense "contemptible religious beliefs" that a new adjective was formed from the basic noun: *superstitiosus* 'one who gives himself up to *superstitio*' or who allows himself to be influenced by it. From this a new idea of *superstitio* arose, the opposite of *religio*. And this produced this new adjective *superstitiosus* 'superstitious', which was wholly distinct from the first and was the antithesis to *religiosus* formed in the same way. But it was the enlightened view, the philosophic view of the rationalizing Romans which dissociated *religio* 'religious scruple', authentic worship, from *superstitio*, a degraded and perverted form of religion.

In this way we can make clear the link between the two successive senses of *superstitio*, which reflect in the first place the state of popular beliefs and next the attitude of the traditional Roman in matters of belief.

9. This solution to the problem has been sketched out in *Revue des Etudes Latines*, 16, 1938, 35ff.

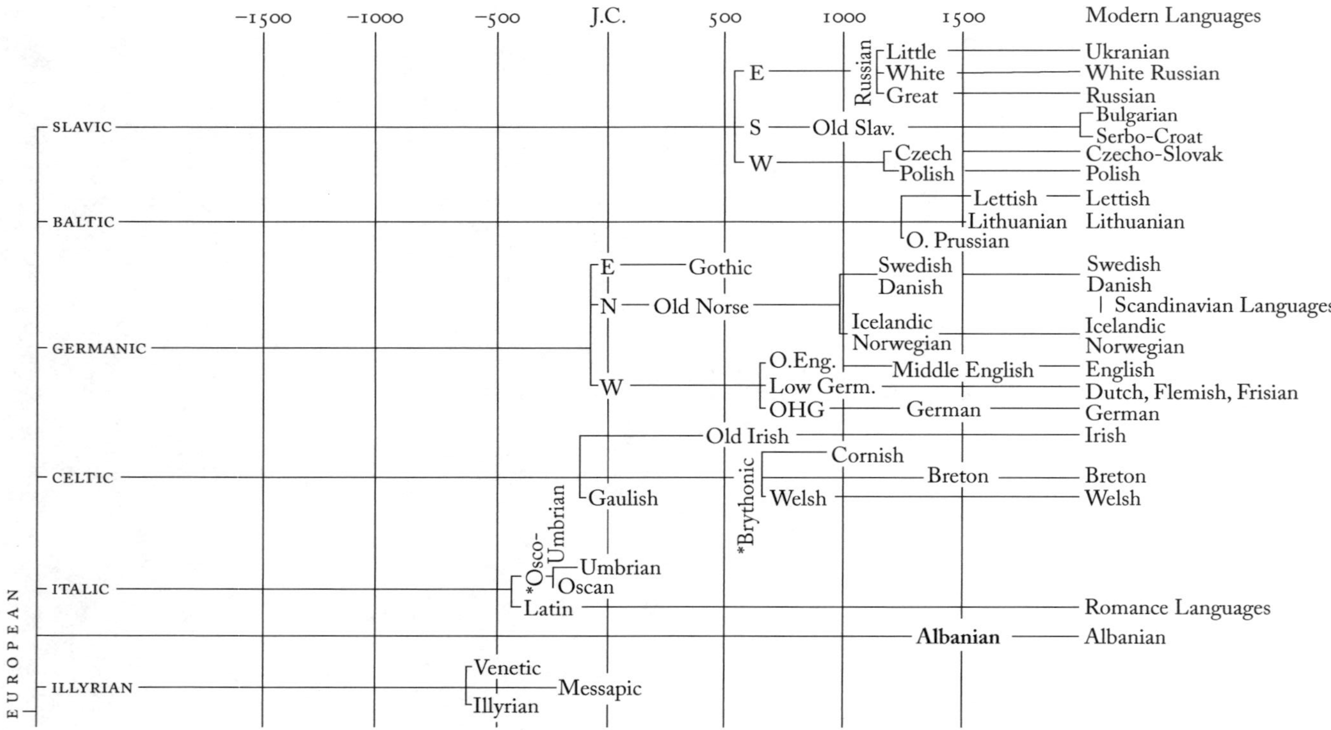

−1500
−1000
−500
J.C.
500
1000
1500
Modern Languages
EUROPEAN
SLAVIC
E
Russian
Little
White
Great
Ukranian
White Russian
Russian
S
Old Slav.
Bulgarian
Serbo-Croat
W
Czech
Polish
Czecho-Slovak
Polish
BALTIC
Lettish
Lithuanian
O. Prussian
Lettish
Lithuanian
GERMANIC
E
Gothic
N
Old Norse
Swedish
Danish
Icelandic
Norwegian
Swedish
Danish
Scandinavian Languages
Icelandic
Norwegian
W
O.Eng.
Low Germ.
OHG
Middle English
German
English
Dutch, Flemish, Frisian
German
CELTIC
Old Irish
Irish
Gaulish
*Brythonic
Cornish
Breton
Welsh
Breton
Welsh
ITALIC
*Osco-Umbrian
Umbrian
Oscan
Latin
Romance Languages
Albanian
Albanian
ILLYRIAN
Venetic
Illyrian
Messapic

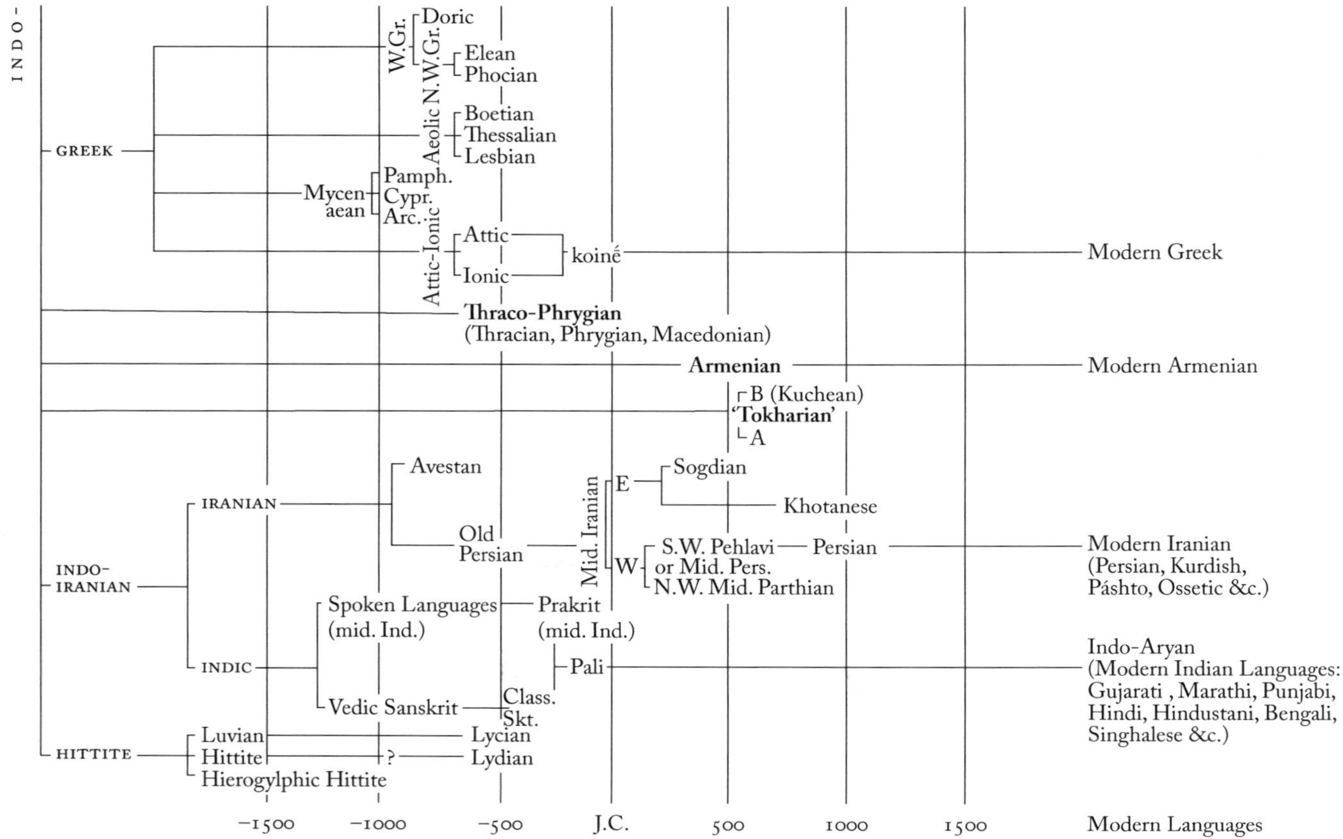
INDO-
GREEK
W.Gr.
Doric
N.W.Gr.
Elean
Phocian
Aeolic
Boetian
Thessalian
Lesbian
Mycenaean
Pamph.
Cypr.
Arc.
Attic-Ionic
Attic
Ionic
koinḗ
Modern Greek
Thraco-Phrygian
(Thracian, Phrygian, Macedonian)
Armenian
Modern Armenian
B (Kuchean)
'Tokharian'
A
INDO-IRANIAN
IRANIAN
Avestan
Old Persian
Mid. Iranian
E
Sogdian
Khotanese
W
S.W. Pehlavi or Mid. Pers.
N.W. Mid. Parthian
Persian
Modern Iranian (Persian, Kurdish, Páshto, Ossetic &c.)
INDIC
Spoken Languages (mid. Ind.)
Prakrit (mid. Ind.)
Pali
Vedic Sanskrit
Class. Skt.
Indo-Aryan (Modern Indian Languages: Gujarati , Marathi, Punjabi, Hindi, Hindustani, Bengali, Singhalese &c.)
HITTITE
Luvian
Hittite
Hierogylphic Hittite
Lycian
?
Lydian
−1500
−1000
−500
J.C.
500
1000
1500
Modern Languages

Bibliographical Note

The preceding table, in which the languages are listed according to the date of their first attestation (see the chronological scale in the right and left margins), has been drawn up after the work of A. Meillet and M. Cohen, *Les langues du Monde*, new edition 1952, Ch. I: "Langues indo-européennes" (written by J. Vendryes, 1st edition 1924, revised and brought up to date by Émile Benveniste). The work should be consulted for its linguistic maps and to supplement the above table and the brief bibliography which follows.

INDO-EUROPEAN AND THE COMPARATIVE METHOD

A. Meillet, *Les dialectes indo-européens*, Paris, 1908, 2nd ed. 1922, new impression 1950.

A. Meillet, *Introduction á l'étude comparative des langues indo-européennes,* 8th ed. Paris, 1937.

A. Meillet, *La méthode comparative en linguistique historique*, Oslo and Paris, 1925.

J. Pokorny, *Indogermanisches etymologisches Wörterbuch*, Bern, 1949–59.

O. Schrader-A. Nehring, *Reallexikon der indogermanischen Altertumskunde*, 2nd ed. publ. by A. Nehring, Berlin, 1916–1929.

G. Devoto, *Origini indoeuropee*, Florence, 1963.

INDO-ARYAN

M. Mayhofer, *Kurzefasstes etymologisches Wörterbuch des Altindischen,* Heidelberg, 1953.

IRANIAN

Chr. Bartholomae, *Altiranisches Wörterbuch,* Strasbourg, 1904.

GREEK

H. Frisk, *Griechisches etymologisches Wörterbuch,* Heidelberg, 1954–1970.

LATIN

A. Ernout and A. Meillet, *Dictionnaire étymologique de la langue latine,* 4th rev. and corr. ed. Paris, 1959.

J. B. Hofmann, *Lateinisches etymologisches Wörterbuch,* Heidelberg, 1938.

GERMANIC (GOTHIC)

S. Feist, *Vergleichendes Wörterbuch der gotischen Sprache,* 3rd ed. Leiden, 1939.

F. Mossé, *Manuel de la langue gotique,* Paris, 1942, 2nd ed. 1956.

BALTIC (LITHUANIAN)

E. Frankel, *Litauisches etymologisches Wörterbuch,* Heidelberg, 1955.

SLAVIC

M. Vasmer, *Russiches etymologisches Wörterbuch,* Heidelberg, 1950.

The following works, which appeared while the book was in the press, could not be consulted:

P. Chantraine, *Dictionnaire étymologique de la langue greque,* Vol. I (A-D), Paris, 1968.

L. Gernet, *Anthropologie de la Grèce antique,* Paris, 1968.

G. Dumézil, *Idées romaines,* Paris, 1969.

Index of Names

Index of Texts/Sources

Index of Languages

F

G

H

I

Index of Key Terms and Concepts

G

H

M

N

O

Q

R

S

T

U

V

W

Z

HAU Books is committed to publishing the most distinguished texts in classic and advanced anthropological theory. The titles aim to situate ethnography as the prime heuristic of anthropology, and return it to the forefront of conceptual developments in the discipline. HAU Books is sponsored by some of the world's most distinguished anthropology departments and research institutions, and releases its titles in both print editions and open-access formats.

www.haubooks.com

Supported by

HAU-N. E. T.

Network of Ethnographic Theory

University of Aarhus – EPICENTER (DK)
University of Amsterdam (NL)
University of Bergen (NO)
Brown University (US)
California Institute of Integral Studies (US)
University of Campinas (BR)
University of Canterbury (NZ)
University of Chicago (US)
University College London (UK)
University of Colorado Boulder Libraries (US)
CNRS – Centre d'Études Himalayennes (FR)
Cornell University (US)
University of Edinburgh (UK)
The Graduate Institute, Geneva Library (CH)
University of Helsinki (FL)
Indiana University Library (US)
Johns Hopkins University (US)
University of Kent (UK)
Lafayette College Library (US)
London School of Economics and Political Science (UK)
Institute of Social Sciences of the University of Lisbon (PL)
University of Manchester (UK)
The University of Manchester Library (UK)
Max-Planck Institute for the Study of Religious and Ethnic Diversity at Göttingen (DE)
Musée de Quai Branly (FR)
Museu Nacional – UFRJ (BR)
Norwegian Museum of Cultural History (NO)
University of Oslo (NO)
University of Oslo Library (NO)
Pontificia Universidad Católica de Chile (CL)
Princeton University (US)
University of Queensland (AU)
University of Rochester (US)
Universidad Autónoma de San Luis Potosi (MX)
SOAS, University of London (UK)
University of Sydney (AU)
University of Toronto Libraries (CA)

www.haujournal.org/haunet